An Anthology on Tongues

A Compilation of Articles by Church of God Authors on the Topic of Tongues.

**Compiled By
Dr. James L. Fleming**

Reformation Publishers
Prestonsburg, KY

Perfect Bound
ISBN 978-1-60416 -318-6   Item #02217

Printed on Demand

Reformation Publishers
242 University Drive
Prestonsburg, Kentucky 41653
1-800-765-2464
Fax 606-886-8222
rpublisher@aol.com
www.reformationpublishers.com

Contents

SECTION II: TRACTS / BOOKLETS / PAPERS 221

Preface

Inspiration comes from many sources. Such is the case for this book. When I was in the process of reading materials for inclusion in another project, I came across several articles written by church of God writers on the topic of tongues. I soon found myself accumulating numerous articles on this topic written by church of God writers. In fact, the number of articles expanded beyond my expectations.

As I collected these articles, I reflected upon the comments of one church of God pastor who said he wanted to read everything he could on this topic by church of God authors to help him determine what he would believe and teach.

It only seemed natural then that these two events would be combined in my mind to see the need of putting all of these articles together into one source for the purpose of helping persons in the church of God to know how we have viewed tongues throughout our history.

And so, here is the result. *An Anthology on Tongues:* A Compilation of Articles by Church of God Authors on the Topic of Tongues. These articles appear just as they were originally written by the authors. No attempt has been made to alter or change their writings. I have, however, made an attempt to put the articles into a chronological order.

Thus, this book is submitted to the church in the hope that it may help us understand the historical, theological position of the church of God on such a controversial issues as tongues.

James L. Fleming

August 2011

SECTION I:
MAGAZINE ARTICLES

Gifts Differing.
H. L. Hargrave.

BUT the manifestation of the Spirit is given to every man to profit withal. For to one is given by the Spirit the word of wisdom; to another the word of knowledge by the same Spirit; 1 Cor. 12:7, 8. In this gift of knowledge their is a clear perception of our privilege. We are rightly informed, have learning, but wisdom is better. The mill may be complete in all its parts, the corn in the hopper, water in the boiler, wood in the furnace, yet everything lays like a lifeless corps: no capacity, no power: but the fireman pours on oil, touches the match, and the machinery is in motion in a short time. Solomon says, "get wisdom." Knowledge when put into motion by the Holy Ghost fire, is quickening. In and through its quickening effects, we have the power to receive, and contain the holy fire, "get wisdom." Verse 9, "To another faith by the same Spirit:" vs. 10, "To another the working of miracles." We frequently hear men and women say, the days of miracles is past; have we not the same right to say the days of faith has past? No! God forbids it, for He says, "Heaven and earth shall pass away, but my words shall not fail." God says to His disciples, "These signs shall follow them that believe." "In my name shall they cast out devils, they shall speak with new tongues; they shall take up serpents; and if they drink any deadly thing it shall not hurt them; they shall lay hands on the sick, and they shall recover." O glory be to God forever! Get wisdom my brother; the wisdom which comes down from above enables me to look into the sect hospital and see the devil pouring into his subjects double doses of unbelief, through the spoon of the day of miracles is past. Says one, this power was given only to the apostles and to whom they laid hands on. But what does the Word say? "It is given to every man to profit withal." What is given to all? These gifts by the same Spirit, these signs, which is to follow them that believe; power through faith to cast out devils, to speak with new tongues, to take up serpents, and if they drink any deadly thing it shall not hurt them; they shall lay hands on the sick and they shall recover. But one says, show me one who can cast out devils, or one who can heal the sick. One instance of the fact will suffice; so the infidels who publish in the Free Pulpit at Waco Texas, say the same thing; they say their is no truth in God's Word, because their is none to be found who follow its precepts. O dreadful dilemma! "Get wisdom;" it enables me to see the unbelieving sect pens, a pitiable hospital. The bunks are all filled with the dead, whom the devil has succeeded in pouring into them this dreadful dose, unbelief. The floor of this hospital is now so full, there is scarcely room for more, but still the old dragon is pulling them in. Some live ones he gets in, clamor for a clean place: but he says, close your mouth on this subject; for, for this very thing, all these whom you see dead, have lost their lives for speaking thus. So they are made to believe that the opening of their mouth on this subject of dead men's bones in the (sects) hospital, will encur a disease, from which, none they say, has ever recovered. When the lunatic was healed, or when the disciples failed to cast the devil out, they had the same right to say the days of miracles was past as we have; but Jesus rebuked the devil and he came out of the child. Matt. 17:18. Jesus said to His apostles, "If ye have faith as a grain of mustard seed, ye shall say to this mountain, remove hence to yonder place, and it shall remove; and nothing shall be impossible to you." The apostles removed no mountains, neither any sycamore tree; but they through faith opened the eyes of the blind, unstopped the ears of the deaf, healed the sick, raised the dead, then failed on the lunatic, not because God's Word was a failure, but because of unbelief. Now there are some who seem to believe a part of God's Word, but that which they cannot comprehend, they say is not for our benefit. God enables me to comprehend promises through the word which was spoken unto me; and as soon as I perceived that I was begotten through the Word, God showed me that He was a God of my body as well as my spirit. Satan tempted me, even said to me, these are impossibilities. But I stood on the Word, and not on impossibilities. Praise God! who gives us these gifts for the completion of His body which is the Church. Now I stand on the promise, washed in the blood of Jesus. Praise His holy name! The blessed Savior has given me more than one of these gifts. One is wisdom, another is the discerning of spirits, and now I am contending for the faith once delivered to the saints. These gifts have enabled me to learn many precious lessons; one is not to walk in the counsel of the ungodly, though his robe may be a priestly one. If he transforms himself into an angel of light, I will know him, God being my wisdom and understanding. Peter says, "add to your faith virtue; and to virtue, knowledge; and to knowledge, temperance; and to temperance, patience; and to patience, godliness; and to godliness, brotherly kindness: and to brotherly kindness, charity. For if these things be in you, and abound, they make you that ye shall neither be barren nor unfruitful in the knowledge of our Lord Jesus Christ." 2 Pet. 1:5-8.

To be virtuous, spiritually, is not to sin. Brother, sister, has the gift which God has given you freed you from condemnation?

If not, "contend earnestly for the best gifts." "For the law of the Spirit of life in Christ Jesus hath made me free from the law of sin and death." God through the mouth of the prophets, declared that Israel had gone off after other gods: we are married to another: now He says, "Little children, keep yourselves from idols." "Have no other gods before me." He that lacketh these things hath forgotten that he was purged from his old sins. 2 Pet. 1:9. "I beseech of you, brethren, suffer the words of exhortation, for I have written a letter to you in few words, and now our Lord Jesus Christ Himself, and God, even our Father, stablish you in every good word and work." "The God of peace make you perfect in every good work to do His will through Jesus Christ." "Unto Him who is able to keep you from falling, and to present you faultless before the presence of His glory forever. Amen!"

H. L. Hargrave.
Nelta Texas.

H. L. Hargrave. "Gift Differing." *The Gospel Trumpet*. Volume 7. Number 17. (November 15, 1885): 4.

Questions Answered.
William G. Schell

Will some of the brethren explain the unknown tongue? Who spoke it? How do we know when it is spoken? Where is it used, and how is it spoken, and who is the interpreter? I can't understand the fourteenth chapter of I Corinthians.

J.J.C.

There is no such a thing taught in the Bible as some deceived souls call the unknown tongue, which is a mere nonsensical smattering of "gibberish," that no living soul can get any sense out of.

The gift of tongues mentioned in the chapter named above, is the power given by the Sprit of God, to speak some established language that we have never learned. For instance, a man who knows only the English language, is enabled by means of the gift of tongues to speak in the German, French, Spanish, Danish, or some other of the languages in actual use upon the earth. Read Acts 2:8.

There are two reasons why this gift was established in the church.

1. It is to be used as a sign to convince unbelievers. I Cor. 14:22.

2. It is to assist the Lord's ministers in preaching the gospel to all nations according to the Savior's command. Matt. 28:19, 20.

In apostolic times those who had the gift of tongues would sometimes speak in some language which the congregation in general did not understand. In such cases another who possessed the gift of interpreting tongues, I Cor. 12:10, would interpret what was being said unto the congregation.

If there chanced to be present one or more unbelievers who understood the language that was being spoken through the Spirit, they could testify to the genuineness of the miracle, and thus the faith of Christ was confirmed in the minds of the unbelievers.

Some of the brethren at Corinth sometimes used the gift of tongues to speak in languages that the church could not understand when there was no one present who had the gift to interpret what they were saying. This was the abuse of the gifts Paul wrote against in I Cor. 14. He commanded, "If any man speak in an unknown tongue, let it be by two, or at the most by three, and that by courses and let one interpret. But if there be no interpreter, let him keep silence in the church; and let him speak to himself, and to God."—Verses 27, 28.

W. G. S.

William G. Schell, "Questions Answered." *Gospel Trumpet* Vol. 16 No 39, Oct. 1, 1896, Page 2.

A Deceptive Fraud.
G. Tufts, Jr

Ever since I started out in this life of faith, I have never limited the power of God, and my favorite stronghold has been Jn. 10:35. It is impossible for the scriptures to be broken, and God has led me in a marvelous way to trust him for all things. Praise his name! I have always contended for, and believed that in the church of God to-day would be manifested the same gifts as were manifested in the morning dispensation, among which was the gift of tongues.

My soul was stirred over a year ago when I read in several faith and popular religious papers telling of one, Miss Jennie Glassy, who had received the gift of tongues and was speaking very plainly several African dialects, and she was on her way to Africa in company with a Mr. and Mrs. Black. Oh, how I longed to see her, for the joy of my life is to meet a man or woman who has real Bible faith. When I arrived in Liverpool, England, in company with Bros. Rupert and Croasdell I went to call on Miss Glassy. When I saw Miss Glassy I shall never forget the awful feeling of disappointment and surprise that came over me. She was a young girl of about eighteen, and was the most dirty, filthy, slovenly looking girl I ever saw, even in the slums of Chicago. All her front teeth were out, and a wild, idiotic, Satanic expression gleamed from her eyes. We tried to converse with her about her gift of tongues, and we were evaded in every question we asked. However, by very close questioning, Mrs. Black told us that no one had ever recognized a single sentence that Miss Glassy had ever pretended to speak, and we also found out that she had been tested by every African sailor that came into Liverpool on ships. We all left much disappointed.

After I arrived in India I read a long article in the Bombay Guardian, written by Mrs. Black, stating their sore poverty and also relating how Miss Glassy had the gift of tongues, and had also received in one night a full set of new, beautiful teeth; also that she had the gift of music, and that God had taught her how to do all kinds of fancy work. I was much surprised again, at this statement, and when I returned to England I again investigated the case, and found that it was all a lie. She had grown no teeth whatever since she had lost her old ones, no one had ever heard of her musical talent or seen any of her fancy work, and even these things were confessed as truth by the very family. So, dear readers of the TRUMPET, it is only another one of the frauds in these last days.

I feel clear in exposing this case, it has spread so broadcast in America, and is calling the sympathy of the people who are sending them means. But, praise God, dear brethren, there never was a real genuine but what the Devil tried to counterfeit the same. I fully believe that among the signs that will follow God's true children is the gift of tongues, but just before God gives it to any of us, the Devil will try to disgust and discourage us and try to reproach the truth by bringing in, these deceptive frauds.

G. Tufts, Jr.

G. Tufts, Jr. "A Deceptive Fraud," *The Gospel Trumpet* Vol. 18 No. 03 (January 20, 1898).

The Baptism of Fire.
By James M'Creary.

WE feel that the Lord would have us sound a note of warning in regard to a doctrine which is being very extensively preached among professed holiness people, called the baptism of fire. Its advocates teach it as a work subsequent to sanctification, some claiming to have received it years after sanctification. We have read about all that has been written in favor of this experience and can conscientiously say that we believe it to be a delusion of the Devil. Those who teach such things are known to reject such portions of the word of God as teach the unity of God's people, as Jn. 17:21-23; 10:16, etc. Also part of the ordinances—baptism, and washing of the saints' feet. The Word says that Jesus gives the Holy Ghost to them that obey him. Acts 5:32. Therefore those who are living in disobedience to any known command of God do not have God's Holy Spirit, and those who reject a part of God's word and still persist in making a profession, make themselves a prey for false teachers and delusions of the Devil. See 2 Thess. 2:9-12. They also bring themselves under the wrath of God. Rom. 1:18; 2:8.

We do not believe that God will leave any honest soul to be deceived by this delusion. Many honest souls have been consecrating for this "baptism of fire," but they did not get it, because God would not allow them to be deceived. But some who are not willing to measure up to the word of God do really get this fiery manifestation. Now why is it? Simply this: if they ever were sanctified, they lost this experience through error or disobedience, and feeling their lack and emptiness, and not being willing to humble themselves and repent, the Devil has taken advantage of them and they are like Nadab and Abihu who put strange fire in their censer and offered it before the Lord. Lev. 10:1, 2. And if they do not repent and get the spirit of obedience their fate will be the same.

The principle text they use in teaching this doctrine is Matt. 3:11, last clause. "He shall baptize you with the Holy Ghost and with fire." They fail to see that the fire is the means used in the work of the cleansing and that the Holy Ghost is the person doing the work; but separate the two and make his work of no effect. The spiritual-minded will see at once that it is not literal fire that is meant, but in symbol or figure just as fire is a cleansing or purifying element, so is the word of God as the Spirit applies it to the soul in its quickening and cleansing power; and as the soul takes hold of it and believes it and obeys, it is purified. "Seeing ye have purified your souls in obeying the truth through the Spirit."—1 Pet. 1:22. "Is not my word like as a fire?"—Jer. 23:29.

"And there appeared unto them cloven tongues like as of fire, and it sat upon each of them, and they were all filled with the Holy Ghost and began to speak with other tongues, as the Spirit gave them utterance."— Acts 2:3, 4.

"Cloven tongues" signifies different languages, and these different kinds of languages came to them and they were enabled to speak to all the foreigners who dwelt in Jerusalem in their own language of the wonderful works of God. Acts 2:11. And as the word of God went forth as a living fire, and men and women were melted down to repentance by it, there were about three thousand souls saved that day. Praise the Lord!

Our God has the same wonderful gifts in store for those who will humble themselves before him. 1 Pet. 5:6; I Cor. 12:7-12. We feel especially led to ask God's people everywhere to pray for the manifestation of the gift of tongues as it was in the church in the morning light. Mark 16:17; I Cor. 12:10, 28. Others besides the apostles received this precious gift. Why should we not have it in the church to-day? Acts 10:46; 19:6.

James M'Creary. *The Gospel Trumpet* Vol. 18 No. 6, February 10, 1898, pp. 5-6.

News From the Field.
J. H. Rupert

With pleasure we write to inform you of our whereabouts and how the dear Lord is prospering our souls in the kingdom of light and truth. We arrived in America Dec. 18, 1897 much worn out in body, but after a few weeks' rest the dear Lord strengthened us, and we are now in the battle again with victory for Jesus. One of our objects in coming to this country is to raise money to purchase a printing-press to be used in foreign fields for the publication of the truth, which is so much needed. Dear ones, we are interested in the work of the Lord. We have labored almost five years in foreign lands as missionaries, and space will not permit and time would fail me to tell you of the many trials and difficulties we were obliged to encounter because we were short of means to carry on the work. So after those years of testing and suffering the dear Lord has said to us, It is enough; go tell your brethren of your needs on this line, and of the thousands of poor little children who are dying daily of hunger and cold through sin, and the thousands of men and women going down to a sinner's hell daily for the want of the bread of life. Therefore we are going to make a missionary tour through part of this country. Those who wish us to visit them in this capacity can write us at Mariasville, Pa.

J. H. Rupert and Wife.

Note.—I wish to say in regard to the article in the TRUMPET of Jan. 20, written by Bro. Tufts relating to a Miss Glassy of Liverpool, England, who claims to have the gift of tongues and so forth, I am a witness to what Bro. Tufts said, and I am informed that some in this country have been duped by her deception and are still loth to believe what Bro. Tufts has written. So let me warn you again that the said Miss Glassy is a rank deception, although I must say I feel a pity for the poor deluded creature, as she is not accountable, nor to be blamed for her hypocrisy as much as those who are with her, who are using her as a sort of Jumbo to their menagerie, and publishing over the world the lie of the Devil to court the sympathies of good-intending people.

Let me say, I conversed with the said Miss Glassy for a few moments, and the subject of tongues was brought up (in which I am a believer). It seemed expedient for her to withdraw from the room and leave it all in the hands of her managers to further explain. They claimed that the girl while under the spirit had spoken words in a foreign tongue. So said a Sister Saylor. Miss Glassy knew nothing of it, nor could she remember anything she said. Mr. Black of Utica, Pa., one of her managers claims that when Miss Glassy is under the Spirit about her work, he can go out and purchase just what she wants, although he cannot understand what she says. The Spirit, he says directs him to get the very things she desired. You see the trick. Next Mr. Black will appear on the carpet as an interpreter of tongues. Let me say they are all a poor lot of deceivers, who are imposing on the public. Yours in defense of the truth,
J. H. Rupert.

J. H. Rupert. *The Gospel Trumpet* Vol. 18 No. 6, February 10, 1898, p. 6.

The Gift of Tongues.
By J. W. Byers.

"FOR to one is given by the Spirit the word of wisdom; to another the word of knowledge by the same Spirit; to another faith by the same Spirit; to another the gifts of healing by the same Spirit; to another the working of miracles; to another discerning of spirits; to another divers kinds of tongues; to another the interpretation of tongues."-1 Cor. 12:8-10. "And God hath set some in the church, first apostles, secondarily prophets, thirdly teachers, after that miracles, then gifts of healings, helps, governments, diversities of tongues. . . . Have all the gifts of healing? do all speak with tongues? do all interpret?"— Verses 28, 30.

These scriptures teach us that the gift of tongues is among those that God set in the primitive church. It was recognized by the apostle as in use at the time of the writing of his epistle, twenty-six years after the Pentecostal establishment of the church. In 1 Cor. 14:18 he acknowledges that he himself speaks with tongues more than they all. The quoted text shows us that not every member of the body of Christ has the gift of tongues. The Holy Spirit may speak with tongues through any one, at times, where such divine manifestation can be for the glory of God; but the gift of tongues is evidently a special endowment of the Spirit in the church to such as can make use of the same in God's appointed manner. The common use of this gift was by those who were endowed with it. But there were special manifestations of tongues upon occasions of unusual seasons of blessing, and important events in the history of the church; such as, the day of Pentecost, the opening of the door of salvation to the Gentiles, and the beginning of the gospel at Ephesus. Acts 2:4; 10:46; 19:6. Upon these phenomenal occasions they spake with tongues regardless of any special or permanent endowment of the gift, but there were evidently those in the church later who possessed this endowment.

TONGUES ARE INTELLIGENT LAN-GUAGES.

They may be the language of angels (1 Cor. 13:1), but whether celestial or terrestrial, they are the expressions of God's wonderful work of redemption in other languages from those commonly in use by the worshipers assembled at the time of such manifestations. "And they were all filled with the Holy Ghost, and began to speak with other tongues, as the Spirit gave them utterance. And there were dwelling at Jerusalem Jews, devout men out of every nation under heaven. Now when this was noised abroad, the multitude came together, and were confounded, because that every man heard them speak in his own language. And they were all amazed and marveled, saying one to another, Behold, are not all these which speak Galilean? and how hear we every man in his own tongue, wherein we were born? Parthians and Medes, . . Cretes, and Arabians, we do hear them speak in our tongues the wonderful works of God."—Acts 2:4-11.

Their use at Pentecost was evidently for a twofold purpose: 1st. To show forth the wonderful works of God and his power. 2d. To the more rapidly publish the gospel to all nations in all languages. Those devout men of God who heard these fire-baptized men of Galilee speak the wonderful works of God in their own language would not be slow to communicate the news and nature of this marvelous event to those of their own tongue and nation. It would be a reasonable conclusion that in this manner the gospel was introduced with Pentecostal energy to every nation under heaven. This divine-manifestation of languages affected two different classes of hearers in two different ways. These devout and believing Jews were filled with astonishment, and were convinced that this was an unmistakable evidence of the presence and power of God, while others who were unbelievers mocked, and said, "These men are full of new wine."—Acts 2:11-13.

THE USE OF TONGUES IN THE CHURCH.

Like the use of all the other gifts of the Holy Spirit, this one would be unprofitable without the richer qualification and grace of charity. The apostle takes special care to instruct the church at Corinth in the proper use of this gift, to which the greater portion of the fourteenth chapter is devoted. The only object of their use is expressed in these words: "Let all things be done unto edifying."—Ver. 26. "If any man speak in an unknown tongue, let it be by two, or at the most by three, and that by course; and let one interpret. But if there be no interpreter, let him keep silence in the church; and let him speak to himself, and to God."—Verses 27-28.

This clearly teaches us that the ordinary use of tongues in the church is different from the special occasion of their use at Pentecost. In that case there was no interpretation needed, for of the different nationalities represented there, each understood their own language; but the ordinary use of this gift required interpretation in order that the church might be edified. Therefore this gift by itself was not considered profitable, and in comparison with the gift of prophecy it was inferior. "He that speaketh in an unknown tongue edifieth himself; but he that prophesieth edifieth the church. I would that ye all spake with tongues, but rather that ye prophesied; for greater is he that prophesieth than he that speaketh with tongues, except he interpret, that the church may receive edifying." —Verses 4-5.

The apostle does not ignore this gift of tongues, by any means, but plainly teaches its proper place and use in the congregation. It no doubt was a source of edification when accompanied by the gift of the interpretation of tongues. It is also evident that it was to no profit to the unbelievers in the congregation, but was simply a sign of God's mysteries. "In the law it is written, With men of other tongues and other lips will I speak unto this people; and yet for all that will they not hear me, saith the Lord. Wherefore tongues are for a sign, not to them that believe, but to them that believe not: but prophesying serveth not for them that believe not, but for them which believe. If therefore the whole church be come together into one place, and all speak with tongues, and there come in those that are unlearned, or unbelievers, will they not say that ye are mad?"— Verses 21-23. The unlearned and unbelievers, therefore, could not be convicted by the use of this gift. It would only be to them a mystery and curiosity, yet at the same time a sign of divine manifestation; but if instead of tongues, the church would prophesy, the sinner would be convinced of his sins, and judged by his own conscience, and would fall down upon his face and worship God. Verses 24-25.

THE PROMISE IN MARK 16:17-18.

"And these signs shall follow them that believe: In my name shall they cast out devils; they shall speak with new tongues; they shall take up serpents; and if they drink any deadly thing, it shall not hurt them; they shall lay hands on the sick, and they shall recover." These promises were given in the commission to preach the gospel to every creature in all the world. The promise that they that believe shall speak with new tongues, was to be made use of in this commission, by those who would come into contact with all languages of the different nations. It was evident that this was the mind of Christ with reference to this promise, and that by faith the divinely appointed missionaries would be able to speak the language of the people to whom they were sent.

This, no doubt, is why the apostle Paul said in 1 Cor. 14:18, "I thank my God, I speak with tongues more than ye all." Being out in the missionary field perhaps more than any other apostle, he had more occasion to speak in other languages. There is no reason why we cannot do the same to-day. It has been done in various parts of the world in recent years. William Taylor, the African missionary, tells of a lady who began preaching to the natives through an interpreter. A few months later he passed through that same place and found the same lady speaking the native language fluently. She had received the miraculous power to preach the gospel to that people in their own tongue.

It is reasonable that this could be instantaneously received, as it was done at Pentecost; while it would also be a miraculous manifestation of God's power, if a foreign language were mastered in a few months, as has been done in different parts of the world. And now as the clear light of apostolic glory and power is shining forth in all the fullness of the gospel, there should be the perfect manifestation of all the gifts of the Spirit in every respect. The missionaries whom God sends to the foreign fields will be able to speak with new tongues; if not always by an instantaneous manifestation of this power, all should at least exercise definite faith for it, and thereby master the difficulties of the language with much more ease, and much less time than could be done otherwise; for the promise is to them, that believe.

The fulfilling of this promise would be the means of spreading the gospel with marvelous rapidity, and together with the apostolic power in every other respect, the church would be able to accomplish more in one year of such missionary work than has been realized in fifty years through the feeble efforts of human evangelization.

While there may have been as yet no clear modern cases of the manifestation of the gift of tongues in the church as mentioned in 1 Cor. 12, and the use of the same in public worship, mentioned in chapter 14, there is no reason why these manifestations should not be brought into effect for the glory of God, in his own manner and time. There have been instances where fanaticism has been practiced; under the pretext of the gift of tongues. But the same can be said of the gifts of healing, or of the grace of sanctification. All inconsistencies which have, by some, been unwisely, and by others, maliciously perpetuated, must not be permitted to stand in the way of the progress of the church of God in the possession and attainments to all the spiritual gifts and graces.

With true humility of heart, and a continual willingness to walk in all the light of the Spirit and Word of God, there is no fear of being led into error in these things. God will qualify his faithful instruments for any gift he may deem proper to bestow. It has been thought by some that the manifestation of tongues always accompanies the baptism of the Holy Spirit as it did at Pentecost, but this is not the case. In Acts 4:31 and 8:17 the baptism of the Spirit was received without any such manifestation. The Holy Spirit himself is a gift, and to possess him as the abiding Comforter and power must be the continual object of every soul. God has ordained that with him there shall be all the manifestations through the individual members of the body of Christ that can profit and edify the same to his own honor and glory.

J.W. Byers, "The Gift of Tongues" *The Gospel Trumpet* Volume 28. No. 25 (June 23, 1898): 1-2.

Reprinted

J. W. Byers, "The Gift of Tongues," *The Gospel Trumpet* Vol. 26 No. 10 (March 8, 1906): 2-3.

These Signs Shall Follow.
The Gospel Trumpet.

The following questions and answers were published in a Dunkard paper entitled *The Gospel Messenger.*

> In Mark 16:17, 18 we read of the
> signs following them that believe—
> casting out devils, speaking with new
> tongues, taking up serpents, drinking
> deadly poison, and healing the sick. Can
> the followers of Christ now do these
> things, or have they lost the power? Can
> a body of people be the true church and
> yet not have these signs to follow? A. C.

These signs or miracles, followed the apostles and
others, until the New Testament revelation was fully
established, then they ceased, not any more being a necessity in order to demonstrate the divine order of
things. Now the New Testament is the authority, and in
that we find ample proof that these signs did follow
those who believed, and that should settle the authenticity of the Christian religion in our minds. As for speaking with divers tongues, or drinking deadly poison, etc.,
not one of those contending for modern miracles can, or
will attempt to do anything of the kind, and so long as
they will not and can not practice what they preach, in
this particular, we think their claims entitled to but little
consideration

It only requires the reading of the foregoing answer
and comparing the same with the word of God to con-

vince a person that the two do not harmonize. It is evident that the writer of that answer has not had his understanding opened to the scripture. If his answer be true, then we may just as well throw away the New Testament as far as it pertains to our salvation in these days, and consider it of no more value to us than a last year's almanac or some history of the past ages. But we are glad to know that such is not the case. In Mark 16:16 are the words of Jesus wherein he gives an account of something else that will take place through the preaching of the word. He says, "He that believeth and is baptized shall be saved; but he that believeth not shall be damned." According to this "Messenger's" interpretation of the Word we would conclude that the "New Testament revelation is fully established." Therefore people will not believe and be baptized, nor be saved.

As it is only the next verse that quotes the words given above, which says, "And these signs shall follow them that believe," we find these signs are manifest among God's believing children, not only in these days, but they were when Christ was here on earth. The same signs followed believers during the days of the apostles, and in the early church after the crucifixion of Christ. The same was continued until the church went into apostasy. History gives us instances of these signs following God's believing children through various centuries afterwards. We are thankful to know that we are still living in the gospel dispensation, in the time when the clear light of the gospel is to shine forth as it did in the morning time of this era. As we read the words of the prophet in Zech. 14:7, where it says, "But it shall come to pass that at evening time it shall be light," our hearts are thrilled with joy to know that the time is now here, that Zion is putting on her strength, and the Lord is delivering his people out of the strongholds of Babylon. We are living in the time when not only one of these signs follow, but when all are manifest.

THE SIGNS DO FOLLOW.

"And these signs shall follow them that believe: In my name shall they cast out devils; they shall speak with new tongues; they shall take up serpents; and if they drink any deadly thing, it shall not hurt them; they shall lay hands on the sick, and they shall recover."— Mark 16:17, 18. The word of God does not say that these signs shall follow them that believe "until the New Testament revelation was fully established," and then cease. Our readers have frequently read and heard testimonies on these lines. We have personally witnessed many cases where devils were cast out. Ofttimes the manifestations were so clear that the whole congregation could not gainsay, but unbelievers and even skeptics acknowledged that such was the case and were caused to believe and yield themselves to the Lord, because of the manifestation of his power. We have heard testimonies from those who have spoken with new tongues, and many have been bitten by serpents, or drank deadly poison, and were delivered through faith in Jesus Christ. This does not mean that a person can intentionally take up poisonous reptiles and serpents, or drink deadly poison, and such like, and thereby tempt God. But if such should accidentally take place, or through compulsion, it is their privilege to exercise faith in Jesus Christ and be made whole.

"And they shall lay hands on the sick and they shall recover." This promise we have seen fulfilled thousands of times. Any one who would deny that these things are the privileges of believers in these days would deny the gifts of the Spirit, as spoken of in the 12th chapter of 1 Corinthians being in the church at the present time; would deny that Jas. 5:13-16 was for us, and claim that it was only for the people who lived in the days of the apostles. The Word there says: "Is any sick among you? let him call for the elders of the church; and let them pray over him, anointing him with oil in the name of the Lord: and the prayer of faith shall save the sick, and the Lord shall raise him up; and if he have committed sins, they shall be forgiven him. Confess your faults one to another and pray one for another, that ye may be healed."

According to the words of the editor of the *Messenger,* many no doubt would conclude that where the Word says, in John 3:16, "For God so loved the world, that he gave his only begotten Son, that whosoever believeth in him should not perish, but have everlasting life," it only means those who believed before the gospel was fully established. Such an idea reminds us of what Jesus said in Luke 8:12-14 concerning the sower. "Those by the wayside are they that hear; then cometh the Devil, and taketh away the word out of their hearts, lest they believe and be saved." When the Devil takes the word out of their hearts, truly they are faithless. The next verse says, "They on the rock are they, which when they hear, receive the word with joy; and these have no root, which for a while believe, and in time of temptation fall away." Some people do really have faith for a time, after they have accepted Christ; but not being fully determined to go through—"have no root," and only "for a while believe"—when temptations come they fall away. They are then among the faithless class described in the answer to the above questions.

Again, we read in the following verse, "And that which fell among thorns are they, which, when they have heard, go forth, and are choked with cares and riches and pleasures of this life, and bring no fruit to perfection." There are many people who start out with good intentions but allow the things of this world to lead them away from Christ, and thus they enter the list of the faithless. At one time Christ spoke to some whose faith was at a very low ebb, and said, "O fools, and slow of heart to believe all that the prophets have spoken!" In the last prayer that Jesus made, after he had prayed for his disciples, he then prayed for all them that believe through the words of the apostles, and said, "Neither pray I for these alone, but for them also which shall believe on me through their word; that they all may be one; as thou, Father, art in me, and I in thee, that they also may be one in us: that the world may believe that thou hast sent me."—John 17:20, 21. He did not mean by this that all the children of God should cease to believe on him, nor cease to be one, that the world may believe, but he meant that this should be true throughout the entire gospel dispensation. If we are believers, then we are the ones through whom this prayer is to be answered.

If so-called "Gospel Messengers," editors, and those claiming to teach the people the word of God would labor as hard to lift up the standard of Bible truths, teach people how to get a Bible experience, teach them the ways of salvation and their privileges through the word of Jesus Christ, and do it as earnestly as they try to do to the contrary, thus destroying the faith of the children of God and those seeking to know God, the world would soon be evangelized, and sinners would come earnestly seeking help through Jesus

Christ; Zion would be a praise in the earth, and the name of the Lord glorified, with the children of God earnestly contending for the faith once delivered.

The Gospel Trumpet. "These Signs Shall Follow." *Gospel Trumpet*. Vol. 18 No. 48 (December 1, 1898): 8.

The Gifts of the Spirit.
Gospel Trumpet.

Taberville, Mo., Jan. 20.

Dear Editor: Please give me an explanation of 1 Cor. 12:4-11. I have noticed in the Trumpet that the Church of God teaches the gifts and power of God today as it was in the days of the apostles. Does any one possess the gift of tongues and interpretation of tongues as mentioned in the 10th verse? I have to meet many different opinions on the scripture in this place and especially with the Latter Day Saints. Your paper is a most valuable one and I am always glad to receive it.

Also please explain to the readers of the Trumpet concerning sending out anointed handkerchiefs and what the charge's are, or if there are any charges made except for the cost of the handkerchief. It has been reported that you charge fifty cents for them; also tell us how much money you would require to be sent to you and you purchase the handkerchief and send it. Please answer these questions, for anything that can be brought up against the church of God is brought up. Your sanctified brother,

L. J. Bishop.

ANS. The scriptures referred to read follows; "Now there are diversities of gifts, but the same Spirit. And there are differences of administrations, but the same Lord. And there are diversities of operations, but it is the same God which worketh all in all. But the manifestation of the Spirit is given to every man to profit withal. For to one is given by the Spirit the word of wisdom; to another the word of knowledge by the same Spirit; to another faith by the same Spirit; to another the gifts of healing by the same Spirit; to another the working of miracles; to another prophecy; to another discerning of spirits; to another divers kinds of tongues; to another the interpretation of tongues: but all these worketh that one and the selfsame Spirit, dividing to every man severally as he will."

There could be many pages written concerning these verses of scripture; however, the scripture explains itself in these verses. All these gifts are in the Holy Spirit and he bestows them upon whomsoever he will, for the edification and benefit of the church. A person may have one or more of them, as he can use them to the glory of God. Different persons having different gifts will not make a confliction in the church of God, as these are given by the same Spirit. There are different ways in which the Spirit of God works for the benefit of the children of God and those who are seeking to know his will. There are different administrations and manifestations. One person when filled to overflowing with the Spirit at God may leap and shout, another may laugh, another weep, while some one else sits in quietude, yet all are filled with the peace and glory of God.

As to people having the gift of tongues and interpretation of tongues, the Spirit still manifests itself in that way in these days. Just to what extent it is manifested in a similar manner as it was on the day of Pentecost, we are unable to say.

Two or three years ago, while at the camp-meeting at Grand Junction, Mich., we met a brother who claimed that while in prayer one day the Lord gave him the gift of the Holland language. He had moved to a community of Holland people and was unable to speak their language and they were unable to understand either the English or German, which he spoke. He stated that one day while communing with the Lord he felt impressed to ask the Lord to give him that language, that he might be a help to those people. He at once procured a Holland Bible and found that he was enabled to read it readily, and not only read it but translate and speak the language, and also was able at once to write it. He sat down and wrote a letter to the Holland minister. After talking with him a while I asked him if he would read from his Holland Testament, which he did. Then I had him interpret the same into the English language. His wife verified his statements. After testing him to my satisfaction I requested him to be in the meeting that day and bring his Bible. While reading from Mark 16:16 I told the people that there was a man present who claimed the Lord had given him the gift of tongues. And I asked him to rise and read that passage in the Holland language. He did so, and then he was asked to interpret it, which he did. The audience was then asked to select any scripture and have him interpret it. Then selections were made, and the name of the Lord was glorified.

I informed the audience that he could also write the Holland language. A minister in the congregation who knew nothing of our former conversation arose and stated that he was the man to whom the brother had written soon after receiving the gift, and that it was well written and the composition was good.

At another time I was traveling with a brother who could only speak English and he was called upon to take charge of a service among the Germans, who were unable to understand the English language. Before going he stated that he could do nothing more than open his mouth and have the Lord fill it with German, and it was marvelous, the aid that he received that night by the Holy Spirit. And those Germans who were present were greatly edified. Doubtless many brethren may have witnessed greater things on these lines that what I have been privileged to witness. Doubtless as the church advances in the knowledge of the truth there will be greater manifestations on this line.

Concerning the sending of anointed handkerchiefs, there are no apologies to make on this line. There is only one reference to anything of the kind in the Bible, and that is Acts 19:11, 12—"And God wrought special miracles by the hands of Paul: so that from his body were brought unto the sick, handkerchiefs or aprons, and the diseases departed from them, and the evil spirits went out of them." There is no statement as to whether Paul anointed the handkerchief, neither do we read that he laid on hands. Doubtless Paul did with them as he would have done to the sick had they been present. There were many sick folk throughout the country and some at such a distance that Paul was doubtless unable to visit them, as so much of his time was occupied by preaching the gospel, and those who could not come had the handkerchiefs from Paul, and the Word says that the diseases departed from them and those who were possessed with evil spirits were delivered. We are glad to know that the same Holy Spirit who worked through Paul in that way will still manifest his power in a similar manner. There are many sick people living in isolated places, away from any elders or those who believe in divine healing, who are in this way enabled to grasp the promises and receive the healing touch. We have read of some who claim to be children of God and yet object to the sending of handkerchiefs. Such people have but little pity for the suffering. There are others who object to the laying on of hands and anointing a handkerchief, because it is not plainly stated in connection with this, that Paul laid his hands upon the handkerchief and anointed it with oil. However, there is more in the word of God in favor of it than against it. In fact there is nothing against doing the same. Furthermore, it says that these miracles were wrought by the hands of Paul, and it is evident that Paul anointed the sick and laid hands upon them. People can go to extremes and oppose such until their spirituality runs at a very low ebb. There are some that oppose the anointing of oil and laying of hands upon the sick at the same time, because there is no place in the Bible where it speaks of both being done at the same time. However, in the fifth chapter of James the sick are instructed to be anointed with oil. In the last chapter of Mark it says, the sick shall have hands laid upon them. In the sixth chapter of Mark we read that the apostles "anointed with oil many that were sick and healed them." In the twenty-eighth chapter of Acts we read that Paul laid hands on the sick; therefore by the reading of these scriptures we can see that it is proper to do one or both.

As to charging for the sending of handkerchiefs, we have never made any charge. The only expense is enough to purchase a handkerchief and pay return postage. This is always left for the one to decide who sends for it. If the handkerchief is sent by the one who is sick or by their friends, there is no added expense except the necessary return postage. This is not a money-making affair, and the one who would undertake it as such would soon find himself shorn of the power of God the same as those who oppose the working of the Spirit of God on these lines.

Gospel Trumpet. *The Gospel Trumpet*. Vol. 22 No. 6 (Feb. 6, 1902): 4.

The Gifts of Tongues.
By Jennie C. Rutty.

GOD'S ways are not our ways, nor his thoughts our thoughts, therefore it is necessary that we should not lean to our own understanding, but depend upon God to lead us into his way of truth. Several years ago a company of religious people at Topeka, Kans., claimed to possess the gift of tongues, and chattered an incomprehensible jargon that was claimed to be first one language and then another, but not understood by those naturally speaking the language claimed. For instance when French was claimed, the French-speaking people could not understand it, and when Swedish was claimed the Swedes could not understand it. Neither could the interpretation be made by any one. This people did not obey the whole word of God, were not in love and unity with God's true children, and manifested a spirit contrary to the Spirit of Christ in various ways, thus proving that what they claimed as the gift of tongues was a counterfeit.

While studying this pretension, my soul was stirred concerning the true gift of tongues as promised to the church of God, and a careful study of God's word concerning the same has brought out some points that will do us good to consider prayerfully. In 1 Cor. 12:7-12 we are told that "the manifestation of the Spirit is given to every man to profit withal. For to one is given, by the Spirit the word of wisdom, to another the word of knowledge by the same Spirit; to another faith by the same Spirit; to another the gifts of healing by the same Spirit; to another the working of miracles; to another prophecy; to another discerning of spirits; to another divers kinds of tongues; to another the interpretation of tongues; but all these worketh that one and the self same Spirit, dividing to every man severally as he will."

From the seventh verse we learn that every manifestation of the Spirit in bestowing these spiritual gifts is for profit, therefore, is needed in the church. Bringing this thought into connection with the gift of tongues we must observe that it is needed in the church today just as much as when placed there by infinite wisdom in its organization on the day of Pentecost. Its use is not that which belongs to any one of the other gifts. It is not to take the place of the gift of prophecy for the edifying of the church, but in 1 Cor. 14:2, we may see what its profit is: "He that speaketh in an unknown tongue speaketh not unto men, but unto God, for no man understandeth him: howbeit in the Spirit he speaketh mysteries." 4th verse, "He that speaketh in an unknown tongue edifieth himself." Here we observe the gift is a source of profit between the giver and receiver as spiritual mysteries are revealed and the receiver is benefited. There is one precious thought right here especially needful of expression. Whatever is a means of edifying one member in the church is a profit to the whole church that much, for we are members one of another. But to give a greater profit to the entire church the gift of interpretation of tongues is given: "'would that ye all spake with tongues, but rather that ye prophesied: for greater is he that prophesieth than he that speaketh with tongues, except he interpret, that the church may receive edifying." Verse 5. "Even so ye, forasmuch as ye are zealous of spiritual gifts, seek that ye may excel to the edifying of the church. Wherefore let him that speaketh in an unknown tongue, pray that he may interpret." Verses 12, 13.

From a careful study of this chapter we see that the gift of tongues was not given as a preparation to go to some foreign land; but to be used in the congregation of the saints where it was not understood, as there was need of the gift of interpretation to bring it to their understanding that they might be edified, thereby. Also, "to others divers kinds of tongues" shows that to one person was given various and numerous tongues, for each of which was an interpretation. Paul said, "I spake with tongues more than ye all," and he praised God for the great gift; yet, was so desirous of assisting others in the church that he would rather speak five words with his understanding for their edification, than ten thousand in an unknown tongue. But because it does not serve equally with the gift of prophecy shall it be discarded from among us? Nay, but we will accord it the place and honor given by the Holy Spirit. "In the law it is written, With men of other tongues and other lips will I speak to this people: and yet for all that will they not hear me, saith the Lord. Wherefore tongues are for a sign, not to them that believe, but to them that believe not; but prophesying serveth not for them that believe not, but for them that believe." Verses 21, 22.

God had promised thousands of years before the Holy Ghost was given that a marvelous, glorious, powerful day of time was to come in the end of the world. One of the glorious things that should come to pass was that he would speak to the people with men of other tongues—that is, that men naturally able to speak but one language should be so anointed by the Holy Spirit as to speak in tongues before unknown to themselves, as it came to pass on the day of Pentecost when they who were filled with the Holy Ghost spake with other tongues as the Spirit gave them utterance. And when this was noised abroad the multitude came together and were astonished to hear Galileans speaking all their different languages and questioned, "What meaneth this?" While some "mocking said, These men are full of new wine." This gave Peter the opportunity to tell them boldly of the great blessing of God in pouring upon his people the Holy Spirit. And many souls were saved.

Here is given us the proper use of the great gifts of God. The people attracted by the power of God manifested in a way to arouse hearts questioning for truth; and then this questioning answered by one anointed of the Spirit to speak the wisdom of God. Some will say: "We see the need of it at that time, but it is different now." Dear saints, will you use the same argument against the gift of tongues that the sectarians have used concerning the other gifts of the Spirit? Nay, we trow not, lest indeed you fail of your high calling. One of the signs that is to follow those who believe is that "they shall speak with new tongues." Mark 16:17. And now, dearly beloved children of God, who serve God in all humility of mind, does this sign—Gift of tongues— abide in our midst to-day? If not, why not? Have we been taught to seek for it by the ministry? Have they been ensamples to the flock? Have we all the humility and consecration to bear more persecution and be a more separate people? "I would that ye all spake with tongues." "Wherefore, brethren, covet to prophesy, and forbid not to speak with tongues." 1 Cor. 14:39.

Jennie C. Rutty. *The Gospel Trumpet* Vol. 22. No. 38 (September 18, 1902): 3.

The Gift of Tongues.
By J. E. Forrest.

TO WHOM GIVEN, AND WHY, THE USE OF THEM, ETC., ETC.

As it is a trick of the devil to deceive souls by mis-quoting and misapplying the scriptures in various ways, it seemeth good that something be said regarding the gift of tongues. Some vainly suppose that the gift of tongues played out with the first apostles, and even teach that the baptism of the Holy Ghost which they received was a special one only adapted to that special occasion and no other. Now we would be without anything to say were it not for the plain Word of God which is given for our instruction in righteousness. The truth is its own defense, therefore, we will hear it speak for itself.

"And when the day of Pentecost was fully come, they were all with one accord in one place. And suddenly there came a sound from heaven as of a rushing mighty wind, and it filled all the house where they were sitting. And there appeared unto them cloven tongues like as of fire, and it sat upon each of them. And they were all filled with the Holy Ghost, and began to speak with other tongues, as the Spirit gave them utterance. And there were dwelling at Jerusalem Jews, devout men out of every nation under heaven. Now when this was noised abroad, the multitude came together, and were confounded, because that every man heard them speak in his own language. And they were all amazed and marveled, saying one to another, Behold, are not all these which speak Galileans? And how hear we every

man in our own tongue, wherein we were born? Parthians, and Medes, and Elamites, and the dwellers in Mesopotamia, and in Judea, and Cappadocia, in Pontus, and
Asia, Phrygia, and Pamphylia, in Egypt, and in the parts
of Lybia about Cyrene, and strangers of Rome, Jews
and proselytes, Cretes, and Arabians, we do hear them
speak in our tongues the wonderful works of God."
Acts 2:1-11.

From the foregoing account we easily learn that together with the pouring out of the Holy Ghost upon that
assembly of "about one hundred and twenty men and
women" (See chap. 1:13-15) was given the gift of
tongues so that every man heard them speak in his own
language wherein he was born. Now can we tell why
they received and spoke in the different languages?
Well, in the first place Jesus had promised the Holy
Ghost and had commissioned them to preach the gospel
to every creature, "beginning at Jerusalem." See Matt.
28:18-20; Luke 24:47-48. Now since the gospel must
be preached to them, it was needful that the preachers
be qualified to preach it so that they might understand
it. The account mentions at least sixteen different languages which were spoken there in Jerusalem at that
time, hence, the consistency of them being endued with
the gift of tongues on that occasion.

People that are unsaved scarcely get interested
enough in their soul's welfare to learn other languages
for the purpose of hearing the gospel preached to them.
The Lord God is the author and finisher of the gospel,
and all the preparation that is necessary that the world
may hear the good news of salvation the Lord is making
himself. He does not ask men to do anything but accept
it. The Lord God is continually preparing men and
women to preach the gospel, as many as will let him of

those whom he can use, yes, to preach it in the different languages needful. But mark you, men do not preach the gospel in English to those who speak only French. It would be folly. And God does not bestow the gift of tongues on preachers who speak English, for the purpose of preaching to English speaking people. When God promised the Holy Ghost he never promised that a great noise, or a windstorm, or cloven tongues, as of fire, would accompany its descension. Of course we read that such did occur on Pentecost, but that does not warrant that it is always to be the case. The Holy Ghost was promised to all believers, but the gift of tongues was not specified. Because we (Americans) do not speak the Spanish, German, and other foreign languages, is no warrant that we have not received the gift of the Holy Ghost. If God should send me to preach to the French nation while as yet I could not speak that language I would expect him to give me that speech through the Holy Spirit. But since he has not made choice of me for that purpose, I do not expect to receive the gift, for if I had it I would be unable to exercise it, there being no French in the immediate territory in which I live, but yet more English than I can possibly reach; hence, the inconsistency of the gift of tongues in my own case.

It is recorded in Acts 10:46 that Cornelius and his kindred spake with tongues immediately after the Holy Ghost fell upon them. It is also recorded in Acts 19:6 that the twelve upon whom Paul laid hands for the reception of the Holy Ghost spake with tongues and prophesied. Paul spake various languages more than the Corinthians. 1 Cor. 14:18.

The gift of tongues is not the Holy Ghost itself. Some pretend that they can not separate the two. We will look into God's Word again for instruction. Speaking with tongues as the apostles and others did in the early church, is a gift of the Spirit. "Now concerning spiritual gifts, brethren, I would not have you ignorant. . . . Now there are diversities of gifts, but the same Spirit. And there are differences of administrations, but the same Lord. And there are diversities of operations, but it is the same God which worketh all in all. But the manifestation of the Spirit is given to every man to profit withal." 1 Cor. 12:1-7. Here is the secret that some have not seen into. There is profit attached to the bestowing of the gift of tongues upon men. "And to each is given the manifestation of the Spirit for the benefit of all." *Emphatic Diaglott.* 1 Cor. 12:7. If there is no benefit to be derived from the gift of tongues why expect it "But," says one, "you speak with tongues and I will believe that you have the Holy Ghost." No, you would not. Your heart is so deceitful that it would not allow you to believe. God never proposed to force men into faith on such terms. There are too many other ways in which he may confirm his Word, and use his followers, than for him to resort to such whimsical ways to satisfy the selfish notions of man. The speaking in different tongues at Jerusalem was not given to make them believe, but to make them hear. Those who wait for signs before they believe run a great risk. Jesus said: "An evil and adulterous generation seeketh after a sign." God's promises are made to those who believe his Word, and his blessings are pronounced upon those who believe yet have not seen. Most of us can believe what we see without real Bible faith. Those who can not believe only that which they see are of the "no faith" sort indeed.

We have noticed that the "manifestation of the Spirit is given to every man to profit withal," "for the benefit of all." It does not matter what gift or gifts God bestows upon man, he does it only when it is profitable or beneficial to do so. He does not bestow gifts in vain. "For to one is given by the Spirit the word of wisdom [a very needful gift indeed. God has commanded us to be wise as serpents]; to another the word of knowledge by the same Spirit; to another faith by the same Spirit; to another the gifts of healing by the same Spirit; to another the working of miracles; to another prophecy; to another discerning of spirits; to another divers [various] kinds of tongues; to another the interpretation of tongues: But all these worketh that one and the self-same Spirit, dividing to every man severally as he will." 1 Cor. 12:8-11.

We have clearly seen from the above scripture that the various gifts are spiritual, and are given for profit, being given to one and another by the same Spirit just as he wills. "And God hath set some in the church, first apostles, secondarily prophets, thirdly teachers, after that miracles, then gifts of healings, helps, governments, *diversities* of *tongues.*" Now Paul asks the question: "Are all apostles? are all prophets? are all teachers? are all workers of miracles? have all the gifts of healing? *do all speak with tongues?*" Can you answer it? Who is so ignorant and unlearned in the Scriptures and of the mind of God that he can not see at a glance that the gift of tongues is only given in cases where the gospel needs to be preached in other languages, and there is no other way suitable to God save imparting the gift or rather he sees it more profitable to do so for the occasion, and that the gift of tongues does not accompany the pouring out of the Holy Ghost in any other case? People are met occasionally who demand us to perform some miracle so that they might be convinced that we are really what we claim to be, but such unreasonable demands are wicked and blasphemous.

Some demand us to speak with tongues, and yet they will not believe the truth in their own tongue, and I am sure it would be just as contrary to their wicked hearts in one language as in another, as it is just the same gospel truth in all languages. Others demand us to heal some person who is a cripple, or of some other incurable disease, probably referring to some one with whom they are acquainted, and say if they are healed they will then believe. The rich man (Luke 16) died in unbelief and went to hell, and he had a conversation with Abraham regarding his five brethren, which were yet alive, asking Abraham to send Lazarus back down there to warn them against that place of torment, but Abraham told him they had Moses and the prophets let them hear them. But the rich man said, Nay, but if one would go to them who had risen from the dead they would believe, however he was told that if they would not believe Moses, neither would they believe though one rose from the dead. It does not become necessary for us to perform miracles contrary to the Word of God for the purpose of convincing: [or trying to convince, I should say], wicked men and devils of the truth of the Bible or to establish or approve ourselves. The devil himself said to Jesus, "If thou be the Son of God, command that these stones be made bread," but his petition was not granted. The Son of God was not in a mission performing miracles to make devils believe that he was the Christ the anointed one. No, the devils all believe and tremble. Art thou more wicked than they? See James 2:19.

We read in Acts 8:5-17 about the gospel being preached in the city Samaria; that they received it, were baptized, and afterwards hands were laid on them and they received the Holy Ghost, but nothing is said about them speaking with tongues. Paul teaches us in 1 Cor. 14, that the gift of prophecy is greater than the gift of tongues, and he says in verse 12, "Even so ye, forasmuch as ye are zealous of spiritual gifts, seek that ye may excel to the edifying of the church." The church there at Corinth or at least a part of it was a sanctified church (See 1 Cor. 1:1-2 and 1 Cor. 6:11), yet they were not able to speak the different languages, for Paul writes: "I would that ye all spake with tongues." The Holy Ghost is the sanctifier (Rom. 15:16), and they had received him (1 Cor. 6:19), yet they could not speak with tongues as Paul who had preached to them and had led or turned them from the power of Satan unto God. As I have already said so say I now again: The Holy Ghost is promised to all believers, but the gift on tongues is not. The different gifts of the Spirit are given out according to divine wisdom just as he sees proper and profitable, but this may be true and yet neither you nor I possess the gift of tongues. Amen.

J.E. Forrest, "The Gift of Tongues," *Gospel Trumpet*, Volume 24. No. 14. (April 7, 1904): 1-2.

Questions Answered.
George L. Cole.

Ques. Are all the spiritual gifts manifested among God's preachers to-day, as described in 1 Cor. 12th chapter? T.R. S.

ANS. There is no change in God's plan, but it is according to the faith of each individual to receive and use to the glory of God what the Holy Spirit imparts. All the gifts except tongues and interpretation of tongues have been and are being effectually demonstrated, and there have been a few instances of remarkable demonstration of tongues. At Grand Junction, Mich. camp-meeting some years ago, a German brother on whom God had bestowed some measure of the gift could talk, read, and translate the Holland language quite satisfactorily to the Holland brethren who were present. More especial attention should be paid by the ministers to the demonstration of the gifts, and they should be more earnestly sought by the church. Mormons and many others under antichrist spirits, have made high claims of the gifts, including tongues, etc.; but I never saw or heard of any such that bore investigation. The antichrist spirit can not produce a good counterfeit that will pass among sensible people.

G. L. C.

George L. Cole. "Questions Answered." *Gospel Trumpet* Vol. 26, No. 9 (March 1, 1906): 4.

Questions Answered.
Jacob W. Byers

Ques. 1. Is there any difference between the Holy Ghost and the gift of the Holy Ghost? If so what? Does the gift always accompany the Holy Ghost? If not, why not? What is the gift of the Holy Ghost?

2. Why do not the saints to-day who receive the Holy Ghost speak with tongues?

3. What were the tongues with which they spoke?

4. Does not perfection accompany the wholly sanctified life?

5. What is meant by "infirmities" so often used in the Bible, and did Adam have infirmities before he fell?

6. What is the book "Osea" mentioned in the Bible?

7. When and where was Paul sanctified?

8. What is the difference between baptism in the name of the Father, Son and Holy Ghost (Matt. 28:19), and baptism in the name of the Lord Jesus ? Acts 19:5; 8:16.

9. Why are not the dead raised to-day as in the days of the apostles?

Ans. 1. Yes. The gift of the Holy Ghost is the Pentecostal endowment of sanctification, such as the apostles experienced in the upper room and as the household of Cornelius experienced, and is for every justified believer to-day upon the scriptural condition of consecration and faith. This is called the gift of the Holy Ghost. Acts 2:38; 10:45; 11:17. While the Holy Ghost is a gift, he also bestows gifts. Heb. 2:4; 1 Cor. 12:4. The nine gifts mentioned in 1 Cor. 12 are gifts of the Holy Ghost.

2. There is no reason why not, where it would be to the glory of God.

3. Evidently they were foreign languages.

4. Yes. Perfection in reference to spiritual life as used in the scriptures and associated with the grace of sanctification does not mean human perfection nor maturity nor infallibility. It signifies perfect love, perfect obedience, perfect unity, perfect purity, etc.

5. The general use of the term in the Bible signifies weakness, but in some instances, is applied to sickness. No, it is not likely that Adam had infirmities before the fall.

6. Hosea.

7. At Damascus. Acts 9: 17.

8. Not any: The expression "baptized in the name of the Lord Jesus," (Acts 19:5; 8:16) is used in contradistinction to the baptism of John.

9. There is no reason why not, where it is clearly manifested to be God's will.

J.W.B.

Jacob W. Byers, "Questions Answered." *The Gospel Trumpet*. Vol. 26 No. 13 (March 29, 1906): 4-5.

Bear Ye One Another's Burdens.
By Lydia Meyer.

FOR some time a burden has been upon my heart, and I feel the time has come when the Lord would be pleased to have me unburden the same and give others a chance to bear a part of it as their own. If each member of the church of God would put forth an effort to do his part, there would be equality—one would not be over-burdened and weighed down, while the others would be disinterested because of their not working and bearing their part of the responsibility. For some time, only a few have been trying to push the work in the different languages. They have been pulling, tugging, praying, digging, night and day, so to speak, to do the work that all should have had a hand in doing; while some in-stead, have been sitting by with their hands in their laps, as it were, without any care, interest, or responsibility.

Beloved, the time has come when all nations must hear this wonderful gospel, and who will take it to them, if we do not awaken to a sense of duty? Let us not permit it to be a one-sided affair; but instead let us put heart and hand into the work of the Lord in every way possible. As the work opens in the different coun-tries and languages, there are many hindrances, difficul-ties, and discouragements, to contend with, that the work in general will know nothing of unless we begin to enter into and bear these burdens as our own. Let us lift up the hands of those who are having to go ahead. Every beginning is like unto pulling up stream. There are Danish, Swedish, Norwegian, and German papers. Have you been interested in the same and prayed for their success in spreading the gospel? I am persuaded to believe that some of our dear Danish, Norwegian, Swedish, and German brethren, who are able to read their own paper, have not taken even enough interest in the work to encourage the dear ones who work on the same, by subscribing for the paper and reading it, to say nothing about their writing spiritual articles and testimonies. Dear ones, are you enjoying this truth? Do you love your people? Then awaken to your duty and do what you can to get this glorious gospel to them. Those who can speak these languages, who perhaps have come from foreign lands some time ago and have become used to the English tongue through practise, begin to practise reading and speaking in your own language and thus return to the old land-marks. I am sure that if you will put forth the same efforts to return to your own language that you put forth to learn the English, you will soon be a master of the same. Ask the Lord to show you your responsibility in getting the truth before your own people. What if some one would not have taken interest in your behalf, would you have enjoyed your freedom in the Lord now? "For every man shall bear his own burden." Ga. 6:5. Our people ought to be our first and own burden. If we who are able to converse with them and to get the truth to them do not do it, whom can we expect to do it? Are we going to let them grope in darkness until some one who can not speak the language get so burdened for them that he will learn the language or get the fit of tongues? If we are decided to get the truth before our own people, we must first do all we can, then we can with a clear conscience, confidence, and faith, ask the Lord to help others learn the language or to get the gift of tongues to help move the work along. I wonder how many of those who write testimonies for the Trumpet, can read, write, and speak the German, Swedish, Danish, or Norwegian language, but who have not interested themselves enough to write a good spiritual testimony in their language. Our German paper is suffering for good spiritual reading material. Why is it? Because you and I have failed to be as interested in getting the truth to all nations as we ought to be. Perhaps you think the paper is not interesting enough for you to read or to give it much attention. Perhaps it is not, especially to those of us who have not spent the time, effort, and care on it that the Lord would have us to do in order to make it interesting. Perhaps it needs testimonies and prayers. Care and labor increase one's love and interest for a thing. Let us labor harder, and our interest will increase, and the work will be more spiritual and interesting, and not only that, but it will help to make us more spiritual. Thus we can lighten the burden of our overburdened brethren. Let all cooperate. Those who can read, write, or speak can encourage with their prayers.

My attention has been called to the fact that some who understand these languages are seldom present at non-English meetings for the benefit of getting the truth to those who can not understand the English. Or sometimes when they do come they come with the feeling or spirit of its being a burden to them to do so, and, their presence is no benefit to the meeting. Let us be interested and deem it a privilege that we are able to understand, and are able to get the truth to more souls than we could otherwise do. Even those that can not understand the language of the meeting will find a benefit to themselves and to others to occasionally attend the same. It will at least stir up a missionary spirit in themselves and in others. I know from experience that if we interest ourselves in the work that the Lord would have us have first and next to our hearts, it will only enlarge our hearts to be able to have more interest in the work in general. May the Lord help us to stir ourselves up to reach out and take hold of God for the salvation of the nations of the earth. The only way we can do this is by doing our duty, and by grasping the opportunities that lie next to our doors. Then little by little others will be provoked by our zeal which will result in their doing what they can in getting the truth to their people. Let Zion travail so she will bear children in the different nations.

There are few places where the sectarians have not sent their missionaries and established their creeds, and obtained followers or children; but, alas! the church is yet barren in many of these places. Let us awaken and cry aloud so we can, when we read the following text, forget our widowhood. "Sing, O barren, thou that didst not bear; break forth into singing, and cry aloud, thou that didst not travail with child: for more are the children of the desolate than the children of the married wife, saith the Lord. Enlarge the place of thy tent, and let them stretch forth the curtains of thine habitation; spare not, lengthen thy cords, and strengthen thy stakes; for thou shalt break forth on the right hand and on the left; and thy seed shall inherit the Gentiles, and make the desolate cities to be inhabited. Fear not; for thou shalt not be ashamed: neither be thou confounded; for thou shalt not be put to shame: for thou shalt forget the shame of thy youth, and shalt not remember the reproach of thy widowhood anymore. For, thy Maker is thine husband; the Lord of hosts is his name, and thy Redeemer the Holy One of Israel; the God of the whole earth shall he be called." Isa. 54:1-5. Let all shake themselves from the dust and rust. This is a work that the entire church should be interested in, and not only ministers and workers. The spirit of Christ is a missionary spirit. Let us get filled with the spirit and the love of Christ and our souls will year more for those who are still in darkness.

Lydia Meyer, "Bear Ye One Another's Burdens," *The Gospel Trumpet* Volume 26 No. 23 (June 14, 1906): 3.

Seeking Pentecost.
Gospel Trumpet

Along the Pacific coast and in a few other places there has been considerable agitation on account of the manifestations among some people who claimed to have received their Pentecost, and are urging others to seek their pentecost, and with the same are seeking the gift of tongues. Some have asked whether or not this is the real workings of the Holy Spirit or a deception. So far as we can learn through the papers and literature which they publish, giving their experiences and teaching, and noting the results of the same, it is an easy matter to conclude that it is a deception, and not an operation of the Holy Spirit.

These people publish some papers—one called the Apostolic Faith, another, Apostolic Light. They teach that after a Person is sanctified, they should then seek their pentecost, or the baptism of the Holy Spirit, and that they should speak with tongues. There are many other things regarding their teaching that are out of line with the Word of God.

There is no question but that they do, some of them, speak with tongues, or at least get some kind of a gibbering that can not be understood; and we doubt very much if it is edifying either to themselves or any one else.

The Word of God teaches that we are justified by faith through Jesus Christ (Rom. 5:1), and sanctified by the Holy Ghost (Rom. 15:16). Sanctification and the reception of the Holy Ghost takes place at the same time. The special gifts of the spirit may or may not be manifest at that time. People, under a wrong teaching of doctrine, drifting along in the ways of error and under this influence seeking for special gifts of power, from God, are almost sure to get a deception and get others into a deception; and when seeking the gifts of tongues under such circumstances, the devil can very easily give them some kind of mutterings and gibberings and good feelings, and carry them away into trances and show them wonderful visions in order to deceive them.

In the meetings herein mentioned, many have sought and obtained the so-called gift of tongues and chattered away without any one understanding what they were saying, or even knowing themselves what they were saying. Paul taught that if any one speak with tongues in public that he should pray to interpret the same. 1 Cor. 14:13.

"Therefore if I know not the meaning of the voice, I shall be unto him that speaketh a barbarian, and he that speaketh shall be a barbarian unto me," Verse 11. "Yet in the church, I had rather speak five words with my understanding, that by my voice I might teach others also, than ten thousand words in an unknown tongue. If therefore the whole church be come together in one place and all speak with tongues, and there come in those who are unlearned or unbelievers, will they not say that ye are mad? If any man speak in an unknown tongue, let it be by two or at the most by three, and that by course; and let one interpret. But if there be no interpreter, let him keep silence in the church; and let him speak to himself, and to God." 1 Cor. 14:19-28.

The people in the places mentioned, instead of following Paul's advice and having not more than three speak with tongues without the interpretation, or if there is no interpreter, then keeping still, do not follow this instruction. The fact is their teaching on other lines is out of harmony with the Word, their experiences are not according to the Word God, and those who seek such things under their teaching and influence get something that is contrary to the Word of God, and is only a delusion and a deception.

God does give some people the gift of tongues in these days and doubtless desires many more to speak with tongues, and the devil is trying to push his messengers ahead and disgust the people insomuch that they will turn against the true messengers of God when his power is manifested through them, the same as they rejected, Moses and Aaron in the presence of the magicians of old. On the day of Pentecost, there was speaking with tongues, but there were people of many languages present, and they were enabled to understand what was spoken.

Gospel Trumpet, "Seeking Pentecost," *The Gospel Trumpet*, Vol. 26 No. 51 (December 27, 1906): 8-9.

A Craze for Tongues.
By E. E. Byrum

The gift of tongues is one of the gifts of the church of God. I Cor. 12:10. It was manifest in the early church at various times and in various places. Probably the most noted of these was on the day of Pentecost. Acts 2:7-11. When this gift was first bestowed upon the church it was at a time when the believers were all of "one accord." They believed and taught the same doctrine, all belonged to the same church—the church of God, had the same kind of an experience of salvation, and were one in spirit. It was then, and is at the present time the same, that the power of God was manifested by the Holy Ghost. It was when "a multitude of them that believed were of one heart and one mind" that "great grace was upon them all." Acts 4:32, 33. It was at this time that they showed their liberality and the power of God was manifested in a different way than by speaking with tongues. They did not speak with tongues on all occasions and at all times, but when necessary to the glory of God.

At the present time there seems to be a regular craze in various parts of the United States to speak with tongues. At a number of places along the Pacific coast, in Texas, at Alliance, and Cleveland, O., and in a number of other places are headquarters of societies who are making a specialty of seeking their Pentecost and speaking with tongues. Several papers are published by them to that end, and in most all places that we have investigated we find them far from being what the believers were in the early church. Their assemblies are filled with division and a lack of unity. Their doctrines differ, some belong to one so-called church, some to another; some believe in the ordinances of the New Testament, some do not; some teach a millennium, others oppose it. Some of them are to be found mourning, mortifying their deeds and bewailing their condition, distorting themselves or almost anything in order to get their Pentecost and speak with tongues. And they keep this up until many of them actually speak with tongues; but the source of the same can easily be imagined. It reminds us of the magicians, and soothsayers and sorcerers who worked their miracles and enchantments before Pharaoh in the presence of Moses and Aaron, or (the 450) priests of Baal in comparison with the power of God.

Now we believe in the manifestation of the gift of the Spirit, and gift of tongues as well as others, but there is such a thing as seeking the power and gifts in a wrong way and obtaining such from a wrong source. A few years ago at St. James, Mo., were a number of persons who had received considerable light on the Word of God, and doubtless most of them were saved. They learned that some brethren were calling from the East who possessed several gifts of the Spirit, such as prophecy, gifts of healing, casting out devils, etc. The elder at the place mentioned said to his company of believers: "This brother and company of workers who are coming here have a great deal of light, but they do not claim to speak with tongues. Now we must show them that we have more light and power than they have. We must speak with tongues."

They began with all earnestness seeking the "power," and "manifestation" as they called it. They began leaping and shouting, and those who could not show the power and manifest the same by leaping and shouting, or going through some maneuvers of the body, were invited to the altar to seek the "power." One after another sought it until they actually got under the influence of the same and they could leap about over the seats, fall under the power, or bounce around on their backs, jerking, twisting themselves with very unseemly actions. As none of them had yet been able to speak with tongues, the leader and two of the others agreed that when the company from the East came, that one of them should arise to his feet and begin talking in an unknown tongue, after which the other one was to arise as an interpreter, and whatever words came into his mind were to be the interpretation, and he was to speak the same to the audience.

The brethren and company of workers arrived, and those who were at that place began their operations, manifesting their power. At that time nearly the whole congregation had drifted under the power of the devil, but they were calling it the power of the Holy Ghost. During the services, one of the men mentioned arose and began to speak with tongues, or rather give vent to his premeditations for a few minutes in unintelligible "jibberings." The other man arose and tried to interpret by saying the things that came to his mind, but became confused, and it was clear that it was only a put-up job. The minister who had arrived from the East discerned by the Spirit of God the situation of the affair, rebuked the spirit of it in the name of Jesus, and stated publicly that it was a concocted scheme of the devil, that the power manifested was the power of the devil. It caused quite a stir in the camp, but the power of God prevailed, and when the spirit was rebuked, many who were merely under the influence of the power could clearly see it and broke loose from its power, while others had to have special prayer, and some even had to have hands laid on and the evil-spirits cast out, and when they sought, and obtained the real experience of salvation it was quite a different power from that which they had received before.

God does and will manifest himself as in times past, but it must be in accordance with his Word. The devil is just as shrewd now as he was in olden times and will work through such ones as Simon the sorcerer, or the maid with the spirit of divination, magicians, sooth-sayers, enchanters, spiritualists, Christian scientists, etc.

All the gifts of the Spirit mentioned in 1 Cor. 12 are in the church to-day and have been manifested, some more than others; but, unquestionably, God wants them all to be manifested more than they have been. The gift of tongues has not been manifested so much, probably because it was considered it was not so much of a necessity. This, the same as the other gifts, is given for a special purpose and for the benefit of humanity.

A few years ago while at the Grand Junction, Mich., camp-meeting we met a brother who said he had received the gift of tongues. Some time before this he had located in a community of Holland people, and, not knowing their language, he was unable to be of any help to them in giving them the truth and light of the gospel. One day while in prayer he was impressed to ask the Lord for the gift of the Holland language. He had before procured a New Testament in that language, but was unable to read it. After praying he took up his Testament and found that he could read and understand the language. When he came in contact with the people, he found he could talk to them freely on subjects relating to salvation and explain the Word of God to them. He then felt led to send for a Holland minister, and when he wrote the letter he wrote it in the Holland language. At this camp-meeting, which convened a short time after this, while talking to a large audience from Mark 16:17, we informed the audience regarding this brother and his claim that the Lord had given him the gift of tongues. We had him arise and read that verse in the Holland language, and then give the interpretation in the English, which he did very fluently. Then the request was made that any one in the audience select passages of Scripture for him to read and translate into English. Different ones in the audience selected scriptures which were read and interpreted to the satisfaction of all. The Holland minister to whom he had written arose and said he was the man who had received the letter in the Holland language, which was well written in that language. As long as this brother remained among the Holland people, he had command of that language. For several years this same brother has been engaged in the publishing work at our office.

When the Lord gives any one the gift of tongues, or any other gift, it will be given in accordance with his Word and for his glory.

E. E. Byrum, "A Craze for Tongues," *Gospel Trumpet* Vol. 27 No. 3 (January 17, 1907): 1, 8.

The Tongues Spirit.
J. W. Byers

The more thoroughly we become acquainted with the modern tongues movement, the more we see the fallacy of its claims. From the very first manifestation of this spirit upon souls with whom we were acquainted, there was sufficient evidence to us that this was not the work of the Holy Spirit.

One of the first causes of question, was the spiritual condition and fruits of those who claimed to have received this wonderful baptism of the Holy Spirit.

Not one of the saints who ever had a clear experience of sanctification, and were in the fellowship of the Spirit in Zion, have, to our knowledge, had anything to do with this movement; but on the other hand, some who never did fit in Zion because of lack of spiritual life, and because of self exaltation, conceit, and pride, have gone into this movement, received their baptism and tongues, and are among the most prominent in the movement. These, either had first separated themselves from us because they were not of us, or had to be dealt with, and set aside as unworthy of the confidence of the saints, and were held to repent before they could be accepted as saints, because they had spirits that were foreign to Zion.

Others of our acquaintance had proved enemies to the truth and had taken a strong stand against it, being full of erroneous doctrines; and others of like spirits who had fellowship with all kinds of Babylon holiness movements, were among those to get their baptism and tongues. This in itself was abundant proof that there was something decidedly wrong with this tongues movement.

Honest enquirers came to us to know of the truth of this matter, and we felt it our duty to look into it from an intelligent and unbiased standpoint, which we did as opportunity came to us. We went to some of their meetings and conversed with some of the leaders, and also read the literature carefully to get the truth of their teaching. We went into the meetings to testify to the truth of sanctification and the Holy Spirit baptism that God had given, which we know is the genuine Bible kind, but our testimony was not received because we did not speak in some unknown tongue. We found the leaders self-conceited and unteachable, and they would not recognize us as having received the Holy Spirit baptism, and held this down upon us in such a manner that would have brought condemnation and accusation had it not been that we knew what we had in our hearts.

We find among them all manner of spirits and crooked lives in different respects. It is not strange among them to have some one speak blasphemous words, and all manner of evil things while they are seeking their baptism. The teachers say that this is a sign that the devil is coming out of them, and all that they need to do, is to keep on, and in due time they will cease speaking such things and they will get the baptism.

One dear brother, who is now free from this awful thing, while he was among them, and urged to seek till he could speak with tongues, and that he was not baptized till he did speak with tongues, while earnestly seeking, began to curse and swear in an awful manner. He had been a good man, and had been living up to all the light that he had but this was something that he could not endure; for he knew that it could not be of God, and he took a stand against it and left the meetings. Later he went to a meeting among the saints of God, got clear of the evil influences of the tongues spirit, repented of the thing, made his consecration, believed for the cleansing and infilling of the Holy Spirit, and rejoiced in the sanctifying grace.

DIFFICULTY IN GETTING HELP TO THEM.

It is very difficult to get any help to the people in this delusion, for they are entrenched in the doctrine that one can not receive the Holy Spirit baptism until he speaks in tongues. To go among them to help them is useless because of this; for if you cannot speak in tongues, and have never done so, they will turn away from you, or else feel that they are commissioned to teach you. It matters not what else you may bring to them on the line of truth, they will first have to know that you can speak with tongues.

There are some good, honest souls among them who must become enlightened, and we believe they will be if they continue to be honest; but for the above reason, it is very hard to get any help to them.

There are many features in this work that plainly tell from whence it is, but there are three plain points that prove it to be wrong. 1. It is wrong in doctrine. 2. It is wrong in spirit. 3. It is wrong in fruits.

1. WRONG IN DOCTRINE.

There is much confused teaching among these people, for the movement has broken into multitudes of factions, and each teaches its own doctrine; but there are a few points that they agree upon so far as we have been able to learn.

They teach that one can not be baptized with the Holy Spirit until he speaks with tongues, and that the baptism is a separate work distinct from sanctification, that the apostles were sanctified before Pentecost. Speaking with tongues is the infallible sign to them that the baptism has come. Some deny this, but a careful observation of their teaching and testimonies prove that they do hold this. In fact, it is the speaking with tongues that forms the basis of fellowship, for without this they hold a person as in need, and he can not have recognition among them in full till he speaks the tongue. It matters not how little one can speak, just so it sounds different from anything that the individual has known before. I know of one who said she could only sing one little sentence, but this was so satisfactory to her that she rejoiced that she could speak in tongues. She would sing it over and over in the deepest of ecstasy, and thought she had something wonderful, for it was a sign to her that she had the baptism of the Holy Spirit.

They take the examples of Pentecost and the household of Cornelius and the twelve disciples at Ephesus for their examples, and claim that this is a sure evidence that the Holy Spirit can not come without the sign of the tongues. The tongues are for a sign, and until this sign is given, the Spirit is not there.

Now, as to these teachings, we can see at once that the basis is wrong. It will not do to hold that one can not receive the Holy Spirit baptism without tongues, for we have two instances in the early church record where this baptism was received without any mention of such a sign, viz, Acts 4:31; 8:14-17. There are three instances where the tongues were manifest, viz, Acts 2:1-11 ; 10:44-46; and 19:1-6, and in this there is no room for controversy; but to make the tongues the standard, and basis of the baptism of the Holy Spirit, is laying a foundation that God does not lay, and building a structure that God does not build. This is not only wrong and unscriptural, but very, very dangerous. There is something significant here that few comprehend as they should.

It matters not what basis may be built, or what foundation may be laid that God does not lay, the devil will be satisfied, and souls can be deceived into error.

The Mormons make the book of Mormon the basis, and the world has a class of people deceived into Mormonism. The Sabbatarians make the Seventh Day the basis, and the world has a class of deceived Seventh Day Adventists. Another class makes Mrs. Eddy's book, *Science and Health*, the basis, and the world has a class of people deceived into Christian Science, and thus there are multiplied doctrines and sects of religion suited to every thing that can be imagined to deceive souls and keep them from the knowledge of the truth of God's only plan of salvation.

This tongues movement makes tongues the basis, which is something that God does not do, and it is not to be wondered at that we see the disgusting spectacles of fanaticism and reproach that this thing has brought with it.

Twenty-five years ago, Mrs. Woodworth was the center of attraction on the Pacific coast for a season, and the cause of Christ was reproached shamefully, simply because she held and taught a wrong doctrine. She taught that one is justified and sanctified at one time, but that the power of the Holy Spirit comes as a separate and subsequent experience. She taught this to thousands of people who believed it. They were taught that they should come forward and call on God for the power, and should not cease till they got it.

The result was, that many people who were not even justified came and fell down and called for the power. The power came to such an extent that many were prostrate for hours and sometimes days, and many went through the most unreasonable contortions, that were not only indecent, but disgraceful, and many fanatical visions and revelations were received to such an extent that the meetings finally broke up in disgrace to the cause of Christianity.

The reason for all this was, this woman taught wrong doctrine. Instead of holding every one to repent of all sin, and then to seek for heart purity and the baptism of the Holy Spirit, she taught that you are cleansed in justification, and this left the heart in possession of depravity. To expect to be filled with the Holy Spirit in this condition, and to open the door for all people, to expect to be filled with power without the important and necessary cleansing preceding it, gave the devil the opportunity to impose a power spirit upon the people, which he was ready to do, and hence the awful error of the Woodworth movement.

Now, the point where the enemy has succeeded the greatest imposition upon the tongues people is to teach that sanctification is a separate work from the Holy Spirit baptism and urging everybody on to the only sure sign of the baptism, namely, tongues. This is nothing less than a tongues spirit that has imposed itself upon the poor people who think they can not have the baptism without the tongues. They seek and seek till they get the tongues, and the devil does not fail to give them what they seek. In Mrs. Woodworth's teaching, the people were possessed with a "power spirit." In the tongues movement they get a "tongues spirit."

2. WRONG IN SPIRIT.

A wrong doctrine is generally the effect of a wrong cause, a wrong spirit. In order that a wrong spirit may be able to deceive souls, it must have some scripture to hide behind, or, to be clothed with. It may take some plain scriptures, and interpret them properly to a certain extent, but it will only do this so that it may be able to take other scriptures to pervert. A false spirit will not exist in the midst of sound doctrine. It is the work of the Holy Spirit to teach us all things, and to guide us into all truth, and out of all error, and no spirit of error can thrive in the atmosphere of the Holy Spirit. The Word of God is the production of the Holy Spirit, and it is impossible for a spirit of error to impose itself upon a soul who has the true knowledge of the Word, and is decided to obey it.

Spirits of error will somewhere pervert the Word of God to those who lose sight of the importance of the strictest obedience to the Word, or who get their eyes on something else than Christ. In the tongues movement the people get their eyes on tongues. It is the tongues spirit that teaches them this, and they must seek for it till they get it. Very few of these people will admit this, however, for they will say that one must seek for the baptism; but the substance of all their teaching is the tongues. Now, if we seek tongues, and lose sight of Christ to the extent that we are willing to give up all our former experience no matter how good it might have been (this is a doctrine that many of the tongues people teach. You must give up everything that you ever had and seek for what we have to show you) we open the door to this spirit of deception and get a deception.

This spirit holds and teaches that one can not be baptized with the Holy Spirit without the manifestation of tongues, and that the apostles were sanctified before Pentecost. Both of these points make a good place for the soul to lose the sound doctrine and give way to something else, to seek for tongues. This is just what the tongues spirit wants. It wants to be honored and worshiped. It robs God of the honor that he has bestowed upon the Holy Spirit. It exalts itself above the Holy Spirit, and exalts the person who possesses it, or, rather, whom it possesses, above all who do not have this experience. It binds itself upon all who give way to it and holds them in an iron grasp of bondage.

At our recent camp-meeting, while casting out this spirit from an honest heart who had been deceived into that deception, the Holy Spirit revealed it as clearly that this is a tongues spirit, and the whole tongues movement is the work of this spirit. It is a rival to the Holy Spirit and is in the field for the purpose to overthrow all who will not measure up to the pure word of God, and to deceive all such who have pleasure in unrighteousness. It is one of the finest-spun deceptions of the last days, and has already in a little more thou five years swept the whole earth. There is hardly a tribe or people who has not been visited by this movement. It will deceive the very elect if possible. But there is no need of any one being deceived who will keep his eyes on the Lord and reverence his Word as the only foundation for doctrine. In fact, the Word of God is the doctrine, and the only one that God has ever designed for our safety.

How thankful we ought to be for the plain teaching of the word of God in Zion. God has sent us teachers who have received the pentecostal baptism of the Holy Spirit to teach us the pure Word, showing us how to get saved and sanctified and baptized, so we may be able to understand the Word, and be protected from all spirits of error and destructive deceptions.

With the Word of God, the Holy Spirit, and in the Church of God, we are safe if we follow on in the clear light that is shining, and we may ever know the deceptions of the enemy.

When we compare the fruits of this tongues spirit with the fruits of the pentecostal baptism of the early church, we find a sad contrast, and therefore we do not hesitate to say that this movement is

3. WRONG IN FRUITS.

This was one of the first symptoms that called our attention to this movement. One of the first floods of opposition we met, was criticism. It challenged our salvation and sanctification, and declared that we sere utterly destitute of spiritual power. It has no fellowship with us, and we were sure we did not with it. One poor man who had accepted the spirit, but did not have his baptism yet, was so grieved with our lack of spiritual power that he could not endure to sit within the sound of our voice; for we so sadly lacked the power. We knew that we were sanctified and filled with the Holy

Spirit, but there was no fellowship with that spirit. Jesus says, "By their fruits ye shall know them", and it is easy to know this spirit in this way.

One of the prominent characteristics of this movement is fanaticism. Very few of these souls know anything about consistency. They are governed by impulse and guided by impressions. We do not say this of all, for there may be some who are naturally more cautious and thoughtful, but the most that we have any acquaintance with, are void of the real leadings of the Holy Spirit, and are given to impressions and leadings of feeling. Some are making great efforts to become more consistent than formerly, but their meeting are usually full of the wildest confusion and inconsistencies. The disgraceful gestures and falling and rolling and tumbling that accompanied the Woodworth meetings are among the demonstrations of this movement.

Sometimes when they meet in worship, their tongues become so controlled that nearly all speak at once, and the confusion is something inexpressible. No one understands what he says, but just gives vent to the spirit. When this finally subsides, they sometimes have testimony and sometimes reading, and teaching, but the most of the teaching tends to bondage, rather than freedom.

It is impossible for many of them to remain together very long, for dissension and division is one of the principal features of this movement. The meetings break into factions, and like a swarm of bees they keep swarming as long as there is more than one leader among them. This may not be the case in every place, but we speak only from observation. In the city of Oakland, Cal., we do not know how many rival factions have held separate missions for a time, but the scene has been disgusting.

The presence of the Holy Spirit will effect peace and unity, as it did among the pentecostal saints; but this spirit bears the fruits of division and confusion. We pity these poor souls in their blind efforts to hold together. There is nothing to hold them together, but much to separate and divide.

One of the first men in this movement on the Pacific Coast, perhaps the very first, has recently been like a wandering star, seeking to find something to bind a little company of them together. He has paid several visits to our home, claiming to enquire into the teachings of Zion, so he might know how to teach others himself. He has attended some of our meetings and tried to learn something about unity, and confesses that they are not united. This is the poor man that a few years are was the attraction of Los Angeles because of the wonderful things that he could do, especially that he could so wonderfully speak with tongues. He is too self exalted to harmonize with any one else, and is trying to learn now how to save the wrecked craft that is shattered and sinking out of sight.

With all that any of these people have ever received that they call power, they are utterly void of spiritual power in the presence of the saints in Zion. There is nothing that they have with all their boasted claims, that a real saint would have. Recently there were three of them came to the camp-meeting, and were not there long till they found that they did not have anything as they thought, and it is satisfactory to say that these dear souls had honesty of heart enough to confess their lack, and were in due time relieved of the awful oppression and possession of the tongues spirit, and rejoiced in the freedom front its bondage.

This is truly a tongues spirit, and its fruits are, bondage, confusion, fanaticism, and division. May God in his mercy deliver every honest soul from its cruel grasp.

J. W. Byers, "The Tongues Spirit," *The Gospel Trumpet* Vol. No. (June 30, 1910): 2-3.

Babel and Pentecostal Tongues
By George N. Stewart

Much speculation and spiritual confusion exist because of the tongues' question, and sincere souls are sometimes carried away with the sweeping influence. Truly, we are living in the "perilous times." Let us with unbiased and unprejudiced minds look at this question.

Having searched a few translations, I find that they all harmonize when understood in their true light. I have before me three—the common, or King James Version, the Emphatic Diaglott, and the Revised. The American Version is the only one using the term "unknown", and it is printed in italics, showing that it has been supplied by the translators. The Revised Version uses the term "a tongue," which implies a means of conveying thought; and the Emphatic Diaglott says, "a foreign language," "in different languages" (1 Cor. 14:1-5).

THE ORIGIN OF TONGUES

In Genesis 11:1 we read: "And the whole earth was of one language, and of one speech." Here God tells us that there was but one language in the whole earth at that time. All spoke in one tongue. It seems that man became discontented and desired to do something great, to get to heaven by his own ingenuity. "And it came to pass, as they journeyed from the east, . . . they said one to another, Go to, let us make brick, and burn them thoroughly . . . let us build us a city and a tower, whose top may reach unto heaven; and let us make us a name.

. . . And the Lord came down to see the city and the tower, . . . and the Lord said, Behold, the people is one, and they have all one language; . . . and now nothing will be restrained from them, which they have imagined to do. . . . Let us go down, and there confound their language that they may not understand one another's speech. So the Lord scattered them abroad from thence upon the face of all the earth. . . . because the Lord did there confound the language" (Genesis 11:2-9). This is the origin of the multitude of the different tongues in the world; and by this confusion of languages the people were scattered geographically over the world.

A MEANS TO RESTORE UNITY

What seemed to be a curse to man, God in the process of time utilized in bringing the human family back to one spiritual speech—the word of God. On the day of Pentecost, the disciples "were all filled with the Holy Ghost, and began to speak with other languages, as the Spirit gave them utterance. And there were dwelling at Jerusalem Jews, devout men, out of every nation under heaven [Many languages were represented there that day]. Now when this was noised abroad, the multitude came together, and were confounded, because that every man heard them speak in his own language. And they were all amazed and marvelled, saying one to another, Behold, are not all these which speak Galileans? And *how hear we every man in our own tongue*, wherein we were born?" (Acts 2:4-8). If you notice, we are told in the foregoing scriptures that every nationality was represented there that day; and they said, "How hear we every man in *our own tongue*?" They heard the disciples speak in other languages, not in some unintelligible language; for they understood what was being said, "We do hear them speak in *our tongues* the wonderful works of God" (v. 11). In Genesis 11 we have seen that the multitudes were dispersed abroad in the land because their language was confounded: and in Acts 2 we learn that by that same means many nations under heaven, speaking various languages, heard the gospel narrative by an incident as miraculous as that by which they had been scattered. This speaking in other languages instantaneously was not by mere chance; for it is a special gift of the Spirit (1 Cor. 12:10). No doubt Paul had the gift to speak in almost every language of his day, considering his extended missionary journeys. He said of his own gift: "I thank my God, I speak with tongues more than you all" (1 Cor. 14:18). On the day of Pentecost the disciples had the privilege to preach to representatives from all parts of the world; in one day the gospel began its course to every nation. No doubt this was the means to open the door for the gospel in many places.

At that time means of conveying messages other than by oral language was slow. Modern inventions of printing were unknown. Had the apostles been required to master other languages before getting the truth to the people, their success would have been greatly retarded. But in Paul's day he declared that "their sound went into all the earth, and their words unto the ends of the world" (Rom. 10:18). This gift of other languages was not given them merely as a sign to convince unbelievers; but to convey to them the gospel message.

This unheard-of occurrence did arouse the curiosity of the people, but there was something else that did them more good than the excitement; they heard them tell in their own language of "the wonderful works of

God." What was the result? "The same day there were added unto them about three thousand souls" (Acts 2:41). If you will notice, there is nothing said about there being an interpreter there that day; for every man heard the gospel in his own tongue. They had and exercised the real gift of the Spirit.

INTERPRETATION

An interpreter is necessary when one does not possess the gift of the language of those to whom he is speaking. "If any one speak in a foreign language, let it be by two, or at most three [sentences] and in succession, and let one interpret: but if there is no interpreter let him be silent in the Congregation" (1 Cor. 14:27, 28, E. D.). This is too plain to need comment. One who is led and influenced by the Holy Ghost, can exercise good judgment and has perfect control of his own will and mind. He does not necessarily lose his head and speak in a gibberish that he nor any one else can understand. He has power to keep himself orderly and yet grieve not the Holy Spirit. "The spirits of the prophets are subject to the prophets" (1 Cor. 14:32). This text exposes the fallacy of this "tongue" power that gets men in its grip and causes them to act unbecomingly. Paul closes this fourteenth chapter of First Corinthians by saying, "Let all things be done in a becoming manner, and according to order" (v. 40, E. D.).

In every instance in the Acts of the Apostles where those who received the Holy Ghost spoke with tongues, there was evidently no need for an interpreter, for they spoke intelligible languages. All who heard understood clearly what was said. First, at Pentecost: "They were all filled with the Holy Ghost, and began to speak with other tongues, as the Spirit gave them utterance. . . . We do hear them speak in our tongues *the wonderful works of God"* (Acts 2:4-11). Second, the household of Cornelius: "While Peter yet spoke these words, the Holy Ghost fell on all them which heard the word, . . . for they heard them *magnify* God" (Acts 10:44-46). Third, the Ephesians: "And when Paul had laid his hands upon them, the Holy Ghost came on them; and they spoke with tongues, and prophesied" (Acts 19:16).

In the light of these texts I want to ask the reader, What did they do with these tongues; did they "speak into the air"? No; they spoke "the wonderful works of God"; they "magnified God"; and "prophesied." The Word of God says the people that heard them said, "We do hear them speak in our own language" (Acts 2:6, 11).

George N. Stewart, "Babel and Pentecostal Tongues," *The Gospel Trumpet* (March 29, 1917): 6-7.

Sources and Nature of Speaking in Tongues.
By Russell R. Byrum

Is It Always from God and in What Does it Consist?

The supernatural ability to speak a language which the speaker has not learned has always been a subject of interest to Christians since the outpouring of the Spirit at Pentecost. Special interest concerning tongues manifestation has been aroused during the present century by the claims and practises of those of the modern tongues movement. The question has often arisen, "What is the true speaking in tongues as taught in the Bible?" A first step to answering this question is to determine

The Possible Sources of Tongues Manifestations

These may be described as three, (1) Divine, (2) Satanic, (3) Human. That the Spirit of God may speak through those he possesses is not incredible for all those who believe in the Bible and the miraculous. "They were all filled with the Holy Ghost, and began to speak with other tongues, as the Spirit gave them utterance" (Acts 2:4). The same God who caused the dumb ass to speak Hebrew to the false prophet Balsam is certainly able to cause one of his people to speak that or other languages not known to the speaker.

That Satan can speak through those he possesses is clear from the words spoken by the Gadarene demoniac to Jesus, "What have we to do with thee, Jesus, thou Son of God? art thou come hither to torment us before the time?" Here the demon spirit in the man used the man's vocal organs to speak to Jesus, we understand. See Mark 5:6-10. So we find demoniacs today whose tongue the indwelling spirit uses entirely independent of the will of the man, and we have sometimes heard the man immediately deny a false statement of the demon made thus through him. This is not uncommon in those possessed of demons. And doubtless demons know not only English or Aramaic but all the languages of men and angels, and can as well cause a man possessed by devils to speak a language unknown to him as to speak his own language through their agency.

Spiritualistic mediums as well as priests of heathen religions are known to sometimes speak in tongues. That such are possessed of demon spirits is certain. Not only their practises as mediums but their looks and actions at such times are such as become a demoniac. The writer is personally acquainted with those who according to their own words were practising as mediums, and at the same time were recognized as preachers in the tongues movement and who spoke in tongues and also interpreted. Such tongues are doubtless not of God and are probably from the devil. Also some whose tongues were understood by those present, have been known to speak without knowing it the vilest and most blasphemous things against God. Such could not be by the spirit of God, and judging from it malignity is evidently from the devil. This seems to be the very point Paul was discussing in 1 Cor. 12:3, "No man speaking by the Spirit of God calleth Jesus accursed." There is a close analogy between being possessed by the Holy Ghost and by a demon. The person baptized by the Holy Ghost is possessed by him, and the Spirit may work through him as an instrument in miracles, teaching, prophesying, or in speaking a language unknown to the person. Closely analogous to this is the case of one possessed by a demon spirit who may counterfeit almost every operation of God's spirit. Human nature, the third possible source of speaking in unknown tongues, furnishes a psychological ground for it. Knowledge once gained by the mind is never lost, it is said, even though it is not always possible to remember it. But excitement may cause an abnormally awakened memory. All the principal acts of a man's life may flash before his mind in an instant when he is in imminent danger. The subconscious mind works especially in times of sleep, excitement, danger, or illness.

Coleridge tells the story of a servant girl who when ill with fever in her delirium talked continually in Hebrew, Greek, and Latin with very distinct enunciation. Those educated in these languages wrote several sheets of her talk and found it to be long quotations from classical and rabbinical authors. People who heard her were astonished, because it was known she had not learned those languages. By inquiring into the history of her life it was found that she had formerly been a servant in the home of an old and learned minister, and that he had been in the habit of walking up and down a passage of the house near the kitchen reading aloud to himself portions from the very volumes from which the afflicted girl had been quoting. She had heard them, and though they were unintelligible to her yet the sounds had impressed themselves upon her mind and in her delirium her subconscious mind had reproduced them. Other similar examples might be given. So one may possibly thus gather foreign words and phrases and in a state of religious frenzy may repeat such even though he does not know the meaning of them.

Nature of the New Testament Speaking in Tongues

We first call attention to what is not the gift of tongues. The pentecostal tongues were not new literal physical tongues in the mouths of the disciples as certain commentators have absurdly conjectured, for Acts 2:6, 8 describes them as languages. They were not mere strange, archaic, or poetic words as held by Baur and others, because the term tongue has no such use in other places in the Bible. Neither can we suppose these tongues were only a new interpretation of Old Testament prophecies, for the text states that they were languages and not interpretations. They were not a miracle of hearing as was held by Gregory Nazianzus, Bede, Erasmus, and others of the present. In other words we do not suppose the disciples spoke their usual language, and that the Holy Ghost caused their auditors to hear in their own tongues. Such a miracle is claimed for certain of the Roman Catholic saints and is certainly possible, but such is not described in the text because the miracle is said to be in the speaking not in the hearing for they spoke with "other" tongues (v. 4), and their hearers doubtless heard them in the language in which they spoke, in their "own" tongues (v. 6).

We learn also by a careful consideration of the various texts on tongues that one's speaking in tongues does not imply that he has a knowledge of that language as he has of a tongue he has learned. He is not only unable to understand one speaking the same language which he is thus supernaturally enabled to speak, but he does not understand what he himself says, unless he has the gift of interpretation. He speaks only as "the Spirit gives utterance" (Acts 2:4). His "understanding is unfruitful" (1 Cor. 14:14).

The New Testament speaking in tongues may be defined as an endowment by the Spirit of God with ability to speak a real language unknown to the speaker, but only as the Spirit operates through him. The speaker may not understand what he says (1 Cor. 14:14), yet it is a real language and not a mere jargon or succession of unintelligible sounds. The expression "as the Spirit gave them utterance" (Acts 2:4) may be understood to refer to the language spoken rather than to the time or manner of speaking as some have supposed. The language spoken may be one of men or of angels (1 Cor. 13:1). Speaking in tongues was usually in a state of ecstasy (Acts 2; and 10:46), but there is no reason whatever to suppose they fell prostrate and lay "under the power" nor that their speaking was accompanied by violent jerking, straining, writhing, groans, and contortions. Such manifestations are more becoming to one possessed of a demon spirit than the Holy Spirit. Neither must we suppose the accusation that they were full of new wine was because of their "reeling bodies" as some have put it who would justify their falling prostrate. This was doubtless because of their language not being understood and their expressions of ecstasy, and so we may understand the charge of madness in 1 Cor. 14:23.

Some would allow tongues manifestations to be genuine only as there is some one who can understand the utterance as at Pentecost. Such fail to consider other texts bearing on the subject. There is a manifestation of tongues that is proper in public consisting in a language known to some present and for which no interpreter is required as was true at Pentecost (Acts 2). There is also a speaking in tongues as described in 1 Cor. 14:2 which is forbidden, in the public assembly unless there be an interpreter, and which must therefore be exercised in private only (v. 28). A failure to clearly distinguish between the public and private phases of speaking in tongues has led to much misunderstanding. From the foregoing facts we conclude (1) that speaking in tongues is not necessarily a proof of deep spirituality or of Holy Ghost baptism, but it may be a result of demon possession or of religious frenzy, (2) that God's spirit speaks through some he possesses words not understood by the person speaking but which may be addressed to men or to God according to the nature of the utterance.

Russell R. Byrum, "Sources and Nature of Speaking in Tongues," *The Gospel Trumpet* (September 16, 1920): 5-6.

The Tongues-Evidence Theory Versus Scriptural Deduction.
By A. L. Byers

(An Answer to the Advocates of Modern "Tongueism")

1.) *It is held that speaking in tongues as the Spirit gives utterance (Acts 2:1) is to be distinguished from the gift of tongues of I Cor. 12:11.*

Answer: The true speaking in tongues as the Spirit gives utterance is necessarily a manifestation of the Spirit, self-implied in the words, "as the Spirit gives utterance." Into this one word "manifestation" therefore, all instances of tongues must converge—all are necessarily the manifestation of the Spirit. Also, since the true tongues are *given* of the Spirit they are therefore the "gift" of the Spirit. If the Spirit gives the utterance it must be one of the spiritual gifts. Any one should see that the above distinction is a strained one, a mere childish juggling of the Scripture. Would the Lord permit such a distinction, if true and if so much depends upon it, to appear so unwarranted and unsupported by Scripture? God's way is a highway and is easily seen by men who are not already blinded by false teaching. The distinction, made to support the tongues-evidence theory, was introduced by Charles P. Parham in the year 1900. No apostle or any great soul-winner during the 1900 years intervening since the Pentecostal outpouring ever taught such a thing.

2.) *The term "baptism of the Holy Ghost" is stressed as being something more than receiving the Spirit or being filled with the Spirit.*

Answer: The distinction here is as unwarranted as the one just considered. Baptism is used figuratively to imply a submerging into the Holy Spirit. Are we not to allow the Scriptural use of figures of speech as a little different manner of conveying a meaning from that of the ordinary manner of expression? It matters not whether the expression is baptism of the Spirit, filled with the Spirit, or receiving the Spirit, all are equivalent. In John 20:22 he who was to baptize with the Holy Ghost breathed on the disciples and said, "Receive ye the Holy Ghost." When this was fulfilled about forty days later we are told that they were all "filled with the Holy Ghost" (Acts 2:4). This same outpouring was referred to in Acts 1:5 as a baptism of the Holy Ghost. And so what matters it which expression be used?—all mean the same. Baptism of the Holy Ghost can be nothing more than being filled with the Holy Ghost or receiving the Holy Ghost, and it may apply either to the initial, or to any subsequent, infilling. The infilling mentioned in Acts 4:31 was just as much a baptism as the initial one at Pentecost. Is a system of teaching worthy of our acceptance whose support rests upon such flimsy and strained distinctions?

3.) *The baptism of the Spirit is in every instance attended by the initial physical sign of speaking in other tongues as the Spirit gives utterance. Acts 2:4.*

Answer: This is the teaching that does the damage, and as another has said. "Will split any church wide open." Being not only dependent upon false premises, as we have seen, it is also utterly refuted by direct Scripture. Paul asks, "Do all speak with tongues?" (1 Cor. 12:30). The implied answer is no, because he had just been explaining that in the manifestations of the Spirit there are "differences of administration" and "diversities of operations" (vss. 5, 6), that to one is given one kind of manifestation and "to another divers kinds of tongues" (vs. 10). The question, "Do all speak with tongues?" was an appeal to facts for confirmation of what he had been teaching, namely, that the manifestations are various in different persons. It is a fact that all were not apostles, all did not prophesy, all had not the gifts of healing and all did not speak in tongues (vss. 29, 30), hence his teaching in the verses preceding was confirmed. And we may say here that in his question, "Do all speak with tongues?" the answer to which is no, he could just as well have included the words "as the Spirit gives utterance," for speaking in tongues could only be as the Spirit gave utterance.

F. F. Bosworth, a man of many years' experience in the Pentecostal movement, says on this point, "I am certain that many who received the most powerful baptism for service did not receive the manifestation of speaking in tongues. And I am just as certain that many who seemingly speak in tongues are not nor ever have been baptized in the Spirit." He says of the latter class that instead of having "form without power" they have "noise without power."

4.) *It is as the Bible evidence of the Holy Spirit baptism that speaking in tongues "as the Spirit gives utterance" is always manifest.*

Answer: If this be true, then in seeking the Holy Spirit baptism we naturally desire to have this evidence supplied and we virtually are made to seek for the tongues. And when in seeking the Holy Spirit we begin to look to a physical manifestation as evidence of his reception we begin a serious departure from the divine plan of salvation and we open the door for counterfeiting agencies to work havoc with human souls. All the divine salvation operations are spiritual and are wrought in the heart by faith. Eph. 2:8. Faith is of such character that during its operation it cannot share its evidence with physical considerations else it were displaced by seeking for those very considerations. Faith is believing (receiving) where there is already no sight or physical assurance. Faith itself is "the evidence of things not seen." (Heb. 11:1). "He that believeth . . . hath the witness in himself" (I John 5:10). The Holy Spirit is to be received by faith. Gal. 3:14. Faith's operations are independent of physical sense. When therefore we accept the idea that there must be speaking in tongues to evidence the baptism of the Holy Spirit we set aside faith as accomplishing the end for us and begin to look to the manifestation of tongues as our goal, for under such a delusion we are not to be satisfied until we receive the tongues. When we set faith aside we set God's plan aside and expose our souls to Satanic deception.

If such a doctrine were true would it not be highly important that it be clearly and positively taught in the Scripture? On the contrary there is absolutely nothing in Scripture about any physical evidence in connection with receiving the Holy Spirit or his gifts, and we are told that faith itself is the evidence. God has established the relation with men that when an individual believes and appropriates to himself a thing God has promised he actually receives the thing promised. To try to receive things from God by any other than the faith method is not to receive them at all, though it is altogether possible to receive a substitute. Speaking in tongues, prophesying, and the other gifts of the Spirit, may he regarded as evidences of the Spirit variously distributed among individuals, but they are manifestations *after* faith has completed its work, appropriated the promise and become its own evidence. Such gifts of the Spirit are not to be regarded as *deciding* evidence of the Spirit's reception but as standing in the relation merely of additional evidence.

5.) *That speaking in tongues was to be the God-intended evidence of receiving the Holy Spirit baptism is established by the Scriptural examples recorded in Acts, where tongues actually served as such evidence. See Acts 2:4; 10:11-46; 19:6.*

Answer: Looking at this from every possible angle we see it is purely assumption. The fact that tongues were given in three instances mentioned is by no means a conclusive proof that God gave the same manifestation to all the multiplied thousands who received the Holy Spirit during that period of the church. It is nowhere taught that speaking in tongues is required as evidence that the Holy Ghost is received. The instances mentioned in Acts are historical accounts of things as they happened, and they do not appear in the light of possessing doctrinal content. It is not safe to ascribe to anything historical the strength of Scriptural teaching and to conclude that the Holy Spirit cannot be received at all without the manifestation of tongues. It is just as consistent to assume that there should be cloven tongues as of fire in visible form, because mentioned in Acts 2:3, or just as reasonable to assume from the historical accounts in Acts 2:44, 45 and 4:34, 35 That it is doctrinally incumbent upon Christians to have all things common. It is also worthy of note that even as a historical consideration no mention is made of speaking in tongues in the instance of the apostle Paul's receiving the Holy Ghost (in Acts 9:17, 18), neither in the case of the Samaritans, recorded in Acts 8:14-17.

6.) *These examples in Acts show that speaking in tongues was to be the sign of a believer to the unbelievers.*

Answer: In Mark 16:17, 18 we have these words of Jesus; "And these signs shall follow them that believe; in my name shall they cast out devils; they shall speak with new tongues; they shall take up serpents: and if they drink any deadly thing it shall not hurt them; they shall lay hands on the sick, and they shall recover."

Here we find that speaking in tongues stands in the same relation to the believer as do casting out devils, taking up serpents or healing the sick. The fulfillment of these shows that they are distributive, manifest with different persons and upon different occasions throughout the Spirit dispensation.

7.) *The baptism of the Spirit, as evidenced by the speaking in tongues, is supposed to be tarried for.*

Answer: The first disciples were told to tarry at Jerusalem until endued with power from on high. Luke 24:49. This was because the outpouring promised had to be delayed (in obedience to Old Testament type) until the day of Pentecost should come. All that tarrying could possibly mean was simply to await the day of Pentecost. Acts 1:5. When that day came the outpouring came readily and the Spirit dispensation began, which opened the door for the Spirit's ready reception by faith to all generations following. Acts 2:39. The command to tarry related only to the first disciples before the day of Pentecost. What is now required is not tarrying, but meeting the conditions, for the reception of the Spirit. It is this tarrying, instead of appropriating by faith, that favors the working up of the false physical demonstrations which many have believed to be of God.

8.) *Power that prompts speaking in tongues should not be resisted, referring to Rom. 13:1,2.*

Answer: The reference to Romans 13 is to political powers. We are told plainly in I Corinthians 14 that tongues are to be kept under control, and made subordinate to the interests of the congregation. See verses 27, 28, also verse 32.

In addition to the above it should be noted that the tongues-evidence theory exalts spirit and gives it precedence over the word, whereas exactly the contrary is to be recognized if we are to be safe. The word is magnified by God himself above his very name. Ps. 138:2. Its testimony is to be preferred to that of angels (Gal. 1:6-9), and it is the arbiter of all questions. (Isa. 8:20). It will judge us in the last day. John 12:48. The spirits are to be tried, for there are many false ones in the world. I John 4:1. The Holy Spirit in his manifestations takes a subjective place. I Cor. 14:32.

Again, the gift of speaking in tongues is exalted out of true proportion in its relation to the other gifts. From I Cor. 14, as well as from the order given in I Cor. 12:8-10, 28-30, we learn plainly that tongues are the least important of the spiritual gifts,

The most dangerous feature of the tongues-evidence teaching is that it makes no allowance for counterfeit manifestations. There are counterfeit spirits. I John 4:1. Satan can and does counterfeit the physical manifestations of the Spirit, and for this reason alone the tongues as an evidence is not safe. Nothing can be taken as an evidence that is not reliable. Demon-possessed persons often speak in tongues, and Satan could not wish for a better opportunity to enter and possess souls than is afforded him by this tongues-evidence theory. The true evidence of the Holy Spirit possession is the Holy Spirit himself, whose godlike qualities soon manifest themselves. The fruits of the Spirit—love, joy, peace, longsuffering, gentleness, goodness, faith, meekness and temperance (Gal. 5:22, 23)—when given time to work out in the life cannot be successfully counterfeited.

A. L. Byers, "The Tongues-Evidence Theory Versus Scriptural Deduction," *The Gospel Trumpet,* (December 11, 1930): 11-12.

Is Speaking in Tongues an Evidence?
By William Thomas Seaton

*And when the day of Pentecost was fully come
(Acts 2:1).*

UNDER the old covenant there was a Pentecost every year occurring fifty days after the Passover. For the New Testament church there has never been but one Pentecost, that which occurred fifty days after the resurrection of Christ. That was a special day to the church. It was its birthday. It was a day when the Holy Spirit came into the world to dwell in the hearts of men. It was the beginning of the reign of the Holy Spirit in the world. While men may now receive the Holy Spirit at any time, since He is in the world, it is not proper to speak of "our pentecost," because there has never been but the one Pentecost.

The Coming of the Holy Spirit

The coming of the Holy Spirit had long been promised. He came as the third person in the Godhead. God the Father, God the Son, had well performed their task, now God the Holy Ghost came to complete the work of the Godhead on earth. This is the last dispensation of time because it is under the administration of the Holy Ghost, the third and last person in the Trinity. The Holy Ghost came to fill a definite need in the souls of men. He came in answer to the craving of the soul after God. He brings man into vital and personal contact with God—contact which the soul has craved since sin drove

God out of the human heart. He came to give man power to subject the human to the divine. The Holy Spirit also came to fill a definite need in the church, to enable the church to witness for Christ (Acts 1:8). He enables men to live sinless, victorious lives.

Visible Manifestations

Various manifestations accompanied the outpouring of the Holy Spirit. He came as a rushing, mighty wind which filled the house. Cloven tongues of fire rested upon each person assembled. It is to be observed that such things, from their very nature, are but temporary and must soon pass away. The real benefits of the Holy Ghost must be permanent, abiding. Our need of the Holy Ghost is such that we must have Him constantly. He must abide with us forever. The manifestations of the Holy Spirit, to be beneficial, must be of a permanent nature.

The temporary manifestations of the Day of Pentecost drew mocks and jeers from the crowd. The disciples were accused of being drunk. But the deeper and more fundamental elements of the Holy Ghost that enabled Peter to preach the gospel and to testify of Christ brought conviction to hearts, and three thousand persons were converted.

Sin brought confusion of tongues into the world. Men cannot understand each other's speech. The Holy Ghost brings unity of thought, unity of tongues. That which is designed of God for the benefit of men must not be confusing. Sin separated and divided nations; the Holy Ghost was sent to unite them under one gospel banner and enable them to speak the same thing.

Tongues Not an Evidence

Speaking in other tongues cannot be an evidence of the presence of the Holy Ghost. If so, we must admit that everyone who speaks in another tongue has the Holy Ghost. The facts are that many do speak in tongues who are not recognized by their own brethren as having the Holy Ghost. Evidence of the Holy Spirit must not be of such a doubtful character. It must be something which Satan cannot duplicate, or counterfeit.

Not Mentioned in Prophecy

It must be admitted, that every fundamental thing relative to God's plan was mentioned by the prophets. The prophecy of Isaiah contained so much of gospel principles that he is called the gospel prophet. The fact that speaking in tongues was mentioned by none of the prophets must be evidence that tongues are not a fundamental part of the gospel system. "They shall prophesy," said the prophet, but nothing is said of speaking in tongues. No Bible character, so far as we know, ever sought to speak in tongues or expected to do so.

Cravings of the Soul

It is natural for the soul that has been awakened by the Holy Spirit to crave God. There is then a natural longing after God, a thirsting after God. David said. "As the hart panteth after the water brook, so panteth my soul after thee, O God." God has so constituted man that he craves and longs after God's presence.

God has placed within man a desire and a craving for everything which his soul needs. There is in man a craving for holiness, peace, love, righteousness, unity, joy, and every fundamental element of salvation. The fact that there is nothing in man, nor in the nature of speaking in tongues that any man craves, is proof that it is not a constituent part of the Holy Ghost. To be sure, there are many seeking to speak in tongues but such desires arise, not from the need or inner craving of the soul, but from wrong teaching. Convince a man that he must have one certain manifestation before he can have the Holy Ghost and he will naturally desire that which to him is an evidence that he has the Holy Ghost. Hungering and thirsting after God and his righteousness are the natural cravings of the soul, and God has promised to satisfy that craving.

Evidence of the Holy Spirit's Presence

In view of the foregoing facts it is easy to discover whether or not one possesses the Holy Spirit. First, the Holy Spirit answers the need of the soul. He satisfies that craving which God has put in man. Second, He enables man to live the life which God demands, and one which is pleasing to man himself.

Do men have any evidence of conversion? If so, what is it? Is not evidence the satisfying of the first need of the soul—the knowledge and satisfaction that sins are all forgiven? Does not the Spirit of God witness to one's spirit, bringing that satisfaction and joy that he has been delivered from the guilt of sin and restored to favor with God? No special manifestations are necessary to convince one that he is converted. The peace, the joy, the satisfaction of being saved and in favor with

God, and the witness of the divine spirit seem to be all the evidence that is necessary. In fact this is all the evidence that God has promised.

What, then, is the evidence of the baptism of the Holy Ghost but the completion of the experience of salvation in the soul? Baptism of the Holy Ghost brings a full and complete satisfaction, supplies every need and longing of the soul. It fully satisfies the soul which has craved the divine presence of God. The Spirit can witness to this experience as well as to the forgiveness of sins.

Not only this, but the Holy Ghost gives power to go out and witness for Christ. He gives special power over sin and power to live victorious lives. He gives inspiration and zeal to work for God and the church. Neither salvation nor the Holy Ghost were designed of God to be merely a temporary, superficial sentiment soon to spend its force, but something lasting, abiding, satisfying, and permanent—something that will keep us holy, blameless, and harmless, busy and active in His service until death or until Jesus comes.

William Thomas Seaton, "Is Speaking in Tongues an Evidence?" *The Gospel Trumpet* (December 28, 1940): 5-6.

Fire!
By Ralph E. Morton

FIRE, when not controlled by man, can become a wild, raging thing. HAVE YOU EVER TRIED TO PUT OUT A BRUSH OR GRASS FIRE? If so, you know how much like a ferocious beast it can be. One of the greatest fires in history was the burning of Hamburg, Germany, during World War II. Winds, caused by the rising of the tremendous heat, reached gale forces of over one hundred miles an hour.

Many years ago a different kind of fire broke out of the control of man to spread throughout the then known world. It started in Jerusalem on a Jewish holy day called Pentecost. It was ignited by the Holy Spirit "with cloven tongues like as of fire" and burned furiously, destroying sin and wickedness and radiating the light of truth and righteousness.

After a few hundred years man was able to bring this fire under control, and for about a thousand years it was all but extinguished. One of the strange things about it was that it was the church which brought the fire under human control and nearly extinguished it.

But today this fire of holiness and righteousness is burning again, and wherever it can get out of the control of man is spreads quickly, burning out sin and carnality, giving light to those in darkness.

The psalmist said, "He maketh . . . his ministers a flaming fire" (Ps. 104:4). Jim Elliot, one of five missionaries recently martyred in Ecuador, South America, commented on this scripture by asking, "Am I ignitable?" Then he wrote as his prayer, "God deliver me from the dread asbestos of other things" (in *Through Gates of Splendor* by Elisabeth Elliot, published by Harper and brothers).

How much light is the world getting from you? Can the Holy Spirit touch you and cause you to burn into a flame that will burn furiously for God?

In areas where there is great possibility of fire breaking out, men insulate with asbestos. This world, controlled by Satan, is fearful of the fire of the Holy Spirit. At those places where such fire is likely to break out—in the church—Satan sees to it that these areas are insulated with the asbestos of "other things."

Nothing stifles the work of God, the burning of the Holy Spirit, as much as "other things." More than likely a thick padding of "other things" is right now holding down the growth of your congregation.

If your congregation is average, then about twenty percent of more of you Sunday school enrollment is absent each week. The reason is "other things." And about half of your church group does not come to prayer meeting. The reason, "other things." Also half or more of your people do not carry a proportionate share of the financial load of your church. The reason, "other things."

Live in a physical, workaday world, and some people are bound to get involved in "other things" from time to time. However, regardless of how well we can justify these "other things," the cold fact is that our personal part in the work of the Kingdom does not get done.

Individually or as a congregation we cannot expect to be ignited by the Holy Spirit and burn furiously for God as long as we are shielded by the asbestos of other things. A piece of paper soaked with water will not burn until a specific, scientific percentage of the water has been removed. It is impossible for it to be immersed in water and to burn at the same time. It is impossible for a person to ignite and burn for God until a specific percentage of "other things" has been removed.

Remember, you are not waiting for the Holy Spirit to break through into your life. Rather, the Holy Spirit is waiting for you—waiting for you to break free from the asbestos of "other things." When you do, you will ignite and burn for God.

Ralph D. Morton, "Fire!" *Gospel Trumpet* Vol. 79. No. 7 (February 14, 1959).

The Baptism of the Holy Spirit.
Hillery C. Rice

WE CAN have real peace right here and now in this troubled world of ours. It is sad that millions of people seek peace in that which cannot give peace. Some seek peace through worldly pleasure and financial security. Others seek respite from the worries of life through alcohol, dope, or nicotine. All of these are false sources of peace and can at best afford only temporary relief.

How glorious it is to realize that the Christian has access to an unfailing source of supply! God offers to him the Holy Spirit. Christians have at their disposal the unlimited Power of God!

The Bible says, "Ye have not, because ye ask not" (Jas. 4:2). "Ask and ye shall receive" (John 16:24).

The early church had two powerful symbols in the "rushing mighty wind" and "tongues like as of fire" which accompanied the outpouring of the Holy Spirit on the Day of Pentecost. We today are long on wind but short on fire!

God wants to give the Holy Spirit to his children. God receives more joy in giving the Holy Spirit to his redeemed race than parents receive in giving good gifts to their children.

The Christian should ask himself some pertinent questions: Am I satisfied with myself? Am I all I know I ought to be? Am I often lonely, longing for the Divine companion? Am I burdened with problems which need solving?

If our need is bread, we must not settle for a stone. If you have a need, perhaps God has inspired this article for you.

MY MINISTRY is much like that of other ministers, I am sure. Never before have I witnessed as much stress and strain in the homes of people as there is today. In the homes of even professing Christians we sometimes find marital impediments—husband and wife going in opposite directions. The Holy Spirit is needed in the home. He unifies, solidifies, restores families.

A steady stream of confused, hurt, and frightened people come to my office. Some of them are disturbed by the lifeless religious experience they have. Some lack victory in their Christian lives. They are powerless against temptation, have no appetite for what God offers. These folks are like a crippled ship at sea, purely at the mercy of the sea.

Paul asked some of the brethren at Ephesus, "Have ye received the Holy Ghost since ye believed?" (Acts 19:2). Many translations give this, "Did you receive the Holy Spirit when you believed?" The Holy Spirit must be present to convict the sinner and motivate him to repent and turn to Christ. After conversion, the Holy Spirit is available to come and fully possess the newly redeemed life and do mighty and wonderful things for him.

I am convinced that the Holy Spirit brings men to Christ. I am equally satisfied that the Holy Spirit comes in a greater measure to the redeemed as a subsequent experience.

Some men have given years of study to technicalities regarding the Holy Spirit. They have debated as to the number present in the upper room preceding Pentecost. Some say there were one hundred twenty present, while others differ. It does not seem to me that we need to know.

The devil uses such means as these to strand us in confusion. There is only one element important in our relationship with God—the actual experience of receiving the Holy Spirit. It is vital that we have that experience and keep it in good working order at all times.

I am deeply concerned about what the Holy Spirit can mean to us now and what he desires to mean to every child of God. The supreme question to me is, "Do you have the Holy Spirit?" I mean now!

Often our bickering over technicalities in God's economy irritate[s] the older saints and confuse[s] the younger ones. We need less emphasis on time and place and more accent on the experience of the Holy Spirit. Jesus told the disciples not to fret about times or the seasons, but said, "Ye shall receive power, after that the Holy Ghost is come upon you" (Acts 1:8).

AT PENTECOST the Holy Spirit came. Never before had he been offered to all who would receive him. As a matter of fact, the masses of people had not even heard of the Holy Spirit.

This experience had come to a few persons in Old Testament times—a Joshua here and a Daniel there. But at Pentecost the Holy Spirit baptized *all* who would qualify to receive him.

The Holy Spirit is urgently seeking to find those today in whom he can dwell and through whom he can do his work. I am convinced that the hope for drooping, defeated, discouraged Christians is the baptism of the Holy Spirit.

What can the Holy Spirit do for you? Ills, doubts, and struggles haunt all of us. Much of this is loaded upon us by our own selfish desires. Week by week I am able to help folks open their hearts to the Holy Spirit, and the victories I witness are encouraging.

It is a real joy to tell you, dear reader, just what I am constantly telling many others, and they are discovering the solution that brings hope, peace, and victory to them—the infilling by the Holy Spirit.

The Holy Spirit will purify the heart, the hub and center of all life. "God . . . giving them the Holy Ghost . . . purifying their hearts by faith" (Acts 15:8-9). I know of no other power which makes the heart pure. Neither do I know of any area which is so badly in need of being purified as is the heart.

Malachi speaks of the refiner's fire and fuller's soap (Mal. 3:2). Think of the souls of apparently clean people that are dragged through the Skid Row of jealousy, hatred, malice, fear, doubt! The Holy Spirit as a refiner's fire and fuller's soap is what man needs. The human soul needs scrubbing! The Holy Spirit will cleanse the soul, purify the heart.

Jesus said also that the Holy Spirit will guide into truth. Like an understanding father who takes his son by the hand, saying, "I will lead you," so the Holy Spirit leads those who are willing to be led.

The good father desires to lead and counsel his son as he reaches for maturity. So the heavenly Father wants to lead his children by the Holy Spirit. The Holy

Spirit will lead, if given an opportunity, the vacillating, indecisive person into mature Christianity, the postgraduate kind. No Christian can be happy with a Christian experience which does not grow and progress.

Surely every Christian is eager to be led into more truth. Can you think of a greater need for your life than that of being filled with the Holy Spirit?

The Holy Spirit empowers the Christian. I used to drive an automobile which had no power. When I approached a hill, my car would slow to almost a stop. I would step on the accelerator to no avail, there just was no power. Now, who wants an experience in the spiritual realm which runs out of power at the foot of the hill?

Jesus said, "You are going to receive power when the Holy Spirit comes upon you." You may have power for living, power for service, power for witnessing, power for soul winning."

"Ye have not, because ye ask not" (Jas 4:2). "It you have a Christian experience which stalls at the foot of the hill, as my old car did, why not seek the baptism of God's Holy Spirit? He will fill you with power. Personally, I refuse to be satisfied with insufficient power to live on the victory level which my soul desires.

When I was a young minister I preached about the Holy Spirit quite often because I felt it was my duty to do so. I knew that such an experience is biblical, but I did not have the experience as fully as I should have had it. I was powerless, frightened.

I still preach the Holy Spirit experience because it is biblical. But I now know also what he does for my own life, and I see vividly the need of this experience for every Christian.

If we ministers and our church leaders will operate under the direction, counsel, and power of the Holy Spirit, there is no limit to the success we can have for God and his church!

Why not go to your pastor and tell him you are tired of a powerless, ineffective Christian life? Ask him to pray with you that you may receive the Holy Spirit into your life. The Holy Spirit will make a great difference in your life.

Hillery C. Rice, "The Baptism of the Holy Spirit," *The Gospel Trumpet*. (May 16, 1959).

The Greatest Unused Power.
Zula Evelyn Coon

Dr. A. J. GORDON frequently told the story of an American who with an Englishman was viewing Niagara Falls. Taking the Englishman to the foot of the falls, the American said, "There is the greatest unused power in the whole world." The Englishman replied, "No, no, my friend. The greatest unused power in the world is the Holy Spirit of the living God."

In *Worship Services from the Hymns*, by Zula Evelyn Coon, Fleming H. Revell Co. as quoted in *Gospel Trumpet* Vol. 79 No. 18 (May 2, 1959).

What Happened in the Upper Room?
By Milburn H. Miller

Ten days after the ascension of Jesus Christ, the promised Holy Spirit came upon the 120 disciples in the upper room. They came down from that place different than when they went up.

Before, they were fearful, confused, and sorrowful. Afterward they possessed boldness, love, unity, and gladness of heart.

Not long before, Jesus and his disciples had eaten the Passover supper in an upper room, perhaps the very same room. After the Passover experience of salvation, we need the Pentecost experience of the Holy Spirit baptism.

They were instructed by Jesus to tarry until the power of the Holy Spirit came upon them. After that, the tarrying was to be over. They were to go witnessing.

Some people will not hold still long enough for God to do anything for them or with them. Others tarry throughout their whole Christian profession. It is inconceivable that one could remain silent and idle, once the Spirit of God came upon him.

The upper-room disciples were of one accord. Whatever adverse personal relationships may have existed as they trudged up the stairway to the room of waiting, these differences melted away as they prayed sincerely and made honest confession. A sense of togetherness swept over the entire congregation.

As they waited in eager anticipation, the room was filled with the sound of a mighty, rushing wind, forked flames of fire sat upon the head of each person, and certain of them spoke in other languages. The Holy Spirit had come! They were never the same again.

The Holy Spirit came as wind blowing away excesses. He came as fire burning out impurities. He came as tongues giving the infant church a new language and a new message.

When the Holy Spirit comes upon a person, he will never be the same gain. The wind and the fire and the tongues may not be present, but the experience of the reception of the Holy Spirit can be just as real and realized just as much as when he came upon the 120 disciples in the upper room.

Milburn H. Miller, "What Happened in the Upper Room," *The Gospel Trumpet* Vol. 79 No. 20 (May 16, 1959).

The Baptism of the Holy Spirit.
By Boyce W. Blackwelder

THE baptism of the Holy Spirit is received when there is consecration and appropriating faith.

THE work of the Holy Spirit embraces the whole of the Christian life, every aspect and development of the believer's experience being included in His activity. (As a matter of fact, in all manifestations of Deity, the Father, the Son, and the Holy Spirit are co-active). While the Spirit is present in the converted heart, he takes possession in a greater way in the Pentecostal enduement of power. To the disciples before Pentecost, Jesus said of the Holy Spirit's presence, "Ye know him for he dwelleth with you, and shall be in you" (John 14:17).

In the redemption of an individual there is a difference between the birth of the Spirit and the baptism of the Spirit. That is to say, there is an operation of the Holy Spirit which is distinct from and supplementary to his regenerating work.

The two definite works of the Holy Spirit in human redemption are necessary because of the nature of sin. According to the Scriptures, sin exists in two basic forms: committed and inherited; or willful transgression and a perverted moral nature.

Thus a distinction is made between sin and sins, between sin as root and sin as fruit, between sin as state and sin as act. Because of these two types of sin man has a twofold need. First he needs forgiveness for committed sins, And, second, he needs to be made pure in heart.

CONVERSION meets the first need. It deals with man's willful sins, the believer being justified before God (Rom. 5:1) and regenerated in his own heart (II Cor. 5:17), these being the objective and subjective aspects of the new birth (John 3:7).

But a deeper experience is required to deal with the principle of sin, the innate tendency or proclivity toward evil. The general belief of Christians is that inbred sin or depravity in some sense remains in the believer after regeneration.

Does not every converted person soon become aware of an intense spiritual struggle? Is there not within him the vestige of original sin, a foreign element not yet expelled, a usurper, an actual ally of Satan, a traitor in the camp, always ready to open the soul's door to the enemy? Is not the regenerate man still a needy man?

Paul describes the battle which once raged in his life:

> Accordingly I find this principle [The apostle here uses the present tense for vividness]: While I want to practice the good, the evil is constantly present with me. In my inmost self, I endorse God's law, but I find another principle of a different kind operating in my bodily faculties, warring against the force of my reason, and bringing me into captivity to the power of sin which is expressive in my bodily faculties. What a miserable man I am! Who can deliver me from this dead-

ly slavery? Thank God! It is through Jesus Christ our Lord! Accordingly, then, I of myself with the reason, truly serve the law of God, but the old nature the law of sin (Rom. 7:21-25, as translated by the author).

God's redemptive grace meets the utmost human need. John foretold the method of divine deliverance from the contamination of sin when he contrasted water baptism with the fiery baptism of the Holy Spirit (Matt. 3:11-12). Water baptism symbolizes the regenerating work of the Spirit. Fire is the emblem of the purifying effected when the Spirit is received in his fullness.

BIBLE students agree that on Pentecost the disciples of Jesus received an extraordinary spiritual experience. One of two theological positions must be taken: Either the disciples were not converted until Pentecost, or, having been converted previously, they received at Pentecost a deeper work of grace—the baptism of the Holy Spirit.

It is clear from the New Testament context (Matt. 10:1; Luke 10:17-20: John 14:17; 17:9, 12, 16) that the disciples were converted before Pentecost. That is to say, prior to Pentecost they were born of the Spirit. At Pentecost they were baptized with the Spirit, an instantaneous experience whereby their hearts were purified (Acts 2:1-4; 15:9).

The New Testament records other occasions when believers received the baptism or infilling of the Holy Spirit. The Samaritans after becoming baptized believers in Christ through the preaching of Philip, received a deeper work of the Spirit under the ministry of Peter and John (Acts 8:12-17).

Paul, after his conversion on the Damascus Road, was filled with the Holy Spirit during the visit of Ananias, who came for that purpose (Acts 9:17). After the twelve disciples at Ephesus had participated in baptism characterized by repentance, Paul instructed them more fully, and they received the deeper work of the Holy Spirit (Acts 19:1-7).

That the baptism of the Holy Spirit received at Pentecost was a representative experience—the norm or standard for the gospel dispensation—is indicated by Peter's words: "The promise is unto you, and to your children, and to all that are afar off, even as many as the Lord our God shall call" (Acts 2:39).

Therefore, we conclude that the baptism of the Holy Spirit is God's plan for believers, that it is an experience to be received after conversion, and that it is the means by which the believer's heart is cleansed from all sin. Thus the believer is brought into full salvation, the privilege of Christians under the gospel.

Holiness (sanctification) begins in conversion and reaches its culmination in the baptism of the Holy Spirit. The Apostle Paul prayed for justified persons that God might sanctify them wholly (I Thess. 5:23). By divine inspiration, Paul adds to his petition the words of assurance: "Faithful is he that calleth you, who also will do it" (I Thess. 5:24). Entire sanctification is a New Testament doctrine.

Let us notice how to receive the Spirit's baptism. The baptism of the Holy Spirit is received when there is consecration and appropriating faith. Consecration means complete surrender to the Lord—unconditional yielding to his will. It means following the Savior with unswerving devotion and being loyal to truth at any cost, regardless of the consequences. Surrender must be complete, final, constant. Faith must be definite, personal, vital.

When the conditions are met, we can expect to receive because we have the promise, "If you then, imperfect as you are, know how to give your children gifts that are good for them, how much more will your Father who is in heaven give the Holy Spirit to those who ask Him!" (Luke 11:13, Weymouth).

The words of D. S. Warner, from a hymn of pioneer days, express graphically the truth for the seeker of heart purity:

> *If your all is on the altar laid,*
> *Guard it from each vain desire;*
> *When your soul the perfect price has*
> *paid,*
> *God will send the holy fire.*

THE baptism of the Holy Spirit involves both crisis and growth. Grace is not static but is always dynamic. Crises in spiritual experience characterize beginnings, not terminations. No doubt many Christians have failed to make spiritual progress because they have been content with obtainment and have not realized the importance of attainment. In the highest Christian life growth and development continue in the grace that is received instantaneously.

On occasions after their Pentecostal baptism, the disciples are said to have been filled with the Holy Spirit (Acts 4:8, 31). These incidents indicate that in addition to their original baptism or infilling, believers may receive special anointings of the Spirit from time to time, and that the normal, Spirit-filled life is one which is constantly motivated by the Holy Spirit

After the crisis work of the Holy Spirit by which the believer is made pure in heart and endued with power for service, progress is necessary to achieve one's maximum potential in Christian fruitfulness.

We should remember that in this glorious experience man has a part to do as well as God; that there are both the gift and the task, both realization and aspiration. The Christian experience is a matter of a moment and a matter for a lifetime.

Boyce W. Blackwelder, "The Baptism of the Holy Spirit," *The Gospel Trumpet*. (May 19, 1956).

Editorial.
By Harold L. Phillips

"My Anxious Concern"

Memorable passages are scattered all through the correspondence of the Apostle Paul with the churches which he founded during his career as a missionary to the Gentile World of his day. Each Bible reader likely has a favorite or two among such passages.

Let me suggest that you take your Bible and turn to 1 Corinthians 11:21-33. Here is the catalog of what Paul went through because of his love for Christ and his church, the people of God. It is a moving record and one likely to bring to any of us a sense of shame for any words we have spoken concerning sacrifices we have been called on to make, or burdens we have been asked to bear for the sake of the Kingdom. Paul has topped us all in this matter of selfless devotion.

The other day I was reading this passage in The New English Translation. It is vividly translated here with its catalog of Paul's manifold perils in connection with this work. But verse 28, in particular, struck home: "Apart from these external things, there is the responsibility that weighs on me every day, my anxious concern for all our congregations." Here speaks the man with a shepherd heart who rushes on past his physical dangers to put on record his sense of anxious concern for all the congregations.

It is indeed a part of Christian consecration to be anxiously concerned about the welfare of the church. This is not to say that we are to go around crying "woe,

woe" all the time, or that we are to appoint ourselves as "watchmen" over the work of others. But it does mean that we are to carry a burden for the growth, outreach, and spiritual quality of the church's life and work in all areas where we can bring wholesome, helpful, and healing insights to bear upon it.

Certain anxious concerns have been churning about in my mind in recent months. It is my intention to set down a few of them here in brief form. Maybe you have some concern at some of these points, too.

The problem of keeping vitality in the life and work of the church is a perennial one. We have to do some organizing to get things done in an orderly fashion. This we know and should not decry. But the subtle danger is always present of settling down into a "just-keep-the-wheels-greased-and-turning" sort of church life—dull, irrelevant, time-consuming, traditionalized.

It's quite a shock to those who think of themselves as a "movement" to find spots here and there where the wheels seem to be spinning as fast as ever but not much forward motion is in evidence!

The church is ever in need of revitalizing and renewal. This takes humility. This takes concern. This takes wisdom in perceiving the difference between the temporary and the timeless, the kernel and the husk, the truth and tradition.

Much fresh grappling with the nature and mission of the church in New Testament terms is needed in our time. Fresh insights here could lead to a thrilling revitalization of life and witness among all who call themselves the people of God.

Just take Ephesians 4:12 as one example. It is very easy to read right past the real and exciting import of this verse. It is commonly thought of as addressed to and of concern only to "the ministry" (meaning ordained clergy), as if the total task of the church were the responsibility of the ordained alone.

This point of view is widely prevalent. It is one of the marks of "gone-to-seed" institutionalism. The underlying idea is that the laity are supposed to "hire" clergymen to take care of the church and its mission in the earth.

But this verse, when understood correctly and in its true depth, speaks of equipping God's people (the total church) for work in his service. The difference is both vast and vital. The mission of the church in terms of evangelism, nurture, witness, and service is the responsibility of the whole body. Each surrendered life is "gifted" by the Holy Spirit for a suitable role in the ongoing life and work of the church.

This leads to brief mention of a related concern. The temptation is always great to substitute physical signs and externalized emotions as supposed evidences of the presence of the Holy Spirit in the life of a consecrated and sanctified believer. There are sad and slippery pitfalls along the route of such an approach. Let those who are tempted to take this route beware. We are "gifted" for witness and service, not for ecstasy and personal glorification.

Harold L. Phillips. "Editorial." *Vital Christianity*, (March 24, 1963): 5.

What Did Paul Mean?
Kenneth E. Jones

When Paul speaks of "speaking in tongues," does he mean the same thing as Luke meant in Acts 2, 10, 19?

ONE purpose of 1 Corinthians 12 seems to be to set the gift of tongues in a proper perspective in relation to the other gifts and to the whole life and work of the church. Paul continually puts the gift of tongues at the end of the list of gifts and minimizes its importance and value in relation to the other gifts.

First Corinthians 13 declares that to have and to manifest real Christian love is not only more important than to speak with tongues but more valuable than all the spiritual gifts together!

First Corinthians 14 makes even more explicit the relative unimportance of "tongues" and the necessity for so keeping it under control that it causes no problems in the church.

LET us study 1 Corinthians 12 and notice what Paul says about spiritual gifts. He introduces the subject of spiritual gifts in the first verse: "Now concerning spiritual gifts, brethren, I would not have you ignorant."

(There is no significance in the omission of the word "gifts" in the Greek, indicated by the italics in the King James Version. *Pneumatikoi* must be translated "spiritual men" or some kind of "spiritual things." The context clearly shows that the subject is "spiritual gifts," and it is so translated.)

After this Paul states that all of the gifts, whatever their nature, are the result of the working of the same Holy Spirit. Paul then lists some of the gifts of the Spirit—that is, the abilities, useful in the church, conferred upon persons by the Holy Spirit.

The last two gifts in this list are "divers kinds of tongues" and "the interpretation of tongues." (In each of the three lists of gifts in this chapter, Paul puts "tongues" last.)

When Paul speaks of "speaking in tongues" or "speaking in a tongue," does he mean the same thing as Luke meant in Acts 2, 10, 19? Some scholars have made a distinction between the two and say that while Luke described speaking miraculously in foreign languages, what Paul describes is mere "ecstatic babbling" and must be explained as a result of excitement rather than inspiration.

Charles B. Williams is an example of the translators who make this distinction. (It must be remembered that every translation is of necessity something of a commentary.) Williams consistently translates *glossa* as "language" or "foreign language" in Acts. But in First Corinthians he always translates the same Greek word as "ecstatic utterances" or "speaking in ecstasy."

It cannot be stated too emphatically that this difference in translation is not caused by a difference in the Greek wording. On the contrary, it is based on a theory of interpretation which *assumes* that the descriptions of Luke and of Paul are so different that they are irreconcilable.

This theory itself is an attempt to explain the difficulties in 1 Corinthians 14. Actually, the theory that Paul is speaking of "ecstatic utterances" or unintelligible babbling raises about as many difficulties as it solves.

Admittedly, 1 Corinthians 14 is very difficult, no matter how it is interpreted. But in a case like this, one should accept the interpretation which seems most consistent with the rest of the Bible.

A fuller study of 1 Corinthians 14 will come in a later article, but since chapters 12 to 14 are one unit and must be interpreted as a whole, some general remarks must be made here.

THE whole passage (chapters 12 to 14) is a discussion of the problems which had arisen in the Corinthian church in relation to the gift of tongues or *glossolalia* (Greek: *glossa,* "tongue," and *lalia*, "speaking"). Evidently the Corinthians, in addition to having other serious problems, had put so much emphasis on this gift and its exercise that it had become a source of division. Even their worship services had become disorderly, just as had their observances of the Lord's Supper (1 Cor. 11:17-22). They sought for this gift above all others.

Paul suggested, and then firmly stated, that prophecy is the most important gift and that tongues and their interpretation are the least important because they are the least valuable. First Corinthians 13 is a beautiful expression of the fact that Christian love (*agape*) is more to be desired than all the gifts.

Then, in 1 Corinthians 14, Paul answers specific questions and problems in relation to speaking foreign languages and gives rules to be followed. This discussion would be far easier to understand if we only knew the exact conditions at Corinth and had a list of the questions Paul was answering.

The best solution does not remove all the difficulties, but it seems to be this: Luke, in Acts 2:4ff. makes it clear that by "speaking in tongues" he means speaking in foreign languages by means of the miraculous power of the Holy Spirit. This is so evident that if there is nothing in First Corinthians which as clearly indicates that Paul meant anything else, we must assume that Paul was speaking also of speaking in foreign languages by the Holy Spirit.

There is one other theory which makes a distinction between the "gift" of tongues in Acts and First Corinthians and the "sign" of tongues in Mark 16. This is a strange interpretation which begins with the non-biblical theory that all who are filled with the Spirit will speak in tongues as proof of this fact, and finds an insuperable difficulty in 1 Corinthians 12:30.

First Corinthians 12:30, by means of a series of rhetorical questions, makes it clear that all do not speak in tongues, just as all do not have the other gifts of the Spirit. In order to get around this clear contradiction of their belief that all speak in tongues when they are filled with the Spirit, some have speculated that Paul was here speaking of the gift of tongues, while the passage in Mark refers to the *sign* of tongues. Those who accept this theory say, then, that while it is true that all do not have the gift of tongues, all who are filled with the Holy Spirit will manifest the *sign* of tongues.

This is a purely artificial distinction which has no basis in the New Testament. The chief reference to tongues as a "sign" is in Mark 16:17-18, where four other things are also called "signs." No one of the signs is singled out as being special.

If one of these things is to be called the proof or evidence that one has been filled with the Spirit, then the others must serve the same purpose, because no distinction is made. They are all equally called signs.

The fact is that Mark, as we have seen before, did not mention the Holy Spirit in connection with these signs. They are not anywhere called signs or evidences of the Holy Spirit. Jesus was saying to his disciples that while he was to depart from them physically, the miraculous working of God with them "confirming the word" would prove to them that he was still in their midst, as he had promised.

The whole argument of Paul in First Corinthians is against considering the gift of tongues as more important than the other gifts. He compares the church with individual members manifesting various gifts, to the physical body, with the different parts of the body serving various purposes.

Just as we must not emphasize one part of the body to the exclusion or neglect of others, we must not emphasize one gift to the exclusion of others.

Paul concludes 1 Corinthians 12 with a plea to "covet earnestly the best gifts." Yet, he says, there is a far better way. That is the way of Christian love. This is the theme of chapter 13.

LET us notice 1 Corinthians 13.

Here we find only two references to "tongues." The first is in the first verse: "Though I speak with the tongues of men and of angels, and have not charity, I am become as sounding brass, or a tinkling cymbal."

Paul reminds the Corinthians that if their seeking for "tongues" were so amply rewarded that they could speak in the languages of men and of angels too, all they said would be empty sounds if it were not said in love.

The other reference to "tongues" is in verse 8, where Paul says that even though tongues, and even prophesying, will pass away, love will never cease to be. He magnifies the gift of prophesy but declares that even it will lose its necessity (in heaven), but love will never change.

Paul is here trying to get the minds and hearts of the Corinthian brethren off of their concentration on the gift of tongues. He realized that this was a gift which, if not thoughtfully controlled, would not benefit the church but rather divide it.

Paul clearly indicates (1 Cor. 14:27-28) that the gift can be controlled and that the speaking must be done in an orderly manner. We can judge from the tone of the instructions that the Corinthians had allowed their services to become disorderly and that each was trying to outdo the others in his speaking in tongues. They may have felt that in doing this they were demonstrating superior spirituality. Paul rebuked this attitude.

Kenneth E. Jones, "What Did Paul Mean?" *Vital Christianity*, September 8, 1963, pp 3-4.

Paul's Attitude Toward Glossolalia.
Boyce W. Blackwelder

MOST persons seem to understand that the "other tongues" of Pentecost were intelligible languages (Acts 2:4-11), but some individuals are puzzled by Paul's comments in 1 Corinthians 14. Is the gift of *glōssai* sanctioned by the Apostle homogeneous with that described in Acts 2, or are there two categories of this charism?

Paul nowhere says that he or anyone else, under the impetus of the Holy Spirit, spoke in an unintelligible utterance. First Corinthians 14, from which some instructors have sought support for a theory of "unknown tongues," contains no basis for such a doctrine. Among the pertinent facts revealed by a study of this chapter are the following:

1. Paul does not use the expression "unknown tongue." In every instance in which the King James Version inserts the term "unknown" before the word "tongue" (vss. 2, 4, 13, 14, 19, 27), the term "unknown" is printed in italics, a procedure which indicates that the equivalent of this term is not in the Greek text.

2. The statement, "No man understands" (vs. 2), is not to be taken in the absolute sense, for the interpreter would understand (vs. 5b), or the speaker himself might give the meaning (vs. 13). Verse 2 does not say that it is the *aim* of the speaker to address only God. However, if he speaks in a foreign language which some people do not understand, the Lord does.

3. Paul writes in verse 5, "I wish," or "I might wish" (*theō*) is the form of the subjunctive, the mode of doubtful assertion, as well as the form of the indicative, the mode of positive assertion) "all of you to speak with *glōssais,* but rather that you might prophesy." *Glōssais* here means languages, for Paul does not approve the expression of senseless sounds (vss. 6-9). The Apostle's contrast, "I could wish . . . but rather," is a master stroke of rhetoric to lead the Corinthians to maturity of thought (cf. vs. 20).

4. Every language is meaningful (vs. 10). In classical Greek the term *phōnai* ("voices," KJV) at times indicates languages, and this seems to be its connotation here. See the RSV.

5. "If I pray in a *glōssa,* " i.e., foreign language (vs. 14), is a supposable case, expressed by the conditional particle *ean* and the subjunctive mode. Paul does not sanction devotions in which reason is ignored. If the emotions supplant intelligence, worship loses its Christian character.

6. "I speak" (vs. 18) renders *lalō* as indicative. However, *lalō* is also the form of the subjunctive. In 13:1 Paul uses this same form with the conditional particle *ean* where the verb is unquestionably the subjunctive in a hypothetical statement, "If I speak with the *glōssais* of men and angels. . . ." Accordingly, 14:18 may be rendered, "I might speak," i.e., "I have the ability to do so." Even if Paul spoke in *glōssais,* his speech would be intelligible in harmony with his consistent emphasis in this chapter.

7. Paul says that if he were to speak in a *glōssa,* he would speak words (vs. 19) . The Greek *logous, words,*

embodies thoughts, ideas, or concepts. That is to say, the *glōssa,* or language, would have meaning.

8. Strange languages are not a persuasive, saving token, but a sign with a negative effect upon unbelievers (vss. 22-23). Paul's illustration from the Old Testament (vs. 21) shows that faith is not produced in unbelievers by speaking to them in strange languages (cf. Isaiah 28:11-12, where the reference is to the Assyrian invaders and their barbarous speech).

9. True prophets exercise self-control (vs. 32). The spirits of mantes and sibyls were not under their control; utterance continued until the incitement stopped. But persons motivated by the Spirit of God maintain control of their speech.

10. Linguistic content is suggested by the verb *di-ermeneuo* (vss. 5, 13, 27). In Koinē Greek this verb often means to *translate* (e.g. 2 Macc. 1:36; Acts 9:36) . This meaning fits the context of 1 Corinthians 14, where the term *glōssai* consistently denotes languages.

The foregoing observations indicate that the gift of *glōssai* sanctioned by Paul is the same in kind as that which is described in Acts 2. Thus there is but one category of genuine glossolalia. The New Testament gift was not manifested in a babel of voices. It was explicit linguistic expression inspired by the Holy Spirit and appropriately presented to certain hearers who instantly recognized their native dialects. The listeners not only understood perfectly the actual words but also the meaning of the words which extolled "the mighty deeds of God" (Acts 2:11).

Boyce W. Blackwelder, "Paul's Attitude Toward Glossolalia," *VITAL CHRISTIANITY* (September 8, 1963).

Was Luke Mistaken?
By Kenneth E. Jones

Luke makes it abundantly clear that on the first Day of Pentecost after Jesus' resurrection, the men were speaking foreign languages which they had never learned. . . . All of the references, in Mark, Acts, and 1 Corinthians, describe this same speaking in foreign languages.

EVERY normal Christian longs for a deeper walk with God and is seeking for every blessing he knows God wants to give him. So when a Christian is told that some have received the infilling of the Holy Spirit and have "spoken in tongues" to prove it, it is natural for him to wonder if he is missing something valuable. This is especially true if such statements come from groups not usually classed as "Pentecostal."

This seems to be the explanation for the widespread interest in the gift of tongues just now. "Pentecostal" groups have been saying for many decades that speaking in tongues is *the evidence* that one has been filled with the Holy Spirit. This has not unduly disturbed us because some of us searched the Scriptures and declared that the teaching had no scriptural foundation.

But now the discussion on the gift of tongues and/or speaking in tongues has been revived by members of churches which have traditionally been opposed to such manifestations. A closer look shows that these churches themselves have not revised their doctrine but that they have permitted some of their preachers to experiment along these lines. Nevertheless, it is always valuable to review the teaching of the New Testament to be sure that we are accepting all the truth we can find there.

If the New Testament does teach that all of us should "speak in tongues" as the sign that we have been filled with the Holy Spirit, all of us who desire to please God want to know it.

On the other hand, if there is no indication in the New Testament that one must "speak in tongues" to please God fully, then we can continue to yield ourselves to God's will, and let the Holy Spirit decide what gifts to bestow, and when.

THE first important fact about the New Testament teaching is that the references are so few. "Speaking in tongues" is mentioned only in three books: Mark, Acts, and First Corinthians. We shall look at them in that order.

In Mark the only reference is in 16:17-18, "And these signs shall follow them that believe; In my name shall they cast out devils; they shall speak with new tongues." The next verse continues by listing three other signs. This is the only mention in the Gospels of speaking in tongues. It occurs in Mark's version of Jesus' last conversation with his disciples. It is well known that the ending of the book of Mark does not appear in some of the best manuscripts, and therefore may not have been written by Mark. But even if Mark did not write this, it was written very shortly afterwards, and was accepted by the early church as inspired. It is therefore to be taken seriously.

In this passage in Mark, the following five signs are listed: casting out devils, speaking with new tongues, taking up serpents (presumably without being seriously injured), drinking poison without being hurt, and healing the sick. It is not stated here or elsewhere that these are proofs of the working of God or of the infilling of the Holy Spirit. In fact, the Holy Spirit is not mentioned here at all. They are, rather, signs which point out the reality of the kingdom of God on earth.

Advocates of what is called "speaking in tongues" usually point to Mark 16:17 as proof that this particular phenomenon is the *evidence* that one has been filled with the Holy Spirit. But if the text did prove that much, it would also prove much more—that all five of these signs are the evidence of the Holy Spirit. One must not take any one of the five and hold it forth as *the evidence.*

But as a matter of fact, these five "signs" of the Kingdom are not anywhere in the Bible implied to be *evidence* of the infilling of the Holy Spirit! There is no inference in the New Testament that one should look for any kind of physical *evidence* of the Holy Spirit. Faith is the evidence of this blessing, as of others. No other evidence should be sought by the Christian.

THE fulfillment of the passage in Mark is found in Acts 2:1-11, which describes what happened on the first Day of Pentecost after Jesus' resurrection. As always, the fulfillment of the prophecy is the clearest interpretation of it. Jesus said in the prophecy, "They shall speak with new tongues." It is not clear what he meant until we read Acts 2. The people who were gathered in Jerusalem on the Day of Pentecost from various parts of the Empire heard these Spirit-filled men speaking of the glories of God in the native languages of their hearers. This is the clear meaning of the statement of Luke, as is recognized almost universally by scholars.

Verse four states: "And they were all filled with the Holy Ghost, and began to speak with other tongues, as the Spirit gave them utterance." The Greek word translated "to speak" is *lalein.* This is a rather broad, generic, term which can be applied to anything from uttering inarticulate sounds, to the most exalted varieties of speaking. Its exact meaning in any instance is determined by the context.

The meaning of *glossa* (translated "tongue") must also be determined by the context, since it literally means the tongue but also is used to mean a "language." Luke makes it abundantly clear that he meant that the men were speaking foreign languages, which they had never learned, under the inspiration of the Holy Spirit. He does so by using *glossa* (tongue or language) and *dialektos* (language or dialect—compare Acts 21:40) interchangeably in verses 4, 6, 8, and 11. He emphasizes it by listing the native countries of some of the hearers and underscoring the astonishment of these hearers that they were hearing these Galileans speak their own languages.

It is true that many modern commentators do not believe that foreign languages were spoken miraculously on the Day of Pentecost. However, the only argument which has been brought forward by scholars against "languages" is the belief that Luke was mistaken.

William Barclay is an example of such scholars. He denies that "foreign languages" were spoken by the disciples at Pentecost, and states that they simply spoke or uttered ecstatic babbling under the excitement of the moment. But at the same time Doctor Barclay admits freely that Luke meant understandable foreign languages. For those who believe in the inspiration of the Bible and the historicity of Luke's account, this argument carries no weight.

Some who accept the belief that Luke was mistaken use other arguments to support this belief. For example, they point out that it was not necessary to speak in foreign languages to be understood by all the hearers, since all of them would understand Aramaic, as well as their native language.

The answer to this is that Luke did not state that it was necessary, only that it happened. In fact, there is nothing in the New Testament to the effect that the gift of tongues was given to aid the missionary work of the church by making it unnecessary to study foreign languages.

This theory did not find expression, so far as we know, until the second century. It is more probable that the gift of tongues was one of the many ways the Holy Spirit used to demonstrate to the early church what was so hard for them to accept—that the gospel was meant for all the world, not Jews only. So far as we know, this was the first time the Christian message was told in any language other than Aramaic. And this first time it was done, not by the decision of the Christians, but under the inspiration of the Holy Spirit, miraculously. This made a strong impression, not only on the hearers but on the disciples, as soon as they knew what was happening.

Another such argument is that if the disciples were speaking actual, understandable foreign languages, why would anyone say they were drunken? Since they were accused of drunkenness, the argument goes, they must have been babbling incoherently.

Also, if they were speaking languages known to the hearers, why did Peter not use that fact as proof that they were not drunk?

The simple fact is that to anyone hearing a spoken language he does not understand, it sounds like incoherent babbling. This can be inferred from the English word "barbarian" and the Greek word *barbaros*. One who is speaking a foreign language (foreign to the hearer) is as though he were saying "bar-bar-bar." So he is called a "bar-bar-ian."

Furthermore, Peter himself, when he got up to speak, may not yet have understood the full import of what was happening, since he probably spoke only Aramaic. He would not therefore be sure enough to use the reality of these languages as proof they were not drunk. But he was certain that whatever was happening, it was the work of the Holy Spirit. Under the inspiration of the Spirit he preached a heart-searching message that day.

Adolf Meyer, on this point, stated baldly the underlying assumption of those who deny the fact that actual human languages were spoken. He stated that "the sudden communication of a faculty of speaking foreign languages is neither logically possible nor psychologically and morally conceivable." Those of us who believe miracles are possible may choose to disregard this whole position!

The other two statements in the Book of Acts (10:46 and 19:6) throw no new light on the gift of tongues. The same Greek words *(lalein glossais)* are used, but no adjective is used (such as "new" in Mark and "other" and "his own" in Acts 2). There is no other difference. Such a commentator as Alford, in his *Greek New Testament,* states flatly: "There can be no question that the fact which this narrative (Acts 2) sets before us is that the disciples began to speak in various languages, namely, the languages of the nations below enumerated, and perhaps others. All attempts to evade this are connected with some forcing of the text, or some far-fetched and indefensible exegesis."

Alford consistently maintains that all of the New Testament references, in Mark, Acts, and 1 Corinthians, describe exactly this same speaking in foreign languages which one has never studied. Unless one doubts the veracity of Luke, the author of Acts, this is the obvious conclusion.

And if one doubts the veracity of the author, he is therefore arguing not on the basis of what the Bible says, but rather on the basis of what he thinks it should have said! Such an argument carries no weight with the present writer, who prefers to trust the Word of God.

Kenneth E. Jones "Was Luke Mistaken?" *Vital Christianity*, April 21, 1963

Questions for Charismatics.
By Robert R. Lawrence

Well, I've received another one. Another letter from another soul, this time a pastor, deceived by the "charismatic movement." He pleads with the brethren to accept his "gift" as simply the "baptism with the Holy Ghost."

We used to call it "holy-rollers", then it graduated to "unknown tongues"; now it is an "ecstatic language", or from the Greek; "glossolalia". Sophistication and acceptance is sought as this movement has crept out of the main line Pentecostal churches into inter-denominational groups such as "Full Gospel Business-men's Fellowship" and on into the Protestant denomi-nations and even into Roman Catholicism.

It is still "tongues" where the intelligent mind and will is dismissed and vocal hysteria takes control. It is still a misrepresenting of a clear Biblical gift of known historical languages; *and it is still false!*

False doctrine of any nature must be rebuked. With Christian charity we are called on by the Bible to "preach the word; be instant in season, out of season; reprove, rebuke, exhort with all longsuffering and doctrine." (2 Timothy 4:2)

Often we are told that by rejecting the tongues advocates we are somehow less than Christian. Let it be understood that Bible believing Christians eagerly want all God wants to give them, but know that God will *never* violate his word! What He gives will *always* be in agreement with what His Word offers!

Here is the response of those who first heard the Biblical gift of tongues . . . they said; "we do hear them speak in *our* tongues (languages) the wonderful works of God." (Acts 2:11). The Biblical gift is *not* an "unknown" heavenly angelic; or ecstatic language; or Paul would not have insisted that an interpreter be present. (I Cor. 14:27)

Interpreters translate languages, not utterances!

These are some simple questions the "charismatics" have never answered satisfactorily:

1.) Why is that Jesus *never* spoke in "tongues"?

2.) Why is it that Jesus *never* even mentioned "tongues"?

3.) Why do you accept a *physical* sign, "tongues", as an evidence of a spiritual work? You would quickly rebuke the church groups that say a physical sign, water baptism, proves a person is converted. You're right. Baptism does not produce conversion, and "tongues" does not produce a Spirit-filled life.

4.) If a man, for medical reasons, had his tongue removed, and later sought to be baptized in the Spirit, would God refuse to fill him? After all he *could not* speak in "tongues".

5.) Are we to believe that John Wesley, Charles Wesley, D. S. Warner, Martin Luther, George Whitefield, and D. L. Moody were not baptized in the Spirit? Remember, none of them spoke in 'tongues".

6.) On the Day of Pentecost two other phenomena accompanied the infilling with the Spirit (tongues of fire and a rushing wind), why don't you expect them when someone receives the Holy Spirit?

7.) The Corinthian Church was abusing tongues. This was a troubled church where people were even getting drunk at the Lord's Supper, they were carnally inclined, divisive, committing fornication, eating meat offered to idols, and fighting Paul's apostleship. Why do you get excited about *this* group's experience of tongues? It didn't seem to have done them any good!

8.) How is it that psychologists can produce the "tongues" experience in clinics with *no* mention of God, Christ, and the Holy Spirit?

9.) How is it that voo-doo worshippers of the West Indian and South American world speak in "tongues"? They have never even heard of Jesus.

10.) Why is it that for centuries saints have sought sanctifying grace by offering themselves for the baptism of the Spirit, and got it, but never spoke in "tongues"?

11.) A few weeks ago I sat on a plane beside a man who was leaving Tulsa, Oklahoma where he attended a "charismatic" conference. He told me how the Holy Spirit had given him the gift of "tongues". I asked him why he came to the conference. His reply was "to become a Christian". I said, "Great, tell me about how you received the Lord." Then he confessed, "I didn't. I'm not saved yet, but I speak in "tongues"." Do you accept the testimony of those who have the "gift" but do *not* have the Lord?

12.) If the "charismatics" have been baptized by the Spirit, and are obeying Him, why haven't they come out of the Roman Church and the dead Protestant groups? (2 Cor. 6:14-18) (Revelation 18:1-4)

13.) Why do you ignore the Bible scholars who clearly state that the gift of tongues is a gift of historical languages?

14.) Why do you ignore the fact that there is no "unknown" tongue in the Bible? The word "unknown" in the King James Version of the Bible in 1 Corinthians 14 is in *italics,* because the translators supplied it. It is *not* in the *original* language of the Greek New Testament.

15.) Why do you ignore Paul's list of spiritual gifts that puts tongues last and least? Why is it most important to you, when it was least important to God's Word?

Certainly we love all our brethren, including those who fall into error. "Jude, the servant of Jesus Christ . . ." says to us today "earnestly contend for the faith which was once delivered unto the saints." (Jude 1, 3). It is for the benefit of God's dear people that we stand against ecstatic "tongues" to declare: "Let all things be done decently and in order." (I Cor. 14:40) God's gift does not bring confusion, but provides communication.

Robert R. Lawrence, "Questions for Charismatics," *Reformation Witness*. N.D.

[Included by permission of the author.]

A Biblical Perspective on Tongues.
By Barry L. Callen
(Part One)

EVEN THOUGH THERE are only a few instances in
the New Testament where an occurrence of "speaking
in tongues" is mentioned, the meaning of these few instances often is the subject of major dispute by both the
scholarly and lay communities of the Church.

The appearances of a phenomenon of tongues from
at least the late second century to the nineteenth century
are relatively infrequent and often obscure. One certainly can point to such practices among the Montanists of
the second century, some German Anabaptists of the
sixteenth century and occasional other groups and
prominent individuals. But, in general, the practice of
speaking in unknown or unlearned or "angelic" tongues
has not been a characteristic part of the mainstream of
Christian life.

It is only during the most recent decades of the
twentieth century that the Church as a whole has been
confronted by a widespread manifestation of what is
sometimes called the "Pentecostal experience." The
current situation is so saturated with claims and coun-
terclaims on this subject that it is important to give
some serious thought to its meaning and its appropri-
ateness among Christian people.

Regarding the "charismatic movement" of recent
years, something quite positive stands out immediately.
The Christian gospel is one of "new life" now. There is
to be rebirth, new creation, a deep joy, a real rejoicing,

and an abiding hope that together make a definite difference in a Christian's daily existence. But in our materialistic setting the institutional church for the most part has failed to get this message across in believable and compelling ways. Thus, there has arisen a spiritual hunger that has nurtured the roots of renewal movements.

A Hunger for Certainty

Christians in many settings, all the way from the Roman Catholic Church to the large Protestant denominations, have reached out for *certainty* in their spiritual quest. They have sought for the *experience* of joy. They have asked, "How do I *know* that the Holy Spirit dwells within me?" And many of them have found what they have considered a convincing and satisfying answer in a "baptism of the Holy Spirit" which has been marked for them by a "speaking in tongues." Whatever we wish to say by way of evaluation, these have been real experiences for tens of thousands of persons. From it has come everything from love, joy, and peace, to strife, discord, and bitter division.

Our purpose here is to look again at the relevant biblical teachings in order to gain some perspective. Above all, we do not wish our own experiences or prejudices to blind us to whatever it is that God may have in mind for his people in these days. We must be motivated by a deep concern for a right understanding of Christian experience and for the maintenance of a wholesome unity among God's people based upon revealed truth and valid experience.

Experiences referred to as "tongues" appear almost exclusively in the books of Acts and 1 Corinthians. In Acts we learn of the pivotal events surrounding that first Pentecost. The disciples of Jesus were filled with the Holy Spirit "and began to speak in other tongues" (Acts 2:4). In this inaugural setting for the Church, the biblical writer seems to imply that God granted a marvelous linguistic ability whereby persons could manage to speak the wonderful words of salvation in foreign languages they had never learned. These languages, however, were understood by foreign travelers visiting in the Jerusalem area. Such a gift apparently functioned as a sign for unbelievers and, without question, was a dramatic symbol of the universal scope of the redemption which had been made possible in Christ.

A Double Problem at Corinth

Later, in the city of Corinth, we encounter a very young Christian congregation situated in an immoral city and suffering from internal division and spiritual immaturity. Chief among the problems of these young Christians (most of whom were fresh from pagan backgrounds themselves) was a false view of Christian liberty and a spiritual pride that centered in receiving and exercising certain gifts of God, the gift of tongues in particular. Paul chose to address these problem areas through a letter which we now call 1 Corinthians. As he wrote, he faced a double problem. He had founded this congregation himself and certainly did not wish to discourage their obvious enthusiasm for the faith. On the other hand, their present manner of expressing their faith involved some unfortunate elements that Paul felt obliged to correct.

It probably is fair to conclude that Paul's faith centered in the risen Lord while that of a vocal element among the Corinthians seemed to center much more in the experienced ecstasies and supposed privileges of their relationship to the Spirit of God. When Paul saw their orientation and realized that it was coupled awkwardly to a spiritual immaturity and a tendency to selfish boasting, he knew that he must reorder their priorities. Accordingly, he proceeded to demonstrate in chapter 12 of 1 Corinthians that the purpose of spiritual gifts is the edification of the Church. In chapter 13 he explained the supreme role of love in the proper exercise of spiritual gifts. In chapter 14 he contrasted the relative value of particular gifts, especially the supremacy of "prophecy"[1] over tongues.

Any brief overview of the biblical references mentioning tongues will, of course, fail to elaborate upon the many technical questions raised by the texts involved. Nor do we find any point in reviewing here the many conflicting interpretations given to these texts by Christian scholars across the centuries. At best we can make some observations that will give general guidance from a biblical perspective.

Private vs. Public Use

From the viewpoint of Paul there is a potential legitimacy in some kind of gift of tongues in the individual lives of some Christians (1 Cor. 12:10-11). Such a

---

[1] In this context the word *prophecy* refers primarily to the divinely given ability to communicate with force and clarity, through preaching or other forms of communication, the marvelous truths of God.

gift is listed among the possible gifts of the Spirit (1 Cor. 12:8-10). But in 1 Corinthians Paul is very concerned to regulate the public usage of this gift because of obvious abuse. The desirability of its frequent occurrence in public is questioned and its lesser importance as a gift at all is emphasized.

The exact nature of the several experiences of tongues mentioned in the New Testament is not defined easily. It appears likely that the occasions referred to in Acts involved what is known technically as *zenolalia,* the ability for one glorious moment to speak not an unknown, but a well-known human language which the speaker had not learned previously. The phenomenon in Corinth may have been much the same, a position held by the late Boyce W. Blackwelder[2] and more recently by Timothy L. Smith[3] and Fred Fisher. Fisher, after having reviewed the complexity of evidence involved, concludes that, although it is difficult to be overly dogmatic, the weight of the evidence is in favor of giving the "tongues" at Corinth the meaning of speaking unlearned foreign languages.[4]

Even so, we must recognize that many and perhaps even the majority of Christian scholars continue to understand the Corinthian phenomenon to have been an ecstatic, nonhuman "language" (1 Cor. 13:1; 14:2) primarily addressed to God in private praise and useful to the Church as a whole only if interpreted for common

---

[2] Boyce W. Blackwelder, "Thirty Errors of Modern Tongues Advocates," *Vital Christianity* (May 26, 1974).

[3] Timothy L. Smith, *Speaking the Truth in Love* (Kansas City: Beacon Hill Press, 1977).

[4] Fred Fisher, *Commentary on 1 and 2 Corinthians* (Waco, Texas: Word Books, 1975), p. 217.

edification. Of interest is the dual understanding of Frederick G. Smith that "Christian glossolalia, or tongues, is a gift of God bestowed upon an individual whereby, through the operation of the Holy Spirit, he is enabled to speak *Unto God* in a language which the Spirit chooses and which 'no man understands' or to speak *Unto Men* the mysteries of God in a language unknown to him (the speaker) but understood by his hearers."[5] Smith sees Paul correcting unprofitable extremism in the exercise of the gift of tongues, but placing in the process no prohibition or limitation on its *private* exercise, only a corrective discipline to insure intelligibility and group edification should it involve a *public* exercise.

The debate over whether tongues in the apostolic age were real languages or ecstatic utterances or both is not resolved. To put it negatively, the biblical evidence is ambiguous. To put it positively, clarity at this point is not a central concern of the New Testament and thus is an issue left unaddressed. The important point is that Paul was not deciding the question of the *validity* of this gift so much on the basis of its nature as on the manifestation of the *fruit of the Spirit* in the life of the tongue-speaker (Gal. 5:22-23).

Barry L. Callen, "A Biblical Perspective on Tongues," *VITAL CHRISTIANITY* (JANUARY 21, 1979): 9-10.

[Included by permission of the author.]

---

[5] Frederick G. Smith, Tract—"The Gift of Tongues: What It Is and What It Is Not" (Anderson, Indiana: Gospel Trumpet Company, n.d.), pp. 19-20.

A Biblical Perspective on Tongues
by Barry L. Callen

(Part Two)

(In search of spiritual certainty, many Christians have accepted the gift of tongues as evidence of God's working in their lives. How does the Bible speak to this subject? In this issue of VC, Dr. Callen continues to explore questions about the proper role of tongues.)

OFTEN PERSONS who possess such an unusual gift as tongues, so emphasize the few biblical verses relating to the gift that they create a false perspective which argues for the importance of a gift of tongues in a Christian's life. While it is dangerous to try to establish the authenticity or relative importance of any doctrine by the argument of the Bible's silence on the subject, the following observations on the larger scope of New

Testament materials do help to keep the subject of tongues in proper perspective.

Jesus and Tongues

As one reviews the entire life and teachings of Jesus, the subject of tongues arises only once. This occurrence is reported in Mark 16:17-18, a part of a passage not appearing in many early manuscripts and thus questioned by many as possibly not belonging to the original Gospel. In the Gospel of John, where we find a rich body of teaching about the Holy Spirit in relation to the followers of Jesus, there is not even a suggestion that the presence of the Holy Spirit in the life of the believer will be manifested by "speaking in tongues." Paul mentions this subject only in 1 Corinthians. The absence of other references seems significant since Paul is the great theologian of the Holy Spirit. He gave much attention to the Spirit's work in the life of the Church and in the lives of individual Christian believers. In Romans, for instance, Paul includes a lengthy and varied exposition of the work of the Holy Spirit without so much as a hint that such will include the divine inspiration of an extraordinary tongues speaking.

Paul chose to deal with the subject of tongues in 1 Corinthians because he had been asked by the leaders of that congregation to help them with some of their pressing problems and unanswered questions. He chose to sound a warning that people may be inspired by spirits other than the Spirit of God. Obviously, in this context, he was seeking to address the outstanding problem of their spiritual immaturity. He accomplished this in part by discouraging the practice of tongues, not by condemning it outright, but by diverting their interest and attention into other and higher channels of activity within the life of the church.

Fruit vs. Gifts

Despite the fact that biblical writers rarely address the question of tongues at all, the New Testament certainly does present several anchors of truth as we consider the question of tongues in the life of the church today.

There is an important difference between the fruit and the gifts of the Spirit. Love is a central fruit of the Spirit, the natural characteristic of any person possessed by God's Spirit. Every Christian is expected to have the fruit of the Spirit, whatever gifts he or she may or may not receive. There is a direct relationship between sanctification and the fruit of the spirit in one's life. There is a much less direct relationship between one's sanctification and the possession of a certain number or particular selection of spiritual gifts. The Corinthians seem to have had all of the gifts. However, because of the general absence of the fruit of love which leads to group edification and abolishes spiritual pride, their use of these gifts actually fractured their fellowship.

Sanctification (perfect love) will make all of the difference in how Christians will choose to use what gifts they have, but it will not determine *which gifts* they will receive from God. At this very point the Corinthians were in serious error. They gauged peoples' spiritual lives by whether or not they spoke in tongues rather than by the degree to which they possessed and expressed love. Paul taught that, whereas spiritual gifts are good and necessary in the life of the Church, without the governance of love they can become worse than worthless.

There is a premium to be placed on *prophecy*. Our concern as Christians must focus on a successful communication of the good news of God in Christ. The keynote of Paul is clarity of expression for the sake of maximum impact on unbelievers and orderly and intelligent worship among Christians that serves to further establish them in the faith.

The Danger of Spiritual Pride

We must always insist that the focus of Christian attention should be upon the Lord Jesus Christ and not on ourselves with our personal experiences and gifts. It is always the Giver of gifts and not the gifts themselves that we should desire most earnestly. And it is never to be forgotten that there is the danger of spiritual pride that comes so easily to those who possess gifts, particularly an unusual one such as a gift of tongues.

We must emphasize one truth of major significance. F.G. Smith states clearly and rightly that the real danger, too often present among possessors of the gift of tongues, is the assumption that speaking in tongues "is an invariable accompaniment, the one convincing proof or evidence, of the baptism of the Holy Spirit." Such teaching, he concludes, "is chiefly responsible for the vast amount of deception and fanatical extremism found in the [modern tongues] movement."[6] After a

---

[6] Frederick G. Smith, Tract—"The Gift of Tongues: What It Is and What It Is Not" (Anderson, Indiana: Gospel Trumpet Company, n.d.), p. 41.

critical study of all the New Testament evidence concerning speaking in tongues, Frank W. Beare similarly asserts that tongues "is not regarded by any New Testament writer as a normal or invariable accompaniment of the life in grace, and there is no justification in the classical documents of the Christian faith for holding it to be a necessary element in the fullest spiritual development of the individual Christian or in the corporate life of the church."[7]

Love as Our Aim

So we stand with Paul. Above all, we "make love [our] aim" (1 Cor. 14:1). We rejoice in the fruit of the Spirit. Regarding gifts of the Spirit, we receive only as God chooses to give. It is inappropriate to seek a gift of tongues or to encourage others to do so. We do not dictate the giving of God and we dare not boast about anything he does give. For we know that even if we somehow should be enabled to speak in the tongues of men and of angels, but would fail to have love, we would be nothing more than noisy gongs and clanging cymbals (1 Cor. 13:1).

It is truly unfortunate that some Christian fellowships seem forced into a state of near chaos because some members express their spiritual immaturity through the manner in which they seek and use God-given gifts. When the gift in question is tongues, the likelihood of difficulty seems especially high. Dedicated pastors often seek to express patience and love, only

---

[7] Frank W. Beare, "Speaking in Tongues: A Critical Survey of the New Testament Evidence" in *Journal of Biblical Literature* (Sept., 1964), p. 246.

to find themselves facing a Corinthian-like situation. Persons actively seek a tongues experience and, once claiming its reception, feel compelled to encourage others to do the same. It is not uncommon for a group of "gifted ones" to emerge with a sense of spiritual superiority and an inclination to be more loyal to each other than to the church as a whole. Then the pastor is faced with a difficult problem (very much like Paul faced at Corinth).

While New Testament teachings discourage us from limiting the possibility of someone receiving whatever gift God may choose to give, the Scriptures do alert us to the sure signs of faulty experiences that endanger the Christian fellowship. If the persons involved do not evidence the fruit of the Spirit—love, joy, peace, longsuffering, and so forth; if they choose to edify the church by means of boasting about a gift like tongues; if they encourage others to seek such a gift; and particularly if they imply that receiving such a gift is the sure evidence of being baptized by the Holy Spirit, these persons have stepped outside biblical guidelines.

God grants gifts in order that his children might encourage one another in the faith and so that each might fulfill his or her particular ministry. God's blessing rests only on those who receive and employ their gifts in his cause and for his glory!

Barry L. Callen, "A Biblical Perspective on Tongues," Part II, *VITAL CHRISTIANITY* (FEBRUARY 11, 1979): 9-10.

Another Look at "Other Tongues."
Benjamin F. Reid

Seeking a Biblical Understanding of Glossalalia

THE GIFT OF TONGUES

Here's a principle for you.

> "While speaking in tongues *may* accompany the Baptism of the Holy Spirit,
> THE BIBLE DOES NOT SUPPORT
> THE PENTECOSTAL POSITION
> THAT ALL WHO RECEIVE THE HO-
> LY GHOST WILL SPEAK IN
> TONGUES AT LEAST ONCE."

The Bible DOES NOT support the Pentecostal position that all who receive the Holy Ghost will speak in tongues at least one time. This is not BIBLICAL! Now, remember, anyone who receives the Baptism of the Holy Spirit MAY SPEAK IN TONGUES, if that's the way the Holy Spirit deals with him, but there is NO BIBLICAL FOUNDATION FOR THE TEACHING THAT EVERYONE WHO RECEIVES THE HOLY SPIRIT WILL SPEAK IN TONGUES.

Now when I say tongues, I mean Holy Spirit inspired talk or language that has not been naturally learned, whether it is men's language or angelic language or so-called prayer language or heavenly language or whatever. I stress this because there are all kinds of words and euphemisms for tongues these days.

LET'S LOOK AT THE WORD OF GOD!!

In the Second Chapter of Acts there were three distinct manifestations on that First Pentecost Day —

1. The Rushing Mighty Wind
2. The Tongues like as of Fire
3. And speaking in other tongues as the Spirit gave utterance.

These three manifestations occurred at Pentecost. My suggestion to you is, if God intended for everyone to experience Pentecost according to Acts Chapter two, then there should also be the rushing mighty wind and the tongues like as of fire. The Pentecostal Movement tells me that God wants everybody to receive their baptism just like the disciples got it in Acts chapter two. But, I do not see them looking for rushing mighty winds and tongues like as of fire—all they look for is speaking in tongues. Now we know that these manifestations of wind and fire are unnecessary to the *fact* that the Holy Ghost has come and will fill every believer who seeks him. Likewise, I insist that the wonderful phenomenon of speaking in tongues is not necessary to the fact of the Baptism of the Holy Ghost. He who is a deaf mute can experience the Baptism without *any* of the physical manifestations, and so may anyone else.

So Pentecost was an initial thing — YES!! A sovereign act of God which can be repeated whenever God so chooses. But I repeat my position . . . that this does not — I insist —this second chapter of Acts — does not teach that everyone must speak in tongues at least once. In fact the very context denies this.

The next point is that EVERYONE DID NOT
SPEAK IN TONGUES—OTHER TONGUES—ON
THE DAY OF PENTECOST! Proof — first of all, in
verse seven, it is stated that all these who are speaking
are what? — Galilaeans. Where is Galilee? In Judea.
All of the hundred and twenty were Galilaeans. There
were no foreigners in the Upper Room. They were na-
tive-born Judeans, and the native language of native
born Judeans was Aramaic.

In verse eight, the crowd said, "We hear every man
in our own language or tongue in which we were born.
Parthians, Medes, Elamites, the dwellers in Mesopotamia and *in Judaea* Capadocia, in Pontus, Asia, Phrygia,
Pamphylia, in Egypt, Libya and some other folks from
Rome, etc., Cretes, and Arabians." Now, some of those
people that said, "We hear them speaking in our own
tongues" were from the land of Judea. So somebody
heard somebody speaking plain old Aramaic — their
Mother tongue.

One thing that you must always remember when
you read scripture, the Holy Spirit protected the text so
you know all that you need to know. And the Holy
Spirit deliberately, in order to erase this heresy, let us
know that on the Day of Pentecost. EVERYBODY DID
NOT SPEAK IN TONGUES. The Holy Spirit made
sure that when Luke, who was the most careful historian in the Word, recorded that day, he included the fact
that there were some folk from Judea who heard them
speak in their native language. So when someone
comes to me saying that on the day of Pentecost, EVE-
RYBODY SPOKE IN TONGUES, I say NO THEY
DIDN'T! The Bible deliberately and distinctly said that
everybody did not speak in tongues, even on the day of
Pentecost. And if there was any time when everybody

should have — that was the time. But God deliberately states that even on that great day there was somebody praising God in Aramaic, his native tongue!

This is not at all an attempt to be picky about scripture, it's a fact! And just to make sure I was not wresting the text, I went back and got the Greek New Testament to make sure that Judea was in there — in the original manuscript — and it was there! So on the Day of Pentecost, I submit that everybody THEN, DID NOT SPEAK IN TONGUES.

SECTION TWO

Turn to Acts 4:31 — "And when they had prayed, the place was shaken where they assembled together and they were all filled with the Holy Ghost and they spake the word of God with boldness."

So in Acts 4:31 everybody there did not speak in tongues, in fact, the Holy Spirit does not record ANYBODY speaking in tongues. The Holy Spirit only indicates that there was a spoken word with boldness. So here is an incident where the same root words in the Greek are used (pletho - filled).[8] "They were all filled with the Holy Ghost" and they spake NOT with other tongues this time. They simply spake the word of God with boldness . . . and verse 33 says so — "And with great power gave the apostles witness of the resurrection of the Lord Jesus and great grace was upon them all." This is in direct fulfillment of Jesus' words of Acts 1:8 — "But ye shall receive power . . . and ye shall be witnesses unto me." So Acts 4:31 teaches that one can

---

[8] Also Acts 9:17; Acts 13:9.

indeed be filled with the Holy Ghost and not speak in other tongues.

SECTION THREE

Please turn with me to Acts 8:14-18: "Now when the apostles which were at Jerusalem heard that Samaria had received the word of God, they sent unto them Peter and John: who, when they were come down, prayed for them, that they might receive the Holy Ghost: (For as yet he was fallen upon none of them: only they were baptized in the name of the Lord Jesus). Then laid they their hands on them, and they received the Holy Ghost."

The Holy Spirit speaks clearly that here in Samaria they received the Holy Ghost. There is no mention or hint of tongues in this passage. However, some Pentecost people and some Charismatic believers say when Simon saw that by the laying on of the hands of the Apostles the Holy Spirit was given, he offered them money saying, "give me this power". They tell us that Simon had to see something . . . and what he saw, was tongues. This is an argument from silence. This is an argument from that which the Holy Spirit has omitted. You don't know what manifestation he might have seen — for there are many manifestation of the Spirit. Suppose someone fell out, which was common in those days, and which is common in certain segments of our society today. When some Christians get the Holy Spirit, they fall out and yet the Bible does not teach anywhere that when you get the Holy Spirit you have to fall out.

I listen to some evangelists who make a big display about hundreds who were slain in the Spirit — THAT did not even happen on the day of Pentecost. On the day of Pentecost, no one fell out! They *got up* and *went out* and aroused the whole community . . . they did not fall out! But that is one manifestation of the Holy Spirit — sometimes people get overly charged and they fall out under what some people call the Holy Spirit's unction. I sometimes worry about that, because in the New Testament the only people who were falling out were people who were demon possessed. That's a Bible fact! When the Lord baptized me, with the Holy Ghost, I told him I did not want to fall out, because I did not want any evil spirit sneaking in on me while I was out. I wanted to be fully conscious when the Holy Ghost took over my life. And praise God, I was! I was overwhelmed and caught up in the Spirit, but I was fully conscious.

Now Acts 8 does not teach speaking in Tongues . . . I'm sorry, I don't care what anybody tells you and it's travesty on scripture to try to read tongues into that. "What did Simon see?" I heard a man preaching about that the other day —"What did Simon see?" I said "I don't know what Simon saw—you don't know what he saw!" "He must have seen speaking in tongues!" The Bible doesn't say that! The Bible says when they laid their hands on them they received the Holy Ghost. PERIOD! Now God knows where to put his PERIODS!! His COMMAS!! His QUESTION MARKS!! He knows where to end sentences and he knows where to complete them, and add to them!

This is another principle to remember — THE HOLY SPIRIT NEVER OMITS A DETAIL THAT WE MUST KNOW — HE NEVER OMITS A DE-

TAIL THAT WE MUST KNOW!! If it's not there, it's because the Holy Spirit doesn't want it there!

SECTION FOUR

Acts 9:17 — "And Ananias went his way, and entered into the house; and putting his hands on him said, Brother Saul, the Lord, even Jesus, that appeared unto thee in the way as thou camest, hast sent me, that thou mightest receive thy sight, and be filled with the Holy Ghost. And immediately there fell from his eyes as it had been scales: and he received sight forthwith, and arose, and was baptized." Now, in Paul's case, his Holy Ghost Baptism was accompanied by his deliverance from blindness. Here, there is no initial evidence of speaking in tongues mentioned accompanying Paul's Baptism.

SECTION FIVE

Acts 10:44 — "While Peter yet spake these words, the Holy Ghost fell on all them which heard the word. And, they of the circumcision which believed were astonished, as many as came with Peter, because that on the Gentiles also was poured out the gift of the Holy Ghost. For they heard them speak with tongues, and magnify God." Now, finally for the second time in the Book of Acts, the introduction of the Holy Ghost to the Gentiles is accompanied by the self same sign as the introduction of the Holy Ghost to the Jews . . . they spoke in tongues. Now, WHY?

Acts 15 will tell you — they had the council in Jerusalem sometime later, and some narrow-minded Jews were fussing and saying those Gentiles didn't have it — salvation was not for them. Peter said, "oh, no — they have the same thing we have and they got it the same way we got it. That is why I said, in opening, that anyone who receives the baptism of the Holy Ghost MAY speak in tongues, if that's the way the Spirit wants it. There is no Bible support for the teaching that EVERYBODY WHO RECEIVES THE HOLY GHOST MUST SPEAK IN TONGUES at least once.

SECTION SIX

Acts 19:6 — This is the final recorded instance of Holy Spirit Baptism in the Book of Acts. "And when Paul had laid his hands upon them, the Holy Ghost came on them; and they spake with tongues — AND Prophesied." Now, in this 19th Chapter of Acts, there are two manifestations of the Holy Spirit — they spake in tongues and prophesied. Do you know anybody that teaches that everyone who receives the Baptism of the Holy Ghost must prophesy? There's just as much support for that as there is for speaking in tongues. For here in one of the "initial evidence cases", they spoke in tongues and prophesied. So I have just as much right to insist that everybody who speak in tongues must prophesy — as someone else who says that everybody must speak in tongues. The Bible does not support the premise that everyone who gets filled with the Holy Ghost must speak in tongues. The Bible does not support that! Nor does the Bible support the premise that everyone who speaks in tongues is spirit-filled.

Please turn to Corinthians 12. On various occasions, as I have traveled among Charismatic people, I have told them that I received the Holy Spirit's baptism with no initial evidence of speaking in tongues. They have responded that everybody does not have the *gift* of tongues. But they insist there is a difference between the gift of tongues, which only some people have, and the initial evidence of speaking in tongues, which, they say, everyone must have.

I have pleaded with them to show me one scripture that says there is a difference between tongues in Acts (which they call the initial evidence) and tongues in I Corinthians (which they agree is the gift of tongues) — but they couldn't find such scripture.

Since I'm not a Greek Scholar, I went and got the Greek New Testament and Lexicon and I looked up all of the instances of Glossalalia. (Glossa is the word for tongues in Greek). And I said now, that's what is in Acts — GLOSSA — and since they say that there's a different tongue in I Corinthians, I know there will have to be a different Greek word. When I got over in I Corinthians, the word was GLOSSA. So according to the *textus receptus* (that's the Greek text your Bible was translated from) the same word was used in Acts and in I Corinthians and Paul knew no different kind of tongue from Peter, James, or John — according to the text.

"But we don't know Greek." Alright, if we don't want to go back and get the text that we received from the Greek, let's just look at the text we have in English — and there is no distinction. And there is no verbal hint in the Bible that tongues in Acts are different from tongues in I Corinthians — it's not in the Book!! It simply appears that by the time Paul is writing in I Corinthians, he had to give the church instructions and guidelines on how to use the precious gift and control the gracious manifestation that God gave the church in the Acts of the Apostles.

SECTION SEVEN

Now Paul begins teaching Chapter 12:1, 4-6, "Now concerning spiritual gifts, brethren, I would not have you ignorant. Now there are diversities of gifts, but the SAME SPIRIT. And there are differences of administrations, but the same Lord. And there are diversities of operations, but it is the same God which worketh all in all." Now anytime you come to the place where you insist the Holy Ghost plays on only one string — *you are dead wrong!* The Holy Spirit deals with each believer as *He wills.*

There is no place in the Bible that says the Holy Spirit deals with all believers the same way. And you are wresting scripture and insulting the intelligence of the Holy Spirit and denying the revealed word of God when you say the Holy Ghost deals with every Christian in exactly the same way and with the same manifestation.

Differences of gifts, differences of administration, differences of operations, DIFFERENT! DIFFERENT! DIFFERENT!!! The whole point of the Spirit-filled life is no longer do we all have to go through the same rituals! Under the Law we all had to worship in exactly the same way for it to be acceptable by God. Under the Holy Ghost dispensation, there are *differences of administration, differences of operations, differences of gifts—but the same Spirit working in all of them. The Holy* Ghost has more intelligence than to insist that everybody that's filled must speak in tongues. And we dyed-in-the-wool Church of God people — He's got more sense than we have — we won't let *anybody* speak in tongues — and that's wrong too. We cannot condemn nor forbid speaking in tongues. It is a valid and Biblical Spiritual gift and has as much right and place in the church of God as the gifts of preaching, healing, teaching and pastoring.

In the Church of God, too many of us honestly don't want tongues. We don't want them included in our order of worship at all — and that's wrong! I am not opposed to people speaking in tongues, for tongues is a valid New Testament Gift of the Spirit and belongs in the New Testament Church today! As long as the gift of tongues is used in an authentic and spiritual manner, *no one* can forbid its operation in the Church of God.

The ONLY THING I insist upon is, that you *cannot ever teach* Biblically that everybody HAS TO SPEAK IN TONGUES. That's where people go wrong. That's where I oppose speaking in tongues . . . when you teach everybody MUST SPEAK. The Bible doesn't teach that.

SECTION EIGHT

I Corinthians 12:7 — "But the manifestation of the Spirit is given to EVERY MAN to profit withal." Then Paul goes on to show you how he means that — I Corinthians 12:8-11 — "For to one is given by the Spirit the word of wisdom; to another the word of knowledge by the same Spirit; to another faith by the same Spirit; to another the gifts of healing by the same Spirit; to another the working of miracles; to another prophecy; to another discerning of spirits; to another divers kinds of tongues; to another the interpretation of tongues: BUT ALL THESE WORKETH THAT ONE AND THE SELFSAME SPIRIT, DIVIDING TO EVERY MAN SEVERALLY AS HE WILL." Severally means individually. "Dividing to every man individually as he will." *He* decides what gifts he gives. When the Holy Spirit comes into your life you might do any number of different things — he divides your gift to you individually as he wills. (The word "severally", I am translating it correctly . . . Greek — *idios*, to each his own, individually).

I Corinthians 12:27-30 — "Now ye are the body of Christ, and members in particular, and God hast set some in the church, first apostles, secondarily prophets, thirdly teachers, after that miracles, then gifts of healings, helps, governments, diversities of tongues." "Are all apostles?" (No!) "Are all prophets?" (No!) "Are all teachers?" (No!) "Are all workers of miracles?" (No!) "Have all the gifts of healing?" (No!) "Do all speak with tongues?" (No!) "Do all interpret?" (No!)

Now that's what made the Pentecostal theologians believe there had to be a different kind of tongues — because Paul so emphatically states that ALL DO NOT SPEAK WITH TONGUES!! Now there is no way in the world you can take the Bible and read it and understand it clearly and go out of here saying everybody who receives the baptism of the Holy Ghost must speak in tongues at least once. The Bible just got through telling you that all do not speak with tongues READ THE WORD, PLEASE. READ THE WORD! I don't care what kind of experience you have, you can't twist the word to meet your experience . . . you must adjust your experience to the word and the word says all DO NOT SPEAK WITH TONGUES — THE WORD says that!!

I didn't say it!! And until God takes it out of the word, don't preach or teach that everybody has to do it. And the Bible isn't as nice as I am about this, I said everybody doesn't have to do it — but the Bible says EVERYBODY DOES NOT!! It's in the Bible, I'm not trying to teach you something out of my head.

I Corinthians 12:31 — "But covet earnestly the best gifts: and yet show I unto you a more excellent way." Now that is the thing that scares me on this whole problem of charismatic phenomenon. "I show unto you a more excellent way!" "There is something in the church," Paul says, "that is more important than all the gifts of the Spirit . . . whatever they are. The grace of LOVE exceeds all spiritual gifts." I'm going to say something that none of you is going to like, but I am going to say it anyway. I would rather have a church without any spiritual gifts at all that is filled with love than to have a church filled with spiritual gifts that has no love. That's why the Church at Corinth was in the mess it was in — because the members had tongues and all the rest of the outward expressions and manifestations of the Holy Spirit but they didn't have basic Christian love. I'm going to tell you something that you are not going to like, but it is a whole lot easier to twist your tongues up and come out with some ecstatic utterance than it is to show consistent Christian love. It's a whole lot easier to come out with a message in tongues or prophecy than it is to show basic Christian love to an unlovely person. So a lot of folk in the Church of God as well as other churches repeatedly go through their emotional orgasms and their external manifestations and their so-called spiritual expressions, and yet remain loveless and mean and cantankerous and hateful and biting and deceitful and jealous!

You see, it is easier to roll on the floor than it is to love somebody in the next pew that doesn't love you. It is easy to stand up and say "thus said the Lord in these last days God is sending a new thing in the world, yea, yea thus said the Lord . . ." It is easier to say that than to stop being resentful and bitter and mean toward other people. So often we attempt to use spiritual endowments as a spiritual escape hatch!

So Paul says, "I am trying to teach about spiritual gifts, and you should have them. Covet them, and covet the best ones — and whatever you think is the best one, is the best one for you. I'm not trying to say that tongues is worse than anything else, or that it is the least of the gifts. But I am trying to show you a more excellent way. I want you to have the love of God abounding in your nature and in your actions, if you don't have *any* gift." Have you not seen loveless pastors who can preach you into next year and they step out of the pulpit and they can't even relate to you a brother? Being gifted isn't the last word, the last word is LOVE. And what shakes me up is Paul doesn't leave you hanging up in space wondering what he is talking about. He tells you how love acts. Love is more than sappy sentimentality, love is action!

Love suffers long and is kind. That wipes out half of the church! Because you and I are not going to suffer too long before we become unkind. And then you see, we turn around and try to justify our unkindness by our suffering. "But you don't know what I'm going through."

Whatever you are going through, love suffers long. They hung Jesus between heaven and earth after racking his body all night long, and running him from judgment hall to judgment hall. They whipped his back, shoved thorns on his head, nailed him to the cross, and he still had enough love to say, "Father, forgive them." I get so disgusted with all this noise about, "Honey, what gift do you have?" "Honey, I have the gift of discernment . . . I see." Why don't you see yourself! A loveless, mean and vengeful person is not spiritual no matter what gifts he possesses.

Please continue reading I Corinthians 13:4-7 — Jesus says through Paul in this chapter, love is the primary thing. LOVE IS NOT ENVIOUS, LOVE DOESN'T PUSH ITSELF FORWARD, IS NOT PUFFED UP WITH PRIDE, LOVE DOES NOT MISBEHAVE, LOVE IS DISCIPLINED. Biblical love is not an emotion — that is natural or human love. *That is EMOTION!* Biblical love is a disciplined response to the inner working of the Holy Spirit. (Some day I will teach on that). DOES NOT SEEK HER OWN, IS NOT EASILY PROVOKED, DOESN'T EVEN THINK EVIL. You know, every time I get a little upset because I don't have as many spiritual gifts as some preachers claim, I say to myself let me go back and read this and work on this love some more. REJOCETH NOT IN INIQUITY, REJOICES IN TRUTH: BEARETH ALL THINGS . . . you see that's why it is so much easier to dance in the spirit than to love. "BEARETH ALL THINGS" — but Lord, I can't put up with any more of this — "BEARETH ALL THINGS" — Lord, I don't even have to put up with these things and I am *not* going to put up with it — "BEARETH ALL THINGS" — And despite our dismal failure to love, the church is running around seeking gifts. "Everybody lift your hands and ask the Lord for your gift." If the Lord would give some of us the gifts we want — He would have to kill us the next day! We would get so proud, so out of control, so stuck on ourselves, so filled with our own importance that we would be of no use to Him. Still, the Lord is saying, "Why don't you let me give you some love?" Some of you don't need *another* tongue, you can't control the one you have! Why don't we learn to look at the word and get our directions from the word of God, and that direction is to pursue love and then whatever gift the Holy Spirit bestows on you will be a blessing to the body of Christ and to you.

I love the exercise of spiritual gifts. I try hard as a Pastor not to be repressive — I really do. I give some folk in our local assembly too much freedom because I want to provide an atmosphere in the church in which there is freedom to use spiritual gifts. But, Lord have mercy, the more gifts we get, the less love we exhibit!

LOVE BELIEVES! Some of us don't believe in anything. And it doesn't mean doctrine. It's talking about believing in people. If you can't trust people — you need to get more love! HOPETH! Love is eternally optimistic. That's why some of God's people yet reach out for some folk you have fallen out with and will not talk with any more as long as the world stands. And even though you have given up on them and refuse to even pray for them — thank God, there is someone else who loves them and keeps on trying. Love is still hoping — "Lord, you are going to help them." LOVE ENDURES, puts up with all things. Can you see why it is so much easier to speak in tongues than to love? It takes no special grace to speak in tongues, but it takes God's grace to LOVE!! I Corinthians 13:8 — "Love never stops trying." Isn't that beautiful! "Whether there be prophecies, they shall fail; whether there be tongues, they shall cease; whether there be knowledge, it shall vanish away." There is going to come a time where there are going to be no spiritual gifts — AT ALL!! And the only thing that will be left is LOVE! And if you don't have love now, you will not have *anything* later. Paul tells you he wants to show you a MORE EXCELLENT WAY. *The man, the woman that walks in love is far more excellent than the person who has all the gifts of the Spirit.*

I Corinthians 14 — All I have done here is to take each verse that has the word "UNKNOWN" tongue and drawn a line through "UNKNOWN" because "UNKNOWN" was not in the original Greek text. "UNKNOWN" is an editorial gloss in the King James Version. There are some words in the Translated Bible that were added by editors and they are always in italics so you will know that this was added. In most cases, the translators added the words to make the passage clearer. But, in this case the word "unknown" makes the meaning more obscure. This word "UNKNOWN" confuses folks. Now there is a language unknown to all of us. We speak English, so we know that. French is known to a few of us, but unknown to most of us. Spanish is known to some of us, but unknown to most of us. So this is what the editor had in mind. There is no such thing as an "unknown" tongue in the spiritual realm. While it may be unknown to you, an authentic tongue is not unknown to our Lord.

Paul deals in the 14th Chapter of I Corinthians with the use of tongues and prophecy IN THE CHURCH. I don't care what you do at home in your secret closet. Whatever you do or however you pray is your business. There are things that you might do in your secret closet that might be unseemly in the church. Paul says what you do in the church must be decent and in order.

That's why some fanatical folk have brought reproach on the Spirit of God, because of their unseemly behavior and often the worse they do, the more they say the Holy Ghost is to blame! It upsets me for people to blame their unseemly behavior on the Holy Ghost.

Remember this, "He that speaketh in tongues, speaketh not unto men, but unto God." If the Lord gives you a message in tongues, you have not said anything to me yet; until you or someone else interprets it. "He that speaketh in tongues edifieth himself." This is where my Charismatic brethren get their prayer language concept from, and it is a valid concept.

"Oh, I go in my closet and I pray in tongues and I'm so edified." Right! Nothing is wrong with that!! You can't fuss with anyone for doing that. YOUR PRAYER LANGUAGE EDIFIES YOU!! But, when we come to the house of God, we are not here to edify ourselves — we are *here to edify the Body!* You come to church to hear the word, but you also came to EDIFY THE BODY.

Paul says in I Corinthians 14:5 — "I would that ye all spake with tongues; (I WISH YOU ALL COULD, BUT I KNOW YOU CAN'T! God didn't plan it that way). "But rather that ye prophesied: for greater is he that prophesieth than he that speaketh with tongues, except he interpret, that the church may receive edifying." Tongues are out of order in *the church* unless they are interpreted! That is why I do not accept the concept of everyone speaking in tongues when he receives the Holy Ghost. Someone would have to interpret what he is saying in church or he would have to keep silent.

I Corinthians 14:6 — "Now, brethren, if I come unto you speaking with tongues, what shall I profit you, except I shall speak to you either by revelation, or by knowledge, or by prophesying, or by doctrine?" Now, what he's saying here is that even when I interpret, it cannot be foolishness — it must be in revelation, knowledge, prophesy, or doctrine! That's how tongues are supposed to build up the church. Give the church a revelation from God — give the church some knowledge they don't know about — give the church a prophetic word from God — or teach the church about some doctrine they are confused about. NOW THAT'S THE PROPER USE OF TONGUES IN THE CHURCH!

I Corinthians 14:12 — "Even so ye, forasmuch as ye are zealous of spiritual gifts, seek that ye may excel to the edifying of the church." I don't preach to make myself happy —I'm trying to edify the church. When I speak, I'm trying to reveal truth to you — to edify or build you up. THAT'S THE PURPOSE OF TONGUES IN THE CHURCH!

I Corinthians 14:13 — "Wherefore let him that speaketh in a tongue pray that he may interpret." If you are afraid there are no interpreters present, say, "Lord, since I feel this thing coming, please Lord, help me to interpret it."

I Corinthians 14:14 — "For if I pray in tongues my spirit prayeth, but my understanding is unfruitful." Unfruitful — you don't know what you are praying — you may feel all kinds of goodies inside, but you don't know what you are praying about. Again, there is nothing wrong with this. God may very well want you to intercede for someone or something beyond your human understanding. So the Spirit would then pray through you in tongues.

I Corinthians 14:15 — "What is it then? I will pray with the spirit, and I will pray with the understanding also." Here Paul is saying he doesn't want to pray in the spirit only, without understanding — but at other times he wants to understand what he is praying about. "I will sing with the spirit, and I will sing with the understanding also." In private devotions, praying and singing in tongues is personally edifying for those in whom the Spirit works this way. At God's house, however, I must seek to pray and sing so that others can understand me.

I Corinthians 14:16 — "Else when thou shalt bless with the spirit, how shall he that occupieth the room of the unlearned say amen at thy giving of thanks, seeing he understandeth not what thou sayest?"

I Corinthians 14:17 — " . . . thou givest thanks well, but the other is not edified." Now look at Paul's statement here —

I Corinthians 14:18 — "I thank my God, I speak with tongues more than all of you!" 'What Paul is saying — "If you want to be Super-Spiritual, I have more tongues than all of you! Isn't that something?" You see, Paul had tongues-speaking ability both spiritually and naturally. So he says, "If you just want to swap tongues, I'll leave you in the shade, for I can speak more than all of you."

I Corinthians 14:19 — "Yet *in the church* I had rather speak five words with my understanding, that by my voice I might teach others also, than ten thousand words in a tongue." Did you read that in your Bibles as I did? I want to make sure we both have the same thing! You see that's why the Pentecostals had to come up with a difference in those tongues. They had to say the tongues in Acts was different from the tongues in Corinthians. But Paul just wiped them out. Paul says he would rather speak five words in church in understanding —in whatever language of the vernacular is than ten thousand words in other tongues! You see that disturbs all these super spiritual folks that think tongues is a sign that they are very spiritual. Paul appears here to be actually down grading tongues, unless they are accompanied — in the church — by interpretation.

I was listening the other night to one of those radio talk shows and this sister called in and said she got her prayer language. Oh, she was so happy! "Thank God, I got my prayer language!" And I said, "What is that all about? Will someone please ask the woman DID SHE GET THE HOLY GHOST?" Your prayer language doesn't mean "beans" ... *did you get the Holy Spirit!* Jesus said you shall receive POWER — NOT NECESSARILY TONGUES when the Holy Spirit comes upon you.

I Corinthians 14:20-21 — "Don't be children in understanding. In the law it is written with men of other tongues and other lips will I speak unto this people; and yet for all that will they not hear me, saith the Lord." That takes care of those folk that say you can't hear from the Lord until somebody gives a message in tongues. God said, "I'm going to do it and still some hard hearts will not hear!"

I Corinthians 14:22 — "Wherefore tongues are for a sign, NOT TO THEM THAT BELIEVE, BUT TO THEM THAT BELIEVE NOT!" So when you jump up in church trying to impress me with your spirituality by speaking in tongues, you are not impressing me ... *it's not for me.* It's for a sign to unbelievers, demonstrating in a special way, the Power of God. And in Acts that was true, when the UNBELIEVERS heard these un-learned Galileans speaking languages they had not learned, the UNBELIEVERS were impressed and gathered together.

The UNBELIEVERS said, "What does this mean?" Then what happened? The tongues did not save them! Then Peter stood up and preached the word!! I want you to understand clearly that *tongues don't save folks . . . the Word preached in the Spirit saves!!* "Wherefore tongues are for a sign to them that believe not . . . but prophesying serveth not for them that believe not, but for them which believe."

I'll give you an example of what he is saying here. When God spoke prophetically in one of our services recently, he dealt specifically with the problems of the believers. You heard God speak to YOUR problems, to YOUR struggles, to YOUR heartaches, to YOUR fears, to YOUR doubts, to YOUR uncertainties. That's prophecy, a word from the Lord for his people.

So when I get ready to edify the church, I must prophesy. And if I speak in tongues, it *must* be interpreted! I must . . .

Benjamin F. Reid, ANOTHER LOOK AT "OTHER TONGUES," *Vital Christianity* (June 30, 1985), [Included by permission of Sylvia Reid, daughter of Benjamin F. Reid.]

Bible Truth About Today's Tongues.
By Richard M. Bradley

IN the last score of years, there has been an unusual growth in a phenomenon known as "speaking in tongues." It has cut across all denominational lines with manifestations among Roman Catholics, Lutherans, Methodists, Presbyterians, and many Evangelicals including many congregations of the Church of God reformation movement.

Through enthusiastic evangelism this phenomenon has been propagated as the single most important need in an individual's life and that without it, that person will have at best only an emaciated experience with the Lord.

This experience has been enhanced in great part by its promotion by slick programming on cable television networks on which big name evangelists and Hollywood stars appear who advocate that their lives have been drastically changed through the receiving of this so-called gift. (However, it seems strange that a night or two later they are back on the nightclub circuit doing their worldly entertainment for the accolades of men and women!)

Many congregations have been torn apart with strife and division generated as a result of divisive characteristics of this phenomenon. In some cases pastors were forced to resign prematurely because of the confusion and contention accompanying tongues speaking.

With this in view, many honest-hearted believers are wondering if they should seek to speak in tongues to enhance their spiritual lives. Plagued with uncertainty, they ask, "Have I received all that God has for me? Am I resisting the Holy Spirit? Am I in danger of blaspheming the Holy Ghost by my refusal to seek the gift of tongues?"

Amid this confusion it is time to sound a clear note. The answer to these questions can be found only in the pages of God's eternal Word! It is imperative that *all* these questions be answered by the Bible, and not by someone's experience.

To avoid confusion at this point we must examine this so-called experience in the light of eternal truth, and there is no greater source of truth than God's wonderful Word! Permit me to share a most important rule of thumb regarding spiritual matters: Always work from the Word of God to the experience, never from an experience to the Word of God! This is a Bible principle that will stand the scrutiny of time and the test of eternity.

The so-called gift of tongues was never a subject mentioned in any other church in all of the New Testament *except the Corinthian* church. Surely a gift as important as many would have us believe tongues speaking is today would have been mentioned to other congregations. But the fact is, the Scriptures are silent except for the church at Corinth.

Here are the statistics: Out of the sixty-six books of the Bible, only *three* of them have direct reference to tongues. Out of the 1,189 chapters in the Bible, only *seven* chapters have a direct reference to tongues. Out of the 31,162 verses in the Bible, only *eighteen* verses make a direct reference to speaking in tongues.

Surely, these facts indicate that tongues speaking is not nearly as important as many would have us believe. In fact, Jesus himself nowhere commanded his followers to speak in tongues. This phenomenon of tongues speaking is a Johnnie-come-lately teaching and should be properly classified as a neo-charismatic phenomenon.

No issue in the Church of God is as potentially divisive as tongues-speaking. On the one hand some believe that all who have been filled with the Holy, Spirit must speak in tongues. Others believe tongues-speaking has nothing to do with the baptism of the Holy Spirit—a few believe tongues-speaking to be demon possession.

It would be far easier for the editors to keep silence on this topic. We believe, however, that to do so would betray our responsibility to our readers, our church, and ultimately to our God. The three articles on tongues-speaking represent various beliefs held by significant groups within the church. They reflect the opinions of the authors and not necessarily the opinions of the editors.

It is our prayer that you will read all the articles with an open mind. They will provide information and food for thought. One thing is clear—we are to seek the Giver above any gift. We pray that the Holy Spirit will be given freedom to work in your life as he wills.

—The Editors

The next natural question would be "Where did it all begin?" The modern neo-charismatic movement came out of the early 1900s with the greatest single eruption taking place in 1906 at the Azusa Street Mission in Los Angeles. From these unpretentious beginnings there has sprung the modern neo-charismatic movement. Suddenly terms such as *charismatic* and *glossolalia* have surfaced in our conversations. The word *glossolalia* is a compound word made from two Greek words: *glossais* meaning *tongue* and *lalia* meaning *speech.* Therefore compounded the meaning is "tongues-speech" or "speaking in tongues." The second word, *charismatic,* comes from the Greek word *charisma* meaning gift. The basic idea is that of a gift freely given and freely received without merit.

Since the scriptures in the Bible in which reference is made to speaking in tongues are really few, we need to begin by looking at the first test in which the subject is mentioned, and I might add, the *only time* it is referred to by Jesus.

> "And he said unto them, 'Go ye into all the world, and preach the gospel to every creature. He that believeth and is baptized shall be saved; but he that believeth not shall be damned. And these *signs* shall follow them that believe; In my name shall they cast out devils; they shall speak with new tongues; They shall take up serpents; and if they drink any deadly thing, it shall not hurt them; they shall lay hands on the sick and they shall recover.' . . .
> "And they went forth, and preached everywhere, the Lord working with

them, and *confirming the word with signs following"* (Mark 16:15-18, 20, italics added).

The main teaching here was that the disciples carry out the Great Commission and preach and teach the gospel to the lost. The *signs* and *miracles* that accompanied the disciples as they obeyed that commission were a confirmation of the message that they preached being from God. In essence they were the credentials of those early disciples.

"How shall we escape, if we neglect so great salvation; which at the first began to be spoken by the Lord, and was confirmed unto us by them that heard him; God also *bearing them witness, both* with *signs and wonders, and with divers miracles, and gifts of* the *Holy Ghost,* according to his own will?" (Heb. 2:3-4, italics added).

Keep in mind if you will that Jesus said these signs would follow the believers—and *they did!* On the Day of Pentecost, the phenomenon of speaking in tongues was a definite sign to the unbelieving Jews and it amazed them that they heard the disciples speaking in their own *heterais glossais* (native languages)! This *sign* of speaking supernaturally in another language stayed right in line with Jesus' teaching in Mark 16:17 and Paul's teaching in 1 Corinthians 14:22: "Wherefore tongues are for a *sign,* not to them that believe, but to them that *believe* not."

In the contextual structure of the Scriptures, in each biblical account where the gift of tongues is given (Acts

2, 10, 19), the tongues spoken were understandable dialects and not inarticulate jargon or unintelligible gibberish that could not be understood either by the speaker or by the hearers! In every instance without exception, when tongues were spoken they were positively understandable languages to those present and never an unknown, unintelligible speech requiring the aid of interpreters!

Now, why did it happen? It was the Day of Pentecost—a day at the end of the wheat harvest which commemorated the giving of the Law on Mount Sinai. It was the fiftieth day after Passover and the beginning of the great festival of harvest. (This prefigured the greatest harvest of all the world—the harvest of souls!)

Jesus had said the fields were white unto harvest. Jews from all over the then-known world had gathered into Jerusalem for this high and holy day. It was the beginning of festive offerings and sacrifices. Great associations of joy were anxiously anticipated and the Jews thronged their beloved Jerusalem to be a part of it all. The multitude was alive with excitement and it was the perfect moment for the designs of God's providence. God's appointed day had arrived.

The Roman government had built roads reaching the most remote areas of the Empire. The Greek language was the universal means of communication across Rome's domain. It was the perfect moment for the wisdom of God to unfold and there they were—multitudes of devout Jews out of all the nations of the earth, gathered to commemorate that great moment in Jewish history when God brought them out of Egypt and gave them the Law through Moses on the mountain filled with thunder and lightning and fire and smoke.

This was the end of a dispensation and the beginning of another. This was the precise moment in elapsed time that God had chosen for his prophetic clock to ring out the great transition from the age of the Law and the Prophets and the earthly ministry of Jesus who was the Final Prophet, and the ringing in of the Holy Ghost dispensation and the age of divine grace.

What was going to be a convincing argument to persuade this multitude of Jews that this was God speaking?

What was the providence of God going to order to arouse the interest of this multitude of party-spirited Jews on holiday to this tiny group of 120 uneducated people?

What was going to be an evidence of the validity and the divine authority and content of their message coming from God?

How were these disciples going to be able to convince these skeptical and analytical-minded Jews that a new word was coming from the great Jehovah?

Remember if you will that this gathered multitude of Jews were not in Jerusalem to hear Peter's sermon. They had not gathered to worship Jesus, for indeed most of them had never heard of Jesus. They were not there to learn of New Testament salvation, for they were still very much satisfied and enamored with their Old Testament Covenant with their Father Abraham. They were gathered to celebrate the old law and had no inkling that God had a new law, a better dispensation, in store for them!

By allowing this to happen on the Day of Pentecost with all nations under the sun present—the good roads, the common language, the *Pax Romana* (Roman Peace)—the climate was perfect for the broadcasting of the gospel over the entire Roman Empire. (The record of Philip and the Ethiopian eunuch is an example of this.)

With this background in view, the purpose of speaking in tongues is clear: the biblical purpose was that it would be a sign-gift/sign-miracle to attract and to authenticate and affirm God's presence with his disciples and it would get the attention of all the nations gathered in the city on that Holy day.

The gift of tongues was a supernatural demonstration intended by God to perform the specific function outlined by Paul in 1 Corinthians 14:22: To be a sign to unbelievers.

This was God's way of convincing the unbelieving, skeptical, sign-seeking Jews that the message proclaimed by these men was of God. Acts 2:6-8 verifies this truth:

> "Now when this was noised abroad, the multitude came together . . . (this is what God wanted) and were confounded, because that every man heard them *speak in his own language.* And they were all amazed and marvelled, saying one to another, Behold, are not all these which speak Galilaeans? And how hear we . . .

in our *own tongue wherein we were born?"* (italics added).

Verse twelve asks, "What meaneth this?" Here was the golden opportunity for which the Holy Spirit was waiting. These 120 disciples had come flooding out of that upper room singing and praising God and glorifying his holy name. They were blessing God in the native tongues of that multitude of Jews gathered in Jerusalem. Suddenly ears began to perk up and heads began to turn and hearts began to race, for someone was singing about God in the very native tongue of their childhood hometown. Someone was praising God in a tongue they had not heard for many years, in that tongue of back home!

Speaking in tongues served as the attracting sign and springboard for Peter's sermon—and immediately Peter stood up and preached (Peter alone). Peter preached in the universal language of the empire, Greek, and everyone heard and understood.

Peter referred to the Joel prophecy in verses 18, 22, 32, and 33 and says that the manifestation of speaking in tongues was the receipt of the promise of the Father which was a sign to the unbelieving Jews. The Jews were sign-seekers. "For the Jews require a sign, and the Greeks seek after wisdom" (1 Cor. 1:22). "Master, we would see a sign from thee" (Matt. 12:38). "What sign shewest thou then, that we may see, and believe thee?" (John 6:30).

It is plain to see by these texts the sign of speaking with tongues was to the unbelieving Jews—to show them that God was initiating something new. Jesus summed up perfectly the point we are trying to make in Mark 16:17 and verse 20 when he said, "And these signs shall follow them that believe; In my name shall they cast out devils; they shall *speak with new tongues*. . . . And they went forth, and preached everywhere, the Lord working with them and confirming the word with signs following."

The primary purpose of speaking in tongues on the Day of Pentecost was evidential, being God's stamp of approval accompanying the disciples and their message to attract and convince the unbelieving Jews. The gift was given in the opening days of the Christian era to provide the initial thrust and lift to successfully launch New Testament salvation.

In Acts 10, at the house of Cornelius, it is plain to see by an honest examination of the Scriptures that the gift of tongues functioned again as a sign of evidence to Peter and his Jewish friends how the gospel was being given to another nation and in essence to all nations. God was saving uncircumcised Gentiles through faith in Jesus Christ and again the wisdom of God used the sign of speaking in tongues to convince Peter and those unbelieving Jews that a Gentile could be brought into the body of Christ.

You see, the surprise was not because the gift of the Holy Spirit was given—but that it was given to the Gentiles! Had there not been a strong sign from God, that crowd of Jews would never, never have believed that salvation was for anyone outside of the Jewish nation.

Is this not exactly where the Jewish attitude is today? It was the Holy Spirit's gift of speaking in tongues which astonished and persuaded the Jews to the authenticity of accepting Gentiles into the family of God. Is not this once again in line with the scriptures of Mark 16:17 and 20 and 1 Corinthians 14:22? Not only did tongues convince Peter and the Jews with him, but it also convinced the Jewish leaders at Jerusalem! That is why God impressed Peter to take some Jewish witnesses along with him on this mission.

The leaders at Jerusalem called Peter on the carpet to explain why he went into a Gentile house with the gospel. In the eleventh chapter of Acts, Peter defended his actions by rehearsing the matter and in verses 15-18 he gives his testimony. If one reads this account it is plain to see and logical to understand that the purpose of the gift of tongues as manifested at the house of Cornelius was a sign-evidence to convince the Jewish Christians.

In the final account of Bible tongues recorded in Acts 19:1-7 we find that Paul had come to Ephesus, where he met twelve men who were the disciples of John the Baptist. Paul questioned them about receiving the Holy Ghost and found that they were not even aware there was such a thing as a Holy Ghost experience available. They had been baptized only unto John's baptism. Upon hearing of this experience, Paul preached to them, laying his hands upon them, and they received the Holy Ghost and spoke with tongues and prophesied.

Tongues, on this occasion, did not serve as a sign to lead these disciples to Christ, as in Acts 2, nor did it serve to convince Paul of truth that he had not yet known or received as in the case of Peter in Acts 10. In this case, the tongues manifested was to give evidence to John's disciples to confirm to them the reality and the validity of that which Paul spoke to them concerning this one called Jesus.

Think with me, if you will, at this point. Here had come one whom they had not heard of, reaching to them in the name of one they knew not of, and telling them of one who was greater than their great teacher, John the Baptist! Now if someone came to you under similar circumstances, would you not have a touch of doubt and question as to whether he or she were on the up and up—especially if what he or she had to say was foreign and different to what you had been taught?

Paul had told them of what had happened to the Gentiles of the Italian band in Cornelius' house. Now Paul laid his hands on them and prayed in the name of this one called Jesus Christ, and suddenly they began to speak in other tongues and prophesy.

I think it is important here to note that the same word used in Acts 2 and Acts 10, *glossais,* is the same word used here in Acts 19. They *prophesied,* and if this were not an intelligent, understandable language, then how did the listeners know that they *prophesied?* It is elementary to me to easily see that the Bible gift of tongues as manifested in each record as tongues speaking in Acts 2, 10, and 19 was in each case an *understandable, plain, intelligible language* given supernaturally by the Holy Ghost for the purpose of a *sign-gift* and a *sign-miracle* to convince *unbelievers* of God's presence in their midst. It was the attracting sign accompanying the message of the disciples and giving thrust to the expansion of Christianity in its early days.

At no time in the Book of Acts was the gift of tongues manifested to be an evidence that one had received the Holy Ghost but instead it was a gift given by the Holy Ghost to testify of Jesus Christ. Neither was it in a language that could not be understood. The Bible nowhere supports the idea that the Holy Ghost will lead a person to speak or pray in an uncontrollable, unintelligent language. The Holy Spirit is an intelligent, operating personality that uses us instead of our using him!

The Holy Spirit never yet gave himself to be used by humanity, but rather, he came for the purpose of using humanity according to his will. Remember, the Holy Spirit does not give gifts for the purpose of self-edification, but rather they are given to build up the Church, to edify the body of Christ, the Church. Paul makes it very clear by saying: "But the manifestation of the Spirit is given to every man to profit withal."

That *all* may profit is a far cry from the idea of privately praying in tongues for the purpose of *self-edification.* That which is being represented as the gift of the Holy Spirit today is a far cry from what the Bible truth about tongues has to say. May God help us always to work from the Word of God to the experience, never from the experience to the Word of God!

Richard M. Bradley, "Bible Truth About Today's Tongues," *VITAL CHRISTIANITY* (JUNE 30, 1985): 8-11.

[Included by permission of the author.]

Doctrine, Desire, and Deception!
By Arlo F. Newell

Historically, church doctrine has been both desirable and deceptive. When divinely revealed and obediently lived out, doctrine is most desirable. But when human opinion or interpretation has been declared as the doctrine of the Church, it is deception at its worst. Such is much of the modern emphasis on the theology of the Holy Spirit, or pneumatology. I refer particularly to the interest in the charismata, or the gifts.

God has revealed the Giver and the gifts, and both are authenticated in the Word and needed by the church. However, when the human opinion that the "gift of tongues" is the initial evidence for having received the infilling of the gift of the Holy Spirit, it is no longer doctrine but deception.

C.W. Naylor and Andrew L. Byers joined together to challenge us in the heritage hymn "Are You Adorning the Doctrine?" While not used too often in our services of worship, it does confront us with a much-needed question.

Theologically the word *doctrine* is applied to teaching and the content thereof. It is the impartation of faith that God has revealed to his body, the Church. Rather than dogma, decreed by religious bodies, doctrine is being confronted by the divine will of God.

Usually the doctrine implies the ethical instruction needed to comply with the purpose of the Lord of the Church. So, Paul could write, "Speak thou the things which become *sound doctrine*" (Titus 2:1, italics added). His intent was to remind them of the deposit of truth committed unto the young church and their responsibility to share that truth with others. As a movement we have been given much truth; therefore, much is to be required of us.

It was the truth we taught that attracted people to this movement—truth that told of freedom from sin and sectarian division, truth that revealed the glorious Church and God's power to give victory over the world, the flesh, and the devil. Such truth, "spoken in love," attracted people and made them desire to be a part of such a fellowship.

Cautiously we have avoided the temptation to let these teachings become the vain traditions of our elders. Truth is always alive and dynamic, confronting our lives, calling us to full stature in Christ.

While not being locked in with legalistic creeds, we have been given great freedom in discovering the doctrines revealed in the Word. True doctrine is that which God has made known to us through the Word and the Spirit.

Such truth does not contradict the nature of God and does not violate the nature of Christ. Both in belief and behavior, the doctrines entrusted to us are always to be tested by the Word. We are cautioned not to be "carried about by every wind of doctrine" (Eph. 4:14).

Bible doctrine becomes the foundation for a strong church, the texts for great sermons, and the guide for holy living. Doctrine determines our direction for the future and is essential if we are to be God's Church.

Coupled with *doctrine* must also be the right *desire* to live out that teaching so that others see Christ in us.

Some along the way have heard and even memorized the doctrines we hold dear but seemingly had no desire to apply them to human relationships within the church, the home, and the world.

Doctrinal correctness does not necessarily mean that we have the right spirit or that we are always right in the interpretation or application of the truth. For doctrine to be rightly interpreted and applied to life there must be the *desire to be like Jesus*.

Such an attitude must be the criterion for understanding the doctrine of the Holy Spirit. Christ becomes our model, the example of what the Christian should be and how we should conduct ourselves. When at his baptism, the Holy Spirit came upon him, witnessing to the approval of the Father, it was all decent and in order. And when standing up to read from Isaiah, he stated that "the Spirit of the Lord is upon me" (Luke 4:18). Once again the example is that of humility, servanthood, and sensitivity to the needs of others.

Jesus alone could communicate the right understanding of the Holy Spirit and at no time did he demonstrate anything like the "gift of tongues." Jesus was not a *charismatic* in the common use of that term today. The spirit of the Holy Spirit is the very nature of Christ, whom we desire to be like.

Deception must always be guarded against when we desire sound doctrine. Even well meaning persons like preachers, teachers, and close friends can sometimes be very mistaken regarding truth that affects our eternal destiny.

Only recently a strong TV evangelist stated with deep conviction, "The true evidence of receiving the

Holy Spirit is speaking in other tongues." And in one of the religious journals that comes to my desk, the writer stated, "As shoes have tongues, so the Spirit-filled person receives the gift of tongues."

How tragic—tragic because it is deceptive. Let us acknowledge that there is a true gift of communication addressed in the gifts of the Spirit. But when this particular gift or any other is used as a standard by which we measure one's spirituality, then it is no longer *sound doctrine* but human deception.

—Arlo F. Newell

Arlo F. Newell, "Doctrine, Desire, and Deception!" *VITAL CHRISTIANITY* (JUNE 30, 1985): 6-7.

[Included by permission of the author.]

Slain, But By What Spirit?
By Donald W. Neace

Experience cannot be denied.

In the court system in the United States, one of the critical components of any witness is the ability to say, "I was there. I am an eyewitness. I experienced it." The legal system gives great weight of believability to persons who have personal experience.

In that regard, the "experience" of being "slain in the spirit" cannot be denied. There is little doubt that persons who have "fallen" under the spirit have had a very real event in their life.

However, the experience begs the question, "slain, but by what spirit?"

The Bible tells us many "spirits" are in the world that can influence a person's life. We are eyewitnesses to varying "spirits" everyday.

At many sporting events, commentators continually speak about the athletes being caught up "in the spirit of the games." It is well documented concerning citizens who have been part of community riots that they honestly never intended to wreak havoc, yet they got overwhelmed by "the spirit of the moment."

I have often heard it preached, "The Holy Spirit is blamed with things for which He is not guilty." Such is the case, I believe, with persons being slain in the spirit and claiming a true Holy Spirit experience. While the experience of being overwhelmed to the point of falling on the floor is very real, one must question the spirit that caused the experience.

Nowhere in Holy Scripture do we see people finding "weakness" after an encounter with the Holy Spirit of God. Rather, the Scripture promises that when we are weak, He will be strong. His Spirit will give us strength to stand—not to fall over in helplessness.

We are challenged by the Apostle John, "do not believe every spirit, but test the spirits, whether they are of God; because many false prophets have gone out into the world." 1 John 4:1

In the Gospel of John, chapters 14 through 16, Jesus goes into great detail to explain the ministry of the Holy Spirit. John points toward at least six elements of the Holy Spirit ministry.

- He will abide with us. 14:16
- He will teach. 14:26
- He will testify of Christ. 15:26
- He will convict the world of sin. 16:8
- He will guide into truth. 16:13
- He will glorify Christ. 16:14

Nowhere in Jesus' discourse does He say that when the Holy Spirit comes upon a person that person will speak in an "unknown" tongue, fall backwards in helplessness, bark like a dog, or crow like a chicken!

Jesus does say the Holy Spirit will point away from self to Christ. Never will the Holy Spirit simply gratify the flesh in an attempt to display or glorify His self. "He will not speak on His own authority ..." Jesus said. John 16:13

I have been asked, "What difference does it make … So what if God has some children who practice some strange, maybe questionable habits … Why make such a formidable issue of the experience?"

The formidable issue is that we are to become accustomed to following the true leading of the Holy Spirit. The danger of such practices is that people become "tuned in" to the spirits of the flesh, spirits of the world, spirits, other than the Holy Spirit, that they begin to do and practice things very foreign to the truth of the Scripture.

The practice opens the door to all manner of fleshly practice that can, and often does, lead to sin. It is a slippery slope of fleshly experience that is foreign to the Holy Scripture.

A Second Work of Grace

Any writing about Holy Spirit truth would be incomplete without discussing sanctification.

Sanctification as used in the Scriptures means to make holy, to consecrate, and be set apart from sin in order that we may be in close fellowship with God and serve Him.

The Gospel writers record that believers in Christ would be "baptized with the Holy Spirit and with fire." (Matthew 3:11, Luke 3:16) The symbolism of fire found its fulfillment in Acts 2 when "cloven tongues like as fire," announced the coming of the Holy Spirit.

The teaching of sanctification as a second definite work of the grace of God is found throughout the New Testament. When Jesus described the work of the Holy

Spirit in the above-described verses, he was laying the foundation for the cleansing, infilling, sanctifying work of the Spirit in the lives of believers.

The promise of Jesus to send the Holy Spirit was a promise made to and intended for those whom Jesus had saved. Jesus was saying that in his physical absence he would send the Holy Spirit to work in the daily life of the redeemed. This work is described in the New Testament as a work of grace subsequent to the redemption of the soul.

In the New Testament, sanctification is not a slow process of forsaking sin little by little; rather, it is taught as a definitive act by which the believer by grace makes a clear break with sin in order to live in holiness before God.

Sanctification involves a definite crisis experience after initial salvation. Believers receive a clear revelation of the holiness of God as well as a consciousness that God is calling them to separate themselves from sin, the world, and to walk closer with Him (2 Corinthians 6:16-18). Through this awareness, believers present themselves to God as living and holy sacrifices. They receive from the Holy Spirit grace, purity, power, and victory to live holy lives, acceptable to God (Romans 12:1-2).

The sanctified life is a holy life. This implies an ethical righteousness of character lived out in purity before God, obedience to His word, and virtuousness before the world. The believer in Christ, by the grace of God, has died to sin and is set free from the power of sin; therefore, believers need not and ought not to sin. We find victory in Jesus. Through the Holy Spirit, we are able to keep from continuing in sin (1 John 3:6) even though we never come to the place where we are free from temptation and the possibility of sin.

Two areas in the discussion of sanctification have always troubled me. My first issue was with holiness in terms of Christian perfection, and secondly, the need for a second work. In my spiritual journey, I believe the Lord has used two simple events to help me understand the scriptural teaching.

In understanding holiness as to Christian perfection, I had to discover the difference between the common definition of perfection and the biblical observation of perfection. Perfection as commonly understood means, "without flaw." That definition does not meet the biblical expectation. Indeed, in the flesh we will never be without flaw.

I believe the biblical call to perfection means to be "fit for the task." To be complete, wholeness, and equipped to do the work God has called you to do.

As a pastor, I have been involved in several building projects. In one building as we worked to build walls inside the new facility, we encountered an area that required us to cut an angle on a two-by-four wall brace. We miss-measured two times, but on the third try we got it right. When we stood the wall up, we declared with excitement that it was "perfect."

To be sure, that piece of lumber was far from without flaw. It had been cut; had knotholes in two areas, and had been damaged by the hammer. However, it was perfect for the task it was intended to do.

I discovered my life was similar to that piece of lumber. The ravages of sin have cut me. I have a few holes in my soul caused by hurt and infirmities. Moreover, I have been hammered by the world (and sometimes hammered by the church!). Yet, by the empowering of the Holy Spirit, I am fit for the task to which God has called me. I am far from without flaw, yet wholly equipped, "perfect" for the calling of God.

Another simple experience showed me the need for a second work.

I collect coffee cups. I routinely use one particular cup as a favorite. One afternoon as I prepared to take out the trash, I discovered my favorite cup among the garbage. I was disappointed that someone had broken my cup and thrown it away. However, upon closer inspection I found no damage to the cup. I reached into the garbage and recovered my cup.

Upon taking my cup out of the garbage, I then carried it to the kitchen where it underwent a complete cleansing. It had to be cleansed before I could fill it and use it again.

In the same fashion, I believe, God works in our lives. He reached into the garbage of sin and saved us from the trash of destruction. Subsequent to the saving event, He must then cleanse us before he fills us with the Holy Spirit and uses us for our intended purpose. Salvation and then sanctification; a two-fold work for a two-fold need.[9]

---

[9]Donald W. Neace, *The Expanded Editorials* (Reformation Publishers; Prestonsburg, KY 41653, 2005; 2008), 14.

Donald W. Neace, "Slain, But By What Spirit?"
Reformation Witness (February 2001).

[Included by permission of the author.]

The Manifestations of the Holy Spirit.
by Bill Konstantopolous

The Bible contains the mystery of the power of the Holy Spirit and the manifestation of His ministry in the world, in the church and in the life of the individual believer. There is no other theme so interwoven from the first chapter of Genesis to the last chapter of Revelation.

Quite often He is addressed in the language of the Bible as the "Holy Spirit"; the "Spirit of Wisdom"; the "Spirit of Christ"; the "Spirit of Revelation" and the "Spirit of Fire." The Bible says, "And the Spirit of God moved upon the face of the waters" Gen. 2:2.

Again it says, "For the letter killeth, but the Spirit giveth life" 2 Cor. 3:6. It was, therefore, the Holy Spirit that breathed into the nostrils of man and he became a living soul; for the Spirit is the breath of God. Thus God says, "Not by might, not by power, but by my Spirit, saith the Lord of hosts" Zachariah 4:6. It is not an accident that the human heart always prays, "And take not thy Holy Spirit from me" Ps. 51:11. And the hymn writer expresses the longing of every believer when he says, "With thy Spirit fill me, make me wholly Thine, I pray."

Yet, the conflict and the confusion over the Holy Spirit are greater today than they were at the church of Corinth. There are so many things which are attributed to the Holy Spirit that some of them boarder blasphemy. Since we lack the discernment of the Spirit the danger exists in our thirst for excitement to attribute things to Him which are contrary to His nature. The irony of our day is that the great controversy is not so much over the Holy Spirit, but over His manifestations. It appears that so many are after His manifestations than they are after Him.

The controversy is over the *chrisma* or the anointing of the Spirit. Those who promote it give the impression that the place and the person are in control of the anointing. It is Jesus' prerogative who will receive the anointing through the Spirit. The Greek word *chrisma* from *chrio*, to anoint, specially the anointing of oil in the Old Testament (Ex. 29:7; 30:25) is used only four times in the New Testament, in I John 2:20, 27 and is combined with the words *echete* (you have), "*elabete*" (you received); "*menei*" (abides in you) and "*didaskei*" (teaches you). It appears to give preeminence to what the readers had experienced as well as referring to the Old Testament practice; but more so he reminds them of their calling and work (I Pet. 2:5, 9). The anointing of God is indispensable in our life:

> a. The anointing of the Spirit comes upon our life as a calling to be separated for God to an office of service or ministry. Simply, it is a call to serve God. The Spirit of God came upon Samson. The Spirit of God came upon John the Baptist and the Spirit of God came upon Paul identifying him as the apostle to the Gentiles.

> b. The anointing comes in order to equip us to speak boldly at the moment with revelation, clarity and authority, unfold-

ing the word of God. Jesus says, "The spirit of the Lord is upon me, because he has anointed me to preach the Gospel to the poor. He has sent me to heal the brokenhearted," Luke 4:18-19.

The great deception of the day is that people are in control of the anointing of the Spirit and that they can manipulate it or even impart it to others. You can be faithful, obedient and totally submissive to the Lord, but you do not have control over the anointing of the Spirit. It is like the wind. It will invade your soul at the time of God's choosing. It will not make you get out of the order of God. It is not intended to give you a super spiritual hype or make you feel super spiritual. The anointing of the Spirit comes to fulfill the purpose of God and that is all. It is not a self gratification experience.

The second area of controversy is over the charismata or the gifts of the Holy Spirit.

The singular is charisma which derives from *charizomai*—"to show grace." "It is a gift of grace or undeserved benefit." In the N.T. it is only used for gifts and graces imparted from God, I Cor. 7:7. Charisma is the instantaneous enablement of the Holy Spirit in the life of any believer to exercise a gift for the edification of others or the church. The Bible speaks freely of the gifts of the Spirit, and it is evident that when these are in operation, only then the church is both edified and perfected and disciples are equipped for ministry.

The apostle Paul states the primary gifts of the Spirit in Ephesians 4:11-13: "And He himself gave some to be apostles, some prophets, some evangelists, and some pastors and teachers." The purpose of these gifts is to edify the body of Christ, to disciple believers, to equip them to do the work of the ministry.

Then you have the secondary gifts of the Spirit whose purpose is again to edify the body of Christ and complement each other for the work of the ministry and the glorification of Jesus Christ. The apostle Paul says in I Corinthians 12, "But the manifestation (Singular— *phanerosis*) of the Spirit is given to each one for the profit of all." Then he begins to name those gifts: wisdom, knowledge, faith, healing, working of miracles, prophecy, discerning of spirits, and different kind of tongues. But all these are helps to the ministry, and the focus should be placed on the giver who is the Spirit. Their purpose is to edify the church, to improve its life and direct it; but all work in harmony with each other.

The third area of controversy is in the area of the phenomena of the Spirit or the manifestations. A phenomenon is known through the senses rather than through knowledge or intuition. You cannot fully understand or explain it. We must confess that at times there is a great mystery when it comes to the manifestations of the Spirit. Some people appear to be confused between the gifts and the manifestations of the Spirit. Even though there is a relationship between the two, yet, there is a distinct difference.

In our days there is the claim of four manifestations of the Spirit which causes controversy, division and confusion across the body of Christ. These manifestations are promoted as the evidence of the Holy Spirit and as His authentic work. Two of these are the slain in the Spirit and the holy laughter. In the slain of the Spirit some one touches you on the forehead and you fall practically unconscious. There is no Biblical foundation for such a practice and it is strange to the New Testament as a manifestation of the Spirit. The holy laughter again it has no Biblical foundation and nowhere in the N. T. seems to be the activity of the Holy Spirit.

The manifestation in speaking in an unknown tongue or prayer language has some scriptural validity; not as such, but as a genuine gift of the Spirit in speaking in other languages. The Biblical gift of tongues or other languages has two purposes according to the N. T. One is the means that God chooses to communicate His Word where there is no other means; and the other serves as a sign to the unbeliever. But nowhere in the N.T. states or implies that in speaking in tongues is the evidence that one has the Holy Spirit. On the day of Pentecost it was said by the audience, "We hear them speak in our own tongues the wonderful works of God." Acts 2:11

The apostle Paul says to the Corinthians, "Therefore tongues are for a sign, not to those who believe but to the unbeliever," I Cor. 14:22. God is not the author of confusion or division. But the promotion of the so called manifestations of the Spirit is causing both confusion and division in the body of Christ. We are so hyped with the counterfeit manifestation that we ignore the true ones which contribute to the unity of the body and the spreading of the Gospel. It will be helpful if we review these.

It is painted clear in the N.T. that the first manifestation of the Spirit is conviction. Jesus said, "And when He has come, He will convict the world of sin, and of righteousness, and of judgment," John 16:8. The Holy Spirit reveals convicts and rebukes sin. He reminds us of sin and its consequence in one's life. Conviction is the exclusive work of the Holy Spirit. This is why on the day of Pentecost people cried out, "Now when they heard this, they were cut to the heart (*katenygesan*), and said to Peter and the rest of the apostles, 'Men and brethren what shall we do?' " Acts 2:37.

It is interesting to note that the second manifestation of the Spirit is the unity of believers or the church. He breaks down the barriers that divide people. He baptizes with fire and love; and he changes human nature to the extent that we are drawn to each other. Thus it was said about the believers after the Pentecost, "Now all who believed were together. . . ." Acts 2:44. "Now the multitudes of those who believed were of one heart and one soul" Acts 4:32. The apostle Paul admonishes us to live in the unity of the Spirit when he says, "endeavoring to keep the unity of the Spirit in the bond of peace," Eph. 4:3. Wherever the Holy Spirit is at work people are united and live harmoniously for the cause of Christ. He draws people, who believe, to Christ and to each other.

Praise is another manifestation of the Spirit. It is His purpose to exalt and lift up Christ. Since the Holy Spirit puts joy in our heart, for joy is the fruit of the Spirit, then He fills our lips with praise. Jesus makes it clear that the Holy Spirit will speak of Him and that He will glorify Him, John 16:14. There is no dull worship, dull singing and dull living when the Holy Spirit is at work among God's people. His praise fills their lips with psalms and spiritual songs.

It will not be strange and inconsistent with the N. T. to say that another manifestation of the Spirit is prayer. Prayer is the activity of the Holy Spirit. He teaches us to pray, but also helps us to pray and makes intercession on our behalf. "Likewise the Spirit also helps in our weaknesses. For we do not know what we should pray for as we aught, but the SPIRIT HIMSELF MAKES INTERCESSION FOR US WITH GROAN-INGS WHICH CANNOT BE UTTERED." Now he who searches the heart knows what the mind of the Spirit is, because He makes intercession for the saints according to the will of God" Rom 8:26-27. Any individual or group movement of prayer is influenced by the Spirit and He makes the discipline of prayer to come alive.

There is another manifestation of the Spirit which decorates the life of God's people and that is holiness of life. He is our purifier and sanctifier. The absence of holiness clouds out any other manifestation of the Spirit. Holiness is the nature of the Spirit and whosoever He possesses lives in the spirit of holiness. It is unrealistic to expect the manifestations of the Spirit where holiness is absent. It is He who helps us to be partakers of Christ's holiness (Heb. 12:10) and enables us to perfect holiness in the fear of God (2 Cor. 7:1). Besides He produces in us the fruit of holiness to the extent that all our members become servants of holiness. You may not have many gifts or other things when the Holy Spirit possesses your life, but you cannot be possessed by Him and remain unholy.

It is evident, to a student of the Bible, that the manifestations of the Spirit are several, but I would like to mention one more which is twofold in nature. The one is the manifestation of spiritual power which is the ability to stand or do the will of God and fulfill His purpose. The other is authority over the enemy. This is spiritual authority to subdue and overcome the enemy. It is to the authority of the Spirit that the powers of darkness are subjected and His power that enables us to be effective in the ministry of the Gospel. To that effect, the Lord Jesus Christ said to His disciples not to leave Jerusalem till they received power from on high, and then He stated, "But ye shall receive power when the Holy Spirit has come upon you, and you shall be witnesses to me in Jerusalem, and in all Judea and Samaria and to the uttermost of the earth" Acts 1:8.

The manifestations of the Spirit are as essential as the gifts are, but not as essential as the Holy Spirit. Too often we get enamored with the gifts that we forget the giver. God wants to give us the giver of the gifts; thus His promise, "Ye shall receive the promise of the Father," and "I will not leave your comfortless, I will send you another comforter." This is the most explosive promise of the Bible. Also notice the prescription that God gives concerning the Holy Spirit: "Be filled with the Spirit"; "Walk in the Spirit'; "Live in the Spirit" and "Grieve not the Holy Spirit with which you have been sealed." Then He outlines the purpose of the spirit to deal with our needs, to be our helper, and to help us in our struggles. He is to help us in our weaknesses, to teach us, guide us, empower us and sanctify us so that we could effectively edify His church and confront the world with the Good News of the Gospel. God wants us to experience His Spirit, His conviction, His sanctification, His power, His peace and His joy. Have you experienced Him? The Lord says "It is not by power nor by might but by my Spirit saith the Lord." No doubt such a genuine experience is needed in the church today.

Bill Konstantopolous, "The Manifestations of the Holy Spirit," *Reformation Witness*.

[Included by permission of the author.]

Counterfeit Gifts of the Spirit.
By William P. Means

Leviticus 10:1 says, "And Nadab and Abihu, the sons of Aaron, took either of them his censer, and put fire therein, and put incense thereon, and offered strange fire before the Lord, which he commanded them not" (KJV).

In the Bible, fire has always been represented of the Spirit of God. The word "strange" in this text means "foreign, alien or unfamiliar," and also "unholy, unauthorized or profane." The fire they offered to God was not authorized; it was not holy; it was fake and counterfeit, as far as God was concerned.

I'm concerned that there is a lot of strange fire being offered to God today in the name of the Holy Spirit. We need to be warned of those who are offering strange fire to Him which produces counterfeit gifts of the Spirit. There are countless non-biblical things being done in the name of the Lord today. To name a few there is: surfing in the Spirit, holy uncontrollable laughter, barking and oinking, being drunk in the Spirit, being stuck in Holy Spirit glue, unknown tongues, slaying in the Spirit, jerks and pawing on the ground like an angry bull, and something called Holy Spirit "backfiring." All of these things are being attributed to God, however none of them can be found in His Word.

Where did these teachings originate? Many of them began with the Azusa Street Revival in California in April of 1906. A former Church of God minister by the name of William Seymour, who believed that tongues, not sanctification, was the evidence of the baptism in the Holy Ghost, hosted these meetings.

During these meetings, devotees fell to the floor in religious ecstasy. They spoke in unknown tongues. They treed the devil and they engaged in "jerks." Soon, spiritualists and mediums were attending, and it was all out of control. You can follow the influence of these meetings forward to Aimee Simple McPherson, Kathryn Kuhlman and E. W. Kenyon. Today the influence of these early "pioneers of spiritual excess" is far reaching, spawning new leaders of this movement including Kenneth Hagin, Richard Roberts, Benny Hinn, Kenneth Copeland, T. L. Osborn, Paul Crouch, Paul Yonggi Cho, and Rodney Howard-Brown, to name a few.

All of these false teachings emanate from one of three sources: false prophets, false teachers, and distortions of truth. Deuteronomy 18:21-22 informs us how to determine false prophets. It says, "And if thou say in thine heart, How shall we know the word which the Lord hath not spoken? When a prophet speaketh in the name of the Lord, if the thing follow not, nor come to pass, that is the thing which the Lord hath not spoken, but the prophet hath spoken it presumptuously: thou shalt not be afraid of him" (KJV).

Let me provide details regarding some of these counterfeit gifts of the Spirit. Holy laughter began from the outpouring in Lakeland, Florida. Barking and oinking came from The Toronto Blessing. They are all disruptive in church services, whereas Paul taught, "Let all things be done decently and in order" (1 Corinthians 14:40 KJV).

Being stuck in Holy Spirit glue involves people falling down and not being able to get up, or even move for a period of time. Surfing in the Spirit involves going from one spiritual high to another. Being drunk in the Spirit is getting so high on God that one can't control oneself and does not want to. Some become frozen in place in the Spirit and stay that way for a period of time. Speaking in tongues and praying in the Spirit is rampant with the excuse that "God understands, even though I don't." Holy Spirit backfiring occurs through involving the power of the Spirit rebounding on the one praying if the recipient is not spiritual enough to receive what the Spirit is trying to give to them.

Then there is spirit-slaying. This is not as new as some of these, for it went on in the early days of this movement. What was not biblical then is not biblical now. What is new is how it is being done. One evangelist blows on a section of the audience or throws his coat and they all go down. Or, the evangelist strikes a person on the head and down they go. They try to justify this practice by Paul's Damascus Road experience, or Peter falling into a trance on the rooftop and John the Revelator falling at the feet of Jesus as a dead man. Not a shred of evidence can be found in the Bible to justify these experiences, but out of context some sound credible.

These leaders go on to teach that confusion is of God. They conclude that caution is a mistake. They even suggest that, if salvation is preached at these meetings, the Spirit is quenched. They teach that Christians ought to "party first" and emphasize holiness later. Some even go so far as to preach "death to all those who oppose us."

Why are these outlandish teachings believed? Because those purporting these beliefs are talented and gifted charismatic individuals with enormous followings. So, from the beginning, the susceptible are engaged by their very gifted oratorical ability. They keep people standing for long periods of time, sometimes as long as three hours and bring them to a state of ecstasy through a combination of sociological and psychological manipulation, mass hypnosis, gross emotionalism and crowd control. They advise the worshipers to "put your mind in neutral and just let the Spirit take over." The Bible warns us about these counterfeit gifts and false prophets.

There are four things we must know in dealing with these things:

First, seduced spirits will become worse. Paul warns, in 1 Timothy 4:1, ". . . in the latter times some shall depart from the faith, giving heed to seducing spirits, and doctrines of devils" (KJV). He goes on in 2 Timothy 3:13 to say, "But evil men and seducers shall wax worse and worse, deceiving, and being deceived" (KJV).

Second, false prophets will arise. Jesus said in Matthew 24:24, "For there shall arise false Christs, and false prophets, and shall shew great signs and wonders; insomuch that, if it were possible, they shall deceive the very elect" (KJV). 1 John 4:1 teaches, "Beloved, believe not every spirit, but try the spirits whether they are of God; because many false prophets are gone out into the world" (KJV).

Third, Confusion is not of God. In 1 Corinthians 14:33, it states, "For God is not the author of confusion, but of peace, as in all churches of the saints" (KJV).

And fourth, Distortion of truth is wrong! Paul said in Acts 20:30, "Also of your own selves shall men arise, speaking perverse things, to draw away disciples after them" (KJV). Power over people is a very heady narcotic. Too many preachers, who start out to be genuine, become drunk with power to the point that they will do anything and say anything to keep it. During the Jim Jones tragedy one commentator noted, "It's sad when the power of love turns into the love of power."

Let me complete this article with a warning from God's Word: "Thus saith the Lord of hosts, Hearken not unto the words of the prophets that prophesy unto you: they make you vain: they speak a vision of their own heart, and not out of the mouth of the Lord" (Jeremiah 23:16 KJV). "I have not sent these prophets, yet they ran: I have not spoken to them, yet they prophesied" (Jeremiah 23:21 KJV). "I have heard what the prophets said, that prophesy lies in my name, saying, I have dreamed, I have dreamed. How long shall this be in the heart of the prophets that prophesy lies? yea, they are prophets of the deceit of their own heart; Which think to cause my people to forget my name by their dreams which they tell every man to his neighbor, as their fathers have forgotten my name for Baal. The prophet that hath a dream, let him tell a dream; and he that hath my word, let him speak my word faithfully. What is the chaff to the wheat? saith the Lord" (Jeremiah 23:25-28 KJV). "Therefore, behold, I am against the prophets, saith the Lord, that steal my words everyone from his neighbor. Behold, I am against the prophets, saith the Lord, that use their tongues, and say, He saith. Behold, I am against them that prophesy false dreams, saith the Lord, and do tell them, and cause my people to err by their lies, and by their lightness; yet I sent them not, nor commanded them: therefore they shall not profit this people at all, saith the Lord" (Jeremiah 23:30-32 KJV). Be warned of counterfeit gifts of the Spirit.

(Sources: "Counterfeit Christianity" by Hank Hanegraaff. "Christianity in Crisis" by Hank Hanegraaff. "Another Gospel" by Ruth Tucker and "Seducing Spirits" sermon by Rev. Richard Bradley).

Bill Means. "Counterfeit Gifts of the Spirit." *Reformation Witness* (May 2010): 9-12.

[Included by permission of the author.]

SECTION II: TRACTS / BOOKLETS / PAPERS

The Baptism Of The Holy Ghost

Is Speaking in an Unknown Tongue the Evidence?

The Baptism of the Holy Ghost
A Bible Doctrine.
By Harold Barber

The Bible is very plain in its teachings concerning the baptism of the Holy Ghost. In St. John 14:15-18 Jesus makes a promise to His disciples before the crucifixion. He says, "If ye love me, keep my commandments. And I will pray the Father, and he shall give you another Comforter, that he may abide with you for ever; Even the Spirit of truth; whom the world cannot receive, because it seeth him not, neither knoweth him: but ye know him: for he dwelleth with you, and shall be in you." This promise was made to the disciples of Jesus; those who had forsaken sin and received Him, thus becoming sons of God by virtue of the new birth as taught in St. John 1:11-13. They were not of the world (having been born of God) nor was promise made to those who are of the world. The promise was that after His departure another Comforter, the Spirit of truth would come and abide in them forever. This Comforter or Spirit of truth is the Holy Ghost (John 14:26) the third Person of the Godhead and every true "born again" child of God needs to be baptized of Him subsequent to their conversion. After the crucifixion and resurrection of Jesus He appeared to the same group of disciples showing himself to be "alive after his passion by many infallible proofs, being seen of them forty days, and speaking of the things pertaining to the kingdom of God: And, being assembled together with them, commanded them that they should not depart from Jerusalem, but wait for the promise of the Father, which, saith he, ye have heard of me. For John truly baptized with water; but ye shall be baptized with the Holy Ghost not many days hence." (Acts 1:3-5) In these verses Jesus commands these disciples to wait in Jerusalem for the promise He has made unto them.

Now let us look to Acts 2:1-40 which gives us a full account of the fulfillment of this promise of the coming of the Holy Ghost. When the day of Pentecost was fully come these disciples were all with one accord in one place and God poured out the Holy Ghost upon each of them and they began to speak with other tongues as the Spirit gave them utterance. "And there were dwelling at Jerusalem Jews, devout men, out of every nation under heaven. Now when this was noised abroad, the multitude came together, and were confounded, because that every man heard them speak in his own language:" (verses 5-6) Now when some of the mockers accused the disciples of being full of new wine Peter stood up with the eleven and preached a sermon to them which pricked their hearts and they said, "Men and brethren, what shall we do?" Then Peter said unto them, "Repent, and be baptized every one of you in the name of Jesus Christ for the remission of sins; and ye shall receive the gift of the Holy Ghost. For the promise is unto you, and to your children, and to all that are afar off, even as many as the Lord our God shall call." (verses 37-39) This promise reaches the disciples of Jesus today. It is the will of God that every "born again" person be baptized with the Holy Ghost.

THE BAPTISM OF THE HOLY GHOST IS A WORK OF FAITH

Receiving the Holy Ghost as an abiding Comforter in your heart is a work of faith. Being baptized with the Holy Ghost is an operation of God in response to our obedience to Him in seeking this experience and the exercising of faith in Him. All salvation operations are spiritual and are wrought in the heart through and by faith, distinct from all physical manifestations. By this, I mean you cannot gauge or judge the work of the Spirit by any particular physical demonstration or manifestation. The Apostle Paul said, "For by grace are ye saved through faith." (Ephesians 2:8) It's the grace of God that saves us from sin and it operates through our faith in God's promises. There is no scripture that gives you, or me, the right to say everyone who is saved by this grace of God will have certain physical demonstrations or manifestations. One may laugh and rejoice when saved, another may weep out loud for joy, another may leap and shout for joy and still another may be rather quiet about it and be as much saved as any of the others. The operations of the Spirit of God within our hearts are independent of physical sense and cannot be gauged by any particular demonstration physically. However, I'm constrained to believe there will be some kind of physical demonstration.

When spiritual life comes to the inner man I believe the outer man will feel some effects of it and demonstrate in some manner. Receiving the baptism of the Holy Ghost is realized through obedience to God's Word and exercising of faith in His promises. Paul says that Christ redeemed us from the curse of the law that the blessing of Abraham might come on the Gentiles through Jesus Christ; that we might receive the promise of the Spirit through faith (Galatians 3:13-14). Again let me say, the baptism of the Holy Ghost is an operation of God within us in response to our obedience to Him and exercising faith in His promises.

THE DEVIL HAS A COUNTERFEIT TO THIS EXPERIENCE

In the realms of the spiritual the devil has a counterfeit for the true and genuine article. He has a counterfeit experience for the true experience of Holy Ghost baptism, and has multitudes promoting his false theory. The counterfeit and unscriptural doctrine of speaking in an unknown tongue as the evidence of the baptism of the Holy Ghost is deceiving millions today. The so-called Pentecostal churches of our land are teaching this false doctrine and deceiving people by the thousands. Their doctrine is without scriptural foundation. There is not one text in the Bible that teaches the idea that everyone who receives the baptism of the Holy Ghost must speak in an unknown tongue. There is not one text in the Bible that teaches everyone who receives the baptism of the Holy Ghost will come into possession of any one particular gift of the Spirit. This is all a misinterpretation of the scriptures. We acknowledge there is a true gift of tongues but nowhere does the Bible teach that all who receive the baptism of the Holy Ghost will possess this one gift any more that it teaches all will possess the gift of Prophecy, or the gift of healing, or miracles, or any of the other mentioned gifts of the Spirit. It is possible to be baptized with the Holy Ghost, and have Him abiding within your heart, and yet not possess any one of His gifts.

Someone may say, "What then is the witness or evidence we are baptized of Him?" Beloved, the Holy Ghost Himself is the witness as Paul states in Hebrews 10:14-15. How absurd to think or teach a particular gift of the Spirit is a witness. If the Spirit Himself can't bear witness to us I'm sure one of His gifts couldn't because the Giver is far greater than His gifts. In 1 Corinthians 12 the Apostle Paul teaches us the gifts or manifestations of the Spirit are not the same in each person. In verses 4-7 he teaches there are diversities of gifts, but the same Spirit. There are differences of administrations, and diversities of operations but it is the same God, the same Spirit that worketh in all. He continues speaking of the body of Christ, the church, being many members yet only one body. "For by one Spirit are we all baptized into one body, . . . and have been all made to drink into one Spirit." This he speaks of the church.

Now he says, "If the foot shall say, Because I am not the hand, I am not of the body; is it therefore not of the body? And if the ear shall say, Because I am not the eye, I am not of the body; is it therefore not of the body? If the whole body were an eye, where were the hearing? If the whole were hearing, where were the smelling?"

Going farther into this truth he says, "And God hath set some in the church, first apostles, secondarily prophets, thirdly teachers, after that miracles, then gifts of healings, helps, governments, diversities of tongues. Are all apostles? are all prophets? are all teachers? are all workers of miracles? Have all the gifts of healing? do all speak with tongues? do all interpret?" He has already answered these questions in the foregoing verses. He pictured a body with all its various members yet constituting only one body. Now if all are demanded to prophecy we have not a body, if all demanded to possess the gifts of miracles we have not a body, if all required to speak in unknown tongues we have not a body. If the Spirit gave the same gift to every believer, and operated identically the same in each we would not have a body but a monstrosity, and those religious groups which teach the gift of tongues as evidence of Holy Ghost baptism are nothing more than a spiritual monstrosity. They are not the true body of Christ. The groups which teach speaking in tongues is evidence of the Holy Ghost baptism tell us this is a sign to the believer, evidence or proof he is baptized with the Holy Ghost. This idea is contrary to the scriptures. The Apostle Paul says, "tongues are for a sign, not to them that believe, but to them that believe not. If therefore the whole church be come together into one place, and all speak with tongues, and there come in those that are unlearned, or unbelievers, will they not say that ye are mad?" (1 Corinthians 14:22-23) Is not such a scene portrayed before the eyes of many unbelievers today that causes them to frown upon all religion. They go to church and soon a spirit falls upon some who lose control of themselves and go into a physical demonstration which is immodest and oft times indecent and finally lose consciousness. In this state of unconsciousness they begin to jibber-jabber and make sounds that is not a language, and is not understood by anyone, and it's called the gift of speaking in tongues. This same spirit sweeps over others and soon there are a number taking part in the demonstration which would lead one to believe they are mad as Paul stated. In such a state of frenzy they have lost complete control of their mind and body.

Beloved, this is not the work of the Holy Ghost within people: He doesn't operate in this manner. The true gift of tongues has its counter-part in the true gift of interpretation of tongues and if operating properly they operate together. "If any man speak in an unknown tongue, let it be by two, or at the most by three, and that by course; (one succeeding the other and not all at once) and let one interpret. But if there be no interpreter, let him keep silence in the church; and let him speak to himself, and to God." (1 Corinthians 14:27-28) This injunction is not carried out in the nominal Pentecostal meeting of our day, but rather it is ignored, and many are jabbering at the same time in what is called an unknown tongue and without an interpreter. Such creates a state of confusion and God is not the author of confusion. If it be the true manifestation of the gift of tongues why doesn't it work according to the scriptures which were written by men filled with the true Spirit of God? What is commonly witnessed in such Pentecostal meetings is the devils counterfeit for Holy Ghost baptism. God doesn't have to knock us unconscious to prophecy through us. In fact He'll give us the spirit of a sound mind that we may know whereof we speak. Paul placed a low premium on such things when he said. "In the church I had rather speak five words with my understanding, that by my voice I might teach others also, than ten thousand words in an unknown tongue." (1 Corinthians 14:19)

Someone might say; "Did not the disciples speak in tongues on the day of Pentecost?" Yes they did, but not in unknown tongues. The Bible says they spake with "other tongues, as the Spirit gave them utterance," and not with an unknown tongue for all those people gathered out of every nation under heaven heard them speak the wonderful works of God in their own language and understood what was being said. It was not a scene of confusion for they were pricked in their hearts by the Spirit of God and sought salvation. On that particular occasion there was need for a manifestation of the gift of speaking in "divers kinds of tongues" because there were people present who spoke divers kinds of languages. Where one common language is spoken the need is not so great for a manifestation of the gift of divers kinds of tongues. Far greater is the need of the gift of healing and miracles.

Other than the day of Pentecost there are only two accounts of speaking in tongues in the New Testament and we have no grounds to conclude they were "unknown tongues" for an interpreter is not mentioned in either case. According to Paul's teaching in 1 Corinthians 14 speaking in an unknown tongue must be accompanied by an interpreter and if no interpreter is present then the speaking must be withheld in public. If it be the true gift it will operate in accord with the Holy Scriptures and the fact it doesn't do this is proof it is false.

Beloved, if you are a twice born person the promise of the Spirit is yours if you'll yield your all to God and seek Him for the experience, but don't be misled in believing the gift of speaking in tongues is the evidence.

[Included by permission of Harold Barber Jr.]

The True Holy Spirit Gift of Tongues.
By Harold Barber

The true Holy Spirit gift of tongues is being slandered today more than it has ever been before in all recorded history. Millions of people are claiming to speak in "unknown tongues" by the power of the Holy Ghost. The truth of the matter is that they couldn't be more wrong! To be able to clearly see their error you must understand: (A) what the true Holy Spirit gift of tongues is, (B) how it is used, and (C) who God gives it to.

(A) What The True Gift Is

The true gift of tongues is the ability to speak in foreign languages without ever having been taught those languages. It's not an "unknown" jibber-jabber or bibbel-babbel. It's a plain, simple to understand, language. It's spoken by an individual who knows and understands exactly what he or she is saying. When someone speaks to you using the gift of tongues, you will understand them perfectly in the same language you have used since you were born. Acts 2:4-11.

(B) How It's Used

The gift is used to communicate the gospel message of salvation to people of all different kinds of languages (tongues). As recorded in the book of Acts, the only time the gift was used was in an area where there were people from different areas who spoke different languages. In Acts the 2nd chapter, on the day of Pentecost: "there were dwelling at Jerusalem Jews, devout men, out of every nation under heaven . . . And they were all amazed and marvelled, saying one to another . . . how hear we every man in our own tongue, wherein we were born?" Acts 2:5-8

The only other places in Acts where mention is made of the use of the gift of tongues is in the cities of Caesarea and Ephesus. These cities were major seaport cities. People from many different nations and tongues would pass through them regularly. The gift of tongues was very much needed to enable the church to testify and preach the message of salvation to the many travelers from many different nations. When everyone already speaks the same language, the gift of tongues is not needed and God does not give it.

The claim by many today is that speaking in tongues is the witness that you have received the Holy Ghost. But in at least 46 places in the New Testament where it tells or teaches of people being filled with the Holy Ghost, it says nothing about speaking in tongues. 1 Corinthians the 12th chapter plainly states that there are many gifts of the Holy Ghost, but different people have different gifts and not everyone has the gift of tongues.

Let's consider the most Holy Ghost filled individual that ever walked on the face of the earth: the Lord Jesus Christ. (Luke 4:14, Mark 1:8-12, Matthew 12:28) In the power of the Spirit, Jesus healed multitudes, performed miracles, cast out devils, prophesied and taught many the wonderful word of God. But while doing all this Jesus never taught the people in a foreign tongue. And most certainly he never jibber-jabbered in an "unknown tongue"! Jesus said his mission while on earth wasn't to the Gentiles, but to the Jews. "I am not sent but unto the lost sheep of the house of Israel." (Matthew 15:24) The people that Jesus taught while on earth all spoke the same language. Therefore there wasn't any need to use the gift of tongues. By example, Jesus showed that the gifts of the Spirit are only used when there is a need. This is so God might be glorified in their use and not man!

Later Jesus sent his disciples into all the world to preach the gospel. When there was a need to speak to people of different languages, the Lord provided the gift of tongues to do so.

(C) Who God Gives It To

Finally, the Bible plainly teaches us that not everyone can receive the gift of the Holy Ghost. Only those who are saved, obeying God and who commit no sin. (Acts 5:32, Hebrews 6:4-8, I John 3:3-10, Hebrews 10:26-31)

Many try to argue that I Corinthians the 14th chapter supports the teaching of "unknown tongues" and the need for someone to translate these "tongues." First of all, it should be noted that the word "unknown" in this chapter was never in the original! In the King James Version it is specifically italicized to show that it was a "supplied" word in the translation. The interpreters did it this way to describe a language not known by a majority of the congregation. The phrase "unknown tongue" isn't used anywhere else in the Bible! The city of Corinth was another major seaport city with many people from different nations passing through regularly. This chapter deals with the problem caused when people of different languages come together to try to worship God together. People of different languages were coming to the congregation at Corinth and trying to use their native language in the worship services. The majority of the congregation did not speak their language. That is why they were in need of an interpreter. The problem dealt with in this chapter is not people using the gift of tongues. The true Holy Spirit gift of tongues does not cause problems, it solves them!

Now if you are one of those who believes that the Holy Ghost has given you the power to bibble-babble in an "unknown tongue," you do have some very serious problems that you should be seriously considering:

(1) Multitudes of different churches and sects are claiming to speak in "unknown tongues" but yet are divided into different bodies and doctrines. They know nothing about Holy Spirit directed Bible unity where the body is one, with one name in God, and where the ministry sees eye to eye on the doctrine. (John 17:9-23, I Corinthians 1:10, Ephesians 4:1-6, Isaiah 52:7-8) The best these "unknown tongues" ministers can produce is a union of churches still holding to their own names and their own doctrines.

(2) While having this power to speak in an "unknown tongue," you, and everyone else with the same power, cannot live without committing sin. A strong characteristic of all who speak and pray in these "unknown tongues" is the sin nature still working inside. Multitudes of church members and preachers still have to sin once in a while, but yet are able to still speak in an "unknown tongue." But the true Holy Ghost causes people to be holy and live free from sin all the time! (I Corinthians 3:16-17, Romans 8:1-5, Galatians 5:16-26) And the Holy Ghost will never lead you to act in a way that is contrary to the Word of God.

(3) Finally, it is a well known fact that even in open heathen, pagan, religious ceremonies they speak in "unknown tongues." These people do not even believe in the Lord Jesus Christ!

Isaiah the prophet foretold of God's church this way: "Thou shalt not see a people, a people of a deeper speech than thou canst perceive; of a stammering (*ridiculous*) tongue, that thou canst not understand." (Isaiah 33:19)

Once people get drunken on the "good feeling" satanic "unknown tongue" spirit, it is rare that they ever get free from its deception. But yet, by the mercy of God, some have. Will you hear the true Bible message of deliverance from all sin, from all satan's power; even freedom from the deceptive, binding, "unknown tongue" spirit

[Included by permission of Harold Barber Jr.]

The Gifts of the Spirit.
By Boyce W. Blackwelder

Warner Press   Anderson, Indiana

I

IN A general sense the blessings of the gospel are called gifts because they cannot be purchased or merited by man but are conferred upon believers by the gracious favor of the Lord. Salvation through Jesus Christ is God's supreme gift, and all other endowments issue from this basic gratuity.

Terminology

In the New Testament several terms are employed to indicate the gifts that God bestows upon men. *Dōrea,* a word which expresses generosity or freeness, is used eleven times, in each instance of a divine gift. In some contexts the *dōrea* is righteousness (Rom. 5:15, 17); in others it is the Holy Spirit (Acts 2:38; 10:45; 11:17); and in one instance it is the water of life (John 4:10). Paul uses *dōrea* to denote the immensity of the sum total of redemptive blessings mediated through Christ when he speaks of God's "indescribable gift" (2 Cor. 9:15).

In Philippians 4:17, *Doma* signifies a gift of financial assistance, while in Matthew 7:11 and Luke 11:13 the plural *(domata)* indicates good gifts in general. According to Ephesians 4:11, individuals endowed with certain leadership abilities are themselves Christ's gifts (domata, cf. vs. 8) to the church.

Dōron is used in Ephesians 2:8 of the gift of salvation, but *dōron* frequently signifies an offering or a presentation made by men (e.g., Matt. 2:11; 5:23-24; Luke 21:1, 4).

The Apostle James reminds us that every good *act of* giving *(dosis)* and every perfect or complete *thing given (dōrēma)* have their source in the heavenly Father (James 1:17).

In Hebrews 2:4, the plural of *merismos,* an action noun from *merizō,* to *divide* or *distribute*, denotes the *apportionings* of the various gifts imparted by the Holy Spirit.

The common New Testament term for spiritual gift is *charisma.* The suffix -*ma* denotes result. Hence *charisma* means something graciously or freely given. This term is used of the gift of righteousness (Rom. 5:15-16), of the blessing of eternal life (6:23), and of help in response to prayer (2 Cor. 1:11). But in its characteristic usage it denotes an extraordinary ability bestowed by the Holy Spirit to equip a Christian for special service. The plural noun, *charismata,* is also used mainly in this technical sense. These nouns are formed from the verb *charizomai,* which means to *show favor*, to *give freely* or *graciously.* The word and the thought of *charis, grace,* are embraced in the term *charismata,* the literal rendering of which is *grace-gifts.*

The singular expression *charisma,* with but one exception (1 Pet. 4:10), occurs in the New Testament only in Paul's Epistles (Rom. 1:11; 5:15, 16; 6:23; I Cor. 1:7; 7:7; II Cor. 1:11; I Tim. 4:14; II Tim. 1:6). The plural, charismata, is found in Romans 11:29; 12:6; and in 1 Corinthians 12:4, 9, 28, 30, 31. These expressions usually stand alone, but *charisma* in Romans 1:11 is modified by the adjective *pneumatikon, spiritual.*

The Nature of the Gifts

Like so many other spiritual realities, the nature of the *charismata* does not lend itself to full logical definition. Nevertheless we may say that spiritual gifts or charisms include any notable capability which operates for the edification of the church and the winning of souls to Christ. Obviously the *charismata* are not to be regarded as mere natural talents. Such a concept is excluded by the designation, "gifts of the Spirit." They are supernatural endowments, but it seems that they are usually given in accordance with the innate aptitudes of the recipients.

Perhaps in certain instances the Holy Spirit may impart entirely new skills, but we believe that generally he works with those proficiencies which already exist, energizing and heightening them to a more effective expression. It may be assumed that the *charismata* are given, both as to kind and number, as were the assets in the parable of the talents, "to each man according to his own ability" (Matt. 25:15). The parable reminds us that the use which a person makes of his opportunities is the measure of his competency for more (vss. 20-29).

Certainly Christian experience is a vital aspect of the background of spiritual gifts. Through his encounter with God, the believer has entered a new dimension of life. The indwelling of the Holy Spirit enhances all his intellectual and moral powers. The most profound inclinations of his personality are ennobled and challenged by this lofty communion and the responsibility which it imposes. As a servant ready for the Master's use, the Christian goes forth eager to serve God in every capacity of his being. His particular gift or gifts will be commensurate to the task which he is called to perform.

Our view of the *charismata* is in harmony with the principle that God usually works with human instrumentality, and not independently of it. This interpretation corresponds with what we know of God's method of coaction with human personality in other circumstances.

For example, divine and human elements were involved in the writing of the Scriptures. Other illustrations of the divine-human inter-working are the preaching of a sermon under the unction of the Holy Spirit (Acts 2:37; 4:8, 31; I Pet. 1:12), and the offering of the prayer of faith (James 5:15; Jude 20).

God deals with different persons in different ways. Paul says that Timothy received a *charisma* by the laying on of the Apostle's hands (cf. 2 Tim. 1:6) The use of the preposition *dia* with the genitive case, a construction which expresses instrumentality or means, suggests that the imposition of Paul's hands was the instrument of God in the communication of this special gift. In 1 Timothy 4:14, the preposition *meta*, which refers to the imposition of hands by the elders, denotes the accompanying circumstances, not the means by which the gift was conferred.

Timothy was gifted in grasping the truth, and of course in discerning spurious doctrine. His *charisma* included the ability to preach and teach the gospel, and to train other workers in the congregations where he labored. He was prepared for this service under the tutelage of the Apostle Paul, and the elders recognized the competence which Timothy exercised. The mention of Paul and the elders in connection with Timothy's gift emphasizes the fact that often God uses the influence of established leaders in calling and developing recruits for the ministry.

Distribution of the Gifts

Both in the natural and in the spiritual realm, life is complex and calls for many kinds of service and corresponding abilities. Accordingly, the Lord has placed a variety of gifts within the church. In I Corinthians 12:4-6, we read of "distributions of *charismata*," "distributions of services," and "distributions of energies." In Roman 12:6, Paul says that we have "*charismata* differing according to the grace that is given to us." The gifts are apportioned and distributed by the Holy Spirit as he wills (I Cor. 12:11).

Every member of the church has one or more of these endowments (12:7, 11; I Pet. 4:10). It is possible that some Christians may possess many or even all the gifts. It seems that all were given to the apostles because all were needed for their work.

Inasmuch as all Christians do not have the same gifts, all do not possess all the gifts. Furthermore, no one of the gifts is intended for every Christian. Paul, in this regard, views the human body as analogous to the church. He argues that it would be as absurd to contend that every Christian has all the gifts, or that all possess the same gift, as to contend that every member of one's physical body can hear, see, or taste, or that the hand can perform the function of the foot (cf. I Cor. 12:44ff.).

In explaining this point, Paul asks a series of rhetorical questions. He introduces each question with the Greek negative particle *mē*, a procedure which indicates that in each instance a negative answer is expected: "All are not apostles, are they? [No, of course not!] All are not prophets, are they? All are not teachers, are they? All are not [workers of] miracles, are they? All do not have charismata of healings, do they? All do not speak with *glōssais* [i.e., different languages], do they? All do not interpret, do they? [Certainly not!] (12:29-30).

Every member of the church has some excellency in him, and he should discover what his particular gift is and how he may contribute to the common good. When a Christian possesses a gift from God, not only will he recognize it, but the church will share his conviction and be benefited by his life and his gift.

Unity of the Gifts

Although there is a variety of spiritual gifts, they are characterized by a marvelous unity. The basis of this unity is the oneness of the Godhead, which is the source of the charismata. Paul reiterates this thought in I Corinthians 12:4-6. Then, after mentioning some of the gifts, the Apostle says, "All these are wrought by the one and the same Spirit, who distributes to each man separately as he purposes" (vs. 11).

The harmonious functioning of the various organs of the human body illustrates the united action of the church which is the body of Christ. "For as we have many members in one [physical] body, and all the members do not have the same function, so we, who are many [believers], are one body in Christ, and we are individually members of each other" (Rom. 12:4-5). The physical body is one because it is animated by one spirit. Likewise, the church is one because of the indwelling of the Spirit of God. Again the mutual dependence of the organs of the physical body is illustrative of the church: no member exists for himself alone.

II

THE twofold task of the church is the edification of the saints and the salvation of the world. Accordingly, the purpose of the *charismata* is to aid us in carrying out these responsibilities.

In the context of Ephesians 4:11, where Paul's emphasis is upon the persons themselves, he does not use the term *charismata,* but he indicates that Christ provides leaders (*domata*, cf. vs. 8) with a view to fully equipping the saints for the work of ministering for the upbuilding of the body of Christ (vs. 12). Anarthrous *diakonias* in the latter verse indicates that the reference is not to the ministry in any technical or limited sense, but to the service of Christians in general. In other words, evangelism is the task of the total church, not of the preachers alone. Certainly the *charismata* are vital in the activities required in soul winning.

Furthermore, the gifts of the Spirit are to aid believers in spiritual growth. Paul says that "the whole number" of disciples are to arrive at Christian maturity, which includes the oneness which belongs to the faith and to the full knowledge of the Son of God (Eph. 4:13).

Jesus prayed for the oneness of all his followers (John 17:20-23). Christian unity exalts the Savor (vs. 21). Conversely, any defect in our oneness weakens our witness for him (vss. 21, 23). Therefore we should endeavor with all diligence to approximate and maintain New Testament unity.

Let us make sure that we ourselves are in this oneness and that we seek to overcome anything that might hinder its full expression. A reckless attitude is doubly sad because a disturber usually takes other persons with him in his tragic course. Factionalism and dissention which create disruption are condemned in the Word of God. The apostles warned the church against doctrinal departures from revealed truth (cf. Acts 20:28ff.; Rom. 16:17f.; Gal. 5:20; Titus 3:10; II Pet. 2:1). Grave ethical implications are involved. No person who turns away from the truth can do so with moral integrity.

In the third place, spiritual gifts are for ornaments to beautify the church of God. Where would be the splendor of the heavens and the earth if our eyes were compelled to look always upon the same things without the refreshing stimulus of variety?

The God who has put so much loveliness in the natural world has done likewise in the spiritual realm. What is more magnificent than the church, radiant with the divine presence, reflecting the inimitable graces and the manifold gifts of the Spirit? I think of three stanzas from the hymn, "O Church of God":

> *The Church of God one body is, one*
> *Spirit dwells within;*
> *And all her members are redeemed, and*
> *triumph over sin . . .*

God sets her members each in place, according to his will—

Apostles, prophets, teachers, all, His purpose to fulfill . . .

In beauty stand, O Church of God, with righteousness arrayed;

Put on thy strength and face thy foes with, courage undismayed.

In the fourth place, we must note that the *charismata* are not given for any selfish purpose, and certainly not for showmanship, but for service. They are not bestowed for private enjoyment, nor for any advantage or gain of the recipients, but to promote the common good. Paul says, "To each one is given the manifestation of the Spirit for a useful purpose" (I Cor. 12:7). Peter emphasizes the same principle. He indicates that each person has received a *charisma* as a sacred trust to be exercised for the benefit of others (I Pet. 4:10).

To be an excellent steward, an individual must administer his gift as the Bestower intended. There should be no thought of self apart from the joy of service to the cause of Christ. Obviously there can be no basis for pride with regard to that which is entirely a matter of grace.

The Relative Importance of the Gifts

Paul wishes his converts to see the *charismata* in their proper perspective. He makes it clear that the graces or fruit of the Spirit are more important than the gifts. He maintains a distinction between the outward (and in some instances non-moral) expressions such as prophecy and languages, and the inward and essentially moral qualities. In Paul's thought, the value of a person's gift or gifts depends upon the quality of the person's character. In I Corinthians, chapters 12-14, the Apostle reproves individuals who make extravagant claims about communion with the Spirit while their conduct is detrimental to the harmony and influence of the church.

With tact and persuasion Paul shows that the *charismata* have a definite order of importance. He places the more spectacular gifts in a secondary position to prophecy (by prophecy he means the clear presentation of God's word; cf. I Cor. 14:3), and he shows further that there is a higher gift of the Spirit than any of the spectacular ones. Without it, all the other gifts are worthless.

The supreme gift is *agapē*, the love exemplified in the Lord Jesus (I Cor. 13). In Romans 15:30, Paul calls *agapē* "the love of the Spirit" (i.e., *the love which the Spirit imparts;* subjective genitive). Cf. Romans 5:5, where Paul says that "the love of God has been poured forth into [and *continues inundating,* force of *ekkechutai,* perfect passive indicative] our hearts through the Holy Spirit who has been given to us." The lesser gifts have their place for a time, but faith and hope and love are graces which abide, and love is the greatest of the three (I Cor. 13:13).

We are saved through faith by grace alone (Eph. 2:8). The *charismata* have nothing to do with our personal salvation, but constitute our equipment for the salvation of others. Gifts have sometimes been conferred, at least momentarily, upon wicked men. For example, Caiaphas, the Jewish high priest who advised the death of Jesus as a matter of expediency, uttered prophetic words (John 11:49-52). Balaam, the Mesopotamian false prophet, received a gift of prediction (Num. 24:2-9, 15-19), but he was a covetous person and lost his life fighting against God's people (31:8). Even Balaam's donkey, which had no soul to save, received a gift of tongues. Notice that what the donkey spoke was intelligible, for the record says that Balaam understood the utterances and carried on a conversation with the animal (Num. 22:28-30).

The point is taken that God bestows gifts on whom he chooses, saved or unsaved, man or beast, and that the gifts are a matter of relative importance. It may be added that the normal condition for the reception of God's endowments is faith.

The ethical implications of the work of the Holy Spirit call our attention to the timing of the Spirit's advent at Pentecost. Why did the Holy Spirit come *when* he did? He came as "a rushing mighty wind" (Acts 2:2), as if for a long time he had been waiting, anxious to come, but for some reason was held back. It may be said that his descent was chronologically according to Old Testament typology; that the festival of Pentecost came seven weeks after the Passover, hence fifty days after the death of Christ the antitypical Lamb, we have the outpouring of the Holy Spirit.

Of course, this is true, but there is something more significant about the time element. It is this: The Holy Spirit could not come until the norm of spiritual experience and conduct had been revealed in the Lord Jesus Christ. That is to say, mankind must first see how a Spirit-filled person acts. Otherwise, all sorts of weird claims could have been made and attributed to the power of the Spirit, thus creating deception difficult to answer. How thankful we are that Christ has exemplified the authoritative standard of spiritual behavior! From his unmistakable disclosure we know how a Spirit-filled person will conduct himself. Spirituality always follows the pattern demonstrated in the life of the Savior.

The relation of the Holy Spirit to Christ is very intimate. Christ dwells in the believer by the presence of the Holy Spirit (Gal. 4:6; Rom. 8:9; II Cor. 3:17). The coming of the Spirit is not thought of apart from the person of Christ himself. Although there is a distinction between the Paraclete and the one who sends him (John 16:7; 15:26), there is no discontinuity in the life of the church after the ascension of Jesus. The triumphant Lord continues to be with his people (Matt. 28:20; John 14:16-18; Rev. 1:10-18).

The work begun by Jesus during his incarnate ministry penetrates deeper into the world as the Holy Spirit energizes the disciples (Acts 1:8). The Holy Spirit, who is the revealer and interpreter of the truth, speaks not of himself, but he testifies of Jesus and glorifies him. He brings to remembrance Jesus' teachings as he guides believers into the whole truth (John 15:26; 16:13-14).

Paul exhorts the Corinthians to desire the most important *charismata:* "The higher gifts are those you should aim at" (I Cor. 12:31, NEB). The greater, or superior, gifts are those that bring the most benefit to the general body of Christians. Paul illustrates what he means when he ranks prophecy far above the ability to speak with various languages (cf. 14:3-5; 23-25).

But how do we strive for the greater gifts? Such striving requires more than asking or praying. It involves the cultivation of fitness on our part.

Of course, the Spirit effects the preparation, but he does so in those individuals who give him full control of their lives. Actually, then, we should seek the Giver, the Holy Spirit himself. The gifts are creatures of God. Therefore it is idolatry to worship them, just as it is idolatry to worship any other creature.

When people seek some mysterious "power" instead of wholeheartedly following the Lord, they open the door for evil spirits to come in and place a deception upon them. Communion with such spirits has been more or less prevalent in every period of history.

Credulous people fall easy victims to the Satanic devices promulgated by false prophets. God's people should keep alert and put every preacher and his message to the acid test of the Word of God (cf. I John 4:1ff.). Paul himself mentions "discernings of spirits" as an important gift among the *charismata* (I Cor. 12:10; cf. I Thess. 5:21).

III

GENUINE religion has always been harassed by imitators. In ancient Israel, tests were established for distinguishing the true prophet from the false (cf. Deut. 13:1-5; 18:20-22; Isa. 28:7; Jer. 23:16-32; Ezek. 13:1-23; Micah 3:5-11; Zeph. 3:4). In the apostolic period when ecstasy was a common feature of non-Christian religions, and when the pagan mantis or frenzied prophet was a well-known phenomenon, it was obvious that all mystical expressions could not be ascribed to the Holy Spirit. Prophets were not to be given indiscriminate credence (I Thess. 5:21; I Cor. 14:29; I John 4:1). Now, as then, the church must differentiate between authentic and spurious manifestations. There are four basic criteria by which the genuineness of any religious expression may be ascertained:

1. *Doctrinal soundness.* An authentic utterance is in harmony with the revealed Word of God. Conclusions should not be based upon how an individual feels or how many persons believe a certain tenet, but upon the teaching of the Scriptures. The test of a true prophet, or of the trustworthiness of any man who lays claim to spirituality, is that he respects God's Word as the objective standard of experience and conduct (cf. I Cor. 14:36-37; Isa. 8:19-20). The Holy Spirit inspired the Scriptures, and he does not lead anyone contrary to what is thus recorded.

2. *Moral integrity.* The New Testament writers steadily concentrate attention on the inner qualities of character, which the popular mind tends to ignore. Paul associates the Holy Spirit with spiritual power, assurance, joy, and exemplary deportment (I Thess. 1:5-10); and with moral purity (4:8) and dedication to the truth (II Thess. 2:13).

That is to say, Christianity is essentially ethical and moral (cf. Rom. 14:17). Its abiding significance is not to be found in the form of turbulent outward phenomena, but in the consistent influence of transformed lives. The charismata are not the chief blessings or the most permanent benefits. The normal product of the Spirit is the virtues which constitute the fullness of the Christian life (Gal. 5:22-23; cf. Matt. 7:15-20; Rom. 8:9; I Cor. 12:31). The incomparable triad of the Holy Spirit's presence is faith, hope, and love (I Cor. 13:13).

3. *General edification.* A gift from God will contribute to the well-being of the church. If we are moti-

vated by the love of Christ, we will not be misfits or schismatics (I Cor. 12:25). It is in terms of the nine-fold cluster of the Spirit's fruit, headed by *agapē* (Gal. 5:22-23), that the gifts are to be evaluated and employed.

The same spiritual dynamic which regenerates and indwells the individual Christian is the cohesive bond of the church's unity. The Holy Spirit distributes the *charismata* in a manner which promotes oneness in the bond of peace (Eph. 4:3).

4. *Intelligent self-consciousness.* No activity under the influence of the Holy Spirit, whether exercised publicly or in private devotion, ever suspends any person's rationality. The diviners of heathenism underwent intense psychophysical disturbances in which they became unconscious under the power of the gods that had taken hold of them. Thus deprived of their reason, the subjects exhibited outward signs of violent excitement resembling symptoms of insanity. Such a state was regarded as a necessary evidence of inspiration.

The Hebrew prophets did not display such peculiarities. They were not placed in a completely passive relation to supernatural influence but maintained the full possession of their mental powers. In the declaration of their message from God, they spoke with a maximum awareness of their surroundings.

The New Testament, like the Old, emphasizes the intelligibility of spiritual expressions. Genuine prophetic activity is characterized by the sensible presentation of truth. The statement, "no man understands" (I Cor. 14:2) is not to be taken in the absolute sense, for the interpreter would understand (cf. vs. 5b), or the speaker himself might give the meaning of the language spoken (see vs. 13).

Paul is against any tendency that would induce mental confusion or deprive anyone of self-control. The Apostle insists that "the spirits of the prophets are subject to the prophets" (I Cor. 14:32). He means that each speaker who is of God is in possession of his faculties and is able to restrain the impulse to speak if the maintenance of order so requires (vs. 33).

Conclusion

We need balance and clear thinking with regard to the *charismata* in order to avoid extreme emotionalism on the one hand and rigid formalism on the other. We should maintain both an attitude of candor and an attitude of caution, so that we may be receptive to all God's blessings and at the same time guard against extravagances and false doctrines.

Charismatic expression is not left to the caprice of subjectivism. The Word of God delineates the lofty framework in which the Spirit's power and gifts operate. The biblical standard must not be perverted by peripheral or incidental emphases, questionable innovations, and compromises. We know that the Holy Spirit is the Spirit of truth, and that we honor him by devotion to the truth, the inscripturization of which he has directed. Let us pray that we may be spared errors of judgment which would distort our perspective.

According to the New Testament, the power of the Holy Spirit is attested not primarily or necessarily by spectacular manifestations, but by the portrayal of inviolate character. Miracles may have been the chief attraction of attention in the early days of Christianity, but even then it was practical wisdom, holiness of life, and the joy of service which were recognized as the evidences of the Spirit's presence (cf. Acts 6:3; 13:52; James 1:27; I Pet. 1:15-16).

The basic work of the Holy Spirit, as he glorifies Christ, is illuminating and regenerating souls, sanctifying Christians, empowering disciples with evangelistic fervor, bringing conviction to the world, strengthening the church, and guiding believers into the fulness of the truth. We must let nothing engage our attention which would tend to focus our eyes off the Savior and the task to which he has called us (Matt. 28:19- 20).

While exercising care not to limit the operation of God's power by any lack of obedience and faith, it is important for us to remember that the Scriptures, speaking of the last days preceding the anticipated return of the Lord, declare that Satan will work with great effectiveness by means of deceptive signs and false miracles (Rev. 13:13-14; II Thess. 2:9-12).

The devil uses the "wonders of a lie" (vs. 9) to make credulous individuals believe they have seen genuine miracles. Thus by his counterfeit prodigies he leads many persons astray. Complete obedience to God's Word and perfect submission to the Holy Spirit will prevent us from being deluded by fake performances. When people seek anything but God, they miss his highest blessing, and unless they recover their spiritual discernment they are sure to become confused by side issues and fall into serious errors.

From the consistent affirmation of the New Testament, we know that *agapē* is the dominating motive, the supreme gift, the preeminent grace, and the indispensable quality in the entire expression of the charismatic ideal. This is true because the love which the Ho-

ly Spirit inspires always makes us Christ-like. Therefore we are sure that here is where our emphasis belongs.

[Included by permission of Alice (Blackwelder)
Allen.]

"Why the Church of God Does Not Believe In An Unknown Tongue."
By R. C. Caudill, D. D.

ACTS 2:4. "AND THEY WERE ALL
FILLED WITH THE HOLY GHOST
AND BEGAN TO SPEAK IN OTHER
TONGUES, AS THE SPIRIT GAVE
THEM UTTERANCE."

1. Who Wrote About This Marvelous Experience In The New Testament?

Paul and St. Luke, and neither of them were in the
upper room on the day of Pentecost, when the Holy
Spirit came upon the awaiting company of 120. Paul
wrote fourteen books of the 27 in the New Testament.
And he mentions "Tongues" only in one. (1 Cor. 14) St.
Luke was not in the upper room, for he was a convert of
Paul's and Paul was not converted until three years after the Pentecost. Here are the New Testament writers
who were there when it happened. Matthew, James,
John, Jude and Peter. These five writers, wrote ten
books of the New Testament. And not one of them in
the ten books, mentions speaking in Tongues. James
tells us what Pure Religion is, (James 1:27). John tells
us what it is. (1 John 4:7-8). Peter tells us about it in II
Peter 1:4-10. None of them mention "Tongues."

2. Tongues Were Languages Of Earth.

(Acts 2:8) "How hear we every man in our own "tongue" (language), wherein we were born?" On the day of Pentecost, when the Holy Spirit came upon those in the upper room. He spoke through them in the language of those who were present. Here is the real example of "Tongues." 1 Cor. 14 is no example. For there Paul is trying to correct the abuse this Corinthian church was making of the gift. He wasn't setting forth "Tongues," he was correcting "Tongues."

3. There Is No Such Thing As An Unknown Tongue.

"Unknown Tongue" is a contradiction of terms. If it's a tongue it has to be known. If it's unknown it can't be a tongue. Hence, there is no such thing as an "unknown tongue." Every time the word "Unknown" occurs in the 14th Chapter of 1st Cor. it occurs in script form, (italics) and this means it was added by the translators, and was not found in the manuscript from which they translated the 14th Chapter. The word "unknown" comes from the word, *agnosto*, and this word does not occur in the Greek text.

Man has always approached God in his mother tongue. And when God talked to man he always approached man in his own language. What non-sense, that there is power to be able to speak something that the speaker nor any one else knows anything about. God wants us to know. (see 1 Cor. 14:15).

4. No Gift Of The Spirit Is A Test Of Christian Fellowship.

The abiding presence of the Spirit is the only test there is. (Romans 8:16) There is no Scripture that even intimates that this gift or any of the Spirit is to be taken as an evidence that we are Christian. Jesus said, "By their fruits ye shall know them." (Matt. 7:16). Paul would have us believe that it was the LOVE of God shed abroad in our hearts. (Romans 5:5) And to this Jesus agrees, when he said, "By this, shall all men know that ye are my disciples, if ye have LOVE one to another." (John 13:35).

The Scriptures do not teach that we are saved by gifts, but, by grace *are ye* saved through faith. (Ephesians 2:8).

5. Tongues Were For A Sign.

A sign of what, and to whom? Modern Holiness Folk says, its a *sign* they have the Holy Spirit, and they make this a test of fellowship. When Paul says, "Its a sign to them that believe not. " (1 Cor. 14:22). And in this same verse he says, "tongues are not a sign to them that believe." It means nothing to the believer, as far as fellowship and confidence is concerned. Note that this Corinthian Church, though they talked in tongues, they did about every thing sinful that you can think of, and in spite of their sinful condition, they all talked in "tongues." You can't do this and have the real Bible Gift of Tongues, as they had on the day of Pentecost.

6. Tongues Were Given An Inferior Place In The Church.

"Whether there be tongues, they shall cease." (1 Cor. 13:8) "I would that ye all speak with tongues, but RATHER that ye prophesieth, for greater is he that prophesieth that he that speaketh in tongues." (1 Cor. 14:15). So we see that speaking with tongues were given no prominence in the early church. The emphasis was not placed on talking, but on living.

7. The Purpose Of Tongues In The Early Church.

The purpose was to enable the speaker to speak in a language he did not learn, in order to get the gospel to the world. For at Pentecost, there were people there celebrating the Feast of Pentecost, from all over the world. This is why the speakers on this day spoke the language of those who were present. It was for the purpose of convincing and converting the unbeliever. (1 Cor. 14:22, 23, 24, 25).

8. Do All Speak With Tongues?

In 1 Cor. 12:29-30, we read, "All are not apostles." "All are not prophets." "All are not teachers." "All do not speak in tongues." (Moffett) It would be just as logical and Scriptural to say all are preachers, as to say that all do speak in tongues. Or to say that all have any of the other gifts. For no gift is to be made a test of Christian fellowship. For it is the Holy Spirit Himself, and not any gift that He may give that is the test. Rom. 8:16. In the Greek Text, the negative participle "ma" prefaces each statement in I Cor. 12:29-30, and reads thus, "No, All Do Not Speak In Tongues."

9. Can One Be Baptised With The Holy Spirit And Not Speak In Tongues?

Why not? Even if they all spoke in tongues on the day of Pentecost, there is no Scripture that says all will speak in tongues, or must speak in tongues when filled with the Holy Spirit. Jesus referred to this experience more than any other teacher or preacher, and not one time did he say they would speak in Tongues. Read the Beatitudes, his explanation of Christian Living. Matt. 5.

Jesus mentions eight distinct things that the Holy Spirit would do when he came, but not one time does he mention tongues. If it was so important, don't you think he would have said something about it? Jn. 16:7-14.

10. You Can't Tell What People Are By Hearing Them Talk.

You might tell whether or not they were Catholic or Protestants, but you would not know whether or not they were Christians. Some one said, "The Religion you LIVE is the Religion you HAVE, regardless of what you profess." How true. You must know the life. The only way to tell a tree is by its nature, and by its fruit. The same is true with Christians. Paul said if he could speak with the tongues of men and angels and had not LOVE he was nothing. (1 Cor. 13). Tongues are not the need of the hour but grace to keep the tongue we have.

By R. C. Caudill, D. D. MIDDLETOWN OHIO

Some Clear Statements About the "Tongues" Issue.
Max R. Gaulke

The following excerpts are published to help clear up the thinking of many in our day who are constantly made to wonder about the nature of "tongues," and the constant confusion the proponents of this false teaching create in the body of Christ — the Church. When prominent people crusade for such carnal evidences of the Holy Spirit, and monetarily-motivated publishers spread the error, the church must take its stand firmly before it becomes rent by divisive people and practices.

I took the liberty to publish these excerpts in rougher form ten years ago, but there is constant request from the College for more material on this subject. Therefore, we are publishing it for pastors and laymen in the interests of Biblical unity, truth, and holy living, the emphases for which Gulf-Coast Bible College exists.

— Max R. Gaulke, D.D. President

Carnality and the Modern "Tongues" Scourge

Dr. Charles Inwood in Keswick's Authentic Voice, pp. 75-79, Zondervan Press, 1959.

Ever and anon carnal man lapses into the grossest sins, sins that make us blush, not only for religion but for humanity and morality. One other thought in this connection, and it is lodged in the first sentence of the Epistle to the Church of God at Corinth. A feature of the carnal is this — its susceptibility to evil environment. The carnal is always the easy prey to the latest error or to the most popular sin. Like the sand on the seashore, it is always ruled by the last wave. Place a carnal Christian where spiritual influences surround him, and where all is in his favor, and you keep him a decent person. But let him go to lands where there is no Christian influence, no Christian public opinion, and oh! how quickly your carnal Christian succumbs there! Oh, they go down terribly! I have met moral and spiritual wrecks by the dozen and the score in every land I have visited. It is traceable to this — the man was only a carnal Christian, and was leaning more than he knew upon healthy environment.

I have not forgotten, in the life of Bishop Creighton, one sentence in a letter he wrote to one of his clergy. He said: "It is far easier to be an ecclesiastical partisan than to be a straightforward Christian." And God wants us to be straightforward Christians. Now, one other feature I must touch on — the craving for the abnormal. You have it in I Corinthians, chapters 1 and 14 —the craving for something which powerfully appeals to the senses, something you can see and feel, and handle, aye, and photograph; something that will startle the people. And I do think the religious Press of our times is somewhat to blame in this matter.

The phenomena of the earthquake and the fire make good "copy"; and if there be anything startling, abnormal, or peculiar, it is flashed all over the world. If, during this convention, some extraordinary light fell on the face of any one of us on the platform, there would be more talk about that than about all the body of Christian truth which will be spoken by the lips of His servants in this convention.

Signs, signs! I meet it in unexpected quarters. I read, with pain of heart, of a convention where, to emphasize the presidency of the Holy Spirit, an empty chair was left on the platform in the chairman's place. That is carnal! If there is a craving for something spectacular, that shows it is of the flesh.

I know a pastor who, on more than one occasion, declared that in that sadly famous prayer meeting of four years ago visible tongues of fire were seen to descend and rest upon the heads of the group who met, and waited, and prayed there. And that went out everywhere, as if God had done some extraordinary thing.

Now, beloved, one reason why Spiritualism is working such deadly havoc inside Christian circles is that very thing. If you want to see the unseeable and to know the unknowable, the devil will take care that there is somebody to give you something strange to look at, and something strange to fear. In the Acts of the Apostles, on one occasion, the disciples prayed for certain signs. The signs they sought were not given; God gave them something infinitely better — God filled them with the Spirit. You never hear of their asking for those signs again.

One thing more: chapter 14, with its strange, sad record of what we would call a tongues movement in the early Christian Church. I believe that we have in that chapter the strangest and saddest phase of the carnal presented in the whole Epistle; and if we laid its teaching truly to heart, we should be saved from much today. I do not believe there was much in common between the fiery tongues on the Day of Pentecost and the tongues movement in the Church at Corinth. I believe an alien movement had come in, and was working havoc in their midst. And what hurts me most is this: that I am forced to the conclusion that there is a painful identity between the worst phase of the tongues movement in the Church at Corinth, and the so-called tongues movement of our own time.

If one-tenth of what I have learned from credible Christian witnesses in Australia, in California, and in England, be true, there is nothing in common between the fiery tongues of Pentecost, and the movement of today; but this latter movement is the latest child of the carnal, and is leading hundreds of earnest, unwary souls astray. If it only took the worst, one would not grieve so much; but some of the best of souls are caught by that snare who would not be caught by any other.

I want you to lay these statements to heart. First, all animal, and nervous psychic excitements lend themselves readily to the carnal, but they do not lend themselves to the spiritual. Again, a disordered condition of mind or body is no condition of the fulness of the Spirit, no proof of the presence of the Spirit in power. By a very singular providence, which I did not at the time understand, I was permitted last year to see the howling dervishes in Asia Minor; and one thing I noticed was this — that the psychic laws manifested by those men were the same as those manifested in Australia and some other places I could mention. The dervishes were probably ignorant of the laws, but they obeyed them; and it is obedience to the law, not knowledge of it, that conditions the result.

One other thing. There are natural psychic leaders, and, if they are in earnest, they lead you far, far astray. Two things have impressed me deeply in this connection, and the first is this — I believe we are on the eve of a new conflict with the forces that come from that quarter; and I believe also, we are woefully ignorant of their disguises, and their peril, and their power. Will you believe me when I tell you that it is a rare thing to meet a Christian of such unerring spiritual intuition that he can distinguish between the power which is psychic and natural, and the power which is the power of the Holy Spirit alone? Only as you learn to distinguish the carnal in this occult region, will you be saved from the melancholy tragedy of the tongues movement as it appeared in the Church at Corinth.

"Tongues" Can Be A Curse

by Professor E. I. Carver

The onward surge of the modern "tongues" movement, and particularly the recent rash of "tongues speakers" within various denominations, has made it imperative that the Church consider carefully and prayerfully the implications this has for her. What may we expect if this comes to our congregation? How should we react when one of our leaders becomes involved? How can we tell whether it is to prove a blessing or a curse? These are not idle, senseless questions. These questions are vital ones right now,

First of all, the one who speaks in tongues is likely to lean over backwards to prove that he has not partaken of the excesses that are usually associated with the "tongues" movement. Do not be fooled by this. In most cases it will prove to be short lived. The reason for this is that most "tongues" is a purely psychological phenomenon which by its very nature tends to release the inhibitions which Christian culture has imparted to us. With controls removed through the lifting of one's inhibitions, it becomes natural for one to act uninhibited. Gradually the enforced controls are relaxed, and the true nature of the "tongues" experience manifests itself in the excesses for which it is noted.

Another temporary feature is the way any effort to impose this experience on other is avoided. Ordinarily such a person will be very careful to refrain from insisting that you must also speak in "tongues." The usual approach is to simply glorify his experience. He isn't apt to downgrade your experience except by implication. If his experience is superior to yours, this does imply that yours is inferior, but at first this may be done in an inoffensive manner. The feeling of superiority that usually accompanies "speaking in tongues" will gradually assert itself through a patronizing or a condescending attitude toward those who have not received an experience similar to his own. Pressure is then applied. An effort to force everyone to seek this experience becomes a standard procedure. This inevitably produces division and all the evils which accompany it, unless the congregation goes "tongues" in which event the excesses of the "tongues" movement reach full fruition.

Another usual concomitant of the "tongues" experience is more difficult to camouflage. This involves such an one's personal relations and fellowship with his brethren. That which he tends to rigidly control in public worship, temporarily, is difficult if not impossible to control in private relationships. The feelings of superiority which his experience genders in him cause him to react coldly to brethren who formerly were very close to him. He can no longer enjoy full fellowship with those who have not attained to his exalted (?) experience. He expects, yea, demands, that he be fellowshipped fully by others, but he cannot return the fellowship which he expects of others. Brethren with whom he previously enjoyed a real intimacy of spirit are now pushed aside. Suddenly, "tongues" becomes more important than love. "Speaking in tongues" becomes the criterion by which spiritually is judged, rather than the fruit of the Spirit. Another may have the gift of prophecy or healing, but this has small significance to the "tongues speaker" unless the other also speaks in "tongues."

One of two things usually happens in a church that has a strong "tongues" proponent arise within it. The one who has "received the tongues" may recognize the deception that has led him astray. If he does, and takes corrective action to restore the fellowship which he has broken, the breach is usually quickly healed. But when the usual course is followed, he grows more insistent that all speak in "tongues," and that those who do not "speak in tongues" are spiritually deficient. His attitude toward the brethren becomes more and more unchristian until continued fellowship is impossible. This is unfortunate, but nevertheless it is true.

The deceptiveness of "tongues" is built around the assumption that it is a miraculous manifestation of God's power in the individual. This is a fallacious promise. Various people out of whom demons have been cast were "tongues" speakers. Hence it may proceed from the Devil. But most speaking in "tongues" is a psychological phenomenon which sinners and even heathens demonstrate with equal facility as Christians. Professed Christians who are spiritually bankrupt, being destitute of a soul-satisfying relationship with God, are the most susceptible to this deception. The deadness of their experience causes them to seek a satisfying portion. But instead of Living Water, an induced, self-imposed psychological state is accepted as the answer to their seeking. This is a cistern without water.

The psychological experience of speaking in "tongues" releases certain inhibitions. Timidity and self-consciousness are removed. Boldness becomes natural. New power "seems" to come to the individual. The power is not new, however. What has happened is that the controls of powers already possessed are removed, just as alcohol, certain drugs, or hypnosis may do. But bear in mind that uncontrolled power is dangerous.

When inhibitions are released, one may find it impossible to control the areas of release. Loosing controls which make it easy to speak or shout in church may seem advantageous, but when it makes one act the fool, it is bad. Alcohol may increase sociability, but it also makes for increased sexual promiscuity. The release which comes through "speaking in tongues" is similar to this. Extreme emotionalism which is a natural outgrowth of the release of inhibitions leads to bizarre conduct which has no place in Christian worship. It is only a step farther to moral and sexual laxity and license. The reason the modern tongues movement has been so plagued with immorality within its ranks is found in these facts. Release of inhibitions is dangerous. Paul retained his for he wrote, "I was with you in weakness, and in fear, and in much trembling" (I Cor. 2:3)

An Internationally-Respected Evangelist on "Tongues"

The following excerpts are from an article by Dr. E Stanley Jones, writing in THE HERALD, Wilmore, Ky

The type of tongues appearing today is the Corinth type, an unknown tongue, and not the Pentecost type where the speaking was in a known tongue. "Every man heard in his own language the wonderful works of God." This un known type appearing in Corinth and appearing today was one of the gifts of the Spirit. But the gifts of the Spirit are not to be confounded with the gift of the Spirit. The gift of the Spirit He "divides severally as He wills" (I Cor. 12:11). Paul asks: "do all possess gifts of healing? Do all speak with tongues? Do all interpret? (I Cor. 12:30), meaning, they do not. And yet they have the gift of the Spirit. This gift of tongues was one of the lower gifts and Paul said that they were not to exercise it unless there was an interpreter.

Paul says that the Corinthian type of tongues could not be used as an evangelistic agency. "If a non-believer comes among you and hears you speaking in tongues he will think you mad." But at Pentecost it was an evangelistic agency and a very effective agency.

In the great Uganda, Africa, revival Dr. Church, a medical missionary, was the moving spirit, greatly used of God. Thousands were converted, whole villages and sections transformed. Dr. Church went off to another group which spoke in tongues, came back and began to speak in tongues in the Uganda revival. The African leaders took him aside and said, "This has made you proud. You will divide the people over this." He saw they were right. He gave up the speaking in tongues and gave himself to the main business, creating changed people, and the revival went on with power and unity.

In these modern manifestation of speaking in tongues it is not only taught — it is often induced. A group will gather around the seeker and lay their hands on his head and the seeker is sometimes urged to use some foreign words he may know to start the flow. Or he is instructed to hold his jaw loose and let his tongue be limp. Or he is told to repeat the name of Jesus over and over and then urged to go faster and faster until he goes so fast that he begins to stammer. "Now," he is told, "you are getting it." For the Scripture says, "I will speak to them by men of stammering lips."

In a brief coverage such as these three discerning Christian teachers and leaders herein give us, we can only point out the dangers in the erroneous Corinthian-type modern-day "tongues." The reader is urged to walk close to God, be much in His Word, and the Holy Spirit will protect him from spurious tongues, while helping him win others to Christ as Lord and Master.

(MRG)

Additional copies available from Gulf-Coast Bible College, 911 W. 11th St. Houston, Texas 77008. Five cents each, 25 for $1.00, 100 for $3.00 postpaid.

The Modern Tongues Experience.
Virgil L. Good

ACTS 2:4 is the key or foundation verse of all modern tongues movements. It is the one verse which they quote above all others as an example of what they believe to be the Bible experience for all Spirit-filled people. When conversing with members of these movements they will almost invariably ask, "Have you been baptized with the Holy Ghost according to Acts 2:4?" Why do these modern tongues people use only the fourth verse of the second chapter of Acts, and not the other verses also, which are so closely related to it? Why do they not ask, "Have you been baptized with the Holy Ghost according to Acts 2?" instead of "according to the fourth verse" only? When one reads the first eleven verses of the chapter, the reason is evident. The modern tongues experience does not tally with the record in the second chapter of Acts.

The only fair and honest way to study the Bible is to approach it with an open-minded attitude, desiring to learn rather than to search for something to support an already existing theory one might have. Also, we should not take one individual verse and try to establish a doctrine by that alone because doing so will lead to confusion and error. We must read all the preceding and succeeding verses relating to the text. These constitute the context.

Neither is the text with its context sufficient alone to establish a doctrine when there are other scriptures in the Bible pertaining to the subject. To be thoroughly honest and absolutely sure that a doctrine is definitely taught in the Bible, one should read everything in the Bible on the subject, and then teach accordingly. All true Bible scholars will admit that this is the only safe way to interpret the Bible. No doctrine should be accepted unless it is in harmony with the whole Word of God. This, the modern tongues people do not do. They stick to Acts 2:4 and utterly ignore other teachings of the Bible on the subject.

When the Book of Acts was written, as well as the rest of the Bible, it was not written in the chapters and verses with which we are acquainted, but was one continuous narrative, without the modern divisions as we know them. The dividing of the Bible into chapters and verses was done several hundred years later for more convenient Bible study. This division into verses has proved very convenient to certain religious teachers in these modern times, who take portions of Scripture out of their setting in order to substantiate their teachings. The Apostle Peter said in one of his epistles that there are some who are unlearned and unstable, who wrest the Scriptures to their own destruction (II Pet. 3:15-16).

It is surprising how people will allow the wool to be pulled over their eyes, so to speak, and fail to read the other verses of Acts 2. Upon the instructor's suggestion, they will look at Acts 2:4, and fail to see the verses before and after.

Please consider Acts 2:2 for a while: "And suddenly there came a sound from heaven as of a rushing mighty wind, and it filled all the house where they were sitting." Notice that there was a sound "of a rushing mighty wind." Do the modern tongues people have this manifestation with their tongues? If their experience is truly according to Acts 2:4, then this manifestation of a rushing mighty wind will also accompany the tongues, for that is the way it happened then. Why not insist on the wind manifestation and not the tongues? If Acts 2:4 proves that a person will speak in tongues when he is baptized with the Holy Spirit, then it also proves that a sound will always be heard as of a rushing mighty wind. On that day they *heard* the Holy Spirit come into the room.

This verse also says, "They were sitting." This point may seem trivial, and yet it is too valuable to overlook for it at least throws a little light upon the scene of this assembly. There is no doubt but what these disciples spent time praying during the ten days they were waiting for the Holy Spirit; however, it is very doubtful if the tarry room on that day had any resemblance to many tarry rooms of today.

Please consider Acts 2:3, "There appeared unto them cloven tongues like as of fire, and it sat upon each of them." If people insist upon speaking in tongues as the manifestation of the baptism of the Holy Spirit according to Acts2:4, they must also insist on the appearance of small flames of fire upon their heads, according to Acts 2:3. Those two verses cannot be separated as two different experiences, for they were not two occasions but one.

Please consider Acts 2:4 itself. Those who spoke in tongues, as mentioned in Acts 2:4, did not speak in a mere babble which no one understood, but they spoke intelligent and understandable languages which were understood by people of sixteen nations present: "They were all filled with the Holy Ghost, and began to speak with other tongues, as the Spirit gave them utterance.

And there were dwelling In Jerusalem Jews, devout men, out of every nation under heaven. Now when this was noised abroad, the multitude come together, and were confounded, because that every man heard them speak in his own language. And they were all amazed and marveled, saying one to another, Behold are not all these which speak Galileans? And how hear we every man in our own tongue, wherein we were born? Parthians, and Medes, and Elamites, and the dwellers In Mesopotamia, and in Judea, and Cappadocia, in Pontus, and Asia, Phrygia, and Pamphylia, in Egypt, and in the parts of Libya about Cyrene, and strangers of Rome, Jews and proselytes, Cretes and Arabians, we do hear them speak in our tongues [languages] the wonderful works of God" (Acts 2:4-11). The so-called speaking in tongues by modern tongues people does not compare with Acts 2:4, for seldom today does anyone else understand what is being said by them

The Day of Pentecost spoken of in Acts 2 was the beginning of the Holy Spirit dispensation. It was the initial outpouring of the Holy Spirit on the church. It was the opening day of the church age and the last dispensation of time. It was the opening day of the era to which the Old Testament prophecies pointed. It was the opening day of the dispensation that God had been preparing since before the foundation of the world

The great plan of all the ages was to build a spiritual church. Jesus Christ came into the world to build a church out of all the redeemed of all nations. He said. "Upon this rock I will build my church, and the gates of hell shall not prevail against it" (Matt. 16:18). No wonder that at this opening of the church dispensation there was such a demonstration of God's power.

Nowhere else in the Bible do we read of a day like the Day of Pentecost. We read of people receiving the Holy Spirit and of great revivals, but no occasion like that recorded in Acts 2. There was a day that was somewhat similar—the day God filled the tabernacle of Moses when it was being dedicated. The tabernacle was a type and shadow of Christ's spiritual church. At no other time did God ever demonstrate his presence in the tabernacle as he did on that occasion, and at no other time subsequent to Pentecost do we find such a demonstration of the Holy Spirit's power as on the opening day of the church.

Before Jesus left this world he told his disciples that when he went away he would send them another comforter who would abide with them always (John 14: 15-18; 16:7; 20:22). Just before he ascended to the Father he told his disciples to wait in Jerusalem. The record in Luke 24:49 says: "Behold, I send the promise of my Father upon you: but tarry ye in the city of Jerusalem, until ye be endued with power from on high." Acts 1:4-5 says: "And, being assembled together with them, [Jesus] commanded them that they should not depart from Jerusalem, but wait for the promise of the Father, which, saith he, ye have heard of me. For John truly baptized with water; but ye shall be baptized with the Holy Ghost not many days hence."

The word "tarry" in Luke 24:49 means the same as the word "wait" in Acts 1:4. There is nothing even hinted at in any of the promises or commands of Jesus that their tarrying in Jerusalem, or even their asking, was to bring the Holy Ghost upon them. It was part of the plan of God that these disciples should be filled with power so as to be able to witness to the fact of Christ's resurrection and saving power. Jesus said that after he was gone away he would send the Holy Spirit (John 16:7), and the one important thing for the disciples to do was "that they should not depart from Jerusalem" (Acts 1:4). Jerusalem was to be the place of the outpouring of the Holy Spirit just as Jerusalem was the place where Christ was to be crucified. If the disciples were to receive the "promise of the Father," they were to fulfill the one and only command of which we have record. and that was to wait in Jerusalem. The act of waiting itself was not the reason why the Holy Spirit came, for Jesus promised that He would come, *but the disciples were to be there at Jerusalem where the initial outpouring was to be given.*

It is implied by many people today that we have to beg and plead and even make loud noises and go through divers contortions in order to receive the Holy Spirit. This is contrary to the teaching of the Scriptures and is even contrary to the record of Acts 2:4. Jesus said that our heavenly Father is more willing to give the Holy Spirit to those who ask than earthly parents are to give good gifts to their children (Luke 11:13). The Scriptures also teach that God will give the Holy Spirit to those who obey him (Acts 5:32). As has already been said, tarrying does not help to persuade God. The disciples tarried to wait for the time the Holy Spirit was to be given.

Now the Holy Spirit is already present in the world and is ready to come into the heart of any believer who is ready to receive him. The reason people have to wait so long today for the Holy Spirit to come in is either because they have not invited him, or else they have not fully consecrated. The Holy Spirit will come into any believer's heart the moment that person is perfectly surrendered. There need be no more noise or outward manifestation that he has come in than the fact that we know our sins are forgiven. "When he is come" our lives will be victorious.

—Virgil L. Good

This tract can be purchased at the rate of 30 cents a hundred or $1.00 for 500, postpaid. From the Gospel Trumpet Company. Anderson, Indiana

Printed In U. S. A.   No. 350

Bible Teaching About Speaking With Tongues.
Gospel Trumpet

In the last great commission Jesus said concerning those who believe on him. "In my name . . . they shall speak with new tongues" (Mark 16:17).

The view taken by many is that speaking with tongues is the invariable witness of the baptism of the Spirit. They encourage people to seek and seek for this manifestation until many, after weeks and even months agonizing, have literally worn themselves out or become either mental or nervous wrecks.

What saith the Scriptures on this subject?

1. There is a genuine speaking with tongues taught in the New Testament.

2. The promise was fulfilled in some in apostolic days. On the day of Pentecost, when the Spirit was first poured out, the disciples "began to speak with other tongues, as the Spirit gave them utterance" (Acts 2:4). When the Spirit fell on the household of Cornelius, they were heard to "speak with tongues, and magnify God" (Acts 10:44-46). And when Paul laid his hands on the twelve disciples at Ephesus, "the Holy Ghost came on them; and they spake with tongues, and prophesied" (Acts 19:6, 7). There were also tongues manifestations in the church at Corinth (1 Corinthians 14).

3. Paul clearly identifies speaking with tongues with the gift of tongues; so that there is no difference between them. Compare 1 Cor. 12:20 with verse 10 and

its context. In this chapter, the argument of the apostle is that the Holy Spirit bestows various gifts on the members of the church, distributing them as he sees fit. These gifts may or may not accompany the operation of the Spirit in a particular individual. Since all these gifts are "by the same Spirit," no one of them is to be exalted over the others as the evidence of the Holy Spirit's presence and operation.

4. There is no evidence that in apostolic times all who received the Spirit baptism spoke with tongues. There is direct evidence of three instances only, and these no more prove the universality of this manifestation than the fact that prophecy was in two instances manifested with the baptism of the spirit proves that that gift should invariably accompany the Spirit's reception.

5. When tongues were spoken by the Spirit in the presence of those who were able to understand the languages uttered, as on Pentecost, they became a powerful "sign" to unbelievers.

6. When tongues were employed in the public congregation where no one understood them, unbelievers, far from being convinced thereby, were inclined to say that the speakers were mad (1 Cor. 14:23).

7. Paul restricted the exercise of tongues in the public congregation to "two or three" persons, and then one at a time—provided there was some one present to interpret (1 Cor. 14:27).

8. "But if there be no interpreter, let him keep silence in the church" (1 Cor. 14:23).

9. Paul teaches that there is a private use for the gift of tongues wherein one "that speaketh in an un-

known tongue speaketh not unto men, but unto God" (1 Cor. 14:3); and that such an individual, thus exercising, "edifieth himself" (1 Cor. 14:4).

10. Paul further teaches that it is better for the person exercising the gift of tongues to possess also the gift of interpretation, so that what he says or does may be with the understanding also (1 Cor. 14:13-15).

11. This gift is only one of the gifts of the Spirit, and is far from being the most important one. Prophecy is of greater importance (1 Cor. 14:1, 5, 19); it is something we are exhorted to "covet," while tongues are simply not to be forbidden (1 Cor. 14:39).

(For additional literature on this subject. see "The Gift of Tongues: What It is, and What It Is Not," by Gospel Trumpet Company. Anderson, Ind.)

The Doctrine of the Holy Spirit.
Gospel Trumpet

The primary passage of Scripture for this study is found in John's Gospel, chapter 16, verses 7-14, which reads:

> "Nevertheless I tell you the truth; It is expedient for you that I go away, for if I go not away, the Comforter will not come unto you; but if I depart, I will send him unto you.
>
> And when he is come, he will reprove the world of sin, and of righteousness, and of judgment:
>
> Of sin, because they believe not on me;
>
> Of righteousness, because I go to my Father;
>
> Of judgment, because the prince of this world is judged;
>
> I have many things to say unto you, but you cannot bear them now. Howbeit when he, the Spirit of truth, is come, he will guide you into all truth: for he shall not speak of himself; but what soever he shall hear, that shall he speak: and he will shew you things to come. He shall glorify me: for he shall receive of mine, and will shew it unto you. All things that the Father hath are mine: therefore said

I, that he shall take of mine and shall
shew it unto you." (KJV)

For a better understanding of this declaration by
Christ, let us review briefly chapters 13 through 17 of
John's Gospel. Here we have the longest recorded dia-
logical discourse of Christ with his first disciples. The
scene has its setting in a large upper room in Jerusalem,
a place personally selected by Christ for the occasion. A
careful reading of the account reveals that Christ is
quite aware of what He is saying and doing even though
his disciples do not fully understand. In chapter 13, the
mood is set for what is to follow; the dual theme of self-
giving service and brotherly love are augmented by the
simple act of our Lord washing his disciples feet and
announcing a new commandment of love.

Faith and prayer are exalted in chapter 14 as God's
answer to troubled hearts. Christ promises here: "What-
soever ye shall ask in my name, that will I do." (vs. 13)
This unlimited promise is followed with the affirmation:

> "And I will pray the Father, and He will
> give you another Comforter, that he may
> abide with you forever; even the Spirit
> of truth; whom the world cannot receive,
> because it seeth him not, neither
> knoweth him: but ye know him; for He
> dwelleth with you, and shall be in you. I
> will not leave you Comfortless: I will
> come unto you." (John 14:16-18)

Do we grasp the import of these words? Our Lord
has complete knowledge that the dark shadows of Calvary are falling quickly upon his life, nevertheless, he
devotes his thought to his disciples and the bringing of

hope into their hearts. Rather than spend his time evoking sympathy from them for what is soon to happen to him, he bolsters them for the venture ahead. After exalting again the principle of love as the distinguishing characteristic of discipleship, Christ speaks further of the Holy Spirit in these words:

> "But the Comforter, which is the Holy Ghost, whom the Father will send in my name, he shall teach you all things, and bring all things to your remembrance, whatsoever I have said unto you." (John 14:26)

Note particularly the identification which Christ gives to the Comforter: ". . . the Comforter, which is the Holy Ghost." In his preceding statements he had identified the Comforter, as "the Spirit of Truth." It would appear that our Lord wants his disciples to clearly understand that the Holy Spirit and the Spirit of Truth are one and the same.

The intimacy and vitality of Christ's relationship with his disciples are described in chapter 15. Here he speaks of the vine and the branches, and of the fruit of those who abide in him. He talks about their being chosen and ordained to bring forth fruit. He describes the persecution and hatred which his disciples will encounter, even from those who think they are doing God's service. Once again he comes to the theme of the Comforter, and attests:

> "But when the Comforter is come, whom I will send unto you from the Father, even the Spirit of Truth, which proceedeth from the Father, he shall testify of me: and ye shall also bear witness,

because ye have been with me from the beginning." (John 15:26-27)

In chapter 16 Christ describes the work of the Holy Spirit in more detail. He talks of the expediency of his departure from them, and outlines for them the manner in which the Holy Spirit will initiate and carry forward his work in the world. As he draws his discourse to a close, he tenderly announces to his disciples:

> "I have yet many things to say unto you, but you cannot bear them now." (John 16:12)

His disciples are momentarily perturbed by his words:

> "A little while, and ye shall not see me: and again, a little while, and ye shall see me, because I go to the Father." (John 16:16)

Perceiving their lack of understanding, Christ uses an illustration to make the meaning clear:

> "A woman when she is in travail hath sorrow, because her hour is come: but as soon as she is delivered of the child, she remembereth no more the anguish for the joy that a man is born into the world. And ye now therefore hath sorrow: but I will see you again, and your heart shall rejoice, and your joy no man taketh from you." (John 16:21-22)

This illustration is followed with a promise:

"The time cometh when I shall no more speak out in proverbs, but I will shew you plainly of the Father."

To these words, his disciples respond:

"Lo, now speakest thou plainly, . . . now we are sure that thou knowest all things. . . . and we believe that thou camest forth from God."

Jesus replies:

"Do ye now believe? . . . In the world ye shall have tribulation: but be of good cheer; I have overcome the world." (John 16:33)

The discourse now ended, Christ prays for his disciples and for those who shall become disciples, earnestly petitioning the Father:

"That they may all be one; as thou, Father, art in me, and I in thee, that they also may be one in us: that the world may believe that thou hast sent me." (John 17:21)

And here we are some 1945 years later trying to fulfill our Lord's commission and help answer his prayer. In doing so, our hearts yearningly cry out for the coming of the Holy Spirit upon our lives to make our witness more effective and fruitful. If it was expedient for our Lord's first disciples, men who had lived three years in his daily presence, to receive the Holy Spirit for carrying forward his work in the world, how much more essential that we open our hearts toward God for the reception of his Spirit into our lives?

Against the background of what our Lord has taught and promised about the sending of his Holy Spirit, let us consider some of the significant ways in which the Holy Spirit, our hope, comes to us.

THE HOLY SPIRIT COMES TO US AS THE COVENANT PROMISE OF GOD

When Jesus Christ announced to his disciples: "I will pray the Father, and he will send you another Comforter," he did so with full knowledge that this was something which the Father had long ago promised to do in the effecting of his new covenant in the hearts of men. Jeremiah the prophet had foretold:

> "Behold, the days come, saith the Lord, that I will make a new covenant with the house of Israel, and with the house of Judah." (Jer. 31:31)

Ezekiel had declared:

> "A new heart also I will give you, and a new spirit will I put with you." (Ezekiel 36:26)

The prophet Joel had proclaimed:

> "And it shall come to pass afterward, that I will pour out my spirit upon all flesh; and your sons and daughters shall prophesy, your old men shall dream dreams, your young men shall see visions: and also upon the servants and upon the handmaids in those days will I pour out my spirit." (Joel 2:28-29)

The expediency of Christ's departure from his disciples is better understood in the context that a new covenant between God and man was being inaugurated. In the upper room with his disciples, Christ took the cup and blessed it with these words:

> "For this is my blood of the new testament, which is shed for many for the remission of sins." (Matt. 26:28)

He knew then, as was later declared by the writer of Hebrews:

> "For where a testament is, there must also of necessity be the death of the testator. For a testament is of force after men are dead: otherwise it is of no strength at all while the testator liveth." (Hebrews 9:16-17)

Jesus Christ, the testator of God's new covenant, willingly accepts death in order that the covenant might be put into effect and the inheritance which is his with the Father might be shared with those who believe on him. Just as a will is of no effect until the death of the testator, an executor has no function until the death of the testator. Jesus Christ has named his own executor, the Holy Spirit, and he spells the provisions of his last will and testament which he knows the Holy Spirit will administer.

After his resurrection from the dead, Jesus Christ spoke frequently with his disciples about "the promise of the Father." He promised to send to them "the promise of the Father" and he enjoined them to "wait for the promise of the Father." The Apostle Peter, in his great and effective sermon on the day of Pentecost, proclaimed:

> "Repent, and be baptized every one of
> you in the name of Jesus Christ for the
> remission of sins, and ye shall receive
> the gift of the Holy Ghost. For the prom-
> ise is unto you, and to your children, and
> to all that are afar off, even as many as
> the Lord our God shall call." (Acts 2:38-
> 39)

God's covenant promise is made effective through the atoning death of Jesus Christ and by the work of the Holy Spirit as the executor of his will. If we are to ben-efit from the provisions of God's will and enjoy the in-heritance among those who are sanctified we must claim our hope through the gift of God's Holy Spirit. God has remembered us in his will and shares his glori-ous estate with us through the death of His son and the executive administration of the Holy Spirit. What God has so graciously and abundantly willed to us through his son is our[s] — if we will appropriate it in faith. The promise is unto us let's claim it!

THE HOLY SPIRIT COMES TO US AS THE CONVICTING PRESENCE OF GOD

Concurrent with his announced departure from the world, Jesus Christ assures his disciples: ". . . if I go not away, the Comforter will not come unto you; but if I depart, I will send him unto you." The work of the Holy Spirit, when he is come, is to be directed toward the world and the fulfillment of Christ's mission in the world. Christ here both personalizes and universalizes the work of the Holy Spirit. "I will send him unto you" is a personal promise repeated here for double emphasis. Earlier Christ had assured his disciples: ". . . ye know him; for he dwelleth with you and shall be in you." But this personal indwelling of the Holy Spirit is for the purpose that the world will more pungently be "reproved of sin, and of righteousness, and of judgment." God's Holy Spirit is not limited to do his work only through persons, but his work is enhanced when he is permitted to work in and through the lives of redeemed and spirit-filled men and women.

The Holy Spirit speaks to man in his actual condition. He reproves the world of sin. Christ identifies the reason for this reproof: "Because they believe not on me." Some believe not on Christ for they have never been told the blessed story of his coming, his death in their behalf, his resurrection and ascension, and his continuing mediation at the right hand of God. These must be told, and it is the mission of the church to tell this story to the world. Others have been confronted with Christ and the demands of his Gospel but have refused to believe on him as Savior and Lord, hence they remain in their sins. Some do not believe Christ because they consider his claims too preposterous, the demands of his Gospel too exacting, and his ability to help too limited. Others are always deciding about Christ but never quite able to decide for Christ. The crucial issue in the Holy Spirit's reproof of sin is Jesus Christ; it is by the holiness of his life and the accomplishments of his death that the sinfulness of sin is revealed.

The Holy Spirit speaks to man of his possibilities through the grace of God. He reproves the world of righteousness. Over against the dark picture of man's actual condition the Holy Spirit flashes a description of what life can be like when it is made free from sin and lived to the glory of God. Jesus Christ becomes real and abiding in the heart of the person who really believes on him. Those who believe on Christ become possessed with a new mind and spirit; this new mind and spirit restrains the thoughts and inclinations from sin and sublimates them toward righteousness by making those who believe on Jesus Christ righteous and holy. If we as Christians want the world to know what Christ is like, then, we must let the world see what he has made us like.

The Holy Spirit speaks to man of his future destiny. He reproves the world of judgment. By the manner of his life, the truth of his words, the accomplishments of his death, the power of his resurrection, and the assurance of his return, Jesus Christ passes judgment on "the prince of this world." The Holy Spirit is now carrying forward in the hearts of men a work of judgment of which the judgment on the last day will only be an outward manifestation. Now the Holy Spirit works through reproof for redemptive purposes; in the judgment of the last day retribution will be complete and final. The Holy Spirit reminds us constantly that "We shall all stand before the judgment seat of Christ," but gives to those who believe on Christ the blessed hope of judgment without fear based on the redemption which is theirs through the blood of Christ and the witness of his spirit.

What a lesson there is here for the Christian! The same spirit which Christ sends into the hearts of his followers is the same spirit which brings reproof to the world of sin, or righteousness, and of judgment. The Holy Spirit does not carry forth its reproof apart from, but in cooperation with the witness of Christ's disciples. This is why the discipling of all nations is so vitally important. The world will not find its way out of sin unless it can behold the example of sinless lives. The world will never know the meaning of righteousness unless righteous men demonstrate that such a quality of life is attainable through faith in Jesus Christ. The world will never know the certainty of standing before God in judgment unless holy men of God proclaim this Gospel message to the world. Our hope, and the hope of the world, is found in the Holy Spirit who now carries forward his work in the world as the convicting presence of God.

THE HOLY SPIRIT COMES TO US
THE CERTIFYING POWER OF GOD

Jesus Christ, according to the record, did not use the word "power" in his upper room discourse on the eve of his trial and crucifixion. After his resurrection and before his ascension, he uses the word frequently. He announces to his disciples that the Father has given unto him "all power . . . in heaven and in earth." (Matt. 28:16) He enjoins his disciples to ". . . tarry . . . in the city of Jerusalem, until ye be endued with power from on high." (Luke 24:49) He affirms to them at the time of his ascension:

> But ye shall receive power, after that the
> Holy Ghost is come upon you: and ye
> shall be witnesses unto me both in Jeru-
> salem, and in all Judea, and in Samaria,
> and unto the uttermost parts of the
> earth." (Acts 1:8)

These scriptures express clearly that Christ wants his followers to receive the Holy Spirit.

There is nothing transitory or indefinite about the coming of the Holy Spirit. The promise of Christ is that he will send "another Comforter" who will "abide with you forever." Through the power of the Holy Spirit the disciples of Christ are to give their witness "both in Jerusalem, and in all Judea, and in Samaria, and unto the uttermost part of the earth." The key word here is "both" denoting that the witness must be given simultaneously and subsequently, locally and universally. In the reception of the Holy Spirit there is always a point of beginning; after this initial experience the Holy Spirit will draw the circumference of our live where he wills.

God does not give power merely to amuse or amaze. The power he gives is nothing less than the ability to achieve whatever he commands. It is the power to stand in the face of opposition, if need be, and give a bold and courageous witness for Jesus Christ. It is the power by which man is able to live free from sin and enjoy the "glorious liberty of the children of God." It is the power by which a man wins the battle against inordinate selfishness, inbred sin, racial segregation, and religious sectarianism. There is nothing narrow or bigoted about the work of the Holy Spirit, but there is the "perfecting of holiness (wholeness) in the fear of God." The glorious message revealed to us by Christ and corroborated to us by the Holy Spirit is that *God is not against us for our sins but he is with us against our sins.*

It is the Holy Spirit who bears witness in our hearts that we are children of God and who certifies our adoption into the family of God.

Two words are used by the Apostle Paul to illustrate the work of the Holy Spirit as the certifying power of God. He wants us to understand that the Holy Spirit is the corporate gift of God the Father and Christ the Son to the church. In II Corinthians, chapter 1, verses 21-22, we read:

> "Now he which establisheth us with you
> in Christ, and hath anointed us, is God;
> who hath also sealed us, and given the
> earnest of the Spirit in our hearts."

When a corporate seal is attached to a legal document it certifies its authenticity and its authority; it becomes a pledge that the resources of the corporation are committed to the fulfillment of the contractual covenant. The word "earnest" denotes something of value given by a buyer to a seller to bind a bargain; it is a token or pledge of what is to come. By use of these words, the Apostle Paul affirms that the Holy Spirit is given as God's "guarantee" that he will complete the work which he has begun and bring the sons of God through to certain victory. The Holy Spirit is God's corporate seal upon the heart of a person who makes an absolute and unconditional surrender to the will of God and to the terms of his covenant.

By the power of the Holy Spirit committed followers of Jesus Christ have access to unlimited resources as they fulfill their high calling in God. No greater credentials can be required of any man than that he be "filled with the Holy Ghost and with faith." Given this kind of certification, there is hope for mankind; without it, there is nothing but futility and despair.

THE HOLY SPIRIT COMES TO US AS THE CONSTRAINING PASSION OF GOD

Love is the dominant theme in Jesus Christ's upper room discourse. He introduces the theme in these words:

> "A new commandment I give unto you, that ye love one another; as I have loved you, that ye also love one another. By this shall all men know that ye are my disciples, if ye have love one to another." (John 13:34-35)

He develops the theme further   by saying

> ". . . If a man love me, he will keep my words: and my Father will love him, and we will come unto him, and make our abode with him." (John 14:23)

It is obvious that Jesus Christ is predicating the whole outcome of his mission in the world on the response of love.

The Christian's love for Christ controls his actions. J. B. Phillips translates II Corinthians, chapter 5, verse 14, in this manner: "The very springs of our actions is our love for Christ." Paul tells us further that "Hope maketh not ashamed, because the love of God is shed abroad in our hearts by the Holy Spirit which is given unto us. (Romans 5:8) The person whose life is filled with the Holy Spirit does not lose his capacity to commit sin; he does become possessed with a new and constraining impulse that keeps him from committing sin he loves Christ too much to sin against him. Through the constraining passion of God, released in the heart of man by the Holy Spirit, all of man's propensities and talents become transformed and sublimated.

Man no longer lives for the satisfaction of selfish ambition but for the glory of God. He finds the indwelling constraint of the Holy Spirit the safety gauge of his conduct, and the spirit level of his life.

The presence of the Spirit of Christ in a man's life is the sole determinant of whether or not he is a Christian. How, then, does a man behave whose life is indwelt and constrained by the Spirit of God? In his description of the work of the Holy Spirit, Christ reminds us that when he is come:

> ". . . he shall teach you all things, and bring all things to your remembrance, whatsoever I have said to you." (John 14:26)

> ". . . he will testify of me: and ye shall bear witness." (John 15:26-27)

> ". . . He shall not speak of himself . . . He shall glorify me: for he shall receive of mine, and will show it unto you." (John 16:13-14)

> ". . . he will guide you into all truth." (John 16:13)

Loyalty to truth is a primary requisite for Christian discipleship. The person whose life is to be filled with the Spirit of truth must be committed to walk in the light of truth which is revealed by a diligent study of God's word and the insights given by the Holy Spirit. Revelation and response, reason and faith, belong together in the life of the Christian.

The Spirit of Christ is the spirit of passionate purity. Purity is not passé for the Christian; it is the basic motivation of his life. St. John declares:

> "And every man that hath this hope in
> him purifieth himself, even as he is
> pure." (John 3:3)

The Apostle Peter describes this as "a lively hope" and uses it as a basis for his exhortation: ". . . as he which hath called you is holy, so be ye holy in all manner of conversation." (I Peter 1:15) Someone has observed that "when truth becomes holy, men become martyrs." This word "Martyr" is one we Christians must reckon with. It comes from the same root word from which we derive the word "witness." To be a Christian witness, in the truest sense of the word, means that we must be willing to lay our lives on the line for the passionate purity of Jesus Christ lest one's words gainsay his deeds.

The Spirit of Jesus Christ is the spirit of sublimated service. When a man becomes a Christian and his life indwelt by the spirit of Christ, he does not cease being a servant — he serves a different master. No longer is he a servant of self and sin, he is a servant of righteousness and has his fruit "unto holiness, and the end everlasting life." (Romans 6:22) His purpose, like that of the Holy Spirit is to glorify Christ and take the things which are Christ's and make them known unto others. His will is to do God's will without stopping to count the consequences.

Such a hope as this, provided by the Holy Spirit, who shares God's love with us, is not mockery. It will never disappoint us. It is the constraining passion of

God in our hearts, which sublimates all our desires and directs out actions.

THE HOLY SPIRIT COMES TO US AS THE COMPLETING PERSONALITY OF GOD

There is something lacking, tragically lacking, in the life of the person who professes to be Christian but whose life is devoid of the Holy Spirit. Human life is depraved to whatever extent it is deprived of the Holy Spirit. The goal toward which God is directing each of his children is that of completeness in Jesus Christ. St. Paul reminds us: "For in him (Christ) dwelleth all the fulness of the Godhead bodily. And ye are complete in him, which is the head of all principality and power." (Colossians 2:9-10) God wills that we "be conformed to the image of his son." (Romans 8:29) He would have each of us to "put off . . . the old man, which is corrupt according to deceitful lusts; and be renewed in the spirit of your mind; and that ye put on the new man, which after God is created in righteousness and true holiness." (Ephesians 4:22-24)

If our personalities are to be transformed and made complete through the Spirit and grace of God, then, there are some things we must put off and some things we must put on. As Christians, we are to put off lying and speak the truth in love. We are to give no place to the devil, but give full occupancy to God. We are to cease stealing and begin laboring with our hands that which is good. We are to put away corrupt communication and speak that which is edifying and graceful. We are to put away all bitterness, wrath, anger, clamor, evil speaking, and malice, and become kind one to another, tender-hearted, forgiving, even as God for Christ's sake has forgiven us. (Ephesians 4) What a standard of conduct! Left on our own we can never attain it, but through the gift of God's Spirit we can appropriate it. This we must do if we are to experience the fulness of God in our lives.

Jesus Christ, in his high priestly prayer, gives to us the clue when he petitions the Father: "Sanctify them through thy truth; thy word is truth." (John 17:17) He prays further: "And the glory which thou gavest me I have given them; that they may be one, even as we are one: I in them, and thou in me, that they may be made perfect in one; and that the world may know that thou hast sent me, and hast loved them, as thou has loved me." (John 17:22-23)

Christ's words, "I in them, and thou in me," call use to a new height of moral relationship with God and with man. He calls us to sanctification and glorification. It is a plus experience for the Christian who identifies his life with that of Christ. "Christ in you, the hope of glory." This experience has a beginning and is capable of infinite increase, here and hereafter.

The Holy Spirit, our hope, comes to us as the covenant promise of God; let us claim our inheritance!

The Holy Spirit, our hope, comes to us as the convicting presence of God; let us accept his reproof!

The Holy Spirit, our hope, comes to us as the certifying power of God; let us appropriate his resources!

The Holy Spirit, our hope, comes to us as the constraining passion of God; let us follow his impulses!

The Holy Spirit, our hope, comes to us as the completing personality of God; let him make us like Christ.

Tongues Explained.
Selected

You may not believe the dragon has been loosed, but he has been loosed! The first thing he did was kill the realms of Protestantism; they are deader than mackerels. After he got them dead and cold, he threw in the fires of false Pentecostalism with all this flesh and false power; and millions are being deceived because of the stir there. Someone says, "If you could only feel it, you would know that there is a spirit and power there." I know there's feeling there, and spirits, and power, but it's not the Holy Spirit because the Holy Spirit doesn't lead contrary to His Word. What are the minds of men thinking? They want to make room for everything. It makes no difference what the teaching is, just move over a little and make room for it. This is the ecumenical spirit that is taking our nation. May God help the church to arise and tell people what the truth is.

It is the serious fault of many to read their Bibles through their experiences instead of evaluating their experiences through their Bibles. "Beloved, believe not every spirit, but try the spirits whether they are of God: because many false prophets are gone out into the world" (1 John 4:1). In every religious body—it makes no difference what their teaching is—there is a spirit that animates that body and keeps it going. Too many people think if you get a thrill, if something warms your heart and makes tears run down your cheek or goose pimples up your back, it's God. No, we can't tell whether or not it's God by goose bumps. Get back to where we really try the spirits. "Search the scriptures" (John 5:39).

"For there shall arise false Christs, and false prophets, and shall shew great signs and wonders; insomuch that, if it were possible, they shall deceive the very elect." (Matthew 24:24). I don't know of anything that's more deceiving than this false tonguesism. It gets people to thinking they have the Holy Ghost because they rattle off some kind of jibberjabber, all the while smoking cigarettes, drinking beer, and committing adultery. ". . . because they received not the love of the truth . . . God shall send them strong delusion, that they should believe a lie." (2 Thessalonians 2:11). How do we get a strong delusion? My friend, just go along with a great profession of the power of God when you are not living right. "Now the Spirit speaketh expressly, that in latter times some shall depart from the faith, giving heed to seducing spirits, and doctrines of devils" (1 Tim. 4:1). I am not branding everybody in it the same. There are some good people there, but just the fact that there are some good, is no proof that the teaching is right.

You can take a scripture out of the setting and state anything you want. But leave it in the context, and it will say only one thing. Let's get some understanding of Acts 2:38. "Then Peter said unto them, Repent, and be baptized every one of you in the name of Jesus Christ for the remission of sins, and ye shall receive the gift of the Holy Ghost." First of all, we need to understand the difference between the gift of the Spirit and the Spirit's gifts. The gift that God promised is the indwelling of the Holy Ghost—not some certain manifestation of Him, but He Himself. Jesus didn't talk about the Holy Ghost in terms of IT; but as HE. "If ye love me, keep my commandments. And I will pray the Father, and He shall give you another Comforter, that He may abide with you forever; Even the Spirit of truth? whom the world cannot receive, because it seeth Him not, neither knoweth Him: but ye know Him, for He dwelleth with you, and shall be in you" (John 14:15-17). "And, behold, I send the promise of my Father upon you: but tarry ye in the city of Jerusalem, until ye be endued with power from on high" (Luke 24:49). I want to say that the only tarrying they had to do was in Jerusalem until the day of Pentecost came. Then nowhere in the Bible can anything be found where anyone had to tarry and wait for the Holy Ghost if they met the conditions. Since then, people receive the Holy Ghost instantaneously if they are saved. This thing of having to tarry night after night around an altar and foaming like a hog is of the devil. Away with this devilish stuff. It throws people into a terrible shape, losing their minds, going insane trying to get religion, and all the time causing a blasphemous work to be done against the real cause of God. We certainly believe just exactly like the Bible says about speaking in tongues and being baptized with the Holy Ghost, but not this false stuff. Let's lift up a standard against it. This very message is going to judge us in the last day. Let me say again, the gift that God promised is the Holy Ghost. Then He's the giver of many gifts.

1 Corinthians 12:4 "Now there are diversities of gifts, but the same Spirit." Verse 7, "But the manifestation of the Spirit is given to every man to profit withal." What is the manifestation? It is the different ways the Spirit moves or speaks through you as an individual. The Holy Ghost never has you do one thing in a public service because it makes you feel good. Away with this

old devilish stuff of going in a frenzy and no one knows what is wrong with you! But you say, "I am feeling good." That isn't the Holy Ghost. Whenever the Holy Ghost has you move in a public service, it is for everyone's benefit in the service, "But the manifestation of the Spirit is given to every man to profit withal [everyone]," "For to one is given by the Spirit the word of wisdom; to another the word of knowledge by the same Spirit; to another faith by the same Spirit; to another the gifts of healing by the same Spirit; to another the working of miracles: to another prophecy; to another divers kinds of tongues; to another the interpretation of tongues; but all these worketh that [by] one and the self-same Spirit, dividing to every man severally as he will" (verses 8-11). "And God hath set some in the church, first apostles, secondarily prophets, thirdly teachers, after that miracles, then gifts of healings, helps, governments, diversities of tongues. Are all apostles? If they were, who would there be to preach to? Are all prophets? are all teachers? are all workers of miracles? Have all gifts of healing? Do all speak with tongues? Do all interpret?" (verses 28-30). The answer to every one of these is no, no, no, When you have the Holy Ghost, you have the gift of God, and then He passes out the gifts as it pleases Him. So when you receive the Holy Ghost, you don't know what you are going to get in the way of gifts. You shouldn't get down and say, "Now Lord, make me jibber-jabber so I will know when I get it, I will be here till I jibber."

Verse 19 "And if they were all one member, where were the body?" It takes many members to make up a body. He took a natural body to show the different gifts and the working of the Spirit. "If the foot shall say, because I am not of the hand, I am not of the body; is it therefore not of the body?" (verse 15). Even so, my friend, if we are going to have a thriving congregation of the church, we must have different gifts of the Spirit, and no member can say, "Because your gift isn't like mine, you are not of the body." That is why it is false to say, "If you don't have the gift of tongues, you are not of the body."

"And these signs (plural) shall follow them that believe; in my name shall they cast out devils; they shall speak with new tongues; they shall take up serpents; and if they drink any deadly thing, it shall not hurt them; they shall recover" (Mark 16:17, 18). Whenever you say, "Unless you speak in an unknown tongue, I am not going to believe you are a believer." I have every right to say, "Unless you handle a snake, I am not going to believe that you are a believer."

Furthermore, believers are ahead of the signs. In Mark 16:17, Christ said that these signs would follow them that believe. Also in 1 Corinthians 14:22, Paul said, "tongues are for a sign, not to them that believe, but to them that believe not." Why? Believers don't need any signs on what the Bible says. You are getting in bad shape whenever you let the devil work on you till you must have tokens to know that you are saved. Does the Scripture say that the just shall live by signs? No, the just shall live by faith! This work that I am denouncing is nothing more than a work of Satan that has turned people from faith to the flesh. Signs are for unbelievers, but even after unbelievers see signs, they are not going to be saved just because they saw signs. They must come to the place that they believe the Word of God if they are ever to be saved.

There are three instances in the Bible when people were baptized with the Holy Ghost and spoke in tongues, or the Greek says languages. Acts 2 (on the day of Pentecost), Acts 10 (at Cornelius' house), and Acts 10 (the Samaritans down at Ephesus). In every instance where the gift of tongues was given they spoke in an understandable language of the day. They needed no interpreter. That is what the gift is for. When God couldn't find any man to talk to Balaam and He wanted to straighten him out, He talked through a mule and the mule spoke in the Hebrew tongue. "And the Lord opened the mouth of the ass, and she said unto Balaam, What have I done unto thee, that thou hast smitten me these three times?" (Numbers 22:28). He didn't have to get another mule to interpret it. Now if that dumb mule can do it right, we ought to.

There are many instances in the Bible where individuals were filled with the Holy Ghost and didn't speak in tongues. The reason is that there was no need for it. I won't need to go back into the Old Testament but we know that the prophets possessed the Holy Ghost, and did not speak in tongues. Now let us look at some of the instances in the New Testament: Zacharias, who was John the Baptist's father, was filled with the Holy Ghost—Luke 1:67. John the Baptist was filled with the Holy Ghost from his mother's womb—Luke 1:15. Also, Elisabeth, John the Baptist's mother, was filled with the Holy Ghost—Luke 1:41. Another example is Mary, the mother of Jesus—Luke 1:35. Jesus Christ Himself was filled with the Holy Ghost—Luke 4:1. My friend, Jesus never spoke in tongues. Why did He never speak in tongues? He came to His own. He spoke the language of His own people. My! How these preachers blaspheme—saying no one is ever filled with the Holy Ghost unless he speaks in tongues!

In Acts 6:3-8, we read of people filled with the Holy Ghost, and they didn't speak in tongues. Acts 8:14-17 gives another instance. In Acts 9:17-18, Paul was filled with the Holy Ghost, and scales fell from his eyes. In Acts 4:31, a multitude was filled with the Holy Ghost and they didn't speak in tongues.

My friend, the Holy Ghost manifests Himself in speaking in tongues only where there is a need. I just want to make this clear: You can be filled with the Holy Ghost, but as long as you work with English-speaking people, you will never have the manifestation of the Spirit in speaking in another language.

Let us go to Acts 2:1-4, "And when the day of Pentecost was fully come, they were all with one accord in one place. And suddenly there came a sound from heaven as of a rushing mighty wind, and it filled all the house where they were sitting. [Now it wasn't a wind that blew and almost blew the windows out as preachers tell you. No, it was as of a mighty rushing wind—a noise, a power.] And there appeared unto them cloven tongues like as of fire, and it sat upon each of them." Those tongues like as of fire simply show the purifying work. Remember John the Baptist said in Matthew 3:11, "I indeed baptize you with water unto repentance: but he that cometh after me is mightier than I, whose shoes I am not worthy to bear. He shall baptize you with the Holy Ghost, and with fire." Let us read the Bible just as it is.

Acts 2:4, "And they were all filled with the Holy Ghost, and began to speak with other tongues as the Spirit gave them utterance." The first thing that we learn from that fourth verse is this. They were all filled with the Holy Ghost, but they didn't all speak in tongues. They only spoke as the Spirit gave them utterance. It doesn't say that they were all filled with the Holy Ghost and they all spoke in tongues. Also the very fact that they spoke in other tongues shows that they had been speaking in tongues before. They had been speaking in the Galilean language before that. When the Holy Ghost uttered through them, they spoke in another understandable language according to the need of the hearers. "Now when this was noised abroad, the multitude came together, and were confounded, because that every man heard them speak in his own language" (Acts 2:6).

Back in this period of time (AD 33) there was a different dialect every 20, 30, or 40 miles. There were eighteen different nationalities there that day, including the Galileans, that were in walking distance from Jerusalem.

Notice as we study the second chapter of Acts that they didn't ask or expect tongues on Pentecost. The Spirit merely allowed them to express their gratitude for God in another language so the other people could understand and hear them magnify the Lord. The same is true in the other two instances in the Scriptures where they spoke in tongues.

We need to realize that the Bible teaches basically three languages. First, there is the language of the soul. "Likewise the Spirit also helpeth our infirmities: for we know not what we should pray for as we ought: but the Spirit itself maketh intersession for us with groanings which cannot be uttered" (Romans 8:26-27). Someone said, "That is it; that is the unknown tongue." No, no, no. Acts 2:4 said that they spoke as the Spirit gave them utterance. They spoke in languages. Here is a picture of an individual praying, and he doesn't know what the will of God is. Since he doesn't know the will of God, the Spirit of God will help him. Have you ever been under a burden like that; where all you could do is just groan?

The next language is our native language. This is the one that we were born with or learned through education. Paul said in 1 Corinthians 14:18, "I thank my God, I speak with tongues more than ye all:" Did you ever study the life of Paul? He spoke many different languages which he learned through education.

The third language that the Bible talks about is a language that is given by the supernatural working of God's Holy Spirit. Now this gift, or this speaking in what you might call an unknown tongue, is what caused the trouble at Corinth. Corinth was a commerce city with a great populous. Men and women flocked in there from everywhere with every kind of language imaginable. Then in church these people were wanting to pray and testify, but they spoke in a language that none of the congregation could understand. This is why Paul, in 1 Corinthians 14, talks about an unknown tongue not unknown to the one that is speaking, but unknown to the audience.

1 Corinthians 14:1, "Follow after charity, and desire spiritual gifts, but rather that ye may prophesy." Every gift that the Spirit gives is for one purpose—the forwarding of the Gospel. Too many people understand prophesying to mean only the foretelling of some future event. Webster says that prophesying is preaching the Gospel in an understandable language.

1 Corinthians 14:2-4, "For he that speaketh in an unknown tongue speaketh not unto men, but unto God: for no man understandeth him; howbeit in the spirit he speaketh mysteries. But he that prophesieth speaketh unto men to edification, and exhortation, and comfort. He that speaketh in an unknown tongue edifieth himself." [No one gets help but him]. Remember we learned in 1 Corinthians 12:7 that every manifestation of the Spirit is to profit withal (everyone). Every manifestation of the Spirit profits the whole church and edifies the whole body. So what is Paul talking about when he speaks of an "unknown" tongue here? For example, suppose I enter your congregation and begin to testify in the Italian language which you do not understand. Now God understands me. He understands all languages. So I am just speaking to God and not to men, and Paul said that he didn't want any just speaking to God in the congregation. The things I am saying are mysteries as far as you are concerned because you cannot understand my language. It is "unknown" to you.

Verse 5 Paul says, "I would that ye all spake with tongues [other languages] but rather that ye prophesied: for greater is he that prophesieth than he that speaketh with tongues, except he interpret, that the church may receive edifying." For example, I speak Russian and come into your English congregation. I can neither speak nor understand your language. But there is another person there who can speak both English and Russian. Paul is saying he shouldn't speak anything to me in the public service unless he interprets to the congregation what he is saying.

Now let us consider why they spoke in "other" tongues down at Cornelius' house when they were filled with the Holy Ghost. Acts chapter 10 says that

Cornelius' house was full of Italians. Acts 10:1 "there was a certain man in Caesarea called Cornelius, a centurion of the band called the Italian band." They spoke the Italian language. Peter was a Galilean, and he didn't believe that the Gentiles could receive the Holy Ghost. So God baptized them with the Holy Ghost right in front of his eyes, and then let them magnify the Lord in a language that Peter could understand. "For they [Peter and the men with him] heard them speak with tongues and magnify God" (Acts 10:46).

1 Corinthians 14:6-13, "Now, brethren if I come unto you speaking with tongues, what shall I profit you except I shall speak to you either by revelation, or by knowledge, or by prophesying, or by doctrine? And even things without life giving sound, whether pipe or harp, except they give a distinction in the sounds, how shall it be known what is piped or harped? For if the trumpet give an uncertain sound, who shall prepare himself to the battle? So likewise ye, except ye utter by the tongue words easy to be understood, how shall it be known what is spoken? For ye shall speak into the air. There are, it may be, so many kinds of voices in the world, and none of them is without signification. Therefore if I know not the meaning of the voice, I shall be unto him that speaketh a barbarian, and he that speaketh shall be a barbarian unto me. Even so ye, forasmuch as ye are zealous of spiritual gifts seek that ye may excel to the edifying of the church. Wherefore let him that speaketh in an unknown tongue [not unknown to himself, but unknown to the congregation], pray that he may interpret [speak in their language]."

Verse 14 "For if I pray in an unknown tongue, my spirit prayeth, but my understanding is unfruitful." My, how they twist this scripture! Away they go in tongues;

and they say, "My spirit is praying but my understanding is unfruitful; I don't know what I'm saying." That isn't what Paul said at all. Paul is saying that if I pray in the congregation in an unknown tongue which you people cannot understand, my understanding (I understand) is unfruitful. How does my understanding become fruitful? When you understand what I understand.

1 Corinthians 14:15 "What is it then? I will pray with the spirit, and I will pray with the understanding also: I will sing with the spirit, and I will sing with the understanding also." The next verse also shows that the understanding and fruitfulness he is talking about is in regard to the others listening. "Else when thou shalt bless with the spirit, how shall he that occupieth the room of the unlearned say Amen at thy giving of thanks, seeing he understandeth not what thou sayest? For thou verily givest thanks well, but the other is not edified" (verses 16, 17).

Verse 18 "I thank my God, I speak with tongues more than ye all." Remember that Paul learned many languages through education, and may have spoken others as a gift. There wasn't any man who needed to speak in tongues more than Paul. He traveled on one missionary journey right after another where there were different languages of every kind. Listen to him though. I want you to get this. "Yet in the church I had rather speak five words with my understanding, that by my voice I might teach others also, than ten thousand words in an unknown tongue" (verse 19). Putting five words up against ten thousand is a pretty good percentage.

Verse 20 "Brethren, be not children in understanding: howbeit in malice be ye children, but in understanding be men." That is just exactly what a lot of this is, just giving away to emotions and acting like a bunch of children. It is surprising how much of that has to be worked up. There isn't very much of it brought from home. There has to be some singing and clapping of the hands to get it going.

Corinth's mistake was stressing gifts above love to all, holiness of heart, and Christian living. This led to one mass of confusion. "Yet shew I unto you a more excellent way"—LOVE (1 Corinthians 12:31). He described something better than tongues. He showed them a more excellent way to keep the church in harmony as a working force. He put love at the top. Tongues were the least of the gifts. The first fruit of the Spirit is love. Gifts are only secondary. Love, heart purity, and holiness of life are held high above all manifestations of the Spirit of God.

Recently, a sister wanted to testify in one of our services. I asked her privately what she was going to testify about. She said, "Salvation." I asked, "Are you saved?" She answered, "I've got the Holy Ghost." I said, "How do you know that you have the Holy Ghost?" She replied, "Because I can talk in tongues." "Well", I said, "Have you been saved from sin?" She answered, "All but the cigarettes; I still smoke cigarettes." I replied, "Smoking cigarettes and filled with the Holy Ghost? That is not the Holy Ghost in you; that is another ghost. The Holy Ghost doesn't live in an unclean place." She had been duped. Her heart was heavy. This is the thing that grieves me. While she was seeking help, the wrong people got hold of her and got her tarrying until she got this jibberjabber, but there was no power in it to live a clean life. I began to teach her about the thing that Jesus came to do: first of all, to set her free from sin, to break the chains and the habits, and to give her victory. That is just one case. I could go on and on.

It hasn't been very long ago that a young man came to the altar. The minute he started praying I saw what kind of a spirit he was under because he went into that jerking that they go into. I went over and asked him what he needed. He replied that he wanted to get saved. Then I asked him on purpose if he was ever saved before. He reared back and said, "Saved! Man, I preached the Gospel, I spoke in tongues." I said, "But were you ever saved?" He said, "Well, I never did get victory over my cigarettes. I didn't smoke them publicly, but I still smoked them on the side." Still, he continued to speak in tongues. He told me how the spirit would wake him up in the middle of the night even while he was out in sin; he would lose control of himself and go through that terrible frenzy that they go through. Friend, that is the work of Satan. That is not of God. My! my! my!

1 Corinthians 14:21 "In the law it is written, With men of other tongues and other lips will I speak unto this people; and yet for all that will they not hear me, saith the Lord." This refers to Isaiah 28:11, "For with stammering lips and another tongue will he speak to this people." This again proves that when God speaks through other tongues, it is not some ecstasy—just speaking unto God. It was a language that was spoken to the people.

Verse 22 "Wherefore tongues are for a sign, not to them that believe, but to them that believe not: but prophesying serveth not for them that believe not, but for them which believe." You should be able to see that tongues, my friend, were never designed to benefit those that believe. Someone said, "You can talk all you want. I am not going to give up my tongues. There is too much of a blessing in it." I just read with you that tongues were never designed to be a benefit or blessing to the individual. Tongues were designed for you to speak in the language of some unlearned person and tell him about God.

Verse 26, "How is it then, brethren? when ye come together, every one of you hath a psalm, hath a doctrine, hath a tongue, hath a revelation, hath an interpretation. Let all things be done unto edifying. (Not edifying yourself, but edifying the Church.) And if any man speak in an unknown tongue [a tongue unknown to the audience], let it be by two, or at the most three [sentences according to the Greek] and that by course; and let one interpret" (verse 27). That is exactly the way that you work with an interpreter. You speak and he interprets two or three sentences at a time. Verse 28, "But if there be no interpreter, let him keep silence in the church; and let him speak to himself, and to God." Now, if God would give him the gift of tongues he would speak in the language of the people. No interpreter would be needed.

1 Corinthians 14:29-32, "Let the prophets speak two or three, and let the other judge. If any thing be revealed to another that sitteth by, let the first hold his peace. For ye may all prophesy one by one, that all may learn, and all may be comforted. And the spirits of the prophets are subject to the prophets." This shows that whenever a spirit gets hold of you that you can't control, it is of the devil. Someone asks, "Don't you think that the Spirit of God would take hold of you in such a way that you would lose all control of yourself"? No sir! God never does take away your free moral agency until we come to final judgment. Nowhere in the Bible,

where anyone received the Holy Ghost, did they fall on the floor or ground, powerless. Read the 9th Chapter of Mark. It will tell you about someone that did fall on the ground, foamed at the mouth, and made noises like a hog. He was possessed with devils, and Jesus cast them out. Then he stood upright, and walked like a man. I am not saying that everyone that gets in that frenzy are all devil possessed. Some people just get into a nervous hysteria that is worked up by those that have supposedly spoken in tongues. They work them up at an altar, getting them into a nervous hysteria till they don't know what they are saying. As long as they can jibber a little and even if they never do it again, they are accepted.

Brother Brown, an educated man, wanted to know first-hand what was going on. So he attended many services. To convince himself and to be able to write in a convincing manner, he took a man that could speak seven languages with him, and sat in several services. This man said, "There isn't anything being said in any language that I know." Mr. Brown took two others that knew a good number of languages. One of them said, "One woman said two or three words in Russian." The preacher supposedly interpreted it. So one of these gentlemen with Brother Brown stood up and gave the preacher a scripture in a certain language, and said, "Now tell me what language I spoke in, and what scripture did I speak?" The preacher thought he had spoken a scripture in Romans: but he had quoted from I John. Also, he thought he had spoken French, but that was not the case. Brother Brown's companion said, "You missed it a hundred percent." About this time a woman went into a frenzy and carried on and one of the men with Brother Brown said, "She's speaking in Chinese and I wouldn't repeat the vulgar words that are coming out of her mouth." So they took her aside and looked into her case. Brother Brown realized the fact that you can pick up things in your subconscious mind. And when you get worked up in a hysteria, they'll come out. When they began to question the woman they found out that she lived in an apartment in Chinatown, in Los Angeles. Day after day, year after year, she would hear the Chinese on the streets below in the markets. They were cussing and ripping at each other. She didn't know what they were saying, but it made an imprint in her subconscious mind. When they got her to the altar and got her worked up she began to rattle out these Chinese words.

Another false teaching is: if you ever say that speaking in tongues is of the devil, you blaspheme the Holy Ghost. Well, I have said it several times now and I haven't blasphemed the Holy Ghost; because I have given you God's eternal Word.

Friend, the devil has worked a terrible work. This tongues movement is spreading even into Roman Catholicism and many false cults, and they are being accepted as saved; all the while continuing in their idolatry and doctrines of devils. I feel sorry for the people that are deceived by this false movement. You and I are held responsible by God to warn those who are in error and to give them the truth of God's eternal Word. "For I testify unto every man that heareth the words of the prophecy of this book [Bible]. If any man shall add unto these things, God shall add unto him the plagues that are written in this book: And if any man shall take away from the words of the book of this prophecy, God shall take away his part out of the book of life," Revelation 22:18, 19.

Selected

Do All Speak with Tongues?
Ruth Cochran Gunter

The gift of tongues is a supernatural gift of languages whereby the Holy Ghost enables the human voice to speak a language not acquired, but understandable to the listeners. It is one among the gifts of the Spirit, but the Bible does not teach that it is more important or necessary than the others. Paul stressed prophecy or preaching as the most important gift (1 Corinthians 14:1, 19). Joel's prophecy regarding the outpouring of the Spirit mentions prophecy instead of tongues. In 1 Corinthians 12:28 we are told, "And God hath set some in the church, first apostles, secondarily prophets, thirdly teachers, after that miracles, then gifts of healings, helps, governments, diversities of tongues." Here tongues is placed at the end of the list, yet many people today make it first and contend that it is the evidence of the Holy Spirit baptism.

The teaching that everyone must speak in tongues as the evidence that he has received the Holy Spirit is false and contrary to the Bible. Paul says, "Are all apostles?" The answer, of course, is NO. He asks, "Are all prophets? are all teachers?" The answer is NO. "Are all workers of miracles? Have all the gifts of healing?" Again the answer is NO. (All Christians must have some faith in order to be saved and to get answers to their prayers, but all do not possess these special gifts of the Spirit). Then Paul continues, "Do all speak with tongues? do all interpret?" The answer is, emphatically NO! (1 Corinthians 12:29, 30). It would be just as consistent to require every Spirit-filled person to have any one or all of these special gifts as to insist that he must speak in tongues as the evidence that he has received the Holy Ghost.

There are those who try to evade this plain teaching of the Bible by making a distinction between "speaking in tongues" as the initial evidence of the Holy Spirit baptism and the "gift of tongues." However, there is no scriptural proof or authority for such a claim. The gift is the speaking and speaking is but the exercise of the gift. Some refer to 1 Corinthian 12:7 as proof that all speak in tongues. "The manifestation of the Spirit is given to every man to profit withal." But the next verses refute and destroy their whole argument, for Paul shows that the Spirit divides the various gifts severally as He wills and that all do NOT speak with tongues.

Many persons say they received their "baptism" according to Acts 2:4 because they spoke in unknown tongues, but the tongues which the apostles spoke in on the Day of Pentecost were known tongues. "When the multitude came together . . . they were all amazed and marveled, saying one to another, Behold, are not all these which speak Galileans? And how hear we every man IN OUR OWN TONGUE, WHEREIN WE WERE BORN?" (Acts 2:6-8).

In 1 Corinthians 14:22 we are told, "Wherefore tongues are for a sign, not to them that believe, but to them that believe not." Here Paul is teaching just the opposite to what the Tongues people teach. They turn this scripture around and contend that speaking in tongues is the sign that one has received the Holy Spirit baptism. Paul declares that it is not a sign to him nor to any other believers; but, if it is a sign at all, it is to those who believe not. On the Day of Pentecost tongues were not a sign to those who had received the Holy Ghost but to the unbelieving multitude that gathered together and were amazed to hear the gospel preached to them in their native languages.

Some say they do not teach people to seek for tongues, but that they teach them to seek for the baptism with the Holy Spirit. However, when they insist that all must speak in tongues as evidence that they have the baptism, they virtually teach them to seek for tongues. Speaking in tongues is not the evidence, neither is physical demonstration an evidence of the Holy Ghost. Too many people look for and place more confidence in physical demonstration than in spiritual manifestation. The Holy Spirit must be distinguished from His works. To put one of His works ahead of the Spirit, Himself, and then demand that one particular work, is to open the heart to all kinds of deception. We are to seek for and obtain the Spirit, Himself.

Let me point out that the "unknown" tongue, is a language known to the speaker but unknown to the audience except it is translated or interpreted. The fact that the speaker "edifieth himself" (1 Corinthians 14:4) is proof that he understands what he is saying. Edify means "to impart instruction to." If one did not know what he was saying, it would be impossible for him to instruct himself or anyone else. The "unknown" tongue is one that is unknown or foreign to the listeners. It is known to the speaker, because it is his native tongue or language in which he is accustomed to speaking. Hence, he edifies himself.

The Bible forbids speaking publicly in a language that cannot be understood unless someone is there to interpret "If any man speak in an unknown tongue, let it be by two, or at the most three, and that by course; and let one interpret. But IF THERE BE NO INTERPRETER, LET HIM KEEP SILENCE IN THE CHURCH" (1 Corinthians 14:27, 28). John H. Church in the booklet "Which Is Right?" says, "Now do the Tongues people follow this procedure? So far as I have been able to learn they do not. Some of them say they cannot keep from talking in tongues. They claim that the power of God comes on them and they can't keep still. If this is true then I want to say that they are mistaken about what kind of power it is, for Paul plainly says, (1 Corinthians 14:32) "The spirit of the prophet is subject to the prophet"

"God does not make you do something you do not want to do. Certainly He will never make you do something that He has commanded you not to do. He has commanded you to keep silence when others are speaking, and to keep silence in the church. If there is no interpreter. If there is some power that comes upon you, and forces you to go against this plain teaching, then I want to say to you, upon the authority of God's Word, that it is not the power of the Holy Spirit. I would also say that If I were you, I would be afraid of any power that makes you do the very thing God says for you not to do." The Holy Spirit who inspired the writing of the Bible is not going to impel you to do anything contrary to its teachings.

God never forces Himself on anyone. Several years ago a woman of our acquaintance attended a Tongues meeting and got in sympathy with their doctrine. After one of their preachers laid hands on her and prayed, she said a peculiar feeling came over her and from that time on a power would get control of her. Sometimes when she started to leave their meetings, she would become rigid and have to be helped into the car. Finally, she began to fear that this power that was imposing itself upon her was not the power of God. She came to a revival which we were conducting in Western Oklahoma and went to the altar of prayer. As she knelt there with her hands raised rigidly over her head and with a strained look on her face, she asked us to pray God to deliver her. We prayed for some time, but could not get the victory until we laid our hands on her and rebuked the Pentecostal spirit which had control of her. Then she was able to keep her hands down; the strained look left her face; and she returned to her home a free woman.

Any power that gets control of people's bodies, minds and wills, causing them to do things they do not want to do and sometimes things that are indecent and unbecoming cannot be the power of the Holy Ghost, for He never forces Himself on anyone, and He is a Holy Spirit who does all things in decency and in order. We are not blaspheming the Holy Ghost when we expose and condemn false doctrine and practices, for He is not the author of them. Nor are we opposing individuals, but rather the deception that they are in. We have no desire to hurt or offend anyone, but want to help people see the difference between truth and error.

It is dangerous to teach individuals to look for and expect any physical sign or manifestation as an evidence of an inward work of God's grace. The devil can work through the physical and duplicate and counterfeit, thereby deceiving honest souls. Speaking in an unknown gibberish is not an indication of the Holy Spirit baptism. Without casting any reflections on Tongues people, it is a proven fact that people have spoken in tongues who weren't even saved. We have known of

some who were dishonest, immoral and backslidden—
and yet they could talk in tongues. Surely God would
not make a physical manifestation that can be so easily
counterfeited a sign of the inward work of His Spirit!

The Holy Spirit is for all Christians who will consecrate and dedicate their lives to God and ask in faith
believing. He is His own witness. We can know that we
are sanctified by the Holy Ghost, as definitely as we
knew we were converted, when we meet the conditions
laid down in the Word of God and believe. The proof or
evidence that we have the experience is that we manifest the Spirit of Christ, bear the fruit of the Spirit, and
have power to live for God, witness for Him, and work
for Him.

[The compiler believes this article to be in the Public Domain.]

Modern Pentecostalism.
By George E. Harmon

That this is an age of many counterfeit religions, we must admit, and of which the New Testament writers have given us definite warning. 1 Tim. 4:1.

In this writing we do not mean to unkindly criticize any one, but the love for precious souls constrains us to expose this particular error in the light of Bible truth so that honest truth-seekers may make their escape from the realms of deception. Souls who are thus in bondage are to be pitied and persuaded by Divine love and wisdom—not crushed or driven. Strictly speaking, the devil is solely responsible for the error itself, so let us place the blame on the author and rescue the subjects from the error's influence. There is deliverance, praise God!

The latter part of the nineteenth century marked the beginning of the full restoration of God's true Church to her apostolic glory and power, or when she emerged from the "cloudy and dark day" into the "evening light"—a fulfillment of Old Testament prophecy (Jeremiah 32:39; Zechariah 14:6, 7; Ezekiel 34:12). Truth was sent forth, such as sanctification, holiness, divine healing, New Testament ordinances and the one Church separate from human organizations.

Hearing this apostolic truth, numbers began to make their escape from religious confusion and embraced the whole truth. Then the devil saw that his grip was being loosened in the religious world. Therefore, quickly he devised and originated new theories to sidetrack precious souls in their search for truth. The Pentecostal or modern tongues movement, to be plain, is the most outstanding counterfeit in recent years it has swept the country. There are reasons for its spread, which we will notice later.

Dear reader, let us turn to the Bible and see if their teaching and spirit, especially the tongues-evidence theory, harmonizes with the Word and Spirit of God.

Error 1. Speaking in tongues as the Spirit gives utterance (Acts 2:4) is different from the gift of tongues of 1 Corinthians 12:10. There is no distinction in the two expressions, for both refer to the same thing. True speaking in tongues of Acts 2:4 is a manifestation of the Spirit as implied by the words, "as the Spirit gave them utterance." The fact that the true tongues are given of the Spirit necessarily means they are a "gift" of the Spirit. In the 12th chapter of 1st Corinthians both expressions are used interchangeably and speaking of the same spiritual gift. We read, "To one is given by the Spirit . . . divers kinds of tongues," (verses 8, 10) referring to the gift of tongues. Then in verse 30 we read, "Do all speak with tongues?" which also refers to the same gift, just as the "gift of miracles" and "workers of miracles" are equivalent expressions. We understand that this distinguishing theory was introduced in the year of 1900 by C. F. Parham. The early church never taught it, for it is a strained interpretation trying to uphold the tongues-evidence theory.

Error 2. The baptism of the Holy Ghost is in every instance attended by the initial physical sign of speaking in other tongues as the Spirit gives utterance. The Scriptures nowhere teach that speaking in tongues is required as evidence that the Holy Ghost is received. In 1 Corinthians 12:30 Paul asks, "Do all speak with tongues?" No, is the implied answer, for in the preceding verses he had explained that there were "differences of administration" in the manifestation of the Spirit, meaning that the Spirit does not manifest Himself through the same particular gift in every person, "but the manifestation of the Spirit is given to every man to profit withal." 1 Corinthians 12:7. You know that all are not apostles, all are not workers of miracles (verse 29), neither do all speak with true tongues. Speaking in tongues, which could only be "as the Spirit gives utterance," is only a manifestation or gift of the Spirit in common with other special gifts. According to this error, the Holy Spirit is denied unless He chooses to manifest Himself in a certain manner. The Holy Ghost Himself is the satisfactory evidence. "Whereof the Holy Ghost also is a witness" (Heb. 10:15). "The Spirit itself beareth witness with our spirit," Rom. 8:16. If the reception of the Spirit must be evidenced by an outward physical sign, surely one's conversion should be determined by a special sign in all cases. Since such is not true, then there is no necessity of that particular witness for the baptism, or for any other special work or favor from God.

On the day of Pentecost the first disciples exercised the gift of prophecy, as well as the gift of tongues, when they received the Holy Ghost. Also, the twelve disciples at Ephesus prophesied when they received the Holy Ghost and spoke with tongues (Acts 19). Therefore, the special gift of prophecy should be given preference if either of the gifts were to be accepted as the evidence of the reception of the Holy Ghost for "greater is he that prophesieth than he that speaketh with tongues" (1 Corinthians 14:5) and Paul further exhorts, "Desire spiritual gifts, but rather that ye may prophesy." (Verse 1).

Error 3. "We receive the baptism of the Holy Ghost just like they did on the day of Pentecost" (Acts 2). Do the modern tongues people manifest the same signs as then? Let us notice more closely the Pentecost scene. The first outward sign was the coming of "a sound from heaven as of a rushing mighty wind and it filled all the house where they were sitting;" the second outward sign was, "There appeared unto them cloven tongues like as of fire, and it sat upon each of them:" the third outward sign, "began to speak with other tongues [languages] as the Spirit gave them utterance." The modern movement does not reproduce these signs as claimed in the above error. They discard the first two, and emphasize the last. However, the first sign is just as important as the last in this particular scene, being only a literal fulfillment of Old Testament prophecy at the ushering in of the Holy Spirit dispensation. The last manifestation or tongues which people generally receive today are not languages as spoken on the day of Pentecost, but only a false gibber through Satanic power or nervous derangement. Therefore, in no sense do they reproduce the Pentecostal outpouring. No hint is made at this Pentecostal scene that the disciples spoke in unknown tongues, nor to God alone, neither did they need an interpreter, but these languages were spoken direct to the people of different nations and were given specifically for the purpose of spreading the gospel to various nations through prophecy or preaching, a special gift which they also received at this time. The Bible gift of tongues is a language, and is given as an aid to prophecy when needed. Evidently the disciples on this occasion did not talk in different languages a few minutes only, for the incident was noised abroad and the multitude representing different nationalities came together, and each "heard them speak in his own language," (Acts 2:6) which no doubt continued the greater part of the day, each disciple talking in order, Peter's sermon being recorded in this chapter. If speaking these various languages was the only evidence that they had the Holy Ghost, then when they ceased to speak the apostles could have rightly concluded that they had lost the Holy Ghost. How inconsistent! Our Pentecostal friends would endeavor to satisfy us with a momentary evidence, but thank God, the infilling of the Spirit is not dependent upon transitory evidences, for the Holy Spirit in the heart is the abiding evidence Himself.

Error 4. That one should "tarry" for the baptism of the Spirit, evidenced by the speaking in tongues. Jesus commanded the disciples to tarry at Jerusalem until they were endued with power from on high, (Luke 24:49). We know that this refers to Pentecost (Acts 1:8). To fulfill Old Testament type the Spirit would not be given until "the day of Pentecost was fully come" (Acts 2:1). This tarrying applied only to the disciples before Pentecost, meaning for them to await that special time. On that day we find them in "one accord in one place," and they were "sitting"—denoting no physical exertion. Tarrying is not needed so much now as meeting the conditions for the reception of the Spirit. Divine operations are spiritual and are wrought in the heart by faith. Ephesians 2:8. Faith is receiving where there is no sight or physical evidence, for faith is "the evidence of things not seen." Hebrews 11:1. "He that believeth . . . hath the witness in himself." 1 John 5:10. By faith the Holy Spirit is received. Galatians 3:14. Therefore, faith is omitted when one looks to the physical evidence as the goal, and one is not satisfied until they receive the "tongues." Under such conditions of tarrying, physical exertion and omission of faith, wonderful opportunities are afforded the devil to give counterfeit tongues or spirits. 1 John 4:1. It is easy for the devil to counterfeit physical manifestations of the Spirit, and this alone makes the theory unreliable. Then, too, no allowance is made for counterfeit manifestations, many of which the Word of God directly condemns. People who are demon-possessed very often speak in tongues. To my knowledge a number of persons have escaped from the tongues movement, and in order to get Bible salvation they had to have the devils cast out by the power of God. In fact, in every case where they had sought and received the delusion of tongues, the power of the devil had to be broken before they could get salvation. This is a warning to beware of this supernatural power of the devil.

We rightly expect those who have the Holy Ghost to bear the fruits of the Spirit . . . love, joy, peace, long-suffering, gentleness, goodness, faith, meekness, temperance. (Galatians 5:22, 23). On the contrary, we find these fruits lacking in many of those who claim to have "the" evidence. We are commanded to try the spirits, for there are many false ones in the world. 1 John 4:1. How can we try the spirits? By the Word of God, for it alone will judge us in the last day. John 12:48. The spirits must agree with the Word and not the Word with the spirits.

The tongues movement, through this supernatural delusive power, has ensnared a multitude of people. Lying wonders are performed by them. It is also a refuge for those who "receive not a love for the truth."

Dear reader, you who believe these theories, be honest with yourself and seek deliverance from the enemy of your soul.

Selected

THE AFFIRMATION SERIES
"THINGS MOST SURELY BELIEVED AMONG US"

A Word of Warning About Tongues.
Edited by Robert Hazen

Volume I, Series 1

Presented
by
Faculty Members of
Alberta Bible Institute
Camrose, Alberta, Canada

Printed by

Gospel Contact Press
Camrose, Alberta

First Printing - 1979
THE AFFIRMATION SERIES

This is the first of what is hoped will be a series of booklets sharing the research, inspiration, and thinking of faculty and friends of ABI. There is no plan for the series to appear on a regular basis, but it will be shared as the need, inspiration, and money are available.

INTRODUCTION

This booklet shares the study of ABI teachers on the subject of tongues, which complements the writings and teachings of other contemporary Church of God leaders. As current as today, and as far back as our pioneers, is the Church of God stand on: Sanctification, the Holy Spirit Infilling, and the Baptism of the Holy Spirit (and that without the contamination of the *glossolalia* of today). We affirm the teaching of John Wesley—that the Holy Spirit perfects love in the human heart. We dare not surrender the glorious doctrine and experience of being filled with the Holy Spirit simply because some would adulterate it with false emphasis or over-emotionalize it with a pseudo-experience.

The format of what is shared is in six sections:

1. The Pastoral Perspective.

    President Hazen originally presented most of this material to his congregation in Lansing, Michigan when the *glossolalia* issue began to appear some years ago.

II. The Historical Perspective.

    Dr. Froese shares out of his years of study and countless hours of pouring over Church History books, both German and English.

III. The Biblical Research Perspective

Prof. Belter brings to us his biblical research in preparation for his classroom presentations.

IV. A Statement Regarding Church Music.

Prof. Swindells appeals to us to select and use music that will emphasize God-centered worship.

V. There is presented for your reading a collection of excerpts from the writings of our pioneers about tongues.

VI. A short bibliography for your further study.

A WORD OF WARNING ABOUT TONGUES
A PASTORAL PERSPECTIVE

This message is being shared because of the many questions and problems arising out of the present revival of Pentecostalism, tongues, or *glossolalia* within Protestantism and Catholicism today. A sermon against tongues is not new for a Church of God pastor, for in former days, it was important to protect our identity and reputation. Pentecostal groups also used the name "Church of God" and since it was a universal name, we could not incorporate it. For this reason, bulletin boards and letterheads declared us as "The First Church of God non-Pentecostal." This was quite acceptable, for tongues, at that time, was associated with "Holy Roller-ism," store-front churches, tent meetings and brush arbors. But the present revival of Pentecostalism has acquired a sophistication and level of acceptance so that it can boast of followers and prayer groups in the Episcopal, Roman Catholic and Presbyterian churches. And, its greatest proponents are Christian Business Men's Organizations. The sophistication, however, ought not to affect us, for our Movement was not hesitant to point out the areas of doctrine that Protestantism and Catholicism taught and believed which were not supported by Scripture. We have said they were wrong in other practices and doctrine, so why should their acceptance validate tongues?

Our study begins with what happened on the Day of Pentecost when the followers of Christ were together, following His resurrection and ascension. "And when the day of Pentecost was fully come, they were all with one accord in one place. And suddenly there came a sound from heaven as of a rushing mighty wind, and it filled all the house where they were sitting. And there appeared unto them cloven tongues like as of fire, and it sat upon each of them. And they were all filled with the Holy Ghost, and began to speak with other tongues, as the Spirit gave them utterance. And there were dwelling at Jerusalem, Jews, devout men, out of every nation under heaven. Now when this was noised abroad, the multitude came together, and were confounded, because that every man heard them speak in his own language. And they were all amazed and marvelled, saying one to another, "Behold, are not all these which speak Galileans?" (Acts 2:1-7 KJV). Following this account, 15 different countries using different dialects and languages were identified. Here the words, "tongue" and "language" were used interchangeably. It is apparent from these verses that at the initial outpouring of the Holy Spirit upon the believers, there was caused a miracle in witnessing so that as the followers, most of whom were Galileans, told the Good News, people from other countries and other languages understood them.

But, Pentecostalism or *glossolalia* of today is an unknown tongue, an ecstatic utterance, or a prayer language, understandable only to God or to special people with the gift of interpretation. In Acts 2, it was a miracle of understanding, not misunderstanding. People of one language did not understand another language until God caused the miracle. Defenders of the doctrine of *glossolalia,* at this point, direct us to I Corinthians, chapter 14 and say here it is different. But, here, Bible translators disagree. The New English Bible translators using the term "ecstatic utterance" translate the following passages thusly, while our own Dr. Boyce Blackwelder translates the term "foreign language." Here are the same texts for comparison.

To get the full benefit of this comparison study, I would suggest first you read both versions so you can see that the translation "foreign language" is much clearer and makes a lot of sense. Then if you compare each of the verses, again you will see how practical and understandable the Scriptures are when translated "foreign language."

1 Corinthians 14

New English Bible

[2]When a man is using the language of ecstasy he is talking with God, not with men, for no man understands him; ... [4]The language of ecstasy is good for the speaker himself ... should be pleased for you all to use the tongues of ecstasy, but better pleased for you to prophesy ... [6]Suppose, my friends, that when I come to you I use ecstatic language: what good shall I do you, unless what I say contains something by way of revelation, or enlightenment, or prophecy, or instruction? ... [8]if the trumpet call is not clear, who will prepare for battle? [9]In the same way if your ecstatic utterance yields no precise meaning, how can anyone tell what you are saying? ... [11]if I do not know the meaning of the sound the speaker makes, his words will be gibberish to me, and mine to Him ... [13]I say, then, that the man who falls into ecstatic utterance should pray for the ability to interpret. If I use such language in my prayer, the Spirit in me prays, but my intellect lies fallow ... [18]Thank God, I am more gifted in ecstatic utterance than any of you, but in the congregation I would rather speak five intelligible words, for the benefit of others as well as myself, than thousands of words in the language of ecstasy ... [21]We read in the Law: "I will speak to this nation through men of strange tongues, and by the lips of foreigners; and even so they will not heed me, says the Lord." [22]Clearly then these "strange tongues" are not intended as a sign for believers, but for unbelievers ... [23]So if the whole congregation

is assembled and all are using the "strange tongues" of ecstasy, and some uninstructed persons or unbelievers should enter, will they not think you are mad? ... [26]To sum up, my friends: when you meet for worship, each of you contributes a hymn, some instructions, a revelation, an ecstatic utterance, or the interpretation of such an utterance. All of these must aim at one thing: to build up the church. [27]If it is a matter of ecstatic utterance, only two should speak, or at most three, one at a time, and someone must interpret. [28]If there is no interpreter, the speaker had better not address the meeting at all, but speak to himself and to God ... [39]In short, my friends, be eager to prophesy; do not forbid ecstatic utterances; [40]but let all be done decently and in order.

Letters From Paul

By Dr. Boyce Blackwelder

[2]He who speaks in a foreign language speaks not to men but to God, for no one understands him ... [4]He who speaks in a foreign language edifies himself ... [5]Now I might wish that all of you could speak in foreign languages. But I much prefer you to be persuasive preachers ... [6]Now, brothers, if I come to you and speak in foreign languages, what good can I do you unless my words convey some meaning either by revelation, or by knowledge, or by clear preaching, or by teaching? ... [8]Again, if a military trumpet does not sound a clear signal, who will prepare himself for battle? [9]So it is with you—unless you

speak clearly, how will anyone know what you say? ... "If, however, do not know the significance of the language (being spoken), I am a stranger to the speaker and the speaker is a stranger to me ... [13]This is why anyone who speaks in a foreign language should pray that he may interpret (what he says to his hearers). [14]If I pray in a foreign language, my spirit prays but my understanding produces no fruit (for the benefit of others) ... [18]I thank God that I might speak in foreign languages more than all of you. [19]Nevertheless, in church I would rather speak five words which are understood, in order that I might instruct others, than (to speak) ten thousand words in a foreign language ... [21]In the law it stands written, "By men of foreign languages and through the lips of strangers I will speak to this people, and not even then will they listen to me, says the Lord." [22]This shows that foreign languages are a sign not to those who believe but to those who do not believe ... [23]Consequently, if the entire church meets together in one place, and all speak in foreign languages, and uninformed persons or unbelievers come in, will they not say you are crazy? ... [26]What are the implications of what I have been saying, brothers? When you meet together, each man has (a contribution to make): a hymn, a teaching, a revelation, a discourse in a foreign language, or an interpretation. Let all things be done with a view to (the) up-building (of the church). [27]If any speak in a foreign language, let only two or at the most three speak, one at a time, and let someone interpret what is said. [28]However if no interpreter is present, let the one who would speak in a foreign language keep silent in the church, and let him speak to himself and to God ... [39]so then, my brothers, be eager to preach persuasively, and do not forbid anyone who has the gift of speaking in foreign languages to exercise it. [40]But let everything be done in a proper and orderly manner.

There are enough variances in older and modern translations that you can say, "The scholarship is acceptable—take your pick between 'ecstatic utterance' and 'foreign language'." I pick the term "foreign language." Even if the term "foreign language" is not used, the Scripture in I Corinthians 14 gives multiple words of caution, limitation, and control that negate or teach against every Christian asking for or experiencing the "Gift." Since agreeing with Dr. Blackwelder, let me go on to say that only once in my limited ministry have I had to speak through an interpreter to a congregation that understood no English. My English was a foreign language to them and their Chinese a foreign language to me. What a barrier to communication a foreign language is. Except for our mutual trust in the interpreter and the reciprocation of warm smiles, I had no way of knowing if they understood. We here at Pennway can remember the times in prayer meeting that Kostas Kurtis broke out in Greek as he prayed or, P. V. Jacob in his Malayalam language of South India. It meant more to them and the Lord than stammering English; however, neither we nor our visitors understood them.

An interesting question to ask ourselves in this study is "What did Jesus say and practice regarding praying by ecstatic utterances, and the Holy Spirit being evidenced this way?" The surprising answer is "Nothing," but there is much that he did and said that was relevant. At the most intense times of his praying in the Garden when he sweat drops of blood and when angels ministered to him, the words that he spoke were most intelligible, did not need interpretation and, fortunately, were divinely recorded for us. God is all wise. He is the mind behind the universe, and our highest and best communication with Him will be at the most intelligible, practical, sensible level we're able to muster. Jesus taught us that when the Holy Spirit would come he would *not* say, "This is proof it's me," but would remind us of the teachings of Jesus (John 16:13-14; John 14:26).

It is natural for us to long for certitudes in our relationship with God. Doubts and fears plague us all at one time or another. But God has so planned our nature and our relationship with Him that faith is a must. Note the texts: "The just shall live by *faith"(* Hebrews 10:38). "Being justified by *faith* we have peace with God" (Romans 5:1). "Without *faith* it is impossible to please God" (Hebrews 11:6). "This is the victory that overcometh the world, even our *faith*" (1 John 5:4). Yet a person seeking the modern speaking in tongues quite often wants it to certify his relation with God. And, upon finding it, asserts it as such. The Biblical basis for being sure of our relationship with God is to keep His commandments and to love God's people (I John 2:3 and I John 4:14).

As pastor, I will receive criticism for this message in the following vein, "Don't be rough on those who speak in tongues. Many of them are sincere Christians who honestly feel they have the gift of praying or speaking in tongues." I didn't say they were not Christian. But, the same thing can be said of one who believes in eternal security, the millennium, infant baptism, church joining, the infallibility of the Pope, bingo and snake-handling—I don't believe in *these* either. I don't believe the Scriptures teach these things as we commonly understand them and I'll preach against them as long as I feel this way.

Whenever you talk about a doctrine and an experience and say what it is and what it isn't, there is a problem. But, take note—one time I was very ill with a sore throat. One doctor observed spots on my throat and in his diagnosis said I had diphtheria and referred me to another doctor. This doctor took a culture, then informed me, "I don't know what you've got, but it's not diphtheria." If you're talking in a modern unknown tongue, I don't know what you've got, but it's not a miracle of talking and hearing as in Acts 2. And, it's not a gift of a foreign language or many foreign languages.

A common phrase in days gone by was, "Don't get mixed up in tongues." It is still valid. It is my pastoral exhortation to you along with "Accept the Pentecostal as a Christian brother by the same criteria you accept anyone else." Remember, the question is not whether you have the Holy Spirit, but does the Holy Spirit have you? The best evidence of healing is that you get well. And, the best evidence of the Holy Spirit is that you love God and love one another. The primary thing the Holy Spirit will do to you is to cause you to be like Jesus. ❑

NOTE: The above sermon was delivered by Pastor Robert J. Hazen to the Pennway Church of God, Lansing, Michigan, February 3, 1974.

Edited and presented to the class on Doctrine 300, November 24, 1977, Alberta Bible Institute, Camrose, Alberta

GLOSSOLALIA—AN HISTORICAL VIEW

Only with great difficulty can an historical view of *glossolalia* be given. There are still too many questions about the phenomenon of *glossolalia* itself—questions about its characteristics and nature, which should be answered before an historian can grapple with its expressions in the past. For example, is *glossolalia* primarily a psychological or predominantly a religious phenomenon? The clarification of such a question is important if a full study of the development of *glossolalia* is attempted. The best an historian can do at the moment is to list incidents where we know that the phenomenon occurred.

An historical study of *glossolalia* is very difficult, especially for an historian of the Christian Church, since speaking in tongues occurred among people before the birth of Christ and in places where the individuals experiencing *glossolalia* did not uphold the Christian faith. Ancient Egyptian writings contain allusions to what may be called *glossolalia.* Also Greek and Roman writers reveal that they were familiar with it. Consequently, the ability of speaking in tongues is not a peculiarly Christian phenomenon.

Modern tongue-speakers point to the records of the New Testament as their basis for *glossolalia.* Other studies in this series focus their attention on the biblical view of the phenomenon and so we may omit that here.

Among the Christian records from the centuries after the New Testament was written, we find only very few references to *glossolalia.* Montanus, a leader of the second century, who considered himself to be a reform-er but was thought of as a heretic by others, spoke in tongues when proclaiming his prophecies. His predictions did not come true. St. Augustine thought that *glossolalia* had had some value in biblical times but had later ceased among Christians.

During the medieval centuries, the Protestant Reformation period, and the succeeding years, we know of very few recorded cases of tongue-speaking. The events described in some of the biographies of medieval saints might be expressions connected more with exorcism of evil spirits than with *glossolalia*. In the Reformation period, Martin Luther was very critical of extreme enthusiasts, or "Schwarmer," as he called them, among whom spiritual ecstasies were seen to have happened. Later, some Roman Catholic reformers, to whose circle Blaise Pascal may be counted, are said to have practised *glossolalia*. Also among the early Quakers the experience of tongue-speaking occurred, even though George Fox, their early leader, avoided the practice.

In the twentieth century *glossolalia* has gained wide attention, especially, as it emerged and spread in the U.S.A. It has led to firm organizational expressions through the founding of many Pentecostal denominations. The whole Pentecostal phenomenon of our century is generally considered to have begun with Charles Parham, a Methodist minister, and W. J. Seymour, one of his students. Parham founded various Bible schools in the southern U.S.A. with the intention of revivifying the Christian life of believers. After attending one of these institutions, Seymour held revival services in Los Angeles in 1906 and here some people began to speak in tongues. The event attracted much attention. For three years the meetings at 312 Azusa Street in Los Angeles went on and literally thousands of people from all over the world visited the place. They not only saw and experienced the gift of *glossolalia* but also spread it when they returned home and started many Pentecostal churches around the globe. Since the experiences of these Pentecostals had been very subjective with personal conversions and individualistic approaches to faith, their later lives also manifested a subjective approach to holiness. The result was the appearance of numerous independent religious groups, such as the Assemblies of God, the Church of God in Christ, the International Church of the Foursquare Gospel, the Pentecostal Church of God in America, the Apostolic Overcoming Holy Church of God, the Pentecostal Holiness Church, the Pentecostal Assemblies of the World, and many others.

Within the last few decades of our century, a neo-Pentecostal movement has emerged in which believers from various older denominations, such as Roman Catholic, Episcopalian, Presbyterian, Lutheran, Methodist, and Baptist claim to be tongue-speakers. The adherents of this neo-Pentecostal movement generally refuse to abandon their former church attachments. While retaining their older denominational commitments and general theological views, they have added *glossolalia* experiences to their involvements of faith. A large number of priests and pastors claim to have experienced the gift of *glossolalia,* yet many wish to remain anonymous, possibly to avoid being misunderstood or to evade a clear stand. Such neo-Pentecostals frequently meet with fellow charismatics in services apart from their usual meetings. At such special gatherings tongue-speaking is a common occurrence.

Looking at the modern manifestations of *glossolalia,* the church historian is tempted to take one of two opposite positions in evaluating such happenings. If he is sympathetic to the phenomenon he can hail it as an emerging revitalization of the Christian Church. Should he be critical of *glossolalia,* he can consider it as a modern heresy into which misled believers have fallen. On the basis of the historical data, the church historian as an historian cannot as yet give a clear and definite verdict about which of these is the correct interpretation. However, as a Christian believer, he can take a stand and in full agreement with the other studies in this series, this writer considers the current expressions of *glossolalia* a dangerous divergence from the true Christian faith and the proper spiritual life. ❏ — Dr. Walter Froese

PAUL AND THE GIFT OF GLOSSOLALIA

The Christian Church has always had many professing members who know as much about the Holy Spirit in their response as the followers at Ephesus who were asked by Paul, "Did you receive the Holy Spirit when you believed?" and replied, "No" (Acts 19:2). Many Christians throughout time have been in the same state. They have heard in a vague way about the Spirit, but have never seriously acted. On the other hand, there have always been people who are very sure about the Spirit. He is the authority of their particular emphasis in Theology and practice. It is therefore not surprising that at the beginning of this century there were no Pentecostals. Today, if the numbers quoted by those who are caught up in this movement can be believed, there are over 20 million coming from every nation and almost every denomination. The emphasis from the beginning has been the outward expression of speaking in tongues. It has been proclaimed that this is the pathway for power, the new reformation, the sign of God's last great outpouring, the only force generating unity and brotherhood. In opposition has come the cry of apostasy.

What, then, in the midst of the many conflicting voices, is the Christian to make of the Holy Spirit and Tongues. In attempting to answer this question, let us remember that we are mere men talking about God. Unless He is generous enough to disclose Himself, we cannot know anything at all about Him. As Paul writes in I Corinthians 2:11, "No one comprehends the thoughts of God except the Spirit of God." It takes God to reveal God and this He has done through His Son via the witness of His Word. Therefore, it is to His Word we must turn.

The word used for the Spirit of God in both the Hebrew and the Greek is quite notable. *Ruach* in Hebrew and *pneuma* in Greek have the meaning of "wind", "breath" and "spirit." God's Spirit is His life-giving breath. This Spirit is no natural quality of man. It is found in God. As the Old Testament writers often put it, "It is the Beyond that has come into our midst." Isaiah demonstrates this as a violent invading force. It is like the wind that has hurtled across the desert or whistled through the cedars. In its force, nothing can resist it. "The grass withers, the flowers fades when the *ruach adonai* blows upon it" (Isaiah 40:7). The Spirit of the Lord is disturbing and mysterious like the wind. We see this same demonstration on the day of Pentecost in Acts. Here God breaks into human life in a violent and unexpected way and directs the mission of the Church in seemingly unexpected and unorthodox ways. It is here also that one first encounters what seem to be the first incidents of speaking in tongues. Without going into an in-depth study as to what tongues were, suffice it to say that it did not generate much concern or attention. It was an expression of the Spirit's mission, the result of which was salvation for many. It should be noted that in this account the event follows worship. Later, in Acts 13, one sees the same pattern that true worship results in the active demonstration of the mission of the Spirit towards salvation.

This is a lesson that had not been digested at Corinth, and Paul spends three chapters teaching them (I Corinthians 12, 13, 14). Corinth was a gifted church, and they rated very highly the ability to speak in tongues. Plato had written that it was through ecstasy that the greatest blessings came. "No man in possession of his rational mind has reached Divine Exaltation." The Corinthian Church was in grave danger to suppose that the more a man loses self-possession the more inspired by God he must be. This is to deny God a place in the rational. To suppose the non-personal expressions of the Spirit to be a mark of inspiration is to deny the Spirit of Christ. This in turn undermines the ethical because it does not matter how you behave as long as you have the mark of Divine Inspiration upon you. This leads to a cult of experience and excessive individualism which ends in spiritual pride.

In I Corinthians 12:1-3, Paul reminds his readers that not all ecstatic speech is Christian. They knew this from their unregenerate days of worshipping Bacchus or Isis. They had shared feasts in honor of demons and fallen under their influence (10:19f). In fact, the force of the word used in Greek here indicates that they actually experienced demon possession. They had been involved in frenzied speech as they worshipped. Francis Schaeffer, at the 1977 meeting of the Canadian Theological Society held at York University in Toronto, in response to a question asked by a charismatic group concerning the tongues movement in the Church, reminded his audience that Muslims, Buddhists, Hindus, and even Satan worshippers speak in tongues. Perhaps some of the Corinthian Christians even cursed Christ in the ecstatic utterance (12:3). Paul reminds them that the crucial mark of the Spirit's presence is confession that Jesus is Lord. It is content that matters, not religious fervour, or speaking in tongues. Only the Holy Spirit bears witness to this fact.

In verses 4-11, the contrast is made between the variety of gifts and the unity of the giver. The Corinthian body of believers lacked fellowship. They were in competition. Note the repetition of in "the same Spirit . . . same Lord . . . same God." The gifts of grace are linked with the Spirit, the acts of service with Christ and the power with God, the Creator. Now the spiritual gifts are imparted by the gifts of grace, the Holy Spirit. They are not given for personal gain or gratification but for service to others. The Spirit unifies for service and gifts are given to all for one common good. This brings us to the second distinguishing criterion for a genuine gift of the Holy Spirit. Does it build up and benefit the Christian fellowship? Again, content is important.

In verses 12-31, Paul further grounds his argument in the very nature of God's being and action in history. There are indeed various ways of serving the Lord, but it is the same Lord we all serve. There are varieties of ways that He is active in us but only one Lord. All of this is for one purpose and that is to build the body of believers. If the whole body is an eye then it is surely wanting. The Church is no earthly society, but the embodiment of Jesus, the Messiah. Whatever the Church is, it is by virtue of the power and presence and action of its Lord. The Corinthians had to learn that they were not individually "little Christs" with all the gifts but rather, members of Christ with some gifts. No one could afford to be self-sufficient.

Before Paul continues with his concern of the varieties of the Spirit's gifts and its relationship to tongues as a sign of true spirituality, he digresses on the subject of God's love. He stresses that all gifts, inherent and acquired, are brought to a focal point in love, the greatest gift of them all and available to all. The word, *charisma,* which has become a common word among tongues people, literally means a gift of *charis. Charis* in Greek stands for God's unmerited love to us. Thus, Paul is saying that to be a follower of Christ is to be charismatic. All in Christ are equal because they are in debt to the sheer *charis*—charity—of God. If it were not for His charity, all men would be lost. Therefore, the only gift that all should be seeking is *charis*—charity, God-like love. In all else we see and understand like a child. Let us grow up and become mature by seeking to have God's charity demonstrated through us.

In Chapter 14, Paul continues his debate concerning true spirituality. It is this chapter that is used as the foundation of the gift of tongues by those who believe in *glossolalia*—the ability to speak in an ecstatic utterance which is identified as a "Holy Spirit Language" designed to enable one to worship God in greater depth and freedom. This communication may not mean anything but expresses an intimacy and trust between God and man and should become the norm of all worship. This, at first view, seems to agree with Paul's analogies in 14:7-11. Let us look closer.

First, he refers to musical instruments. If the flute or harp gives no meaningful melody in notes, nobody will understand and it will thus have no meaning. Uninterpreted tongues are like musical instruments played at random, in contrast to a few words spoken in clarity, which rouse one to action.

Second, he refers to the human tongue itself. If I do not enunciate clear words, I am not understood and accomplish nothing at all. Paul here plays on the word "tongue." The Greek word *phone* can mean either a part of the body or the language of the people. He very gently rebukes them for their cult of the unintelligible. For Paul, the tongue, as a part of the body, is associated with intelligibility.

Thirdly, an illustration is given from other languages: If I speak in a foreign tongue, people will not be able to understand me. Tongues, contrary to the view of the Corinthians, is not a vehicle for evangelism, but for confusion and laughter. One sounds like a barbarian. This is quite a rebuke to the refined Greeks of Corinth who despised foreigners because their language sounded like meaningless jabber of "bar-bar-bar."

One, however, finds a peculiar conflict. It seems there is a legitimate expression of tongues and yet there isn't. Paul raises the question of the purpose of this gift.

First, it enables a man to speak to God in prayer. He speaks not to men, but to God. Nobody understands him but he speaks mysteries in his spirit (I Corinthians 14:2). The gift of tongues opens up a new dimension to prayer. Whereas prayer had been an effort, now it is a desire. Time is of no importance.

Secondly, it enables one to praise God at a depth unknown previously. One finds himself free to praise and thank and adore and glorify as never before. When God's Spirit is at work, one must give vent to praiseful expression. However, it should be observed that Paul seems to be hinting that only in one's infancy and spiritual immaturity does one speak in unintelligible groanings. As one grows in the Spirit one begins to communicate with clarity. It is with both mind and spirit that one praises God.

Thirdly, it edifies the individual, but here is the rub. Because the inner groanings of the soul are a personal communication with God and only have a personal meaning, they ought not to be made the normal activity of the gathered fellowship. Paul makes it clear that it is of no value in congregational worship, but rather a threat because of the rampant individualism that it supports. Furthermore, it generates anarchy in worship. It will not be understood (14:14) unless there is an interpretation. "I thank God that I speak in tongues more than you all, nevertheless in church I would rather speak five words with my mind in order to teach others than ten thousand words in a tongue." Remember Paul could literally say this because of his ability to speak several languages.

Uninterpreted tongues may even denote God's judgment upon a Christian body (14:22ff). Paul quotes Isaiah 28:11-12 where Israel spurned the message of the prophets. God, by way of punishment, spoke to them through Assyrian tongues. This happened because they were unbelieving. This bespoke God's separation from

His people. Paul is making the point that when God speaks unintelligibly, He does so to hide Himself. So the Corinthians were coming dangerously close to God's judgment. This refutes the oft-used argument of the Corinthian use of tongues as a tool for evangelism.

As one continues to study Paul's debate, it becomes clear that tongues, as the Corinthians taught it, is an inferior gift. It is proclamation with clarity that one should strive for. He who can communicate the truth of God and make it understandable to all has a valuable gift of the Spirit. It is not difficult to detect a note of distaste in Paul's debate. He is not happy with the way things have gone at Corinth with their love of tongues. He bids restraint and is very much aware that *glossolalia* can be psychologically induced. He realizes that there are demonic counterfeits. Men were saying "a curse" on Jesus and were using tongues of their pagan days. Tongues, in fact, are a widely-disseminated phenomenon found in many cultures and religious practices. It is no exclusive mark of the Holy Spirit as the Corinthians proclaimed. Because of its selfishness, incomprehensibility and its non-ethical and extreme character, Paul was unwilling to concur with the Corinthian estimation of it. We would be wise to do likewise. ❏

—Siegfried R. Belter

MUSIC IN RELATIONSHIP TO PENTECOSTALISM

There has been a great upsurge of "Pentecostalism" or "tongues in the past few years. To some, "tongues" is considered a special prayer language, while to others, it is an unknown babble of sounds. Still others consider this to be an evidence of the baptism of the Holy Spirit. Many believe tongues, as referred to in Acts 2 and I Corinthians 14 should be interpreted to mean speaking in a foreign language. I personally indentify with the latter position and, there, view the prevalent concentration on emotionalism and experience-centered activities, as related to the Holy Spirit, to be erroneous.

One might ask what influences Church music has in abetting "Pentecostalism." Too often music is used as a tool to manipulate man's emotions and lead him into an ecstatic experience by a rapid, repetitious phrase on a melody. Thus, there is a need for a greater emphasis on God-centered worship, enhanced by the use of more objective hymns, e.g. "Praise to the Lord, the Almighty" or "Immortal, Invisible, God Only Wise."

Likewise, consider instrumental and vocal music used in worship. Does it direct man's thoughts Godward or does it appeal to the emotional rhythmic sense in man?

Down through history, music has been a powerful instrument wielded either for good or evil. We must seek to discover the integrity in our music that will guide people into the true Spirit-filled worship and not into emotional highs bordering on the demonic. Church music should express man's enjoyment of the fullness of God's grace and true spiritual freedom.

The pressing need of the hour is for man to be filled with the Holy Spirit; not with a manifestation of "tongues" or some emotional high. Oh, that Church music would inspire man to seek God, the fount of every blessing. ❏

Early writings of the Church of God affirm that, as a whole, we do not believe in "speaking in tongues." The term, "Most surely believed among us," certainly applies here, for one after another of our pioneer writers spoke out clearly against speaking in an unknown tongue.

It is very significant that tongues was not a problem or an issue in that day, yet they preached against it. There was an identification problem, however, because our name, "Church of God," was used by Pentecostal groups. Some of the Pentecostal groups taught that speaking in tongues was the evidence of being filled with the Spirit, so a lot of our writings were to refute this.

In these later years, however, the Charismatic Movement is not emphasizing Sanctification, but instead is emphasizing the gift of a prayer language. At this point, it is also amazing that the early writers were emphatic that the gift of tongues was a gift of being able to speak in a foreign language and/or to interpret a foreign language.

This collection is by no means exhaustive, nor are we giving you excerpts from writings that have appeared in the last 25 years. Our writers from the last quarter-century would, of course, attest to what the Pioneers have written as well as would our contemporary writers. ❑

THE FOLLOWING ARE EXCERPTS FROM WRITERS AND PREACHERS OF OUR BEGINNING YEARS FOR YOUR STUDY AND AFFIRMATION

Note: This material is reprinted with permission of Warner Press, Inc., P.O. Box 2499, Anderson, Indiana (formerly Gospel Trumpet Company, Anderson, Indiana).

HOLY SPIRIT BAPTISM AND THE SECOND CLEANSING

Russell R. Byrum (234 B18) p. 30-31.

Those who advocate the theory that all who get the baptism speak in tongues also hold that this speaking in tongues is different from the gift of tongues described in I Corinthians. But a careful consideration of I Corinthians 12 shows that the "gift" and the "manifestation" of the Spirit are identical, and the apostle closes with the clear implication that all do not speak with tongues (see I Cor. 12:28-30). We agree with the apostle that all do not speak with tongues. The best evidence that one has the Holy Spirit is the Spirit himself.

QUESTIONS AND ANSWERS

Charles E. Brown (230 B877) pp. 130-134.

QUESTION: Do you Church of God People at Anderson, Indiana, speak in tongues? If not, why not?

ANSWER: We Church of God People of Anderson, Indiana, do not actually speak in tongues, although we have no rule against it, because we believe that the Spirit of God must have his right of way in our lives; and if he should give one of us the gift of tongues, it would be our duty to take it and to use it boldly at all costs.

The reason why we do not speak in the gift of tongues is because none of us has the true gift of tongues, and we discourage the false gift.

QUESTION: What is the true gift of tongues?

ANSWER: The answer is—or would be if it were given to any individual—the power to speak some foreign historical language without ever learning from a human teacher or by human means. Thus a person with a gift of tongues would have to speak Russian or Chinese or Latin or Greek or some historical language without ever having learned it. Or to put the matter in another way. If a person among us should begin to speak in Spanish or Russian or Chinese or Italian or perhaps in ancient Latin, and there were conclusive proof that this person had ever learned this language by any human means; no teacher or teachers had ever taught it to him, he had never spoken it before—in other words, the language was plainly given to him by the Lord, new and fresh—then we would admit that this man had the gift of tongues, and we would honor his gift accordingly. I have heard of a few cases among us which were said to be like this, but personally I have never met such a person. Moreover, I do not believe that there are any cases of the real gift of tongues among the so-called tongues people, unless it might be possible once in a thousand times, as is said to be the case among us.

QUESTION: If the so-called tongues people do not speak in tongues, what kind of gift do they have?

ANSWER: We do not deny that any of the Pentecostal people ever spoke with the gift of tongues by the Holy Spirit. We feel that such a broadcast universal negative would be improper to make and difficult, if not impossible, to prove. We admit that in the last sixty-nine years of our history there may have been four or five people among us who had the real gift of tongues. We neither deny nor affirm, and we are willing to admit that among the millions of people who profess and have professed the gift of tongues within the last century— we are willing to admit that eight or ten of these people may have had the real gift of tongues. We neither affirm nor deny, because we do not know.

We do affirm, however, with all confidence, that what commonly passes for the gift of tongues among the Pentecostal people is not the gift of tongues described in the Bible. It is, we affirm, only a form of mental excitement commonly called hysteria. The scientific people would probably call it psychoneurosis. In popular language, this babbling and jabbering is the product of hysterical excitement. One evidence of this is the fact that it has often happened that a person who had the gift of tongues backslid and went into sin and still found that his gift was just as good as it ever had been, which was proof that it was of the natural man from the beginning.

Actually I believe that many Pentecostal people have been lured by the enemy of souls into a deceived spiritual condition because they developed this hysterical condition while they were saved. Later on, if they went into sin, and found they could still speak in tongues, the fact of being able to speak in tongues while living in sin deceived them into thinking that they could sin and still be filled with the Holy Spirit, which is a logical impossibility.

QUESTION: Do you think, then, that the gift of tongues as practiced among the Pentecostals is due to the direct inspiration of the devil?

ANSWER: I have heard and read the opinion of brethren who stated boldly that people who spoke in tongues were possessed of the devil and it was due to this devil possession that the tongues speaking was done. But this opinion to me seems to be altogether too harsh and uncharitable towards thousands of earnest Christians who have rejoiced and given place to ecstatic utterance under the impression that they were speaking with tongues in the power of the Holy Spirit. Actually, honest, unprejudiced acquaintance with and observation of these people will often give evidence that they are living sincere and faithful consecrated lives and that they are, in fact, real saints of God. It is a sin to stain the reputation of people like that. It is not a sin, however, to point out their mistakes; and this hysterical excitement, while not directly inspired by the devil, does constitute a snare many times, we think, because it tends to put the work of the flesh in the place of the work of the Spirit of God and thus make confusion. It has often happened that the hysterical excitement of the tongues meetings has been so fierce and extreme that a form of fanaticism has been engendered and developed which actually destroyed Christianity in a district. Such fields are known as burned-over fields, and failure in such situations is due to the fact that human nature commonly cannot be kept on such a strain of fanatical excitement over a long period of time.

In all sincerity we must also add that there is a temptation for seekers of the marvelous and egotistical exhibitions to pretend the gift of tongues and thus lay claim to divine endowment which they do not actually possess. Then if in the course of time they become aware that their claim is not based on reality, there is a temptation to maintain a false claim through a false gift and this, of course, if yielded to, is found to be injurious to the soul of the person who follows this course. In other words, there are certainly educated people among the Pentecostal tongues folks who have fairly well reached the conclusion that their hysterical, excited babbling is not the work of the Holy Spirit. At this point in their development, if these people go on making a false pretense to a spiritual gift which they know they do not have, their spiritual danger is very great, and we hope the Lord will give them strength not to make any such false profession.

Nevertheless we feel that there are thousands of illiterate and uneducated people who will continue to take their own jumping nerves and tortured minds as constituting a special gift of the Spirit, and no words of warning which we could utter would have any beneficial effect, perhaps.

BIRTH OF A REFORMATION

A.L. BYERS, pp. 355-356.

As soon as they arrived at the place of meeting they were accorded a strange reception. Those who were supposed to be saints at that place came to meet them, some dancing on one leg, some rolling their eyes in their head, others gibbering in tongues, or jerking or falling stiff, etc. At first they did not know what to make of the strange performance. At this place also was another attempt by a mob to capture Brother Warner. His report continues:

"We met also a much larger host of saints than we had expected to find in this country. Praise God for this! But oh, how soon we saw and felt that Satan, the deceiver, had passed a dreadful network of deception over them, or nearly all of them! Unseemly and even hideous operations and contortions were carried on and called the manifestations of the Spirit and power of God. We began at once to rebuke it in the name of the Lord Jesus. God gloriously blessed our souls in preaching his word and assured us that he had much people there who were honest and sincere at heart and who would be delivered by the presentation of his word. The supposed gift of tongues was alarmingly increasing. Indian war-dances, etc., had turned the church of God into something quite different, a disgusting maze of confusion. We were helped of God in teaching them "how they ought to behave themselves in the house of God, which is the church of the living God.

"A terrible nervous jerking had seized upon many in the meetings, which in some cases resembled much the St. Vitus' dance. We speak of these things in order to give the saints of God everywhere the benefit of what these precious souls have learned in the dear school of experience. We had never seen such manifestation except in persons possessed with devils, and yet the Spirit of God showed us these were not so possessed, but were, for the most part, still owned of the Lord. We read I Cor. 12, 13, 14 and showed the beautiful harmony of the church under the control of the Spirit of God; that 'love does not behave itself unseemly'; that the gift of tongues was not of general usefulness, and was a sign to the Jews, not generally edifying to the church; that other gifts should be sought in preference, and unless he or some one else interpret, the person having the gift should keep silent or speak to himself; that 'five words with the understanding is better than ten thousand in an unknown tongue'; that spasmodic jerking is not mentioned in the Bible as a manifestation of God's Spirit, but is ascribed to a malignant spirit."

CHRISTIAN THEOLOGY II

Albert F. Gray, (230 G778) pp. 90-91.

THE GIFT OF TONGUES. This gift is declared to be the least valuable of all. It is the power given by the Spirit to speak in a language not previously known. It has no practical value except as a sign to unbelievers. So far as we have record, it was never used in preaching. The gift of tongues is not to be confused with the meaningless, hysterical utterances that are sometimes substituted for it.

THE RECEIVING OF GIFTS. It is clear from the record that spiritual gifts are received in connection with the baptism with the Spirit. Such was the case on the Day of Pentecost and on other occasions. However, it appears that gifts may be received at other times also. They are distributed as the Spirit wills, and hence are not to be sought for at the wish of the individual. It is not to be expected that any one person will possess all the gifts and neither is there any one gift possessed by everyone. The assumption that the gift of tongues is given to all as the evidence of the baptism with the Holy Spirit is without foundation and is contrary to Paul's express statement that not all have the gift of tongues.

STUDIES IN THE NEW TESTAMENT

Otto F. Linn, (225 LI V2) p. 69.

From First Epistle to the Corinthians

In a city where from fifty to seventy-five languages and dialects were spoken, the gift of ecstatic speaking could easily be overestimated. Their utterances were definite languages which could be understood and interpreted, although the one speaking did not himself understand them, and in case no one present was able to interpret they should be reserved for private prayer (14:19-28), and even then it was better to pray with the understanding (vs. 14-15).

In their eagerness to display their gift of tongues there seems to have been a rush for first place (vs. 27), which caused disorder in the service. Paul's estimation of the importance of this gift may be seen in the subordinate place which he gives it in his list—three times he places it last. He urges them to seek the best gifts (12:31), which are to be determined by their use to the church (14:12).

THE HOLY SPIRIT AND OTHER SPIRITS

D.O. Teasley (231 T253) pp. 229-231.

DIVERS KINDS OF TONGUES. Wilson translates this "different language," which is its true meaning. The

Holy Spirit enabled those who had never learned a different language to speak it for the benefit of the hearers. Sometimes a Hebrew would have occasion to preach to a congregation who were mostly Greeks; in such a case the Holy Spirit gave him a different language. We have heard and read of some who claim to have the gift of tongues; but investigation has revealed the fact that they only chatter a kind of gibberish, which no one understands, and by which no one can be benefited. The gift of tongues is not a silly jargon, but an intelligible language, given for a purpose, and by which men may find salvation or be edified in the divine life.

It seems that those who had the gift of tongues could generally speak several languages; but even those who have received only one language by the Holy Spirit should be considered as having a part in this gift. We are acquainted with a brother who received the gift of speaking the Holland language. He being among Hollanders had a desire to tell them of the true Bible way, and after praying earnestly to God over the matter he was enabled to tell them of Jesus in their own language. God will doubtless restore this gift to his true people as they may have special need of it. The Spirit does not bestow this gift without purpose; therefore we shall receive the gift of tongues when we have need of it. For this reason also we should exercise our gifts when we receive them, lest we lose them.

INTERPRETATION OF TONGUES. This was simply the ability to interpret different languages, which ability was a direct gift of the Holy Spirit. This was much needed in the days of the apostles, as often a congregation would represent more than one language; and when such was the case an interpreter could be used to the glory of God to interpret the meaning of the speaker to the part of the congregation who could not understand. This gift will also be restored to the church of God when it has special need of it. God is at this time restoring to his church her pristine glory, and we expect all the gifts of the Spirit just as they were in the morning of Christianity, as far as God sees that we need them. We should at all times be in a humble attitude before God that he may at any time he sees fit bestow upon us any special gift he sees need of.

BOOKS FOR FURTHER STUDY

Myron Augsburger, *Quench Not the Spirit,* Herald Press, 1975.

> This book emphasizes the Lordship of Jesus Christ.

John R. Boyd, *The Holy Spirit and Tongues,* The Gospel Contact Press, Camrose, 1977.

> A short tract written by a Baptist pioneer preacher.

Charles W. Carter, *The Person and Ministry of the Holy Spirit: A Wesleyan Perspective,* Baker House, 1974.

> This is one of the most complete books on the Holy Spirit and fits well into the Church of God tradition.

Michael Green, *I Believe in the Holy Spirit,* Eerdmans, 1975.

> Here is a book written by an evangelical Anglican who writes with a slant towards tongues.

H.C. Heffren, *The Holy Spirit and the Charismatic Movement,* Gospel Contact Press, Camrose, 1975.

David Howard, *By the Power of the Holy Spirit,* Inter-Varsity Press, Downers Grove, 1973.

David Howard is Missions Director of Inter-Varsity Christian Fellowship. He writes in a non-technical way to university students. He writes in a very practical way with a favorable, yet reserved response to the tongues movement.

John Thomas Nichol, *Pentecostalism,* Harper and Row, 1966.

Here is a book written by a Pentecostal. It was written for a Ph.D. dissertation and is remarkably objective. The concern of this work is the story of growth and development of the Pentecostal force in American Protestantism.

From Babel to Pentecost.
By H. C. Heffren

ACCORDING to Genesis 11:1, there was a time on this earth when all men spoke one language. After the flood God commanded men to disperse over the earth but they refused to obey His voice. In defiance of His command they assembled on the plains of Shinar and determined to build a tower reaching from earth to heaven to prevent their being scattered throughout the world.

THE CONFUSION OF TONGUES

WITH consummate energy coupled with amazing ingenuity and skill they commenced their colossal task. Using plenty of slime for mortar they piled brick upon brick, tier upon tier, higher and higher until their building was the wonder of the world. Then a mysterious thing happened. Suddenly they could not understand one another. They became a confused and distracted mob hopelessly incapable of proceeding further with their gigantic enterprise. God's judgment had fallen upon them. Their tongues were confused and thus ended their attempt to defy God's Sovereign Will.

Let us ponder some of the lessons derived from this disastrous failure. First they wanted to make a name for themselves. "Go to, let us build us a tower and let us make us a name." It was "us, us" and God was left out. They forgot that His name is above every name and that He does not recognize the name we make for ourselves. Secondly, they tried to build a tower reaching to heaven that rested upon an earthly foundation. They built on the plain, and they used clay and slime. We learn from this that men cannot reach heaven by their own efforts. All such efforts are bound to fail, and with equal certainty will all human attempts to build a heaven on earth leaving God out lead to abject and total failure. Thirdly, it shows us that men can never thwart the sovereignty of God. They did disperse under God's judgment, leaving for themselves a name immortal in ignominy and tragic in its effect on mankind. The name is BABEL, a word that is synonymous with confusion.

Since the building of Babel men have varied their methods in every conceivable way but they have not deviated from their determination to amalgamate men into some kind of federation that leaves God out. Nations have formed alliances, mutual-aid-pacts. power blocs, economic treaties, have made leagues, formed unions and United Nations and solemnly pledged their word to innumerable peace treaties. But they have all ended in dismal failure. Instead of peace there has been discord, strife, hatred, mistrust, intrigue, confusion, frustration and periodic war. That is the record of men from the dawn of history, and is still in progress to-day, men are still trying to build a temple of peace without God, on the shifting plains of human wisdom, seeking to bind themselves together with ropes of sand in the form of diplomatic agreements. Not bring founded on the rock, it will certainly fail.

THE FUSION OF TONGUES

GOD'S PLAN is entirely different. He sent His Son Jesus Christ into the world and although men rejected and crucified Him He rose again. Obedient to His command, His followers congregated in the great temple at Jerusalem and waited for the promised outpouring of the Holy Spirit. After ten days of earnest prayer the Holy Spirit came and baptized each believer with cleansing fire. Immediately they were constrained to speak. They had to witness. One after another they followed Peter in declaring that Jesus Christ saves from sin. But the amazing thing was that everyone present heard what was said in his own dialect. Hearing the commotion multiplied, thousands of people hastened to see what happened and at least fifteen different language groups were represented in the crowd from various parts of the Roman Empire, and they all heard the gospel in the language of their birth. HERE WAS BABEL IN REVERSE. Men's tongues were unified through the Holy Spirit. The judgment of Babel was confusion; the blessing of Pentecost is unity. Babel typifies the futility of man's disobedience to God; Pentecost demonstrates how God's plan will work through obedience. From Babel's ruins comes mute evidence of defeat, but from Pentecost issues eloquent testimony of victory.

On the sure foundation of the apostles and prophets, Jesus Christ Himself being the chief corner stone, God has raised up the most unique structure in history. In contrast with the clay and slime on the plains of Shinar, God uses living stones, redeemed souls of men and women who are bound together by the love of God that is shed abroad in our hearts by the Holy Ghost as He builds His Church on Mount Zion. Into the walls of His building God places each redeemed member whom He likens to one of earth's rarest gems, cleansed and purified and fashioned to reflect the beauties of Jesus Christ, the Son of Righteousness. Together they present a spectacle of dazzling beauty and exquisite charm. This sacred shrine is the body of Christ, where all men are one and speak the same spiritual language and all bear the same spiritual image the image of the Son.

LIMITATIONS OF TONGUES

IN SUGGESTING a limitation of tongues we do not infer a limitation of the Holy Spirit. We must remember that God did not give us a code of rules setting forth each detail of Christian conduct. God gave us eternal principles which He expects us to apply to our moral conduct. He did not give us a book of theology or a doctrinal statement to chart our belief but He did give us spiritual life through faith in Jesus Christ. All creeds and doctrinal statements are the result of men's efforts to rationalize their spiritual experiences and explain spiritual phenomena. But the gift of the Holy Ghost cannot be reduced to any more formula. By making their personal experience arbitrary and binding on everyone else, men have produced the bewildering labyrinth of conflicting doctrines, sects, factions and contentions that afflict the religious world of to-day.

No one will deny the miracle of tongues on the day of Pentecost, but what Luke records is a FACT, not a DOCTRINE. It is true that one baptized with the Holy Ghost MAY speak in tongues but it is an entirely unwarranted conclusion to assume that one MUST do so. Whether we call tongues a "sign" or a "gift" is not the issue, for we are still confronted with the fact that Jesus told His disciples to wait for the Holy Ghost Himself, and not for a sign of him or a gift from Him. If a man gazed at the sun through a spectrum and beheld the violet rays of light we must concede that his testimony is true; but if he were to contend that no one had seen the sun until he recognized the violet rays thereof, he would be guilty of gross error, namely that the whole is less than its part. But that is exactly the position of those who claim the Holy Spirit does not baptize believers unless accompanied by tongues. Such a doctrine repudiates all the other gifts of the Spirit as not valid evidence, while the Bible definitely says that tongues is the least of the gifts.

It is obvious that the modern tongues movement is unscriptural in claiming to receive the Holy Spirit according to Acts2:4 because the tongues they claim to speak are not intelligible to anyone present, nor even to the person exercised. In Acts 2:4, everyone present understood what was said for it was spoken in his mother tongue. If, as some claim, there is a difference between the gift of tongues in Acts 2:4 and the sign of tongues in 1 Cor. 14, let me point out that their application of the sign is as unscriptural as their claim to the gift. For instance, 1 Cor. 14:22 say "That tongues are a sign to unbelievers." Tongues people make it a sign to themselves to prove to themselves and other members of their group that they have received the Holy Ghost. This is not scriptural. Furthermore, 1 Cor. 14:23-28, says speaking in tongues should never be indulged in by more that two or three, at one meeting and even then, only when an interpreter is present. When no interpreter is present the use of tongues is unconditionally forbidden lest the performance be thought madness by those who are present. Those who have attended tongues gatherings and tarry meetings know how frequently this plain admonition is violated. It is impossible for the Holy Ghost to disobey His own command which He inspired to Apostle Paul to include in the Word of God.

CONCLUSION

It is quite apparent that God did not give tongues to PROVE that the Holy Ghost had come. That momentous fact could not be hidden. God caused the believers to speak in tongues, first to demonstrate the unity of all men in the Holy Ghost in contrast with the confusion of all men at Babel. Secondly, He used it as a medium to spread the gospel to the greatest number of people on the shortest possible time. Again we say, this is a fact, but not necessarily a doctrine. The Holy Ghost cannot be limited in His operation.

God does not look for SIGNS in His people. He looks for FRUIT. 1 Cor. 13:1 say, "Though I speak with the tongues of men and of angels and have not love, I am become as sounding brass or a tinkling cymbal." The characteristics of the Holy Spirit's indwelling are unmistakable. First He fills us with a love for God and the people of God. If love is lacking it is vain to claim the Spirit's baptism regardless of what other experience we may have (1Cor 13). The Holy Spirit will glorify Christ (John 16). He enables us to understand the Scriptures, particularly those relating to the Deity of Christ (Luke 24:27, 44-47). He imparts gifts according to His will for the edification of the body of Christ to enable believers to become Christlike in measure and stature. (Eph. 4:11-13). In other words He will manifest Himself by demonstrations of power best calculated to glorify Christ in any circumstance. Never does He dispense His power or gifts for any selfish cause.

While we repudiate the false doctrines about the Holy Spirit, we contend most earnestly for faith in the Holy Spirit Himself. We believe in all His gifts. Christ enjoined His followers to wait for the Holy Spirit before entering upon their ministry. We cannot do less today. The need for the Holy Spirit is evident and every servant of Christ should seek His sanctifying Presence by consecrating to surrender entirely to do His will. Let Him fill you and bless you with whatever gift He may choose to give—or if He apparently gives none, remember the words of Paul, "Yet show I unto you a more excellent way." That way is love and the love of God is the only thing the Devil cannot duplicate. The devil can speak in tongues, do miracles and even preach, but the devil cannot produce the love of God. That is why love alone is the only ultimate proof of the presence of the Holy Spirit. A church filled with the Holy Spirit is the hope of mankind, the alternative to Babel and the longing of every seeking soul, as well as the joy of each believer.

[Included by permission of Gladys Krueger, the author's daughter.]

Rethinking Biblical Tongues.
By H.C. Heffren

ON THE DAY OF PENTECOST a very special visitation from God came to the believers assembled in Jerusalem when the promise of Jesus was fulfilled. The believers were filled with the Holy Ghost and began to speak with other tongues. Manifestly, they were languages for the listeners were amazed, saying,

> **"Behold, are not all these that speak Galileans? And how hear we every man in our own tongue, wherein we were born?"**

> (Acts 2:7b,8)

Those who advocate "tongues" as a deeper work of the Spirit should ask themselves some questions: "Did Jesus ever speak in tongues?" Did He ever encourage His followers to speak thus?" "Did any of the New Testament writers ever advocate speaking in tongues?" If the answer to these questions is "No," then upon what authority does the phenomenon of "glossolalia" or "speaking in tongues" rest?

In I Corinthians 14, Paul encountered the misuse of tongues and tried rectifying it. He showed that tongues was the least of the spiritual gifts and was always the last and least of the gifts. By comparison Paul said, **"Greater is he that prophesieth than he that speaketh with tongues"** (I Cor. 14:5). To further emphasize his point, he said, **"Yet in the church I had rather speak five words with my understanding, that by my voice I might teach others also, than 10,000 words in** an unknown tongue." (I Cor. 14:19) A rule to go by is I Corinthians 14:9, **"So likewise ye, except ye utter by the tongue words easy to be understood, how shall it be known what is spoken? For ye shall speak into the air."**

We should note the following regulations regarding the use of tongues. **"If any man speak in an unknown tongue, let it be by two, or at the most by three, and let one interpret"** (I Cor. 14:27) The next verse clarifies this by saying, **"But if there be no interpreter, let him keep silence in the church."** The **interpreter** in this case is someone capable of understanding the speaker and giving his message in the language spoken by the congregation in that place. It does not refer to unintelligible sounds which someone may claim to be "Jesus is coming soon" or some such phrase . . . "An interpreter is someone whose business is translating from a foreign language" (Thorndike-Barnhart Dictionary). The point to observe is that an "interpreter" is a "translator." The Bible uses this word in this manner: "Talitha cumi: which is being *interpreted,* Damsel, I say unto thee, arise." (Mark 5:41b) In Acts 9:36, we read, "Now, there was at Joppa a certain disciple named Tabitha, which by interpretation is called Dorcas . . ."

The matter of "interpretation" seems relatively important because Paul refers to it three times in I Corinthians 14. In verse 5b, the last clause says, **"except he interpret, that the church may receive edifying."** In verse 13, **"Wherefore let him that speaketh in an unknown tongue pray that he may interpret . . ."** And in verses 27-28, **"If any man speak in an unknown tongue, let it be by two, or at the most by three, and that by course (in turn); and let one interpret. But if there be no interpreter, let him (the one speaking)**

keep silence in the church; and let him speak to himself and to God." The scriptural limitations of speaking in tongues is such that there should only be a maximum of three during any one service and then only provided that an **interpreter** be present.

An interesting observation is made in *Clarke's Abridged Commentary* (p. 1119), "God grants no ungovernable gifts." In this connection, we read in I Corinthians 14:33, **"For God is not the author of confusion,"** and Paul sums it up by saying, **"Let all things be done decently and in order"** (v. 40).

Paul is not precluding the exercise of the Spirit in any spiritual gifts, provided they are exercised decently (i.e., honorably, modestly, honestly) and in a manner that edifies the church. Order must be maintained for that is the rule of the universe, that all things operate within the confines of God's eternal law and order. If these stipulations are followed, the result is **peace.** If they are not followed, the end result is **confusion** (which is identified as tumult, divisions, fanaticism or want of order). God is the author of **peace and order,** not confusion and discord!

In I Corinthians 14:9-12, Paul exhorts, **Unless you speak intelligible words with your tongue, how will anyone know what you are saying? You will just be speaking into the air. Undoubtedly there are all sorts of languages in the world, yet none of them is without meaning. If then, I do not grasp the meaning of what someone is saying, I am a foreigner to the speaker, and he is a foreigner to me. So it is with you. Since you are eager to have spiritual gifts, try to excel in gifts that build up the church.** (New Internat'l Version)

It will be noticed that Paul recognized the existence of many languages in the world but, interestingly, did **not** even refer to any incomprehensible, incoherent sounds as "language" or the so-called "prayer language." Such a performance may be called "prayer language" but it is definitely not what Paul advocated. He says, in I Corinthians 14:15,

> **"So what shall I do? I will pray with my spirit, but I will also pray with my mind."**

Adam Clarke's comment on this verse is edifying:

"And I will pray with the understanding, also." He says, *"I will endeavor so to pray that others may understand me, and thus be edified and improved by my prayers. And therefore I will pray in a language in the public congregation that may be understood by all present, so that all may join not only in the act but in the spirit of devotion."* (op. cit., p.1118) When a group gives vent to unintelligible speaking, it should be extremely cautious about attributing such exercises to the Spirit of God, for God grants no ungovernable gifts! Furthermore, the tongues to which Paul refers is specifically aimed at convincing unbelievers rather than believers (1 Cor. 14:23). If there is widespread babbling, even in foreign languages, the listeners may regard this as evidence of insanity (see 1 Cor. 14:23).

The identifying hallmark of a Christian is not gifts, but love. Jesus said, **"By this shall all men know that ye are my disciples, if ye have love one to another"** (John 13:35 KJV) Perhaps the most comprehensive statement about the work of the Holy Ghost is given by Christ in John 14:26:

> But the Comforter, which is the Holy
> Ghost, whom the Father will send in
> my name, He shall teach you all things
> and will bring all things to your re-
> membrance, whatsoever I have said
> unto you."

Although Christ gave a detailed account of what the Holy Ghost would accomplish, He did not here, or at any other place, suggest that "tongues" would accompany His coming or give evidence of His presence. Jesus further stated,

> "And when He (the Holy Ghost) is
> come, He will reprove the world of sin,
> of righteousness and of judgment . . .
> He will guide you into all truth . . . He
> shall glorify me." (John 16:8, 13, 14)

The prime purpose of the Holy Ghost is to glorify Christ and to edify the church. No gift of His is given for personal benefit or for manipulative reasons. The instruction given by Paul is definite:

> . . . forasmuch as ye are zealous of
> spiritual gifts, seek that ye may excel
> to the edifying of the church. (I Cor.
> 14:12)

We have no right to misconstrue what Paul is saying, for he says, "If any man think himself to be a prophet or spiritual, let him acknowledge that the things I write unto you **are the commandments of the Lord."** (I Cor. 14:37) Since Paul claims to have divine authority for his instruction on the proper use of tongues, we would do well to follow his words scrupulously!

Paul did not ban or prohibit the speaking with tongues. He is obviously not giving license to any childish prattle, for he says, "Be not children in understanding; howbeit in malice be ye children, but in understanding be men." (I Cor. 14:20) An infant may prattle in unrecognizable childish syllables, but the mark of maturity is exhibited when a person uses his mind and reason to communicate. Paul says, ". . . when I became a man, I put away childish things." The thinking, speaking and understanding of a child is not bad; it just needs to grow up and mature . . .

BEING "SLAIN IN THE SPIRIT"

Perhaps some are troubled about this phenomenon? Is this a genuine spiritual takeover of a sincere seeker after a deeper spiritual life? This is a fair question and it demands an authentic answer.

To be "slain in the Spirit" may quite likely indicate that the person is seeking spiritual help but through the coaching of his advisor or friends yields to some urge within and succumbs to a power that causes him to be unable to control his physical body, thus dropping to the floor where he/she remains inert for an indefinite time.

The following observations seem pertinent: We read in Luke 4:1,

"And Jesus returned in the power of the Spirit into Galilee."

Every act of Christ was an act guided by the Holy Spirit. Even His atonement was effected through the cooperation of the Holy Spirit, for in Hebrews we read,

"How much more shall the blood of Christ, who through the eternal Spirit, offered Himself . . ." The life of Christ, from His humble birth to His ultimate ascension, was lived **in the Spirit**. Yet, we never read of Christ "being slain in the Spirit" or of His advocating others to be "slain in the Spirit!"

Pentecost was the place the Holy Ghost was poured out on all flesh, yet we have no knowledge of anyone there having been "slain in the Spirit." In I John 4:1 we read, "Beloved, believe not every spirit, but try the spirits whether they are of God: because many false spirits are gone out into the world." Does being slain of the Spirit exalt and give preeminence to Christ in such a way that it glorifies Christ? (John 16:14) Does being "slain in the Spirit" *edify* the church? (I Cor. 14:5, 12, 26) When a person "goes under the power" and falls to the floor while some helpers cover him/her with blankets, does this comply with Paul's injunction, "Let all *things* be done *decently and in order*"? (I Cor. 14:40) (i.e., done with becoming reverence, with gravity and intelligent composure and infinite dignity because what we do is offered to Deity).

To conclude, the Holy Spirit will glorify Christ, edify the Church, and produce actions that will result in order, peace and genuine love. □ —H.C.H.

[Included by permission of Gladys Krueger, the author's daughter]

Move When the Spirit Says Move!
A Biblical and Theological Investigation of Selected Phenomena of the Spirit.
By Dr. James W. Lewis

INTRODUCTION

"In the Spirit." This is a phrase frequently used by Christians to describe and authenticate elements of their worship and their own behaviors. Depending on who uses the phrase (or one like it) and for what purposes, the environment of worship might be described as quiet and reflective or loud and ecstatic. In many venues of worship and Christian living, the call to faithfulness requires that the believer "move when the Spirit says move."[10] Christians have been known to label another's Christian experience of the Spirit as authentic, depending on their particular beliefs and practices of the Holy Spirit. At all points in the history of the church, teachings on the Holy Spirit have been crucial in instructing the faithful. Authors have written volumes about the Holy Spirit throughout the centuries. Today is no exception. Academics, pastors, apostles, television evangelists, and others are making their contributions to the growing literature.

What I believe all these writers and thinkers have in common is that what they believe about the Holy Spirit and what they attribute to the Holy Spirit are cru-

---

[10] This is a line from a Spiritual, adapted by Ryan D. Neaveill.

---

cial for what they think promotes the ongoing life of the Christian faith. Yet, no book can presume to capture all that needs to be said and that can be said about the Holy Spirit.[11] In this paper, I am more interested in the "phenomena" of the Holy Spirit. The physical manifestations many attribute to the Holy Spirit prompt the writing of this paper.

As Christians battle for "orthodoxy" concerning the Spirit, what often gets left behind is that love which Christians are commanded to have for one another. I am well aware that the most important witness to a hurting world is the manifestation of God's love in the community of faith and in the world God created (John 13:34-35; 17:23). I write this paper as one who desires to be open to all the Holy Spirit wants to visit upon His church and upon His people. Even as I affirm this desire, I still contend with an inward suspicion that I am less open than I care to admit. In my limited observations of church life, many Christians know much too little and others know far too much about the possible workings and manifestations of the Holy Spirit.[12]

---

[11] There are many theological positions and paradigms out of which Christians think and live their lives. It is not the scope of this work to address all these positions. I gladly leave it to others to speak more forthrightly from their particular theological and ecclesial traditions.

[12] John Wimber – a former Fuller Seminary professor and Missionary – provides an enlightening discussion of worldview, which might inform the Spirit-filled life. A proponent of Signs and Wonders, Wimber's discussion is a wonderful attempt to suggest how worldviews influence one's openness to the possibility of Signs and Wonders in the material world. Those of us in western societies tend to be more secularized, Wimber argues, walling off this world from divine and spiritual interventions. As Christians,

So I do not write this paper to suggest that those who disagree in whole or in part with the intent of the paper are not Christians. I realize there are brothers and sisters whose beliefs, practices, and experiences of the Spirit differ from my own. Yet they might display in compelling ways a love for God and for others. My emphasis here is different. The specific concern I address in this paper instead is the troubling tendency of claiming biblical and theological warrants for certain phenomena of the Spirit, when no clear biblical and theological warrants seem to exist. Too frequently this tendency in the church produces widespread confusion, blatant distrust, and inconsistent practices in our worship experiences and daily walk of faith.[13]

---

our worldview should not be determined by the logic and criteria of scientific rationality. Wimber is right also that our worldview as Christians determine our expectations and our theology in the area of Signs and Wonders [Spiritual phenomena]. See John Wimber [with Kevin Springer], *Power Evangelism: Signs and Wonders Today* (Toronto: Hodder and Stoughton, 1985), see especially chapter 5, "Signs and Wonders and Worldviews." *I acknowledge here that my attempt to do this work is not immune to such western tendencies. However, I doubt if anyone can separate themselves totally from cultural influences. I do hope, however, that my efforts here are guided by nobler purposes to be in service to the church. All who care about these matters are under the same requirement to exercise humility and to expect the Trinitarian God to guide.*

[13] My reading of Scripture is primarily as Narrative. The Bible is fundamentally a true story of God's dealings with God's creation. While I will reference many Scriptures in this book, I do so in view of their contributions to the overall story of God-with-us. My colleague, Dr. Sharon Pearson, presents a compelling case for this in her inductive study of Luke-Acts that the descriptions of the phenomena surrounding Pentecost are several and mixed. As fundamentally a narrative, Luke-Acts does not intend to be doctrinal in the limited sense of that term. This is one weakness, in my

One can ask: Can't God through the Spirit do a new thing? I refuse to insist that God can not do this. Such an insistence would be arrogant indeed. However, my purpose in this paper is to focus on a "biblical and theological" assessment of selected phenomena of the Spirit. The phenomena covered in this assessment include Speaking in Tongues, Being Slain in the Spirit, and Laughing in the Spirit (Holy Laughter).[14] These three phenomena of the Spirit were the topics I addressed in a shorter paper delivered at the North American Convention of the Church of God in Anderson, Indiana. This doctrinal dialogue convened in the summer of 2005. From my initial research for the presentation until the present moment, I have sensed the continuing relevance of this topic for the church.

Though I stand firmly in the Wesleyan-Holiness tradition of the Church of God (Anderson, IN.), I wish to speak to all Christians. Admittedly, all Christians will not resonate with my particular readings of certain texts or the implications drawn from certain texts. While I could hope for agreement, I do not even expect

---

opinion, in much of the discussion regarding the phenomena of the Spirit. Rather, Pearson understands Luke's primary purpose in the book of Acts is to highlight the church's empowerment to witness, the joy the gospel brings, the signifying power of baptism as a norm for all Christians, and the theme of Luke-Acts as God's good news for all people. I agree with Pearson's understanding of the basic message of Luke-Acts. I believe it to be just the right kind of emphasis which preserves the truth of Scripture and promotes Scripture's intention to produce disciples of Jesus in a dynamic community of the Spirit.

[14] I have chosen not to include Divine Healing. This is a historical teaching of the Church of God (Anderson), and, on the whole, does not generate the kind of confusion other phenomena do.

---

total agreement from those who do share my particular church tradition. Nevertheless I write this paper to be accessible to all Christians who believe that this subject is important to their vocation as disciples of Jesus Christ.

Except for purposes of clarity, then, this paper will not involve a systematic study of the person and work of the Holy Spirit. First, such a task would go well beyond the scope of this book. Second, there are significant earlier and later works by Church of God (Anderson, Indiana) authors on this subject.[15] I believe it is crucial to acknowledge upfront that the Church of God early pioneers appeared to be open to all that the Holy Spirit might visit on them. There was a yearning for real experiences of the Holy Spirit. Certainly this desire included the acknowledgment and legitimacy of a variety of phenomena of the Spirit. While they would not do so in an uncritical manner, they did make space, it seems to me, for a variety of experiences.

I have chosen to focus my primary search on the earlier periods of the Church of God. I do this for two reasons. First, the more recent works by Church of God authors provide excellent theological and biblical discussions of the Holy Spirit. Yet, very little space is given to the physical, demonstrable phenomena associated

---

[15] Merle D. Strege, *I Saw the Church: The Life of the Church of God told Theologically* (Anderson, In.: Warner Press, 2002); John W. V. Smith, *The Quest for Holiness and Unity* (Anderson, In.: Warner Press, Inc., 1980; Barry L. Callen, *Contours of a Cause: The Theological Vision of the Church of God Movement (Anderson)* (Anderson, In.: Anderson School of Theology, 1995); Gilbert W. Stafford, *Theology for Disciples* (Anderson, In.: Warner Press, 1996).

with the Spirit; perhaps the exception might be Speaking in Tongues. It just seems to me that it would be interesting to connect with the period in our evolving tradition where more space seems to have been given to such phenomena of the Spirit. Second, this attention to the earlier tradition invites us into fresh conversation about issues that we otherwise might keep on the periphery.

If disciples today truly care about faithfulness to the Spirit, then we cannot neglect to give attention also to how those who preceded us in the historic faith have thought about these matters. May we honor their faithfulness and their efforts to "move when the Spirit says move." To assist me in this, a principal source that I will use for documenting Church of God responses, direct or indirect, is the respected work of the late Kenneth Tippin, whose extraordinary labors in mining these responses remain a gift to the broader church.[16] Of course, a variety of other sources also will be utilized in this paper.

In the July 1, 1884 issue of *The Gospel Trumpet*, D.S. Warner said, "God will lead us much farther out into the deep things of God, and put upon the saints a power and glory that has never yet been reached....Yea we are not only looking for the return of the 'early

---

[16] Kenneth R. Tippin, ed., *Powerful Words: Radical Words Then and Now* (Sturgis, MI.: Douglas Carr, Gateway River of Life Ministries, 2001, First Printing). This is a completed volume covering approximately the first four chapters of a broader manuscript. Both these sources are located in the Church of God Archives, Anderson University, Anderson, Indiana. In this paper, the book will be cited according to convention, but references to the manuscript will be noted as **Tippin Manuscript.**

rain,' the Apostolic power; but in addition the 'latter rain' also...." In another article in *The Gospel Trumpet*, "The Spirit's Indwelling," Warner says:

> [T]he Holy Spirit can calm down in the soul, but because the Holy Spirit resides in us, his mighty power is always ready to spring forth into "vehement" action, and "thrilling" flashes through our consciousness....[17]

E.E. Byrum also observed and commented on the legitimacy of diverse responses to the move of the Holy Spirit:

> There may be a number of persons converted at the same time, yet their actions or operations of the Spirit may be widely different. While one may leap and shout and manifest great physical performances, another one may sit quietly down without a word or outward manifestation, and yet be just as thoroughly converted, just as free from the guilt of sin, and with as positive knowledge of an acceptance with God as the one who makes such an outward manifestation.[18]

H.M. Riggle also expresses assurance that God is up to something. According to Riggle, "...God is nurs-

---

[17] *GT* (April 1, 1887) quoted in Tippin, *Powerful Words*, 113-114.

[18] E.E. Byrum, *The Secret of Salvation*, 76, quoted in Tippin, *Powerful Words*, 116.

ing a storm in the heavens, and I pray God it may soon break upon us. Oh, that heaven's lightning would strike the church and burn up the dry sticks! Let it come, Lord. I can hear the distant thunder-roll."[19] Further, J.W. Byers, in an 1895 *Gospel Trumpet* article wrote that "today the great need of the church is the power and accompanying manifestations of apostolic days....We must receive the endowment of holy boldness, and dare to declare the whole truth of the gospel. Brethren, we have been weak on this line."[20] These few historical reminders make our present concerns both necessary and relevant.

I acknowledge that this paper might prove more helpful to some by taking into account the social, economic, cultural, and psychological influences on these manifestations. This is a hard task and would make the scope of this book unnecessarily broader than it needs to be. So I have chosen to limit my investigation more to a descriptive discussion. I try, however, to provide a broader context in which to place my more specific examination of Church of God responses. It is not a detailed historical account preferred by professional historians. Yet, I hope that readers still see some value in this method, despite its limitations.

I have placed this historical context in chapter two. In each chapter that follows, I will focus more on how particular authors within the context of the Church of God (Anderson, Ind.) have reflected on the phenomenon under examination, and then offer my personal reactions or assessments. Chapter three will focus on

---

[19] H.M. Riggle, *Pioneer Evangelism*, 55-57; quoted in Tippin, *Powerful Words, 119.*

[20] Quoted in *Tippin Manuscript*, 396.

Speaking in Tongues. Then, I will examine the phenomenon of Being Slain in the Spirit in chapter four. The final phenomenon in chapter five is Holy Laughter and its attendant phenomena[21]. I will conclude in chapter six—perhaps the most important chapter--with a reminder about how we are commanded by Jesus to relate to each other, even in the midst of different perspectives on the phenomena of the Spirit. In many ways this is the most crucial of all the chapters. The previous chapters are important, but may for many people raise more questions than they provide answers. The final chapter seeks to provide the most fundamental context in which all discussions on the phenomena of the Spirit should rest. While all Christians must move when the Spirit says move, this obedience to the Holy Spirit becomes displayed always in a lifestyle of love for our sisters and brothers – the body of Christ, the church.

PHENOMENA OF THE SPIRIT: HISTORICAL OBSERVATIONS AND CONNECTIONS

Talking about the role of the Holy Spirit in historic and contemporary revivals is not an unusual association. It is crucial. Yet, the discussions are diverse and complex. How does one know it is the Holy Spirit actually working in people's lives? Are there other legitimate factors to consider when describing manifestations of the Spirit? How can one be sure that those who experience the move of the Spirit are describing the experience accurately and adequately? Should descriptions of

---

[21] This work will not include the chapters on Being Slain in the Spirit or Holy Laughter.

these manifestations always rise to the level of doctrine or orthodoxy?

Anyone seeking to grapple with this whole area of the phenomena of the Spirit must face these daunting questions. As stated in the Introduction, this work is intentionally limited to a biblical and theological investigation of selected phenomena.

There is little doubt that these outward manifestations occurred. Whether they are in all cases products of the Holy Spirit may be much less certain. The case can be made that these manifestations or phenomena were not pervasive. Also, in reading accounts of some of the revivals, one cannot be completely certain that the manifestations today refer identically to the earlier phenomena or to phenomena described in the Scriptures.

In addition, as a reminder, the limitation associated with this work does not account for social, economic, political, and psychological factors that might contribute to or influence these manifestations. There are also regional and denominational factors that provide varying explanations of what and how phenomena of the Spirit are talked about and acted out.

William G. McLoughlin provides a helpful analysis of revivals and awakenings by placing them within broader contexts of human interactions: (1) the First Great Awakening [1730-1760], (2) the Second Great Awakening [1800-1830], (3) the Third Great Awakening [1890-1920], and (4) the Fourth Great Awakening [1960-90 (?)].[22] To keep this chapter manageable, I will

---

[22] William G. McLoughlin, *Revivals, Awakenings, and Reform: An Essay on Religion and Social Change in America, 1607-1977*, Chicago History of American Religion, ed. Martin E.

focus primarily on the First and Second Great Awakenings, with even more space given to the Second Great Awakening. Within the Second Great Awakening, I will examine particularly what sometimes is named The Great Revival, with Cane Ridge in Kentucky being an illustrative representative. I do this because this period seems to capture "similarities" with more contemporary phenomena.

The First Great Awakening [1730-1760]

Representatives of this period include giants like George Whitefield, Gilbert Tennent, Jonathan Edwards, John and Charles Wesley. McLoughlin indicates that this period includes "direct, visualized experiences of the senses."[23] Note Charles G. Finney's description of a "mighty baptism of the Holy Ghost" that overwhelmed him:

> The Holy Spirit descended upon me in a manner that seemed to go through me, body and soul. I could feel the impression, like a wave of electricity.... Indeed it seemed to come in waves and waves of liquid love....It seemed like the very breath of God. I can recollect distinctly that it seemed to fan me, like immense wings....

Marty (Chicago: University of Chicago Press, 1978). His is an excellent example of accounting for such influences on how and why people responded as they did. For example, he offers five broad categories of explanation of the First Great Awakening. See McLoughlin, 52-53.

[23] Ibid., 65.

I wept aloud with joy and love; and I do
not know but I should say, I literally bellowed out the unutterable gushings of
my heart....[24]

This account by Finney definitely contains evidence of a dynamic move of the Spirit: *wave of electricity, liquid love, the very breath of God, loud weeping,
the unutterable gushings of the heart.* Feelings, impressions, weeping, the unutterable, and so forth are all part
of the landscape in these early revivals. However, we
are less certain about how these manifestations actually
looked. We do not have videos.

Furthermore, according to McLoughlin—Jonathan
Edwards, labeled as the "leading theologian" of the
First Great Awakening—based his analysis of conversion on 'sensational' [sensory perception] psychology.[25]
If McLoughlin is right, he further argued that Edwards
believed humans' affections must be touched. "The
physical manifestations are side effects, symptomatic of
an inner change of heart."[26] Take note of this. While
Edwards certainly embraced the role of the religious
affections, he linked this understanding to "an inner
change of heart." One could argue—and some did and
still do —that being moved by the Spirit in ecstatic
ways is not an end-in-itself. They evidenced changed
lives. What of the memorable line by John Wesley indi-

---

[24] Charles G. Finney, *Memoirs of Rev. Charles G. Finney
Written By Himself* (New York, 1876), 18-21, quoted in Bernard
A. Weisberger, *They Gathered at the River: The Story of the Great
Revivalists and Their Impact Upon Religion in America (Boston:
Little, Brown and Company, 1958), 92-93.*
[25] McLoughlin, 71.
[26] Ibid., 74, 75.

cating that his heart was "strangely warmed"? What
followed that experience of being "warmed" proved to
be the ongoing depth of transformation in his life.

The Second Great Awakening [1800-1830]

Key representatives during this period include
Charles Grandison Finney and Peter Cartwright [in the
South]. I will focus on the southern expression of this
revival, since it appears so illustrative of some of the
phenomena under examination. A few words about
Charles G. Finney are in order. His impact in American
religious life through mass revivals is undeniably powerful. There are some accounts indicating "that inhabitants became so thoroughly wrought up that they literally fell off their seats in a state of shock and ecstasy."[27]
Thousands of converts were won to the Lord by Finney's faithful efforts. Many onlookers, however, labeled such conversions as "emotional excesses."[28] "Yet
Finney was not an advocate of emotionalism for its own
sake."[29] Finney believed that religion was to turn human attention to God and God's claims on their lives.[30]
Even with the emotional responses to the moving of the
Spirit, Finney in his *Memoirs* cited some "striking characteristics" of these revivals:

> (1) The prevalence of a mighty Spirit of
> prevailing prayer. (2) Overwhelming
> conviction of sin. (3) Sudden and power-
> ful conversions to Christ. (4) Great love

---

[27] McLoughlin, 123.
[28] Ibid.
[29] Ibid., 126.
[30] Ibid.

and abounding joy of the converts. (5)
Intelligence and stability of the converts.
(6) Their great earnestness, activity, and
usefulness in their prayers and labors for
others.[31]

It seems clear that even while many experienced
powerful manifestations of the Spirit's presence, Finney
is just as clear above about the "striking characteristics"
of the revivals. Let us turn our attention to a well-
documented revival in the South. In the area of Cane
Ridge, Kentucky, persons experienced powerful manifestations that they attributed to the Holy Spirit.[32] Peter
Cartwright is one interesting figure who narrates some
of the experiences of Cane Ridge. Other sources will
round out this discussion.

The Great Revival in the South

In his analysis of The Great Revival [like at Cane
Ridge, Kentucky], John B. Boles identifies six distinct
varieties of "exercises"[33]: (1) the falling exercises, (2)

---

[31] Charles G. Finney, *The Memoirs of Charles G. Finney*.
Garth M. Rosell and Richard A.G. Dupuis, eds. (Grand Rapids,
MI.: Zondervan, 1989), 239, quoted in Wesley Duewel, *Revival
Fire* (Grand Rapids, MI.: Zondervan Publishing Company, 1995),
105.

[32] While the emphasis centers on Cane Ridge, similar descriptions of the purported move of the Spirit would apply to portions of Tennessee, North and South Carolina, Virginia, and Georgia.

[33] John B. Boles, *The Great Revival, 1787-1805: The Origins of the Southern Evangelical Mind* (Lexington, KY.: The University Press of Kentucky, 1972), 67-68.

the rolling exercises, (3) the 'jerks', (4) the barking exercise [see chapter 5], (5) the dancing exercises, and (6) the laughing and singing exercises [see chapter 5]. Some firsthand accounts appear to support Boles' conclusion.

In his autobiography, Peter Cartwright provides an insider's view of frontier camp meetings. The outpouring of the Spirit at Cane Ridge Camp-meeting between 1800 and 1801 in the upper part of Kentucky is a case-in-point. It is here that Cartwright saw "hundreds fall prostrate under the mighty power of God, as men [sic] slain in battle."[34] As the revival spread throughout the Cumberland area, Cartwright recalls how ministers of different denominations came together and preached night and day, four or five days at a time.[35] According to Cartwright, there were camp meetings that lasted three to four weeks.

He makes an interesting observation. "He saw more than a hundred sinners fall like dead men under one powerful sermon, and heard more than five hundred Christians shouting aloud the high praises of God at once."[36] In his autobiographical account, Cartwright appears to value "moderation": He says, "In this great revival the Methodists kept moderately balanced; for we had excellent preachers to steer the ship or guide the flock. But some of our members ran wild, and indulged in some extravagances that were hard to control."[37]

---

[34] W.P. Strickland, ed., *Autobiography of Peter Cartwright: The Backwoods Preacher* (Cincinnati, OH.: The Methodist Book Concern, 1856), 30.
[35] Strickland, 45.
[36] Ibid., 45-46.
[37] Ibid., 46.

What were some of the "extravagances" to which Cartwright alludes? What he called the "great revival" from 1801 well into the following years, Cartwright writes about certain "powerful exercises."[38] Among these powerful exercises were the 'jerks,' which was overwhelming in its effects upon the bodies and minds of the people. "Saints or sinners" apparently engaged in these exercises.[39] A warm song or a sermon could lead people into convulsive jerking all over, which they could not stop. The only way, according to Cartwright, to find relief from jerking required that "they rise up and dance."[40]

"Other strange and wild exercises" included the "running, jumping, barking exercise."[41] In addition, there was what he considered "the most troubling delusion of all." This involved some that fell into trances and saw visions. They could lie motionless for days or weeks at a time, without food or drink. Upon awakening, they would claim to have seen heaven and hell, to have seen God, angels, the devil and the damned. "They would prophesy, and, under the pretense of Divine inspiration, predict the time of the end of the world, and the ushering in of the great millennium."[42]

In his book, Boles reported eyewitness descriptions of "the common falling exercises [as] the collapse into a semi-conscious state, after which many arose to shout praises to their God."[43] During this time period, Barton

---

[38] Ibid., 48.
[39] Ibid.
[40] Ibid.
[41] Strickland, 51.
[42] Ibid., 51-52
[43] Boles, 68.

W. Stone of Cane Ridge also narrated some of the events of the earliest outpourings at Logan County, Kentucky. According to Stone, "many, very many, fell down as men slain in battle, and continued for hours…in an apparently breathless and motionless state….After dying for hours they obtained deliverance."[44] He further reports that when such people later offered their testimonies, others might "fall down into the same state from which the speakers had just been delivered."[45]

Cartwright viewed the *jerks* as judgment sent from God, first, to bring sinners to repentance. Secondly, to show believers that God could work with or without means, and do whatever seems good to Him.[46] Interestingly enough, Cartwright saw them all as delusions for weak-minded, ignorant, and superstitious persons. For jerking, Cartwright indicated he would recommend fervent prayer as a remedy. According to him, fervent prayer "almost uniformly proved an effectual remedy."[47] Cartwright's paradoxical view of these exercises finds some support from others.

Barton Stone's account of the revival's spread throughout Kentucky, Georgia and the Carolinas included his observation of what he called "extravagances and vagaries."[48] According to Barton Stone, the preachers did not attempt to suppress these actions as might

---

[44] Frank G. Beardsley, *A History of American Revivals*, 3rd ed. (New York: American Tract Society, 1904 and 1912), 92-93.

[45] Ibid.

[46] Beardsley, 51.

[47] Ibid.

[48] Ibid., 94.

have been done in areas where people were more learned. The preaching services, he writes, "were attended with outcries, faintings, convulsions, 'falling under the power of God,' *hysterical* weeping and *laughter* [emphasis mine], and a peculiar species of exercise called the 'jerks.'[49] Weisberger recounts one man's experience at Cane Ridge who was not by nature a mystic nor a zealot. Doing all he could to resist the impulse of frenzy surrounding him, he finally went to his knees, gave a shout and fell prostrate. Some neighbors put him to bed. When he awoke, feeling release, he went home *"uncontrollably laughing* [emphasis mine], weeping, and shouting most of the way."[50]

It is interesting to note that these manifestations were understood by many as part and parcel of a mighty move of the Holy Spirit. Others permitted them but saw most as excessive. Still others pointed to them as justification to discredit the entire revival. John B. Boles believed that many persons pointed to these "exercises" to discredit the revival. Yet, he also believed that these "grossly exaggerated revival exercises … were probably restricted to a comparative few."[51]

Another basis on which some sought to discredit the revival rested on denominational and regional perspectives. Weisberger argued as such: "The Atlantic

---

[49] Ibid., 94-95.

[50] James B. Finley, *Autobiography of Rev. James B. Finley, or Pioneer Life in the West*, ed. W. P. Strickland (Cincinnati, 1853), 15-16, 99-118, 147-70, quoted in Weisberger, 33-34.

[51] Boles, 68. I do not believe we can know for sure about the numbers. It does appear, however, that many were not willing to discount what probably was a legitimate move of the Spirit due to any "excesses" that manifested themselves.

phase of the Great Revival of 1800 was characterized by leaders considered better bred and cultivated."[52] According to McLoughlin,

To New Englanders the camp-meeting revivals of the years 1798-1808 were barbarous emotional outbreaks ....The revivalistic excesses of the frontier (which later psychologists were also to attribute to the primitive quality of wilderness life) were crude appeals to 'the animal emotions' of illiterate half-educated, half-savage men and women who had strayed too far from the institutional order of decent society.[53]

These value-laden descriptions above indicate the belief of many that such displays were more indicative of crass emotionalism and illiteracy, than a legitimate move of the Holy Spirit. No doubt this is the view of many today in relation to any emotional display attributed to the Holy Spirit. Just as instructive is the conclusion of some eyewitnesses that these fervent displays attending the revivals calmed with the passing of time.

For example, in his influential work on frontier camp meetings, Charles A. Johnson argues that "the 'falling exercise' was the most common of all forms of bodily excitement...."[54] In a revival at Providence, Kentucky in 1801, during a falling exercise, "women in their frantic agitations sometimes 'unconsciously tore open their bosoms and assumed indelicate attitudes'."[55] In Johnson's work, he includes a chapter subsequent to

---

[52] Weisberger, 50.

[53] McLoughlin, 107.

[54] Charles A. Johnson, *The Frontier Camp Meeting: Religion's Harvest Time*, Dallas, Texas: Southern Methodist University Press, 1955); 57.

[55] Ibid.

these descriptions entitled "The Camp Meeting Matures." In this chapter he indicates that "Thomas S. Hinde, untiring reporter of western Methodism in its earlier years, did not make a single mention of 'barking, running, jumping, or falling' taking place after the Great Revival."[56] Furthermore, from 1834-1844, reports from the *Western Christian Advocate* regularly reported the following: "'Good order and solemnity prevailed throughout.'"[57] Weisberger comes to a similar conclusion in his work. He agreed that this revival was "characterized initially by tears and shouts and such wild dances as David performed before the ark of the Lord."[58] However, according to Weisberger, the revival had become institutionalized for the most part in what came to be known as the "camp meeting." He said that "by 1830 the genuinely frenzied and spontaneous frontier revival was largely a memory. It survived…in remoter mountain counties, and among certain Negroes."[59]

The Third Great Awakening [1890-1920]

This is the period of personalities such as Billy Sunday and the emergence of the Social Gospel Movement under Washington Gladden and Walter Rauschenbush. For purposes of this book, attention is directed to the Azusa Street Revival, which began in 1906. The manifestations evident in this revival may share some resemblances to former revivals. Yet, the descriptions

---

[56] Ibid., 95.
[57] Ibid.
[58] Weisberger, 20-21.
[59] Ibid., 21.

of the earlier revivals capture more vividly manifestations like laughing, dancing, falling, etc. They do not give much direct insight into speaking in tongues. This is not to say it did not happen, but just that if it did the eyewitnesses I will identify do not bring it to the forefront. The Azusa Street Revival, on the other hand, does make more visible the phenomenon of speaking in tongues. It is also believed by many to be the birth of the modern Pentecostal movement, where speaking in tongues is prevalent.[60]

Vinson Synan claims that Agnes Ozman was baptized in the Holy Spirit at a small Bible school in Topeka, Kansas. Charles Fox Parham, a former Methodist pastor and holiness teacher, recalls that "he laid [his] hands upon her and prayed…when a glory fell upon her, a halo seemed to surround her head and face, and she began speaking the Chinese language and was unable to speak English for three days."[61] Some have claimed that this event triggered the worldwide Pentecostal charismatic movement. With regards to actual languages spoken, Gaston Barnabas Cashwell of North Carolina received the baptism of the Holy Spirit in 1906 and, by his own account, spoke perfect German.[62]

---

[60] Merle Strege rightly states that "this revival and the Pentecostal movement that it spawned claimed far more than the ecstatic experience that many consider its trademark." Strege, *I Saw the Church*, 121-3. Vinson Synan reminds us that the Azusa Street revival meetings were noted for their interracial gatherings and harmony. [*The Century of the Holy Spirit: 100 Years of Pentecostal and Charismatic Renewal, 1901-2001* (Nashville, TN.: Thomas Nelson Publishers, 2001), 4]

[61] Vinson Synan, ed., *The Century of the Holy Spirit*, 1.

[62] Synan, 108.

In the Azusa Street revival, their worship and praise could be described best as expressive, including dancing and shouting. These expressions certainly were known among the African American Christian tradition; yet, Synan noted that these expressions were common also among Appalachian whites. By some accounts these revival services included as many as nine a day—from morning to late night. They often lasted for weeks —twenty-four hours a day.[63] Besides speaking in tongues, one might find persons prophesying and exorcising demons. Some described some manifestations as "falling under the power."[64] A newspaper account described it like this: "Pandemonium breaks loose, and the bounds of reason are passed...."[65] "Many labeled the Pentecostal practices as by-products of religious ignorance and unbridled enthusiasm."[66] The inclusion of tongues and other gifts along with the expressive worship "created a new and indigenous form of Pentecostalism."[67] The tongues movement especially spread as those who received tongues at Azusa in 1906 went back to their own people.

There appear to be commonalities in how persons described what was happening in Azusa Street and how persons described the happenings in previous revivals. I say "appear" because we can not be absolutely certain. There often appears a common or shared vocabulary. We are just less sure that the vocabulary used intends to convey a one-to-one correspondence with the vocabu-

---

[63] Ibid., 149.
[64] Ibid.,55.
[65] Ibid., 56.
[66] Ibid.
[67] Ibid., 4-5.

lary employed in previous revivals. Those who resist these manifestations also seem to share a common vocabulary for voicing their denial of them. So, one might certainly envision similar actions on the part of worshipers and similar denunciations for those who reject what they see and hear.

This brief and admittedly incomplete survey of the landscape is an attempt to provide an account of a broader context into which to examine the phenomena of the Spirit selected for this paper. Specifically, manifestations attributed to the Spirit did occur. They are not new on the scene of the historic Christian faith. Despite their adherents, the demonstrations of Spirit phenomena frequently produced confusion and controversies among many people. From specific locations, it often seems that what is happening is a "new thing" or a "new move" of the Spirit. This brief overview reminds us that what we witness may be, in fact, a new awareness of the Spirit in new and changing contexts. We now begin our examination of selected phenomena of the Spirit with Speaking in Tongues.

SPEAKING IN TONGUES

On the Baptism of the Holy Spirit

The Baptism of (by) the Holy Spirit goes by other names, also. A few of the more familiar alternative terms used by the Church of God (Anderson, Ind.) include "Entire Sanctification," "Holiness Perfected,"

"Perfect Love," "Christian Perfection," "Second Work of Grace," and "The Second Crisis in Redemption." Simply, we have defined Baptism in the Holy Spirit as a second work of grace [subsequent to regeneration] that destroys the inbred depravity inherited from Adam.[68] For the Church of God (Anderson), Baptism of the Holy Spirit is the same reality as Entire Sanctification and its synonyms above.

In *We Preach Christ*, Charles Ewing Brown aligns his basic understanding of the doctrine of Sanctification with the Wesleyan doctrine. Brown wrote that "the justified believer may consecrate himself [sic] fully to God and receive in this life full deliverance from the remains of original sin in his nature by one definite act of faith and one immediate work of grace" (95). Brown is in basic agreement with his historical predecessors Daniel Sidney Warner and F.G. Smith.

The biblical proofs of the "Baptism" as a subsequent, instantaneous work of the Spirit rest in the following passages: Acts 2:1-12 [Pentecost], Acts 8: 5-13, 17 [the Samaritans], Acts 9:17 [the conversion of Saul/Paul], Acts 19:6 [the twelve disciples at Ephesus], and Acts 10:44 [the Gentile, Cornelius, and his household]. All these passages serve as proof-texts to support

---

[68] See William G. Schell, *The Better Testament: Or The Two Testaments Compared* (Moundsville, W. Va.: Gospel Trumpet Publishing Company, 1899), 199, 200; Charles E. Brown, *We Preach Christ* Anderson, In.: Gospel Trumpet Company, 1957), 1957; F.G. Smith, *What The Bible Teaches: A Systematic Presentation of the Fundamental Principles of Biblical Truth,* condensed by Kenneth E. Jones (Anderson, In.: Warner Press, Inc., 1945, condensed edition, 1955), 63; Albert F. Gray, *Christian Theology*, vol. II (Anderson, In.: The Warner Press, 1944), 281-284.

the view of sanctification as a second, distinct work of grace.

In contemporary discussions surrounding the Baptism of the Holy Spirit in some church traditions, one must be clear about a distinction between the Baptism of the Holy Spirit and "Entire Sanctification." While the Church of God (Anderson) and "Holiness" Pentecostals[69] —like the Church of God (Cleveland, TN) and the Pentecostal Holiness Church—equate the two biblical notions, other Pentecostals, like the Assemblies of God, see them as different realities. They generally classify themselves as "Non-Holiness" Pentecostals.

Holiness Pentecostals hold to the belief that Entire Sanctification is a second, distinct work of the Spirit.[70] However, they generally argue for a "Baptism of the Spirit" as a "third" work of grace, subsequent to Entire Sanctification, with tongues as the "initial evidence."

Non-holiness Pentecostals originate from Baptist, Presbyterian, or other non-Wesleyan Holiness groups.[71] They believe that there is an initial sanctification that comes with the conversion experience. So they go directly from the conversion experience to the baptism in

---

[69] Holiness Pentecostals embody what is sometimes called "classical Pentecostalism," for its roots trace more directly to the Wesleyan-Holiness tradition, starting with a basic Arminian-Wesleyan theology. The historic Azusa Street testimony was 'I am saved, sanctified, and filled with the Holy Ghost" [Synan, 98-99].

[70] The "first wave" of Pentecostal churches began in the second blessing holiness movement before 1901: the United Holy Church (1886); the Fire-Baptized Holiness Church (1895); the Church of God of Cleveland, Tennessee (1896); the Church of God in Christ (1897); and the Pentecostal Holiness Church (1898) [Synan, 3].

[71] Synan, 123, 124.

the Holy Spirit, evidenced initially by the speaking in tongues, without the intervening 'second blessing' of sanctification.[72] They believe further that there is "progressive" sanctification.[73] Their subsequent, distinct work is not entire sanctification, but rather it is the Baptism of the Holy Spirit, evidenced by speaking in tongues. Again the Baptism of the Holy Spirit for the Church of God is Entire Sanctification, as a second, distinct work of the Spirit after conversion. For non-holiness Pentecostals, Baptism in the Holy Spirit at Pentecost was an "empowering" experience for Christian service. It was not an act of Entire Sanctification.[74] They also believe that the Baptism of the Holy Spirit is a distinct experience that is still available to all believers today.[75]

Often the event of the Baptism in the Spirit is associated with the initial evidence of "Speaking in Tongues." Before the discussion of this, there is another distinction to which one must attend: the distinction between the Acts 2 phenomenon and the I Corinthians gifting phenomenon.[76]

---

[72] Synan, 123.

[73] Ibid. According to Synan, William H. Durham popularized this view. It is known as the "Finished Work of Calvary." Their testimony evidences this belief in only two works: "Saved and baptized in the Holy Ghost." The Assemblies of God embraces this theological view.

[74] Stanley M. Horton, "The Pentecostal Perspective," in *Five Views On Sanctification*, ed. Stanley N. Gundry, Counterpoints (Grand Rapids, MI.: Zondervan, 1987), 51.

[75] Ibid., 52.

[76] I am indebted to my colleague, Gilbert Stafford, for helping me to clarify this and other distinctions relating to the phenomena of the Holy Spirit.

Acts 2 is Luke's narrative of the church's beginning and growth. Pilgrims had gathered in Jerusalem from diverse places for the festival of Pentecost. People of many countries, speaking diverse dialects, had made the journey to Jerusalem. The promised Holy Spirit descends, especially on the assembly of 120 people who had gathered on one accord in an upper room. Luke's vivid description of this event highlights the phenomena associated with the Spirit's descent on all those gathered in that room. Suddenly "[they heard] a sound like of a violent wind..." (2:2). They saw "tongues of fire that separated and came to rest on each of them" (2:3). They were all filled with the Spirit and began to speak in other languages.

The Holy Spirit communicated the mighty acts of God through them within the languages/dialects of the various people groups present in Jerusalem. They all marveled at the fact that they heard the mighty acts of God proclaimed in their own language, even though these disciples were all Galileans. So the tongues of Acts 2 promotes the missionary agenda of God who desires—as God always has—a people who will love him and serve him wholeheartedly in the world. There is widespread consensus that the tongues in Acts 2 are known languages at that time. The speaking of these languages or dialects was a sign of the Spirit's presence for being and doing the will of God in the world.[77]

---

[77] I agree with those who interpret Acts 2 Pentecost as God's reversal of the phenomenon of Babel in Genesis 11. Acts 2

I Corinthians is, on the other hand, Paul's letter to the Church at Corinth. These believers lived in a city of brazen immorality. Many of them were participants in immoral behavior before their new life in Christ. The worshipers in the pagan temple were known to engage in ecstatic utterances or speech. Paul understood clearly that not all ecstatic speech is charismatic or a gift of divine grace. As so often happens even today, these Corinthian Christians were in need of apostolic instructions about how their new life as disciples of Jesus contrasted with the ecstatic excesses of their pagan neighbors. Paul then proceeds to give them positive instructions about the gifts of the Holy Spirit and to offer them a divine corrective to the errors they perpetuated in their worship life together. One of these grace gifts is the gift of tongues. A close kin is the gift of interpretation of tongues. The corporate worship of God appears to be the principal context where the confusion regarding the gift of tongues is manifested.

What are the phenomena of speaking in tongues as the initial evidence of the Spirit and the gift of tongues? Are they the same phenomena? Are they different?

Speaking in Tongues as Initial
Evidence of the Infilling

This phenomenon is held by many as different from "Speaking in tongues as a gift of the Spirit." According to Pentecostal writer, L. Thomas Holdcroft, "the difference between sign and gift is one of function

---

demonstrates unity in the midst of diversity. I am grateful to Mr. Jason Varner—a former student who reminded me of this perspective.

and purpose, not of nature or quality."[78] The conviction of speaking in tongues as the "sign" of the infilling of the Holy Spirit is embraced by many of our brothers and sisters in Pentecostal and neo-Pentecostal or "charismatic movement" groups. Some of the same texts we use to support the Baptism as a second, distinct work of God's Spirit are used by many in support of their belief that speaking in tongues in the book of Acts is the sign of the initial filling of the Holy Spirit. Also, for many who hold to this view, the Baptism of the Holy Spirit is subsequent to the salvation experience, but identified as a "third work" of grace, subsequent also to "sanctification" as a "second work." There have been writers who have insisted that justification and sanctification were distinct realities, clearly separated in time. Others have agreed but strongly exhort the church that while these realities may be separate, it must not be argued dogmatically that they cannot happen simultaneously. It is the prerogative of the Holy Spirit.[79]

What is the nature of the "tongues"? Who should speak in tongues? "Speaking in Tongues" refers to actual known languages. It is not some "unknown," unintelligible voices. The miracle is that one speaks in a language, previously unknown or untaught to him or her. The fundamental purpose for speaking in tongues as the initial evidence of the Baptism is to promote the missionary agenda of God. Who is to speak in tongues as the "sign"? The answer for those who see speaking

---

[78] L. Thomas Holdcroft, "Tongues and the Interpretation of Tongues," in *Conference On The Holy Spirit*, vol. 2, ed. Gwen Jones (Springfield, MO.: Gospel Publishing House, 1983), 253.
[79] See Arlo F. Newell, *Receive the Holy Spirit* (Anderson, In.: Warner Press, 1978).

in tongues as the initial evidence of the baptism of the Spirit would be that *every Christian* should speak in tongues as the initial physical evidence of the Baptism of the Holy Spirit.

While the tongues of Acts 2 at the church's beginning in Jerusalem appear to be evidence of the Holy Spirit, the tongues in I Corinthians is a gift and, by definition, is not expected to be for all Christians. Some scholars believe that the nature and experience of tongues are identical in Acts 2 and I Corinthians. Many others do not view them as identical phenomena.

For those who affirm that Acts 2 and I Corinthians "tongues" are identical argue along the line that the tongues are a gift for building up the body of Christ. In a setting where one is present who speaks a certain language [the speaker might not realize this], the one with the gift of tongues may be led to speak in that language previously unknown to him or her. In this way, the whole body is edified or built up. There is then one among the body who can "interpret" the language—if the speaker himself or herself is unable to do so. The purpose of the gift of tongues is not solely for private edification, especially if one seeks to do it publicly, without any interpretation given. In this case, Paul is quick to say that no one can say "amen." Paul indicates in his letter that he is glad that he speaks in tongues, but would rather prophesy in a language known to the hearers. In this way, even unbelievers might be convicted and come to know the truths of the gospel.[80]

On the other hand, for those who see a significant distinction between the tongues of Acts 2 and I Corinthians, the tongues of I Corinthians is not known languages, but a "heavenly," "angelic," or "prayer" language. I Corinthians 13a appears to contrast "the tongues of men" with "the tongues of angels." In chapter 14 we read the following phrases which seem [on its face] to point to a non-human language or a human language unknown to others: "[A]nyone who speaks in a tongue does not speak to men but to God" (verse 2); "He who speaks in a tongue edifies himself…" (verse 4); "For this reason anyone who speaks in a tongue should pray that he may interpret what he says" (verse 13); "For if I pray in a tongue, my spirit prays, but my mind is unfruitful" (verse 14); "So what shall I do? I will pray with my spirit, but I will also pray with my mind…" (verse 15); "If you are praising God with your spirit, how can one who finds himself among those who do not understand say "Amen" to your thanksgiving, since he does not know what you are saying?" (verse 16).

The proponents of this difference argue that it is a language of heaven supernaturally given to the speaker. There is no limit on the "private" use of the gift, but there is a limit on its public expression. There must be an interpreter, whether that is the speaker or another person in the congregation with the gift of interpretation. If this is the case the gift of tongues is equal to the

---

[80] There are other ways biblical scholars compare similarities between Acts 2 and I Corinthians. For my purposes here, this line of reasoning suffices for one dominant strand of thought.

more intelligible form of prophecy delivered in a language known to the hearers.

A Confusing Example: Oral Roberts

Whatever theological or church tradition one might embrace, one must admit to Oral Roberts as a man of great faith. He and others like him can remind all of us about the living power of faith in the Trinitarian God. Yet, in relation to the phenomenon of speaking in tongues, much of his teaching is confusing at best and unscriptural at worst. In one of his writings, Oral Roberts literally equated Acts 2:4 tongues with speaking in a "prayer language of the Spirit."[81] The prayer language is "a true communication of your spirit with Him."[82] Oral Roberts viewed the gathering of the one hundred twenty (120) as "a very private affair, devotional scene."[83] How can he simply describe the gathering of 120 people as only a private, devotional scene? This appears even more an interpretive stretch when he then sees the gathered crowd in Acts 2:7-8 as hearing the 120 speak in actual "languages" they obviously [as Galileans] had not learned.

Oral Roberts' discussion at this point is very baffling. He does highlight tongues as a prayer language of the spirit. This is clear enough. However, I am confused as to how he connects this with known languages. Could he be saying that the prayer language is for private, devotional purposes and that unlearned languages

---

[81] Oral Roberts, *The Holy Spirit in the Now I* (Tulsa, Oklahoma: Oral Roberts University, 1974), 40.

[82] Ibid.

[83] Ibid.

are the more public display or act? I do not know with certainty. Does he see the private, devotional context as including public worship of expecting believers? This question is a reasonable one, since he did describe the 120 people in the upper room as a private, devotional scene. If he equates the private with the 120, then the use of a "prayer language" is permissible in any assembly of believers in corporate worship. Yet, this seems to expressly contradict Paul's teachings in 1 Corinthians 12-14. Oral Roberts seems to take speaking in tongues as "gift" into the arena of "obligation" for every believer. Such an emphasis also goes against the teaching of Paul in 1 Corinthians 12-14.

Specifically, Oral Roberts says that,

> Now if you have repented and believed on Christ the Holy Spirit has already come in and you have an open door to a deeper level of communication with God. You can, *if you will to do it* [emphasis mine], speak directly to God in a new prayer language of the Spirit. You can communicate with Him, beginning with your spirit. This means you can speak directly to God with your SPIRIT and then WITH YOUR UNDERSTANDING (1 Corinthians 14:15). You can pray much better with your understanding AFTER first praying with your spirit in tongues.[84]

---

[84] Roberts, *The Holy Spirit in the Now I*, 43.

I agree with Oral Roberts here that when one has repented and believed on Christ the Holy Spirit has already taken up residence in one's life. His next move, however, is a wrong one. He seems to assume that "speaking in tongues" is not a gift for some believers as much as it is a privilege for every believer. He says as much in his discussion on 1 Corinthians 14:5:

> In all these years that I have had this experience and have prayed for people to receive it, in every case where there was any openness at all or lack of tension and inhibition, every one has received it. . . . It's my experience that he can release the prayer language of the Spirit immediately if he knows how to open up his inner self.[85]

Roberts' teaching here is not in tune, it seems to me, with the biblical teaching given by Paul in 1 Corinthians. Roberts' "experiences" tend to drive his interpretation and his desire for everyone to have this experience. Paul desired that all speak in tongues as he did, but Paul's emphasis was that this was a gift, and, thereby, not for everyone. Roberts, on the other hand, appears to put on human beings the burden of initiating this experience. In doing so, it is clear that the sovereign move of the Holy Spirit is minimized and the will of humans is elevated: "if you *will to do it*, says Oral Roberts. So everyone who *wills* to experience this, according to Roberts, will experience praying with one's

---

[85] Roberts, *The Holy Spirit in the Now I*, 48.

spirit in tongues. Hence, he believes it is normative for everyone to desire or *will* this.

In a prior book he authored ten years earlier, Oral Roberts appeared to make a clearer distinction between the prayer language which all believers should have and the "gift and interpretation of tongues possessed by some Christians.[86] Roberts' teaching on the baptism with the Holy Spirit intends to be more comprehensive, yet his discussion still appears to suffer from interpretive ambiguity and distortions.[37] He appears oblivious to any problems with arguing that in 1 Corinthians 12 and 14 Paul embraces 'simple tongues' and the 'gift form' of speaking in tongues.[88] For Roberts in this 1964 work, "the simple tongues of prayer and praise are for personal edification and release in [one's] own spirit after [one has] received the infilling of the Holy Spirit."[89] On the other hand, Roberts argues that in "its gift form, Speaking in tongues has a larger purpose altogether. . . . [One] exercises the gift of tongues when he is with a body of believers either in a church meeting or a smaller group."[90]

---

[86] Oral Roberts, *The Baptism With The Holy Spirit: And the Value of Speaking in Tongues Today* (Tulsa, Oklahoma: Oral Roberts), 1964. See especially 52-58.

[87] Ibid. Oral Roberts does provide interesting suggestions for exercising the gift of tongues (chapter 6); the motive of love for its exercise (chapter 7); the nature of and rules for interpretation of tongues (chapters 9-10).

[88] Ibid., 52.

[89] Roberts, *Baptism with the Holy Spirit* , 52. Roberts uses 1 Corinthians 12:10 as a proof-text.

[90] Ibid., 52. Here Roberts uses 1 Corinthians 14:26-28 as a proof-text.

While Roberts provides much more instruction than I have cited here, the point is that he believes all Christians should seek and exercise "simple tongues." For him, simple tongues take on a "gift form" which is exercised only by those with the gift. Yet, the gift does function to edify the whole body. I sense, in addition, that my discussions on these two works by Oral Roberts indicate the confusing nature of his beliefs about the relationship of the baptism with the Holy Spirit, simple tongues, and the gift and interpretation of tongues.

This brief discussion maps out the general arguments, and even highlights some of the difficulties introduced by those who bend the interpretation of scripture to justify their experience. These experiences may require, as Oral Roberts testifies, the willingness of people to lose "inhibition." Let's now see how some of this plays out within the historic connections of the Church of God.

Historical Connections in the Church of God

Kenneth Tippin highlights the early tongues story in the Church of God.[91] The early tongues emphasis spans the beginning years to just before the end of 1926. However, there is not much said about the gift of tongues during much of the early decades of the Church

---

[91] The information on "The Early Tongues Story" in the Church of God is found in Appendix C of Tippins' manuscript, 399ff.

of God.[92] Yet, the historical testimony is clear in many respects.

For the early writers, it is clear that Speaking in Tongues was not evidence of the Baptism of the Holy Spirit. F.G. Smith says that "to ask for our evidence that we have the Holy Spirit is like asking for an evidence of the existence of the sun overhead. The sun does not need a witness to testify for it, it stands for itself . . ."[93] The fundamental teachings embraced the view that there are many manifestations or evidences of the Holy Spirit. From Hebrews 10:15 and Romans 8:16, for example, F.G. Smith argues that the Holy Spirit is the evidence.[94] In fact, for F.G. Smith, the Pentecostal emphasis of speaking in tongues as the initial evidence of the Holy Spirit was a major theological departure of the Church of God from many of the Pentecostal churches at that time. Smith believed that the vast amount of deception and fanatical extremism in the Church of God reformation movement could be attributed to this belief.

The early writers certainly do seem to secure their teachings on the gift of tongues on Paul's first letter to the Corinthians, specifically chapters 12-14. From these passages, writers like J.W. Byers, Jennie C. Rutty, F.G. Smith, H.M. Riggle, D.O. Teasley, J.M. Nichols-Roy, and E.E. Byrum appear to share a fundamental consen-

---

[92] Merle Strege's discussion on "The Early Church of God and Glossalalia" is very well done. He nicely summarizes positions of key leaders on this phenomenon, while situating this discussion, in part, within the broader modern charismatic movement during this period. See Strege, *I Saw the Church*, 121-33. My emphasis here includes some of this content, but attempts, in addition, to highlight other dimensions of this discussion.

[93] Smith, *What the Bible Teaches*, 71-72.

[94] Ibid., 73.

sus. Specifically, the scripture does not prohibit speaking in tongues. However, not every member has this gift. For the most part, many of the writers understood tongues as being intelligible human languages [J.W. Byers, F.G. Smith, Russell Byrum, J.M. Nichols-Roy]. The gift of tongues requires the gift of interpretation, or else the public display of tongues will not edify or build up the body of believers. These writers understood that the gift of tongues as "gift" required limits and was subordinate to the gift of prophecy.

There are, in addition to what appears to be a consensus, some interesting departures. While J.M. Nichols-Roy agreed that tongues included human languages, he appeared to extend the definition of languages to include other than human language.[95]

In the early years, F.G. Smith appears to have provided an influential contribution to the Church of God's understanding of the gift of tongues. On June 14, 1918, he gave an address to the General Ministerial Assembly on "The Gift of Tongues." It was based on Paul's first letter to the Corinthian church, chapter fourteen. R.L. Berry wrote a follow-up account of Smith's message. Smith finally made this teaching available to all in the church, not just to the ministerial leadership. Smith promoted a "Double Phase" of the gift of tongues: a "Private" phase [a Christian's personal devotional use] and a "Public" phase [corporate worship].[96]

---

[95] Tippin Manuscript, 422.

[96] F. G. Smith, *The Gift of Tongues: What It Is And What It Is Not* (Anderson, Indiana: Gospel Trumpet Company, 1918 (?). Quoted material for this section will maintain the male pronoun so characteristically used in denoting any gender. The reader should

F. G. Smith advocates that the Acts 2 and I Corinthian tongues are identical phenomena. More specifically, he sees no distinction between "speaking in tongues" (Acts 2) and the "gift of tongues" (I Corinthians 12-14). He believes that the gift of tongues serves a useful purpose for the church and, therefore, deserves a claim to permanency.[97]

Smith describes, on the one hand, the "personal, private phase of tongues," as including the following dimensions:[98] (1) "Is by the Spirit" (I Cor. 14:2), (2) "Is addressed to God, not to men" (14:2), (3) "Is not understood by men (14:2, 28), (4) "Speaker himself does not understand" (14:14), (5) "He receives interpretation" (14:13), (6) "The prime object is to EDIFY HIMSELF" (14:4), (7) "If brought into the congregation is not edifying" [unless interpreted] (14:5, 19), (8) "Is prohibited in public unless interpreted" (14:28), (9) "Is not profitable for public use, even if interpreted" [it is restricted to two or three persons in one service—no such limits on prophecy] (14:26-27).

Smith emphasizes the use of prophecy without the limits imposed on the use of tongues (14:31). Prophecy possesses a directness and a power to convince unbelievers in a way that uninterpreted tongues cannot do (14:23-25).

On the other hand, Smith then focuses on the "public" phase of the gift."[99] According to Smith, "this phase of the gift is designed primarily for the express

---

keep in mind that in all appropriate cases the gender use should be extended to include feminine references also.

[97] Smith, *The Gift of Tongues,* 6.
[98] Ibid., 13-17.
[99] Ibid., 17-19.

benefit of the public."[100] This public phase of the gift of tongues includes the following: (1) "Real languages of earth" (Acts 2:6, 11), (2) "Being intelligible, they require no interpretation" (Acts 2), (3) "They constitute a real 'SIGN'" for unbelievers. The real sign is "the ability to speak *by the Spirit* languages that the speaker himself does not understand"[101], and (4) "Is neither prohibited nor limited."

Smith sees the Pentecostal experience of tongues in Acts 2 as being identical in nature to the "public" use of tongues Paul describes in I Corinthians 12-14. Remember that for Smith, the tongues as a gift can be manifest in no other way than by "speaking." He sees Acts 2 as a very "public" display of the Spirit, having the elements just identified above. From this Smith defines more clearly the gift of tongues as follows:

> Christian glossalalia, or tongues, is a gift of God bestowed upon an individual whereby, through the operation of the Holy Spirit, he is enabled to speak UNTO GOD in a language which the Spirit chooses and which 'no man understands,' or to speak UNTO MEN the mysteries of God in a language unknown to him (the speaker) but understood by his hearers.[102]

---

[100] Ibid., 17-18.
[101] Smith, *The Gift of Tongues*, 18.
[102] Ibid., 19-20.

Furthermore, Smith provides a summary of the distinguishing features of the gift of tongues.[103] First, the gift of tongues is a special gift given sovereignly by the Holy

Spirit. This is in line with the dispensation of other spiritual gifts Paul identifies in I Corinthians 12. Second, this gift enables a person to speak to others in a language he or she understands, although unknown or unlearned by the speaker. This gift also enables a person to speak to God in a language which no human understands—unless interpreted.

In addition, Smith's summary brings further clarity to the use of the gift in public and private contexts. When the gift of tongues is used in a "public" way [corporate worship], there are two permissible avenues. First, in a language unlearned by the speaker, the speaker is uttering prophecy in the language of the hearers. Hence, no interpretation for the benefit of the hearers is required. The very intelligibility of the language is its primary divine witness. Second, speaking in a language unlearned by both the speaker and the hearers, the speaker may speak in this language publicly only if interpreted for the benefit of the gathered congregation. Only in this way will the "tongues" serve as a "sign" to any unbelievers present and as a confirmation to any believers present.

It is understandable, then, that Paul insists that the speaker pray for the interpretation also, so that the speaker and congregation's understandings might be enhanced to the glory of God. If this does not happen,

---

[103] Ibid., 20-26.

then Paul insists that the use of the gift of tongues must be limited to the private phase.

Continuing his summary, Smith highlights the scriptural evidence that the gift of tongues may be used at the will of the speaker. So the gift is subject to abuse in its exercise, if the speaker is not led by the Spirit. While Paul does not condemn the use of this gift, he does promote appropriate limits to its use, even as he himself does in exercising the gift privately [See 14:18-19.]. Paul's main emphasis is maintained: the promotion of a clear word of prophecy for the building up of the body of Christ, to the glory of God.

Reaction and Assessment of Speaking in Tongues

Of all the phenomena or manifestations, speaking in tongues is both biblically attested and tenaciously ambivalent within the thought and practices of the Church of God (Anderson, Ind.). It seems to me that our movement is not served well by categorically denying the validity and exercise of the legitimate use of tongues. I believe that there is no sound scriptural basis for advocating the cessation of this gift. Whether it should be used given our current context is another issue of note. Yet, the abuse of this gift does not justify its exclusion as an authentic gift of the Spirit. While we have an obligation to be discerning and pastoral in our responses toward the legitimate use of the gift of tongues, we also have another fundamental obligation to embrace the truth attested in Scripture. The teachings on the gift of tongues we affirm from Scripture are clear that not every believer should be expected to have this gift.

The nature of the gift must be carefully expressed. There appears to be sound biblical warrant to affirm that the public use of tongues is indeed known human languages. The gift of tongues exercised in public worship agrees with the thrust of what Paul teaches in 1 Corinthians 12-14. The speaker previously may not have learned the language, so interpretation within the language of the hearers must be forthcoming. If not, the speaker is instructed to remain inaudible or silent in the exercise of this gift within public worship.

If the speaker does not know the language, then someone in the congregation is expected to have the interpretation, so that the congregation might be able to say "Amen" to what is said or that non-believers might be convicted to assent to the gospel. Still it must be said that, according to Paul, the gift of tongues is still subordinate to prophecy—even if interpreted.

The gift of tongues in its private devotional use presents some interesting interpretive challenges. On one hand, the tongues spoken in private are languages unfamiliar and unlearned by the speaker. This can be the case, even if the language spoken is a known human language—just unknown by the speaker. The speaker may have no way to tell. What the speaker does know is that he or she is edified personally and God is glorified certainly. Even F.G. Smith's discussion does not explicitly contradict this. In a similar line of reasoning, the exercise of the gift of tongues privately also might allow for a "heavenly" or an "angelic" language—although the true nature of this language is not completely devoid of mystery.[104] F.G. Smith, in warning of deception in the use of this gift, clearly says that the very nature of the tongues is "mystical, mysterious, and outside of the ordinary range of human activities."[105]

Those who affirm the role of Scripture and the on-going move of God in the world should be careful in their categorical denial of an experience of an "angelic" or a "heavenly" utterance to God for edification of oneself. In any event, proper weight in this matter should rest on Scripture. Also, we should emphasize what Scripture emphasizes. For Paul, his emphasis is not on the validity of the gift itself—though much teaching is needed here—but rather on its problematic use in corporate worship.

Specifically, priority in corporate worship must be given to the clear use of intelligible words. Further, there is no biblical justification for everyone speaking in tongues—whether at the same time or separately. First, not everyone has the gift of tongues or their interpretation. Second, a stranger in the midst of all this will not be edified, but would only label this speaking as indecipherable gibberish. Third, when everyone wants to exercise this gift without limits—together or sepa-

---

[104] We need not suggest a complete mystery in this. There is the biblical instance of angelic language: the angelic praise at the birth of Jesus. I am indebted to Gilbert Stafford for bringing this biblical event to my attention. Yet, I am uncertain that this removes all "mystery." Specifically, how does Luke interpret what the angels were singing in their praises? Did the triune God gift Luke with an "interpretation" of an angelic language? In contrast, was this "angelic language" simply a known language—contextualized to the language pattern of the writer Luke and his audience?

[105] Smith, *The Gift of Tongues,* 56.

rately, it may be proof of the lack of love for others and for God's missionary agenda to spread good news to the world.

The "public" use of a "language"—whether known or unknown ("heavenly" or "angelic")—is a deceptive use of the gift of tongues. It only "edifies" the speaker. It may edify others, however, if they, too, embrace such speaking as an expectation for themselves as part of the congregational culture. Yet, this is a dangerous expectation to have because, in part, it assumes a hierarchy of spiritual persons that 1 Corinthians 12-14 does not support. It assumes, in addition, a view that perhaps everyone should strive for this gift. By the nature of spiritual gifts, this is not an expectation supported by the Scriptures.

In the broader scheme of worship, contexts matter. God through the Spirit is free to do whatever God wants to do. One might envision a scenario where the miraculous use of another language may accompany a missionary's efforts to witness boldly to unbelievers and believers. One also might envision an opposite scenario where the exercise of such a gift may prove counterproductive or too contentious for building up a particular congregation. Paul's emphasis is on the community of faith, not on fostering the spiritual excesses of individualism so rampant in western societies. Paul is clear where he corrects the abuse of this gift in insisting that the pursuit of the more "extraordinary" gifts is no substitute for the earnest pursuit of the Gift-giver.

Pastorally speaking, congregations are justified in insisting on these biblical guidelines in the exercise of this gift in public worship. Yet, they must permit its legitimate biblical use. What mature believers do in private devotions must also be consistent with Scripture.[106] While we should care that sound teaching, earnest prayer, and spiritual maturity surrounding this and all gifts can guide the exercise even of the private use of this gift, there is less concern that strict limits to its use must apply. Therefore, the believer is free to glorify God privately in this way and to experience all the blessings that this might bring. However, what we can affirm publicly as "doctrine" or the "church's teachings" for increasing believers' knowledge of and love for God should not apply to the private use of tongues. We cannot elevate to the level of doctrine for the whole church what clearly is limited as a gift to a few in private devotions.

LIVING IN THE SPIRIT

I have covered a lot of territory in this paper, but there is still so much more to consider in any serious examination of the phenomena of the Spirit. I understand that perhaps more questions have been raised than answers have been realized. I will offer some concluding observations and pose some questions raised by this overview of phenomena of the Spirit. This chapter hopefully delivers on the expectation that readers will go beyond just puzzling questions or easy explanations of phenomena of the Spirit to a faithful living out of the

---

[106] If what we do in "private" is to be governed by Scripture, then our actions—even in private—is subject to communal expectations. The church, as the community of faith, has much to say about the faithful use and interpretation of Scripture. I do not claim here that the community is all-pervasive, but rather that spiritual practices of the church cannot be disconnected from the very community which give them intelligibility.

fullness of the Spirit. I will venture to offer some explanations to some of these questions. Then, I will conclude with a final exhortation and concluding Pastoral Notes. This final exhortation and these pastoral notes I cannot help but believe bear the key to experiencing the power of the Holy Spirit among us and in us.

Some Observations and Questions

From this paper, I come humbly to several broad conclusions or inferences from this limited investigation of selected phenomena of the Spirit. First, physical phenomena of the Spirit did occur in the early years of the Church of God and were not categorically rejected. While a case could be made for this, one should not infer that the early years of the Church of God experienced a groundswell of spiritual manifestations. The Church of God sources I quoted often did not give much in-depth description of the phenomena. In addition, I was impressed by their persistent openness to and yearning for the move of God's Spirit in significant ways. Moreover, while phenomena of the Spirit did appear to enjoy a great degree of acceptance, they were always subject to scrutiny. The consequences of a "Spirit-led" testing many times resulted in judging much of the phenomena as ordained by Satan. Again, while many of the writers mentioned in this paper appeared accepting of many manifestations, I did not get any sense that they believed that these manifestations constituted the major work of the Holy Spirit. In much of what I read, the major work of the Holy Spirit was still in preparing both the saved and the lost to hear the Word, respond to the Word, live out the Word in the world, and share the Word with the lost.

As a result of this work, I also ask myself some "interesting" questions. Is talking about and discussing the phenomena of the Spirit viewed more favorably than experiencing the Spirit in corporate worship and in daily living? When was the last time that our camp meeting services witnessed persons responding to the preaching and the singing with loud weeping, high praises, falling on their faces, laughter borne of the Spirit, and so forth? We have observed the solemn, the blessed quietness, the "thoughtful" gaze, the nodding of the head, and the scatterings of "Amens." Why do these responses appear to be normative? Do we "program" around the Spirit at times? Do we already have preconceived notions of what are acceptable expressions of the Spirit? Have we become so modern that we radically separate our "human reason" from our "passions"? Are we bound by cultural norms or expectations that limit the visible moving of the Spirit to certain acceptable phenomena?

These observations above may be symptomatic of other fundamental concerns. This calls for more elaboration about possible reasons for the tension or fear we experience in the body of Christ in relation to the phenomena of the Spirit. Have we considered the roles which fear plays both in our articulation of some of the teachings on the Holy Spirit and in our responses to our brothers and sisters who might embrace another perspective?[107] I believe that our status as "moderns" have

---

[107] I am indebted to Mr. Arthur Kelly, former Coordinator of Christian Education of Church of God Ministries, Anderson, Indiana, for his suggestion that I pursue the role that fear plays in the degree to which we seem willing to embrace the various phenomena of the Spirit.

shaped us and our expectations in ways we generally do not and often cannot acknowledge. I find it absolutely interesting in this research that historically we seemed to be a people more open to the move of the Spirit or the move of God. As long as experiences could be biblically validated, the church of God tended—and the exceptions are real—to be open to new light. Yet, this is nothing new with the Church of God Reformation movement. Much of church history is full of examples of how the church's responses have been varied, depending on the spirit of the times.

The Church of God Reformation movement was an anti-Enlightenment movement. That is, while the spirit of the times might have called for more "reasoned" approaches to living the Christian life, the reformation movement appeared to justify the immersion of the whole self into the life of faith. As Barry Callen reminds us, the church always lived its life within various tensions or polarities. Yet, the Church of God did acknowledge that tensions existed and often—not without pain—purposed to exist in light of them.

What happened? On one hand, we acknowledged like most western people that human reason and the explanatory power of science become the gatekeepers for the real and the authentic. Therefore, we see the continuation of the effects of the Enlightenment period. We are uncomfortable with mystery, seeking to overcome it with the power of our human reason and intellect. We are people having been shaped by the necessity of the modern, western mind to explain the unexplainable.

On the other hand, we live in the times when relativism replaces absolutism. While that is not always a bad thing, it does breed a kind of fear, having no firm foundation upon which our lives can be built. In a world of fear and uncertainty, cynicism and hopelessness appear to be the reigning dispositions. The habits of cynicism and the power of human reason become like the air we breathe. In our western Christian tradition, the individual is the authority and human reason is supreme. What does this have to do with phenomena of the Spirit? I offer this as a response. We learn to exist in a fragmented world. With the supremacy of the individual and of human reason, we often see no problem separating our "reason" from "our body," along with the passions expressed through it. Rather than seeing the holistic nature of our lives [we are "one"], we see instead our reason as fundamentally separate from our bodies and from our passions. Living fragmented lives runs the risk of our living too comfortably on the extremes. Emphasizing reason, on one hand, believers may equate reason and cognitive responses with the truthfulness of the faith. Consequently, feelings and passions in partnership with our created bodies get devalued. Bodily expressions might get viewed as "premodern" responses, and that such expressiveness contributes little to the essence of the Christian faith. Historically, this response to phenomena or to expressiveness is well documented.

Emphasizing feelings and bodily movement, on the other hand, believers may equate expressiveness or phenomena as the only reliable evidence of being changed or being Spirit-filled in any authentic sense. Muted expressions and reasoning through the faith might get viewed as "static" and "stale" faith. Historically, this response to the rational is also well documented.

What I have just described—admittedly in a simplistic manner—also influences our understanding of Christian doctrine surrounding selected aspects of the Holy Spirit. Doctrine is separated from its true end. Doctrine should be rooted in the richness of our Christian story. The teachings of the faith are meant to help us to know God and to serve God in the world. This can be construed as its true end. Yet, when doctrine is disconnected from its true end, it becomes propositional faith—a faith expressed in rational statements, subject to proof or disproof. Yet, this dependence on the rational is too frequently viewed as the prerequisite or foundation to living holy lives. If first we just "think right," then we can act right. In view of the New Testament understanding of what constitutes genuine belief, this way of separating thought and action, belief and practice, and so forth, is severely limiting. One can reason propositionally or can have "head knowledge" of Christ without their whole person being transformed. The separation of our minds, body, and passions into a compartmentalized existence seems rational, but it is not the way we humans are fundamentally constituted. When human reason is so fragmented from the totality of our being, we are rendered less human, regardless of what extreme we emphasize. We are called to be "one." Jesus, in response to the question about the greatest commandment, says this in Mark 12: "Hear, O Israel, the Lord our God, the Lord is one. Love the Lord your God with all our heart and with all your soul and with all your mind and with all your strength. The second is this: 'Love your neighbor as yourself." [Vss. 29-31, NIV] Our minds, soul, body, passions must be integrated—must be one. The mind and body are not to be in opposition to one another, but rather should mutually interpenetrate each other with the aim of doing the will of God more perfectly. We must be "one." Our "oneness" must be seen in the context of the body of Christ, the Church. Can't we see how "unity" of Christ's church is so essential in helping us all to discern and to move rightly in the Spirit of the triune God?

The Church of God speaks of unity of all believers. We have done well in more recent years of challenging ourselves to live out this fruit of the holy life. Yet, there are still pockets of divisions among us. Continuing divisions [arguments for legitimacy aside] are Anderson here, Hispanic Concilio yonder, the American Indian Council and West Middlesex over there; and *One Voice*[108] here and the *Reformation Witness* there; there is the North American church here and the broader international diversity of the church yonder. Why have I witnessed less demonstration of the phenomena of the Spirit in Anderson than in West Middlesex or Kampala, Uganda? How do we or should we hear our brothers and sisters outside North America about their reflections and experiences on the phenomena of the Spirit?

Even given the diversity of our movement, why is Anderson seen as predominantly Anglo and West Middlesex as predominantly African American? Do these distinctions contribute to or explain in any meaningful way the degree of openness to certain phenomena of the Spirit? Do such varying contexts present us with differing interpretive lens for imagining the possibilities of spiritual phenomena? It just might be that only as we experience the authentic unity the Holy Spirit brings—which we affirm as a distinguishing mark—will we

---

[108] Unfortunately, publication of *One Voice* has ceased.

then grasp with our whole selves—mind and body—
what the Spirit is doing in the world today, and be more
willing to go where the Spirit leads. Now these concluding exhortations

Concluding Exhortations

This brings me to my concluding exhortations. It
should be of utmost concern that we are more willing to
divide over manifestations of the Spirit than we often
are willing to demonstrate love of God and love of
neighbor. In light of this central biblical teaching, I offer the following. First, our teaching and preaching surrounding the phenomena of the Spirit must always be in
the context of God's ultimate and broader agenda to
reconcile the world back to God. God is not just concerned about our movement or denominations, or about
the necessary but not sufficient attention to doctrinal
faithfulness. The story of God-with-us, from Genesis to
Revelation, supports the view that God's primary agenda is always much broader than ours seem to be. Whatever our spiritual passions and convictions, they ought
to direct our life together in embracing God's main
agenda of calling a people who will serve and love him
with all of their heart, soul, mind, and strength.

Second, our teaching, preaching, and daily living in
the Spirit must always be in the context of our distinguishing doctrines of holiness of lifestyle and its fruit—
the unity of all believers. This must hold true as an ongoing willingness to engage all our brothers and sisters,
wherever they may worship—and in spite of the uncharitable labels we often apply to one another.

A third encouragement is that we need to be reminded that the Spirit fills our heart with God's love (Romans 5:5), which produces spiritual fruit (Galatians 5:22-23), and God's love-bearing Spirit dispels all fear (I John 4:18). We need not allow fear and suspicion based on differences to produce unholy responses within the body of Christ. It is no accident that 1 Corinthians 13—Paul's extended discourse on agape, God's love—is the appropriate bridge between Paul's instructive teaching on gifts in chapter 12 and his corrective teaching on their abuse in chapter 14. The fruit that the Spirit brings is the very character of Jesus Christ. Unless the gifts of the Spirit are motivated and nurtured by the fruit of the Spirit, then their effectiveness for kingdom work will be undermined. While not every Christian possesses *all* the gifts, each Christian is called and expected to embody the fruit cluster in Galatians 5:22-23. The fruit displayed within Christian community and within the believer's life is the best evidence of a life surrendered to the Holy Spirit.

Further, in humility, we must be willing to "test" the spirits, understanding that the goal of this testing is true knowledge, trust, wisdom, and obedience. Its goal is not unwarranted suspicion and spiritual rigidity. The church is charged with the responsibility to test the spirits to discern whether they are of God. Charges leveled by some Christians that any question or analysis of phenomena of the Spirit is a sign of unbelief and disobedience are inappropriate and unbiblical.[109] I would

---

[109] While Oral Roberts would fall into this category, he also is not in total opposition to the role of examining biblical truth. He says: "I'm very interested in our *understanding* the teachings of the Holy Spirit throughout the Bible until the baptism in the Holy

agree, though, that if one's desire is not sincere in the pursuit of truth, then that person also is outside God's will. Such attitudes among Christians are also a distortion and serves to deny the move of the Spirit in the body of Christ and in the world.

In addition, as our own writers in the Church of God have instructed us, we are not simply "individuals" wanting our own individual experiences validated at all cost. We are the body of Christ, the family of God, and, as such, our apprehension of the Spirit's work should be a communal responsibility. We are wise, therefore, to remember that Paul's teachings on all the gifts of the Spirit in 1 Corinthians 12-14 focus first and foremost on the building up of the body of Christ. Unlike the contemporary display of much of the phenomena of the Spirit, Paul is relatively unconcerned with the inward, psychical expressions associated with rampart individualism. The community of faith in corporate or public worship—in one accord—is the context in which the Holy Spirit works to produce an embodied witness to a rebellious and disbelieving world.

Finally, there are times when we do "walk in the dark," but in prayerful submission to our God, may the Holy Spirit help us to "walk in the light."

Benjamin F. Reid wrote passionately about the need for a priority of teaching on the Holy Spirit, in the context of a willing spirit of obedience. Reid said, "We

---

Spirit explodes in your being. I want you not only to have the experience of the baptism in the Holy Spirit in your life, but *equally important* [emphasis mine] to you also is to have an *understanding* of it – to have a workable knowledge of it." [Oral Roberts, *The Holy Spirit in the Now I* (Tulsa, Oklahoma: Oral Roberts University, 1974), 9.]

must let the wind blow!"[110] As the wind of the Spirit blows, how might we go forward together?

Going Forward Together:
A Pastoral Note to Christians Who Are Resistant to These Phenomena

In light of the biblical emphasis of a church united in the Spirit, we should exercise humility and care in what final judgments we make about how the Spirit works. Also, we should be just as diligent to practice the love of God in our relationships with one another—especially toward those with whom we disagree. Let's remember that God is not finished with any of us yet—and that's a good thing!

As I have demonstrated in this book, I do not advocate that all displays of Spirit phenomena are permissible or that all doctrinal teachings on the phenomena of the Holy Spirit are equally valid. I urge church leaders, however, to resist the quick move to squash all actions you personally dislike, but which you have committed little or no effort to study or examine. Taking a cue from Matthew 18:15ff, a leader might pray earnestly and study diligently (See 2 Timothy 2:15). Assuming such a posture allows you to exercise pastoral oversight that first guides rather than condemns. Certainly, Godly discipline may be in order at times, too. Only God's wisdom can guide the leader or leaders into what is proper in the circumstances. Whatever you conclude is

---

[110] See Benjamin F. Reid, *Glory to the Spirit* (Anderson, In.: Warner Press, 1990).

a necessary response, the ultimate purpose of your actions should be that God is glorified. Truth-telling, forgiveness, and reconciliation always will bring honor and glory to our God.

An ongoing pastoral strategy might include teaching about the gifts of the Spirit within the broader context of the character of Jesus. The character of Jesus is demonstrated best by the cultivation of the fruit of the Spirit in the lives of disciples (Galatians 5:16-18, 22-23). Many congregations have assumed this responsibility faithfully. Others have done little or nothing in this respect. For those congregations, I urge you to take this step as soon as possible. Be Alert! You just might be blessed to learn more about the works and wonders of the Holy Spirit from the very people you now energetically oppose. There are Christians who endorse and practice a myriad of Spirit phenomena who support their practices within the context of God's love and out of the character of Jesus—as evidenced by the fruit of the Spirit.

Going Forward Together:
A Pastoral Note to Those Who Practice and Endorse These Phenomena

All Christians are called to practice the love of God to their brothers and sisters in Christ. This is a non-negotiable command of our Lord Jesus Christ (John 13:34-35). In the midst of this love, you might assume a defensive posture against those Christians who would dismiss your exercise of the phenomena of the Spirit [of any kind] as ignorance at best and as demonic at worst.

On the other hand, you must confess that so many who practice these and other phenomena of the Spirit often view themselves as spiritually superior to those Christians who do not practice them. While this might oversimplify matters, I believe it is the case that too many "Charismatics" embrace a two-tiered view of the body of Christ—those who have already arrived and those who have not. Paul certainly appeared to respond negatively to such ideas.[111] We all live "between the times."

It is also the case that Christianity has much still to learn from our brothers and sisters who take with utter seriousness the work of the Holy Spirit today. I urge you to pray without ceasing for the church. We owe one another love and that is a debt we can never payoff (Romans 13:8). Also, be ready always to unite with other Christians to build bridges by the power of the Spirit that works in us (Ephesians 3:20). Be Alert! You just might discover additional insights into how the Spirit works from the very people you now tenaciously dismiss. Everyone who disagrees with you are not resistant to the move of the Holy Spirit in their and others' lives. Neither are they simply hindered by a hardened "religious traditionalism" and "religion-as-usual."

Furthermore, in our pursuit of truth, might you also, like all Christians must, remain open to the work of the Spirit in the heart and in the body of Christ. As you fervently practice what you believe the Spirit leads you to do, practice also the law of love—put on love which binds us all together in perfect unity (Colossians 3:14).

---

[111] See examples of Rodney Howard-Browne's cynical and abrasive responses to those who question him and his experiences of the Holy Spirit in *School of the Spirit* (Tampa, Florida: Revival Ministries International, 1995), 17-18, 42.

Let the Church Move When the Spirit Says Move!

Therefore, we—all of us—are God's holy nation and royal priesthood in a world who lives by other gods (1 Peter 2:9). May God's Spirit ever guide us into all the truth (John 16:13) that our communal and personal lives might conform to the image of Jesus Christ (Romans 8:29). As the church of God, inclusive of all the redeemed, let us submit to the law of love and *move when the Spirit says move.* Without the practice of the phenomenon of the love of God, a disbelieving world can and will discredit all else we do and say. Only as we love one another and our enemies with the love of God will the world know that we are disciples of Jesus Christ. Then there will be little doubt in the presence of an unbelieving society that we exhibit the unity of all believers for which Jesus prayed (John 17:20-23). Our unity, born of the Spirit, will be at its most profound heights. The move of the Spirit will point beyond us to Jesus Christ.

So let's go forward into God's future. In doing so, let us passionately shun the false, even as we just as passionately embrace the authentic. For those who have an ear, let them hear what the Spirit says to the church. The distant thunder-roll is nearer than ever before! May the Church move when the Spirit says move! May all believers move when the Spirit says move!

[This article included by permission of the author.]

A Challenge Answered.
By J. W Lynch

An Open Letter to the
CHURCH OF GOD
Reformation Movement
Anderson, Indiana

(Ten years with that movement)

Cry aloud, spare not, . . . show my
people their transgression. Isa. 58:1.

Before rejecting this little brochure
or committing it to the flames, please
read Prov. 18:13 and Jer. 36:20-32.

CHALLENGE ANSWERED

An Open Letter to the Church of God, Reformation
Movement

To the Editor, contributors and readers of the Gospel
Trumpet, and to all adherents of that faith.

Brethren:

For some time I have desired to write you; in fact,
for a number of years I have watched with interest your

repeated attacks on the Pentecostal Movement, as you have through tracts and articles in the Gospel Trumpet, warned your people and all others against them, as being of the devil; not realizing that in this you are fulfilling the prophetic words of Jesus and thus proving who are the true people of the Lord, for Jesus says (Matt. 10:25), "It is enough for the disciple that he be as his master, and the servant as his Lord. If they have called the master of the house Beelzebub, HOW MUCH MORE SHALL THEY CALL THEM OF HIS HOUSEHOLD?"

It is surprising that you who claim to surpass all others in unity, and claim to be the last reformation to bring the whole Church into the unity of the faith, and sing, "We reach our hand in fellowship to every blood-washed one," can show so little love, and condemn in such strong terms a movement made up of blood-bought, blood-washed and Spirit-filled people.

I wish as briefly as possible to mention a few of your many articles, and especially to answer your challenge; and place in the balance your teachings with the Word of God. I cannot mention all you have said, for I do not wish to write a volume.

Taking a few extreme cases of those whom you say were demon possessed, etc., and setting them up as the standard of the Pentecostal Movement and using the words of demons to support your claims, is not consistent with the Scriptures which you so strongly insist that others adhere to.

Remember that one of the twelve had a devil; the early Pentecost Church at Jerusalem had its Ananias and Sapphira; at Samaria its Simon; and at Corinth (the one church mentioned as "enriched in everything" and "come behind in no gift") had some whose conduct was below anything that was even named among the Gentiles.

In your tract "An Experience with Demons" the writer claims to have cast a number of demons out of two poor backslidden women who had once been with the Pentecostal Movement, and says these demons called themselves by the names of some of the "tongues leaders" and said they were "leading hundreds of souls to hell." Is the devil divided against himself like that? Not according to the words of Jesus.

The devil is indeed a poor source from which to get information concerning the ministry. A "thus saith the Lord" is preferred before a "thus saith the devil." Do the Scriptures anywhere justify you in taking the words of demons and using them against your brethren in the ministry? It says, "Preach the Word" (God's Word). I have no confidence in what the devil says. He is a liar and the father of it, the great accuser of the brethren. He lied on Job (Job 1:11); he even lied on God (Gen. 3:4, 5) and he will lie on a minister of today. If he said what you say he did about these ministers it would but strengthen my confidence in them, for any people that the devil would thus speak against would seem a good people to line up with. I now direct attention to the testimonies of these two women as printed in your tract.

Mrs. Palmer, according to her testimony, first attended services at the "Church of God" (your movement), knelt at the altar, taught Sunday School class, courted a young man and says she "disobeyed the Lord and married him;" her home was broken up—this was while she was with your movement. Then as a sinner, she went to a Pentecostal meeting, and instead of going to the altar and getting right with God, she went to the "tarrying room" to deceive herself and others: came there with a devil, went in for deception and got what she went after. Apparently she became demon possessed while with your movement and before attending the Pentecostal meetings.

The other woman, Elsie M. Hughes, says she "prayed earnestly" for the Lord to direct her to a church, and she "felt impressed to go to a certain church." This was a Pentecostal Church, and she was led there in answer to prayer. She was "under the power" and was TOLD that she had spoken in tongues and had received her baptism. (No one had to tell me when I received my baptism, for I knew about it).

She says that what she received was devil possession, but says "I was so happy." I do not know what she received, but I must say that it is my first time to hear that the devil makes one happy.

She says, "I watched others and found them living in sin and speaking in tongues." (Yes, Sister, if I had kept my eyes on people instead of the Lord when in the Reformation, I too could have become discouraged and perhaps filled with devils.)

After she became devil possessed and had got to the place where she "did not believe in God, and was desperate," she just "noticed a little Church on the corner; it was the Church of God" and she went in. She didn't pray about it—was in no condition to pray—was demon possessed and led by the devil; and this is how she was led to your movement. It was three years before she could take her stand with you. Doesn't sound much like the truth and power of the early church, when three thousand accepted the Pentecostal message in one day and it took only a few words from Philip to cause the eunuch to see the truth and take his stand (see also Cornelius' house and others).

She says she found the Church of God the "only true church" (your movement) and "found they did not believe you had to speak in tongues in order to receive the Holy Spirit." Now because folks don't believe the Bible, this does not destroy the truth of the Word; but let me say that we do not believe you must speak in tongues in order to receive the Holy Ghost; you first receive the Holy Ghost and then speak with other tongues as the Spirit gives utterance (Acts 2:4). He is first to "testify" and "ye also shall bear witness" (John 15:26, 27). One may receive the Holy Ghost in a measure, as the disciples did before Pentecost (Jn. 20:22), may preach with a degree of power, heal the sick, cast out devils, etc., and yet not have received their full Pentecost, with the evidence of speaking in tongues. When He is come, Jesus said, "He shall testify of me." This is why you hear so much praising and exalting Jesus in the Pentecostal meetings, and why people are flocking to them as at Pentecost.

You preach "the church," sing "the church," praise "the Church," exalt "the Church," (your church), when if you would let the Holy Ghost come in, you would be praising Jesus, and He said, "If I be lifted up will draw all men unto me." How many times does it say in the Word to preach the Church? If the Church is the bride of Christ, should the bride exalt self or exalt Him?

Now, I would not like to admit, as Sister Hughes does, that I was serving a God who, when I "prayed earnestly" for Him to lead me to the right church, led me to the wrong one, and when I sought the Holy

Ghost, gave me a devil. I could not serve a God like that and recommend Him to others. If He led her into the wrong church once, perhaps she is not in the right one yet.

That these women failed to seek and obtain the real baptism of the Holy Ghost but professed something they did not have, is not at all impossible (and especially since Sister Hughes says she took another's word, for her baptism); or having obtained it and failing to keep true to God and going on professing and putting on a sham or imitation of what they once had until they became filled with sin and the devil, is also possible. But if this is proof that the Pentecostal movement is wrong, then the fact that some have knelt at your altars and testified to being saved and sanctified and afterwards living in sin would prove your movement false also. Neither of their testimonies would convince any sane, reasonable person that, should an honest soul seek the Holy Ghost and (like the 120) tarry until He came, according to Acts 2:4, there would be any danger of his becoming devil possessed.

There are many abominable doctrines and false teachers in the world, even denying the Lord Jesus and the atonement, teaching commandments of men and doctrines of devils; and it seems strange that these demons who converse with you never represent themselves as any of these, or refer to them as "leading souls to hell;" but rather refer to a people who obey the command of the Lord to "tarry until," and who are marked as the early Church was, the way that "everywhere it is spoken against," and who are called devils as Jesus foretold.

The casting out devils is a good work and we are glad the poor women got deliverance; but why hold a jubilee over it when Jesus said "in this rejoice not." Charity vaunteth not itself, is not puffed up. Jesus said, many will say, Lord, Lord, have we not cast out devils in thy name? and then will I profess unto them "I never knew you, depart from me." Paul said that in the last days men would be "boastful" and would "creep into houses and lead captive silly women;" from such he says "turn away" (2 Tim. 3:2, 5, 6). These two women are not the first to be turned from the true way; in the book of martyrs we read of two women who were induced to recant and when their former pastor was tied to the stake they applied the torch to the faggots.

You may quote a minister to support your arguments against "tongues" who once preached the Pentecostal message in all its fullness, but who has compromised; but remember that some holiness preachers have ceased to hold up the standard; likewise there are evangelists who once used the mourners bench to get folks saved in the old fashioned way, who have for popularity's sake adopted a "hit-the-sawdust-trail," a "handshake," or a "card-signing" method. But are the compromisers a safe crowd to follow? Remember Pilate and King Saul.

Had you been at Samaria when it was discovered that Simon the sorcerer was not right with God, you could have published a tract saying that these Pentecostal ministers, Philip, Peter and John, were devils and used Simon as an example, and had not Judas Iscariot committed suicide so soon, you might have secured his testimony also as having become devil possessed while in company with these ministers, and one Jesus of Nazareth; and you could have had a large company of

Christ-rejecting Jews to join with you in calling the Master of the house Beelzebub and those of His household, devils. You might have got the demons in Judas to call themselves by the name of Jesus or some of the Apostles and to say they were leading souls to hell.

Now brethren, please reverse the matter and see how it will appear. Supposing the Pentecostal movement was putting out such literature against your movement, saying that people became devil possessed in your meetings; calling your ministers devils, etc.; and backing their claims by a "thus saith the devil"—would you expect any reasonable, thinking person to accept such and believe it?

THE CHALLENGE

Fay C. Martin, author of the tract referred to in a series of articles in the Gospel Trumpet, under the title of "Do All Speak with Tongues," waxes very warm and becomes very adept in the use of abusive terms, giving vent to his displeasure by calling the Pentecostal movement the "modern tongues delusion," "unseemly," "indecent," "rankest," "most deceptive," "net," "devilish," "diabolical trap," "originated in the lower regions," "deceptive," "tricky," "fraudulent," "delusioning," "cunning," and says that "many of the very elect are being deceived and dragged into its relentless clutches to the regions of torment" (all the above extracted from a space 2 ¼ x 3 inches and is a sample of the overflow of the love (?) and unity (?) from the heart of a Reformation minister). Perhaps he means by the "very elect," those of his own movement, from which so many have gone to the Pentecostal movement to receive a deeper experience and freedom of spirit. But he flatly contradicts Jesus who shows that even the false christs and false prophets cannot deceive the very elect nor pluck them out of His hand (Matt. 24:24; John 10:27-29).

Mr. Martin not only criticizes the speaking in tongues, but sets himself in array against all demonstrations of the Spirit. He says in regard to people becoming prostrate under the power of the Spirit, "Again" (repeating) "we CHALLENGE any and all Pentecostal tongues contenders to produce in the New Testament where any person went under some so-called power and became helpless, senseless and prostrate, or even the hint of their going down onto the floor," and adds, "there is not even a hint of such unseemly, unbecoming, indecorous, unsuitable and indecent conduct." My! What a Challenge! Is it through ignorance of the Scriptures that you publish such, or is it that you think your readers so ignorant as to be deceived by such a challenge or statement and frightened into staying away from all Pentecostal meetings?

Is Mr. Martin so modest as to become shocked at the so-called "indecorous, unsuitable and indecent conduct" which he charges us with? and yet your congregations go on bathing parties and your ministers (women preachers included) practice promiscuous bathing, which is granted and justified through the pages of the Gospel Trumpet, as I have in my possession to show. Jesus speaks of some who strain at a gnat and swallow a camel, and who bind heavy burdens on others but touch them not with one of their fingers. So do you demand and CHALLENGE others to give Scripture for everything they do; yet you do many things that there is no Scripture for doing; and even do that which it forbids. It emphatically says "Forbid not to speak with tongues" (1 Cor. 14:39), yet you forbid it. It nowhere says they built meeting houses and put the name "Church of God" over the door; but you do this and get people to where they cannot go in and worship or fellowship God's people if it is otherwise; it nowhere says that people knelt at an altar for either regeneration or sanctification, or that they sang with an uplifted hand, or that the apostles prostrated people when baptizing them, yet you do these things. The Scriptures say nothing about the apostles putting on church shows (pageants) with paid admissions, or even the hint of their approval of such. It nowhere says that devils when being cast out represented themselves as some living person (minister or others), but you claim they do in your séances. It doesn't say that the apostles ever took the words or messages of demons and used them against their fellow-brethren in the ministry; yet you do this. Can you show where the demons ever called the names of any, other than some holy person, as Jesus or Paul? The devil was well acquainted with Job, but refused to recognize those who were not of God (Acts 19:15). You bestow honor on those whom you would destroy by saying that the demons call their names.

Now since Mr. Martin so vehemently directs attention to the position of those in the upper-room and assume that because the word "sitting" is used, they were all sitting upright during the tarrying and outpouring of the Spirit, I ask, why in the name of reason do you not insist that people in your services remain in their seats to be sanctified (or filled with the Spirit as you call it) instead of going to the altar for a few minutes to be argued into saying that they are sanctified?

Your "Challenge" is to produce "EVEN A HINT" in the Scriptures of anyone falling down or lying prostrate before the Lord. You shall have plenty of proof, Scripture too, not a "thus saith the devil." You admit there is one instance (only one)—that of Saul on the Damascus road—but try to explain it away by saying "he had murder in his heart and was not yet lined up with Christ." But notice that he surrendered when he fell and talked to the Lord and received his instructions from Him while lying there. Three days later we find him again down before the Lord, tarrying and praying, for the account says he "arose" (Acts 9:18). Again when he was caught up to the third heaven (2 Cor. 12:1-4) and was under the power of the Spirit so that he did not know if he was in the body or out of the body, can you prove he was sitting upright, beholding and knowing all that was going on about him? Are you sure Peter when in a trance on the housetop was not prostrate when the voice said "Rise"?

Come now and take a little trip with me through the Scriptures. In Luke 5:12 we find a leper falling down on his face before Jesus and begging to be made clean. In Luke 17:16 we see another leper lying on his face and thanking Jesus for his cleansing. We go up on the Mount of Transfiguration and there we find Peter, James and John lying right down on their faces (Matt. 17:6). We go over to Gethsemane and there find Jesus on His face (Matt. 26:39). We go to the Isle of Patmos, where John is under the power of the Spirit (Rev. 1:10), and as Jesus appears he falls at His feet as dead (v. 17). My! such "unbecoming and indecent conduct," says Mr. Martin. He calls this a "new counterfeit of Christianity," and tells us that the devil invented it. Well, let us see how "new" it is.

Before finishing with the New Testament, we will drop back a few thousand years and begin with Abraham, and shock his modesty (?) and pride with the actions of a few thousands (or millions) of Old Testament characters. We read, "And Abram fell on his face and God talked with him" (Gen. 17:3). Then it isn't so "new," is it? "Then Moses and Aaron fell on their faces before all the assembly of Israel" (Num. 14:5). Again "they fell upon their faces and the glory of the Lord appeared unto them" (Num. 20:6). (See also Ch. 16:4, 22, 45; Deut. 9:18, 25.) "And Joshua fell on his face to the earth and did worship" (Josh. 5:14; 7:6). Worshipped whom, the devil? You might say so. Even the ass on which Balaam was riding, when it saw the angel of the Lord, had reverence enough to fall down (Num. 22:27). Balaam also "fell flat on his face" (v. 31). Elijah and Elisha both prostrated themselves in raising the dead (1 Kings 17:21; 2 Kings 4:34). Many times when Ezekiel saw the glory of the Lord, he says, "I fell upon my face" (Ezek. 1:28; 3:23; 11:13; 43:3; 44:4.) Daniel too was guilty of this "unbecoming" (?) conduct (Dan. 8:17, 18; 10:8, 9.) "All Judah and the inhabitants of Jerusalem (thousands of them) fell before the Lord" (2 Chr. 20:18). Again "All the people shouted and fell on their faces" (other thousands) (Lev. 9:24). When the fire fell and consumed Elijah's sacrifice at Carmel, "and when all the people saw it (still other thousands), they fell on their faces" (1 Kings 18:39). When the Spirit of God (not an evil spirit) came on Saul, Israel's first king, he lay down all day and all night and prophesied (1 Sam. 19:23, 24). Very "unbecoming," but Samuel witnessed it and never rebuked him. King David also, a man after God's own heart, with the elders of Israel "fell on their faces" (1 Chr. 21:16).

Now back to the New Testament, but first permit me to quote from "Deeper Experiences of Famous

Christians" (a book sold and highly recommended by the Gospel Trumpet Co.) what Chas. G. Finney says about the power falling in his meetings. He says "The people began to fall from their seats in every direction—nearly all were prostrate within a few minutes." We wonder what class Mr. Martin would put these people in, and also the numbers that I have seen in my boyhood days, in the good old Baptist revivals when many would lie prostrate for hours, and some even lay all night. This was before the coming of the present Pentecostal outpourings; the latter rains of the evening light; the speaking with stammering lips and other tongues, which the prophet foretold and said "This is the rest, and this is the refreshing;" this is the "sign" also (read 1 Cor. 14:21, 22 with Isa. 28:11, 12 and Acts 2:16-18 with Isa. 44:3-5; Joel 2:28, 29). It is the receiving of the full baptism of the Holy Ghost and speaking in tongues that causes the "unbelievers" to become hardened and to speak evil of the way (Acts 19:6-9).

We will now let Mr. Martin pass judgment on another blood-washed company of a few hundred millions. Let someone good in multiplication and enumeration count them while he closes his eyes, or takes his congregation to a bathing beach to prostrate themselves half nude in the water or on the sand along the shore. Please read Rev. 4:8-11; 5:8-14; 7:9-17. Chapter 5:8 says the elders and four beasts fall down before the Lamb. V. 9 shows that these represent the redeemed of all nations, (so agrees F. G. Smith and Adam Clark). Ch. 7:9-14 says that this company that fall down before the Lamb, "NO MAN CAN NUMBER." Ch. 5:11 shows a host of angels, and their number was ten thousand times ten thousand (one hundred million) and thousands of thousands (no small company is it?); Ch.

7:11-12 says that all these angels fall down before the throne on their faces and worship God "saying, Amen: blessing, and glory, and wisdom, and thanksgiving, and honor, and power, and might, be unto our God for ever and ever, Amen." I want to be among that number, don't you? Hallelujah. Praise God and the Lamb for ever!

If the devil "invented" this, his patent has expired and he and Fay C. Martin both cannot stop God's people from using it. If it is a "counterfeit of Christianity," Mr. Martin will have to drag all the angels into his court to pass judgment on them with us, for we have all the angels on our side, Glory! Should your people get in there with all their modesty (?) and pride, and hatred toward the Pentecostal people, and behold such a scene as John saw—all the redeemed of earth and all the angelic hosts of heaven lying prostrate on their faces, shouting praises to God—could you join in with them, or would you pull off and start another rebellion in Heaven? Why sing "At the Name of Jesus bowing, FALLING PROSTRATE at His feet" (148 in M. of Z.) and then condemn it in such strong terms?

Reader, I ask you in all sincerity to consider a people who would throw out such a challenge, whether it is because of ignorance of the Scriptures, or for the purpose of deceiving others; can they be trusted in the handling of God's Word on any point?

C. W. NAYLOR PROPHESIES

Brother Naylor once turned prophet and predicted the death of the Pentecostal movement. He said, "It is rapidly dying out—it doubtless will altogether die out and be only a memory."—(Gospel Trumpet, June 21, 1928).

Now it is not my desire to elaborate on the Pentecostal movement; neither to detract from the good that your movement may be doing; but let us make some comparisons between the two movements, lest your people become blinded by hearing so much about the great (?) "Reformation," the "only true Church," and the only movement in all the world that has the "truth" (?).

You have just celebrated the fiftieth anniversary of your movement, and according to your printed statement have 32,000 members; millions in our land have never heard of it. The Pentecostal movement is just half as old, and numbers into the millions; and where is the man, woman or child in America or any other Protestant country that does not know of it? In this city (Detroit, Mich.) of a million and a half people of all nationalities, your movement has six small congregations (which is fewer than at the time Mr. Naylor predicted the death of the Pentecostal movement) with a total of less than 1000 members; and in all Detroit, you have not a church of any foreign nationality. Moreover, your people sold their church property to get out of a foreign locality, while Pentecostal congregations were springing up all around them among the foreign people. To my knowledge, there are eight foreign nationalities here with from one to four Pentecostal congregations each, besides the hundreds of all nations (including Jews and Indians) who worship in the many American congregations where many have heard messages in their native tongues as the "Spirit gave utterance."

Mr. Naylor says the Pentecostal movement is split into twenty or more "factions," and says "there is a constant warfare among the leaders." The Protestant or Evangelical movement, founded on regeneration, became divided into many groups or bodies. The Holiness movement, founded on sanctification, did the same. And the Pentecostal movement, founded on the baptism of the Holy Ghost, it is true is divided into several groups; but can they be accused of being at "warfare" with each other more than are those of either the Holiness or Evangelical movements? No matter how varied may be the different groups of Pentecostal people, there certainly is no one group more adverse to the others than is your movement toward other groups of Holiness people. Your group, as small as it is, has not been without divisions, and though you hold the title to the original publishing house, etc., my guess is that, should D. S. Warner, its founder, come back now and see the things that you practice, he would take another wing of the split rather than your group.

Now I have not the statistics of all Pentecostal groups (Mr. Naylor says there are more than twenty), but I have before me a report of one branch only (the others may be, some larger, some smaller), but this one group alone far exceeds the whole of your movement. Yet you call your movement "Reformation." They have more than double the number of congregations and three times the members that you have. They don't beg or make money drives as you do, yet they receive more for foreign missions alone than you receive for your associated budgets (five phases of your work). You have only fifty-six foreign missionaries. They have 283, with more in either Africa, China or India than you have in all the world.

Some years ago it was claimed that your movement had 100,000 members against 32,000 now. So it seems that your movement is the one that is dying out, rather than the Pentecostal movement.

A movement that is founded on an experience as are the Evangelical, the Holiness, and the Pentecostal movements, never die out, but are always on the increase; while a movement founded on a mere teaching, as your movement is, may die out.

Mr. Naylor, please prophesy again; but read Rev. 19:20 before doing so.

YOUR MOVEMENT FALLEN

I am new going to make a statement that may surprise and shock you, since you claim your movement is the "only true Church," and that you are the only people who have the truth. I will put it in the form of a challenge (challenges seem in order since you started it) and will back it up by a reward of any ten dollar Bible on the market to the first one to point out any body of holiness people who have apostatized so soon and fallen to as low a plane as your movement. I say this with pity and not to ridicule.

I shall not take individual and extreme cases as the basis, and set them up as your standard (as you do of the Pentecostal movement); but will take that which comes from your leaders and which is published in your literature. Neither do I condemn the honest individuals in your movement until they have the light; but if after reading this they fail to heed the call of God to "come out of her my people," they become as those of other fallen movements who refuse to come out.

If D. S. Warner, the founder of your movement has declared you as fallen (and he has) by saying that your ministers "By following the silly and pompous habit of Babylon lords, these priests actually appear to set themselves in the temple of God, showing themselves that they are gods;" and adds "these men set themselves up to be feared and worshiped"; then you should not censure me for saying that you are fallen.

Though Brother Warner has been in glory many years, yet his words come down to you through the tract "No-Sectism" published by you even since being at your present location. He applied the above words to the ministers of another body of people for practicing that which your ministers practice today, and which your movement approves. Take that tract, read page one and substitute "Reformation" for the other church and see for yourself. If D. S. Warner were here today and preaching as he preached then, would you allow him in your pulpit?

In former days you were so modest as to forbid the wearing of a necktie; and had such fear of pride that your people, I am told, even refused to allow buttons on children's clothes; but alas! you have swung to the other extreme so that your only standard of modesty is the customs of the community in which one lives.

You were once very strict on divorce, not granting that one divorced, no matter for what cause, should marry. Now one may be divorced by his companion and marry another within a week, and still hold important offices in the church; or one may have three living companions, and not divorced from any on Bible grounds and not be condemned. I have in my possession a letter from C. W. Naylor (the man in charge of your Question Department, and considered able to state correctly your position on all matters), who says of one guilty of adultery, "The guilty party, in case the companion divorces him or her and remarries, is left without a companion. We understand that the divorce completely breaks the marriage tie. The Bible does not say anything specifically on the point of the remarriage of the guilty party. IT DOES NOT FORBID IT." This is equal to saying that one with a companion whom he wishes to cast off for another, but in whom he could find no ground for divorce, can commit the offense himself to cause his companion to divorce him that he may marry another and still not be condemned.

Your salaried ministry; money-raising schemes; putting on church shows (pageants) with paid admission and reserved seats; socials; Halloween parties, etc., which you practice now would not have been countenanced by your people in former days; neither by other bodies of holiness people at the present time. The last year I was with your movement, our pastor held two social suppers in the church to one of the Lord's supper.

Is your movement fallen? If not, please tell me what would constitute a fallen movement.

"Come out of her my people."—Bible.

SPEAKING IN TONGUES

I deem it unnecessary in this brief article to set forth a treatise on speaking in tongues. Plenty may be had on this subject from the many publishers of Pentecostal literature. It seems that any Bible student should discern between the speaking in tongues at an altar or tarrying service, as the evidence of the Holy Ghost Baptism as set forth in Acts where a dozen spoke in one instance, a household in another, and 120 in another, with no limit put on it, neither any interpretation mentioned; and that of Corinthians where the gift of tongues with interpretations in the church is dealt with and the control or limiting of it, to within reason, left to those in charge, as is prophecy) so that when a reasonable number of messages have gone forth, they may proceed with the services (singing, etc.) leaving the one speaking to become silent, or to speak to himself and to God, and not to the Church; keeping in mind that in all instances we are commanded to "forbid not to speak with tongues" (1 Cor. 14:39). "He that speaketh in an unknown tongue edifieth himself" (V. 4) and we should rejoice to see another edified. Note that the word "let" occurs four times in Vs. 27, 28 and as in V. 13 means "LET" (not make) one interpret the same as "let" (not make) two or three speak. These scriptures are for the limiting rather than the eliminating of tongues; and given to a church that practiced speaking in tongues, not to one that opposed it. Suppose you try binding V. 34 as you do 27, 28 and see the results.

Much stress is put on the "do all speak with tongues" of 1 Cor. 12:30. Paul says that if the whole church came together and "all" speak with tongues (as though it were possible), will they not say ye are mad? The "unlearned" and "unbelievers" will (Ch. 14:23). They said at Pentecost that they were drunk. He also says, "I would that ye all spake with tongues" (V. 5). Would he desire them to do that which is not Scriptural? He asks "are all prophets," but says "ye may all prophesy" (V. 31). "Have all the gifts of healing?" No, but all may pray for the sick. All do not have the gift of faith, yet all may exercise faith. Do all speak with tongues (the gift)? No, only those who have the gift. Do all speak with tongues (the evidence)? No, only those who receive the Holy Ghost (the baptism) speak with tongues. Do any in your movement speak with tongues? Do any in your services ever receive the Holy Ghost according to Acts 2:4; 10:44-46; 19:6?

You require that the one who speaks in tongues must know that he has the gift of tongues and must know that it is going to be interpreted, and the one that interprets must know the language that is spoken. This kind of man rule, pressure and unbelief would stamp out the operation of the Spirit along any line. Would divine healing stand up under it? Were you as adverse to healing as you are to tongues, would there be any praying for the sick in your services? If you prayed for one in your services and he claimed to get healed, and if after you had published it, he should come out and say it was a mockery on his part to prove your movement false and your healings all a fake (as the one who pulled the "sweet potato" stuff referred to in your wonderful (?) tract), I ask, what would you think of him and of the movement that published it?

To you who write so much about the speaking in tongues—how it should or should not be practiced—I ask, have you experienced it? Would you accept one's teaching on Salvation if he had never been saved? or on divine healing if he had never experienced healing, never prayed for the sick, and only found fault with everyone who did?

Since you admit there is a "true gift of tongues," I ask, have you any of it in your movement? Will you tell us how you practice (not how others should) speaking in tongues in your services? Are your people carrying it to an excess? If you can show us BY EXAMPLE a better way to use the gift of tongues, we will be glad to sit at your feet and learn; but until you do we shall continue to speak as the Spirit gives utterance.

The apostles, before Pentecost, healed the sick; cast out devils; prophesied (Preached); had wisdom, knowledge, faith, etc., but the speaking in tongues was the "sign" reserved to accompany the Holy Ghost "the rest and refreshing" to those who "understand doctrine and weaned from the milk;" a stumbling-block to those who will not hear "that they might go and fall backward" (1 Cor. 14:21, 22; Isa. 28:9-13).

Fay C. Martin says, "There are but three recorded instances where people spoke in tongues at the reception of the Holy Ghost." How many times must the Scriptures say a thing before he will accept it? By the mouth of two or more witnesses, I believe the Word. There are instances galore where people prostrated themselves in worship, yet he says it is "new" and the devil "invented" it. Will he give one instance where any "gift" or "sign," save tongues, is mentioned as first evidence? There are only two references made to anointing the sick with oil, yet you accept this as the Scriptural way. I challenge you to show in the Scriptures where any one ever received the baptism of the Holy Ghost without speaking in tongues.

Men oppose speaking in tongues because they cannot rule over it. The human must give way and the Holy Ghost have full sway. They cannot say "now we will have a message in tongues by Miss Popularity and the interpretation by Dr. Collegebred;" neither can they say to the one speaking "thus far and no further" without disobeying the Word and driving the Spirit away. The message may come from some humble child of God, unlearned in the wisdom of the world and may be a rebuke to Dr. DeDee (for God is no respecter of persons); and so they are constantly telling how tongues should not be used, meaning that it SHOULD NOT BE USED. Many commit the "folly" by answering and saying "I don't believe in tongues the way you practice it," when they have never heard a real message in tongues with interpretation, or seen anyone receive the Holy Ghost according to Acts 2:4. (See Prov. 18:13).

THE REFORMATION

Regeneration brought the Sixteenth Century Reformation and the Evangelical movement; Sanctification brought the Eighteenth Century Reformation and the Holiness movement; the Holy Ghost baptism has brought the Twentieth Century Reformation and the Pentecostal movement. (Within eighteen months from the time of the general outpouring of the Spirit in 1906 the Pentecostal movement had encircled the globe and its missionaries were in all parts of the world). It takes an experience—that which changes the lives of people—to work a reformation. A mere teaching about the Church, baptism, the keeping of a day, etc., may produce a sect, but not a reformation. Webster defines "sect" as a "body of people who unite in holding some particular religious view." It is as much of a sect with an unwritten creed as with a written one.

Salvation makes one a member of the family of God; but it does not make one a member of your movement, therefore, your movement is not the Church of God. Naming a thing "reformation" does not make it such. A reformation is a work, not a teaching; not taught but wrought; not understood, but felt; not explained but experienced; not in word but in action; not an outward form but an inward work; not of men but of God; not built up, but comes down.

Sanctification comes between regeneration and the Holy Ghost baptism, both in the type and antitype; between the Passover and Sinai (Pentecost); between Calvary and the upper-room (Pentecost). In Ex. 12 we have the Passover-type of Calvary. In Ex. 19 the people were sanctified, made ready, waiting (tarrying) for Pentecost. They were sanctified with blood (Ex. 24:8); so are we (Heb. 13:12). When Moses was ready to ascend up into the Mount, he said "Tarry ye" (V. 14). Jesus when ready to ascend said, "Tarry ye" (Lk. 24:49). In the camp the people trembled (Ex. 19:16). In the camp of the saints today there is shaking and trembling. Some look on and say it is of the devil and would stop it, but it meant death to "gaze" or to "touch" even the border of God's mountain (Ex. 19:12, 13, 21). Remember what happened to Uzzah who tried to stop God's property from shaking (2 Sam. 6:6, 7). Many today are dead, but don't know it, because they have laid their hands on God's Anointed. It was not to ungodly sinners that Jesus uttered the warning about the blaspheming against the Holy Ghost (Mk. 3:22-30) but to the religious leaders of the day, and because they charged the work of the Lord to being the work of the devil.

Sanctification is the Bethany experience and comes between Calvary and the upper-room. He led them out to Bethany, lifted up His hands and blessed them. They were already saved; so this was the "second blessing" (Sanctification). While He blessed them He was parted from them (as Elijah was from Elisha, 2 Kings 2) and carried up into Heaven. The blessing (like Elijah's mantle) remained with them. They returned with "great joy," a mark of sanctification; were of "one accord," another mark (Jn. 17); continued in "prayer and supplication—praising and blessing God;" as people do today when seeking the baptism (Luke 24:50-63; Acts 1:14). Clark, commenting on the Samaritans receiving the Holy Ghost (Acts 8:15) says this was "certainly not for the sanctification of the souls of the people; this they had on believing on Christ Jesus; and this the apostles never dispensed. It was the miraculous gifts of the Spirit—speaking with different tongues" etc., and on V. 18 as to what Simon the Sorcerer saw, he says, "By hearing then speak with different tongues and work miracles" (Clark's Commentary). Nowhere do the Scriptures say we are sanctified with the Holy Ghost. We are sanctified "by" the Holy Ghost (Rom. 15:16) but "with" the blood (Heb. 13:12), the Spirit being the agent, as a vessel is washed BY (not with) an individual, and WITH (not by) water.

Regeneration redeems; Sanctification cleanses; the Holy Ghost fills. Regeneration comes through repentance; Sanctification, through consecration; the Holy Ghost through praise. Regeneration brings pardon; Sanctification, purity; the Holy Ghost, power. The results are of Regeneration, peace; of Sanctification, joy; of the Holy Ghost, comfort.

The tide of persecution that has come against each step of this triune reformation, instead of coming from the world, has come from the religious leaders closest behind them—they being too wise (?) to accept anything new—and the others being left too far in the rear to see the light or put up a fight. (It was the Jews—the former light-bearers—who persecuted Jesus). We know who opposed the Luther reformation; and as all Holiness people know, it was the old line Protestant Churches that so strongly opposed the Holiness movement. If you Church of God Reformation (so-called) people wish to see a picture of yourselves as you fight Pentecost, you only need to go to your own literature and read the "Deacon of Dobbinsville." The so-called Holiness people are the ones who abuse the Pentecostal people most and heap all kinds of names on them.

I'm not dogmatizing on seeking each of these experiences separately; I am only showing that they are in the Bible, and the order in which they come. They are for God's people no matter how men may theorize on it. All were lost in the Apostasy, and have been restored a step at a time. They are here now and one may, like those at Cornelius' house, believe and be filled with the Spirit so quickly that onlookers will be "astonished," and of course his Sanctification will be complete, for Calvary and Bethany are on the way to the upper-room, and the temple must be clean before the Holy Ghost will come in. It is a frequent occurrence to see one get saved and filled with the Holy Ghost before leaving the altar. God is able—it matters not if it takes one sixty seconds or sixty years to receive the fullness. It is surprising how easily the little children receive the baptism and it is like heaven indeed to see a little child come through and hear it speak, as it were in the language of heaven, as it seems to be explaining to the angels the wonders of a full baptism. The angels could but fold their wings, hang their harps and listen. If you have never beheld a scene like this, you have surely missed the greatest foretaste of heaven.

There is something radically wrong with a people who are so dead spiritually that there is no demonstration of the Spirit among them and who only find fault with others and charge them as of the devil for not becoming like themselves. Mr. Naylor says that the Pentecostal people "live upon their emotions" and that "the movement is full of emotionalism." This, I assert with all love and kindness, is not true. One instance will suffice as proof. Everyone who attends Pentecostal meetings regularly knows that often our altars are filled with seekers before even an invitation song is sung; while in your services you sing the most emotional and touching songs during the altar calls and with little or no results. We only let God have HIS way and you cannot discern between the power of the Spirit and emotion. Remember that it was the shouting that caused the walls of Jericho to fall. It took the wind, earthquake and fire to get Elijah's attention, and the "still small voice" prepared him for the message that was to follow, (1 Kings 19). The wind, earthquake and fire accompanies the Holy Ghost (Acts 2:2-3 and 4:31), and the still small voice— speaking in tongues—follows, (Acts 2:4). There is no proof that anyone understood them while in the upper-room and apparently there was no need to speak in tongues to be understood, as they were all Galileans (Acts 2:7). Note also Acts 10:44-46, 19:6—no mention of an interpreter or of any understanding the language in either instance. Paul refers to this (1 Cor. 14:2) as speaking unto God, the mysteries that no man understands. This is what caused the people to turn out (like Elijah) (Acts 2:6) and then they heard the message. But there were mockers then, as now, saying they were drunk, when they saw the wonderful demonstrations (perhaps shouting and dancing in the Spirit). Had you been there, which crowd would you have been with?— with those speaking in tongues, acting like drunk, etc.; with those who heard the message; or with those who mocked, speaking evil of the way, saying they were drunk, mad, crazy, of the devil, etc.? I have seen some who could spend the day on a pleasure boat where worldly people were dancing to the flesh and the devil, and enjoy themselves; but when they went to a full Gospel service and saw folks dance in the Spirit, they wanted to get out and could never go back again; yet they claimed to be saved and sanctified (lovers of pleasure more than lovers of God). Are you on the side with God's people, who leap, shout and dance before the Lord; or with Saul's daughters and the prodigal son's brothers who "despise" them in their heart and become "angry" and will not go in because there is re- joicing ("music and dancing") in Father's house? (See 2 Sam 6:16; Luke 15:25-28). The Psalmist David makes dancing as much a part of worship as the playing of stringed instruments and organs. See Ps. 149:3; 150:4; 30:11; Ex. 15:20-21; Jer. 31:4). Notwithstanding, Mr. Naylor says it never was a part of worship, either in the Old Testament or in the New.

What will you do with David when you get to heaven if he should happen to be there? Were the Apos- tle Paul here today and instead of using "enticing words of men's wisdom" he came with "demonstrations of the Spirit and of power and in much trembling" (1 Cor. 2:1- 4) and if he laid hands on people and a dozen at once began speaking in tongues (Acts 19:6-7), I ask, would you go to hear him, or allow him to preach in your pul- pit? The Lord gives the Holy Ghost to those who obey Him (Acts 5:32), not to those who disobey (1 Cor. 14:39) find fault and speak evil of the way. Before you get your baptism, you must stop finding fault with God's way of doing things. You don't get it on one knee and with bowed head. Get on both knees, turn your face heavenward, put your hands up (for lightning rods), let His praises roll. (Lying on your back is a convenient way to turn your face toward heaven). When the power starts coming down and the glory floods your soul, don't be afraid; don't try to stop it—just keep on keeping on; let go and let God. He is able to take care of you, no matter what men and devils say about Him. The God that we are serving doesn't give His children serpents when they ask for fish, or stones instead of bread; neither does he catch them with their mouths open, praising Him and pleading, for the Holy Ghost, and poke devils down their throats. Those who say He does, don't know our God and have either never sought the Holy Ghost earnestly and received Him; or having "tasted the heavenly gift, and been made partakers of the Holy Ghost," have fallen away so that it is impossible to restore them.

Brother, sisters let God have His way. Let the shouts and glories roll. Our Jesus is worthy of praise, Hallelujah! There is rejoicing in Father's house. Jesus is coming soon. He is coming with a shout, and we expect to go up with a shout to meet Him, Hallelujah!

"Tarry Until"

"These Signs Shall Follow"

"This Is That"

SALVATION

Full and free, for you and me.
God thought it,
Love wrought it,
Jesus bought it,

The Spirit brought it,
The Word taught it,
I sought it,
The devil fought it,
Some doubt it,
Others had it,
I got it,
      and
You may have it,
      Hallelujah!

I have no apology to make for the writing of this tract, only that out of a heart of pure love I have written as the Lord laid the burden on my heart; and because I am rejoicing in the wonderful experience which I have received, and desire to help those whom I love to escape from the bondage that I was once in, that they too may enjoy the freedom that I now enjoy.

May He who leads and guides aright,
Lead you on and give you light;
And grant to me what I crave most;
That you receive the Holy Ghost.

In Christian love,

J. W. LYNCH.

An Experience With Demons In "Pentecostal Tongueism." By Fay Martin

Two young women began attending services at the Church of God, one starting some months after the other and neither at that time acquainted with the other. They had both attended one of the Pentecostal (tongues) churches here in Washington, D. C., were both members, and one had been a member for around a period of two or three years.

We at once discerned a spirit which seemed to be foreign to the Holy Spirit, and spent hours laboring with these two girls, as we recognized their honesty and sincerity and strong desires to serve God in a manner pleasing to Him. But in spite of all, it seemed they had an up and down experience, now on the mountain top, then again in the valley, and filled with doubts and fears as to the genuineness of their experience and the infilling of the Holy Spirit.

Some months ago Wife and I spent with each girl separately nearly two whole nights in prayer that they might be freed from this terrible bondage. We discerned they were demon possessed. It seemed that all the blackness of hell settled in the room while we prayed till in each case along toward morning of the second night of prayer the darkness lifted and it seemed crawled off like an old serpent after which the room was lighted with the glory of God, and the presence of Jesus seemed so close and real. It seemed we had complete victory it seemed; but oh, how deceptive is the Devil.

Time went on, the girls realizing that the Movement was wrong and that their experience of getting under the power and speaking in tongues was not the Holy Spirit at all, but was the power of the Devil and yet they were to make a plain, definite statement of this fact and to take a final, decisive stand against it for fear of blaspheming the Holy Ghost. We wish to state right here that this is the reason why many of those who get into the Tongues Movement know it is not right, are afraid to take a stand against it and come out.

The girls would try to take a firm stand against it but in each instance it seemed like all hell would let loose on them. One of them would have the bed quilts jerked off her while she slept with no one in the room at all, and presently she would begin to see forms moving about the room. (This is as near like Spiritualism as can possibly be). This experience would occur after her exposing the movement and trying to take a definite stand against it. Similar experiences on the part of others who have tried to come out have undoubtedly driven them back into it again.

The girls thought they were going insane and we wish to state here that many cases of so-called insanity are nothing more than what these young women had.

They came to Wife and me in confidence as their pastors. We took one of them into our home to live. No one but God knows the battles and victories we have had, as we felt in duty bound not to publish all we knew, knowing that but few could really understand. Finally both girls felt an irresistible, impelling power within forcing them to take their own lives. Devils were possessing and gradually usurping all power and all authority in their lives. Both girls held fine positions, but realized they could continue no longer in their present condition.

We discerned beyond doubt they were demon possessed. Wife and I spent days in fasting and prayer, altogether seven or eight days. During the afternoon of the fourth day of my fasting while one of them lay under the power, Wife and I laid on hands while I commanded the evil spirit in the name of Jesus to come out. Then came the first response from the devil who talked out of her and said, "I will not come out." I asked, "Who are you who dares to defy Jesus' name and to say I will not come out when commanded in the name of Jesus?" The voice shouted back, "I am Lucifer, and you do not have powers to cast me out." The battle was on. Jesus' name has never known defeat and we knew victory was ours through him as the all-powerful, ever-living, ever-present Christ.

We called in one of the spiritual brothers and one sister of the congregation to agree in prayer. Altogether a number of demons were cast out, each calling himself by the name of some of the "tongues" leaders. At last a voice said "We will not come out." We commanded "In the name of Jesus tell us who you are who says, 'We will not come out'." The reply was "We are Legion." When the last one was gone the sister sat up like one raised from the dead and began praising the Lord.

A few nights later we called in some of the church to agree with us for the other young woman. Wife and I went after her in our car. As we entered the front door a shriek which none of us will ever forget came from one of the devils possessing her, while she seemed to plunge head first onto the davenport.

We laid on hands and rebuked the powers of the demons, commanding them in Jesus' name to come out. One after another came out until finally a voice said, "We will not come out." Upon command in Jesus' name, "Who are we?" the voice shrieked out "All hell." Shortly an officer of the law rapped at the door and stepped in. We were seemingly to meet defeat, knowing if she were not delivered it meant a free ride to the police station.

Neighbors had heard the unearthly shrieks and thinking some one was being killed called the police.

He threatened to take the girl "over on the hill" (the insane asylum). Finally he asked her, "Who are you?" A voice shrieked out, "I am the devil." The officer shrank back. He finally desired to use the telephone to call the police station. Calling for the lieutenant he said, "There is something here I do not understand. Please come at once."

As he left the room for the telephone, I said to those present, "If you ever prayed, pray now and give a final command in the name of Jesus, to come out." This they did and as the officer turned from the telephone the sister was delivered and arose like one from the dead, shouting praises to the name of Jesus with the devilish look gone from her face. The glory of God and heaven beaming out. At this the big, burly lieutenant walked in. But the battle was won, the victory was ours in Jesus' name. The "ever present Help in time of need" had risen to the occasion and once more asserted his authority and power.

During the casting out of these demons many of them called themselves by the name of some of the "tongues" leaders. One shrieked, "I am anti-Christ." We commanded "Who are you?" The reply was, [Naming a prominent woman tongues teacher] and I am leading hundreds of souls to hell." Many other things were declared which we do not have space to write.

All this time these girls knew what was going on, but had no power to talk or act. They had a glimpse of hell with the millions falling in and immediately pounced upon and tormented by demons. To hear them repeat their experience we are confident that but few would ever want to go to hell.

The church here for months had been praying for a greater manifestation of Holy Spirit power, but little did we dream of how it might be brought about.

We had read of Martin Luther's experience with personal devils when he grasped an ink-well from his desk and hurled it at the devil, it splashing on the wall, and rather thought perhaps it was imaginary. Needless to say we have a new vision of the powers of personal devils, but thank God, our trust is in the one who has "all power in both heaven and earth."

We have preached the gospel for years and have believed its *theory* and *practise*, but now the *powers* of the gospel, and of an ever-living Christ and the name of Jesus have a new significance and a solid reality to us such as we have never had before.

These two young ladies are now saved and filled with the genuine Holy Spirit and ready for service, their experience based, not on feelings, but this time on real faith in Jesus.

TESTIMONY OF
THE YOUNG WOMEN

Mrs. Lillian Palmer

I was but a girl of seventeen when I went to the Church of God in Erie, Pa. I was hungry for Jesus and when the invitation was given I knelt at the altar and found Jesus precious to my soul. How happy I was. I don't believe I had been happier in my life. Oh, the preciousness and nearness of Jesus. I would walk to work all unconscious of the people, having such a blessed time in fellowship and communion with Jesus. We talked and walked together daily.

When about nineteen, Jesus spoke to me, telling me to start family worship which I did after a struggle and the Lord surely blessed. Then one other time he told me to go to the park and I would find boys to start a Sunday School class. I took a bag of candy and started to the park to do as Jesus bade me to do. When I arrived there was not a sign of a boy anywhere. I was not discouraged but simply told Jesus he had promised there would be boys in the park. As I walked in the park for a few minutes, I turned and there in the centre of the park were three boys. They went with me to the city mission and I started my class. We soon had other boys and it was but a short time until Jesus took one of them home to glory.

As the weeks rolled by I was very happy in Jesus. Then I met a young man whom I liked very much. As I prayed about him I was not sure of the Lord's will about him. It was here that I made the sad mistake of my life, for I disobeyed the Lord and married him. Whoever is reading this just now, I want you to know it does not pay to disobey God, as you will find out a little later. The devil broke up our home and I left Erie with my two children and came to Washington, D. C.

Oh, how I wanted Jesus. My heart was broken, bleeding, and torn. I had never been happy away from Jesus. I did not know what church to go to, so I went here and there. I then went to a Baptist church for about six months. One day Aime Semple McPherson came to Washington and I was asked to sing in her choir which I gladly did. Then after she left I went to a Pentecostal church in Washington.

I went tired, discouraged, empty-hearted, heart broken and heartsick, wanting Jesus. Oh, how I wanted Jesus. So when the altar call was given I went to the tarrying room. As they prayed for me, they said "Now Sister, let go, let go and begin to praise the Lord." So that is what I did, and the next thing I knew I was under the power lying on the floor. I had visions and also a call to go to Japan. They said I was under the power about two hours. After I came out of it I felt so queer. Something had happened to my head. I went to the pastor and asked him what was the matter and he excused the whole thing without giving me a satisfactory answer. Time went on, my mind never clear and always doubting. Life itself began to be unholy and not worth living. I also spoke in tongues and time after time would lie on the floor under the power.

During the time I was in the Pentecostal church I had a very dear aunt who knew the Lord, and she was praying for me. She came to visit us, and it was at that time I stopped going to the Pentecostal church. My mother said I had such a wild look out of my eyes and she was fearful of my losing my mind, which I nearly did.

Once more I was without a church to go to. I went here and there, but none satisfied the longing in my heart. But at last I found the Church of God and started to attend there. Brother and Sister Martin, pastor and wife of the Church of God in Washington, invited me to their home. Before leaving they wanted to know if I wanted them to pray for me, and of course I did. But I could not pray. I had lost all faith, and the devil had me bound. They layed on hands and rebuked the devil, but all that I could do was to groan. When they held on and cast out the devil I was able to break forth and pray.

During the following months I had a struggle to try to live for the Lord. I was up one day and down the next, with the devil at me as a roaring lion. It got so I couldn't sleep good at night. Something would wake me up and startle me. One night I saw a spirit leaving the room as I awakened. Time went on with my trying to live for the Lord, but the devil not letting me. Sometimes I wished I could get out of this world without taking my own life. The blackness and despair and wretchedness of my life was becoming unbearable.

About four or five weeks ago Brother Martin announced that Sister Hughes and myself would give our experience in Pentecost at the Wednesday prayermeeting. Brother Martin had always said it was of the devil, but I had always been afraid to make such a severe statement. The request started the devil up and showed him up in our lives. Brother Martin came to the conclusion we were devil possessed. They layed hands on me to rebuke them and to cast them out, and the devil flew in me. It took several to hold me, and the devils spoke out of my lips. The saints, as true soldiers of the cross, held on to God for my deliverance. Brother and Sister Martin fasted for days and prayed night and day. They held on to God for our deliverance, and if they had not held on and claimed victory through Jesus I doubt if I would be here to write this. The devils were not cast out the first night. Brother Martin and the prayers of God's people saved me from running to the river.

The next day, Brother Martin got together in his home some of the Spirit-filled children of God who knew how to hang on to God until He answered their prayers. They had been praying all afternoon. Then they came over to my aunt's, where I was, and took me to their home. The devils started to cry out of me before I got into the house. When I got in the door they gave blood-curdling screams. Then came the battle. They declared they would not come out of me. They even told who they were. Some of the names were those who went to the Pentecostal church. Then they called themselves "Legion," and "All hell." The devils exposed the Pentecostal movement as the saints would command them to in the name of the Lord. They cried "Impure, Unholy, Lustful, Deceitful," and many other names.

Just about when the victory and deliverance was to come, in walked a policeman. He said it had been reported a woman had been screaming for some time. He questioned them all and took down all names and addresses. He watched for a while and at last said the place for me was on the "Hill," which means the asylum. He went out in the other room to call the lieutenant to come and take me to the asylum. Before he could get back in the other room the Lord made the devils to come out, almost choking me to death. Hallelujah for deliverance. When the Lieutenant arrived I was happy and in my own mind. Praise the Lord forever for such a marvelous deliverance! Our God is an all powerful God, One who is able to deliver from hell itself. For that was what it meant if I was not delivered. Glory hallelujah. I am free tonight with a real experience of salvation and the infilling of the Holy Spirit.

May God help other poor lost souls out of the Pentecostal movement.

I am happy to say tonight that I am now happy in Jesus, willing to do what he wants me to do. I ask all to pray that I may keep true and faithful, humble and low down at his feet, never to disobey again.

Mrs. Lillian Palmer
712 Webster St. N. W.
Washington, D.C.

Elsie M. Hughes

I was a member of the Methodist Church for several years and thought I was saved until about eight years ago, the Lord sent such a conviction into my heart I could not rest day or night.

I attended a revival service and went forward for prayer, but the minister only asked me to shake hands with him and say by that I was saved so I went away miserable. I knew I was not saved so with a hungry heart I attended another revival service where they believed in repentance and the Lord saved my soul.

Praise His name! I know I was saved, because I had joy and peace in my soul and he changed my heart and life.

I then had such a burden for lost souls I went from house to house telling others about Jesus and inviting them to church.

About one year after I was saved I came to Washington, D. C., and prayed earnestly for the Lord to lead me into a church where I could receive food for my soul and work for Him. One Sunday as I was reading the church ads I felt impressed to go to a certain Protestant church. I heard such a wonderful sermon and they made me feel so welcome. They also believed in divine healing, so I thought, "Surely this is where the Lord wants me." One night a sister asked if I had ever received the Baptism of the Holy Spirit or had spoken in tongues. I did not know anything about speaking in tongues, but I knew I needed something in my life I did not have, and I wanted all the Lord had for me. What I did need was the Holy Spirit.

The first time they prayed for me I went down on the floor under what they said was the power of God. Now I know it was the power of the devil.

The pastor of this church was Pentecostal and he told me I would speak in tongues when I received the Holy Spirit. I did not want to speak in tongues or fall over on the floor, but I did want the Holy Spirit. When the people fell over on the floor and spoke in tongues I was afraid of it at first, but they seemed so happy I thought, "Surely this must be the Lord."

One night after praying for me, they said "Sister, you spoke in tongues tonight and have the baptism of the Holy Spirit." If I did I didn't know anything about it. When you receive the Holy Spirit, you know it.

One night while sitting in my seat at the Church both hands went up and I spoke in tongues for about twenty minutes. I was so happy for a while I thought, "Now I know I'm all right BECAUSE I SPOKE IN TONGUES." What I received was devil possession. When the Pentecostal pastor left that church the majority of people left and I with others joined the Full Gospel Assembly, in Washington.

One day an evangelist at this Assembly prayed for my healing and I went down under the power. I could not control my head for about three hours and was trembling from head to foot. I tell you they have power, but it is not the power of God. I would go to church and was happy during the service, but before I got home I was doubting my own experience. After doubting my own experience I watched others and found them living in sin and speaking in tongues. Some would come to church under the influence of liquor and speak in tongues, and the pastor would give the interpretation. Our song director and one of the personal workers were living a life of sin and speaking in tongues. I was so miserable and full of doubts I was afraid to pray for people, for they would fall over on the floor when I prayed for them.

I believe the Lord called me to personal work, but I certainly could not work for the Lord in that place. The Lord does not throw us over on the floor in an unseemly position as they claimed he does in the Full Gospel Assembly. One person decided she would find out if the pastor had the gift of interpretation, so she spoke in a language she understood. What she was saying was "sweet potatoes, sweet potatoes," and the pastor gave the interpretation as a message from God.

I got to the place where I did not believe in God, and I was certainly desperate. One Sunday as I was walking down the street I noticed a little church on the corner. It was the Church of God. I went in and the pastor preached "Sanctification." I found they did not believe you had to speak in tongues in order to receive the Holy Spirit. Praise the Lord for leading me to the church of the living God, the only true church.

I tried to stay away from the services because I thought it was wrong for me to even listen to any one preach against Pentecostalism. The Pentecostal people told me I was sinning against the Holy Spirit if I said their speaking in tongues was of the devil. I know there is a real gift of tongues, but the Holy Spirit does not come into an unclean temple.

I attended the Church of God three years before I could take my stand for the truth. I wanted to be sure this time I was right. Praise God, I know I have the truth now, and a deep, settled experience I never had before.

Brother Martin, pastor of the Church of God, spent hours and hours teaching me the Word of God and praying with me. Praise the Lord for Brother and Sister Martin. They are certainly consecrated to the Lord and do everything they can to lead souls into the blessed truth as it is in Christ Jesus.

After taking my stand against Pentecostalism I had a real battle with the devil. At night the room was full of demons and I could see the devil. This went on until I was ready to take my life. One night, Brother and Sister Martin prayed for me and found I was devil-possessed. I could not stand the name of Jesus. Sister Martin said my throat turned black and the devil was trying to kill me. I had a trip to hell. Dear ones, I can tell you just what hell is like. I saw millions and millions of precious souls falling into hell and millions and millions of demons waiting to receive and torment them. I had a little taste of what it means to be tormented on this earth with them. What must it be to fall into the hands of demons, to be tormented forever and forever?

They prayed for me and fasted for several days and nights, commanding the demons to come out, in the name of the Lord. The devil had me so under his control they could not even move my head. The devils came out, calling themselves by name. One was Lucifer, another Beelzebub, another Nell, and most of them were members of the Pentecostal church. They said, "We will not come out. You will tear down our work and testify against us."

Praise God, they did come out, and today I'm happy and free in Jesus. There is power in the name of Jesus. Oh, if I could only tell you how I suffered, I'm sure you would never go inside of a Pentecostal church.

While under this power I saw a beautiful field and a gate covered with flowers. Thousands of people were going in. When they got inside a large trap-door opened and the people went down. Pentecostalism looks beautiful at first. But oh, the awful darkness precious souls fall into when they once go into this devilish place. The devil said I would testify against him. Praise God, I intend by the help and grace of God to do everything I can to lead precious souls out of this awful darkness. If the Lord calls me and opens up the way I will go from coast to coast, warning precious souls and telling them my experience.

I am writing this for the glory of God and praying it will help keep some precious soul from the "tongues movement."

Elsie M. Hughes,
118 Bryant Street N.W.
Washington, D.C.

"Speaking In Tongues" In The New Testament. By Dr. Gene Miller

I

The concept of "speaking in tongues" and the "gift of tongues" appears at several points in the New Testament. This concept, like all doctrines or ideas to be found in the scriptures, is not to be feared, ignored, or misused. Rather, it is to be read, rightly interpreted, and understood.

The term "tongue" *(glossa)* is employed in the New Testament with at least two meanings — the actual physical organ of speech, and a language or dialect. Examples of the former use may be seen in such passages as Luke 16:24, Mark 7:35 and James 3:1-12. The latter occurs also in a number of passages, and is the one with which we are primarily concerned in discussing the topic at hand. The chief references which bear upon the subject are contained in Acts 2, 10 and 19 and I Corinthians 12, 13 and 14. In Mark 16:17, part of the so-called "long ending" of Mark, Jesus says that certain "signs" shall follow those who believe; among these is "they shall speak in new tongues."

Acts 2:1-13 recounts the initial outpouring or "baptism" of the Holy Spirit after the ascension of Christ, according to his promise to his followers. At this point, the first reference to "speaking in tongues" occurs:

> When the day of Pentecost was fulfilled,
> they were all together in the same
> (place). Suddenly, there was a noise

from heaven like a mighty sweeping
wind, and it filled the whole house
where they were sitting. Divided tongues
like fire appeared to them, and rested
upon each one of them. They were all
filled with the Holy Spirit, and began to
speak (lalein) in other (foreign) tongues,
as the Spirit gave them expression. Now
there were staying in Jerusalem Jews,
devout men, from every nation under
heaven. When this sound came, the
crowd gathered, and were amazed, because each one heard them speaking in
his own dialect (language). They were
bewildered and wondered, saying:
"Look, are not all these who are speaking Galileans? How is it that we hear,
each in his own native dialect (language)? *Parthians,* Medes and Elamites,
and the citizens of Mesopotamia, Judea
and Capadocia, Pontus, and Asia, Phygia
and Pamphylia, Egypt and the area of
Libya around Cyrene, and the visitors
from Rome, Jews and proselytes, Cretes
and Arabians — we hear them speaking
in our own tongues the great works of
God." All were bewildered and perplexed, saying to one another, "What
might this be?" But others, making fun,
were saying, "They are drunk with sweet
(new) wine." (Translation by author, direct from Greek New Testament).

II

Several particular aspects of this passage are worthy of note in the development of the subject at hand. Notice the outward manifestations accompanying the phenomenon — the sound, the appearance of the "tongues like fire", the "speaking in other (foreign) tongues." The first two of these are never repeated in any New Testament account of the occurrence of "speaking in tongues"; apparently their purpose on this occasion was to call attention to what God was doing in fulfillment of prophecy and promise, and to set the stage for Peter's memorable address which immediately followed. At the time of the Pentecost festival, men — "devout men", or men who were ready to receive and to pass on the news of the new age and the unprecedented outpouring of the Spirit —were in Jerusalem from throughout the known world of the Dispersion.

Furthermore, this is the only occasion in the New Testament when the term "other" (*heteros* —another of a different kind, foreign) is employed in connection with "speaking in tongues", with the exception of I Corinthians 12:10, where "different kinds of tongues" are mentioned. In Acts 2:1-11, the result of the Spirit's power upon the recipients was definitely the expression of known languages or dialects; otherwise in the New Testament, even in Acts, this was apparently not the case. In the church (as evidenced in I Corinthians) the gift of "speaking in tongues" or in "a tongue" had to be interpreted by use of another gift, or it was worthless — even harmful, in some circumstances. On the Day of Pentecost, it may be also noted, part of the miracle apparently lay in the hearing as well as the speaking; some of the people ("devout men") heard and understood in their own languages, while others, hearing the same things, said that the speakers were "drunk on sweet (new) wine". (The term "unknown" tongue, employed in the KJV at I Corinthians 14:4, 14, 19, 27, is, like other words in italics in this version, inserted by the translators. It is neither in the Greek text, nor justified by implication or idiomatic considerations.)

The concept of "speaking in tongues *(glossais)*" appears in two other passages in Acts — 10:44-48 and 19:1-6. In the first, Cornelius and his household heard the gospel from Peter, and received the Holy Spirit. (Literally, he "fell upon them"). Immediately, they were heard "speaking in tongues and praising God." It is interesting to note that praise to God resulted from their speaking, as in Acts 2; also, that they received the Holy Spirit and gave manifestation of it before being baptized, "in the name of Jesus Christ." In the second instance, Paul met some believers ("about twelve") at Ephesus who had been baptized only with "John's baptism" (i.e., the baptism of repentance, but had "not even heard if (whether) the Holy Spirit is." (The probable meaning of this statement is not a reference to whether or not the Holy Spirit, existed, but rather that they had not heard of the outpouring of the Spirit on the Day of Pentecost, and so of the fact that God had fulfilled prophecy and promise by making the Spirit available in full measure to every believer. Some early manuscripts even contain a variant reading which includes the words "if anyone has received" the Holy Spirit). Under Paul's guidance, these men were "baptized in the name of the Lord Jesus", and the Holy Spirit "came upon them." As a result, they "spoke in tongues and prophesied."

The phenomenon of "speaking in tongues" appears in I Corinthians as one of the so-called "spiritual gifts."

This phrase translates two terms in the Greek New Testament which are, literally, "Spiritual things" *(pneumatika)* and "things of grace" *(charismata)*. The first mention of such a "gift" is in I Corinthians 12:4-10. Several significant aspects of the matter appear in this passage. First, note that Paul insists that all gifts are given and controlled by the same Spirit, inspired by the same God. Thus, they must all work toward the same ends and objectives within the Christian body — the church. Furthermore, all manifestations of these gifts are for the common good. In mentioning the various "gifts", note that "tongues" and the "interpretation of tongues" are listed last of all. This will gain added significance in other passages to be considered.

In I Corinthians 12:28-13:1, these gifts or types of service in the church again come under consideration. Again, "speakers in various kinds of tongues" are listed last of all, and in verses 30 and 31, Paul says: "Do all speak with tongues? Do all interpret? But earnestly desire the higher gifts." Furthermore, love is a more excellent way — than even the highest gifts! "Tongues" of "men and of angels" are of no use without love! In 13:8, it is pointed out that tongues — and the other gifts — will "cease" or "pass away", but "love never ends."

Further counsel concerning the "gift of tongues" and its use in the church is given in I Corinthians 14. The Christians are urged to "desire . . . especially that you may prophesy (that is, speak out for God)" because: it upbuilds, encourages and consoles the hearers; it is understood by all at all times; and the whole church is edified. Note verse 5 — "Now I want you all to speak in tongues, but even more to prophesy!" The one who prophesies is greater than the one who Speaks "in tongues", unless someone interprets — so that the church may be edified. Prophesying is more to be desired and sought than "speaking in tongues." Unwise or indiscriminate use of "tongues" results in confusion, uncertainty, and false guidance! If this was true in the first-century church at Corinth — how much more so in our own day and our own congregations! If any Christian is "eager for manifestations of the Spirit," let him strive for those gifts which "upbuild the church." The one who "speaks in tongues" is to pray for the power to "'interpret." Notice that this is not left to chance; the person who possesses the "gift of tongues" is to seek also that which will enable him to use the gift for constructive purpose in the body of Christ —the gift of "interpretation"! Otherwise, those who are hearing, not understanding what is spoken, cannot agree, with or appreciate or be blessed by the manifestation of the gift.

Paul states the case strongly, effectively, and personally in verse 19 — "In church, I would rather speak five words with my understanding (mind), in order to teach others, than ten thousand words in a tongue." Furthermore, he goes on to point out to the people that "tongues," which, like other "gifts" of the Spirit, should serve to impress, teach, attract, and convict unbelievers, as well as to build up the church itself, if used carelessly, selfishly, or indiscriminately will have the opposite effect!! ("Will they not say that you are mad?") These words are being attested to and proven repeatedly in our day when numerous persons, congregations, and denominations are abusing and misusing the "gift of tongues" in flagrant violation of New Testament teaching and principle.

Some very specific directions are given in the remainder of this chapter for the use of this particular gift, in light of what Paul has already said on the matter. It is obvious that the abuse of this "gift" or manifestation of the Spirit had become a serious problem in the church at Corinth; it can quickly become the same for any congregation in our day which disregards scriptural admonitions and instructions regarding its exercise. Notice that at any one meeting of the church ("when you come together"), only two or three at the most are to "speak in tongues." These are to speak one at a time — "each in turn", and one is to interpret. (Usually, this would be expected of one of the speakers themselves; see comment above.) In case there is no one to interpret, "Let him keep silent in the church." This is not a suggestion — it is a command *(sigato),* given in the imperative mood in the Greek New Testament. This is not a command, let us be careful to note, against "speaking in tongues" as such, or against all exercise of the gift; it speaks specifically concerning the public worship services of the church. If there is no one present who can exercise the gift of "interpretation," let the person exercising the gift also exercise control — and speak "to himself and to God." Notice the contrast in 14:39 — the Christians are instructed to "earnestly desire to prophesy", but "not to forbid speaking in tongues." Of primary significance in the total picture are the admonitions in 14:40 and 14:33 — "Let all things be done decently and in order" and "God is not (a God) of confusion, but of peace."

It is worthy of note that in a list of spiritual gifts in Romans 12:6-8, there is no mention of "speaking in tongues." In Galatians 5:22-23 the "fruits" (results, products) of the Spirit are set forth — love, joy, peace, patience, kindness, goodness, faithfulness, gentleness, self-control. While these are certainly not the same as the "gifts of the Spirit," it is just as certain that the genuine and scriptural exercise of any true gift of the Spirit in the church will have this kind of result or "fruit," not an opposite kind.

Some commentators have held that all references to "speaking in tongues" refer to the use of known human languages. The considerations above, however, particularly those regarding I Corinthians 14, point definitely to the conclusion that the "gift of tongues" and "speaking in tongues", as exercised and known in the early Church, consist of the manifestation of spiritual or "ecstatic" language or utterances, rather than known human languages or dialect. In 14:2, Paul points out that one who speaks in a tongue "speaks not to men, but God; for no one understands him, but he utters mysteries — in the Spirit." If there is no one to interpret, "tongues" are not to be spoken at all in the church, but reserved for "speaking to himself and to God." In 14:10-11, human languages are used as an analogy or comparison with "speaking in tongues." While the employment of known human languages by the Spirit served a very real and significant purpose on the Day of Pentecost, it obviously would have no logical meaning or purpose in a local assembly of Christians. These facts and others lead to the conclusion that the phenomenon of "speaking in other (foreign) tongues" on the Day of Pentecost was either entirely different from other occurrences of this manifestation recorded in the New Testament, or it was the same, with God in this case being the interpreter and using the manifestation to make known his "mighty works" and so his gospel to men of every nation.

III

Regardless of the position taken concerning this question, there are no grounds in the New Testament for the abuses and false teachings which have become prevalent through the years in connection with the "gift of tongues" or "speaking in tongues." Particularly misleading is the doctrine that "speaking in tongues" is the *sina qua non* of religious experience, and of the infilling or baptism of the Holy Spirit. From the passages already considered, it is very evident that not all Christians are expected to manifest the same "gifts," or any particular "gift." Furthermore, numerous instances of conversion and of persons being "filled with the Holy Spirit" are recorded in the New Testament, at which there is no mention of "speaking in tongues." See, for example, Acts 2:41; 4:4; 4:8; 4:31; 5:14; 8:12; and 13, 8:15-17; 9:17 and 18; 11:21; 13:2; 13:48; 14:1; 16:14. and 15, 16:30-34; 17:12; 18:8.

Several pertinent conclusions may be expressed regarding the "gift of tongues" and "speaking in tongues" in the New Testament, as a result of this careful consideration of scriptural teaching concerning the subject. It is the least of all the "gifts" in importance, value, honor, and effectiveness. It is less to be desired than "prophesying" (speaking forth for God). Both New Testament admonitions concerning it and human experience bear irrefutable testimony that this "gift" or spiritual manifestation lends itself particularly to personal pride, confusion, misunderstanding, misuse, and offense. Its exercise or use is severely regulated and restricted, especially where public worship services are concerned. Speaking in tongues is tolerated —while prophesy and other gifts are encouraged, and to be desired. Speaking in tongues requires the possession and exercise of another "spiritual gift" to make it of any use to the church; this is not true of any other. Any person or congregation or group who desires, "seeks," claims, or attempts to exercise the "gift of tongues" ought to understand and give full attention to all of these facts and to the plain New Testament directions concerning it. Failure to do so will result (as it has in many instances) in disobedience to the word of God and detriment to his church.

[Included by permission of the author.]

A Biblical Position
In Respect To Tongues.
By Dr. Leslie Ratzlaff

The Church of God and Warner Southern College seek to be truly Biblical in respect to tongues. The Bible is the basis for distinction between true and false tongues. The attempt here is to permit the Scriptures to speak on the subject and then to make some general observations.

I. The Gospel and Tongues

The Gospels are silent on the subject except for a spurious passage in Mark 16:17, "They shall speak with new tongues." Even if this passage were authentic it still could be interpreted as referring to the change of a converted life in respect to speaking habits.

The absence of tongues in the midst of obvious manifestations of other gifts of the Spirit is significant. Apparently tongues was of no importance to Christ and never used by Him Who is our supreme example. Neither did He attach any significance to it in His teachings to the disciples.

II. The Book of Acts and Tongues

The key verse of Acts (Acts 1:8) stresses the Holy Spirit's power as the ability to witness effectively, which, in short, is the ability to communicate Christ as the Truth of the Gospel and this means to disclose or disseminate facts so that they are understood by the hearers.

The baptism of the Holy Spirit is the important gift! The Holy Spirit then works by manifesting Himself both through the fruit and the gifts of the Spirit. The former is always present as abiding qualities of the Holy Spirit and the latter as special abilities to meet the demands of occasions. One of these gifts, the gift of tongues (γλώσσαις) translated as tongues or languages) was mentioned as present on three of five occasions in Acts when the Holy Spirit baptized the believers. (Acts 2:1-11, 10:44-46 and 19:1-7) Two other incidents of Holy Spirit baptism make no mention of tongues (Acts 8:14-17, 9:17-19).

The following observations are in order:

1. Tongues was a genuine current language. Although previously unknown to the speaker it, nevertheless, was a means of effective communication to some persons present, particularly on the Day of Pentecost where each heard "in his own native dialect." (Acts 2:8)

2. The reverse of the experience at the Tower of Babel took place at Pentecost. At the Tower of Babel selfishness led to confusion and inability to communicate. In Acts the Spirit-baptized believers were one in spirit and communicated effectively, extolling God with His mighty works.

3. The progressive manner in which the Holy Spirit baptism experience extended geographically in Acts demonstrated that God is no respecter of persons (Acts 15:8-9). The Baptism of the Holy Spirit came first to the Jews; then to the Samaritans who were ethnically Jewish but a mixed people; then to Paul, a Jewish-

Roman citizen; then to the Gentile Cornelius and his Italian band who were apparently Jewish proselytes, and then finally to full Gentiles in the city of Ephesus. God is absolutely impartial and therefore the Holy Spirit with His ability to communicate effectively was shared without any favor to those who responded to the Promise.

III. First Corinthians and Tongues

Paul discusses the gifts of the Spirit in First Corinthians 12 - 14. But first we need to examine the cultural background of the Church of God at Corinth. Corinth was a cosmopolitan commercial center located on the lower portion of a strategic isthmus separating lower from upper Achaia. It was noted for debauchery, religious syncretism, including mystery religions and the worship of Aphrodite with her thousand temple prostitutes.

Among the pagan practices, no doubt, was the phenomenon of ecstatic utterances, imitation of false tongues—the practice of uttering sounds and syllables that were unintelligible to others. These utterances may have been learned or cultivated; they may have come from high states of emotional frenzy; they may have been the results of hypnotic trances or psychic powers or even demonic influences.

Members of the Corinthian church apparently were so captivated by these practices that they either brought some of them into their public and private worship or paganized a valid gift of the Spirit by treating it in a pagan fashion.

Paul proceeds to correct the situation but does so with tact, courtesy and gentleness: the principle of appreciation before criticism is obviously being practiced.

Paul lays down broad principles in Chapter 12 which are clearly understood; he then strategically brings in the great chapter on love stressing the primacy and the eternity of love as against the temporariness of prophecies, tongues, etc., which have their day and cease to be. The 14th Chapter where "our beloved brother Paul" zeros in on tongues has in the words of Peter "some things in them hard to understand," unless a wise hermeneutical principle is followed. This principle states that obscure passages of Scripture must be interpreted in the light of clear passages. Thus Chapter 14 must be interpreted in the light of Chapter 12. With this in mind, II Corinthians 12, 13 and 14 say essentially the following:

1. He who is genuinely influenced by the Spirit of God always acts in harmony with God's nature. Christ is acknowledged as Lord and certainly not cursed. (I Cor. 12:1-3). Apparently some unintelligible utterances had been interpreted as curses against Christ.

2. God (the Holy Spirit) is the giver of all gifts and distributes them according to His pleasure "for the common good." (I Cor. 12:4-11). The gifts are to edify the total body rather than for private or selfish use.

3. The Holy Spirit, who obviously knows all languages, gave the gift of tongues as a valid gift to certain persons on occasion. However, for all persons to have the same gift of any one of the spiritual gifts would result in gross distortion of the body of Christ. (I Cor. 12:14ff).

4. Each divinely given gift is for a specific purpose even as each body organ has a specific function. A gift in no way is to be regarded as necessary for any or all believers, (I Cor. 12:27-31). The point that all persons do not have the same gift including tongues is strongly stressed in the Greek language of the New Testament.

5. The absolute requisite for the Spirit baptized believer is the fruit of the Spirit. The grace of "love" is primary followed by "joy, peace, patience, kindness, goodness, faithfulness, gentleness and self-control." The fruit of the Spirit provides the climate in which the gifts of the Spirit are to operate. (I Cor. 13, Gal. 5:22).

6. The gifts to be desired are those that edify the church. The gift of tongues even though it could bring about personal enrichment as can the other gifts has no place in public worship unless it is a means of effective communication as a living language. Even though tongues is a possible gift for all, its practical value is so doubtful that a gift like prophecy is favored. (I Cor. 14:1-5). Paul is saying in effect "Yes, I allow tongues as a valid gift that could on occasion manifest itself but I really don't want you to be concerned about it because other gifts that always communicate are the important gifts." (I Cor. 14:6-12),

7. Tongues when meaningless is a foreign element that leads to confusion. Any manifestation of the Spirit would build up the church. (I Cor. 14:6-12).

8. Tongues in prayer is unfruitful both to the person praying and to the outsider hearing it and is to be shunned in favor of intelligible communication. (I Cor. 14:13-19).

9. Tongues is a sign for unbelievers but even then is of doubtful value unless it is intelligent communication. (I Cor. 14:20-25).

10. Tongues, if used at all in public worship, must be used only when it communicates and then sparingly. (I Cor. 14:26-33).

11. Tongues is recognized as a valid gift but must be used "decently and in order." (I Cor. 14:39).

General Conclusions:

1. The Scriptures clearly teach that tongues when mentioned in Acts and I Corinthians is a genuine language with communication value for the purpose of witnessing.

2. Tongues had no part in the ministry of Christ and was mentioned only incidentally in Acts and discussed in I Corinthians in an attempt to resolve a problem resulting from its abuse in the church.

3. Tongues is clearly a minor manifestation of the Spirit and <u>definitely</u> not to be experienced by all.

THEREFORE

4. Although one should always be open to the Holy Spirit and His activity, no biblical basis can be found for promoting, stressing or seeking tongues in particular.

5. However, the indispensable evidence of Holy Spirit baptism is the fruit of the Spirit. Without the manifestation of "love, joy, peace, patience, kindness,

goodness, faithfulness, gentleness, self-control" anything that passes for a gift of the Spirit is to be held in suspect and is of no avail. With the genuine fruit of the Spirit in evidence, the gifts will be used for the common good to equip the church for its task of ministering so as to bring God into the human scene with His judgment, healing and holiness.

6. If perchance the Holy Spirit in God's pleasure does choose to manifest Himself in tongues, it is then a genuine language with practical communication value and to be used decently and orderly for communicating the Gospel and not for display or private enjoyment.

7. Apparently most of what is commonly called tongues in the modern charismatic movement must be explained on other than biblical teachings. The phenomenon of unintelligible utterances (imitation or false tongues) may be explained as a result of: (a) learning or cultivation, (b) high states of emotional frenzy, (c) hypnotic trances, (d) psychic powers, (e) demonic influences.

8. Warner Southern College as a Christian community following the holiness tradition of the Church of God reaffirms its stand on the baptism of the Holy Spirit as the gift necessary and available for all believers. We recognize "tongues" (a language) as one of the gifts of the Spirit that God may give on occasion to certain individuals. The College sees no Biblical basis for stressing, seeking and promoting the gift of tongues in particular. Therefore, in obedience to the Scriptures, the College cannot condone any activity which stresses or promotes ecstatic utterances (imitation or false tongues) by and within the campus community.

9. The College urges all members to seek spiritual maturity based upon a deep abiding faith resulting in a living relationship with God.

10. This let us do: Let us follow Christ our example, Savior and Captain and with Him witness to the Kingdom of God — the Kingdom of "righteousness, peace and joy in the Holy Spirit" (Romans 14:17) by readily understood, intelligent communication.

[Included by permission of Grace (Selent) Ratzlaff, wife of the author.]

Learning About The Holy Spirit.
Claire W. Shultz

TABLE OF CONTENTS

LEARNING ABOUT THE HOLY SPIRIT

The subject of the Holy Spirit is of extreme importance to the Christian. We all need His presence and

His power and, without Him, it would be utterly impossible to live an effective, fruitful Christian life.

Some people are entirely ignorant about the ministry of the Holy Spirit. They are like the Christians at Ephesus who, upon being asked, "Have you received the Holy Spirit since you believed?" replied, "We have not heard whether or not there be any Holy Spirit." (Acts 19:2) Some Christian people have never taken the time to give much attention to a study about the Holy Spirit.

Again, some people would like to find the truth about the Holy Spirit but have not seemed to get clear understanding in their minds. They are saying, "What is one to believe about the Holy Spirit? What really is the truth?"

Let us ask the Lord to guide us in our study by the same Spirit about whom we shall speak, and to renew our inner life and our testimony through the truths which He will reveal to us.

Chapter I

WHY LEARN ABOUT THE SPIRIT?

Let us examine important reasons why we should study about the Holy Spirit and His work.

First, Jesus taught much to His disciples about the coming of the Holy Spirit.

In John 14:16-17 He said, "And I will pray the Father, and he will give you another Counselor, to be with you for ever, even the Spirit of truth, whom the world cannot receive, because it neither sees him nor knows him; you know him, for he dwells with you, and will be in you."

Jesus gave explanations about the Holy Spirit in John 14:26, 15:26, 16:7-8, 16:12-14.

Too, Jesus explained to the disciples the urgency of receiving the Holy Spirit into their lives. He explained that they were to be His witnesses in the world but warned them not to start this important task until they had first received the Spirit into their lives. We read in Luke 24:48,49:

> "You are witnesses of these things. And
> behold, I send the promise of my Father
> upon you; but stay in the city, until you
> are clothed with power from on high.'

Christ's last words to His disciples as He left them were these:

> "But you shall receive power when the
> Holy Spirit has come upon you; and you
> shall be my witnesses in Jerusalem and
> in all Judea and Samaria and to the end
> of the earth." (Acts 1:8)

Jesus knew His disciples would need great strength if they were to be successful in their task. They would not be able to stand in their own strength alone but the Holy Spirit would abundantly help them. Jesus warned His disciples of the great difficulties they would face as they started their work:

> "Behold, I send you out as sheep in the
> midst of wolves; so be wise as serpents
> and innocent as doves. Beware of men;

for they will deliver you up to councils,
and flog you in their synagogues, and
you will be dragged before governors
and kings for my sake, to bear testimony
before them and the Gentiles . . . Brother
will deliver up brother to death, and the
father his child, and children will rise
against parents and have them put to
death; and you will be hated by all for
my name's sake. But he who endures to
the end will be saved." (Matt. 10:16-17,
21-22)

If the early disciples needed the Holy Spirit to help
them in their work, we, living in a hard, cruel world,
will still need this same power.

Secondly, the early disciples received the Holy
Spirit into their lives and experienced His presence and
power.

The story begins in Acts 2 where it is explained
how the Holy Spirit came into the lives of the early believers but the story continues throughout the entire
book of Acts.

Before the Holy Spirit came into the lives of the
disciples they were discouraged, fearful and about
ready to give up their faith. During the crucifixion all of
the disciples deserted Jesus and fled. (Matt. 26:56)
Even after the resurrection seven of the disciples went
back to their fishing business again. (John 21:1-3)
However, after the presence and power of the Holy
Spirit was manifested in their lives, the disciples were
wonderfully strengthened and empowered to do the
work they had been called to do. With the Spirit's unseen presence in their lives, they were able to face per-

secution, hardships, and accomplish seemingly impossible tasks. A few scriptures which especially show the presence and power of the Holy Spirit at work are: Acts 2:14-40, Acts 4:10-12, Acts 4:31, Acts 4:32-37. The early disciples, through the power of the Holy Spirit in their lives, had great witnessing power, praying power, yes, and even "giving" power. The Holy Spirit's power even helped to release their money to be used by the church.

Obviously we need this same power today. We need witnessing power, praying power and giving power. We need Christians in the church who will be able to face their problems and difficulties and have strength to live a victorious Christian life. We still need the presence and power of the Holy Spirit in our lives.

Thirdly, we need to study carefully about the Holy Spirit and His work so we can find the truth about the Spirit.

What really is the work and ministry of the Holy Spirit? How does one know he has received the Holy Spirit? How does one receive Him into his life? The Christian must know the answers to these questions before he begins his search or he may be deceived. It is possible for one to find, not the "Holy Spirit" but a "spirit of deception." John, the Apostle, warned the early converts to "test the spirits." He said,

> "Beloved, do not believe every spirit, but test the spirits to see whether they are of God; for many false prophets have gone out into the world." (I John 4:1)

If one is searching for the wrong thing, he may not recognize the right thing when he sees it. For example, after Jesus was crucified, Mary went to the tomb very early on Sunday morning to see the tomb of Jesus but when she got there she saw that the stone was rolled away and the body of Jesus was gone. She ran and reported the news to Peter and John and they both ran to the tomb to see. Mary stood outside the tomb weeping. Two angels asked her why she was weeping and she complained that the body of Jesus was gone. Then she turned around and saw the resurrected Jesus standing close to her but she did not know it was Jesus. She thought he was the gardener. Why? Only a few days before she had been with Him but now she did not recognize Him. The reason is that she was looking for a dead Christ rather than a living Christ. Because of the wrong set of her mind, she did not recognize Jesus even when He stood before her. (See John 20:1-18)

This same idea is shown in the lives of the two disciples on the Emmaus road. (Luke 24:13-22) They walked along, sad and discouraged, thinking only of the dead Christ. Thus, when Jesus came and walked with them, they did not even know who it was.

We also note this same truth in the life of the Jews. Jesus, their long-awaited Messiah, had come and was standing among them but, instead of receiving Him, they crucified Him. (John 1:11, 26) Why was this so? Because they were looking for the wrong kind of a Messiah and did not recognize the true one when He came to them.

Now this same thing is very true of receiving the Holy Spirit. Unless one has the correct idea of who and what the Holy Spirit is—of His work and mission and how the Christian receives Him—one may search for the wrong thing. He may have a "spirit" but not the

"Holy Spirit"; he may have a kind of "power" but not really have an experience of the real power of the "Holy Spirit." Therefore it is very important that Christians study and learn about the Holy Spirit and know what they are searching for before they begin their search for Him.

Chapter II

ASCERTAINING THE TRUTH ABOUT THE HOLY SPIRIT

John wrote to the early Christians that they should test the spirits.

". . . but test the spirits to see whether they are of God; . . ." (I John 4:1)

Obviously John recognized that there was a danger of falsifying the truth about the Holy Spirit. Where and how does one learn the truth about the Spirit?

On first thought, one would probably answer this question by saying, "Why, the Bible, of course: The place to learn about the Holy Spirit is the Bible." This is true but it is true only if one looks in the right places in the Bible and has the right attitude in his search. There are many false religions and teachings in the world and many of them have their origins in the Bible. Some of the cults like Jehovah's Witnesses and Christian Science have their origins in the Bible. The problem is that they ignore many plain teachings in the Bible which would help them and they twist certain passages of scripture to suit their own thinking. (See II Tim. 4:3-4, II Peter 3:16)

In finding the truth about any teaching, one must first turn to the Gospels to see what Jesus said and taught about the subject. Jesus was the "author and finisher of the faith." (Hebrews 12:2) Jesus did talk about the Holy Spirit as recorded in John 14, 15 and 16. What did He say about the Holy Spirit? According to Jesus, what would the Holy Spirit be like? What would He do? How would one receive Him? The Christian does not start in the book of Acts or the epistle to the Corinthians to study about the Holy Spirit. The Christian *must start with the plain simple teachings of Jesus.*

Secondly, after ascertaining what Jesus taught about the Holy Spirit, one should then turn to the Acts and then to the Epistles. In Acts he will note how the early followers of Jesus responded to the teachings of Christ about the Holy Spirit. How did the early Christians experience the Holy Spirit? Did any of the churches have any problems in their understanding about the Holy Spirit? How were these problems handled? What can we learn about the mistakes of the early Christians in their experiences?

We must be very careful we do not base our belief on superficial evidence about the Holy Spirit which is being advocated by some church groups unless such teaching can be authenticated by the clear teaching of Jesus. For example, some Pentecostal movements in several places in the world have had an unusually fast growth in their membership. Pentecostal groups always stress speaking in tongues. Therefore, according to some, speaking in tongues must be right for the Pentecostals are seeing a fast rate of growth. Is the evidence of the Holy Spirit necessarily a fast rate of growth? This is faulty logic indeed. Did Jesus teach that the evidence of the Holy Spirit is a fast rate of growth? If we argue that the Pentecostals are right with their stress on tongues and that this is the cause of their growth, we would do well to ask the question also as to what is causing the rapid growth of the Jehovah's Witnesses movement? The Roman Catholic Church is by far the largest single denomination in the world. Its membership will equal the total membership of all the Protestant churches. What has caused their phenomenal growth? What about Christian Science? What about the Mormon faith? Evangelical Christians fully believe that some of these groups are utterly false in many of their doctrinal teachings but, even so, most of them are making progress. Obviously there are many reasons why different movements grow and it is not necessarily the fact that they are teaching truth which causes it. All movements spread and grow because of strong conviction, whether it be Communism, Catholicism, Jehovah's Witnesses, or what.

It must be stated again that the truth about the Holy Spirit must be discovered and seen through the life and teachings of Jesus. Any teaching or belief about the Holy Spirit which cannot be found in Christ's ministry, either by word or inference, must be rejected no matter how good or plausible it sounds or seems. Jesus said very clearly to His disciples that the Holy Spirit would compliment and amplify His work—the work and ministry of Jesus.

> "But when the Counselor comes, . . . he
> will bear witness to me;" (John 15:26)

"When the Spirit of truth comes . . . he will not speak on his own authority, but whatever he hears he will speak, and he will declare to you the things that are to come. He will glorify me, for he will take what is mine and declare it to you." (John 16:13, 14)

Christ does not have one ministry and the Holy Spirit another.

Chapter III

THE MINISTRY OF THE HOLY SPIRIT

Quite briefly it may be said that the main ministry of the Holy Spirit is to help the Christian to become a dynamic witness for Jesus Christ. (Acts 1:8) However, if the Christian is to become a forceful witness, he must be helped and developed in several different ways or his witness is meaningless. How does the Holy Spirit minister and assist the Christian to become an effective witness?

First, the Helper

First, the Holy Spirit becomes the Christian's day-by-day helper in all of his affairs and difficulties empowering the Christian to cope with whatever difficulty he may meet.

In John 14:15-16 Jesus told the disciples that after He would go away, He would not leave them alone but, rather, He would send the Holy Spirit to stay with them. The word He uses to describe the Holy Spirit is a word which is hard to translate. In the King James Version

He is called the "Comforter." In the Revised Version, the "Counselor." In Moffatt's translation, "Helper." The original word used in the Greek language was "paraklētos." "Paraklete" is the English version of the word. What Jesus said was, "And I will pray the Father and He will give you . . . the Paraklete to be with you forever." The problem is that there is no one word in the English language which means the same thing. Hence, scholars try to pick words which mean almost the same. William Barclay describes the work of the paraklete as follows:

> "The word paraklētos really means 'someone who is called in'; but it is the reason *why* the person is called in which gives the word its distinctive associations. The Greeks used the word in a wide variety of ways. A *paraklētos* might be a person *called in* to give witness in a law court in someone's favour; he might be an advocate *called in* to plead someone's cause when someone was under a charge which would issue in serious penalty; he might be an expert *called in* to give advice in some difficult situation. He might be a person *called in* when, for example, a company of soldiers were depressed and dispirited to put new courage into their minds and hearts. Always a paraklētos is *someone called in to help* when the person who calls him in is in trouble or distress or doubt or bewilderment. Now the word *Comforter* (word used in the King James Version) was once a perfectly good

translation. It actually goes back to Wycliffe; he was the first person to use it. But in his day it meant much more than it means now. The word *comforter* comes from the Latin word *fortis* which means *brave*; and a comforter was someone who enabled some dispirited creature to be brave. Nowadays the word *comfort* has to do almost solely with sorrow; and a comforter is someone who sympathizes with us when we are sad. Beyond a doubt the Holy Spirit does that, but to limit the work of the Holy Spirit to that function is sadly to belittle Him. We have a modern phrase which we often use. We talk of being able to *cope* with things. That is precisely the work of the Holy Spirit. The Holy Spirit comes to us and takes away our inadequacies and enables us to cope with life. The Holy Spirit substitutes victorious for defeated living.

"So what Jesus is saying is: 'I am setting you a hard task, and I am sending you out on an engagement very difficult. But I am going to send you someone, the *paraklētos*, who will guide you in what to do and who will make you able to do it. The Holy Spirit will bring you truth and will make you able to cope with the battle for the truth.' "

The Holy Spirit wants to become the daily helper of the Christian to enable him to be victorious in all of the difficulties and perplexities of life. This is the kind of power the Christian needs to help him become an effective witness in this world.

Second, the producer and developer of Christian virtues

The activity of the Holy Spirit in the lives of the Christian people is to produce Christ-like qualities or characteristics in their day-by-day living. Paul refers to these characteristics as "fruit of the Spirit." In Galatians 5:22-23 we read:

> "But the fruit of the Spirit is love, joy, peace, patience, kindness, goodness, faithfulness, gentleness, self-control. . . ."

A Christian cannot be a good, effective witness for Christ unless he bears Christ-like characteristics in his day-by-day living. The work of the Holy Spirit is to help activate and produce this fruit—love, joy, peace, kindness, goodness, etc. When a Christian can show forth these qualities in his life, then, and only then, his life becomes a powerful witness for Christ.

When we speak of becoming an *effective witness,* it means more than just being able to speak words for Christ. Our witness for Christ involves what we say and what we are. It is reflected in our manner of speech, in our attitudes, in our dealing with people. It is reflected in what we do when we are under stress and trial. It is reflected in how we treat our neighbours, our employees, other members of our families, our wives, our husbands, and our children. The Holy Spirit wants to make us have an effective witness in all of life. He wants to give us power to live a victorious life for Christ in all things and under all conditions and circumstances. He wants to change us and equip us so that our lives can be of effective service in the church.

Paul and Silas gave a powerful witness to the jailer and other prisoners when they were in the Philippian jail. Even though they had been beaten badly and had bruises on their bodies, yet they manifested peace, love and joy. At midnight they were so happy they sang songs and praises to God. After the earthquake had freed them of their bonds they could have run away but they didn't try to escape. Instead, they spoke reassuring words to the jailer, telling him not to harm himself or to fear. This whole experience was so different than the jailer had known that he was amazed beyond words and fell down in front of Paul and Silas and asked them, "What shall I do to be saved?" (Acts 16:19-32)

As the Holy Spirit produces love, kindness, goodness, self-control, etc., in the life of each Christian, that life then becomes a powerful witness for God. This is the kind of power the world needs and will appreciate.

When a person manifests one part of the fruit of the Spirits goodness, in his life, it gives power to his life as a witness. A person who is honest and pays his debts, who forgives and forgets, who is faithful and can be trusted, is one who shows the power of the Holy Spirit in his life. Right living gives powerful witnessing to Christ. Thus, the Holy Spirit is to produce a good life in the life of every Christian.

Third, endowment for service

Part of the Holy Spirit's ministry is to bestow special spiritual gifts to each Christian so that each life can be used for effective service in the church.

One important way in which the Holy Spirit equips the Christian for effective witnessing is to give him special service gifts, special abilities, which prepare him for service in the church. Jesus explained that the Spirit would help the Christian to become a "river of living water." (John 7:38-39) Just as rivers of living water bless, refresh and help maintain good life, in the same way, through the Spirit, the lives of Christian people will be transformed to become like rivers of living water, refreshing and blessing the world with Christian love and effective service.

What are these gifts? To whom are they given? How are they to be used?

In several places, especially in the writings of Paul, the Bible speaks about spiritual gifts. We read about them in Ephesians 4:11, I Cor. 12:4-11, 14:28-30, and Romans 12:6-8. In Ephesians we read of ". . . some should be apostles, some prophets, some evangelists, some pastors and teachers. . . ." In I Corinthians we read of the gifts of wisdom, knowledge, faith, healing, miracles, prophecy, administrators, helpers, tongues, interpretation of tongues. In Romans we read of prophecy, service, teaching, exhortation, giving of money, giving of aid and doing acts of mercy. Obviously, God wants the church to have leaders who are adequate for any problem or need.

Several things should be noted concerning the usage of these gifts.

1.The purpose of these gifts. The Holy Spirit bestows these gifts to different members of the church so that the whole church may be strengthened.

a. Each gift should benefit the *whole church.* "To each is given the manifestation of the Spirit *for the common good."* I Cor. 12:7

b. Christians should desire gifts which will build up and bless the church as a whole. ". . . since you are eager for manifestations of the Spirit, strive to excel in building up the church." I Cor. 14:12

c. Each gift should contribute to the good of the church in the same way each member of the physical body contributes to the good of the whole body. I Cor. 12:14-26.

In Corinth, the Christians were majoring on the gift of tongues and seemed to be ignoring the importance of the other gifts of the Spirit. Too, their use of the gift led only to confusion and disorder and apparently did not lead to the edification of the church. Things were so bad that Paul suggested that people who came into their worship might think they were mad. (I Cor. 14:23) Paul cautioned them that ". . . all things be done for edification." (I Cor. 14:26) He warned them that ". . . God is not a God of confusion but of peace." (I Cor. 14:33) In concluding his teaching he said, ". . . all things should be done decently and in order." (I Cor. 14:40) Paul explained that they should not forbid people to speak in tongues but that their use of the gift should be to edify the church, not bring disgrace upon the church by making people think the church was full of "mad people." Paul warned them that anything spoken in the church had to be intelligible so that it had a useful meaning to the whole church. (See I Cor. 14:6-19)

It should be noted that on the Day of Pentecost, when the disciples received the Holy Spirit and spoke in tongues, this manifestation helped in communicating the Gospel to people who did not know Christ. The crowd of people who were from many places and spoke many diverse languages, were amazed that they were able to understand what was being said by people from Galilee, by those who spoke a different language from theirs. (Acts 2:8-11) They said, ". . . we hear them telling in our own tongues the mighty works of God." (Acts 2:11) Thus, this first experience of tongues was something which had great meaning to the people. They heard and understood about "the mighty works of God."

Some people advocate that the gift of tongues is not for the general use of the church but, rather, for private use. They believe this because Paul said that "He who speaks in a tongue edifies himself, but he who prophesies edifies the church." (I Cor. 14:4) And, previously, Paul had written, "For one who speaks in a tongue speaks not to men but to God; for no one understands him, but he utters mysteries in the Spirit." (I Cor. 14:2) Thus, it is said that the tongues speaker "speaks only to God and utters mysteries in the Spirit" and in using the gift the speaker is "edifying himself." Could Paul have meant that the main use of the gift of tongues is for private use and personal edification? Paul argued that if tongues had any use, they should be interpreted and if they were not interpreted, the speaker should keep quiet for if no one understood, then the speaker was uttering mysteries in the spirit for he was not being understood by anyone except God. Truly, if a person speaks in an unknown language, then it is God alone who understands him and he may be edifying himself but certainly not the church. Paul's main argument is that we should strive to edify the church, not ourselves. (I Cor. 14:12)

2. How the Holy Spirit Distributes the gifts among the Christians

First, each and every Christian can expect to receive one or more of the gifts. "*To each* is given the manifestation of the Spirit for the common good." (I Cor. 12:7)

Second, all Christians do not necessarily receive the same spiritual gifts. "To *one is given* through the Spirit the utterance of wisdom, and to another the utterance of knowledge according to the same Spirit, *to another faith* by the same Spirit, *to another* gifts of healing . . ." (I Cor. 12:8-11)

Paul explains that not all are apostles or prophets, or miracle workers or speakers of tongues in I Cor. 12:29-30.

There is no evidence that all people will have the gift of tongues. Paul says just the *opposite* in his teaching.

Third, the Holy Spirit Himself decides which gifts should be given to each individual Christian.

> "All these are inspired by one and the
> same Spirit, who apportions *to each one
> individually as he wills*." (I Cor. 12:11)

The Holy Spirit chooses which gift each Christian needs and can use in God's service. We read the same thought in Hebrews 2:4.

Paul did say to "covet the best gifts," which are *prophecy* (inspired preaching), and *teaching* but it is still God's business to decide. Paul did say that "now I want you all to speak in tongues . . ." (I Cor. 14:5) but, even so, he recognized this was not something he could control. This matter of giving gifts is entirely God's business. ". . . to each one individually as he wills."

3. Christians are advised to desire the higher gifts

First, the higher gifts are prophecy (inspired preaching) and teaching. Even teaching is higher than the gift of healing or the working of miracles. (I Cor. 12:28-31) But higher than any gift is the manifestation of love. Christians are to make love, first and foremost, the highest goal of their lives. Love will outlast tongues and prophecies. (I Cor. 13:1-3) God is love and if a person is to become like God, he must have love in his life. The humble child of God who manifests God's love in all of his relationships has the highest manifestation of the Spirit of God in his life. Christians are to make love their main aim and earnestly desire the spiritual gift of prophecy. (I Cor. 14:1) The next highest gift is teaching. (I Cor. 13:28) The reason why Paul suggests that preaching and teaching are the highest gifts is quite obvious. It is the preaching and teaching of the Word of God which leads men to be saved. Therefore, they are the most important and should be the most desired.

Some of the spiritual gifts mentioned in the Scriptures are not noticed as much in the church today as they were possibly seen in former times. For example, we do not see as many miracles now as in the day of Jesus. In the day of Moses there were many miracles but in other times not so many. The important thing to remember is that God must decide when and what particular kinds of gifts are needed. The Christian's job is to seek the Holy Spirit and allow Him to decide which gift he should receive.

Fourth, sanctifier

The Holy Spirit's work is to sanctify and empower the Christian so he has power to live a holy life, to have victory over sin and evil.

Christian people are commanded to live a holy life and not allow sin and evil to overcome them. Paul wrote to the Roman Christians, "Let not sin reign in your mortal bodies, to make you obey their passions. Do not yield your members to sin as instruments of wickedness, but yield yourselves to God as men who have been brought from death to life, and your members to God as instruments of righteousness. For sin will have no dominion over you, since you are not under law but under grace," (Romans 6:12-14) Paul wrote to the Ephesians, "Put off your old nature which belongs to your former manner of life and is corrupt through deceitful lusts, and be renewed in the spirit of your minds; and put on the new nature, created after the likeness of God in true righteousness and holiness." (Eph. 4:22-24)

While Christians are commanded to live holy lives, yet we are aware of the fact that the forces of evil are ever present to defeat us. Paul explained to the Roman Christians how he had a mind to do good but evil was ever present with him and that the good things he wanted to do he could not do. (Romans 7:13-24) In desperation he cried, ". . . Who will deliver me from this body of death? Thanks be to God through Jesus Christ our Lord!" (Romans 7:24-25) Paul had great trouble with evil but there was hope in Christ. It was through Christ and His Spirit that deliverance from evil would come. (Romans 8:1-4) This deliverance would come to those ". . . who walk not according to the flesh but according to the Spirit." Paul said, "While we were living in the flesh, our sinful passions, aroused by the law, were at work in our members to bear fruit for death. But now we are discharged from the law, *dead to that which held us captive*, so that we serve not under the old written code but in the *new life of the Spirit*." (Romans 7:5-6)

Paul explained about the law of sin which bound him. (Romans 7:21) However, he further explained about another law – "For the law of the Spirit of life in Christ Jesus has set me free from the law of sin and death." (Romans 8:2) Here one powerful law which worked in his body was canceled out by another law which operated in his body. This greater law was the "law of the Spirit." As an illustration let us think of the law of gravity. Everything is held to the earth by the law of gravity. Throw up a stone and it falls back to the earth. There is always an unseen power which pulls downward. However, there are other laws, too, which may cancel out the law of the pull of gravity. A bird has wings which help it to stay in the air and the power of gravity is superseded. An airplane flies through the air and is being pulled down to the earth at all times but there are other laws which hold it up and permit it to fly. Thus it is with the Christian life. The forces of evil are pulling down but the law of the Spirit of life is holding us up from falling into sin and evil.

Paul explained that the Holy Spirit gives us power to resist sin and evil so that we can live holy lives for God. Paul wrote, "Likewise the Spirit helps us in our weakness; . . ." (Romans 8:26) It is through the power of the Holy Spirit that we "put to death the deeds of the body." (Romans 8:13) The Holy Spirit puts strength in the inner man. (Eph. 3:16) If one will "walk by the Spirit" he will not gratify the desires of the flesh. (Gal. 5:16)

Thus, when Jesus told the disciples, "Ye shall receive power after that the Holy Spirit has come upon you," it was this kind of power He was speaking of. A Christian has no Christian witness unless he lives a holy life. Pure, righteous living by all Christians is what brings about a positive witness for Christ, the blessed Redeemer, who came to "save His people from their sins." (Matt. 1:21)

Thus, we see something of the character of the Holy Spirit and how He gives us "power to witness." He helps us day by day to have victory over the difficulties and perplexities of life. He helps us to know what is right and wrong and sees to it that our lives bear the true fruit of the Spirit. He gives various kinds of gifts so that the complete work of the church can be done. *Some* are apostles, *some* prophets, *some* evangelists, and *some* pastors, and *some* teachers, for the work of the ministry. Some are given gifts to pray for the sick; some are empowered to administrate in the affairs of the church; some are endowed with gifts of mercy and charity; some have gifts of wisdom and knowledge.

All of this, and more, is what the Holy Spirit wants to do as He comes into our lives. No wonder Jesus said to His disciples, "Stay in the city until you are clothed with power from on high."

Chapter IV
RECEIVING THE SPIRIT

Receiving the Holy Spirit was never meant to be a burden or difficulty for the Christian. However, some Christian people seem to feel that receiving the Spirit into their lives depends on their continued seeking, searching, and begging in order to prevail upon God to send His Spirit to them. According to the plain teaching of the Scriptures, this is in no way the case. How does one receive the Holy Spirit?

1. A Christian receives the Holy Spirit through believing faith in the same way he was saved through faith.

> Note: "Christ redeemed us from the curse of the law . . . that we might receive the promise OF THE SPIRIT THROUGH FAITH." (Gal. 3:13-14)

> ". . . you . . . who . . . have believed in him, were sealed with the promised holy Spirit." (Eph. 1:13)

> "He who believes in me, as the scripture has said, 'Out of his heart shall flow rivers of living water.' Now this he said about the Spirit, which those who believed in him were to receive; . . ." (John 7:38-39)

> ". . . whatever you ask in prayer, *believe that you receive it, and you will*." (Mark 11:24

Obviously the Scriptures teach that the Holy Spirit comes into the life of the Christian through simple faith and trust. It does not depend on any "works" we may do in special times of seeking, searching, or begging. The Holy Spirit enters the heart when faith takes hold of the promise of God.

Sometimes the laying on of hands was practiced in New Testament days. This is told about in Acts 8:17-18, Acts 9:17, Acts 10:6, II Tim. 1:6. It may be that this act may strengthen the faith in the life of the Christian and there is nothing wrong in doing it. However, it is not the laying on of hands that counts but, rather, it is BELIEVING FAITH.

2. While FAITH is the door which admits the Holy Spirit into the heart, yet His coming is conditioned by our obedience to God.

> a) "If you love me, you will keep my commandments. And I will pray the Father, and he will give you another Counselor, . . ." (John 14:15-16)

> Here the Holy Spirit's coming is dependent on keeping the words of Christ.

> b) "And we are witnesses to these things, and so is the Holy Spirit whom God has given to those who obey him." (Acts 5:32)

> c) God's continuing presence in our lives depends on our obedience.

> "Jesus answered him, "If a man loves me, he will keep my word, and my Father will love him, and we will come to

him and make our home with him."
(John 14:23)

Christ recognized the presence of God to be with Him because of His obedience.

"And he who sent me is with me; he has not left me alone, for I always do what is pleasing to him." (John 8:29)

God has promised the Holy Spirit to every Christian, but the sending of His gift depends on obedience.

Let us take an example. A student may have the promise that he can enter secondary school but his admittance is conditioned by his paying of school fees. A person may obtain a loan of money but the loan is conditioned on his agreement to pay it back within a certain length of time at a certain rate of interest. In the same way God offers His Holy Spirit to us on a conditional basis. We must give Him absolute obedience. If one has not received the Holy Spirit and he has been seeking and searching, what he should do is to begin to examine his commitment to God, his willingness to obey the revealed Word of God. Shortly after Paul was converted, God showed him his special mission was to go to the Gentiles "to open their eyes, that they may turn from darkness to light and from the power of Satan to God, that they may receive forgiveness of sins and a place among those who are sanctified by faith in me." (Acts 26:18) Paul's secret of Holy Spirit power was in these words, "I was not disobedient to the heavenly vision." The question of receiving the Holy Spirit is not a matter of long, hard praying but rather, a close examination of one's commitment to God, of one's absolute obedience to Him. To one who is obedient, the Spirit will come immediately. To one who is struggling and fighting against God's will and purpose for his life, the time of the Spirit's coming may be long delayed.

3. The Spirit is a gift which must be accepted.

Six times in the book of facts the Holy Spirit is called the "gift" of God. (Acts 2:38; 5:32; 8:20; 10:45; 11:17; 15:8) How does one receive a gift which has been offered? He has only to accept it. One has only to ask for the Holy Spirit, give complete obedience, and accept Him.

> "If you then, who are evil, know how to
> give good gifts to your children, how
> much more will the heavenly Father give
> the Holy Spirit to those who ask him?"
> (Luke 11:13)

Peter explained that God would give the Holy Spirit to all Christian people. He said, "For the promise is to you and to your children and to all that are far off, every one whom the Lord our God calls to him." (Acts 2:38-39)

Thus, receiving the Holy Spirit is accepting God's gift through faith and trust, and believing God's Word. God has promised the gift of the Holy Spirit to all of His children, through all ages to come.

> "Therefore I tell you, whatever you ask
> in prayer, believe that you receive it, and
> you will." (Mark 11:24)

It may not be a simple matter for some people to accept the gift of the Holy Spirit. When the Holy Spirit comes into a life, He revolutionizes everything in that life. He wants the Christian to become an effective witness in speaking, in his business affairs, in the affairs of his home life, in the affairs of his neighbours and also with his wealth and property. Many people are not interested in any revolution taking place in the way they use their money, property, time, etc. Therefore it may not be an easy matter for some people to accept the gift of the Holy Spirit because certain changes will have to be made which are not easily made. In accepting the Holy Spirit a real dedication will have to be made to God to be obedient to His will and it is at this point that many Christians fail to find the presence of the Holy Spirit in their lives. Christ was obedient "unto death, even death on a cross." (Phil. 2:8) Paul told the Roman Christians that it is our obligation as Christians to "present our bodies to God as a living sacrifice." (Romans 12:1-2)

Chapter V

THE EVIDENCE OF THE SPIRIT

What is the evidence that one has been filled with the Holy Spirit? How does one know that he has been filled with the Holy Spirit?

First, the Holy Spirit gives us *an inner witness* of His presence.

"*It is the Spirit Himself bearing witness with our spirit* that we are children of God." (Romans 8:16)

"Now we have received not the spirit of the world, but the Spirit which is from God, *that we might understand the gifts bestowed on us by God.*" (I Cor. 2:12)

When a sinner repents of his sins and is converted, the Holy Spirit witnesses to him inwardly that he is forgiven and is saved. The same is true when one is receiving the Holy Spirit. Paul said the Holy Spirit helps us "to understand" about the gifts. (I Cor. 2:12) When one has agreed with God to meet the conditions which are required for receiving the Spirit and to accept the gift of the Spirit, then the Spirit comes and *He, Himself, brings an inward witness* that His presence is there. This cannot always be explained in human words or seen with the human eye but God reveals this truth through the inward man of the spirit. Note Paul's clear words to the Corinthians,

"But, as it is written 'That no eye has seen, nor ear heard, nor the heart of man conceived, what God has prepared for those who love him,' God has revealed to us through the Spirit. For the Spirit searches everything, even the depths of God. For what person knows a man's thoughts except the spirit of the man which is in him? So also no one comprehends the thoughts of God except the Spirit of God. *Now we have received* not the spirit of the world, but *the Spirit which is from God, that we might understand the gifts bestowed on us by God.* And we impart this in words not taught by human wisdom but taught by the Spirit, interpreting spiritual truths to those who possess the Spirit. *The* unspiritual man does not receive *gifts* of the Spirit of God, for they are folly to him, and he is not able to understand them because they *are spiritually discerned.*" (I Cor. 2:9-14)

Note carefully, ". . . the gifts of God . . . are spiritually discerned."

Secondly, if the Spirit has filled a life with His presence and power, there should be some evidence of the Spirit's work and ministry there.

a. There should be some evidence of the fruit of the Spirit in a person's life. The fruit of the Spirit is love, joy, peace, kindness, self-control, patience, goodness and gentleness. (Gal. 5:22-23) Obviously the Spirit will not be able to do all of His work in a minute. He is with the Christian always, to keep working with him, so that all of the fruit of the Spirit may be manifested.

b. The Christian should sense the Holy Spirit guiding him, directing him, helping him to understand more and more about spiritual things. Didn't Jesus say that when the Holy Spirit is come He will guide you, teach you? The Christian should sense the Spirit guiding the plans and purposes for his life, his work, his marriage, his relationships. (John 15:13)

c. There should be a greater sensitiveness to wrongdoing and a winning of the battle over evil and sin. (John 16:8-10)

d. The Christian should begin to show forth a fruitful life which is useful in the church. The Holy Spirit equips the Christian for service and this should be noted. ". . . Out of his heart shall flow rivers of living water." (John 7:38)

e. There will be a sense of burden and conviction to share the Good News of Christ with others. The Holy Spirit is to help the Christian to become an effective witness. Part of this witness will be to

share with others what Christ has meant
and what He can mean to others. (Acts
1:8)

One group of people say that you will have the evidence of the Holy Spirit when you manifest a certain
gift – the gift of tongues. No one can doubt but that
there was an accompaniment of speaking in tongues to
some who received the Holy Spirit in New Testament
days. The tongues experience is mentioned three times
– in Acts 2, 11:15, and 19:6. Those who advocate
tongues as the evidence of the infilling of the Holy
Spirit like to quote these texts as their proof for today.
However, what does it really prove? At the first outpouring of the Holy Spirit on the day of Pentecost the
disciples spoke in languages which were used in those
days. Over ten different languages are mentioned in
Acts 2:8-11. Do people who argue for "tongues" mean
real languages which are spoken by people of today? Is
this the kind of accompaniment they mean? There were
other experiences of speaking in tongues, such as when
the Gentiles received the Word of God – Acts 10:34-36.
In explaining what happened at a later time, Peter said,
"As I began to speak, the Holy Spirit fell on them just
as on us at the beginning." (Acts 11:15) If this experience was the same as happened in the "beginning," then
these tongues mentioned were also languages. It is
doubtful if the advocates of "tongues" today are thinking of real languages as they put forth their arguments.

The accompaniment of tongues with the coming of
the Holy Spirit on the day of Pentecost undoubtedly had
a symbolical meaning. This was a symbol of the fact
that, from that time on, the Gospel would be taken to all
people of all nations and languages. With the coming of
the Holy Spirit God's blessing would be extended to

"all flesh," all people. (Acts 2:17) It was the Holy Spirit who would give power to take the Gospel to all peoples in all parts of the world.

What is the meaning, then, of other places in the Scriptures where it says that Christians spoke in tongues? (Acts 10:45, 19:4) With the Gentiles, the meaning is quite clear. In order to get the Gospel to the Gentiles, God had to first get a revelation to Peter, who was a Jew, to help him to go to Cornelius, a Gentile. (Acts 10:9-29) After Peter preached, these Gentiles believed the Gospel and the Holy Spirit came upon them. (Acts 10:34-36) Now, when these Gentiles had the same kind of experience as did the Jews at Pentecost, it helped to prove to the early church that the Gentiles were just as much Christian as were the Jews. Because of this, these Gentile Christians were given the right hand of fellowship into the church. (Acts 11:17-18)

There are only three instances mentioned in the book of Acts of speaking in tongues which accompanied the coming of the Holy Spirit. It should also be noted that, in the book of Acts, there are other instances when the speaking of tongues did not accompany the coming of the Spirit.

> a. In Acts 4:31 nothing is said about speaking in tongues. "And when they had prayed, the place in which they were gathered together was shaken; and they were all filled with the Holy Spirit and spoke the word of God with boldness."

> b. In Acts 8:17 nothing is said. "Then they laid their hands on them and they received the Holy Spirit."

c. In Acts 2 there is no evidence that all of those who received the Holy Spirit received the gift of tongues at that time. One hundred and twenty people were waiting in the Upper Room. (Acts 1:15) It was only the Galileans who spoke in tongues. "And they were amazed and wondered, saying, 'Are not all these who are speaking Galileans?' " (Acts 2:7) The disciples were from Galilee but there is no evidence to make us think that all of those in the Upper Room were from Galilee.

d. Nothing is said about the three thousand who were converted on the day of Pentecost speaking in tongues. They were saved and baptized. (Acts 2:41)

Too, since Paul thoroughly explained that the gift of tongues is only one of the many gifts of the Spirit, and one of the lesser gifts at that, why should people look for the receiving of this gift as the evidence of the infilling of the Holy Spirit? We must understand that not one of the gifts of the Spirit is to be substituted for the Spirit Himself. We should not be seeking a "gift' of the Spirit but, rather, we should be seeking the Holy Spirit Himself.

In thinking about the infilling and anointing of the Holy Spirit in our lives, we must ever keep in mind the experience that Jesus Himself showed us. We read in Acts 10:38, "how God anointed Jesus of Nazareth with the Holy Spirit and with power; how he went about doing good and healing all that were oppressed by the devil, for God was with him." Jesus Christ is the object of our earthly journey and our Companion in the way, the only pattern we have to follow and imitate. How did the Holy Spirit cause Jesus to act and react? How did He live? What kind of an example did He show us? Do we have any reference that Jesus, in His experience, ever spoke in tongues? Our goal in seeking the Holy Spirit is to seek an experience which will bring glory and honour to Jesus Christ and any thing which is akin to the Holy Spirit must bring glory to Jesus. (John 16:14)

Chapter VI
LIVING IN THE SPIRIT

In the beginning of this study it was pointed out that every Christian needs to experience the continuing presence and power of the Holy Spirit in his life. Living in the power of the Spirit is the need of every Christian for it is this experience which brings the fullness of the Christian life to him. The Holy Spirit is the one who makes victorious living possible. He is the one who equips and empowers the Christian so that "out of his heart shall flow rivers of living water."

Therefore, every Christian ought to examine himself to see whether or not he has received the Holy Spirit into his own life. If there is any doubt that he has experienced the fullness of the Holy Spirit, then he should get in earnest at once and take those steps which makes the coming of the Holy Spirit possible.

For those Christians who are now ready to receive the fullness of the Holy Spirit into their own lives the following steps are suggested.

Step 1 - Expect

Expect the Holy Spirit to come into your life. Remember that God has willed that you receive the Holy Spirit as a part of His plan for you.

> "For the promise is to you and to your children and to all that are far off, every one whom the Lord our God calls to him." (Acts 2:39)

If God has called you to Himself and has saved you, then this promise is to you.

Step 2 - Obedience

Bring your life into full obedience to God's will.

Remember the Holy Spirit comes to those who obey Him. (Acts 5:32) Examine your life very truthfully to see if you are completely obedient to God's revealed will for your life. Has He showed you anything to do which seems difficult? Are you ready to do whatever He says, to go wherever He leads, and be whatever He wants you to he? Are you willing to become a "living sacrifice" in God's service? (Romans 12:1-3) This point is the main key which unlocks the door for the coming of the Spirit. Deal carefully with this point. Take a few days, if necessary, to search your heart. Then, if from your heart you feel you are ready to live in complete obedience to God, you are ready for the next step.

Step 3 - Ask

In simple faith pray and ask God for the Holy Spirit to become your companion for life. Tell God you will accept His gift which is offered. ". . . HOW MUCH MORE will your heavenly Father give the Holy Spirit to those who ask him?" (Luke 11:13) Some people might like to ask a senior Christian – a pastor perhaps – to pray with them when they are seeking the Holy Spirit. Some may even wish for some of the brethren to lay their hands on them in prayer as was done in several instances in the early church. There is nothing wrong in this and some may find more assurance in this method. Others may wish to pray on their own. The main objective is to have a deep assurance that the presence of the Holy Spirit is in the heart.

Step 4 - Receive

God has offered the Holy Spirit as a gift. Receive the gift through humble faith.

God has promised the Holy Spirit to the obedient Christian. Now believe His word and trust God that the Spirit comes to you personally. God would not lie to you.

> ". . . that we might receive the promise of the Spirit through faith." (Gal. 3:14)

> "Therefore I tell you, whatever you ask in prayer, believe that you receive it, and you will." (Mark 11:24)

Thank God for answering your prayer and making it possible for you to experience the fullness of the presence of the Holy Spirit in your life.

Step 5 - Live by the Spirit, walk by the Spirit (Gal. 5:25)

If you have received the Holy Spirit into your life through faith, you must now begin to recognize His presence. As Paul said, ". . . live by the Spirit. . . ." Live your life in consultation with Him. He is there so talk to Him in the spirit. In the difficulties which arise day by day, ask Him to help you to find the best way out, to stand beside you and help you to be equal to the difficulty of the problem. In important decisions you must make in all the affairs of life – your home, family, work, vocation, journeys, marriage, etc. – you should quietly talk to the Holy Spirit for His counsel and guidance. Some answers do not come immediately but, with a little time, prayer and meditation, the Holy Spirit will help you find the right course of action.

The Holy Spirit may point out sin in your life, mistakes you are making which hinder your witness for Christ. He may speak to you showing you better ways to use your time and talent. He may direct you into some form of Christian service you had never thought of. He may talk to you about the money you make and suggest how you should use it for the best things in relationship to eternal values. He may tell you to break some of your friendships with those who have a bad influence on you. He may speak to you about bad habits which need to be changed. The work of the Holy Spirit is to sanctify you and bring forth holiness in your life.

Some answers He may give you may seem hard but, no matter, be obedient to your Counselor for He knows the way better than you do. As He shows you sin and wrongdoing in your life and changes which should be made, then seek the Holy Spirit's power to gain victory over that which is evil and that which is not best for you.

Paul suggested that we should "walk in the Spirit." This seems to suggest that we should make our goings and comings so that the Spirit is in all we do. "Walking in the Spirit" means living and being where the Spirit is. In order to understand and know His way for us we need to listen as He speaks through the Scriptures. Therefore, take time each day to read the Bible. As you read ask Him to help you with problems which seem difficult to understand. Make special times for meditation and prayer. The Holy Spirit speaks to us through His gathered church, through other mature Christians we may meet and counsel with.

The Holy Spirit may speak to you about something at any time – at work, on the road, at night when you are not able to sleep, in time of sickness, etc. "Walking in the Spirit" means that we keep an open ear to the Spirit of God at all times for His counsel and guidance and then walk as He directs.

[Included by permission of David Shultz, son of the author.]

What a Christian Should Know About The Gift of Tongues.
Claire W. Shultz

Published by:

Church of God Publications
Mwihila, P.O. Yala

Printed by:
Mwihila Press
P.O. Yala
6-66-7C

OUTLINE

INTRODUCTION

The subject of this study is: 'What a Christian Should Know About the Gift of Tongues.' This booklet is written for Christians, those who have a deep interest in Bible teaching, and desire to achieve a better understanding of what Christians should believe and practice. It is a known fact that there are different views concerning the meaning and use of 'tongues.' Those who teach that Christians should seek and use the gift of tongues are convinced that there are good reasons for believing as they do. Likewise those who do not stress speaking in tongues also believe there are good reasons for not doing so. The problem comes to those who are undecided and would like to know more about this teaching.

Understanding about the gift of tongues, and all of the other 'gifts of the Spirit', is very important to the Christian. Paul, in writing to the Corinthians concerning the nature and use of spiritual gifts, said: 'Now concerning spiritual gifts, brethren, I do not want you to be uninformed' (1 Corinthians 12:1). And again, 'Do not be children in your thinking, brethren; be babes in evil, but in thinking be mature' (14:20). Thus it is right that we should study these matters, and know why we believe as we do.

In making any kind of Biblical study it is not a good practice to take only one or two verses of Scripture and formulate a belief from them. Rather, it is necessary to look carefully at all that the Scriptures have to say on a subject, and then draw a conclusion as to what is the correct belief. Thus, in this study, we shall look briefly at different passages wherein the subject of tongues is mentioned, and endeavor to discover exactly what is taught in each passage.

I. IN THE BEGINNING

1. On the Day of Pentecost - Acts 2:1-21

The Scriptures definitely teach that on the day of Pentecost, when the Holy Spirit came to the church, the disciples spoke with 'other tongues' (Acts 2:4). No one who loves the Scriptures could doubt the truth of this statement. Hence this idea is readily admitted at the beginning and should be accepted by all Christians.

Looking more closely at the Scriptures, we should try to discover the exact meaning of the 'other tongues' spoken of. What was this experience which was manifested? The Scriptures are quite clear at this point, and there is not much room for argument. Those who were there understood these tongues to be nothing more than the many languages of the people who lived in that part of the world. The writer says,

And they were amazed and wondered saying, 'Are not all of these who are speaking Galileans? And how is it that we hear, each one of us in his own native language?'

Looking further we find that the Scripture lists the languages which were spoken:

Parthians and Medes and Elamites and residents of Mesopotamia, Judea and Cappadocia, Pontus and Asia, and Phrygia and Pamphylia, Egypt and the parts of Libya belonging to Cyrene, and visitors from Rome both Jews and proselytes, Cretans and Arabians, we hear them *telling in our own tongues* the mighty works of God (Acts 2:9-11).

Thus, on the day of Pentecost, definite languages were spoken and all the people understood what was being said. They said, . . . we hear them telling in our own tongues the mighty works of God' (Acts 2:11). When the Holy Spirit came on the day of Pentecost those present heard the mighty works of God being proclaimed in their own native languages, and understood what was said.

Looking further into this experience of the disciples we should try to discover the reason for this experience of speaking in different languages. First, it should be noted that what happened on that day was said to be a fulfillment of prophecy from the book of Joel. In explaining the experience Peter said, '. . . this is what was spoken by the prophet Joel' (referring to Joel 2:28-32). That which was experienced at Pentecost was a part of God's plan for the world and was, at that moment, beginning to come to pass. What was there in Joel's prophecy that had relevance to these experiences?

Acts 2:2-3 tells of some strange happenings which took place on the day of Pentecost. There was a sound from heaven like the 'rush of great wind' and 'tongues of fire' resting upon each of them, and different languages being spoken. This was indeed strange to those who were there on that day. Peter saw in these phenomena a fulfillment of Joel's prophecy. In Acts 2:18-19 Peter quotes the words of Joel: '. . . I will pour out my Spirit, and they shall prophesy. And I will show wonders in the heaven above and signs on the earth beneath, blood, and fire, and vapor of smoke . . .' Joel spoke of 'wonders' and 'signs'. Truly the 'rush of mighty wind' and 'tongues of fire' and the 'speaking in other tongues' were signs and wonders. No record is given of other things which Joel said would happen, but even so, Peter said, '. . . this is what was spoken by the prophet Joel' (Acts 2:16).

Joel said there would be 'signs and wonders'. What did he mean? Undoubtedly all three of the wonders mentioned in Acts—the sound of wind, the tongues of fire, and speaking in other languages—had symbolical meaning. Joel referred to them as 'signs'. Of what were they signs? It is probable that they were signs of what was taking place in the lives of the disciples and the infant church. They were signs of the supernatural power of the Holy Spirit at work.

Of what was the 'rushing mighty wind' a sign? In olden days wind had often been likened to a messenger of God, or a means by which he spoke. The Psalmist said, 'Who makest the clouds thy chariot, who ridest the wings of the wind, who *makest the winds thy mes-*

sengers, fire and flame thy ministers' (Psalm 104:3-4). When God spoke to Job it is said that He spoke to him out of the 'whirlwind' (Job 38:1). God used '. . . a great and strong wind (which) rent the mountains and broke in pieces the rocks . . .' (1 Kings 19:11) when he was preparing to speak to Elijah in a still, small voice. In the New Testament Jesus compares the working of the Holy Spirit to the wind (John 3:8).

Thus, on the day of Pentecost, the sound of the mighty wind indicated that God was doing something of unusual significance, and the people should, therefore, be alert to what God was doing. It indicated that God was about to speak, and that powerful influences and operations of the Spirit of God would be released, and would be at work upon the hearts and minds of men all over the world.

Of what was the 'tongues as of fire' a sign? As wind was often a sign of calling attention to some special message of God, so fire was also a sign of God's presence. Psalm 104:4 called attention to the fact that 'fire and flame' were ministers for God. In olden days God's people had been led by a pillar of fire by night. When the Law of Moses was given, the mountain was '. . . wrapped in smoke, because the Lord descended upon it in fire' (Exodus 19:18). Malachi referred to the coming of Christ as a time of cleansing like 'refiner's fire' (Malachi 3:2).

Thus, fire was a sign to God's people of His presence with them, giving light for the journey, direction and guidance in life, and cleansing and refinement of the soul. It does seem fitting, then, that with the coming of the Holy Spirit, the manifestation of 'tongues as of fire' should accompany it, as a beautiful symbol showing that God was still at work in the world, and was in the process of fulfilling another of his promises to the church. It was fitting that John the Baptist, in speaking of the ministry of Jesus, should say, '. . . He will baptize you with the Holy Spirit and with fire' (Matthew 3:11-12).

We come now to the 'other tongues', and ask, 'What did these mean?' Was this also a sign which had reference to the coming of the Holy Spirit? In explaining this unusual manifestation to the Peter called attention to the words in Joel's prophecy: 'And in the last days it shall be, God declares, *that I will pour out my Spirit upon all flesh . . .'* (Acts 2:17). This was good news indeed! All flesh! Up until this time the Jews alone had been God's chosen people and all other people had been left outside of God's covenant. But now, under the new covenant of Christ, the grace of God was to be shared by all people of the whole world. All people, all races, and all nations—all were to receive the blessings of Christ. This was to take place with the coming of the Holy Spirit. Hence, what a fitting and beautiful sign that on the day of Pentecost the 'mighty works of God' were heard being proclaimed, not only by the Jews, but by all people in their own languages. Thus the manifestation of languages was a sign that the Gospel was now being shared by all tribes and nations.

On the day of Pentecost the disciples were enabled by the Holy Spirit to speak in the various languages of the people present so that the good news about Christ could be made known to them. This resulted in a great harvest of souls being won to Christ on that very first day, and it may be that some of those converts carried the message even to Rome. We know this because in Acts 2:10 it is stated that there were visitors from Rome in attendance on the day of Pentecost. It is likely that they returned home, carrying the message with them.

In reading this passage in Acts 2 the reader should not only notice the 'tongues' experience but also the sound of the 'mighty rushing wind' and the 'tongues as of fire'. All three of these were important happenings on the day of Pentecost.

2. Other References in the Book of Acts

After the experience on the day of Pentecost speaking in tongues is mentioned only twice in the book of Acts. We read of speaking in tongues in connection with Cornelius, a Gentile, (Acts 11:15), and also with the Ephesian Christians (Acts 19:6).

In reading carefully what is said it should be noted that Peter, in explaining the experience he had had with the Gentiles in the house of Cornelius, said that they had the same experience with the Holy Spirit as did he and the other disciples in the beginning, on the day of Pentecost. Peter said, 'As I began to speak, the Holy Spirit fell on them *just as on us at the beginning'* (Acts 11:15). Peter, who was present on both occasions, said the manifestation was the same. Further, there is no reason to believe that the experience recorded in Acts 19 is any different than that recorded in Acts 11. It then follows that if they are the same as that which happened on the day of Pentecost then the 'other tongues' were intelligible languages which were spoken. 'And as Paul laid his hands upon them, the Holy Spirit came on them; and they spoke in foreign languages and prophesied' (Acts 19:6, Amplified Version).

These manifestations of 'tongues' among the Gentile Christians prove that what was signified on the day of Pentecost, namely that the Holy Spirit and the Gospel would be shared by all people was coming to pass. Thus, the Holy Spirit, in prompting this 'speaking in tongues', or in different languages, was trying to impress upon the minds of the early Christians that the Christian faith was not a faith to be squeezed into the mold of Judaism, but was to be taken to all tribes and nations under the sun. Tongues were a sign that the Holy Spirit would be 'poured out on all flesh.'

3. Mark 16:17

In this passage we read once more about signs and one of those mentioned is speaking in 'new tongues'. What is this particular passage saying, and what help can we get from it in seeking to understand the 'tongues' problem?

First of all, it should be borne in mind that the majority of outstanding Bible scholars do not believe that the passage commonly known as Mark 16:9-19 was part of the original Gospel of Mark. They hold this belief because the oldest and best Greek manuscripts in existence today do not contain this passage. In these original manuscripts Mark 16 ends with verse 8. In the Revised Standard Version of the Bible these verses are not included in the printed text, but in a footnote. Footnotes in several other versions also confirm this (See New English Bible, Amplified Version of the New Testament, J. B. Phillips New Testament in Modern English). Thus, if one accepts this view, then the reference in verse 17 to 'new tongues' is not a question for discussion. However since some texts do include these latter verses in Mark 16 it would be well to examine them carefully to determine if they have any real relevance to the doctrine of speaking in tongues, as it is taught by some groups.

In Mark 16:17 we read, 'And these signs shall accompany those who believe . . .' Then several things are mentioned in verse 18 which were to be signs to those who believe: drive out demons; speak in new languages; pick up serpents; not be harmed by deadly poison; and heal the sick. How is this passage to be interpreted?

In interpreting this passage, most commentators would say that all people, even though they believe, will most likely be harmed if they pick up deadly snakes or drink poison. Hence, these 'signs' of drinking poison or handling deadly snakes are not usually stressed as 'signs' that should [be] demonstrated to prove one's belief in Christ. Yet those who teach the importance of speaking in 'tongues' usually refer to this one sign alone, that is, speaking in 'new tongues', as being one of the signs that is to be demonstrated to prove that one has received the Holy Spirit. But if this [is] necessary, why should not all of the other 'signs' mentioned in the ending of Mark's gospel also be demonstrated as proof that one has been called by God, and filled with His Spirit? I doubt that anyone in his right mind would insist that all of these 'signs' would have first to be demonstrated in a person's life to prove that he is a believer and has received the Holy Spirit.

Some commentators would, perhaps, say that the 'new languages' refers to the new language which would come from the mouth of a converted man after his heart has been cleansed from sin and evil. Others would insist that the 'new languages' has reference to historical languages which formerly had not been used in preaching the gospel of Christ, but would, under the control of the Holy Spirit, be learned and used in the proclamation of the Gospel. As more and more people were won to Christ, the gospel story would spread into different lands, and be spoken in 'new tongues.' Thus, to say that this passage teaches that one must speak in 'tongues' as an evidence that he has received the Holy Spirit is to read something into it that is not there.

II. IN THE CORINTHIAN CHURCH

1. Difficulty and Disorder

The people at Corinth had entirely the wrong idea concerning the use of the 'gift of tongues'. Paul stated that he did not want them to be uninformed concerning the right use of spiritual gifts. 'Now concerning spiritual gifts, brethren I do not want you to be uninformed.' Before their conversion they had been led astray by their heathen practices, and Paul wanted to make sure that, as Christians, they were not led astray in their understanding of spiritual gifts, and their use.

They had, apparently, developed a wrong view of the use of the 'gift of tongues' Paul urged them to become mature in their thinking and not be like little children. 'Brethren, do not be children in your thinking; be babes in evil but in thinking be mature' (1 Corinthians 14:20). Paul warned them that by the way they were behaving outsiders or unbelievers coming into their church might think they were mad. 'If, therefore, the whole church assembles and all speak in tongues, and outsiders or unbelievers enter, will they not say you are mad?' (1 Cor. 14:23). Because of the confusion and disorder which had developed as a result of their wrong understanding of 'tongues', Paul warned them that they should be sure that what they were doing was done 'decently and in order' (1 Corinthians 14:40).

It must be kept in mind that the only place where tongues is mentioned in any of Paul's letters is in 1 Corinthians, and the reason it was dealt with there was because those who were trying to use this gift did not fully understand its use, and, as a result, the church had been led into great difficulty and confusion. If this happened in the early church, it is no marvel that the same teaching may be misunderstood in our day, and likewise result in disharmony and difficulty in the church.

In order for the Corinthian Christians to gain a proper understanding of this matter, Paul gave a very long explanation concerning the use of the gifts of the Spirit, and then showed how the one gift of tongues was related to the whole. In this study we shall not deal at length with all of the gifts, but we will examine what Paul wrote as it is related to this one gift alone, We shall note several facts which are important to a proper understanding of Paul's teaching about tongues.

2. Tongues Only One of the Gifts of the Spirit

First, we should note that Paul explained to the Corinthians that tongues was only one of the many gifts of the Spirit. He said, 'Now there are varieties of gifts . . .' (1 Corinthians 12:4). These different gifts are given to different people (1 Corinthians 12:7-11). The people at Corinth had not grasped this truth. No Christian has all of the gifts, nor do all have the same gifts. Paul asks: 'Are all apostles? Are all prophets? Are all teachers? Do all work miracles? Do all possess gifts of healing?

Do all speak with tongues? Do all interpret?' (1 Corinthians 12:29-30).

3. Tongues is the Least of the Gifts

Paul also pointed out that the gift of tongues is the least important of the gifts In chapter 12, verse 28, Paul sets forth the different gifts in their proper order. He said, 'first apostles, second prophets, third teachers, then workers of miracles, then healers, helpers, administrators, speakers in various kinds of tongues.'

In the work of the church the most important gifts are those which strengthen and edify the whole church. Paul said in 1 Corinthians 14:12, 'So with yourselves, since you are eager for manifestations of the Spirit, strive to excel in building up the church.' Note what Paul said: . . . *strive to excel in building up the church'* (verse 21). Seeking for spiritual gifts should be in the direction of those gifts which would lead to this goal. Which gift would be most likely to accomplish this? Speaking in unknown tongues? Using words which no one understands? No, certainly not! In 1 Corinthians 14:1-28 Paul explained this at great length. In verse 1 he said, 'Seek especially that you may prophesy.' Why? because this gift leads to the upbuilding of the church. '. . . He who prophesies speaks to men for their upbuilding and encouragement and consolation.' Those speaking in tongues did not help or profit the church, for their contribution could not be understood, and was therefore meaningless to the church. 'For one who speaks in a tongue speaks not to men but to God; for no one understands him, but he utters mysteries in the Spirit' (vs. 2). 'He who speaks in a tongue edifies himself, but he who prophesies edifies the church' (vs. 4). In verses 9-11 Paul explains even further:

   . . . If you in a tongue utter speech that is
not intelligible, how will anyone know
what is said? For you will be speaking
into the air. There are doubtless many
different languages in the world, and
none is without meaning; but if I do not
know the meaning of the language I
shall be a foreigner to the speaker and
the speaker a foreigner to me.'

Again, Paul did not give a high place to the gift of
tongues because it was of no spiritual value to unbelievers. Unbelievers who witnessed the tongues activity
as it was manifested among the Corinthians would look
upon it as madness. Paul said, 'If . . . outsiders or unbelievers enter will they not say that you are mad?' On the
other hand, prophecy would be of some benefit to the
unbeliever by bringing him under conviction that he
ought to become a Christian.

Further, Paul counted the gift of tongues last because it caused so much disorder and confusion in the
church This point is fully explained under the heading,
Paul's Final Appeal Concerning the Use of Tongues.

Still again Paul counted this gift last because it is a
manifestation which can be very easily counterfeited.
At the beginning of chapter 12 of his first letter to the
Corinthians, Paul reminds them that formerly they had
been led astray to dumb idols, and they needed to be
well informed in the matter of spiritual gifts so that they
would not fall into error again. It is a known fact that
those who have the 'tongues' experience usually have it
during a time of high emotional feeling and excitement,
and it would be very easy for a person to fall into mere
ecstatic speaking, and think this is the Biblical gift of

tongues. Satan would be very well pleased if he could get an earnest Christian to experience some kind of ecstatic speaking as a substitute for a genuine experience of the Holy Spirit in his life. Jesus warned that there would be 'great signs and wonders so as to lead people astray' (Matthew 24:24).

Thus, the gift of tongues is of little value to the church as a whole. This is why Paul puts it last on the list. Those who speak in tongues may be understood by God, even though men do not understand, and there may be some benefit to the person himself, for 'he who speaks in tongues edifies himself . . .' (verse 4). But Paul's great stress is on manifestations of the Spirit which bless and help the whole church.

4. Tongues Not to be Earnestly Sought After

If we examine carefully what Paul wrote to the Corinthians we will find that he did not stress that Christians should seek the gift of tongues. It is true that in chapter 14, verse 5 Paul said he wished they would all speak in tongues, but even before he finished his sentence he changed it and said, '. . . *but even more to prophesy.*'

After setting forth the gifts of the Spirit in their order of importance in chapter 12, verse 28, and stressing that all Christians do not receive the same gifts (verses 29-30), he said very clearly, 'But earnestly desire the higher gifts' (verse 31). Since tongues is not one of the higher gifts, what reason, then, is there for seeking it? Even more, why should people teach that one must seek this manifestation to prove that he has received the Holy Spirit?

In order to make himself perfectly clear, Paul said the same thing again and again in different ways. In 14:1, after showing the Corinthians the great importance of love over all the gifts, he said, 'Make love your aim, and EARNESTLY DESIRE the higher gifts, ESPECIALLY THAT YOU MAY PROPHESY.' Previously, in 12:28, he had put this gift at the top of the list of the gifts which are available for Christians. He said, '. . . first apostles, second prophets, third teachers . . .' His main theme in chapter fourteen is that the gifts which have real meaning to the church are those which will help all the people of the church to be built up in the faith.

> For one who speaks in a tongue speaks not to men but to God; for no one understands him for he utters mysteries in the Spirit. On the other hand, he who prophesies speaks to men for their upbuilding and encouragement and consolation. He who speaks in a tongue edifies himself, but he who prophesies edifies the church. Now I want you all to speak in tongues, but even more to prophesy. He who prophesies is greater than he who speaks in tongues, unless someone interprets, so that the church may be edified. Now, brethren, if I come to you speaking in tongues, how shall I benefit you unless I bring you some revelation or knowledge or prophesy or teaching? If even lifeless instruments, such as the flute or the harp, do not give distinct notes, how will anyone know what is played? And if the bugle gives an indis-

tinct sound, who will get ready for battle? So with yourselves; if you in a
tongue utter speech that is not intelligible, how will anyone know what is said?
For you will speaking into the air. There
are doubtless many different languages
in the world, and none is without meaning; but if I do not know the meaning of
the language, I shall be a foreigner to the
speaker and the speaker a foreigner to
me. So with yourselves; since you are
eager for manifestations of the Spirit
strive to excel in building up the church
(1 Corinthians 14:2-12).

Nothing could be more clear in this passage than
what Paul is saying about the value of the different spiritual gifts. He exhorted those at Corinth again and again
to listen to his words. Look at verses 13-20:

Therefore he who speaks in a tongue
should pray for the power to interpret.
For if I pray in a tongue, my spirit prays
but my mind is unfruitful. What am I to
do? I will pray with the spirit, and I will
pray with the mind also; I will sing with
the spirit and I will sing with the mind
also. Otherwise, if you bless with the
spirit how can any one in the position of
an outsider say 'Amen' to your thanksgiving when he does not know what you
are saying? For you may give thanks
well enough, but the other man is not edified. I thank God that I speak in tongues
more than you all; nevertheless, in
church I would rather speak five words

with my mind, in order to instruct others,
than ten thousand words in a tongue.
Brethren, do not be children in your
thinking; be babes in evil, but in thinking
be mature.

If one is seeking especially for a spiritual gift, his first choice should be prophecy and his second choice teaching. Why is this so? Many people seem to think that the gift of prophecy is a gift of the past and is not given today. Their idea of a prophet is one who is able to foretell the future. Some of the Old Testament prophets foretold some future events, but prophecy means more than foretelling future events. It means to forthtell God's Word to people today. Paul explained this in 1 Corinthians 14:3 when he said, '. . . he who prophesies speaks to men for their upbuilding and encouragement and consolation.' Paul is not thinking of foretelling future events, but of inspired preaching. Christ has already revealed the great truths of God, and the prophet of today is to preach it. In Revelation 19:10 we read, '. . . For the testimony of Jesus is the spirit of prophecy.' Therefore the two gifts of prophecy and teaching are the two gifts which do the most to explain the faith and lead people to salvation. The body is doomed to die and therefore healing, as wonderful as it is, has only a temporary value to people. But finding Christ as Savior, and understanding the way of salvation and the great truths of the Christian faith have everlasting value. Thus, the gifts of inspired preaching and teaching are the two gifts which head the list of the gifts of the Spirit, and have the greatest value for the church.

5. The Holy Spirit Bestows Gifts as He Wills

Christians may desire the higher gifts, but in the main, they should not be trying to choose the gifts they think they should have. They must realize that the Holy Spirit bestows his gifts according to His own plan. In 1 Corinthians 12:11 Paul said, 'All these are inspired by one and the same Spirit, who apportions to each one individually as he wills.' Again, in Hebrews 2:4: '. . . by gifts of the Holy Spirit distributed according to his own will.' In Ephesians 4:11 Paul said, 'And *his gifts* were that some should be apostles, some prophets, some evangelists, some pastors and teachers.' When the apostles were called in the beginning it was not because they had asked to be made apostles. Christ saw in each of them certain qualities that would enable them to be apostles. Thus, while Paul did say that Christians should seek the highest gifts, that is, inspired preaching and teaching, he also said that is not necessarily one's asking which determines the gift to be received. The distribution of the gifts is in greater hands. It is important to note here that in no sense did Paul indicate that people should be urged to seek the gift of tongues, or for any gift for that matter, other than for the highest ones.

People who are pressing and seeking for certain gifts according to their own desires and ideas may definitely hinder the work of God and the operation of the Spirit in their own lives. It may be that God has already given a certain gift to a Christian, which, if used properly, will become a vital force in the overall work of the church. However, if one sets his mind on a special gift, which he thinks to be important, he may overlook the very gift God has already given him to use. Paul told Timothy to . . . rekindle the gift of God . . .' According to what Paul wrote in 1 Corinthians 12:7, 12, every sincere Christian already has some gift given to him. He should look at his life to see what God has put there, be thankful, and begin to use it. Paul pointed out that some parts of the body, like some of the gifts of the Spirit, may not always be looked upon as important, but if the body is to function properly, they are of great importance.

6. Is the Gift of Tongues to be Sought for Personal Edification?

On the basis of what Paul wrote, there is nothing to indicate that a Christian should seek the gift of tongues for personal edification. Paul did say that if a person speaks in a tongue he edifies himself. However, Paul also said in the same breath, 'but he who prophesies edifies the church.' As has been pointed out already, Paul's main concern was that the church should be built up and strengthened. In chapter 14, verse 12, he says, '... strive to excel in building up the church.' Nowhere does Paul suggest that the gifts of the Spirit were gifts of God to bring help to oneself. He taught that the gift of tongues was was to have meaning for the whole church. His words in verses 13-15 are quite clear:

> 'Therefore, he who speaks in a tongue
> should pray for the power to interpret.
> For if I pray in a tongue, my spirit prays
> but my mind is unfruitful. What am I to
> do? I will pray with the spirit, and I will
> pray with the mind also; I will sing with
> the spirit and I will sing with the mind
> also.'

Thus, Paul taught that in using this gift it is not right to pray in a tongue without using the mind properly. One can pray 'in the spirit' and still pray with the mind. It is pointed out that the tongues speaker may give thanks in a mysterious language, and God may understand him, but this does not help God's people as a whole. In verse 17 Paul said, 'For you may give thanks well enough, but the other man is not edified.'

It should be emphasized that nowhere is the slightest teaching given that tongues, or any other gift of the Spirit, is to be used for personal benefit alone. In 1 Corinthians 12:14-31 Paul gives the illustration of the human body, and shows how all of the various parts work together to enable the body to function properly. The purpose of each part is to assist the body in achieving its fullest development. The nose does not exist for its own benefit. The eye is used to bring light and direction to the body. The gifts of the Spirit are for the same purpose. Hence, the value of the gift of tongues is to be measured by its value, its usefulness, to the whole body, the church. There is no indication that this gift is to be sought for personal use and edification.

7. Paul's Final Appeal Concerning the Use of the Gift of Tongues

The careful reader of 1 Corinthians 14 will discover that most of Paul's teaching in the chapter was set forth in order to minimize the value of the gift of tongues, and to discourage its use. Even so, he did say in verse 39, '. . . do not forbid speaking in tongues', and laid down rules as to how the gift should be used in the church. He said: 'If any speak in a tongue, let there be only two or at most three, and each in turn; and let one interpret. But if there is no one to interpret, let each of them keep silence in church and speak to himself and to God' (1 Corinthians 14:27-28). Since we believe the words of Paul to be a part of the inspired Scriptures, how then do we explain these words, and what meaning do they have for us today? If Paul wrote, '. . . do not forbid speaking in tongues', then what right do people today have to restrict the use of tongues?

In order to have a correct understanding of these words, it is first necessary to understand that the Bible sets forth two kinds of truth. First, there is the abiding foundational truth of the Christian faith which never changes. For example, Matthew 5:1-15, Jesus gave certain teachings known as the 'beatitudes'. In these teachings Jesus mentions certain personal qualities which characterize the godly life. These truths will never change, and will always be important to the Christian In Romans 12 Paul writes concerning many of the basic principles which govern the Christian life. These are abiding truths, and will always be binding upon the Christian.

However, in addition to these foundational truths there are also certain teachings which apply only to temporary problems. Such teachings are a part of Scripture, but their value is conditioned by time and circumstance. For example, in 1 Corinthians 7:27 Paul asked: 'Are you free from a wife? Do not seek marriage.' Again, in verse 38, 'So he who marries his betrothed does well; and he who refrains from marriage will do better.' Is it an abiding truth, 'It is better not to marry'? Clearly, what Paul was writing was for that time only, because of the uncertainty of the times (see verse 26). He did not give a rule which was to be in force for all time and all people. What he said was conditioned by time and circumstance.

In the very same chapter in which Paul dealt with the problem of tongues, he told the women to keep silent in the church, and if they had any questions to ask their husbands at home (1 Cor. 14:34-35). Why did Paul write this? In that day the women at Corinth were not well-educated, and may have been rather uncultured and ill-mannered, and when they entered into the church they behaved in an unbecoming manner. Thus, Paul wrote that it was wrong for them to speak, and therefore they should keep quiet. What Paul had written was Scripture, and it was true, but it had value particularly for the women at Corinth and only so long as they were in that condition.

In our day women are cultured and educated, and know how to behave, and to participate in the worship services of the church. Hence, if we were to take this scripture and try to make it binding today, we would violate one of the basic truths of the Scriptures, that 'There is neither Jew nor Greek, there is neither slave nor free, there is *neither male nor female . . .'* (Galatians 3:28). In Christ's day the women were very well accepted, and were found to be faithful, but at Corinth there was a different problem, and for that reason Paul commanded the women to keep silent in the church. This is not one of the foundational truths of the Bible.

In the same chapter Paul warned the Corinthians that they should not forbid speaking in tongues (verse 39). It was the Corinthians who were making so much of the tongues issue, and Paul gave them permission to carry on with manifestations of this 'gift', if and providing they followed certain procedures. Even so, he reminded them in several places that their aim in worship should be to strengthen and edify the church. Paul asked, 'What then brethren? When you come together each one has a hymn, a lesson, a revelations, a tongue, or an interpretation. Let all things be done for edification.' Paul's main concern was that what was done should edify the whole church.

Their previous use of the gift of tongues had not helped the church very much. Three times in chapter 14 Paul mentions this. In verse 23 he asked them, 'If, therefore, the whole church assembles and all speak in tongues, and outsiders or unbelievers enter, will they not say that you are mad?' In verse 33 he inferred that their meetings had been in a state of confusion for he said, 'God is not a God of confusion but of peace.' Again in verse 40 he inferred that things had not been done properly, for he said, 'Let all things be done decently and in order.'

But because the people at Corinth had seemingly made such a great issue of this problem and because it might have created more trouble and division in the church had Paul forbidden the use of tongues completely, he made a concession to them that they might use this gift, providing it was done in a way that would help and edify the whole church. This was his major concern, and he mentions it seven times in this chapter (verses 5, 12, 17, 26, 31, 33, and 40). True, he told them 'Do not forbid speaking in tongues', but he said it conditionally. Their use of the gift was to build up the church, and not to bring confusion and trouble.

What Paul wrote to the Corinthians, that they should not forbid speaking in tongues, was valid for that particular church, and was contingent upon the mutual help and benefit derived from its use. However, at Corinth—the first and only church where Paul had to deal with the use of this gift—it caused a great deal of trouble and division, and required the great Apostle Paul himself to deal with it.

What about the use of this 'gift' today? In most places, as at Corinth, instead of bringing about unity, love, peace, and edification to the whole church, it most often produces discord, division, disharmony, and wild-fire emotionalism which weakens the church rather than strengthening it, and building it up. It cannot be believed that the Spirit of God is responsible for this.

At Corinth not only the activity of the tongues speakers was called into question, but also that of the 'prophets'. Apparently, some of their activities were not all that they should have been, and perhaps some of them were not teaching the true teachings of the church. Paul pointed out to them that, 'the spirits of the prophets are subject to the prophets.' And so it is that what any leader does or says in the church may be judged by his fellow leaders, as to whether or not it is Biblical, constructive, and edifying to the whole church. In the church it is necessary that the activities of those who are causing confusion and discord be controlled by the leadership of the church.

Thus, Paul's words, 'Do not forbid speaking in tongues' are words which were directed to a special church at a special time, and under very special circumstances. Paul's approval for the Corinthians to use tongues depended upon 'all things being done decently and in order.' It is not right to quote Paul's words to prove that speaking in tongues is permissible, if, at the same time, the use of tongues is causing strife and division among the brethren.

8. If All of the Gifts are not Manifest in the Church Today, Does This Not Indicate that the Church is No Longer Under the Control of the Holy Spirit?

The answer to this question is NO! Paul most emphatically says that the gifts of the Spirit are given to each person as He, the Holy Spirit, chooses. Several Biblical passages prove this: 1 Corinthians 12:11; Hebrews 2:4; and Ephesians 4:11. As times change, and conditions in the world are different, it maybe that the methods of the Spirit's operation will likewise change in making the church a vital force in the world, able to fulfill its God-given mission. It is a known fact that at certain times God has made greater use of miracles than at others. In the days of Moses God used many miraculous events to warn Pharaoh, and to free the Israelites from their bondage. However, at other times, the working of miracles was not especially needed. God most often works through natural means, and only does the unusual under extraordinary circumstances.

It is true that a few of the gifts of the Spirit are not as noticeable in the church now as they were at one time, but the 'higher gifts' are just as much in evidence as they ever were. There are many great preachers in these days who are able to proclaim the message of God prophetically. They have the gift of prophecy. There are many wonderful Bible teachers, who are able to explain clearly the teachings of the Scriptures. They have the gift of teaching. There are many with gifts of wisdom and knowledge—and many of these have never gone to school. Paul speaks of the gift of 'administration', and what an important gift that is! The business of the church is very important, and some churches break up because they do not have a proper organization or effective administration. Then there is the gift of 'helps'. This must be one of the more important gifts, for there are so many who have it. Many more people are called to be 'helpers' than are called to be pastors or church leaders.

It is very dangerous to presume that the Holy Spirit is no longer working in and through the church simply because some of the gifts may not be manifested as much as formerly. Since the distribution of the gifts is entirely the work of the Holy Spirit, it is not good for mere human beings to sit in judgment on the way God does His work, and, in effect, criticize him for what they believe to be a lack in his work. The prophet Jonah was one who sat in judgment on the work of God and suffered exceedingly for his narrow thinking.

III. IN THE LIFE OF THE CHRISTIAN

1. Is 'Tongues' the Evidence of the Baptism of the Holy Spirit?

The answer is NO! Several facts support this answer. First, there is no indication in Scripture that all of those who received the Holy Spirit spoke in 'tongues'. In Acts 4:31 we read, 'And when they had prayed, the place in which they gathered together was shaken; and they were all filled with the Holy Spirit and spoke the Word of God with boldness.' Also, in Acts 8:17, we read: 'Then they laid their hands on them and they received the Holy Spirit.' Nothing is said in these passages which would lead us to believe that the 'gift' of tongues was manifested on these two occasions.

Secondly, Paul states positively that all do not receive the same gifts, and this includes the 'gift' of tongues. In 1 Corinthians 12:8-10 Paul states: 'To one is given through the Spirit the utterance of wisdom, and to another the utterance of knowledge . . . , to another faith . . . , to another gifts of healing . . . , to another working of miracles, to another prophecy, to another the ability to distinguish between spirits, to another various kinds of tongues, to another the interpretation of tongues. Paul's inference in verses 29-31 of the same chapter is that different people receive different gifts from the Spirit, *and the gift of the Spirit is not to be thought of as the Spirit Himself.*

Thirdly, in 1 Corinthians 14:22, Paul says, 'Thus, tongues are a sign not for believers but for unbelievers . . .' People who hold the belief that one must speak in tongues to prove that he has received the Holy Spirit find these words of Paul difficult. In this verse he seems to contradict the idea that the tongues manifestation bears witness to Christians that the Holy Spirit has come upon them.

2. What is the True Evidence?

What is the evidence or proof that the Holy Spirit has come into the heart and life of the Christian? It is the *ministry* of the Spirit in his life. What did Jesus say the Holy Spirit would do after coming into the life of the Christian? Here again it is important to look carefully into the Scriptures. Jesus had much to say about the ministry of the Spirit in the life of the Christian. In John 16:13, 'When the Spirit of truth is come, he will guide you . . .' The evidence of the Spirit in the life of the Christian is a sense of His guidance in day-by-day activities.

Again Jesus said, 'When the Holy Spirit comes . . . he will teach you . . .' (John 14:26). The evidence of the Spirit is that there should be growth in spiritual understanding. The work of the Holy Spirit is to teach the Christian.

In John 16:14 Jesus said, 'When the Holy Spirit comes . . . he will glorify me . . .' The evidence of the Spirit in the life of the Christian is a growing desire to glorify Christ in all that he does. The work of the Holy Spirit is to glorify Christ.

In John 16:8 Jesus said, 'When the Holy Spirit comes . . . he will convince the world of sin and of righteousness . . .' The evidence of the Spirit in the life of the Christian is a greater sensitivity to wrong-doing. When the Holy Spirit is living in the heart of a Christian there is a willingness to live right, and when he does wrong, to make that wrong right.

Jesus also said that 'When the Holy Spirit comes . . . you shall receive power . . . and you shall be my witnesses . . .' (Acts 1:8). And again, '. . . He shall bear witness of me' (John 15:26). The evidence of the Spirit in the life of the Christian is a yearning to share the Gospel message with others, that they might come to know Jesus.

Paul also had something to say concerning the evidence of the Holy Spirit in the life of the Christian. In Galatians 5:22 he said, 'But the fruit of the Spirit is love, joy, peace, patience, kindness, goodness, faithfulness, gentleness, self-control.' The evidence of the Holy Spirit is that there is a desire for, and development of, the fruit of the Spirit.

The believer should progressively see manifestation of the fruit of the Spirit in his life. Fruit on a tree does not all mature at the same time. The fruit of the Spirit may not all be perfectly manifest at once, but the work of the Spirit is to work with the Christian, as his helper, until he is able to show forth these fruits in their fulness. How soon the full manifestation of the fruit appears will depend upon how closely the Christian is able to walk with Him in fellowship and communion.

Again, Paul points out that the evidence of the Holy Spirit in the life of the Christian is that there is an increasing victory over all forms of sin. The work of the Holy Spirit is to empower the Christian to overcome sin (Romans 8:2, Galatians 5:16).

No Christian will necessarily show that he has all of these marks of the Holy Spirit in his life at the beginning when the Holy Spirit first comes, but if the Holy Spirit does dwell in him He will work in every area of his life, and he will be pliable, enabling the Holy Spirit to accomplish His work.

The Holy Spirit's work is to stay with each Christian, and help him to attain the glory and beauty of Christ (2 Corinthians 3:17-18). As the Holy Spirit works, slowly and surely, an increasing fullness of the fruit of the Spirit will be seen in the life of the Christian, and the perfect life of Christ will be revealed in him.

3. How Does One Receive the Holy Spirit?

The Christian should remember that everything God gives to him is a GIFT, and is to be received simply by faith.

God intended that the plan which he has for helping his children should be clearly understood by them. However, sometimes men, because of their human limitations, make the teachings of the faith much more difficult than they are.

The way of receiving the Holy Spirit was never intended to be difficult, or beyond the understanding and faith of men. Receiving the Holy Spirit is not a question of saying certain phrases again and again, or of working oneself up into a special emotional state. What do the Scriptures say? What is the simple way of receiving the Holy Spirit into one's life? Several things are mentioned in the Scriptures. These are:

a. The Christian should understand that the Holy Spirit is his promised due.

Jesus said that those who believed in Him would receive the Holy Spirit (John 7:37, 39). He also said that the Father would send the Holy Spirit to His followers (John 14:16, 26). And then in Luke 11:13 he assured His disciples that the Father will give the Holy Spirit to those who ask Him.

God is always ready to give each and every Christian the Holy Spirit, because it is His plan for all Christians to receive Him. The Holy Spirit is as available to the Christian as air is to our lungs.

b. Certain conditions must first be met before one can receive the Holy Spirit.

The President of a country goes to a certain part of the country to visit only after certain conditions have been met by the people who are to receive him. Likewise, a student is admitted to a university only after having first fulfilled certain requirements made by the university. An individual seeking a large loan from a bank with which to build a new home receives the money only after having met certain conditions required by the bank. Thus, much of what one receives in life comes only after stated conditions are met.

Thus it is with the Holy Spirit. He can infill the life of the Christian only if and when certain specified conditions are met by that person. When these conditions are met, the Holy Spirit comes in all of His fulness, without begging, waiting, or emotional frenzy.

The Christian must earnestly desire the Holy Spirit to possess him completely, and to live his life completely under the control and guidance of the Spirit. Until the Christian has this desire the Holy Spirit cannot enter into his life. But his desire must not be superficial or insincere, but a deep yearning in the heart for the Holy Spirit to direct and use him. The Holy Spirit will not go where he is not really welcomed.

Also the Christian must have an obedient heart, and a willingness to do the will of God which has already been revealed to him. Jesus said, 'If you love me you will keep my commands and I will pray the Father, and He will give you another Counselor, to be with you forever' (John 14:15-16), Obedience to Christ's commandments precedes the giving of the Counselor, the Holy Spirit. Peter also points out that the Holy Spirit is given to those who are obedient to God (Acts 5:32).

A third condition which must be met before the Christian can receive the Holy Spirit is that he must have a desire to glorify Christ in all of his thoughts and actions. The ministry of the Holy Spirit in the life of a Christian is to glorify and magnify Christ always (John 15:26, 16:4). Thus, the Christian must endeavor to follow Christ the best he knows and glorify Him in his mind and actions. Everything which is not Christ-like should be put away from the Christian. If his desire is to enthrone Christ in his heart as Lord of his life, the Holy Spirit will come in all of his fullness to perform His ministry, according to the promises of Jesus.

c. Having fulfilled the conditions, the Christian should immediately claim the experience of the indwelling Spirit, by faith.

Every Christian can immediately claim the promise of the Holy Spirit as soon as he has met the conditions, for, as we have already pointed out, the Holy Spirit is God's promised gift to every Christian. Peter said, 'For the promise is to you and to your children and to everyone whom the Lord our God calls to him' (Acts 2:39). And the Lord himself has said, '. . . how much more will the heavenly Father give the Holy Spirit to those who ask him?' (Luke 11:13). The Christian must believe these promises and begin living with full assurance that the Spirit is there ready to begin His ministry in his life. Paul told the Galatian Christians, 'Christ redeemed us from the curse of the law . . . that we might receive the promise of the Holy Spirit through faith.' God has promised! Believe God!

How badly God must feel—the loving Father who has promised the Holy Spirit to his people, and who desires to give Him as a free gift when the proper conditions are met—to hear Christians shouting and pleading, and saying meaningless words over and over again, such as some people instruct one to do, saying, 'Let yourself go; let your tongue say Abba, Abba, Abba, Abba . . . for as long as you can,' for they say that when the Spirit enters into us he cries 'Abba', that is to say, 'Father.' Is not praying of this kind just the opposite of what Jesus taught in Matthew, chapter six? 'And in praying do not heap up empty phrases as the Gentiles do; for they think that they will be heard for their many words' (Matthew 6:7).

4. Is the Laying on of Hands Necessary?

The answer is NO! It is true that when the apostles went to Samaria to observe what God had done through Philip they laid their hands on the believers and prayed for them that they might receive the Holy Spirit (Acts 8:14ff). It is also true that Paul did likewise in Ephesus (Acts 19:6). But this does not mean that this is a rule which the church must follow. Nor does it mean that a Christian must have others lay their hands on him and pray for him before he can receive the Holy Spirit.

Peter's experience in the house of Cornelius (Acts 11) indicates that the laying on of hands is not necessary to receiving the Holy Spirit. While Peter was still preaching the Word of God the Holy Spirit fell upon all who heard him. Nor is the laying on of hands mentioned in Acts 2, and 4:31. In neither instance were the disciples even praying for the baptism of the Holy Spirit.

As we have already said, the Holy Spirit comes to the Christian as soon as he fulfills the requirements set forth in God's word for receiving the Holy Spirit. If he has an earnest desire to receive this gift of God, if he is obedient to the known will of God, and if he yearns to glorify Christ through his life, he can receive the Holy Spirit THE VERY MOMENT HE ASKS IN FAITH!

[Included by permission of David Shultz, son of the author.]

The Gift of Tongues.
By F. G. Smith

What It Is and What It Is Not

The writer preached on the subject "The Gift of Tongues" to the Ministerial Assembly of the Church of God at Anderson, Indiana, where hundreds of ministers and gospel workers were gathered together. So well was the discourse received and so numerous were the requests that it be put in tract form; that I have felt constrained to present it to the church in general.

THE GIFT OF TONGUES

In the last commission given by our Lord to his apostles, we read "Go ye into all the world, and preach the gospel to every creature. He that believeth and is baptized shall be saved; but he that believeth not shall be damned. And these signs shall follow them that believe; In my name shall they east out devils; *they shall speak with new tongues;* … they shall lay hands on the sick, and they shall recover" (Mark 16:15-18) .

The subject of speaking with other tongues has attracted considerable attention in recent years. The modern tongues movement has placed great stress upon it, but in many places the teaching has been accompanied by such wild disorder, confusion, unseemly demonstrations, false teaching, fanaticism and extravagances of various kinds, that many pious souls are unduly prejudiced against the very word "tongues" as relating to super-natural speaking by the Spirit.

The supreme test of truth; however, is not the inconsistencies or extravagances of some who profess it. If it were, almost every doctrine of the Bible could be thus summarily set aside as of no value. The Word of God is the standard. "To the law and to the testimony: if they speak not according to this word, it is because there is no light in them" (Isa. 8:20). We should always approach the truth with open minds, ready to give it careful, prayerful, unprejudiced consideration. Speaking with other tongues is one of the signs which Jesus declared should follow believers. This fact alone should create in us a desire to know what is the Bible standard of teaching concerning this supernatural gift.

The first fulfilment of Jesus' prediction relative to speaking in tongues is recorded in Acts 2. "And when the day of Pentecost was fully come, they were all with one accord in one place. And suddenly there came a sound from heaven as of a rushing mighty wind, and it filled all the house where they were sitting. And there appeared unto them cloven tongues like as of fire, and it sat upon each of them. And they were all filled with the Holy Ghost, and began to speak with other tongues, as the Spirit gave them utterance.... Now when this was noised abroad, the multitude came together, and were confounded, because that every man heard them speaking in his own language. And they were all amazed and marveled, saying one to another, Behold, are not all these which speak Galileans? and how hear we each man in our own tongue, wherein we were born? ... We do hear them speak in our tongues the wonderful works of God" (vs. 1-11).

A Gift Set in the Church

This remarkable phenomenon on the day of Pentecost marked the initial work of the Holy Spirit in setting in order the Christian church as a visible working force in the world. This particular manifestation was not, however, limited to that one occasion. Christian glossolalia, or speaking in tongues, was set in the church for a useful purpose and therefore has a just claim to permanency, like the other gift of the Spirit. The apostle Paul says, "By one Spirit are we all baptized into one body" (1 Cor. 12:13). And he proceeds to show that to these various members of Christ, constituting the one body, God has by his Spirit distributed gifts for the profit of all.

"Now there are diversities of gifts, but the same Spirit.... And there are diversities of operations, but it is the same God which worketh all in all. But the manifestation of the Spirit is given to every man to profit withal. For to one is given by the same Spirit the word of wisdom; to another the word of knowledge by the same Spirit; to another faith by the same Spirit; to another the gifts of healing by the same Spirit; to another the working of miracles; to another prophecy; to another discerning of spirits; *to another divers kinds of tongues;* to another the interpretation of tongues: but all these worketh that one and the selfsame Spirit, dividing to every man severally as he will" (1 Cor. 12:4-11).

Same as Speaking in Tongues

An attempt has been made to draw a distinction between the gift of tongues and speaking with tongues. Some say that the gift of tongues is special, being bestowed upon certain persons only, and that it is under the control of the individual possessing it; but that speaking in tongues is general, being the invariable accompaniment of the Holy Spirit baptism, and is therefore an uncontrollable overflow of exhortation and warning to men or of thanksgiving and praise to God. The relation of "tongues" to the Holy Spirit baptism will be considered later. Just now I wish to show that there is no Scriptural warrant for making such a distinction between the gift of tongues and speaking in tongues.

In every chapter and place in the New Testament where the tongues are mentioned, they are referred to simply as "speaking in tongues." Christ's prediction was, "they shall speak with new tongues." The Pentecostal fulfilment was, "they began to speak with other tongues." In 1 Cor. 14, where Paul exhorts the Corinthians to "follow after charity, and desire spiritual *gifts*," and to be "zealous of spiritual *gifts*" (vs. 1-12), devoting almost the entire chapter to the tongues subject, defining their use, control, and limitations, he refers to that gift constantly as merely speaking in tongues. In fact, in chapter 12 the same apostle classes the "diversities of gifts"—miracles, prophecy, tongues, etc.—as merely *"manifestations of the Spirit."* Gifts of the Spirit and manifestations of the Spirit are therefore the same. There is no possible way in which tongues can be manifested except by speaking. Therefore, in the very nature of the case, there can be no difference between the gift of tongues and speaking with tongues, for the "manifestation" or "operation," speaking, *is the exercise of the gift.*

Notice, also, how Paul in a more explicit way uses the gift of tongues and speaking in tongues interchangeably in this same chapter. In verses 8 to 10 he mentions the gifts—wisdom, knowledge, faith, healing, miracles, prophecy, discernment, tongues, interpretation of tongues; in verses 28 to 30 he refers to the same list again—miracles, healings, tongues—and then asks, "Are all apostles? are all prophets? are all teachers? are all workers of miracles? have all the gifts of healing? do all speak with tongues? do all interpret?" Any one should be able to see that "speaking with tongues" in verse 30 corresponds to "divers kinds of tongues" (the gift) in verse 10, just the same as "do all interpret" In verse 30 corresponds to "the interpretation of tongues" in verse 10. The reason why modern tongues teachers have forced an unscriptural distinction between the gift of tongues and speaking, in tongues will be made apparent hereafter.

Double Phase of the Scriptural Gift

We have seen that the attempt to distinguish between the gift of tongues and its only possible method of manifestation — speaking — is forced and unscriptural, for the New Testament constantly refers to speaking in tongues and speaking with tongues as the gift. The Scriptures do, however, describe two orders of tongues, or rather two phases of the gift, and when these are clearly discerned, the entire subject and all the texts pertaining thereto are easily harmonized. We read of "divers kinds of tongues" — "tongues of men and of angels." We know that the Spirit of God is not limited. He can speak through man, if he so chooses, every language, whether of heaven or of earth; but, according to the Scriptures, in the manifestation of this supernatural gift in the church there is a phase designed particularly for PUBLIC use and another phase intended for and more particularly adapted to the Christian's PRIVATE devotional exercises.

This distinction is in harmony with the Spirit's operations in other respects. He works in one manner in the individual, and he works in another manner in the collective body of individuals, the church. Now, just as the Spirit works salvation in the heart of the individual in uniting him to God, and works divine fellowship in the collection of individuals, uniting them to each other and directing their course as workers together, so also the same Spirit, through the gift of tongues, manifests himself in one way, privately, for the special benefit of the individual, and in another manner, publicly, for the benefit of the church or as a "sign" to the unbelievers. This distinction I shall now proceed to draw, and the reader will please observe how beautifully all the scriptures harmonize when this double phase of the gift is recognized.

Personal, Private Phase of Tongues

1. *Is by the Spirit.* "In the Spirit he speaketh mysteries" (1 Cor. 14:2).

2. *Is addressed to God, not to men.* "He that speaketh in an unknown tongue speaketh not unto men, but unto God" (v. 2).

3. *Is not understood by men.* "He … speaketh not unto men, but unto God: for no man understandeth him; howbeit in the spirit he speaketh mysteries" (v. 2). "Let him speak to himself [privately], and to God" (v. 28).

4. *Speaker himself does not understand.* "For if I pray in an unknown tongue, my spirit prayeth, but my understanding is unfruitful" (v. 14). (Note: Ordinary speech, which is with the understanding of the speaker, is contrasted with the tongues in verse 19.) In tongues, therefore, the speaker does not himself understand, unless—

5. *He receives interpretation.* "Wherefore let him that speaketh in an unknown tongue pray that he may interpret" (v. 13).

6. *The prime object is to EDIFY HIMSELF.* "He that speaketh in an unknown tongue edifieth himself" (v. 4).

7. *If brought into the congregation is not edifying* (unless interpreted). " Greater is he that prophesieth than he that speaketh with tongues, except he interpret, that the church may receive edifying" (v. 5). "In the church I had rather speak five words with my understanding, that by my voice I might teach others also, than ten thousand words in an unknown tongue" (v. 19).

8. *Is prohibited in public unless interpreted.* "If there be no interpreter, let him keep silence in the church; and let him speak to himself, and to God" (v. 28).

9. *Is not very profitable for public use, even if interpreted,* hence is restricted to two or three persons in one service, and then only one at a time. "How is it then, brethren? when ye come together, every one of you hath ... a tongue, hath a revelation, hath an interpretation. Let all things be done unto edifying. If any man speak in an unknown tongue, let it be by two, *or at*

the most by three, and that by course; and let one inter-pret" (vs. 26-27).

Prophets. are allowed greater liberty. While the apostle instructs also that the prophets "speak two or three," he does not say, as regarding the tongues, "at the most by three"; but he does say, "Ye may ALL prophesy one by one" (v. 31). Prophecy is direct and convincing. "He that prophesieth speaketh unto men to edification, and exhortation, and comfort … he that prophesieth edifieth the church" (vs. 3-4). *Such* tongues are regarded by the unbeliever as a sign of madness. "If therefore the whole church be come together into one place and all speak with tongues, and there come in those that are unlearned, or unbelievers, will they not say that ye are mad? But if all prophesy, and there come in one that believeth not or one unlearned, he is convinced of all, he is judged of all and thus are the secrets of his heart made manifest; and so falling down on his face he will worship God, and report that God is in you of a truth" (vs. 23-25). Thus Paul shows the great advantage prophecy has over this phase of tongues manifestation. Prophecy is to be coveted, whereas tongues are to be held within the limits specified, and then merely to be not forbidden (v. 39)

Public Phase of the Gift

There are times when the Holy Spirit chooses to manifest the gift of tongues in a different manner and for a different purpose. Instead of being intended particularly for personal devotion and edification, this phase of the gift is designed primarily for the express benefit of the public. A Scriptural example is the Pentecostal experience, when the disciples spoke in other tongues as the Spirit gave them utterance. Under this phase of the gift, the tongues are—

1. *Real languages of earth.* "Every man heard them speak in his own language." "We do hear them speak in our tongues the wonderful works of God" (Acts 2:6, 11).

2. *Being intelligible, they require no interpretation,* if persons acquainted with such forms of speech are present (Acts 2).

3. *They constitute a real "SIGN,"* helpful' unbelievers. The sign does not, however, consist in the mere fact of speaking, but in the ability to speak *by the Spirit* languages that the speaker himself does not understand.

4. *Is neither prohibited nor limited.* The Pentecostal experience of tongues was not limited to two or three persons and they speaking through an interpreter. The language was direct from God to the multitude of unbelievers; they understood it; they were convinced by it; it was a real sign to them. I fail to see how any other manifestation of tongues can be a convincing sign to unbelievers. Paul says unintelligible tongues are to unbelievers a *sign of madness*; that is, they regard them as such.

The Gift Defined

The foregoing Scripture deductions as to the manifestation and use of the tongues prepare the way for a particular definition of the gift itself. *Christian glossolalia, or tongues, is a gift of God bestowed upon an individual whereby, through the operation of the Holy Spirit, he is enabled to speak UNTO GOD in a lan-*

guage which the Spirit chooses and which "no man understands," or to speak UNTO MEN the mysteries of God in a language unknown to him (the speaker) but understood by his hearers.

Summary of Distinguishing Features

1. The gift of tongues is a special gift of God through the Spirit.

2. It enables a person to speak to men in language known to them but unknown to him, or enables a person to speak to God in language which "no man understands" unless interpreted.

3. It is used as a means of personal edification in private prayer and devotion, in which exercise of tongues the individual *"speaketh not unto men* but unto God" (1 Cor. 14:2). It may also be used publicly with some profit if the speech is interpreted. It may also be used publicly with great profit and as a "sign" to unbelievers when the language is *spoken to the people,* at which time no interpretation is required. "With men of other tongues and other lips will I *speak unto this people....* Wherefore [such] tongues are for a sign, not to them that believe, but to them that believe not". (1 Cor. 14:21-22).

4. May be used at the will of the speaker, hence may be abused, as at Corinth. It is evident that the Corinthian church was indulging in unprofitable extremism in the exercise of tongues. Paul did not condemn the gift itself as a bad thing. On the other hand, he said that he himself exercised it privately (vs. 18-19). And he placed no prohibition or limitation whatever on its *private* exercise; but when the tongues were unintelligi-

ble to the hearers, he did endeavor by corrective discipline to limit their *public* exercise.

At this point I wish to call attention to the fact that in 1 Corinthians 14 the apostle draws a sharp contrast between "with the spirit" and "with the understanding." "With the spirit" refers to the mysterious "tongues," and "with the understanding" represents plain, intelligible human language, or "prophecy." Admitting that he spoke in tongues abundantly, the apostle nevertheless declared that in the church he would rather speak five words with his understanding (prophecy—see vs. 3-4) than ten thousand words in an unknown tongue (vs. 18-19). In verse 13 he exhorts the one who speaks in an unknown tongue to pray that he may interpret; and then he adds, "If I pray in an unknown tongue, my spirit prayeth, but my understanding is unfruitful. What is it then? I will pray with the spirit [that is, *in tongues*—see v. 18; and I will pray with the understanding also [in ordinary language]; I will sing with the spirit [in tongues]; and I will sing with the understanding also" (vs. 14-15).

The private phase of tongues is designed as a special means of spirit communication, a language of the spirit and of the emotions, in the exercise of which the soul of man overflows in rapturous praise and thanksgiving to God. To man understandeth him," but "in the spirit he speaketh mysteries." He "edifieth himself."

The contrast between tongues and prophecy is very pronounced, yet not to the disparagement of either when exercised within their respective bounds. In verses 2 and 3 of this wonderful chapter, the apostle speaks very highly of both; in verses 14 and 15 he shows that both are permissible under certain circumstances; in verses 18 and 19 he shows their comparative importance in public use: "I thank my God, I speak with tongues more than ye all: yet in the church I had rather speak five words with my understanding, that by my voice I might teach others also, than ten thousand words in an unknown tongue."

5. The true gift is under control, the same as the spirits of the prophets: "And the spirits of the prophets are subject to the prophets" (v. 32). "If there be no interpreter, *let him keep silence* in the church" (v. 28). Paul told us that true love "doth not behave itself unseemly" (1 Cor. 13:5). Therefore we may expect that the true operation of the Spirit will be in harmony with the law of fitness and propriety. We may set it down as a fact that those unseemly contortions of body, apparent signs of awful agony and distress, that some people undergo while professing to speak in tongues, are not the operation of the Spirit of God at all, but are due either to psychological causes or to Satanic influences. If, as the apostle Paul plainly teaches, the true gift of tongues is designed as a medium of heart-communion with God, through which the joyful emotions of the soul are expressed in lofty ecstatic praise, how can any one conceive the physical and mental attitude of its possessor to be other than in perfect unison with such joyful emotionalism? Can we believe that the one whose very heart is so in tune with God that his spirit overflows in such exalted rapturous praise as can be expressed only by the use of "the tongues of men and of angels"—can we believe, I say, that he will at the same time *look like a demon*—twisting, writhing, groaning, a picture of darkness and despair, sometimes even frothing at the mouth, and uttering shrieking cries like one possessed

with evil spirits? Perish the thought. "The tree is known by its fruits."

Not THE Evidence of the Holy Ghost Baptism

Another erroneous doctrine urged by most teachers of the modern tongues movement is that speaking in tongues is an invariable accompaniment, the one convincing proof or evidence, of the baptism in the Holy Ghost. What says the Word of God? In 1 Corinthians 12 where the apostle Paul mentions "speaking with tongues" in connection with miracles, prophecy, healings, and other divine gifts (vs. 28-30), he classes them, all together as "manifestations of the Spirit" which may or may not belong to a particular individual, since all these "worketh that one and the selfsame Spirit, dividing to every man severally as *he will"* (vs. 7-11). "Are all apostles? [No.] are all prophets? [No.] are all teachers? [No.] are all workers of miracles? [No.] have all the gifts of healing? [No.] *do all speak with tongues?* [NO.] (vs. 29-30). Notice that the very thing which modern teachers affirm is the invariable accompaniment of the Holy Ghost baptism and its positive evidence, namely, speaking in tongues, is one of the things that Paul affirms is not given to all the members of Christ. Rom. 3:3 lays down a principle as to how we should regard those who thus contradict the Word of God.

Speaking in tongues, like prophecy, miracles, and the other things mentioned, is simply a "manifestation of the Spirit." Now, the Holy Spirit himself should always be carefully distinguished from his works and never confounded with any one of his works. The evidence of the sun's existence is not particularly any one thing done by it, but all its effects testify to the great central fact. The evidence that I possess a watch does not rest in any particular thing that the watch is able to accomplish. It may run correctly; it may run too fast or too slow, or possibly may be out of order and not run at all; but no one of these things constitutes the real evidence of its existence nor of my possession of it. *The watch itself is the evidence.* So also the evidence that I have received the Holy Spirit baptism does not depend on any one particular thing that the Spirit may or may not accomplish through me. *The Holy Spirit himself is the evidence.* He is personal. He dwells in the heart. "The Holy Ghost also is a *witness*" (Heb. 10:15) . All his works in me testify *to me* his presence and power. Others; however, can know of the presence of the Holy Ghost in my heart only by means of his outward manifestations—whatever those manifestations may be, in one form or another, whether in tongues, prophecy, special enduement of power, or in other ways.

The Jews who accompanied peter to Caesarea were convinced that Cornelius and his household had received the baptism of the Holy Ghost, "for they heard them speak with tongues and magnify God" (Acts 10:46). Tongues was to them an evidence; but when the twelve men at Ephesus received the Holy Spirit, they "spake with tongues, and *prophesied*" (Acts 19:6). In that case prophecy was an additional evidence. Philip the evangelist, a man who was "full of the Holy Ghost," "had four daughters, virgins, *which did prophesy"* (Acts 21:9). Paul classes prophecy, as well as tongues, as a "manifestation of the Spirit"; therefore Philip's daughters had the Holy Ghost. If in this dispensation prophecy is a manifestation of the Spirit, then people can not prophesy without the Spirit, and true prophecy becomes an evidence of the Spirit's presence. Prophecy is the very evidence that Joel predicted should declare the baptism of the Holy Spirit—the prediction to which Peter appealed on the day of Pentecost: "I will pour out my Spirit upon all flesh, and your sons and your daughters shall prophesy." If any particular work of the Spirit must be regarded as the evidence of the Spirit baptism, then prophecy has a distinct advantage over tongues; for, as we have clearly seen, the apostle Paul shows the decided advantage that prophecy holds over tongues in public usefulness in convincing unbelievers.

There is, in the nature of things, an essential, inseparable connection between the Holy Ghost and holiness. One can not have true holiness without the Spirit of holiness that produces it. Neither can one have the Holy Ghost without possessing holiness. But any one should be able to see that there is no essential, inseparable connection between the Holy Ghost and tongues, prophecy, or other manifestations of the Spirit. They may or they may not be manifested, and yet the Holy Spirit remains the Holy Spirit, and his work in other respects remains just as clear and distinct.

I have produced Scripture texts stating that all Christian believers who have the Spirit *do not* "speak in tongues I have also given reasons why tongues are not necessarily an accompaniment of this baptism. Now where are the tests which affirm that tongues must in all instances accompany the baptism as its invariable evidence? *They can not be found.* Such is only an inference. To this some one may reply, "Tongues accompanied the baptism and gave evidence on Pentecost, at the house of Cornelius, and at Ephesus." Prophecy also gave evidence on Pentecost (the prophet Joel predicted that it should) and at Ephesus. These instances of tongues are admitted by all, but there is a vast difference between the historic record of three specific instances and that species of broad generalization by which it is affirmed that since the tongues were an accompaniment of the Spirit baptism three times, therefore they must be such in every instance of the Holy Ghost baptism down to the end of time. The fallacy of such reasoning, of such sweeping generalization, is evident to every logical mind.

Allow me to illustrate the point just mentioned. Suppose that a wealthy man was accustomed to making a trip to a certain town every day in the week, and suppose that for twenty consecutive days he gave a dollar to a blind man who sat on a certain street-corner. Here we have a particular succession of events producing an inference that this man will continue giving a dollar to that blind man every day. But does this or can this inference amount to a certainty? No. And why not ? Because in the very nature of the case there is not an essential, inseparable connection between the man and his gift. Giving the dollar was an arbitrary act. Although the gift was made twenty times in succession, there is not the least actual proof that it will be repeated on the twenty-first day, nor will the absence of that particular action or gift on the twenty-first day, *be any proof whatever that the wealthy man has not come to town.*

Now, the fact that speaking in tongues accompanied and was evidence of the Holy Spirit baptism in three instances, is no proof whatever that tongues should accompany all baptisms of the Spirit, nor is the absence of that particular manifestation of the Spirit any proof whatever that the Holy Ghost has not come in power and glory into the heart of the loving, surrendered, trusting, believing child of God. The multitude of believers in the church at Jerusalem were "filled with the Holy Ghost." But there is not the slightest intimation that any of these, aside from the one hundred and twenty on Pentecost, ever spoke with other tongues (Acts 4:31-32). The church at Samaria received the Holy Ghost through the laying on of the apostles' hands, but no mention is made of any tongues manifestation on that occasion. "But great power was manifested," says one; "it must have been the tongues." Healings, prophecy, and miracles are classed by Paul among the "manifestations of the Spirit," and these may have occasioned the incident concerning Simon. Where is the proof that it was tongues? "It was omitted," some say. Well, I propose to base my teaching on what is in the Bible rather than on *what was left out.*

The prediction of Jesus gives no more ground for supposing that every individual believer should speak with tongues than for supposing that he should take up serpents, lay hands on the sick for physical healing, or cast out devils. When it comes to attempting to establish doctrine on the mere testimony of historic incidents, the experience of multiplied thousands in our own day has some bearing on the subject. Multitudes have, without the particular tongues manifestation, experienced the baptism of the Holy Ghost—purging and cleansing the heart from the nature of sin, filling with holy power and boldness, granting faith in abundance, the discerning of spirits, the gifts of healing, and the working of miracles. All these things are abundant in the church by the power of the Spirit of God. They are the "manifestations of the Spirit." To deny them is to deny the Spirit, and to deny, on account of the absence of tongues, the Spirit by which these works are done, is to commit an offense corresponding to that of the Pharisees in denying the works of Christ (which also were done without tongues), an act which Christ closely associated with blasphemy against the Holy Ghost.

In a single divine healing testimony service of the church of God held in Anderson, Ind., recently, the following number of instances of healing and miracles were represented:

Total blindness 5
Partial blindness 4
Weak eyes 41
Deafness 2
Partial deafness 21
Heart-trouble 62
Stomach-trouble 155
Liver-trouble 21
Kidney-trouble 149
Spinal 10
Catarrh of head 51
Catarrh of stomach 6
Consumption 51
Rheumatism 149
Paralysis 19
Typhoid fever 62
Scarlet fever 47
Diphtheria 28
Tonsillitis 53
Cancer 36
Goiter 13
Broken bones 46
Walking on crutches 13
Walking with braces 7
Ruptured 13

John the Baptist was filled with the Holy Ghost from his birth, but he did not speak in tongues. The Holy Spirit of God rested on Jesus, yet he did not speak with tongues, but he did affirm, "I cast out devils *by the Spirit of God"* (Matt. 12:28). So also thousands today are performing the works of the Spirit of God who have never yet experienced the particular manifestation of speaking in tongues. In this respect at least they are not above their Master, and it is possible for them to be perfect by being as their Master (Luke 6:40).

The mighty works wrought by God's people before Pentecost were performed by the Spirit of God, but in that dispensation the Spirit came upon them at intervals, and they spoke, or wrote, or wrought mighty works *"as they were* moved by the Holy Ghost" (2 Pet. 1:21). According to the teaching of Jesus, however, the baptism of the Spirit, in the new dispensation, was not to be of this intermittent type: for the Comforter, the Holy Ghost, should "abide with you forever" (John 14:16) . In the very place where this blessed promise is given, we are told that the Comforter, the abiding, indwelling Holy Spirit should be sent for the purpose of *performing the works of Christ;* that is, to take his place, as a result of this baptism. Jesus said, "He that believeth on me, *the works that I do* SHALL HE DO ALSO" (v. 12). "It is expedient for you that I go away for if I go not away, the Comforter will not come unto you; but if I depart, I will send him" (John 16:7). Now, inasmuch as in this dispensation, since Pentecost, the works of Christ are wrought by the Holy Ghost in Spirit-baptized believers, therefore the presence of such works with those that "believe" is evidence of the Holy Spirit baptism.

Deceptive Features of Tongues Doctrine

The teaching just considered, held by most teachers of the modern tongues movement, that speaking in tongues must accompany the Holy Ghost baptism, is chiefly responsible for the vast amount of deception and fanatical extremism found in the movement. The reason is obvious. Although many affirm that they are not seeking "tongues" but are seeking the Holy Ghost, it is a fact, nevertheless, that since they teach that tongues constitute the evidence, they will not accept any experience as the baptism until the tongues come. This attitude opens an avenue for deception. Seeing that they can not or will not be satisfied with anything less than tongues, the enemy can easily step in and give them a manifestation of tongues of some kind or other. That this is true is proved by a fact which the leaders ofttimes admit—that they have among them many tongues-speaking people who are positively ungodly and hypocritical in their lives, or immoral in conduct, some even being possessed with devils. So bad have some of these cases become that the leaders of the movement have been obliged to reject them openly. Under such conditions the teaching that speaking in an unknown tongue is the one decisive evidence of the Holy Spirit baptism breaks down by its own weight.

The Bible doctrine of justification, and entire sanctification as a second work of grace, has been taught in many quarters and professed by many people who are now identified with the modern tongues movement. But the erroneous teaching just considered has given rise among them to another doctrine that is at variance with the truth. When they were led into the belief that tongues constitute *the* evidence of the Holy Spirit baptism, and they did not have that evidence, they were obliged either to surrender their profession of sanctification as a second work of grace and seek for it, together with the tongues, or else to provide in their theology for a third experience—the baptism as subsequent to entire sanctification. They chose the latter. The majority of those in the movement today teach such a threefold experience—justification, sanctification, Holy Spirit baptism. In accordance with this position, it is affirmed that people "receive the Holy Ghost" in sanctification and that they are subsequently baptized with the Holy Ghost, tongues being the evidence of such baptism.

This theory is urged with great boldness, but the careful student of the Bible can see that the theory was made to suit the doctrine that tongues always accompany the baptism. The difficulty with the theory is that it not only lacks Scriptural proof but is actually contrary to the truth, as I shall now show.

The records of the New Testament show a twofold experience received by primitive Christians, but not in a single instance is there a record of a threefold experience. For example, take the church at Samaria (Acts 8). Philip preached Christ to them, and they believed and were baptized. At a later time Peter and John came down and prayed for them that they might receive the Holy Ghost. "Then laid they their hands on them, and they received the Holy Ghost." Only two experiences here—acceptance of Christ under Philip, and the Holy Spirit baptism under Peter and John.

Again, consider Cornelius (Acts 10:11) . He was a devout man, a man whose prayers were heard and who was already accepted of God (10:35). Peter came and preached to this man and his household. While he preached, the Holy Ghost fell upon them, and they spoke with tongues. A twofold experience only.

The disciples at Ephesus (Acts 18:24-28; 19:1-7). Apollos preached to them, and they became believers. Then Paul came and laid his hands upon them, and the Holy Ghost came upon them. A double experience only.

These disciples did not "receive" the Holy Ghost in a second work called sanctification and then in a third experience receive the Holy Ghost baptism. No such distinction is made. The receiving of the Holy Ghost is identical with the baptism. Paul asked those disciples at Ephesus, "Have ye *received* the Holy Ghost since ye believed?" Then when he laid his hands on them, the Holy Ghost came on them, and they spoke with tongues and prophesied (Acts 19:1-6)

Peter and John visited the Samaritan church referred to, "that they might *receive* the Holy Ghost," and "through laying on of the apostles' hands *the Holy Ghost was given.*" It was "the gift of God"—the gift of the Holy Ghost (Acts 8:15-20).

After Cornelius and his house-hold received the Holy Ghost baptism, Peter said, "Can any man forbid water, that these should not be baptized, which have *received* the Holy Ghost as well as we?" Referring to this event later, Peter said, "As I began to speak, the

Holy Ghost fell on them, as on us at the beginning [Pentecost]. Then remembered I the word of the Lord, how that he said, John indeed baptized with water; but ye shall be baptized with the Holy Ghost" (Acts 11:15-16). The primitive church knew no difference between receiving the Holy Ghost and being baptized with the Holy Ghost, for they received only one definite experience after their regeneration.

Sanctification and the Holy Spirit Baptism

What about sanctification? In the experience of the primitive Christians, entire sanctification was identical with the Holy Spirit baptism. Sanctification means cleansing. Jesus prayed for his saved apostles, "Sanctify them through thy truth" (John 17:17). Paul declares that men are *"sanctified by the Holy Ghost"* (Rom. 15:16). When did the apostles receive such heart-purification? "When they were baptized with the Holy Ghost on Pentecost. Proof: Peter, referring to his experience with the household of Cornelius, said, "And God, which knoweth the hearts, bare them witness, giving them the Holy Ghost, *even as he did unto us;* and put no difference between us and them, *purifying their hearts by faith"* (Acts 15:8-9). This shows that these Gentile disciples received entire sanctification, or heart-purification, when they by faith received the Holy Ghost. And it also shows that their experience was identical with that received by the apostles on Pentecost; for God "put no difference" between them.

So there were only two works of grace, or a twofold experience, in the apostolic church. They received "forgiveness of sins, and inheritance among them which are sanctified" (Acts 26:18). They were "saved … by the washing of regeneration, and renewing of the Holy Ghost," which was shed on them abundantly (Tit. 3:5-6). The work of entire sanctification was wrought in them by the baptism of the Holy Ghost, but there were " diversities of operations," different "*manifestations* of the spirit"; for in one the Holy Spirit manifested himself in "healing" gifts, in another in "miracles," in another in "prophecy," and in another in "divers kinds of tongues" (1 Cor. 12:6-11). Not all prophesied, nor worked miracles, nor *spoke with tongues*; for in the same chapter Paul positively shows *that they did not* (vs. 28-30).

Why Not More General Now?

The question naturally ariscs, If speaking in tongues as a "manifestation of the Spirit" was worthy of a place in the apostolic church, why is not the gift more generally exercised now? One reason is, the manifestations of the Spirit through us are in a great measure regulated by the light and understanding that we have concerning God's plan and will. Gifts of healing, miracles, and other gifts were also neglected for centuries, but with the advent of light and understanding concerning them, new interest in them has sprung up, and they are now being manifested for the glory of God.

Another probably cause for the lack of interest in this particular gift is found in the constitutional make-up of the Occidental mind. Although gifts of the Spirit are sent from God to men, a careful study of the whole subject seems to show that God's supernatural working in the human heart harmonizes with the quality of mind possessed by the individual. In other words, Spirit manifestations rest upon, or correspond to, a psychic background in the human consciousness. In the person of predominating emotional temperament, the Spirit operates especially through the emotions, but the operation differs in the person of practical, logical tendencies.

Certain gifts of the Spirit are no exception to this rule. Those who through the Spirit possess faith in a remarkable degree, entitling them to claim the "gift of faith," were naturally strongly predisposed to believe. The gift of healing and of miracles belong in the same category as faith, specifically applied. The gift of wisdom is more apt to be developed in the one whose natural tendency is toward great discretion. And discernment reaches its fruition in the person of keen intuitions.

Now, the Oriental mind naturally inclines to the abstract and the mystical, and this particular psychic state is peculiarly adapted to the revelation and manifestation of the divine in the mysterious speaking in tongues. It is not altogether to our credit that the practical, matter-of-fact, logical Western mind naturally inclines away from the divine, insomuch that earnest, corrective discipline is necessary even to the development and maintenance of real spirituality.

A particular case for the neglect of the tongues manifestation has been the general misapprehension of the nature of the gift. The general idea has been that the principal use, or the only use, of the gift of tongues was a public one, as a medium of communication with people of foreign languages; and this belief has made tongues appear as of little practical value today among a people already possessing an easy means of universal communication. A wrong view or an unsympathetic attitude is always a hindrance to the development of spiritual truth.

The Gift Manifested Today

However, the gift of tongues is being manifested in the church of God today. To some who are in a proper receptive attitude toward manifestations of the Spirit, it comes with a joyful overflow of thanksgiving and praise to God at the time of their Spirit baptism. Others who had already experienced the work of entire sanctification in the baptism of the Holy Ghost, have sought for and obtained this gift of the Spirit at a later time. Many more will doubtless experience the ecstatic joy found in this form of Spirit edification.

Only the spiritual minded can understand the benefits of this gift to the soul. Only such can appreciate the blessedness of being thus wholly surrendered to, and for the time being wholly used by, the Spirit of the living God. It is one office of the Spirit to declare the things of God. "He shall not speak of himself," said Jesus, but "he shall glorify ME" (John 16:13-14). "He shall *testify of me*" (John 15:26). The Spirit speaking in the individual, independently, for the time being, of the intellectual faculties, testifying of Jesus and declaring "the wonderful works of God," elevates the human soul to the highest possible plane of unison with the divine, thrilling the soul with holy joy, edifying it, and strengthening its hold on things infinite and eternal. This is the true Christian glossolalia. And when the tongues employed by the Spirit in thus declaring "the wonderful works of God" are *addressed to men,* and are real languages of earth, as on Pentecost, they constitute a marvelous "sign," which cause men to fear and trem-

ble on account of this visible display of divine power
and glory. Oh, for more of the Spirit's power and manifestation!

The True and the False

The devil has always sought to counterfeit every
principle of truth; hence we must learn to distinguish
between the true and the false. Thousands profess an
experience of salvation who are deceived. Many are
healed supernaturally by a power other than the Spirit
of God; for these are the days in which there were to be
"spirits of devils, working miracles" (Rev. 16:14),
"signs and lying wonders" (2 Thess. 2:9). We need not
be surprized, therefore, to learn that most of the work
passing under the profession of tongues in these last
days is the work of a false, deceptive spirit. When men
who are really filled with the Holy Ghost come in contact with such and rebuke the evil spirit, either audibly
or silently, the "tongues" immediately cease. Many of
us have had personal experience in dealing with this
deception and know whereof we speak. But such experiences should only increase in our hearts the longing
for a greater manifestation of the true work of God's
Holy Spirit in his redeemed saints.

Admonition and Warning

The very nature of the tongues, being mystical,
mysterious, and outside of the ordinary range of human
activities, exposes the soul particularly to the danger of
deceptive influences possibly more than any other one
thing. I have already shown that the modern tongues
people have opened the door wide to such deceptions
by adhering to the false doctrine that every one must

speak in tongues as the evidence of the Holy Spirit baptism. To obtain the experience of speaking in tongues, requires the most complete yielding of oneself; the absolute, unconditional surrender even of the mental powers—and every other faculty of one's being—*to an unseen, mysterious, psychic force.* How easily deception may come in when the mental power, man's natural protector, is thus surrendered! Is it any wonder, then, that in seeking tongues under the strong influence of deceptive doctrines and false teachers, many become possessed with devils, twisting and writhing like demons and *looking like demons?* My brother, let me warn you. If you are anxious for this gift of the Spirit, then before surrendering yourself unreservedly to any unseen, mysterious force, be sure that your heart is right with God, that you are obeying his Word faithfully and walking in all the light that you have; that you are *free from all the deceptive influences of false doctrines and false teachers;* that it is really THE SPIRIT OF GOD TO WHOM YOU ARE ABOUT TO SURRENDER YOURSELF. Then, if it is God's good pleasure to grant the gift, you may "speak with other tongues *as the Spirit giveth utterance."*

Desirability of the Gift

With our understanding of the private use of the gift of tongues as a medium of expressing the heart's deepest emotions, a greater field of usefulness for the gift opens up before us. The essentials of its general exhibition are: (1) A correct understanding of its nature and purpose; (2) Stronger desire on the part of Christian believers for its manifestation in them; (3) Greater emphasis in teaching on the positive nature of the work performed in us by the Holy Ghost.

As to the first, this tract is written for the purpose of giving a better understanding of the gift. Second, prayerful consideration of the truth herein presented will doubtless awaken in many strong desire for the true Bible gift, thus creating a condition favorable to the operation of the Spirit in this respect. Third, the time is here when we as ministers of the gospel must set forth more clearly the positive or divine side of entire sanctification.

Many ministers have presented only one phase of the subject of sanctification, merely the negative work—a cleansing out of evil—until great numbers today hardly know what it is to be filled with the Holy Ghost. How, then, can they experience the gifts of the Holy Ghost? I do not believe that people are really sanctified wholly without receiving the Holy Ghost, but it is a fact that the manifestations of the spirit in us are, to a great extent at least, limited by our faith and expectations. Christian believers should have a greater interest in being filled with the Holy Ghost and power for the accomplishment of a divine work in the world than they have in merely—for their own comfort and satisfaction—getting rid, of a troublesome inward disposition.

Such a negative conception of the second work of grace makes the experience of sanctification a mere historic event, a thing of the past. Greater emphasis on the infilling of the Holy Ghost in entire sanctification and on the Holy Ghost as a personal, abiding presence, a wonder-working power in the soul, will develop in believers a faith that will lay hold on God to the end that all the gifts of the Spirit may flourish in the church as they did in the bright, golden days of primitive Christianity.

F. G. Smith, "The Gift of Tongues," GOSPEL TRUMPET COMPANY, 1920.

An Open Letter
On The Tongues-Evidence Teaching.
G. P. tasker

MY DEAR PENTECOSTAL FRIEND:

Let us hear the earnest exhortation given us by our Lord through his apostle, in Eph. 4:1-6.

"I therefore, as the Lord's prisoner, beg of you to live a life worthy of your calling, with all lowliness and gentleness, forbearing one another in love; endeavouring to keep the unity of the Spirit in the bond of peace: For there is one Body and one Spirit, even as ye are called in one hope of your calling; one Lord (Jesus the Christ), one Faith (concerning Him), one Baptism (immersion into Him, in both water and Spirit), and one God and Father of all, who is over us all, and through us all, and in us all."

Heeding these glorious words, let me now, as briefly and clearly as possible, explain to you why we are not able to accept the teaching that the "speaking with tongues" is the *necessary* sign of the believer's baptism in the Holy Spirit today.

But before I begin, please try to understand, first, that I am not opposing or in the least degree meaning to depreciate the speaking with tongues, when it is kept in its Scripturally ordered place. I am *not* "fighting Pentecost," as the saying is. I would only help to rescue the movement from an idea that is making it less than fully Christo-centric and catholic, which true Christianity is.

Second, that although I do not lengthen out this letter needlessly by taking up all the arguments and texts in popular use among you in support of the said idea, I am perfectly familiar with them all. And, third, that St. Paul, when dealing directly with this very manifestation of tongues, exhorts us to exercise our *minds,* our intelligence, upon it (1 Cor. 14:20), for that is the highest and most God-like thing we possess. "Brethren," he says, "be not children in understanding (Gr. *nous,* the mind, the intellect); "howbeit, in malice be ye children, but in mind be men." See Appendix.

It therefore cannot be Scriptural for anyone to try to evacuate his intelligence or understanding in order to be filled with the Holy Spirit. Nor should anyone be frightened from *thinking* on this matter, by the saying that the Son of God was crucified in "the place of a skull." I "For God hath not given us a spirit of fear, but of power, and of love, and, of a *sound mind.*" 2 Tim. 1:7.

I. First, then, let us be quite clear on one thing, namely, that the Holy Ghost is not a *law,* nor a mere *influence,* but a divine Personality,—the executive of the Godhead. "It seemed good to the Holy Ghost." Acts 15:28. He therefore, as a personality, is not bound to act always in one particular way. He is a free agent.

"Tongues" are admittedly one of his "manifestations" in us, but not his invariable or only manifestation. For Heb. 2:4 tells us that he gives these "according to his own will." He "divides (them) to everyone severally as He will." 1 Cor. 12:7-11.

II. Again, the Scriptures nowhere say that "tongues" were to be the unvarying accompaniment of the gift or baptism of the Holy Spirit, nor is there any *promise* in the Bible that such would be the case. No careful reader of the Book will for a moment deny this fact. There is just no such word or promise to be found anywhere in it.

It is therefore wrong for you to make the point an issue and separate yourselves from others over it. Where the Bible itself has no such doctrine, it would be well for us to make none, lest God reprove us and we be found liars. Prov. 30:5, 6.

In John 14-16 our Lord mentions as many as seven definite things that would characterize the Spirit's coming into us to abide, but "tongues" is not among them. Why not, if it were meant to be *the* sign?

III. That "tongues" did, in the beginning, often if not always accompany the reception of the Holy Spirit, is clear enough from the record in the Book of Acts, and with that we have no contention. But that is *history,* not *doctrine,* and a reason for it I will give presently.

It is also history that on the Day of Pentecost a fire-like tongue "sat upon" each recipient of the Spirit. Ac. 2:3. If then every individual "pentecost" must have the same accompaniments as the first, why not be consistent and say that the tongue of flame should rest upon every one of us too? The answer of course is that the Holy Spirit is a *person* and as such is not bound to manifest himself always in the same way. And so He did not in the early church, and He does not now.

A personal illustration may help to make this point clear. In my pastoral visiting at home, in Canada and in the States, as many people can tell you, I would nearly always seat myself at the piano, as almost every home had one, and play some hymns. That is *history,* and just as true history as any in Acts. But would it not be absurd for anyone to make a *doctrine* out of it and say now to all in whose homes I had not chosen to play on the piano, "Oh, Mr. Tasker has not yet fully come to *you*"? And for anyone to insist that for me to come fully into any home today, I must in every case give that particular manifestation of my presence, because I did so in many or even in all of the *first* homes I visited, would be to deny me any real personality. It would make me a *law,* or a robot, a purely mechanical *thing* that cannot but act always in the same way. And is not that exactly what is being done today with regard to the Holy Spirit in many "Pentecostal" circles, where people are being tutored and "jazzed" and "rail-roaded" into the baptism"?

And, by the way, what really *is* this experience that can be thus psychically induced? No such performances as we see in many "tarrying meetings" today can be found in any of the instances of the baptism given in the New Testament. Surely this should make us pause and *think.* As also should the fact that unity and harmony followed the original Pentecostal outpouring (for "all that believed were *together",* and were of "one heart and one, soul"), while something very different almost everywhere attends these new "pentecosts" to-day. Whatever be the cause of this, it certainly is not God. 1 Cor. 14:33. It is individualism run wild; whereas God has called us into the peace and harmony of "one body," "knit together in love." Col. 2:2, 19; 3:14, 15.

IV. Returning then to our main thought, the fact of the matter is that every *person* is his own sufficient evidence, not what he might be pleased to do or not do. So the Holy Spirit is himself his own evidence within us when he establishes himself there. Thus we read, "He that believeth on the Son of God hath the witness (of God) within himself." 1 Jn. 5:9, 10. And is not this exactly what our Lord himself said, in Jn. 14:16-20? "At that day (when the Spirit would come into believers to abide) ye shall know that I am in my Father, and ye in me, and I in you."

How do we know that Christ is in us, and that he is in the Father? Certainly not by some physical or emotional "sign", but by an inner spiritual consciousness or certainty. Such knowledge is not of the deductive order at all. It is of a purely spiritual character, like our own calm self-consciousness. As Charles Wesley put it: "God, *through himself,* we then shall know, If thou (the Holy Spirit) within us shine." And the beloved apostle says, "Hereby we know that we dwell in him and he in us, because he hath given us of his Spirit",—not because we speak or have spoken in "tongues". This knowledge, I say again, is spiritual in its nature, depending upon a spiritual experience, and not a knowledge standing in or depending upon any physical phenomenon whatever by which a person can say, "I know I have received the Holy Spirit."

This is a very important point, my friend. So please give it your attention, noting well how spiritual and unphenomenal are all the proofs which Jesus and his apostles everywhere give of the Spirit's having come into us to abide. They say that he bears witness within us concerning Christ,—making us Christ-centered, Christ-conscious. Jn. 15:26. That he glorifies Christ and guides us into all the truth concerning him and his relationship to the Father and to us. Jn. 16:13, 14. That he, and not the flesh, dominates and determines the life course. Rom. 8:9, 14. And that he makes us to know that we are children of God. Vs. 15, 16; Gal. 4:6. In all the New

Testament there is not a single passage or text where either Christ or his apostles point us to anything phenomenal as evidence of our having or not having received or been baptized in the Holy Spirit. And in this they are consistent with the nature of spiritual things and have set us an example we shall do well to follow.[112]

V. Again, will not the best and most certain proof of the Holy Spirit's coming into and possessing us be the unchangeable nature of the Spirit himself, rather than some changeable "manifestation" on the physical or emotional side of our own complex nature? The best proof of the coming of oil upon a receptive substance and its presence there, surely is the oiliness it imparts. So the best proof of the Holy Spirit filling anyone is the *holiness* of that person's heart and mind and life. And while we may not exactly identify the baptism in the Spirit with the work of entire sanctification and be Scriptural,—for the Corinthians certainly had received the Spirit baptism but were in sore need of understanding its essentially ethical nature and purpose in the life of the believer, still there assuredly is a most intimate connection between that Spirit of holiness and the expe-

---

[112] When "tongues" had been given at the first coming of the Spirit on the Day of Pentecost it at once became necessary that the same phenomenon should also attend his coming to the Samaritans and the Gentiles, because the Jews of that time could not otherwise have believed that God made *no difference* between them and others, but had bestowed upon these "outsiders" the very same gift they themselves had received. Ac. 10:45-47; 11:15-17; 15:7-9. But once the fact of "no difference" had been established, the *need* of this *uniformity* no longer existed, and so we have had, and will have to the end of time, variation in the accompaniments of the Holy Spirit baptism, the Spirit himself ever remaining the same.

rience of holiness. Is he not distinctively called the *Holy* Spirit because his chief work is to make holy? Rom. 15:16; 1 Pet. 1:2. See also Exod. 29:43; 40:34, 35.

"Tongues," and some other "manifestations" much valued in certain quarters today, are not unknown among idolaters and devil worshippers here in India (See "Kim", p. 256, pocket ed.), just as they are not unknown among the Mormons and the Spiritualists of Europe and America. Like "visions" and "prophecies," "tongues" are by no means peculiar to Christianity. They are found among the devotees in all religions.[113] It is the *content* and the outcome or tendency of an experience which determines for us its origin and utility. And when non-Christians, and manifestly unrighteous, unholy and deceived individuals among us today, speak in "tongues," and help others to do so, how can we, as intelligent people, believe that to us today the speaking with tongues is to be taken as *the* evidence of an immersion in the Holy Spirit?

Will we say that the "tongues" in the unrighteous are "false tongues"? The reply is that they sound exactly the same as the "true tongues" and are accepted as such by "tongues people," until outraged morality,

---

[113] They had them in Rome; for Virgil, in his Aeneid, written about 30 B.C., vividly describes a prophetess speaking in "tongues," with her heaving breast, changed appearance, and preternatural voice. Aeneid VI, 40-101. Plutarch also tells of the prophesying and speaking in "tongues" of the famous Grecian Pythia at Delphi. Even Plato (400 B.C.) refers to much the same phenomenon when he says, in his Timaeus (71), that no one can attain real divine inspiration when he is in possession of his mind, "but only as his intelligence is fettered in sleep or upset either by disease or some divine frenzy." So even the greatest of pagans thought.

sound doctrine and common sense all rise up in protest and expel the individual from the fellowship of clean, sane men and women. The simple fact is, if we would only acknowledge it, we must have some more reliable evidence than "tongues" by which to test what claims to be of the Spirit of God. *Perhaps it is to be found in the fact that the Holy Spirit is always given along the line of Christ's redemptive work as our Saviour from sin.* So it was in the case of Cornelius and his friends, in Acts 10:43, 44. True "believing," we know, is always *"unto righteousness."* Rom. 10:10. And true "receiving" must be, fundamentally, to the same end. "For the fruit of the Spirit (or Light) is in all goodness and righteousness and truth." Eph. 5:9. Satan can counterfeit every *phenomenal* thing, but not goodness and righteousness and truth. For these are all far from him. And we are definitely warned in Mt. 24:24, 25 and 2 Thess. 2:9 not to take "signs and wonders" as being *in themselves* any proof of God.

Two more Scriptural reasons why we cannot accept this peculiar modern teaching of the tongues-evidence, and I close. They are, the example of our Lord's own experience of the baptism in the Spirit, and the Scriptural fact of God's own faithfulness.

VI. That the Lord Jesus, on the threshold of his public ministry, received the full, unmeasured gift of the Holy Spirit, I think no Christian will deny. But the significant fact for us in this connection is that there is not the slightest evidence that "tongues" were associated with it.

The baptism in the Holy Spirit, then, *can* be received in all its fullness without "tongues." And if this be admitted, as it must be in the case of Jesus, then my point is proved, and you can no longer insist that without "tongues" no one has been baptized in the Holy Spirit.

Remember that it was not in his divinity that Christ stood in need of and received that baptism, but in his humanity; for "in all things (except sin) it behooved Him to be made like unto his brethren." Heb. 2:17. In view of *his*" experience," therefore, it is indeed strange that the doctrine should ever have established itself among any Christians that only those who have spoken in "tongues" have been fully baptized in the Spirit.

Finney, the great evangelist, is widely acknowledged among Pentecostal people as having had "the real baptism." But my friend, Charles Grandison Finney never in his life spoke in tongues. Those who knew Mr. Finney personally, including one of his own daughters, have testified to that, His experience of the baptism, which he fully describes in his Autobiography (pp. 18-23), took the form of "waves of liquid love," which swept over him for hours, accompanied by the most intense joy and peace and a remarkable illumination of his understanding. There were no "tongues." But there was power, power to live victoriously and to bring men to God. And that is what every Christian needs. None of us should stop short of knowing in his own heart and life that he has been baptized in the Holy Spirit, and "filled with all the fullness of God." Eph. 3:14-19[114]

---

[114] It is all-important that the center of interest and the stress in teaching should be kept upon the ethical side of the Holy Spirit's work in us as the power of a Christ-like character and walk, rather than upon either psychic or physical phenomena. For *Christ is the pattern Christian.* The Holy Spirit is *his* Spirit, "the Spirit of Jesus." Acts 16:7. And history shows that whenever the

VII. And now, finally, as our seventh reason, we have the grand Scriptural fact that "God is faithful":— faithful, not to give tongues with every baptism in the Spirit, for that He has never promised to do; but faithful to fill with the Holy Spirit every truly consecrated believer in Jesus who asks for, believes for, and *accepts* the gracious gift, for *that* He *has* promised. When therefore I humbly testify to you that years ago, in Chicago, God was faithful even to me and did exactly as He had promised, filling me with the blessed gift of the Holy Spirit through Jesus Christ my Saviour, can you not see that for such an one now to accept this "tongues evidence" teaching would mean the denial both of his own faith and of God's faithfulness to do as He had promised? It would also depreciate and ignore the precious witness of the Spirit himself within such an one today, that He, the Comforter, *has come indeed,* and is abiding.

My dear Christian friend, please consider quietly and prayerfully these seven plain Scriptural reasons why we cannot accept the teaching under review. And if you can then still think we are mistaken or within the grip of any hurtful illusion, please pray for us. And may God bless you and keep you from evil.

Sincerely yours in Christ,
G. P. Tasker.

---

stress has been allowed to fall upon the ecstatic or the phenomenal as marks of the Spirit, excesses of all sorts have come into dishonour His name and hinder His work. Dr. A. L. Drummond's recent book, "Edward Irving and His Circle," affords an interesting and illuminating study in this connection.

APPENDIX

Notes on 1 Cor. 14:1-33.

This section of Paul's great letter to the Church, which seems to have little direct application anywhere today except in "Pentecostal" circles, deals specifically with the relation of the believer's mind and spirit (the *nous* and the *pneuma*) to his speaking with "tongues" and prophesying.

In verses 1-5, (12), the apostle points out that *edification* is the end in view in all the Spirit's "gifts" in the Church, all being "for the common good." 12:7. In verses 6-13, (17), he shows that *intelligence* is an essential condition to church edification; and, in verses 14-20, he explains the necessity of *co-operation* between the mind and the spirit of the speaker if that edification is to be secured. Then finally, in verses 21-33, he gives the *regulations* needed to attain this good end and to establish a sane and wholesome church life. In short, his point is that the faculty of the understanding and the faculty of the religious feeling and activity must both come into play and cooperate if this is to be achieved.

Religious feeling and activity, as in praying or prophesying or speaking in ecstasy, take their rise within the human spirit and normally pass upward into intelligent expression through the mind. The *pneuma* and the *nous* are therefore not to be set over against one another in our experience, as though they were antagonistic. For they are not; but, especially when unctionized by the Holy Spirit, are needed allies in securing the fulfilment of the divine purpose in the "gifts." "What is it then?" the apostle asks, "I will pray with the spirit, and I will pray with the understanding also: I will sing with the spirit, and I will sing with understanding also", the enabling energy in each case of course being the grace of the Holy Spirit.

The tongues-speaker therefore must interpret or be interpreted if the Church is to be edified through him; and where there is no interpreter he must keep silent in the assembly, "speaking to himself and to God." Vs. 27, 28. Likewise also the prophets must exercise their gift in an orderly manner, speaking "one by one", no one's prophesying being prolonged so as to stand in the way of the utterance of a revelation given to another. Vs. 29, 30. And the speaker is fully able thus to give way, as also the other is to withhold, "for the spirits of the prophets are subject to the prophets." Thus God's own orderliness and peace find their expression in the worship of his assembled people.

Anything short of our being actuated at all times by Christ's gentle spirit of meekness and service in these activities, makes for an over-stepping, aggressive individualism in the assembly, with consequent jar to the unity of the Spirit in the one Body. Eph. 4:1-3.

1016-42. Printed and Published by the C. L. S. Press, Bangalore, for the
Rev. G. P. Tasker, 9, Ulsoor Road, Bangalore, S. India.

The Modern Tongues Theory Exposed.
By Cecil M. Washington

"The Modern Tongues Movement," which started in Topeka, Kansas, in a Bible School conducted by Chas. H. Parham, in the Fall of 1900, has been divided into several different factions, such as: "The Latter Rain Movement," "The Assemblies of God," "The Pentecostal Assemblies of Jesus Christ", "The Church of God in Christ", and others.

With reference to the subject of speaking in tongues — they are also much divided, some teaching one thing and some another. One Pentecostal preacher says in his book: "Speaking in tongues is a glorious exercise and a blessed gift of our Lord, but it is not the most important thing. It is the least of gifts". Another Pentecostal minister says: "The idea that the gift of tongues is least, is as erroneous as the 'darkness of the Arabian nights', for that gift absorbs many qualities of the other gifts".

One Pentecostal preacher says: "I was asked to preach the gospel at a certain assembly, and before I had a chance to open my lips the meeting was ruined by eight or ten fragments of other tongues interpreted as fiery judgments of God". Another Pentecostal minister says: "It makes no difference how strange tongues may seem or how peculiar the tongues people do, God Himself is responsible for all of it, for He poured out His Spirit on the people and caused them to act peculiar".

SPEAKING IN TONGUES A GIFT

The Modern Tongues people teach that there is a difference in "Speaking in Tongues as the Spirit gives utterance" and "The Gift of Tongues". If you believe that it is not God's will for all, who are Spirit-Filled, to speak in Tongues and then quote from Paul's writings to prove it, the Modern Tongues people will immediately tell you that Paul was writing about a different kind of tongue. Here is one of their written statements: "It is generally believed that the 'tongues' mentioned in the Acts of the Apostles as on the Day of Pentecost is not the same as in the 14th. chapter of First Corinthians, which is termed 'Gift of Tongues' ".

———Tennessee.

If you should tell the Modern Tongues people that not more than three should speak in tongues during a public service and quote from Paul's epistle to prove it, they would tell you that you had been misinformed. Here is another one of their statements: "There is a difference in the speaking of tongues mentioned in the New Testament. On the Day of Pentecost they all spoke with tongues 'as the Spirit gave utterance'. In the 14th chapter of 1st Corinthians Paul is dealing altogether with the 'Gift of Tongues' ".

———Ohio.

Should you tell the Modern Tongues people that speaking in tongues is not the Bible evidence that one has the Holy Spirit, they would tell you that you are wrong, They teach, "For our information concerning the manifestation given to believers when baptized in the Spirit we are entirely shut up to the instances already noted in the book of Acts".

——Missouri.

The Modern Tongues people teach that, "There is difference between the gift, and speaking in tongues, as St. Paul is not writing about the SAME KIND of 'tongues' as that mentioned in Acts. They say you do wrong to quote the writings of Paul to prove that 'Speaking in tongues as the Spirit gives utterance' is not for all. They say: "Paul is dealing altogether with the 'Gift of Tongues'.

Now that I have made clear the teachings of the Modern Tongues people on this point, I shall prove that they DO NOT believe this teaching. I shall prove that they, in reality, CANNOT consistently believe that there is a difference. Note these six FACTS:

1. Their say, "St. Paul had the SAME KIND of 'tongues' as that mentioned in Acts". For proof of this they go to 1 Cor. 14th Chapter.

2. They say, "Some of the Corinthians had the SAME KIND of 'tongue' as that mentioned in Acts". For proof of this they go to 1 Cor. 14th Chapter.

3. They say, "One MAY NOT understand what he says when speaking the SAME KIND of 'tongue' as that mentioned in Acts". For proof of this they go to 1 Cor. 14th Chapter.

4, They say, "ONE EDIFIES HIMSELF when speaking the SAME KIND of 'tongue' as that mentioned in Acts, even though he doesn't understand what he says". For proof of this they go to I Cor. 14th Chapter.

5. They say, "A person having the SAME KIND of 'tongues' as that mentioned in Acts, may speak more than the one time". For proof of this they go to I Cor. 14th Chapter.

6. They say, "One who speaks the SAME KIND of 'tongue' as that mentioned in Acts, should NEVER be silenced during public service". For proof of this they go to 1 Cor. 14th Chapter.

NOTE: Why do they go to the writings of St. Paul, in 1 Cor. 14th Chapter, to prove these things, that they believe about the KIND of tongues that's mentioned in Acts?

If St. Paul is writing about a DIFFERENT KIND OF "TONGUE" than that mentioned in Acts, they have no proof for the six things above mentioned.

The fact that they CONSTANTLY go to the writings of St. Paul in 1 Cor. 14th Chapter to prove these six things, is in itself conclusive proof that they DO NOT practically, and CANNOT consistently, believe that there is any difference. ACTIONS SPEAK LOUDER THAN WORDS.

The Nationally known Evangelist, Rev. F. F. Bosworth, said: "At a recent State Council of the Assemblies of God, when the Chairman of the Council was asked by one of the young ministers if there was a passage or a number of passages upon which he could base this distinction, he publicly admitted that there was not a single passage".

"Charles F. Parham, who came forward with this doctrine in the year 1900, was the first man in the history of the world publicly to teach this doctrine. He saw that it was not possible to teach that speaking in tongues will in every case accompany the Baptism in the Spirit, unless he could make it appear that the speaking in tongues on the Day of Pentecost was something distinct from the gift of tongues at Corinth. He was also the first to teach that none have been baptized in the Spirit except those who have spoken in tongues".

NATURE OF THE GIFT

Speaking in tongues is mentioned in St. Mark 16:17-18; Acts 2:3-11; 10:46; 19:6; I Cor. 12; 13; and 14. In Acts 2:8, the English word 'tongue' is translated from the Greek word 'DIALEKTOS', and means 'the LANGUAGE of a country, especially the LANGUAGE of a special district'. In 1 Cor. 14:21, the English word 'tongue' is translated from the Greek word 'ETERO-GLOSIS' and means 'A foreign LANGUAGE'. In the other references, above mentioned, the Greek word is 'GLOSSA' and means 'a foreign tongue, a LAN-GUAGE, to speak a dialect'. Webster says: "Tongue means LANGUAGE", Funk and Wagnall's Dictionary says: "A tongue is the speech or LANGUAGE of some one people, country or race". The New Century Dict. says: "The speech or LANGUAGE of a particular people, country or locality (as, the Hebrew tongue; the many tongues of India; the Old Cornish tongue); a dialect". St. Paul says: "There are it may be, so many kinds of voices in the world, and none of them is without signification". 1 Cor. 14:10. "There are so many kinds of LANGUAGES in the world, everyone of them meaning something". —Moffatt.

On the Day of Pentecost, the people spoke a living, intelligent LANGUAGE, and not a jargon, babble, gibberish, or something unintelligible. The multitude came together, and were confounded, because that every man heard them speak in his own LANGUAGE". Acts 2:6.

They said; "One to another, 'Behold are not all of these which speak Galileans? And how hear we every man in our own tongue wherein we were born?" (Acts 2:8-9).

"Then how is it that we each of us hear them in our own LANGUAGE". —20th Century New Testament. "We hear these men talking of the triumphs of God in our own LANGUAGE". —Moffatt.

At Caesarea (Acts 10:46) The people of God spoke a LANGUAGE, and at Ephesus (Acts 19:6), they also spoke a LANGUAGE,

With reference to an 'UNKNOWN TONGUE' there is no such thing. In the 14th Chapter of 1 Cor. the only place where the expression occurs, the word 'Unknown' is italicized in each and every case. Such italicized words were not in the original GREEK. They were placed in the text by the translators. No New Testament writer ever preached, or wrote anything at all about 'UNKNOWN TONGUES'. 'Tongue' means LANGUAGE, and all LANGUAGES are known. All LANGUAGES can be interpreted, "Wherefore let him that speaketh in an tongue pray that he may interpret". 1 Cor. 14:13.

TONGUES THE LEAST GIFT

Concerning Apostles, we read of "The Chiefest" (Mark 10:44; 2 Cor. 13:5); of Prophets "The greater" (Matt. 11:7-11); of saints "The least" (Matt. 25:40-45);

and of gifts "The Best" and "greatest", (1 Cor. 12:31; 13:13).

St. Paul said: "God hath set some in the Church, FIRST apostles, SECONDARILY prophets, THIRDLY teachers, AFTER THAT miracles, THEN gifts of healings, helps, governments, diversities of tongues".

"The Church" is "the mystical body of Christ", and repentant believers are 'in particular, members' of that body. In placing these members, God, in His sovereign and unerring wisdom, "has" appointed some to the FIRST and most honorable office of Apostles", "LASTLY, persons who, having the gift of speaking different kinds of foreign LANGUAGES".—James McKnight's notes.

Matthew Henry says: "They are placed here (1 Cor. 12:28) in their proper rank, those of most value first."

Smith's Bible Dictionary says: "St. Paul places that of tongues , and the interpretation of tongues lowest in the scale".

The Bible Commentary says: "In this list of gifts the utterance of tongues is placed last as being least."

"Greater is he that prophesieth than he that speaketh with tongues EXCEPT (or unless) he (also) interprets". Therefore "covet earnestly the BEST gifts" says St. Paul. Speaking in tongues is not the "greatest", "best" or "superior" gift, but the LEAST Gift.

TONGUES A LIMITED GIFT

St. Mark 16:17-18, is quoted to prove that all will speak in tongues, according to Acts 2:4, when Baptized with the Holy Spirit. Note carefully: St. Mark 16:17-18 does not teach that all FIVE of these signs shall be manifested in every individual the moment they are baptized with the Holy Spirit. St. Mark 16:17-18 does not teach that all five of these signs shall, at some later date, be manifested in every individual believer. Picking up 'serpents' being one of the signs. St. Mark 16:17-18 does not teach that any particular one of these FIVE signs shall be manifested when people are Baptized with the Holy Spirit.

The Modern Tongues people teach, that all should receive the Holy Spirit according to Acts 2:4. Why are they so insistent about obtaining an experience according to Acts 2:4? Why are they not just as persistent about Acts 2:2? For if the Holy Spirit's coming in every case is to be a duplication of Acts 2:4, consistency would require a duplication of conformity, of every one who received him, to Acts 2:2.

According to Acts 2:2 the disciples were SITTING down when they were Baptized with the Holy Spirit.

The Modern Tongues people insist that one must kneel down and say: halleluiah, halleluiah, halleluiah, or glory, glory, glory as fast as he can, sometimes for hours, until by the "co-ordination of mental concentration and vocal conglomeration", you speak some thing that they are pleased to call the 'UNKNOWN TONGUE'. A few years ago, while living in Dayton, Ohio, I attended a tent meeting. An old gentleman went forward for prayer. The preacher in charge told him to say: "Halleluiah, halleluiah, halleluiah, halleluiah." He did, but rather slowly. He was told to say it faster, but the poor man was too old to say halleluiah fast enough to get the so-called "Bible Evidence" of the Baptism of the Holy Spirit. This thing of telling people to say 'halleluiah, halleluiah, or glory, glory' for hours (sometimes), to receive the Holy Spirit, is not right. In fact there is not one book, chapter, paragraph, verse, clause, phrase or word that even intimates that such a thing was ever done. The Modern Tongues people insist on people doing this without one 'Thus saith the Lord' to support it. Jesus did say to the disciples to "Tarry ye . . . until ye be endued with power from on high" (Luke 24:49). But "tarry" means to "STAY", "ABIDE", "REMAIN IN THE SAME PLACE". The disciples were "to remain in Jerusalem".

The word TARRY does not, and never did, mean to sit down, kneel down or stand up, and shout, 'glory', 'glory', 'glory' or 'halleluiah', 'halleluiah', 'halleluiah' for hours.

The Modern Tongues people say: You MUST speak once, if no more. That word MUST is found in only one chapter where speaking in tongues is mentioned. In Acts 19:21, we read where Paul said, "I MUST see Rome".

The Modern Tongues people say: "Speaking in tongues is the Bible Evidence that one has been Baptized with the Holy Spirit. That word 'EVIDENCE' is not found in any chapter where 'Tongues' is mentioned. That word 'EVIDENCE' is not found in any BOOK in the New Testament where "tongues" is mentioned. The first recording of the word EVIDENCE in the New Testament, is in Heb. 11:1 and says: "Now faith is the substance of things hoped for, the EVIDENCE of things not seen".

The Modern Tongues people say: "A baby cries as soon as it is born. This argument is used to prove that when one is Baptized with the Holy Spirit he will talk in tongues. Babies do cry, 'tis true, but they do not 'TALK'.

I heard one preacher say, in a tent meeting, in Indiana: "When you go up town to buy a pair of shoes you do not ask for TONGUES, you ask for shoes. TONGUES said he, come with the shoes. "This statement was made to prove that when one receives the Holy Spirit, such initial Baptism will always be accompanied by speaking in 'TONGUES'. Now let me kindly remind you that many people ask for, and receive shoes, genuine leather shoes, if you please, but do not get any TONGUES with them.

St. John 15:26; and 16:13 are quoted to prove that when the Holy Spirit comes in, He will always speak. We read here: "He shall testify of me, He will guide you into all truth", "He will show you things to come". These verses do not teach that the Holy Spirit will do all three of these things when He comes in, neither do they teach that any one of them will always be manifested when He comes in.

" 'Tongues' are a sign to the unbelievers" says some. 'Tongues' serve as a sign to the unbeliever if what is spoken is understood. On the day of Pentecost the unbelievers understood what was being spoken. If they (the unbelievers) do not understand, will they not say that ye are mad"? I Cor. 14:23. "Will they not say that you are crazy"? —Moffatt.

Some say: "Jesus spoke in 'tongues' while hanging on the Cross". It is true that Jesus in his dying hour uttered some words in the ARAMAIC, which was his mother tongue. This was not an 'unknown tongue' but

an intelligible LANGUAGE, capable of being interpreted, and the Bible has a record of its interpretation.

Speaking in tongues "is not now, nor was it in the
beginning universal in the Church. It is a limited gift to
a limited few".

PURPOSE OF THE GIFT

The primary object in giving gifts is for the edification of the Church. St. Paul says, "The manifestation of
the Spirit is given to everyman to profit withal". 1 Cor.
12:7. "For the profit of all"— Conybeare and Howson.

"For the benefit of all" —Emphatic Diaglott.

Matthew Henry says, "Spiritual gifts are bestowed
only that men may with them profit the church and
promote Christianity.

Dr. Adam Clark says, "God has given no gift to
any man for his own private advantage or exclusive
profit".

Dr. Hodge says, "They are not designed exclusively for the gratification of the recipient; but for the good
of the Church".

Peak's Bible Commentary says, "The edification of
the CHURCH is the governing principle".

NOTE: Speaking in tongues in public services is
not to be permitted unless it can be interpreted. St. Paul
said; "If any man speak in an unknown tongue, let it be
by two, or at the most three, and that by course; and let
one interpret. But if there be no interpreter let him keep
SILENCE in the Church". (1 Cor. 14:27-28).

"If there is no interpreter, let the speaker keep QUIET in the Church".   —Moffatt.

"If there is no one to explain it, HAVE HIM KEEP QUIET IN CHURCH". —Goodspeed.

"But if there be no interpreter, let him who speaks in tongues KEEP SILENT in the congregation and speak in private to himself and God alone".
—Conybeare and Howson.

THE FALSE GIFT

To avoid confusion in the Church, St. Paul said: 1 "Let the prophet speak two or three, and let the other judge. If anything be revealed to another that sitteth by, let the first HOLD HIS PEACE".

"If anything is revealed to another who is seated, the one who is speaking must STOP"— Goodspeed.

"The first speaker must be QUIET" —Moffatt.

"Let the first HOLD HIS PEACE", "STOP", "BE QUIET", "If anything is revealed to another" said St. Paul.

NOTE: St. Paul says a Prophet must "HOLD HIS PEACE", "STOP", "BE QUIET" when another gets a revelation. A true prophet can "STOP", "BE QUIET", "HOLD HIS PEACE" when another should speak, because, "The spirits of the prophets are subject to the prophet".

"Prophets CAN CONTROL their own prophetic spirits". —Moffatt.

"The Divine impulse under which the prophet speaks is not an UNCONTROLLABLE force, which

must have its way irrespective of order or decorum".
—Dictionary of Christ and the Apostles.

If one having a greater gift than 'Tongues' can "STOP", "BE QUIET", "HOLD HIS PEACE" and thus avoid confusion, surely one who has the LEAST gift, the gift of tongues, can "STOP", "BE QUIET", "HOLD HIS PEACE" if there is no interpreter present or while another is speaking, (1 Cor. 14:27-28) UNLESS he is possessed of "an UNCONTROLLABLE force", something not of God.

One man says in his book: "God put 'tongues' in the Church". True, but God also put the "gift of discernment" in the Church; to discriminate between the true and false miraculous manifestations. 1 Cor.12:10.

"The recipient of which could distinguish between the real and the imaginary possessor of Spiritual gifts".
—Conybeare & Howson.

A Pentecostal preacher says in his tract: "'We do not believe that every manifestation in the world called tongues is of God".

"Wesley proclaimed the tongues of his day to be of the devil. The Modern Tongues Movement is the same in spirit and operation as the movement of Wesley's day". —C. W. Naylor.

Rev. E. E. Shelhamer tells of conducting a Camp Meeting in Oregon, some years ago. The leader of the camp became convicted and sought a better experience. He did not get satisfied, so he went to the 'tongues' meeting and there professed to receive his 'Baptism', and declared that God had given him the Japanese language. His wife also professed to be able to write in seventeen different dialects. Fifteen missionaries rallied to them and they went to Japan, but to their dismay the Japanese could not understand their gibberish. They returned home, some became infidels and others temporarily insane. The leader and his wife separated, and he took up with a Japanese woman. Anything that will bring such havoc in its trail is not of God! True every movement has its scandals and fanaticism, but nothing to equal this one".

We read of "false witnesses", Acts 6:13; "false accusers", Luke 19:8; "'false brethren", 2 Cor. 11:20; "false teachers", 2 Pet. 2:1; "false prophets", Mark13:22; "false Apostles" 2 Cor. 11:13 and "false Christs" Matt. 24:24. The Modern Tongue is a FALSE tongue. False, because sinners can get it as well as those who are saved.

In Mark 1:27 we read of "The doctrine of the Pharisees". In Rev. 2:14 of "The doctrine of Baalam; in Rev. 2:15 of "The doctrine of the Nicolaitanes"; in Heb. 1:9, of "Divers and strange doctrines"; in Eph. 4:14, of "Every wind of doctrine"; in Col. 2:22, of "Doctrines of men" and in 1 Tim. 4:1 of "Doctrines of Devils". A doctrine of the devil is one that is unscriptural, divisive, deceptive and directly responsible for many being lost. This Modern Tongues Doctrine may rightly be called, a doctrine of the devil.

The Rev. F. F. Bosworth writes: "After some time in the work on Pentecostal lines —— I am certain that many who receive the most powerful Baptisms for service do not receive the manifestation of speaking in tongues. And I am just as certain that many who *seemingly speak* in tongues are not, nor ever have been Baptised in the Spirit".

"The fact is that hundreds of the greatest soul-winners of the entire Christian era, without the gift of tongues, have had a much greater enduement of power, and have been used to accomplish a much greater and deeper work than has Mr. Parham.

Many illustrious saints, whose lives and usefulness have had no parallel among the advocates of this Modern Tongues Movement, never did speak in tongues.

John Wesley, George Fox, Francis Ridley Havergal, Alfred Cookman, Mrs. Catherine Booth, Dorthea Trudel, John Fletcher, David Brainerd Baxter, "one of the mightiest men of God that ever lived", John Bunyan, the Author of *Pilgrim's Progress*; George Muller, "one of the greatest men of prayer known to history", P. P. Bliss, "one of the greatest gospel singers and Hymn writers", Dr. Adam Clark, "one of the greatest of Bible scholars", John Inskip, "The Father of the Modern Camp Meeting", Sammie Harris, "The Spirit Filled Life", Chas. G. Finney, "Holder of the World's Greatest Revivals", George Whitefield, "The World's Greatest Evangelist", Amanda Smith, "The World's Greatest Colored Soul-Winner", D. L. Moody, "The World's Greatest Lay Preacher, and thousands of others who were Baptized with the Holy Spirit, never did speak in tongues. In fact, speaking in tongues is not the Bible Evidence that one has been Baptized with the Holy Spirit, and in the language of the Rev. F. F. Bosworth, I say, "Many who seemingly speak in tongues, are not, and never have been Baptized in the Spirit".

THE END.

The Truth About Speaking in Tongues.
By Cecil M. Washington

INTRODUCTION

The book entitled "The Truth About Speaking in Tongues" written by Dr. Cecil M. Washington, has come to the press at a time most significant for readers of our day. Brother Washington, in treating the subject of "tongues", has made a scholarly approach that will appeal to all honest thinking people. With his many years of experience as a great preacher and pastor, as well as a student of practical theology, he has examined every inch of ground from the Scriptural standpoint. This makes Dr. Washington's book a very valuable one for every minister's library.

We owe our thanks and gratitude to this man who, through sound reasoning, practical judgment, and Scriptural analysis, has given the plain truth on the Bible gift of tongues. His Spiritual maturity has given great depth to the words found in this book. We thank you, Brother Washington, for this fine work.

Edwin C. Ogle
Executive Vice President
Gulf Coast Bible College
Houston, Texas

SOME OF THE 120 WHO DID NOT SPEAK WITH TONGUES.

In Acts 2:1-13 we have the first account of persons who were baptized with the Holy Spirit speaking in tongues. The account reads:

> "When the day of Pentecost was fully come, they were all with one accord in one place. (2) And suddenly there came a sound from heaven as of a rushing mighty wind, and it filled all the house where they were sitting. (3) And there appeared unto them cloven tongues like as of fire, and it sat upon each of them. (4) And they were all filled with the Holy Ghost, and began to speak with other tongues, as the Spirit gave them utterance. (5) And there were dwelling at Jerusalem Jews, devout men, out of every nation under heaven. (6) Now when this was noised abroad, the multitude came together, and were confounded, because that every man heard them speak in his own language. (7) And they were all amazed and marvelled, saying one to another, Behold, are not all of these which speak Galileans? (8) And how hear we every man in our own tongue, wherein we were born? (9) Parthians, and Medes, and Elamites, and the dwellers in Mesopotamia, and in Judea, and Cappadocia, in Pontus, and Asia, (10) Phrygia, and Pamphylia, in Egypt, and in the parts of Libya about Cyrene, and

strangers of Rome, Jews, and proselytes,
(11) Cretes, and Arabians, we do hear
them speak in our tongues the wonderful
works of God."

Please note that according to Acts 2:9-11, fifteen countries were represented on that occasion. This text reads in the Twentieth Century New Testament:

Some of us are Parthians, some Medes,
some Elamites; and some of us live in
Mesopotamia, in Judaea and Cappadocia, in Pontus and Roman Asia, in
Phrygia and Pamphylia, in Egypt and the
districts of Libya adjoining Cyrene;
some of us are visitors from Rome, either Jews by birth or converts, and some
are Cretans and Arabians—yet we all
alike hear them speaking in our own
tongues of the great things that God has
done.

Thus we can see that fifteen countries in all were represented.

The doctrine that all who are baptized with the Holy Spirit will speak in tongues at least once is a new doctrine, that is, it is not yet seventy-five years old. It was not taught in the days of the Apostles, as we shall see. Too, while some of the early Christians did speak in tongues, many of them did not. I write with direct reference to those who were baptized with the Holy Spirit.

This writer does not want to be understood as teaching that no one today has the same kind of 'tongues' as was given on the Day of Pentecost, at

Caesarea, and at Ephesus. Be that far from me. My contention is that not all the Christians in the early church who were baptized with the Holy Spirit spoke in tongues, and I affirm that thousands who have been baptized with the Holy Spirit since Pentecost never spoke in tongues.

I hold with R.R. Byrum, one-time professor of Systematic Theology in Anderson Bible School and Seminary, Anderson, Indiana. He said:

> Two opposite extremes should be avoided in our attitude toward speaking in tongues. We should not fall into the error of the Corinthian church and of some who profess to speak in tongues today by exalting tongues manifestations out of proper proportions to all other operations of the Spirit. The opposite extreme to be avoided is the excluding of all speaking in tongues as being improper or not of God. Paul very well described the proper attitude when he said, 'Covet to prophesy, and forbid not to speak with tongues' (1 Cor. 14:39). Keep other gifts more prominent because they are of more value, but allow the speaking in tongues, because it is the operation of God's Spirit and for God's glory. Paul does not urge the speaking in tongues, neither should we urge it. It should not be regarded as a proof of deep spirituality in the speaker, as it is the least important of all gifts. The church at Corinth spoke much in tongues, yet it was one of the least spiritual of the New Testament

congregations, being carnal, having division and strife among themselves, tolerating one guilty of incest, and going to law with each other. We should not condemn all speaking in tongues as of the devil nor accept all as being of God.(Byrum)

The language of each of the fifteen countries represented was spoken by the 120 Galileans who were baptized with the Holy Spirit. Palestine was one of the fifteen countries represented; the name "Judea" appearing in the list is conclusive proof of that fact. Because of this we know that the language of Palestine was spoken by some of the 120 Galileans who were baptized with the Holy Spirit. All of the 120 Galileans did not speak a foreign language on that occasion — some of them spoke the language of Palestine, the language of the country in which they had been born and reared, i.e., the Aramaic language.

The following extracts will suffice to show that Aramaic was the popular language of Palestine:

Collier's New Encyclopedia, "In Palestine it (i.e. Aramaic) supplanted Hebrew, and it was it (Aramaic) — that was the tongue of the Jews in the time of Christ."

Schaff-Herzog's Encyclopedia states: "After the exile the Aramaic language gradually became the popular language of Palestine; not only of Galilee, and Samaria, but also in Judea, Christ and the Apostles spoke it."

Weymouth's *Modern English New Testament* (5th ed.) explains "By the time of Christ Aramaic had long been the current speech of Palestine. It was the speech of Jesus and His disciples and probably the earliest preaching of the Gospel was in Aramaic."

The *Encyclopedia Brittanica* (14th edition) says, "It is certain that the language (Aramaic) was firmly established in Palestine in the first century A.D. By that time as we know from many sources, Aramaic was not only the language in common use, but had received official recognition."

Philip Schaff's Popular Commentary on the Bible points out: "The occurrence of this name (i.e. Judea) has occasioned some difficulty. Various emendations have been suggested, but they are purely conjectural, the manuscript authority for "Judea" being decisive. 'Judea' appears in the catalogue of nations as the representative of Aramaic, because St. Luke desired to enumerate all the languages spoken that day by the disciples on whom the Spirit had fallen."

The following extract from Dr. Albert Barnes's Notes is very illuminating.

> This expression has greatly perplexed commentators. It has been thought difficult to see why Judea should be mentioned, as if it were a matter of surprise that they could speak in this language. Some have supposed an error in the manuscripts, and have proposed to read Armenia, or India, or Lydia, or Idumea, but all this has been without any authority. Others have supposed that the language of Galilee was so different from that of the other part of Judea, as to render it remarkable that they could speak

that dialect. But this is an idle supposition. This is one of the many instances in which commentators have perplexed themselves to very little purpose. Luke recorded this as any other historian would have done. In running over the languages which they spoke, he enumerated this as a matter of course, not that it was remarkable, simply that they should speak the language of Judea, but that they should speak so many, meaning about the same by it as if he had said they spoke every language in the world.

Dr. George A. Barton, Ph. D., LL.D., formerly Professor of Semitic Languages in the University of Pennsylvania writes:

Here in America we can tell by the way people pronounce words containing the combination 'ou' whether they come from Philadelphia, Baltimore, or Virginia; and by the way they pronounce certain other words, whether they come from New York. In Palestine the differences of pronunciation between the different parts of the country, and even different villages have always been much greater than here. One of the bystanders, therefore, said to Peter: "You are a Galilean, for your speech betrays you."

—*Jesus of Nazareth*, p. 370

In his Bible Commentary, Rev. John Gill says:

"For though the same language was spoken in Galilee as at Jerusalem, yet it was not so accurate and polite in Galilee as at Jerusalem, not so well pronounced."

On this same point Matthew Henry writes:

". . . though the language of those in Judea was the same with that which the disciples spoke, yet before, they spoke it with the north-country tone and dialect ('Thou art a Galilean, and thy speech betrays thee'), but now they spoke it (Aramaic) as correctly as the inhabitants of Judea themselves did."

The evidence that can be produced in support of the view that both Galileans and the Judeans spoke the very same language in the time of Christ is so overwhelming that even Carl Brumback, an outstanding Pentecostal pastor and author of the book, *What Meaneth This* believes it according to the following extract which appears on page 201 of his hook:

"There is a real basis for the belief that the language spoken by both Galileans and Judeans was the popular Aramaic."

Remember now, the Galileans and the Judeans were born and reared in the very same country (Palestine), and spoke the very same language (Aramaic). When I hear a German, who was born and reared in Germany, speak German, the language of his native country, I know that he is not speaking in tongues. When I hear a Chinese who was born and reared in China, speak Chinese, the language of his native country, I know that he is not speaking in tongues. When I hear a Bostonian, who was born and reared in the northern part of the United States, speak English, the language of the United States, I know that he is not speaking in tongues. When the Judeans heard some of the 120 who were born and reared in the northern part of Palestine, speaking the language of Palestine, (Aramaic), they knew that some of the 120 were not speaking in other tongues. When individuals speak the language of their native country, they are not speaking in other tongues.

The expression, "and the Judeans," in Acts 2:9 proves conclusively that some of the 120 spoke in their native language and not in the language of another country when they were baptized with the Holy Spirit.

The sacred writer declared that "every man" (including the Judeans) "heard them speak in his own language" (Acts 2:6). They said: "How then does each of us hear his own native language spoken by them?" (Acts 2:8)—*Weymouth's New Testament*. ". . . we all alike hear them speaking in our own native tongue the mighty wonders of God!" (*Norlie's Simplified New Testament*.)

Here are three syllogisms that will stand any Scriptural test:

I

1. The language of every country that was represented on the Day of Pentecost was spoken.

2. The country of Palestine was represented on the Day of Pentecost.

3. Therefore, the language of Palestine was spoken on the Day of Pentecost.

II

1. Both the Galileans and the Judeans spoke the popular language of Palestine.

2. The popular language of Palestine was Aramaic.

3. Therefore, both the Galileans and the Judeans spoke Aramaic.

III

1. The Judeans declared that they heard some of the 120 speaking Aramaic when they were baptized with the Holy Spirit.

2. Aramaic, the popular language of Palestine, was the native tongue of the 120.

3. Therefore, the Judeans declared that they heard some of the 120 speaking in their native tongue when they were baptized with the Holy Spirit.

My friend, according to Acts 2:6, 8, 9, and 11, the Judeans heard some of the 120 Galileans who were baptized with the Holy Spirit on the day of Pentecost praising God in their native tongue, not in some foreign tongue. All the wresting and twisting of Acts 2:4 cannot be made to contradict what these four plain texts of Scripture clearly teach. Here we have seen that some of the charter members of the church DID NOT speak in tongues.

SOME OF THE FIRST CONVERTS OF THE APOSTLES DID NOT SPEAK WITH TONGUES

In the Acts of the Apostles, chapter three, we have an account of a lame man who had been miraculously healed and this, in turn, attracted the attention of many, many people to whom Peter and John preached the Word, and many were saved. The Bible says, "the priests, and the captain of the Temple, and the Sadducees . . . being grieved that they taught the people and preached through Jesus the resurrection from the dead . . . laid hands on them, and put them in prison." The inspired historian tells us that "many of them which heard the Word believed; and the number of men was about five thousand" (Acts 4:1-4). "The next day Peter and John, having been released from prison, went to their own company and reported all that the chief priests and elders had said unto them." The Bible Says: "And when they heard that, they lifted up their voice to God, with one accord" ("with one united prayer"). And "when their prayer was ended (Norlie's version) the place was shaken where they were assembled together; and they were all filled with the Holy Ghost, and they spoke the Word of God with boldness (Acts 4:31).

Many good people understand Acts 4:31 to teach that this was a case where people who had once been baptized with the Holy Spirit were refilled. It has never occurred to these people that perhaps some here who had NEVER been filled with the Holy Spirit may have been baptized on this occasion. This is exactly what happened. Bear this fact in mind there were at this time at least five thousand Christians in Jerusalem (Acts 4:4). Three thousand of these were converted on the Day of Pentecost. According to Acts 4:23, the Apostles were by no means the only ones present. Dean Henry Alford writes: "There is nothing in verse 31 to mark that only the Apostles were present on this occasion." Dr. Phillip Schaff says: "The Greek word here translated 'their own company' . . . has been understood by some to signify 'their brothers Apostles,' by others, 'the church in the Apostles's house, 'or' those with whom the Apostles were accustomed to unite in prayer.' The term, however, is a far more inclusive one, and comprehends a large number of the believers then in the city." In the Homiletic Commentary, we read: "Their own company, not the Apostles' merely, but their friends in the faith generally." Says Dr. A. T. Robertson: "To their own company (*pros tous idious*). Not merely the Apostles only (all the disciples)." Therefore, some persons, certainly not the Apostles, received a second work of grace or were baptized with the Holy Spirit on this occasion.

Dr. John W. Watson says: "This does not refer to the preliminary work in conviction and conversion; it refers to the permanency of the indwelling Spirit in the heart of the perfected believer. A great mistake is made in the matter of advanced Christian experience, by confounding the witness of the Spirit in conversion with the baptism of the Holy Ghost." —*Holiness Manual*, pp. 86, 87.

Dr. Jasper A. Huffman, one time President of Winona Lake School of Theology wrote:

> While no denial is made of the possibility of failure to be kept filled with the Spirit, the normal Spirit-filled life is a life constantly filled with the personality of the Holy Spirit, and ever led by Him. It was not said of the Apostles in Acts 4:31, they were again filled with the Holy Spirit or refilled with the Spirit, but that 'they were all filled with the Holy Spirit.' Doubtless there were those among the group who had not previously been Pentecostal participants, and they, no doubt, became filled with the Holy Spirit, and were included in the 'all' who were filled. It is only by bringing to such

and similar passages a prejudiced or un-
enlightened attitude concerning the Holy
Spirit and His work, that persons find it
necessary to read into the narrative that
the individuals or groups of the early
church were again filled with the Holy
Spirit. —*The Holy Spirit*, p. 237.

On pages 46 and 47 of the book, *Deeper Experiences of Famous Christians*, by J. Gilchrist Lawson, the
following extract app ears:

The early Christian church believed in
and prayed for the filling of the Holy
Spirit, and this was the secret of its power. It lived in the Spirit, walked in the
Spirit, prayed in the Spirit, and sang in
the Spirit. Its meetings were conducted
in the Pentecostal order, or manner; everyone praying, singing or testifying as
they were moved by the Spirit. Soon after Pentecost they were gathered together in prayer, and the Holy Ghost again
came with such power as to shake the
place where they assembled together and
all who were not previously filled with
the Spirit were now filled, so that 'they
were all filled with the Holy Ghost, and
spoke the Word of God with boldness' "
(Acts 4:31).

May I elaborate on this point for emphasis —Acts
4:31 is not a record of persons who had been previously
baptized with the Holy Spirit being refilled. It is a record of some converted people being baptized with the
Holy Spirit for the first time in a prayer meeting con-

ducted by some who had been baptized with the Holy Spirit prior to this time.

Dr. Paul F. Beacham, Pentecostal President of Holiness Bible College in Franklin Springs, Georgia, was asked the following question: "Does Acts 4:31 include some of the same ones who received the Holy Ghost in the second chapter?" Here was his answer. Read his answer carefully.

"Yes, some of those present here were filled with the Holy Ghost on the Day of Pentecost, but there were others also who were not present on the Day of Pentecost, and they were filled at this time. So all assembled at the place where they were praying were filled with the Holy Ghost. No doubt those who had been filled with the Spirit before were greatly blessed; but we are not to understand they had lost spiritual power and had to be baptized again."

—*Questions and Answers on the Scriptures and Related Subjects*, p. 239

Have you noticed there has not been one word said anywhere about these people who were baptized with the Holy Ghost on this occasion speaking in tongues? They received another gift, as we shall see. Just here, however, we shall add one more extract in support of the view that on this occasion some converted persons received the infilling of the Holy Spirit:

> This seems to have been a more powerful manifestation of the Holy Spirit than was manifested on the Day of Pentecost, for even the very terra-firma was shaken beneath this powerful assembly when this multitude of converts received the

Holy Ghost. This clearly proves the two works of grace in the experience of the first converts of the Apostles.

—*The Better Testament*, by Wm. G. Schell, p. 214.

When these persons, the first converts of the Apostles, were baptized with the Holy Spirit, they received the gift of preaching. They did not speak in tongues. The Bible says: "They spoke the word of God with boldness." Theodore H. Epp; on page 55 of his book, *Gifts of the Spirit* writes:

> The word 'filled' is again used in the aorist tense. In addition to the disciples, other people were gathered together. They were no doubt new Christians; and they were permanently filled with the Holy Spirit. They began to speak, but not in other tongues this time. They began to speak 'the word of God with boldness.' The literal translation of this is, 'they began to prophesy.' This is another of the gifts of the Holy Spirit.

The Twentieth Century Version reads: "When their prayer was ended, the place in which they were assembled was shaken; and they were all filled with the Holy Spirit, and began to tell God's message fearlessly."

The late T. J. McCrossan, one-time eighteen-years' examiner in languages for the Presbytery of Minneapolis, offers the following enlightening comment on Acts 4:31.

"And when they had prayed, the place was shaken where they were assembled together and they were filled (*eplesthesan*—third personal plural, Aorist passive) with the Holy Ghost, and they spake (*elaloun*—third person plural, imperfect tense) the word of God with boldness. 'The word here for filled is the very same identical word that is used in Acts 2:4, and so declares that it is also the aorist tense as in Acts 2:4, and so declares that the filling was completed before they spoke in tongues or prophesied. This proves beyond the possibility of all doubt that 'the infilling' was just as complete in Acts 4:31 as in Acts 2:4; but in Acts 2:4, we read, '. . . and they began to speak with other tongues as the Spirit gave them to utter forth.' Here the word 'gave' ('As the Spirit gave to them to utter forth') is *edidon'* (Imperfect tense), and so tells us very clearly that the Spirit gave to them to speak forth then in other tongues, and continued so to do, as we have so clearly proven. In Acts 4:31 however, 'They spoke the word of God with boldness; after they had all been filled with the Holy Ghost. Here the word, 'spoke' is *'elaloun'* (imperfect tense, and so proves to us, that when they were baptized, instead of speaking with other tongues and continuing to do so, these in Acts 4:31 preached the word with boldness, and continued to do so. Their gift therefore, following their infilling, was 'the gift of prophecy,' while in Acts 2:4 it was the 'gift of tongues.' "

—*Speaking with Other Tongues, Sign or Gift, Which?* pp. 23, 24.

The reference in Acts 4:31 is to persons who received the gift of prophecy, NOT TONGUES, after they were baptized with the Holy Spirit. This was not a case where persons were merely refilled. The Bible says: "And they were all filled with the Holy Ghost, and they spoke the word of God with boldness."

The Twentieth Century Version reads: "and they were all filled with the Holy Spirit, and began to tell God's message fearlessly."

The Centenary Version says: "and began to speak the message of the Lord with boldness."

Reference here is to the first converts of the disciples. It was after they were baptized with the Holy Spirit that they BEGAN to speak the word of God "fearlessly" or "with boldness."

J. B. Rotherham translates, "and A began speaking the word of God with freedom of utterance."

Dr. A. T. Robertson; one of the greatest of Greek scholars, offers this very enlightening comment: "They spake (*elaloun* imperfect active indicative), began to speak, after being (*eplesthesan*, aorist passive indicative) with the Holy Spirit.' —*Word Pictures in the New Testament*, vol. 3, p. 56.

After these persons were baptized (not refilled) with the Holy Spirit they began to prophesy or preach the word fearlessly. "When they had finished praying, the place in which they had gathered rocked to and fro, and they were all filled with the Holy Spirit, and began to preach the Word of God with confidence." —*The New Testament of Our Lord and Savior Jesus Christ,* by Ronald A. Knox.

OTHER CHRISTIANS WHO WERE BAPTIZED WITH THE HOLY SPIRIT

(A) The Samaritan Christians who were converted under Philip's ministry and later baptized with the Holy Spirit under Peter and John's ministry (Acts 8:14-17) may have spoken in tongues, or they may have received the gift of prophecy when Spirit-filled. Most commentators believe they received the gift of tongues and this gift, so Paul says, is not given to all. The gift of prophecy may have been given to some of the Samaritans as on the occasion recorded in Acts 4:31. No one knows what gifts were given on this occasion. On the Day of Pentecost we know all DID NOT receive the gift of tongues and such could have been the case here, who knows?

(B) St. Paul was converted on the Damascus road (Acts 9:1-9) and called to preach at the same time (Acts 26:13-18). Three days after this he ("brother Saul" Acts 9:17) was baptized with the Holy Spirit (Acts 9:17-18) in the city of Damascus. The Bible nowhere says he spoke in tongues when he was baptized with the Holy Spirit. Bear this fact in mind as you read this account: Paul had several gifts, so no one knows what gift or how marry gifts were given to him when he was filled with the Sprint, because the Bible DOES NOT say. The Holy Spirit divides "to every man severally as He wills" (not as we will). When Paul wrote his letter to the Corinthians he was in possession of a number of gifts. The gift of "prophecy" was no doubt the first gift Paul received, as he was called to preach while he was on the Damascus road. It is reasonable to assume that he received the gift of prophecy BEFORE he received the GIFT of tongues. As a matter of fact it is utterly impossible for ANYONE, to prove that he spoke in tongues BEFORE he received the gift of prophecy.

(C) The Caesarean Christians were converted, not under Peter's ministry, but prior to that time. Before Peter went to Caesarea, their prayers and charities had been "an acceptable offering to God" (Acts 10:4). God had cleansed (Acts 10:15) and accepted them before Peter had seen them. In some way, at some time, they had heard the story about Jesus (Acts 10:37, 38). It was under Peter's ministry that they were baptized with the Holy Spirit. These baptized believers received the GIFT of TONGUES, the same as was given on the day of Pentecost. We are sure it was the GIFT OF TONGUES because the Apostle Peter says so (Acts 11:17) and this explains why it was not given to all in the early church.

(D) The Ephesian Christians (Acts 19:2) who had been converted and baptized twice (Acts 19:3-5) received the gift of prophecy and the gift of tongues when they were baptized with the Holy Spirit. Now, this could mean that some received two gifts at the same time, one being as much an evidence as the other that the recipient had been baptized with the Holy Spirit. There is nothing in any of the accounts to support the "tongues-evidence" theory, and for lack of Scriptural support, it must he rejected.

FOUR SPIRIT-FILLED GIANTS
WHO DID NOT SPEAK
WITH TONGUES

(A) D. L. Moody, is said to have addressed over fifty million people during his ministry. He was also the author of several religious publications.

"In 1879 Mr. Moody founded a school for poor girls, at Northfield, Mass., which later grew into the celebrated Northfield and Mt. Hermon institutions."

—*Men and Women of Deep Piety*, pp. 330, 335

In the year of 1871, Mr. Moody went east to New York City to collect funds for the sufferers from the Chicago fire, but his heart and soul were crying out for the power from on high. Said he: "My heart was not in the work of begging."

"I could not appeal. I was crying all the time that God would fill me with His Spirit. Well, one day, in the city of New York—oh, what a day!—I cannot describe it; I seldom refer to it; it is almost too sacred an experience to name. Paul had an experience of which he never spoke for fourteen years. I can only say that God revealed Himself to me, and I had such an experience of His love that I had to ask Him to stay his hand. I went to preaching again. The sermons were not different; I did not present any new truths; and yet hundreds were converted. I would not now be placed where I was before that blessed experience if you should give me all the world."

D. L. Moody, the World's Greatest Lay Preacher, never spoke in tongues.

(2) George Muller, the Greatest Man of Prayer Known to History. It was written of him. "In his labors of over three score years, he built five large orphan houses on Ashley Down, Bristol, England, and took under his care over ten thousand orphans, spending for them almost a million dollars. He gave aid to day schools and Sunday Schools, in Britain and other lands, where nearly 150,000 children have been taught. He circulated nearly two million Bibles, or parts of it, at a cost of $200,000; also three million books and tracts at a cost of about $200,000 or more. In addition to this, he spent about $1,300,000 to aid missionary labors in various lands. The aggregate (sum total) of money he thus handled for the Lord in answer to prayer was seven million, five hundred thousand dollars.

"Of money given to him for his own use, or bequeathed to him personally, he gave $400,000 to the work so dear to his heart. He did not die rich. The total value of his books and earthly possessions at his death was less than eight hundred dollars.

Dr. Harry E. Jessop says:

"In an address given to ministers and workers, after his 90th birthday, Mr. Muller said: 'I was converted in November 1825, but I only came into the full surrender of heart four years later, in 1829. The love of money was gone, the love of place was gone, the love of position was gone, the love of worldly pleasures and engagements was gone. God, God, God alone became my portion. I found my all in Him. I wanted nothing else.

"By the grace of God this has remained, and has made me a happy man, an exceedingly happy man, and it led me to care only about the things of God . . . This change was so great that it was like a second conversion."

—*Foundations of Doctrine*, pp. 247 – 248

Mr. George Muller, the greatest man of prayer known to history, never spoke in tongues.

(C) Amanda Smith, the World's Greatest Colored Soul Winner. Amanda Smith, was born at Long Green, Maryland, January 23, 1837 She was the oldest of nine children, five of whom were born in slavery.

On Tuesday, March 17, 1856, she was soundly converted and twelve years later (September 1868) under the ministry of John Inskip she was baptized with the Holy Spirit. In telling of this experience she writes: "I seemed to feel a hand, the touch of which I cannot describe. It seemed to press me gently on the top of my head, and I felt something part and roll down and cover me like a cloak! I felt it distinctly; it was done in a moment, and O! What a mighty peace and power took possession of me" —An Autobiography, *Mrs. Amanda Smith*, page 79.

In 1869, when she was thirty-two years of age, God called her definitely into religious work.

"She would go from camp to camp, where she would be invited to stay with some friend, and often times these were white people. When not one of the slated preachers, she was mightily used of the Lord in singing. Her fame gradually spread through New York City, to Philadelphia, and Boston, and on to the ends of the earth.

"The fame of the ex-slave evangelist spread to different nations. Through influential friends, she was called to England, where her preaching became a sensation, and hundreds sought the Lord. The largest halls in England's cities were taxed beyond their capacity to seat the crowds.

"The call of God became stronger that she should go around the world. She turned her face to the Orient. Her visits at Rome, Florence, Naples, Alexandria, and Jerusalem were made memorable because people flocked to hear her plead the cause of redemption. The mighty Bishop Thoburn invited her to visit India. Of her visit in that land, the bishop wrote, 'During the seventeen years I have lived in Calcutta, I have known many famous visitors to visit the city, and some of them attracted large audiences, but I have never known anyone who could draw and hold so large an audience as Amanda Smith. She went directly to the heart of a problem and faced the souls of men, as though they were standing before the judgment bar of God.'

"For some eight years, she labored in Liberia, Africa, where multiplied thousands were saved through her preaching. It seemed her faith in God was miracle working. She plead with those savage multitudes with a power that was irresistible.

"When Amanda turned homeward again, her ovation in London was unequaled. Thousands of letters and telegrams were received by her. The wealthiest of homes were opened to her. Back again in America, the arms of the people were extended to the slave evangelist. George Sebring furnished her a beautiful home in Sebring, Fla., which she called home during her revivals. It was here that she died. Her body was shipped to Chicago for burial, all and along the railroad en route, multitudes came to gaze upon the train which bore the remains of the 'world's greatest colored soul winner to their resting place."

—*God's Great Soul Winners*, by Basil Miller, pp. 107 - 110.

Dr. Charles E. Brown says she: "traveled nearly all over the world and enjoyed a fame and success very few scholarly ministers could match." —*The Meaning of Sanctification*, p. 187.

Amanda Smith, the World's Greatest Colored Soul Winner never spoke in tongues.

(D) Charles Grandison Finney, the World's Greatest Revivalist. "It is estimated that during the years 1857-58 (one year's time) over a hundred thousand persons were led to Christ as the direct or indirect result of Finney's labors, while five hundred thousand persons professed conversion to Christ in the great revival which began in his meetings. It is said that at Governeur, New York, not a dance or theatrical play could be held in the place for six years after Finney held meetings there.

"Finney seemed so anointed with the Holy Spirit that people were often brought under conviction of sin just by looking at him. When holding meetings at Utica, New York, he visited a large factory there and was looking at the machinery. At the sight of him one of the operators and then another broke down and wept under a sense of their sins, and finally so many were sobbing and weeping that the machinery had to be stopped while Finney pointed them to Christ.

"In London, England, between 1,500 and 2,000 persons were seeking salvation in one day in Finney's meetings. The great revival of 1858-59, one of the greatest revivals in the world's history, was the direct results of his meetings. That was the greatest work of God and the greatest revival of religion the world has ever seen,' says Dr. Lymon Beecher. It is estimated that six hundred thousand persons were brought to Christ in this revival."

—*Deeper Experiences of Famous Christians*, by J. Gilchrist Lawson, pp. 243-256.

Where was he when he was baptized with the Holy Spirit? In law office. He said:

"I returned to the front office, and found that the fire that I had made of large wood was nearly burned out. But as I turned to and was about to take a seat by the fire, I received a mighty baptism of the Holy Ghost. Without any expectation of it, without ever having the thought in mind that there was any such thing for me without any recollection that I had ever heard the thing mentioned by any person in the world, the Holy Ghost descended upon me in a manner that seemed to go through me, body and soul. I could feel the impression like a wave of electricity going through and through me. Indeed it seemed to come in waves of liquid love; for I could not express it in any other way. It seemed like the very breath of God. I can recollect distinctly that it seemed to fan me, like immense wings.

"No words can express the wonderful love that was shed abroad in my heart. I wept aloud with joy and love; and I do not know but that I should say I literally bellowed out the unutterable gushings of my heart, These wave's came over me, and over me, one after the other, until I recollect I cried out, 'I shall die if these waves continue to pass over me.' I said, 'Lord, I cannot bear any more'; yet I had no fear of death. How long I continued in this state, with this baptism continuing to roll over me and go through me, I do not know."

—*Memoirs of Rev. Charles C. Finney*, pp. 20-21.

Mr. Finney says nothing in any of his writings about speaking in tongues when he was baptized with the Holy Spirit. He certainly would not have been ashamed to say so had he spoken.

And, too, had he spoken in tongues when he was baptized with the Spirit, he would have spoken again in his private devotions because the kind given on the Day of Pentecost is a gift, is something to be repeated. I repeat, had he spoken in tongues once, he would have spoken again, because he would have had the gift of tongues—the same kind as given on the Day of Pentecost, at Caesarea, at Ephesus and at Corinth. God gave him the gift of preaching.

Under the caption, POST APOSTOLIC SAINTS WHO HAVE NOT SPOKEN IN TONGUES, Mr. Carl Brumback makes the following statement in his book:

"It would appear from the available records that most (note he says 'most') of the great saints of this dispensation, who lived previous to this Twentieth Century, did not receive an infilling with the Spirit which included speaking with other tongues."

—*What Meaneth This*, p. 275.

Mr. Brumback is saying here "According to available records" many men of God previous to this generation DID NOT speak in tongues when baptized with the

Holy Spirit. This statement from Mr. Brumback lends some additional support to our belief and teaching that all do not speak with tongues who are baptized with the Holy Spirit. When Mr. Brumback made the foregoing statement he was referring to a number of people who were mightily used of the Lord and "had marvelous spiritual experiences" but had never spoken in tongues according to "available records." Why, then, should one preach that speaking in tongues is the initial, physical evidence of the baptism with the Holy Spirit when one cannot prove it?

My second extract is from the pen of the late T. B. Barrott, the famed Norwegian Pentecostal pastor and author of the book *In the Days of the Latter Rain* (for which he received the King's Prize). He wrote:

> I have known people who, on being filled with the Spirit, have risen quietly to their feet, with beaming faces, and testified to the power of God within; others have sprung to their feet and moved about the hall or church, speaking in tongues and prophesying; others have acted like the man in Acts 3:8-10, leaping shouting, walking and praising God. —p. 105.

And from pages 152 and 153 of the same book we take the following:

"Let me again lay stress on the fact, that although there are other evidences of the indwelling Spirit, it is clearly stated in Acts that the Apostles, when tongues were heard in Jerusalem and Caesarea, considered this to be a sure sign of the baptism of the Holy Ghost. No one can read the account given in the tenth chapter of

Acts with a fair mind and doubt this. Still I believe that many have had, and that people may obtain in our day mighty baptisms without this sign.

"The Holy Ghost may . . . set up His throne within in mighty power where tongues have not been heard. This is seen from the lives and works of many."

My next excerpt is an open letter to the ministers and saints in the Assemblies of God by the late Rev. F. F. Bosworth. Rev. Bosworth, Pentecostal, was an outstanding minister in the Assemblies of God movement. As an evangelist and divine healer, he was nationally known.

After laboring in the Pentecostal Movement for eleven years, preaching and teaching that speaking in tongues is the initial, physical evidence of the baptism of the Holy Spirit he became convinced that speaking in tongues as in Acts 2, 10, 19 is only one of the gifts of the Spirit. And in 1918 he left the Assemblies of God movement and wrote "an open letter to the ministers and saints in the Pentecostal Movement." A portion of the letter reads

"The purpose of this letter is to point out what I consider a serious doctrinal error, the elimination of which will solve many of our difficulties besides opening the way for more of the manifestation of the Spirit, and a much deeper work of God. The error to which I refer is the doctrine held by so many, that the Baptism in the Spirit is in every instance evidenced by the initial physical sign of speaking in other tongues as the Spirit gives utterance, Acts 2:4, and that this is not the gift of tongues, referred to in Paul's letter to the Corinthians, 1 Cor. 12. After some time in the work on Pentecostal lines (during which time it has been my privilege to see thousands receive the precious Baptism in the Holy Spirit) I am certain that many who receive the most powerful baptisms for service do not receive the manifestation of speaking in tongues. And I am just as certain that many who seemingly speak in tongues are not, nor ever have been baptized in the Spirit. Although I have in the past very tenaciously contended for it, as many of the brethren still do, I am certain that it is entirely wrong and unscriptural to teach that the miraculous speaking in tongues on the Day of Pentecost was not the gift of tongues God set in the church, and which is so often mentioned in Paul's first letter to the Corinthians. Not only is there not a solitary passage of Scripture upon which to base this doctrine, but, on the other hand, the Scriptures flatly deny it. That there is no Scripture for this distinction between speaking in tongues as the Spirit gave utterance at Jerusalem, and the gift of tongues at Corinth, is being seen and admitted by many Bible students and teachers in the Pentecostal movement. In fact, some in the movement have never believed this distinction was Scriptural,

"At a recent State Council of the Assemblies of God, when the Chairman of the Council was asked by one of the young ministers if there was a passage or a number of passages upon which to base this distinction, he publicly admitted that there was not a single passage. Charles E. Parham, who came forward with this doctrine in the year 1900, was the first man in the history of the world to teach publicly this doctrine. He saw that it was not possible to teach that speaking in tongues will in every case accompany the baptism in the Spirit, unless he could make it appear that the speaking in tongues on the Day of Pentecost was something distinct from the gift of tongues at Corinth. He was also the first to teach that none have been baptized in the Spirit except those who have spoken in tongues.

"The fact is that hundreds of the greatest soul-winners of the entire Christian era, without the gift of tongues, have had a much greater enduement of power and have been used to accomplish a much greater and deeper work than has Mr. Parham.

"The argument that the miraculous manifestation of tongues on the Day of Pentecost is, distinct from the gift of tongues, called in the Scriptures 'the manifestation of the Spirit,' falls flat when we consider the 7th and 8th verses of the 12th chapter of 1 Corinthians. In the 7th verse Paul says, 'The manifestation of the Spirit is given to every man to profit withal.' Some have taught and written that 'the manifestation of the Spirit here mentioned is always the speaking in tongues as the Spirit gives utterance as on the Day of Pentecost. They claim that this is for all who receive the Baptism of the Spirit, but that not the gift of tongues later mentioned in the same chapter. But in the next verse Paul entirely demolishes this argument by explaining what the 'manifestation of the Spirit' is. 'For to one,' he says, 'is given by the Spirit the word of wisdom; to another the word of knowledge by the same Spirit; to another faith by the same Spirit; to another the gift of healing by the same Spirit; to another the working of miracles; to another prophecy; to another discerning of spirits; to another divers kinds of tongues; to another the interpretation of tongues; but all these worketh that one and the self-same Spirit, dividing to every man severally as He will.' Each one of these nine gifts is called 'the manifestation of the Spirit.' The speaking in tongues on the day of Pentecost was 'the manifestation of the Spirit,' and, therefore is identical with the gift of tongues, about which Paul writes to the Corinthians. These Galileans had no power in themselves, without the Spirit, to speak in these languages, but it was given them by the Spirit to utter words and form sentences not originating in their own minds. We therefore contend that this was the gift of tongues that God set in the church. The fact here mentioned that the gift of tongues is always 'the manifestation of the Spirit,' refutes the theory held by many that the gift of tongues is the ability to speak in tongues at will. The word of God discountenances all speaking in tongues except that which is 'the manifestation of the Spirit.'

"The eleventh verse makes this clear by saying that the Spirit works each of these manifestations, or, as Weymouth translates it, 'These results are all brought about by the Spirit.' In other words, the Holy Spirit uses us instead of our using Him. God, we are told in this chapter, has set these gifts or manifestations in the church. If the speaking in tongues on the day of Pentecost, was not the gift of tongues, I ask you when did God set the gift of tongues in the church? Chapter and verse please. The Scriptures tell us that when Christ ascended up on high, He gave gifts unto men. Eph. 4:8-12.

"Another argument used in the attempt to prove that the gift of tongues is not speaking as the Spirit gives utterance is based upon Paul's instructions to those with the gift of tongues to be silent in the church, unless there is an interpreter. They argue that if Paul told them to keep silent, it is proof that it was not the Spirit's utterance, because that would be rebuking the Holy Ghost. This idea arises from the mistaken notion that the manifestation of the Spirit in tongues is always for the public, whereas Paul said, 'If there be no interpreter (present) let him keep silence in the church, and let him speak to himself and to God.' It is a great mistake to think that the manifestation of tongues must always be spoken to the church, and that it will be quenching the Spirit to obey Paul's inspired instruction to speak 'unto himself and to God.' Ignorance here has made much confusion in Pentecostal assemblies. Many after disobeying these inspired directions say, 'I could not help it.' This is a mistake, for Paul commands silence unless there is an interpreter. Sometimes, when the church is being greatly edified by a sermon, there may be many at the same time who feel like worshipping God in tongues, but this may be controlled without quenching the Spirit, for Paul says that even where there is an interpreter only one should speak at a time.

Even the greater manifestation of prophecy, which is especially for the edification of the church, is to be restrained, so that the prophets shall speak 'one by one that all may learn, and all may be comforted.' The Apostle evidently purposed effectually to cure the Corinthian church, of the can't help it idea, that caused so much confusion in the Corinthian church, and is doing the same thing in these days. He tells them distinctly that God is not the author of this confusion, but that 'the spirits of the prophets are subject to the prophets.' Of course we are always glad when God, in the middle of our sermon, saves and baptizes souls, and gives them the speaking in tongues, as He did while Peter preached to the household of Cornelius.

The Doctrine Is Never Mentioned In Any Epistle

"But once again as to the supposed distinction between tongues in the Acts and at Corinth, after which we will leave you to an impartial searching of the Scriptures touching this point. It is insisted that the speaking in tongues in the Acts was temporary, and that every Christian should speak in tongues as the initial sign of being baptized in the Spirit, while the gift of tongues dealt with in Paul's letter to the Corinthians implies permanence, and that few have the permanent gift. If this theory is correct, with its necessary distinction between tongues and tongues, then we agree that it is the most important doctrine of the New Testament, for what can be more important than for Christians to receive the enduement of power so necessary to accomplish the work that God wants done? Then is it not strange that no one of the inspired writers of any of the epistles to the New Testament Churches, preachers and saints scattered abroad, ever made the slightest reference to that kind of speaking in tongues which, as many allege, is the evidence of baptism? Think of it, and then think again, all the New Testament epistles and not a single mention of this doctrine. We hear in these letters, of backsliding from almost every other doctrine, even the truth of justification by faith, the resurrection from the dead, and the second coming of Christ. They backslid from the great truths of faith and love, and the apostles were careful to line them up and get them straight, but if they ever held the doctrine of 'tongues the evidence,' they never once deviated from it, but held it so tenaciously that not even a word of exhortation was deemed necessary to keep them from letting down on this point. Will any of the brethren make the charge that the writers of these epistles had compromised on the question of the baptism in the Spirit before writing all these letters?

"The doctrine that all are to speak in tongues when baptized in the Spirit is based entirely upon supposition without a solitary 'Thus saith the Lord.' It is nowhere taught in the Scriptures, but is assumed from the fact that in three instances recorded in the Acts they spoke in tongues as a result of the baptism. While this notable fact should serve as an eye-opener to those who contend against any speaking in tongues, it is by no means a conclusive proof that God gave the same gift to all the multiplied thousands added to the church during this marvelous period of church history, extending over more than a quarter of a century.

"God always has a definite purpose and an infinitely wise reason for everything he does. The Day of Pentecost witnessed the grandest and most effective display of the gift of tongues the world has ever seen, And God's purpose was that it should be a 'sign', not to believers, but to the unbelieving Jews dwelling at Jerusalem, 'out of every nation under heaven.' And God's purpose was most wonderfully realized, for three thousand unbelieving Jews were, by the fact that these Galileans spoke in their own languages, forced to believe that Jesus was actually the Messiah. Perhaps there was no other sign that God could have manifested so effectually under these circumstances as the speaking in tongues. Eight years later Peter and the six Jewish brethren who accompanied him to the household of Cornelius were, with all other Jews, unbelievers as to the Gentiles being included in the privileges of the gospel. So God made the gift of tongues a sign to them, thus convincing them to their astonishment, that 'God also to the Gentiles hath granted repentance unto life.' When Peter returned to Jerusalem, the apostles and brethren contended with him, saying, 'Thou wentest in to men uncircumcised, and didst eat with them.' So Peter rehearsed the matter from the beginning and closed his argument by saying, 'As I began to speak, the Holy Ghost fell on them as on us at the beginning.' If the thousands who were saved during that wonderful revival period of eight years between the second and the tenth chapters of Acts, spoke in tongues when baptized in the Spirit, why did Peter say, 'as on us at the beginning?' He could just as well have said, 'As He has been baptizing all from the beginning.' If it was well known that all these spoke in tongues when they were baptized in the Spirit, why should he point back only to the time when they spoke in tongues on the day of Pentecost? Again, years later, when Paul met the brethren at Ephesus who had never heard that there was any Holy Ghost, God gave them both tongues and prophecy when they received the Spirit. And if Luke was so careful to record it when only these few spoke in tongues, why did he not record it when all the many thousands since Pentecost spoke in tongues, if they all did?

"If it be objected here that perhaps the multitudes added to the church during this unparalleled revival period did not receive the Holy Ghost, let it be remembered that in apostolic days converts were not left in the dark concerning the baptism in the Spirit as they are in modern revivals. Peter declared to the multitude on the Day of Pentecost that as many as would repent would receive the gift of the Holy Ghost; that the promise was unto them and to their children, etc., Acts 2:38-39. And it is distinctly stated of the three thousand added to the church on that day, that 'they all continued steadfastly in the apostles doctrine and fellowship', proving that they all received the Holy Ghost. The baptism in the Holy Spirit held an important place in the apostles' doctrine and is clearly stated in Peter's first sermon. We read in the eighth chapter of Acts that as soon as the apostles at Jerusalem had heard about the revival at Samaria they sent unto them Peter and John, who prayed for them that they might receive the Holy Ghost. And when Paul met the brethren at Ephesus, his first question was, 'Have ye received the Holy Ghost since ye believed?' By reading the epistles, we find that all the churches had received the baptism of the Spirit.

"Another argument used in the attempt to prove that all Spirit-baptized believers will speak in tongues is based upon John 15:26, 27; 'When the comforter is come he shall testify of Me, and ye shall bear witness.' It is contended that because two testimonies are here spoken of, one is the Holy Ghost speaking in tongues. But in Heb. 2:4 we are told how the Holy Ghost testifies, or bears witness. 'God also bearing them witness, both with signs and wonders, and with divers miracles, and gifts (not the gift of tongues only) of the Holy Ghost, according to His own will.

"The fact is that it is unscriptural to teach that they all received that one manifestation, and this is the force of all of Paul's argument to the Corinthians. For instance, from the 12th verse to the close of the 14th chapter, Paul teaches the exact opposite of what many today are teaching, endeavoring to show them that all are not to expect the same manifestation of the spirit. He uses the illustration of the human body and its members and asks, 'If the whole body were an eye, where were the hearing?' etc., and then, to make it still more emphatic, he asks, 'Are all apostles? are all teachers? are all workers of miracles? have all the gifts of healing? do all speak with tongues? do all interpret?' Of course, the answer to each of these questions is No. In other words, Paul is distinctly saying that all are not teachers, and all do not speak in tongues. We can't dodge this question by saying that this is the gift of tongues and not the speaking in tongues as on the Day of Pentecost, because as already shown, Paul distinctly states that this is 'the manifestation of the Spirit', making it identical with the manifestation of the Spirit that came on the Day of Pentecost.

Gifts not for Evidence but for Service

"Teaching that tongues is the evidence of the baptism in the Spirit makes it a sign to believers, whereas Paul distinctly says that it is not a sign to the believer, but to the unbeliever. If made a sign to the seeker for the baptism, it not only leaves no place for faith, but on the other hand destroys faith already divinely given. After God has most powerfully baptized the seeker, and with perfect faith divinely inwrought, he is rejoicing with joy unspeakable and full of glory, with every ounce of his flesh quivering under the power of the indwelling Spirit, some one will tell him that he has not yet received the Holy Ghost because he did not speak in tongues. This destroys his faith, which Paul says is both the 'evidence' and the substance', Heb. 11:1, and sends him home discouraged, to continue his seeking as some have for several years. Everywhere I have gone I have met hungry souls who seemingly speak in tongues, but who have not this assuring faith that they are baptized in the Spirit. Nothing short of real faith can satisfy the heart and put the soul at rest.

"The word 'evidence' in the Scriptures is never used in connection with a spiritual gift, or manifestation, making faith to depend upon any sign or physical manifestation, but the Apostle distinctly states that 'faith is the evidence.' Anything that is to be received in answer to prayer is to be received by faith, even the great miracle of the new birth, and Paul expressly states that we are to 'receive the promise of the Spirit through faith', Gal. 3:14. Nothing short of faith can satisfy the heart and give us power. Paul said, Let everything be done with a view to building up faith,' but the 'tongues evidence' teaching reverses this, not only destroying faith, but making it impossible until the gift of tongues is received. This teaching causes people to reject the mightiest baptism in the

Spirit, disregarding the personal Holy Spirit within and puts them from that time on seeking, for years, in many instances for a physical manifestation, that Paul plainly teaches us all are not to expect, for the Spirit is to divide the manifestations 'as he will.'

"This teaching, besides destroying faith, puts some to seeking a hundred times after God has baptized them in the Spirit, in many instances much more powerfully than others who spoke in tongues. It is absurd to suppose that Jesus must pour out the Spirit upon the same persons a hundred times before he succeeds in getting them baptized in the Spirit. There is not a single instance like this in the Scriptures. John the Baptist completed the work the first time he undertook to baptize those who came to him. And so with Jesus, according to the Scriptures. He never had to make two attempts to administer his baptism. Jesus taught that the first time the Spirit comes upon a consecrated seeker he is to 'abide forever.' And I insist that when a consecrated seeker has been correctly instructed, he should receive the Holy Ghost the first time the Spirit falls upon them.

"Again, this telling those who have been baptized in the Spirit that they have not been so baptized because they did not get the gift of tongues also robs them of a testimony for months and even years, and puts them to seeking for a physical manifestation when they ought to be witnessing and laboring for souls. Jesus said, 'Ye shall receive the power of the Holy Ghost coming upon you; and ye shall be my witnesses.' Acts 1:8 R.V. If allowed to believe, their testimony under the power of the Spirit would have led others into the Baptism. Instead of this those who might have been led into the baptism by their testimony, have watched them seek for hours after the Holy Spirit had fallen upon them, and this has discouraged many delaying the revival that much, besides denying Christ's encouraging words. 'How much more shall your heavenly gather give the Holy Ghost to them that ask Him?' Luke 11:13.

"It is a notable fact that many of the deepest and best teachers and preachers in the Pentecostal movement have the poorest success in getting the seekers through to speaking in tongues. The reason is they are too conscientious to use the 'Glory-glory-glory say it a little faster' and other similar methods, which have made some of the shallowest and most fanatical workers apparently the most successful. Proper instruction followed by consecration and prayer will, in every instance, bring down the baptism in the Holy Spirit, but it will not always bring down the manifestation of tongues. Repeated seeking and methods never used in the Scriptures have been employed to get all the seekers through to the 'Bible evidence,' so called, and then I am certain that many who have the baptism and seemingly speak in tongues do not really do so, although they are sincere in the matter. This over-emphasis in teaching tongues and the employment of unscriptural methods is responsible for this. I recently heard a prominent minister in the Pentecostal movement preaching from the tenth chapter of Acts. For nearly an hour he insisted that unless we press the 'tongues evidence' teaching the people will not receive the Holy Ghost. He overlooked the fact that Peter, in this chapter, had better success in getting his audience through to the baptism without even mentioning the subject, than any preacher in modern times has had by preaching that tongues is the Bible evidence. While Peter was Preaching to them, about Jesus, they all received the baptism, to the astonishment of Peter himself."[115]

---

[115] Joybringer Bosworth, *His Life Story*, pp, 56-70. The foregoing is a portion of an open letter that Rev. F. F, Bosworth sent to hundreds of ministers and saints of the Assemblies of God movement after he left it.

SPEAKING IN TONGUES AS IN ACTS 2:4 — A GIFT

The majority—not all, of course—of our Pentecostal friends, some of whom are good, honest, sincere Christians, believe that the tongue we read about in Acts 2:4, 10:46, and 19:6 is something altogether different from that which Paul writes about in 1 Cor. 12, 13, 14. Mr. Carl Brumback, an outstanding author in the Pentecostal movement, says: "if there is a clear distinction") between the tongues phenomenon in Acts and that in 1 Cor., then the Pentecostal argument for tongues as the initial, physical evidence is well nigh irrefutable. If not, then the Pentecostal theology on the evidence teaching suffers a severe blow. This is perhaps the decisive point of the entire controversy." *What Meaneth This?* p. 201.

W. V. Grant writes: "There is a vast difference between other tongues as one speaks when the evidence of the Holy Ghost comes, as in Acts 2:4, and an unknown tongue, as the gift of God set in the church." *The Holy Spirit Baptism*, p. 113.

Our friends in the Pentecostal church labor long and hard trying to prove that Paul in his letter to the church at Corinth is writing about the gift of tongues and not about the kind of tongue that we read about in Acts 2:4, 10:46, and 19:6. Mr. Brumback declares that "the pentecostal theology on the evidence teaching suffers a severe blow" if this be not true. We are indeed sorry that our friends in the Pentecostal movement have taken that position, because it is indefensible. So, in the interest of truth and the cause of Christ, we must expose this false teaching here and now. Here are some of the reasons we know it is false. Our Pentecostal friends believe:

(1) The kind of tongue Luke writes about in Acts 2:4 is a language, an intelligible language that can be interpreted or understood by man. True, and the kind of tongue Paul writes about in 1 Cor. 14 is an intelligible language that can be interpreted or understood by man (see 1 Cor. 14:27). There is no difference.

(2) They believe one who speaks in tongues as the 120 did on the Day of Pentecost may not understand what he is saying. True, but now read 1 Cor. 14:13 where Paul says the same thing about the kind of tongue he writes about. There is no difference.

(3) They believe people who speak in tongues as they did on the Day of Pentecost can edify themselves even when they do not understand what they are saying. True, but now read 1 Cor. 14:13 where Paul says the same thing about the kind of tongue he writes about. There is no difference.

(4) They believe if people speak in tongues as they did on the Day of Pentecost, they often speak "mysteries." True, and according to 1 Cor. 14:2 people who speak the kind of tongues Paul writes about often speak "mysteries." There is no difference.

(5) They believe when one speaks in tongues as they did in Acts 2:4, there may be times when one will speak unto God, as when no man present understandeth him. True, and Paul has this same thing to say about the kind of tongue he writes about 1 Cor. 14:2. There is no difference.

(6) They believe the kind of tongue Luke writes about was a "sign to unbelievers." True, and the kind of

tongue Paul writes about is a "sign to unbelievers." There is no difference.

(7) They believe the kind of tongue Luke writes about is still in the church today. The kind of tongue Paul writes about is also in the church today. Luke and Paul are writing about the same kind of tongue.

There is no "clear distinction" between tongues in Acts and tongues in Corinth. Shall we look a little further into this subject?

(a) If the expression in Matt. 15:11 which reads: "not that which goeth into the mouth defileth a man; but that which cometh out of the mouth—" does not apply to alcoholic beverages—and it does not—then it should NEVER be quoted to prove it is no harm to drink alcoholic beverages.

(b) If Rom. 7:14-24 does not refer to Paul's life AFTER his Damascus road experience—and it does not—then it should NEVER be quoted to prove that after one is converted he will sin more or less every day.

(c) If the passage in 1 Cor. 14:34 is not referring to women preachers—and it is not—then it should NEVER be quoted to prove that a woman should not be permitted to preach.

If in 1 Cor. 12 and 14 Paul is not referring to the same kind of tongue that we read about in Acts 2:4, 10, and 19—then one should NEVER quote from Paul's writings to prove these four things:

(a) That Paul spoke in tongues as the disciples did on the Day of Pentecost.

(b) That one who speaks in tongues as was done on the Day of Pentecost often speaketh mysteries.

(c) That one who speaks in tongues as they did on the Day of Pentecost may not understand what he is talking about.

(d) That one who speaks in tongues as they did on the Day of Pentecost edifies himself even though he does not know what he is talking about.

The main reason, doubtless, that our Pentecostal friends think Paul is writing not about the same kind of tongue we read about in Acts 2, 10, 19 is because more than three persons were permitted to speak at the same time in these three instances related in Acts. Concerning this point, Mr. Carl Brumback writes:

> ". . . at Pentecost there were one hundred and twenty speaking in tongues, all at one time! How many spoke at Caesarea we know not, but surely their number exceeded three, And at Ephesus Paul himself allowed twelve to speak with tongues in one meeting and that not by course! Now if all speaking with tongues is the gift, then all these believers, the apostles included, were out of order, How are we to explain this contradiction between the two phases of tongues? Certainly, the Holy Spirit would not inspire and give utterance in Acts to that which He afterwards condemns in Corinthians!" —*What Meaneth This?* p. 261.

We do not have two phases of prophecy, do we, merely because more than three prophesied in Ephesus at the same time? (Acts 19:6) Is not prophecy a greater gift than tongues? If tongues (the lesser gift) may be a sign or evidence of the Spirit's indwelling, may not prophecy (the greater gift) also be a sign or evidence of the Spirit's indwelling? Was it not said by the prophet Joel that in the last days God's Spirit would be poured out upon "sons, and daughters" and they would prophecy? Two gifts were given at Ephesus. On the Day of Pentecost only one gift was given to some (the gift of tongues); and when the first converts of the apostles were baptized with the Holy Ghost, only one gift was given—prophecy. The Bible does not say which gift was given at Samaria. Here in Ephesus, they received the gift of tongues and the gift of prophecy (preaching). The Bible says: "And when Paul had laid his hands upon, them, the Holy Ghost came on them; and they spake with tongues and prophesies." (Acts 19:6).

T. J. McCrossan said: "These Ephesians received two gifts in place of one, for both these verbs are in the imperfect tense, (1) They spoke '(*elaloun*) with tongues.' *Elaloun*' is the imperfect third plural of '*laleo*,' I speak. This means they spake with tongues then, and it was something that was repeated over and over again, something habitual or a gift. This is the exact meaning of the imperfect tense in Greek. (2) Then too, 'they prophesied.' The verb '*proepheteuon*' is the imperfect tense third plural of '*propheteuo*', I prophesy in the sense of speaking forth or expounding the Word of God. The use of the imperfect tense here means that they began to preach and expound God's word, and they continued to do so—a gift, the gift of prophesy, or the gift of preaching or teaching the Word of God." — *Christ's Paralyzed Church X-rayed*, p. 194,

When the Spirit of God is poured out upon people, six or even more people may be seen or heard doing the same thing at the same time, This can always be expected in the time of a great spiritual awakening, It would not be out of order for a dozen or even more people to call on God for mercy at the same time in a great camp meeting. And, may I say, it would not be out of order for a dozen or more people to leap, shout or praise God at the same time on such occasions. Just because a number of people have done the same thing on three or four different occasions would not justify one in saying that ever after when God's Spirit is poured out upon the people they must all do a certain thing because it so happened on previous occasions. I agree with Rev. Leroy McDowell who wrote:

> "The different manifestations which attend the receiving of the work of grace in the heart are about as varied as the characteristics of the people who receive them. To say that the manifestation would be the same in every case would be to say that all people are alike in disposition and temperament and that God's great purposes run in a rut, neither of which is true. There is nothing in Scripture, to my knowledge, that says God even intends to change the individuality of people, and of one thing we are very certain—God is a God of infinite variety.

> "We stand firmly against the teaching that the sure sign of the 'baptism of the Spirit' is that one speaks with an 'unknown tongue.' Shall we, then insist on

some other manifestation which is based equally upon the emotions or the physical senses? Let me illustrate: on one occasion a young man was seeking the experience of entire sanctification. Two young friends knelt beside him and attempted to lead him into the experience. One of them, calling him (the seeker) by name, said earnestly, 'When He comes into your heart you will feel a tingling clear out to the ends of your fingers!' 'That's right,' said the other, 'that's the way I felt when He came to me.'

"At this the young man sought even more diligently but God did not grant his request. Thank God that He didn't; for had He come in the manner in which He was sought for and expected, there would have been a fair beginning for a new sect among us which might eventually have been called 'The Tinglers'—whose essential demand would have been that all must tingle clear out to the ends of their fingers."[116]

I repeat; the Bible nowhere teaches that speaking in tongues is the initial, physical evidence of the baptism of the Holy Ghost. Paul and Luke are writing about the same thing, the GIFT of tongues. The late Principal George Jeffreys, founder and leader of the Elim Foursquare Gospel Alliance in the British Isle, whose work

---

[116] Rev. Leroy McDowell, in *The Wesleyan Message*, pp. 152-153.

as a Pentecostal minister no doubt surpassed that of any Pentecostal minister in the United States maintained that there is no difference. Here is his statement: "The speaking with tongues that accompanied the disciples at Pentecost was a gift as well as a sign." *Pentecostal Rays*, p, 221.

THE TRUE GIFT OF TONGUES — A REAL LANGUAGE

The word "tongue" when used with reference to the "gift of tongues" is found in the New Testament 28 times. Twenty-six times the word is translated from the Greek word *glossa,* which means "a foreign tongue, a language; to speak a dialect." One time (Acts 2:8) the word "tongue" (when referring to the "gift of tongues") is translated from the Greek word *dialektos,* meaning "the language of a country, especially the language of a special district." And one time (1 Cor. 14:21) this word "tongues" comes from the Greek word *heteroglossos,* meaning "a foreign language."

Webster says, "Tongue means a language, an intelligible language."

Funk and Wagnall's New Standard Dictionary says: "specifically, a language, vernacular, or dialect; as, the Latin tongue."

The New Century Dictionary defines the word thus: "The speech or language of a particular people, country, or locality (as the Hebrew tongue, the many tongues of India, the old Cornish tongue); a dialect."

In 1 Cor. 14:10 we read, "There are, it may be, so many kinds of voices in the world, and none of them is without signification." Moffatt translates: ". . . everyone of them meaning something."

On the day of Pentecost the disciples spoke a language. The inspired writer declares that "every man heard them speak in his own language (v. 6), At Caesarea (Acts 10:46) they spoke a language: "They heard them speaking in foreign languages and declaring the greatness of God." And at Ephesus, those who spoke in tongues spoke a language. The term "unknown tongue" does not appear in the original Greek text—it is not once used by any New Testament writer.

In the King James translation of 1 Cor. 14, the expression "unknown tongues" appears six times (1 Cor. 14:2, 4, 13 14, 19, 27), and in every single instance the word "unknown" has been italicized (i.e., printed in a slender, sloping kind of type) which means, as all real Bible students know, that the word does not appear in the original writings of St, Paul. The true gift of tongues is a real, living, intelligible language. Observation reveals that much of the so-called "speaking in tongues" today is but fanatical gibberish, unintelligible speech, whereas the true manifestation is a real, living, lucid, active, plain and intelligible language. On the day of Pentecost, ". . . every man heard them speak in his own language." St. Paul instructs all who speak in tongues to ". . . pray that he may interpret . . ." (1 Cor. 14:13) because it is "better to speak five words that can be understood"; ". . . so as to instruct others also, than ten thousand words in a tongue." (Weymouth).

THE PURPOSE OF THIS SPIRITUAL GIFT

The primary object in giving gifts is for the edification of the church. St, Paul says, "The manifestation of the Spirit is given to every man to profit withal." (1 Cor. 12:17); ". . . for the profit of all." (Conybeare and Howson); ". . . for the common good." (Weymouth, 5th Edition); ". . . for the general good." (Twentieth Century New Testament); ". . . for the benefit of all." (Emphatic Diaglott).

Matthew Henry says: "Spiritual gifts are bestowed only that men may with them profit the Church and promote Christianity."

Dr. Adam Clarke says: "God has given no gift to any man for his own private advantage or exclusive profit."

Dr. Hodge comments: "They are not designed exclusively for the gratification of the recipient, but for the good of the Church."

Peake's Bible Commentary states: "The edification of the Church is the governing principle."

Notice that speaking in tongues in a public service is not to be permitted unless it can be interpreted. St. Paul said: "If any man speak in an unknown tongue, let it be by two, or at the most three, and that by course, and let one interpret. But if there be no interpreter, let him keep silence in the church." (1 Cor. 14:27, 28); "If there is no interpreter, let the speaker keep quiet in church" (Moffatt); "If there is no one to explain it, have him keep quiet in church" (Goodspeed); "But if there be no interpreter, let him who speaks in tongues keep silent in the congregation and speak in private to himself and God alone" (Conybeare and Howson).

One who has the true gift of tongues should not speak in a public service unless there is an interpreter present, seeing it would cause confusion, and God is not the author of confusion. When God poured out his Spirit on the people at Pentecost and enabled them to speak with tongues, they were understood.

SPEAKING IN TONGUES — AN INFERIOR GIFT

St, Paul places tongues at the bottom of the list in 1 Cor. 12:28. He says: "And God hath set some in the church, first apostles, secondarily prophets, thirdly teachers, after that miracles, then gifts of healings, helps, governments, diversities of tongues."

The *Abingdon Bible Commentary* states: "St. Paul discouraged the seeking of the gifts that would not, of themselves, edify the body of Christ . . . the Church. Paul does not dispute the reality of this experience. But he counts it inferior to prophecy, which is also inspired utterance, for the latter (preacher) edifies, comforts, consoles, while the exercise of tongues, though it may edify the performer himself, brings no revelation of truth, nor insight into spiritual values, nor inspiration, nor instruction to the assembled church (vv. 9-11)."

Matthew Henry wrote: "They are placed here (1 Cor. 12:28) in their proper rank, those of most value first."

The *Bible Commentary* says: "In this list of gifts the utterance of tongues is placed last as being least"

Harold Horton, outstanding Pentecostal preacher, makes the following statement in his book, *What is the Good of Speaking in Tongues*: "We certainly do not look upon this gift as the most important, but rather as one of the least of the supernatural gifts."

Dr. James McKnight writes: "In placing these members, God, in his sovereign and unerring wisdom, appointed some to the first and most honorable office of Apostle . . . lastly persons who have the gift of speaking different kinds of foreign languages."

The conclusion of sound Biblical scholarship may be summed up in the following words as taken from *The People's Bible Encyclopedia*: "The comparison of gifts, in both the lists given by St. Paul (1 Cor. 12:8, 10; 28-30) places that of tongues and the interpretation of tongues lowest in the scale." (See article "Gift of Tongues").

At this point, it is essential to make it crystal clear that it is not the author's intention to minimize, in the slightest degree, the reality of the true manifestation of speaking in tongues as the Spirit gives utterance. God himself set "tongues" in the church the same time He set the other eight gifts in the church, and they are all in the church today. However, I certainly do not believe that all preachers, healers, etc., have a true gift from God. Neither do I believe that all who speak in tongues have a true gift from God. I shall give here reasons why I believe that most people who speak in tongues (as they say) have a false tongue, not a true manifestation of the Spirit:

This new doctrine began with the modern Pentecostal movement, which started in 1906, and at the present time there are over a hundred sects in America teaching this doctrine. Among these are the International Church of the Foursquare Gospel, the Pentecostal Fire Baptized Holiness Church, Calvary Pentecostal, the Pentecostal Assemblies of the World, The Church of God and Saints of Christ, the Assemblies of God, the Pentecostal Holiness Church, The United Pentecostal Church, the International Pentecostal Assemblies, the Pentecostal Church of God in America, the Catholic Apostolic Church or Irvingites, Father Divine's Peace Mission, Apostolic Faith Mission, and other bodies too numerous to mention. They believe that every person who is truly baptized with the Holy Spirit will speak in tongues and that there is no fully Scriptural baptism unless a person speaks in tongues at least once.

Seven reasons I hold that most of the Pentecostal people do not have the true Bible tongues.

First, they did not get what they got the Bible way. Thousands of the people were compelled to say "hallelujah," "hallelujah"; "glory, glory"; "Jesus, Jesus"; "praise Him, praise Him"; or some such words for a long time, yes, hours in many instances in order to get the so-called "baptism." They would not have got it any other way. As one of six rules for people to follow if they would be baptized with the Holy Spirit, Jonathan D. Bright, Pentecostal, says: "Bless God continually! The 120 received the baptism with the Holy Ghost because they were continually in the Temple, praising and blessing God." See his book, *The Baptism of the Holy Ghost*, p, 28.

Mr. Bright read Luke 24:52-53 where it says: "and they worshipped him, and returned to Jerusalem with great joy: and were continually in the temple, praising and blessing God in the temple when they were baptized with the Holy Spirit on the Day of Pentecost,

Mr. Ralph Riggs, Pentecostal, believes as Mr. Bright does that the apostles were in the temple "praising and blessing God" when they were baptized with the Holy Spirit because he writes:

> "The twelve or rather the eleven, were told to tarry in the city of Jerusalem until they be endued with power from on high, Luke 24:49. 'These all continued with one accord in prayer and supplication,' Acts 1:14. 'And were continually in the temple, praising and blessing God,' Luke 24:53. They obeyed and waited; they asked by prayer and supplication (insistent asking); they believed and expressed their faith by praising and blessing God. Did he meet them on this pathway of faith? They were all filled with the Holy Ghost, and began to speak with other tongues as the Spirit gave them utterance. Acts. 2:4"

—The Spirit Himself, by Ralph M. Riggs, p. 108.

Mr. Bright and Mr. Riggs are no doubt sincere in their belief and their teaching that the apostles were in the Temple in Jerusalem "praising and blessing God" for several days before they were baptized with the Holy Spirit. It is on the basis of this false assumption that honest, conscientious, sincere people, many of them Christians, have been instructed to "praise and bless God" (?) for hours, and in some instances days, before receiving what thousands regard as "the initial, physical evidence of the baptism with the Holy Spirit." One dear man said 'I myself, I believe, have spent well over two hundred hours in tarrying meetings, without as yet, I am sorry to say, having received my baptism."

    —By Elmer C. Miller in *Pentecost Examined*, p. 122.

    The truth is the apostles were not in the Temple "praising and blessing God" when they were baptized with the Holy Spirit. The Bible says they were in a "house" (Acts 1:13). Dr. Paul E. Kretzmann writes: "They went to their usual meeting place, to the upper chamber, probably in the house of one of the disciples. The disciples held public meetings in the Temple (Luke 24:53) principally in the interest of mission work. But for mutual consolation and encouragement they met at the house of members of the congregation."

    —*The Popular Commentary of the Bible*, vol. 1, p. 535.

    Dr. Albert Barnes writes: "Some have supposed that the upper room here (Acts 1:13) designated, was one of the rooms of the Temple. But there is no evidence of that; and it is not very probable. Such a room was a part of every house, especially in Jerusalem; and they probably selected one where they might be together, and yet so retired that they might be safe from the Jews."

    —*Notes on Acts of the Apostles*

    Whedon's Commentary: "Probably the same as the room of the Pentecost. Not, as some have supposed, in the temple, for the Jewish authorities would not have permitted so bold proceedings on the part of the disciples of the lately crucified Christ."

Dr. Adam Clark says: "The room here (in Acts 1:13) mentioned seems to have been the place where all the apostles lodged on *esan katamenontes* (where they were staying), and therefore most probably a private house." See his comments on Acts 1:13 in his original edition.

Dean Henry Alford: "It is in the highest degree 'the improbable' that the disciples would be found assembled in any public place at this time. The upper chamber was perhaps that in which the last supper had been taken; probably that in which they had been since then assembled (John 20:19, 26)' but certainly one in a private house."

—*The New Testament for English Readers*, p, 649.

Dr. A. T. Robertson: "It was in a private house as in Luke 22:11 and not in the temple as Luke 24:53 might imply."

—*Word Pictures in the New Testament*, vol. 3, p, 13.

I repeat, the disciples were not in the Temple shouting "hallelujah, hallelujah, hallelujah," or "glory, glory, glory," or "praise Him, praise Him, praise Him," or some other word or words until they were baptized with the Holy Spirit. There is no record of anyone anywhere doing such a thing in Bible times.

2. Thousands of Pentecostal people who supposedly speak in tongues do not speak an understandable language, one that can be interpreted. On the Day of Pentecost the 120 spoke an understandable language when

they were baptized with the Holy Spirit. Luke, the inspired historian tells us plainly that "every man heard them (the 120) speak in his own language." (Acts 2:6) They said one to another "how hear we every man in our own tongue, wherein we were born?" (Acts 2:7) The Parthians, the Medes, the Elamites, the Judeans and others knew that the disciples were speaking an earthly language. Why would Luke tell us the 120 spoke an earthly language when they were baptized with the Holy Spirit if they did not? All this talk about the disciples speaking in "unknown tongues" or speaking an heavenly language—one that is unknown to man, on the Day of Pentecost, is a waste of time and energy because there is absolutely no Scriptural support to be found anywhere for such a statement. We know what the 120 Galileans were talking about when they were "speaking in tongues" because Luke, the inspired historian has told us. He says they were talking about "the wonderful works of God." (Acts 2:11) "The triumphs of God"— Moffatt. "The mighty wonders of God". Norlie, "The great wonders of God," Williams. "The marvelous acts of God"—Feuton. They said "we all alike hear these Galileans speaking in our own languages about the wonderful things which God has done,"—Weymouth 3rd ed. Had they not spoken an understandable language the unbelieving Jews would not have said: "we all hear these men telling in our own language what great things God has done."—Montgomery. "It is probable", says Matthew Henry, "that the apostles spoke of Christ, and redemption by him, and the grace of the gospel; these are indeed the great things of God, which will be forever, marvelous in our eyes."—*Matthew Henry's Commentary*, Vol. 6, verse 11. Dr. Adams Clark thought the expression "wonderful works of

God" could be interpreted to mean "such as the incarnation of Christ, his various miracles, preaching death, resurrection and ascension—and the design of God to save the world through him." Vol. 5, verse 11.

When writing on this point of the 120 Galileans speaking an understandable language on the Day of Pentecost, the late D. N. Buntain, Pentecost, who was "for eight years . . . General Superintendent of the nation-wide fellowship, and traveled across the Dominion of Canada from coast to coast, and afterwards served as Principal of the Canadian North West Bible Institute until the time of his death had this to say:

> "We read that when these folk were filled with the Holy Ghost, they 'began to speak with other tongues as the Spirit gave them utterance.' It is not said that they spoke with unknown tongues, but with other tongues, The expression 'unknown tongues' was never used by an inspired writer. In the Epistle to the Corinthians it is found in the English version but the word 'unknown' is in italics, showing that it is not taken from the original. On the Day of Pentecost God awakened men to listen to the gospel truths. As the awaiting company received the promise of the Father, they burst forth speaking in languages they had never learned. Whether or not they knew what they were saying, God knew and the listeners knew. He caused his people to speak in the very languages ("tongues") that the multitude would understand."

I repeat, thousands of our Pentecostal friends who think they have been baptized with the Holy Spirit and speak in tongues according to Acts 2:4 do not speak an intelligible, understandable language, and, therefore, do not have an experience according to Acts 2:4.

3. Because of the methods they used to get what they call the "initial, physical evidence of the Baptism with the Holy Spirit."

From 1906, the time when the modern Pentecostal Movement began, until 1947 most of the Pentecostal people were told to say "hallelujah, hallelujah", or "praise Him, praise Him," or "Jesus" or some similar ejaculation constantly and persistently for an extended period of time as rapidly as possible until the incoherent sounds which are considered the "speaking in tongues" began.

In 1949 another method was introduced. One could have the Holy Spirit imparted to him by some preacher or layman.

Rev. Paul W. Stewart and Barbara Franzen wrote: "We know that the baptism of the Holy Ghost is a gift of God. But we must face the fact that the Lord administers this baptism by imparting this gift to believers through the laying on of the hands of those who have this ministry."

—Impartation, page 52.

Mr. Theodore Fitch writes: "In . . . great mass meetings where the Lord has poured out His Spirit, hundreds have received their baptism, Those in charge have the seekers seated in rows about five feet apart. This gives the workers a chance to work freely.

"Each day of the revival someone instructs the class, also the workers. When hands are laid on the seekers, about half of them receive their baptism. They usually come through, speaking in tongues, at the rate of about one every minute,

"He who is in charge can address the class in this manner: 'After about ten minutes of instruction, we will all kneel and pray earnestly for three minutes. In this manner everyone can become lost in prayer, as it were, and come into a state of spiritual ecstasy. Then we will all arise and be seated.

"First, you close your eyes and keep them closed. Raise your hands and praise the Lord Jesus until hands are laid upon you. Then you must stop talking. Do not say one more word in English. The Holy Ghost cannot speak in His language if you insist on talking in your language. Just open your mouth, yield to the Spirit, and He will speak."

—*Spiritual Gifts Being Restored*, pp, 42, 43.

Today there is a faster, quicker way to receive the Holy Spirit and speak in tongues "as the Spirit gives utterance" according to Mr. Harold Horton, Pentecost, and author of the book titled, *Gifts of the Spirit*. He writes: "Since Pentecost it is both unnecessary and un-scriptural to tarry. The order now is 'Drink,' p, 3.

"Not one after Pentecost was ever invited or ex-pected to Tarry, or praise or sing or even pray for the baptism, or the coming of the Comforter." p. 6

"If any man thirst, let him come unto me, and drink of salvation or the Spirit, Jesus paid it all. There is absolutely nothing for me to do but to drink of what He in mercy offers. p. 8.

"I have heard some employ a cynical word in reference to this direct route. They say that those who teach seekers the Scriptural way of drinking at once of the Spirit, are 'railroading' them into the baptism. Is not 'railroading better than globe-trotting?' If I could, I would not only 'rail-road' them into the heavenly blessing; I would 'spit-fire,' 'Jet-plane' them into the glorious experience of the Holy Spirit!"

—*Receiving Without Tarrying*, pp. 3, 6, 8, 9.

Speaking in tongues IS NOT the "initial, physical evidence of the baptism with the Holy Spirit" as we have proved.

Bear this fact in mind, men can no more impart the Holy Spirit than they can impart salvation. A Bible experience of salvation or Holy Spirit baptism can only be obtained by counting the cost and paying the Bible price.

4. Sinners can get what most of the Pentecostal people regard as the "initial, physical evidence" of the baptism of the Holy Spirit. I say this because some Pentecostal people baptize sinners; they believe that in water baptism sins can be literally washed away. After the sinner has been baptized he is told to tarry for the Holy Ghost (?) i.e., say "glory, glory;" "hallelujah, hallelujah" or some similar ejaculation constantly and persistently for an extended period of time as rapidly as he can, until the incoherent sounds which are considered the "speaking in tongues" begins. Truly this is a false

and most deceiving doctrine. Some people are speaking the so-called "tongues", but are not so much as living good moral lives.

5. Most people who have received what they call the "initial, physical evidence" of the baptism of the Holy Spirit cannot keep still in church when they should. If a person with the gift of prophecy, which is even greater than the gift of tongues (1 Cor. 14:5), can keep still, surely one with the gift of tongues, the least gift, can keep still. The Word plainly says: "If there be no interpreter, let him (the one who has received the gift of tongues) keep silence in the church; and let him speak to himself and to God." (1 Cor. 14: 28). Now all manifestations of the Holy Spirit are impromptu at the baptism, but afterwards almost entirely under the control of the recipient.

6. The Pentecostal people themselves do not believe that all who "speak in tongues" in the Pentecostal Movement have the baptism of the Holy Spirit. Some who supposedly "speak in tongues" have had to be expelled from the movement because of their being guilty of gross sin, in some cases immorality.

In Matthew 19:8 we read of "false witnesses."
In II Timothy 3:2 we read of "false accusers."
In Galatians 2:4 we read of "false brethren."
In II Peter 2:1 we read of "false teachers."
In Matthew 24:24 we read of "false Christs."
In II Corinthians 11:13 we read of "false prophets."

In Matthew 24:24 we read of "false Christs." And there are "false tongues". I am confident that most of the modern Pentecostal people have "false tongues." It is "by their fruits" that we know those who are baptized with the Holy Spirit. It has been well said, that, "You can hang gifts on a dead tree, but it takes a live tree to bring forth fruit."

Robert Chandler Dalton states in his book: "The power of evil spirits to speak in 'tongues' is an attested fact. This makes the gift of discernment of spirits absolutely a necessity for Pentecostal people."

—*Tongues Like as of Fire*, p. 118.

7. Many members of Pentecostal churches who spoke in tongues when they were fellowshipped into the church, never stopped talking in tongues after they were ex-communicated on account of some gross sins they had actually committed. Thus we see that backsliders can keep what is called the "Bible evidence" of Holy Spirit baptism.

In Bible times when the evil spirit was cast out of a person the man or woman could no longer do the things that he had been doing with the aid of that spirit. When the evil spirit left, the unmistakable evidences of his indwelling went with him. They were seen no more. And so it is, when a person who has been truly baptized with the Holy Spirit loses the Holy Spirit out of his heart and life, the unmistakable signs or evidences or His indwelling can be seen no more. They are gone. Bear this fact in mind when a person can talk in tongues AFTER he has backslid he was definitely deceived in thinking that he had been baptized with the Holy Spirit because he could talk in "tongues."

Dr. Charles E. Brown says: "What commonly passes for the gift of tongues among the Pentecostal people is not the gift of tongues described in the Bible. It is, we affirm, only a form of mental excitement commonly called hysteria. The scientific people would probably call it psychoneurosis. In popular language, this babbling and jabbering is the product of hysterical excitement. One evidence of this is the fact that it has often happened that a person who had the gift of tongues backslid and went into sin and still found that his gift was just as good as it had ever been, which was proof that it was of the natural man from the beginning." —*Questions and Answers*, pp. 131-132.

One minister who speaks in tongues said recently: "We believe persons can, and perhaps some do, speak in 'unknown tongues' who are not saved and have never been filled with the Holy Spirit. This is tragic!"

I repeat, sinners can get the so-called Bible "evidence of the baptism with the Holy Spirit" and backsliders can keep it. And this is tragic.

I hold with Dr. Oswald J. Smith who said: "There are four great results that follow the anointing, four evidences that can neither be disputed nor counterfeited. The first is victory over sin; the second, power in service; the third, the fruit of the Spirit; and the fourth a burden for souls. Now, I care not what else you may have received, even though visions and revelations have been yours—they fade into insignificance in the face of these four tremendous results. You may think you have the gift of tongues, but if these four results are lacking, you have never been anointed with the Holy Ghost."

SOME QUESTIONS ANSWERED

1. Did Jesus speak in unknown tongues while He was hanging on the cross?

Answer: Our Lord did not speak in "unknown tongues" while hanging on the cross. In fact, there is no such thing as an "unknown tongue." We know exactly what Jesus said,— see Matt. 27:46.

2. Does Mark 16:17 teach that speaking in tongues is for all the true people of God?

Answer: No, Since all are not supposed to drink something "deadly," "take up serpents," or "cast out devils," neither are all supposed to speak in other tongues.

3. I heard a preacher say: "When you go down town to buy a pair of shoes, you do not ask for tongues, you ask for shoes; tongues come with the shoes."

Answer: The preacher who made that statement was hard pressed for an argument. Tongues do not always come "with the shoes"; neither does the "gift of tongues" always accompany the baptism with the Holy Spirit.

4. I have been told that you must speak once, if no more, in "tongues" in order to know that you have received your baptism. Is this true?

Answer: It is not true. Speaking in tongues is mentioned in seven chapters in the New Testament (Mark 16:17; Acts 2:10; 19; I Cor. 12; 13; 14); the word "must" appears in only one of these chapters (Acts 19:21) and in that case is used totally irrelevant of the subject of speaking in tongues.

5. Does not John 16:13 prove that when the Holy Ghost "moves in" He will invariably speak in some foreign tongue?

Answer: No, There is absolutely no proof what ever that He will always speak some foreign language such as Turkish, Lappish, Kamba Bantu, Mishito, etc. The doctrine that advocates this type of manifestation is of human origin and misleading.

It is an incontrovertible fact that He (the Holy Spirit) can speak through anyone whom He fills in one's OWN NATIVE TONGUE as He did on the day of Pentecost. (See pages 6 to 12 of this booklet).

6. Does not Paul say that when a person speaks in "unknown tongues" he "speaketh mysteries" and therefore not an earthly language? (1 Cor. 14:2). No.

In 1 Cor. 14 Paul gives ten reasons one should not speak in tongues in public if the message is not going to be interpreted: (1) "He speaketh not unto men but unto God," (2) "No man understandeth him," (3) "He speaketh mysteries," In verses 4 to 23, we can see that seven more reasons given are: (4) he edifies himself alone (vs. 4); (5) he does not edify his hearers (vss. 4-5); (6) he speaks "into the air" (vs. 9); (7) he will be a "barbarian" to his hearers (vs. 11); (8) his understanding will be unfruitful" (vs. 14) (9) those hearing him will not be able to say "amen" to his praying, singing or "giving of thanks" (vss. 15, 16); (10) People will say that he is mad" (vs. 23).

Yes, with no interpreter he would be speaking "mysteries" to the "unlearned" or "unbelievers". "Wherefore, let him that speaketh in an unknown tongue pray that he may interpret. (vs. 13).

7. Where does the Bible say that speaking in tongues is "the initial, physical evidence of the baptism with the Holy Spirit?"

Answer: This statement does not appear in the Bible. Neither are the words "initial" or "physical" to he found in the Bible.

8. Why do some leading ministers suppress all favorable comment on speaking in tongues? Can it be that they do not even believe that speaking in tongues is one of the evidences of the baptism of the Holy Spirit?

Answer: Perhaps those who suppress all favorable comment on speaking in tongues should be called upon to answer this question. However, I personally believe that the true gift of tongues that God set in the church (1 Cor. 12:28) is still in the church (not in every local assembly). In most cases, what is called the "gift of tongues" today is nothing more than an imitation of a true manifestation.

9. Is it possible for one to have the true "gift of tongues" and not understand what he says when he speaks?

Answer: I sincerely believe that one may have the true "gift of tongues" and not understand what he says when he speaks. In fact, I see no other way to explain 1 Cor. 14:13, where Paul plainly says: "So let a man who has the gift of tongues pray for the power of interpreting them." (Weymouth's New Testament in Modern Speech). See also I Cor. 14:27-28.

10. If those who spoke in tongues in the days of the apostles did not understand what they were talking about, was it edifying to them?

Answer: "The edification that came to one possessing the gift did not consist in the fact that he understood the revelation given him, but in the fact that his spiritual experience was built up and quickened by reason of the consciousness that he had been a vessel God had "designed to use, for no man can surrender himself really, truly, and fully to the full purposes of the Holy Spirit and his whole nature not be edified and blessed."

—Dr. William Evans, *Question Box*, p, 78.

THINGS TO REMEMBER

1. Some of the 120 Galileans DID NOT speak with tongues when they were baptized with the Holy Spirit on the Day of Pentecost; they praised God in their native tongue,

2. Some of the first converts of the apostles DID NOT speak with tongues when they were baptized with the Holy Spirit (Acts 4:31). They received the gift of prophecy (preaching,)

3. The Bible does not say which one of the gifts was given to the Samaritan Christians when they were baptized with the Holy Spirit. Some of them, no doubt, received the gift of prophecy.

4. Three days BEFORE "brother Saul" was baptized with the Holy Spirit he received his call to the ministry (Acts 26:13-20). Nowhere is it recorded that he spoke with tongues BEFORE he received the gift of prophecy or preaching.

5. The Ephesian Christians received two gifts, the gift of tongues and the gift of prophecy. For many Christians the gift of prophecy was an initial, physical evidence that they were baptized with the Holy Spirit.

6. According to available records the MAJORITY of the great saints who lived in the nineteenth century

DID NOT speak with tongues when they were baptized with the Holy Spirit.

7. Since the MAJORITY of the great saints who lived in the nineteenth century DID NOT speak with tongues when they were baptized with the Holy Spirit, we know that speaking with tongues does not always accompany the baptism with the Holy Spirit.

8. The doctrine which teaches that speaking with tongues is the initial, physical evidence of the baptism with the Holy Spirit is without Scriptural support.

9. The doctrine which teaches that speaking with tongues is the initial physical evidence of the baptism with the Holy Spirit cannot be supported by church history.

10. Speaking with tongues as on the Day of Pentecost is one of the gifts of the Spirit.

11. Speaking with tongues as on the Day of Pentecost is one of the least of the gifts of the Spirit.

12. Speaking with tongues as on the Day of Pentecost is a living, live, active, intelligent language that can be interpreted.

Undeniable Facts About Speaking in Tongues.
by C. M. Washington

A Sermon Preached at the

INTERNATIONAL CAMP MEETING
of the
CHURCH OF GOD
Anderson, Indiana

PREFACE

This sermon has been prepared and published in response to several requests that came for it immediately after it was delivered at our international Camp Meeting, Anderson, Indiana, June 18, 1936.

Trusting that the inspired truths contained herein will be helpful to those who are seeking light.

I commit it to the public,
C. M. WASHINGTON

UNDENIABLE FACTS ABOUT
SPEAKING IN TONGUES

"God hath set some in the Church, first Apostles, secondarily prophets, thirdly teachers, after that miracles, then gifts of healing, helps, governments, diversities of Tongues.

"Are all apostles? Are all prophets? Are all teachers? Are all workers of miracles? Have all the gifts of healing? Do all speak with tongues? Do all interpret?" (1 Cor. 12:28-30)

Tongues Means Language

There are 260 Chapters in the New Testament and the word "tongue" or "tongues" when referring to one of the manifestations of the Holy Spirit is found in only seven (7) Chapters.

Twenty-seven times the word "Tongue" is translated from the Greek word (Glossa) which means 'a foreign Tongue', a LANGUAGE, to speak a dialect.

One time the word "Tongue" is translated from the Greek word (Eteroglosis) which means "A foreign LANGUAGE."

One time the word "Tongue" is translated from the Greek word (Dialektos) which means 'The LANGUAGE of a country, especially the LANGUAGE of a special district.'

Webster says: "Tongue means LANGUAGE."

Funk and Wagnall's Dictionary says: "A Tongue is the speech or LANGUAGE of some one people, country or race."

St. Paul says: "There are it may be, so many kinds of voices in the world, and none of them is without signification." (1 Cor. 14:10)

Moffatt translates this verse "There are ever so many kinds of LANGUAGES in the world, every one of them meaning something."

"And no one unmeaning"—Emphatic Diaglott,

"Each with its own meaning"—Goodspeed.

"Not one of them without meaning"—Syriac.

"And not one of them fails to convey meaning"— 20th Century New Testament.

The Pentecostal 'tongue' then, was not a jargon, babble, gabble, chatter, twaddle, jabber, gibberish, rapid or unintelligible speech, but a LANGUAGE, an intelligible LANGUAGE.

When God poured out His Spirit on the Day of Pentecost, the people spoke not in an unknown 'tongue' but in a living, an intelligible LANGUAGE. "The multitude came together, and were confounded, because that every man heard them speak in his own LANGUAGE." (Acts 2:6)

"Each one heard them speaking in his own LANGUAGE."—Goodspeed.

"Everyone heard his own LANGUAGE spoken."—Weymouth (3rd Ed.)

"Each of them heard the disciples in his own LANGUAGE."—20th Century New Testament.

The multitude was astounded, amazed, bewildered. "They were all amazed and marvelled, saying one to another, Behold, are not all these which speak Galileans? And how hear we every man in our own tongue wherein we were born?" (Verses 8, 9)

"How then does each of us hear his own native LANGUAGE spoken by them?"—(Weymouth 3rd Ed.)

"Then how is it that we each of us hear them in our own native LANGUAGE."—20th Century New Testament.

And what were the disciples talking about? And was their talk edifying? Yes, Thank God! It was edifying to all who heard it. The multitude declared that,

"We do hear them speak in our tongue the wonderful Works of God."—Verse 11.

"We hear them speak in our LANGUAGES the wonders of God."—Syriac.

"We hear these men talking of the triumphs of God in our own LANGUAGE."—Moffatt.

"We all alike hear these Galileans speaking in our own LANGUAGE about the wonderful things which has done."—Weymouth (3rd Ed.)

I repeat, the Pentecostal tongue, the kind that God's approval rests upon is a LANGUAGE, an intelligible language, capable of being understood and interpreted. Any other kind of tongue is a counterfeit, yea, is not of God.

At Caesarea, the people of God spoke, not an "unknown tongue," BUT A LANGUAGE; and at Ephesus, the sacred writer clearly states that: "When Paul had laid his hands upon them (about twelve men) they spake with tongues and prophesied." Acts 19:6. "And they began to speak with 'tongues' and to preach."— 20th Century. Truly, truly, the kind of 'Tongues' that God gives and the only kind that He recognizes is the kind that is intelligible, such as was given on the Day of

Pentecost, at Caesarea, and at Ephesus. I repeat, any other kind of tongue is not of God, it is a counterfeit.

Someone says: "What about speaking in 'Unknown tongues'?" I ask, where do you find the expression, "Unknown tongues?" St. Mark didn't write anything about "Unknown tongues;" St. Luke, when writing the book of Acts did not say anything about "unknown tongues;" and St. Paul never wrote anything about "Unknown tongues" in any of his epistles. It's true that we see the word 'Unknown' six times in the 14th Chapter of 1st Corinthians, but St. Paul did not write it. The men that translated our Bible from the Greek language into the English put it there. Get your Bible, turn to the 14th Chapter of 1 Corinthians and note carefully how the word 'Unknown' is printed in verses 2, 4, 13, 14, 19, and 27. You can see that the type is different. Such words are not in the original Greek. I repeat, the expression "Unknown tongues" is not to be found in any of the writings of St. Paul. No New Testament apostle ever preached, taught, or wrote anything about "Unknown tongues." "Tongue" means LANGUAGE and all LANGUAGES are known, and may be translated or interpreted. There is no such thing as an "Unknown tongue!"

Conclusive Proof That Speaking in Tongues and the Gift of Tongues Are the Same

The Pentecostal people teach that there is a difference in "Speaking in tongues as the Spirit gives utterance" and the "gift of tongues." They say that the tongues given on the Day of Pentecost is different than that mentioned by St. Paul in his epistle to the Corinthians. If a person should talk in tongues during public worship and you would tell him he should keep still because there was no one present to interpret what was being said, and should you quote where Paul said "If there be no interpreter let him keep silence in the Church" (1 Cor. 14:28), the Pentecostal people would tell you that Paul was not writing about speaking in tongues as the Spirit gives utterance but was giving instructions about the public exercise of the "Gift of Tongues."

Have you ever spoken in Tongues? Did you speak in tongues when you received the Holy Spirit? If not, the pentecostal people will tell you that you have NEVER received the Holy Spirit as an abiding Comforter, and should you quote the writings of St. Paul where he said, "Do all speak with Tongues" (1 Cor. 12:30), to prove that speaking in tongues as the Spirit gives utterance is not for all, they, the Pentecostal people, will tell you that St. Paul meant that all don't have the "Gift of Tongues." They will tell you that St. Paul is not writing about "Speaking in tongues as the Spirit gives utterance." They teach and would have us believe that there is a difference in "Speaking in tongues as the Spirit gives utterance" and "the Gift of Tongues." Here are their own words taken from their own writings.

1—"There is a difference in the speaking of tongues mentioned in the New Testament. On the day of Pentecost they all spake with tongues "as the Spirit gave utterance." In the 14th Chapter of 1st Corinthians Paul is dealing altogether with "the gift of tongues."—Ohio

2—"It is generally believed that the 'tongues' mentioned by the Acts of the Apostles as on the day of Pentecost is not the same as in the 14th Chapter of first Corinthians which is termed "Gift of tongues.""—Tennessee.

3—"It is true," says one, "that St. Paul taught that all should not receive the GIFT OF TONGUES (1 Cor. 12:10, 30), and that in the Church he would rather speak five words with his understanding, that by his voice he might teach others also, than ten thousand words in an UNKNOWN TONGUE (1 Cor. 14:9); and, if there be no interpreter, let him keep silence in the Church (1 Cor. 14:28); but nowhere did Paul condemn TONGUES, and besides; Paul is here writing about an entirely different and distinct kind of TONGUES than that which we have mentioned in the book of Acts."—Ohio.

4—"This doctrine, says another, is sometimes questioned on Scriptural grounds because of Paul's statement in the subjunctive mood in 1 Cor. 12:30 "Do all speak with tongues?" But on examination of the context we find that Paul is dealing here exclusively with the subject of Spiritual gifts as permanently residing in the various members of the body of Christ for the edification of the whole. The question of the proper experience of believers when personally receiving the fullness of the Holy Spirit does not come up here at all, and any attempt to wrest this statement from its proper application must result in confusion.

"To recognize a proper distinction between speaking with tongues as the initial evidence of receiving the Baptism of the Holy Ghost and the gift of tongues in the Church is both justifiable and necessary to prevent confusion in doctrine and application. The book of Acts deals with the first phase of this manifestation; the Epistle to the Corinthians with the second."—Missouri

Now my friends, you can clearly see that the advocates of this Modern tongues theory teach that there is a difference in "speaking in tongues as the Spirit gives utterance" and the "gift of tongues."

They say that St. Paul writes about a different kind of tongues than that given on the day of Pentecost. "St. Paul," they say, "writes about the 'gift of tongues', and not 'speaking in tongues as the Spirit gives utterance'." One of their writers says "For our information concerning the manifestation given to believers when baptized in the Spirit we are entirely shut up to the instances . . . noted in the book of Acts."

"St. Paul," says one, "is writing about an entirely different and distinct kind of tongues than that mentioned in the book of Acts."

Now I shall prove to you that they are COMPELLED to believe that St. Paul is writing about 'Speaking in tongues as the Spirit gives utterance.' They know that St. Paul emphatically declares that all do not speak with tongues, but in order to win more converts, they say, "St. Paul meant that all would not speak with the "GIFT OF TONGUES."

Note how they answer these six questions. (1) Did St. Paul ever speak in tongues as the Spirit gives utterance? They say "Yes." (2) Did any of the Corinthians ever speak in Tongues as the Spirit gives utterance? They say, "Yes." (3) Is it true that one may speak as the Spirit gives utterance and not know what he is talking about? Again they say, "Yes." (4) Does one edify himself when speaking in tongues as the Spirit gives utterance if he doesn't understand what he is talking about? "Yes," so they say. (5) Is it possible for one to speak in tongues as the Spirit gives utterance more than once? They say, "Yes." (6) Should one who speaks in tongues as the Spirit gives utterance be permitted to do so in a public service. The Pentecostal people say, "Yes."

They, the Pentecostal people, say "yes" to all six of these questions, but where do they go to get the proof? They cannot find it in St. Mark's Gospel; they cannot find it in Acts of the Apostles. (1) Where, I ask, do they get their proof for saying that St. Paul spoke in Tongues as the Spirit gave him utterance? I'll tell you, they get it from Paul's writings. (2) Where do they get their proof for saying that some of the Corinthians spoke in tongues as the Spirit gave them utterance? From the writings of St. Paul. (3) Where do they get their proof for saying that one may speak in tongues as the Spirit gives utterance and not know what he is talking about? From the writings of St. Paul. (4) Where do they get their proof for saying that one edifies himself when speaking in tongues as the Spirit gives utterance, even though he doesn't understand what he is talking about? From the writings of St. Paul. (5) Where do they get their proof for saying that one who speaks in tongues as the Spirit gives utterance should be permitted to do so in public worship? From the writings of St. Paul.

My friends, the Pentecostal people go to the writings of St. Paul to prove these six things that they believe and teach about speaking in tongues as the Spirit gives utterance. In fact they CANNOT get conclusive proof for these six things anywhere else, and they know it. I have long since discovered that the Pentecostal people teach some things that are not true but here are six more things to be added to the list if St. Paul is not writing about the same kind of tongues as that mentioned in Acts of the Apostles. I'll admit that there is a whole lot of repetition in what I am saying, but I want all who are seeking for the truth to know that St. Paul IS WRITING about the same kind of tongues as that mentioned in St. Mark 16:17, 18; Acts 2:4, Acts 10:46, and Acts 19:6. If the Pentecostal people insist that St. Paul is not writing about speaking in tongues as the Spirit gives utterance, I kindly ask them to stop teaching these six things, because there is no conclusive proof for them outside of Paul's writings.

(1) You ask me, "How many should speak in tongues as the Spirit gives utterance during public worship?" I answer, not more than three and that by course—one at a time, while some one interprets what is being said.

(2) You ask, "If there is no interpreter present should they speak?" I answer, no! Not even ONE of them. They should all keep "silent," "quiet," "still."

(3) You ask, "Is it true that all who have been baptized with the Holy Spirit, spoke in tongues according to Acts 2:4?" No, it is not true.

"Where is your proof?" you ask. My proof is found in the writings of St. Paul, in the writings of St. Paul.

The Pentecostal people, as I have shown, quote the writings of St. Paul as conclusive proof for six things that they teach about speaking in tongues as the Spirit gives utterance. They cannot get such proof anywhere else, and they know it. But if St. Paul is not writing about the same kind of tongues as that mentioned in

Acts then these six things are all wrong and they should stop teaching them. The undeniable fact is this: St. Paul is writing about the same kind of tongues as that mentioned in Acts 2:4 but he emphatically declares, that it is nor for all. He says "to one is given by the Spirit the word of wisdom" . . . "to another the working of miracles" . . . "to another" (not to all) "divers kinds of tongues." (See 1 Cor. 12:8-10); "Are all Apostles? Are all prophets? Are all teachers? Are all workers of miracles? Have all the gifts of healing? Do all speak with tongues? Do all interpret?" No! Emphatically NO!! Don't forget now, that St. Paul is writing about the SAME KIND OF TONGUE as that given on the day of Pentecost, as we have proven, and as they must admit.

"Speaking in tongues as the Spirit gives utterance," mentioned in Acts 2:4 is nothing more or less than One of the "differences of Administration," One of the "Diversities of Operations," One of the "Manifestations of the Spirit," yea, One of the "Gifts of the Spirit." There is no difference.

The Nationally known Evangelist, Rev. F. F. Bosworth says, "That there is no Scripture for this distinction between speaking in Tongues as the Spirit gives utterance at Jerusalem, and the gift of tongues at Corinth, is being seen and admitted by many Bible students and Teachers in the Pentecostal movement. In fact, come in the movement have never believed this distinction was Scriptural."

"At a recent State Council of the Assemblies of God, when the Chairman of the Council was asked by one of the young ministers if there was a passage or a number of passages upon which to base this distinction, he publicly admitted that there was not a single passage." I say, thank God for some that will dare to tell the truth.

"Speaking in Tongues as the Spirit gives utterance" is not only one of the GIFTS of the Spirit, but it is the LEAST one of the GIFTS. This fact, my friends, is admitted by some of the Pentecostal people. "Speaking with tongues," says one of their authors, "is a glorious exercise and a blessed Gift of our gracious Lord, but it is not the most important thing. It is the least of the Gifts . . ."

"Prophesy" my friends, is greater than "Speaking in Tongues." St. Paul says "Greater is he that prophesieth than he that speaketh with tongues, except ("unless") he interpret that the Church may receive edifying."—1 Cor. 14:5.

"God hath set some in the Church," first tongues? No! FIRST APOSTLES; Secondly tongues? No! SECONDLY PROPHETS; thirdly tongues? No! tongues is the LEAST Gift, THIRDLY TEACHERS; "AFTER THAT miracles, THEN gifts of healings, helps, governments, diversities of tongues." See 1 Cor. 12:28.

Since Tongues is the LEAST, Paul says "Covet earnestly the BEST gifts." "Strive for the GREATER gifts"—20th Century New Testament. "Set your heart on the HIGHER talents"—Moffatt. "The SUPERIOR gifts"—Syriac New Testament.

I repeat, "speaking in Tongues as the Spirit gives utterance" is the LEAST Gift in the Church and for proof, I simply refer you to THE WRITINGS OF ST. PAUL.

The Purpose of Spiritual Gifts

The primary object in giving gifts is for the edification of the Church. St. Paul says, "The manifestation of the Spirit is given to every man to profit withal." 1 Cor. 12:7. "For the profit of all"—Conybeare and Howson. "For the Common good"—Weymouth 3rd Ed. "For the general good"—Twentieth Century New Testament. "For the benefit of all"—Emphatic Diaglott.

Matthew Henry says, "Spiritual gifts are bestowed only that men may with them profit the Church and promote Christianity."

Dr. Adam Clarke says, "God has given no gift to any man for his own private advantage or exclusive profit."

Dr. Hodge says, "They are not designed exclusively for the gratification of the recipient; but for the good of the Church."

Peake's Bible Commentary says, "The edification of the CHURCH is the governing principle."

Note: Speaking in tongues in a public service is not to be permitted unless it can be interpreted. St. Paul said "If any man speak in an unknown tongue, let it be by two, or at the most three, and that by course; and let one interpret. But if there be no interpreter let him keep SILENCE in the Church." (1 Cor. 14:27, 28.)

"If there is no interpreter, let the speaker keep QUIET in Church."—Moffatt.

"If there is no one to explain it, HAVE HIM KEEP QUIET IN CHURCH."—Goodspeed.

"But if there be no interpreter, let him who speaks in tongues KEEP SILENT in the congregation and speak in private to himself and God alone."—Conybeare and Howson.

If there is no interpreter present during a public gathering, "you may sing with the Spirit," but "sing with the understanding also." "You may pray with the Spirit," but "pray with the understanding also." "You may bless with the Spirit," but may I say, bless with the understanding also. "Let all things be done unto edifying." "Let everything be directed to the building up of faith."—20th Century trans.

Speaking in tongues in public is displeasing to God unless it is interpreted, because it only causes confusion and God is not the author of confusion. When God poured out His Spirit on the people at Pentecost and enabled them to speak with tongues, they were understood. There was some one present to interpret what was being said at Caesarea, and also at Ephesus. St. Paul would understand what was being said if no one else would. Furthermore, we are told that at Ephesus two Gifts were manifested, "Tongues and "prophecy" because "they spake with tongues, and prophesied." (Acts19:6) "They began to speak with 'tongues' and to 'preach'.—20th Century New Testament.

Speaking in Tongues as the Spirit Gives Utterance Is Not for All

St. Mark 16:17-18 is quoted to prove that all will speak in tongues according to Acts 2:4 when Baptized with the Holy Spirit. Note carefully: Mark 16:17-18 does not teach that ALL FIVE of these signs mentioned shall be manifested in every individual at the moment of their Baptism.

Mark 16:17-18 does not teach that all FIVE of these signs mentioned SHALL BE manifested the next day, week, month, or year after one is Baptized with the Holy Spirit. Have you taken up any serpents? That's one of the Signs.

Mark 16:17-18 does not teach that any PARTICULAR ONE of these five signs shall be manifested in every individual the moment of their Baptism. Such reasoning is based purely upon supposition without a solitary "Thus saith the Lord" to prove it.

"Have you been Baptized with the Holy Ghost according to Acts 2:4?" asks the Pentecostal people. Yes, I was Baptized with the Holy Ghost as they were on the day of Pentecost, but the Holy Spirit did not manifest Himself through me as on that day. Let me ask them a question; "Were you sitting when seeking for the Baptism (see Acts 2:2) or were you down on your knees saying "halleluiah, halleluiah,   halleluiah, halleluiah, halleluiah, or glory, glory, glory, glory, glory, glory, glory, glory, as fast as you could until by the co-ordination of mental concentration and vocal conglomeration you SPOKE something that you are pleased to call 'unknown Tongues'?

God help the people that are DUMB, that can't talk. What will they do? I say, AWAY with such erroneous teaching!

I remember when I was in Dayton, Ohio, several years ago, while attending a tent meeting an old gentleman went forward for prayer. He was told to say halleluiah, halleluiah, halleluiah. He said "hal-le-lu-iah, hal-le-lu-iah, hal-le-lu-iah." He was told to say it faster. But the poor old man could not say it fast enough to get the so-called "Baptism." My friends, to get what MOST of these modern tongues people call the 'Evidence of the Baptism of the Holy Ghost' you have to talk fast. I repeat, you surely have to talk FAST to get what MOST of these modern tongue folk have, and when you get it, you have not a thing but a FALSE tongue, that is actuated by a FALSE spirit.

God help folk to pray for the Holy Ghost. The Apostles did not tell anyone to get down on his or her knees and say halleluiah, halleluiah, halleluiah for hours at a time in order to get the Holy Spirit. Jesus did not tell anyone to do such a thing. Such advice or instruction is not based upon any book, chapter, paragraph, verse, clause, or phrase in the Bible. I Boldly challenge any Pentecostal preacher in the WORLD to produce one verse, yes, one verse in the Bible showing that any of the early Christians ever did such a thing or taught anyone else to do it. They simply cannot produce it and they know it. There is no mentioning of such a thing in all the Bible. They did not do such a thing. Jesus told the disciples to ASK for the Holy Ghost (Mt. 7:11); "TARRY . . . until ye be endued with power from on high" (Lk. 24:49); "Wait for the promise of the Father" (Acts 1:4). The Disciples obeyed. They went to the upper room and there "waited," or "TARRIED" (tarry means to stay, abide, to remain in the same place). It does not mean to get down on your knees and shout halleluiah or glory for hours.

On the tenth day, "There came a sound from heaven as of a rushing mighty wind, and it filled all the house where they were SITTING." Note: On the day of Pentecost they were SITTING down and not down on their knees shouting halleluiah, halleluiah, halleluiah when they received the Baptism of the Holy Spirit. The "sound" . . . "filled all the house where they were SIT-TING," "Which filled the whole house where they were SEATED"—Moffatt. "And the whole house where they were SITTING was filled"—Syriac. "And there appeared unto them cloven tongues like as of fire, and it sat upon each of them, and they were all filled with the Holy Ghost, and began to speak with other tongues," (LANGUAGES) "as the Spirit gave them utterance," yea, "Every man heard them speak in his own LANGUAGE." The disciples prayed for others that "they might receive the Holy Ghost" (see Acts 8:15, 9:18, 19; 19:6). We have one instance on record where some received the Holy Ghost while the message was being delivered (see Acts 10:44); but there is no mention whatever of our Lord, or the Apostles, telling anyone to say halleluiah, halleluiah, or glory, glory, real fast in order to get the Holy Ghost. The modern Tongues people tell seekers to do that, and many of them do it and receive what they call the UNKNOWN TONGUES, but for the Baptism of the Holy Spirit saved people are to ASK for it. ASK and you shall receive, praise our God!

Some say, "You must speak once if you don't speak anymore." Where, I ask, does the Bible say 'you MUST speak once'? In all of the seven Chapters where TONGUES are mentioned, the word MUST is found in only one of them, namely, the 19th Chapter of Acts, verse 21, and there we read where Paul said, "I MUST see Rome."

Others say, "Speaking in Tongues is the Bible evidence of the Baptism of the Holy Ghost." They make this statement so often that one would think that such a statement could be found several times in the New Testament. The truth of the matter is that such a statement is not made even once in the New Testament. In fact the word EVIDENCE is not found in any chapter where the word TONGUES is even mentioned. Beginning with the first chapter in St. Matthew you will have to go clear to Hebrews before you find the word EVIDENCE, and there in the 11th chapter, verse 1, we read, "now faith is the substance of things hoped for, the EVIDENCE of things not seen."

Another argument that some advance is this: "A baby cries as soon as it is born into the world. If it doesn't cry there is something wrong with it." They mean to teach by this argument that when one is filled with the Holy Spirit he will speak in Unknown Tongues. May I ask them, do babies TALK as soon as they are born? No! Did you cry when you were Baptized with the Holy Ghost? Babies cry, but they don't TALK as soon as they are born.

I heard one preacher say, "When you go up town to buy a pair of shoes you don't ask for TONGUES, you ask for SHOES, TONGUES come with the SHOES." This poor preacher was trying to make it appear that when one receives the Holy Ghost, TONGUES will always accompany such initial outpouring. If I couldn't get a better argument than this one I would go some place and hide. God bless your soul there are a lot of people getting shoes every day, good shoes, real genuine leather shoes if you please, and they don't get any TONGUES with them. I repeat, they asked for SHOES, and they got SHOES, but they didn't get any TONGUES. Thank God, there are hundreds, yea, thousands of people that have asked for and received the Holy Spirit Baptism, but they did not get 'TONGUES.' Thank God, there are hundreds, yea, thousands of people who are gloriously filled with the Holy Spirit but they have never spoken in Tongues and never will.

Another says, "The Holy Ghost will always speak through every individual that He comes into" and they quote St. John 15:26 and 16:13 to prove it. Are we to infer from the grammatical construction of John 16:13 that the Holy Spirit will guide one into all truth the MOMENT he is Baptized? Do these verses teach that He will "testify" in unknown tongues or "Speak" in 'Unknown Tongues' when "He comes into our hearts?" Aren't there some DUMB PEOPLE (people having no power of speech) that are filled with the Holy Ghost? Did the Holy Ghost SPEAK through them? You say, "He could have." The question is, "Did He?"

"Tongues are the sign 'that you have the Baptism of the Holy Ghost'," say some. St. Paul informs us that "TONGUES" serve as a sign to UNBELIEVERS when the UNBELIEVERS understand what is being said, as they did on the day of Pentecost, BUT if the words spoken are not understood, the UNBELIEVERS will say you are "mad", "crazy," "insane." The Church will not be edified, and such demonstrations will only cause confusion and "God is not the author of confusion." "God is not a God of disorder"—Moffatt. See 1 Cor. 14:33.

"Jesus spoke in tongues while hanging on the cross," says another. He certainly did not speak in 'Unknown Tongues.' I am glad we know what He was talking about.

No, my friends, speaking in Tongues as on the day of Pentecost is not for all. The Apostle Paul is writing about 'speaking in tongues as the Spirit gives utterance' as I have proven and as the Pentecostal people MUST admit, but He assures us that it is not for all. "I WOULD that ye ALL spake with tongues" (1 Cor. 14:5) and "do ALL speak with tongues" (meaning as the Spirit gives utterance 1 Cor. 12:30), is proof that all in the early Church, or, at Corinth as well as other Congregations, did not speak with tongues. (See I Cor. 12:30 and 1 Cor. 14:5)

False Tongues

The gift of prophecy is greater than the gift of tongues, for "Greater is he that prophesieth than he that speaketh with tongues, except he interpret that the Church may receive edifying." (1 Cor. 14:5) Prophecy, the greater gift can be controlled. St. Paul says, "The spirits of the prophets are SUBJECT to the prophets." (1 Cor. 14:32)

Weymouth translates (3rd Ed.) "The spirits of prophets yield SUBMISSION to prophets. Moffatt translates, "Prophets can CONTROL their own prophetic spirits." The dictionary of Christ and Apostles says, "The Divine impulse under which the prophet in each case speaks IS NOT an uncontrollable force, which must have its way irrespective of order or decorum."

My friends, a person with the gift of prophecy should keep still sometimes in public worship. We read, "let the prophets speak two or three, and let the other judge. If anything be revealed to another that sitteth by, LET THE FIRST HOLD HIS PEACE." (1 Cor. 14:29, 30) "Let the first STOP speaking."—Syriac. "Let the first be SILENT."—Weymouth 3rd Ed. "The first speaker must be QUIET."—Moffatt. I repeat, a person with the true gift of Prophecy, a gift that is greater than tongues, if talking can "STOP," "be SILENT," "be QUIET," when some one else should talk. Surely, one that speaks in Tongues as the Holy Spirit gives utterance can "STOP," "BE QUIET," "BE SILENT," when there is another speaking in tongues, or if there is no interpreter present, because the hearers would not be edified. I know the Pentecostal people would evade the force of this argument by saying, "St. Paul is not writing about 'Speaking in tongues as the Spirit gives utterance," but as I have already said, if St. Paul is writing about some other kind of Tongues, then the Pentecostal people should stop teaching six things that they have been teaching.

Acts 6:13 tells of "false witnesses."
Luke 19:8 tells of "false accusers."
2 Cor. 11:20 tells of "false Brethren."
2 Pet. 2:1 tells of "false Teachers."
Mk. 13:22 tells of "false Prophets."
2 Cor. 11:13 tells of "false Apostles."
Mt. 24:24 tells of "false Christs."

Observation tells me that there are FALSE TONGUES.

The nationally known evangelist Rev. F. F. Bosworth says, "I am certain, that many, who SEEMINGLY speak in tongues, are not, nor ever have been, Baptized in the Spirit.

"Every place I have gone to help Pentecostal people in revivals some have come to me and said, 'Brother Bosworth, pray for me, I have spoken in tongues, but I am not satisfied'."

One man advanced this argument, "God put 'tongues' in the Church." Yes, He did, but He also put the Spirit of discernment in the Church, to discriminate between the true and false miraculous manifestations. (See 1 Cor. 12:10)

Conybeare and Howson says: "The recipient of which could distinguish between the real and the imaginary possessors of Spiritual gifts."

In Col. 2:22 we read of "Doctrines of Men."
In Rev. 2:14 we read of "The Doctrine of Baalim."
In Mk. 1:27 we read of "The Doctrine of the Pharisees."
In Rev. 2:15 we read of "The Doctrine of the Nicolaitanes."
In Heb. 1:9 we read of "Divers and strange doctrines."
In Eph. 4:14 we read of "Every wind of doctrine."
In 1 Tim. 4:1 we read of "Doctrine of devils."

A doctrine of the devil, is that which separates and confuses the people of God, deceives them, misleads souls and causes many to be lost. This modern tongues theory may rightly be termed a "doctrine of the devil."

A few months ago, I attended a convention conducted by some Pentecostal people. I was given an opportunity to ask these two questions.

(1) Do you believe and teach that speaking in tongues is the Bible evidence of the Holy Spirit? The minister presiding during that service said, "yes."

(2) Do you believe and teach, that there are people who have been Baptized in Jesus name and speak in

tongues that sin? He said, "yes, they lie like anyone else." (He meant some of them did.)

Think of this my friends. People talking in tongues and at the same time SOME of them "Lie like anyone else."

There are people who are Baptized with the Holy Spirit, but NEVER spoke in tongues, that sing, shout, pray, dress modestly, pay tithes, "see Visions and dream dreams," heal the sick and work miracles by the power of God, preach the Gospel, get Divine revelations, live holy, love everybody, witness wonderful conversions, cast out devils, do home and foreign missionary work, "fight the good fight of faith," "endure hardness as a good soldier," "set their affections on things above," "live in the Spirit," "walk in the Spirit," and "bear the fruits of the Spirit." However, there is ONE THING that SOME people who talk in tongues do, that people who are Spirit-filled but never spoke in tongues don't do, and that is, "LIE LIKE ANYONE ELSE."

"Are all Apostles?" No. "Are all Prophets?" No. "Are all Teachers?" No. "Are all workers of miracles?" No. "Have all the Gifts of healing?" No. "Do all speak in tongues?" (as the Spirit gives utterance) No. "Do all interpret?" No.

In conclusion, let me say:

1. There is no such thing as UNKNOWN TONGUES. Those who speak the kind of tongues given on the Day of Pentecost, speak a real, living, intelligible language.

2. St. Paul writes about the same kind of tongues as that mentioned in Acts of the Apostles, because there is no difference.

3. Speaking in tongues as the Spirit gives utterance is not for all, and never was given to all that were Spirit-filled.

4. The primary object in giving spiritual gifts is for the edification of the Church, and they should not be exercised in public unless the Church is being edified.

5. The modern tongues theory is FALSE. Therefore, the TONGUE of MOST of the Pentecostal people is a FALSE TONGUE.

SECTION III:
OTHER SOURCES

Speaking In Tongues.
S. O. Susag

At the State Camp meeting at Wilmar, Minnesota, was asked to preach in Scandinavian as there were some sixty elderly Scandinavian people who did not understand the English language. I agreed to do so. As soon as I had begun to preach the whole camp came in to listen. When the service was over people asked why Brother Susag did not preach in Scandinavian in the afternoon. Brother Ring told them that he had done so. However, they insisted that I had spoken in English, since the whole camp, they said, had come in and heard me preach in English. The fact is: I had spoken in Scandinavian and the Lord interpreted it to them in English.

S. O. Susag, *Personal Experiences of S. O. Susag* (Guthrie, OK: Standard Printing Company, 1948), p. 62.

Guest Editorial.
by Rev. Harold Boyer

There is a lot of talk these days about "tongues." It has always seemed to me that when people began seeking after signs and evidences they were seeking contrary to the will of God because He teaches us that we are to "walk by faith." He also teaches us that a "sinful and adulterous generation seeketh after a sign."

There are all sorts of religious cults that do strange things. There are religious cults, for instance, that attempt to attain righteousness by abusing the body. Some men actually put rocks in their beds and do other things to make themselves as uncomfortable as possible. Now if I were going to give up to a life of sin and deny God's ability to make me anything different, I think I would at least try to be a comfortable sinner. Man gets enough rocks, bumps and bruises in life without putting a few in his bed. Righteousness cannot be induced by physical suffering.

The other extreme of this attempt to attain righteousness by acts of the flesh is man's rather clumsy attempts to gain some physical demonstration or other "sign" or evidence that he is now made righteous. The church at Corinth was like that. The people there were converted pagans (for the most part) and they desired "signs and evidences." Since God had poured out His Spirit on another occasion and given the gift of languages not learned, to enable the Christian to speak to every man in his own language, it seemed quite natural to the church at Corinth to seek after a similar manifestation. Paul wrote them about this and cautioned them about seeking such a "sign."

Every gift that God ever gave was for a purpose. No one should ever seek a gift except he first make the consecration to USE THE GIFT IF GOD WOULD HONOR THEM WITH IT.

The gift of healing is for the purpose of bringing healing to people who are sick. Unless one is consecrated to bear the burden, visit the sick and pray the prayer of faith, then the gift of healing will never be given.

The gift of prophecy is for the purpose of prophesying.

The gift of teaching is for the purpose of teaching..

The gift of tongues is for the purpose of speaking to people about the Gospel, in their own tongue IN ORDER THAT THEY MIGHT BELIEVE AND BE CONVERTED.

I think it is still a pretty well established fact that the greatest manifestation of the power of God and the presence of the Holy Spirit in a man's life is not his ability to speak in another tongue, but his ability to control the one he already has.

If we are to follow the example of our Lord; we are not going to be people who desire to be spectacular or to stand above our fellows; Jesus said, "I am among you as one that serveth." He taught us, "He who would be greatest among you, let him be servant of all."

The evidence of a Spirit-filled life is not found in some gift or manifestation but in our ability to walk humbly before God and man as "examples of the believers."

Harold Boyer, "Guest Editorial," THE OHIO
CHURCH MESSENGER, Vol. I NO. 9 April 1963.

[Included by permission of Ohio Ministries]

SESSION I.
The Biblical Doctrine of the Holy Spirit.
Dr. Adam W. Miller

There is no attempt in the Scriptures to work out a comprehensive account of the nature and activity or the work of the Holy Spirit. To some degree this is true of all the great Biblical doctrines. In the case of the doctrine of the Holy Spirit, we note that the majority of references are to be found in the record or reports of living experiences. It was as the Holy Spirit laid hold of the lives of men that they were constrained to bear witness of that fact. They were persuaded that the power which had invaded their lives had come from God; that what had happened was in the realm of the human spirit. There was nothing abstract or formal about the Biblical doctrine of the Holy Spirit. Everything moves within the Biblical doctrine of the Holy Spirit. Everything moves within an atmosphere of warm and vital experience. We must never forget this when we attempt to work out a general statement of the nature and activity of the Holy Spirit in the individual and in the church. At the same time it should be pointed out that there is value in bringing together the references to the Holy Spirit in the Scriptures, especially in the New Testament, and bring them together as a connected whole. We shall seek to do this as we move ahead in our conferences, with major emphasis on the Holy Spirit in the New Testament.

THE HOLY SPIRIT AND CHRISTIAN EXPERIENCE

Christian experience as described in the New Testament had a thoroughly real meaning for the Christians of the first century. It was something so unique, so distinguishable from everything else in the religious world of that day, that it could not be overlooked or mistaken for some kind of religious experience found in the non-Christian world of that day. The New Testament records describe Christian experience before compromises and approximations had developed. Then it possessed all of its originality and distinctiveness.

If we are ever to find the language or speech of the New Testament meaningful and natural for us today as Christians, it will be only by a return to that originality and distinctiveness of the Christian life and experience which created or gave rise to the New Testament speech and the various terminology used to describe its various aspects or elements.

Important for our consideration in a study of that experience is the Christian's relationship to the Holy Spirit, or the Holy Spirit's relationship to the Christian. For there is no experience possible to us as Christians which is not vitally related to the work of the Holy Spirit.

WHO IS THE HOLY SPIRIT?

How shall we define the Holy Spirit? The Hebrew word used in the Old Testament may help us some. The word is **ruach,** a term originally used to describe loud, violent breathing and very often applied to the wind which swept down the mountain gorges and whirled across the desert. One can well imagine how awe-inspiring this unpredictable and powerful unseen force was. The use of this word **ruach** to designate the work of the Holy Spirit in and through the prophets is quite understandable. **God was in action!**

This same word **ruach** was used to designate man's **ruach,** that part of man's being which was open to the invasion of the divine. Since God's **Ruach** was ever active toward man: man's **ruach** might at any time receive the energizing of that divine **Ruach** from above.

When the Old Testament Scriptures were translated into the Greek language, the word **pneuma** was used and took on the same meanings as the Hebrew word **ruach.**

Jesus never tried to define the Holy Spirit. He did, however, say something that helps us understand that the Holy Spirit is best known by what he does. Here are his words:

The wind blows where it wills, and you hear the sound of it, but you do not know whence it comes or whither it goes, so it is with every one who is born of the Spirit (John 3:8).

We cannot understand the mystery, but we may open our whole being to the Holy Spirit. When he comes in he will do in each of us what he has been do-ing through men and women throughout the centuries.

REVIEW SOME THINGS THE HOLY SPIRIT DOES FOR US

All of us have had some relationship to the Holy Spirit. This includes new Christians, mature Christians and ministers. This review will serve to make us more aware of the continuing work of the Holy Spirit in today's world.

1. Brings Conviction of Sin. This is a profound realization of the sinfulness and guilt of sin, brought about by the Holy Spirit working on the conscience of an individual (see John 16:8).

2. Response to the Holy Spirit: Repentance. When repentance is accompanied by faith in Christ and the act of redemption completed on the cross and through his resurrection, man experiences pardon for sin, the barrier between God and man is removed, and man is reconciled to God. Paul's great word for this is **Justification.**

3. Regeneration. Jesus referred to this as a new birth (John 3:1-8), Paul refers to it as a new creation (2 Cor. 5:17 RSV).

4. The Witness of the Holy Spirit (sonship). It is the Holy Spirit who witnesses to man's pardon and of God's acceptance of him as a child of God. (Romans 8:16-17; I John 4:13; I John 5:10).

THE UNITY OF PERSONAL CHRISTIAN EXPERIENCE

Listing the above separate elements of personal Christian experience seems to suggest that they are successive steps leading to the entry into the Christian life. But there is another way to look at these elements that helps us to see that personal salvation is not so much a complex or compound thing, but an indivisible unit. When the Holy Spirit or the life from God makes itself felt upon the individual soul effectively, the various elements result. These elements then are manifestations of the new life that has taken hold of the individual.

IS A FULLER RELATIONSHIP TO THE HOLY SPIRIT POSSIBLE?

The answer is yes! This fuller relationship is God's promise to every Christian. Wonderful as is the experience of entering the Christian life, it is only the beginning. There is promised to every Christian what has been called the baptism or the infilling of the Holy Spirit. It would be well to note some of the terms used in describing this experience.

Baptized: Acts 1:5; 11:16

Filled   with the Holy Spirit: Acts 2:4; 4:8; 9:17; 13:9 (Note Paul's experience in 9:17).

Giving   (as a gift) the Holy Spirit: Acts 15:8

Fell   on (came upon): Acts 10:44; 11:15.

Received   the Holy Spirit: Acts 8:17.

Note how Acts 2 is a fulfillment of the promise made to the disciples in Luke 24:49 and Acts 1:1-5.

THE MINISTRY (or Work) OF THE HOLY SPIRIT IN AND THROUGH THE CHRISTIAN

1. To empower the Christian for witnessing (Acts 1:8).

2. To make possible the "fruits of the Spirit." (The graces of the Christian life — Gal. 5:22-23).

3. To be a teacher and a guide (John 14:26; 16:13).

4. To awaken in the believer the spirit of intercession (Romans 8:26-27).

5. To create and maintain in the believer a holy life.

   —Jesus prayed for the sanctification of his disciples (John 17:17-20).

   —When the Holy Spirit came on Pentecost the hearts of the disciples were purified by faith (Acts 15:8-9).

   —This experience is part of the redemptive process of restoring the image of God affected by sin.

   —There is also a continuing process, making possible a transformation into an ever increasing likeness of the image of God.

All of us, then, reflect the glory of the Lord with uncovered faces, and that same glory, coming from the Lord who is the Spirit, transforms us into his very likeness in an ever greater degree of glory." —II Cor. 3:18 (TEV)

6. To bestow gifts for services in the church and in the world. (I Cor. 12; Ephesians 4:8-13; Romans 12:3-13)

(No. 1)		(No. 2)	(No. 3)	(No. 4)
I Cor. 12 (A.D. 54)		Romans	Ephesians	I Peter (4:10-11)
List I	List II	(A.D. 55-57)	(A.D. 59-61 [63])	(A.D. 63 or 95)
1. Wisdom 2. Knowledge 3. Faith 4. Healing 5. Miracles 6. Prophecy 7. Discernment 8. Various Tongues 9. Interp. — Tongues	1. Apostles 2. Prophets 3. Teachers 4. Miracles 5. Healers 6. Helpers 7. Admin. 8. Tongues 9. Interpret.	1. Prophecy 2. Service 3. Teachers 4. Exhorters 5. Givers 6. Charity (aid)	1. Apostles 2. Prophets 3. Evangelists 4. Pastors 5. Teachers	As each has received a gift, speak as one who utters oracles of God. Service

NOTE: List II of Corinthians would seem to give the basic Gifts.

Ephesians includes two important additions: Evangelists and pastors.

Romans: four of the six listed could be identified with some in Corinthians and Romans.

For Consideration: Note the differences in the lists given in Romans and Ephesians when compared with those in Corinthians.

Do you see any reason for his?

Session II will deal with **Glossolalia**

Dr. Adam W. Miller
Printed - March 1975

SESSION II.
Glossalalia: Speaking In Tongues.
Dr. Adam W. Miller

Widespread interest and attention has been manifested in a movement which has been designated by a number of names or terms, some of which are here listed.

1. The Charismatic Movement

2. Neo-Pentecostal Movement (distinguished from the older Pentecostal Movement which is usually dated from 1901).

3. Catholic Pentecostalism

4. Glossalaliaists

5. Gift of Tongues; speaking in tongues; speaking with tongues.

LOOK AT THE MEANING OF TERMS

1. Glossolalia (or Glossalalia). This is not a biblical term and is not used in the New Testament. It is however, made up of two New Testament words.

Glossa: Meaning tongue, speech, language.

Laleo: Meaning to speak.

When the two words are combined we have Tongue-speaking.

2. Dialektos. This is another word for tongue or speech. It means speech, manner of speaking, peculiar language of a nation, dialect.

Note the use of dialektos in the book of Acts —

Acts 1:19 — in their own language.

2:6, 8 — talking in his own language (native tongue)

21:40 — speaking to them in the Hebrew language

22:2 — he addressed them in the Hebrew language

26:14 — in the Hebrew language.

Note: The purpose in calling attention to the use of this word **dialektos** in the book of Acts, is to show that its meaning is "language." This same word is used in Acts 2, where the many different nationalities heard the disciples speak in the various languages.

The word used for "tongue" elsewhere in the New Testament in Acts and in Paul's letters is **Glossa** or some form of it.

3. How **Glossa** is translated in modern speech translations.

Note: The word "unknown" in KJV is in italics, which means the translators added that word. They felt it would make clear that it was a tongue or language unknown to the hearers, as on Pentecost.

Goodspeed: Acts 2 "foreign languages." The Greek word is the same. I Cor. 14 "ecstatic speech." Why translated differently?

N.E.B.: Acts 2 "other tongues."

Living Bible In Acts — "languages they had never learned."

I Cor. 14 — "other tongues" —that is, languages they had never learned.

TEV: Acts 2 "talk in other languages"

1 Cor. 14 "speak with strange sounds" (in some places so translated).

vs. 20, 21 — "men of foreign languages" when quoting the passage from Isaiah.

Phillips: Acts 2 "different languages"

I Cor. "tongue" in quotes to indicate he is not giving any paraphrase or explanation.

REVIEW THE NEW TESTAMENT BACKGROUND

1. Two main clusters of references to speaking in tongues

    The Book of Acts 2:4-21 The Day of Pentecost

    10:44-46 Experience of Cornelius

    19:6 The disciples of John at Ephesus.

    Corinthians (I)

    12:10, 28-29

    13:1-8

    14 - Entire chapter

2. Preliminary Comments

    On Acts 2 — The people who heard were from 15 language areas. Most of them Jews of the Diaspora, but some were doubtless Gentile proselytes.

    > All would be well versed in the language of the country from which they came, since that language would be the medium of communication.

    > They would also be somewhat familiar with Aramaic, the spoken language of the Jews in that day. Also Hebrew from hearing the Old Testament read in the synagogues.

It is also possible that Jews from Asia Minor knew everyday Greek.

Note: The text states that the people of the 15 areas heard members of the 120 speak in their own language

Evidently they had moved out from the Upper Room to meet the larger audience that had assembled. When Peter addressed the multitude, he stood with the eleven and must have addressed them in Aramaic (2:14).

On Acts 10 — Cornelius and his household. Cornelius was a Gentile; a God-fearer, acquainted with Jewish Law and teachings, but not as far as to be circumcised for entrance into Jewish faith.

> Was there a special reason for this bestowal?

On Acts 19 — These were disciples of John the Baptist at Ephesus. These were Jews.

On I Corinthians —

> Ch. 12 — listed as one of the gifts

> Ch. 13 — evaluation of love as transcending all spiritual gifts

> Ch. 14 — deals h the improper use of "tongues."

Mark 16:17 Tongues would be one of the signs that would follow the acceptance of the gospel.

SUMMARIZE THE HISTORICAL BACK-GROUND

1. The phenomena among ancient non-Christian religions

2. Among current non-Christian religions

3. Pre-modern manifestations of tongues

4. The Modern Period, 1901 to present

5. The rise of the Charismatic Movement: April 3, 1960

6. Catholic Pentecostalism. Modest beginning in 1950; strong thrust beginning 1967.

7. The Jesus People.

AN INTERPRETATION OF I CORINTHIANS 14

Evaluation, Problems, Attitudes

1. Consider some of the evaluations made by biblical scholars and linguists.

2. What grounds are there for considering modern manifestations to be that of a "prayer language"?

3. Pentecostals and counselors in the charismatic movement use "priming" and tutoring to aid seekers. What is your evaluation of such methods?

4. Do you equate the modern manifestations in Pentecostal and charismatic groups with the

"Gift of Tongues" in Acts 2 and I Corinthians 12?

5. If not, how would you counsel persons from those groups should they come to you for counseling?

Session III will deal with the function of the Holy Spirit in the structure and work of the church.

Dr. Adam W. Miller
March 1975

[Included by permission of the author's daughter, Joyce Jones.]

Pastor's Fellowship
Of The Church of God.

Dear Church Leader:

The following resolution is self explanatory. It is mailed to you at the request of both assemblies, the ministers of the mid-west area who meet at Winchester, Kentucky, and the south-west pastors who convene at Pryor, Oklahoma, This resolution was adopted in both assemblies without a dissenting vote.

With love and concern for the unity of the church,

Lillie McCutcheon, secretary

Whereas, the Neo-Pentecostal movement is making rapid inroads threatening the unity of the Church of God Reformation, we, the ministers of Pastor's Fellowship, in session May 2, 1978 at Winchester, Kentucky, and the Pastor's Fellowship in session May 16, 1978 at Pryor, Oklahoma, adopt the following resolution:

Recognizing our Church of God heritage firmly acclaims believing in the true experience of the Baptism of the Holy Spirit, excluding any practice of "prayer language", "unknown tongues", or "heavenly language", be it resolved that we vigorously reaffirm this conviction. We believe Neo-Pentecostalism advocates unscriptural practices, intimidates sincere Christians and divides believers. We therefore regard the phenomenon of "unknown tongues" to be unscriptural and stand opposed to both preaching and practicing this pseudo experience.

We strongly appeal to leaders of our Educational Institutions, National Agencies, State Assemblies, local congregations, pastors and evangelists to concur with this position regarding Neo-Pentecostal aggression. We advocate the proclamation of biblical truth concerning the Baptism of the Holy Spirit thus producing a genuine experience which negates a false concept.

[Included by permission Pastors' Fellowship]

An Excerpt From the Minutes of the 1985 General Assembly of The Church of God

Page 13   Session #3   June 1985

MOTION — ARTICLES OF INCORPORATION

. . . College," which had been sent to all delegates. These restated articles, he said, represent the smoothest transition from the Texas incorporation known as Gulf-Coast Bible College to the Oklahoma incorporation to be known as Mid-America Bible College. The restated articles also allow for dissolution, should the corporation dissolve. Dr. Conley moved the acceptance of the Restated Articles of Incorporation. The motion was seconded by Richard Bradley. The vote carried without dissent.

COURTESY LETTERS

Chairman Hines recognized Wilber Hatch, chairman of the Business Committee. Mr. Hatch asked that Helen Russell, a newly elected member of the Business Committee, join the rest of the committee on the platform. Mr. Hatch noted that Dr. Tanner has been asked by the Business Committee to write letters of sincere appreciation to the appropriate persons in the city and on the convention grounds who have contributed to the success of the convention.

EXHIBIT S RESOLUTION ON STUDY COMMITTEE ON GLOSSOLALIA

Mr. Hatch then introduced the Rev. James Burchett, a member of the Business Committee, and asked him to present a resolution from the General Assembly of Southwest Ohio to the Assembly (attached to the minutes as Exhibit S). Mr. Hatch asked the tellers to distribute copies of the resolution to the Assembly. James Burchett read the resolution to establish a committee composed of qualified individuals from the academic and pastoral fields to study the work of the Holy Spirit as related to Glossolalia in light of Scripture, our historical perspective and present happenings in the Church of God movement. Mr. Burchett moved the adoption of the resolution. He also asked the Chair to determine whether the . . .

[Included by permission of Ronald V. Duncan.]

Exhibit S

Minutes 1985

Resolution, Ohio General Assembly of the Church of God

Resolution to develop a study committee concerning the work of the Holy Spirit particularly as related to GLOSSOLALIA in light of Scripture, our historical perspective and present happenings in the Church of God Movement.

> Whereas, we are being confronted with a surge of neo-pentecostal charismatic influence which is causing pronounced confusion and division in our congregations and

> Whereas, we have historically avoided being identified in practice or teaching with the "tongues" churches and

> Whereas, the work and ministry of the Holy Spirit in the world today is relevant to our message and ministry and

> Whereas, it could be beneficial, in light of possible further confusion and division, to thoroughly reexamine this issue in light of scripture and also to evaluate the general effect of this teaching and practice on congregations within the Movement, therefore

Be it resolved that the Board of Directors of the Executive Council of the Church of God, Anderson, Indiana, appoint a committee composed of qualified individuals from the academic and pastoral fields to study this subject and to present their findings in written form to the General Assembly during the 1986 Convention of the Church of God convening in Anderson, Indiana,

Presented to and approved by the General Assembly of the Church of God, Southwest Ohio March 12, 1985 and then to the Ohio General Assembly of the Church of God March 22, 1985.

[Included by permission of the Ohio Ministries of the Church of God.]

Glossolalia
By Barry L. Callen

Issues and Perspectives in the Church of God

My assignment was to provide perspective on glossolalia and related issues from the heritage of the Church of God in particular. As assistance to the study process, the intent was for me to be historical, specific, candid.

I. Introduction

The Church of God Movement has been committed to <u>experiencing deeply</u> the work of the Holy Spirit and <u>accepting joyfully</u> the gifts of the Spirit. The "gift of tongues" has been recognized as a valid, biblically-taught gift. However, differing interpretations of the appropriate definition and use of this gift and negative experiences with some self-proclaimed possessors of this gift have led to a range of perspectives and attitudes within the Church of God.

It is difficult to generalize on attitudes within the Church of God towards "tongues people." One obvious reason is that there has been and now is considerable diversity among "tongues people." Many years ago C.E. Brown ("The Confusion of Tongues") was aware of such persons whose meetings, he wrote, were characterized by "the wildest disorder. . . . People sometimes dance wildly, roll on the floor, go into trances, and babble in a pandemonium of insane furry. . . . Fanatics, lost in the wild delirium of religious excess, have committed murder during such periods of excitement." Such a description probably was appropriate for the particular persons then being encountered, but it is very inappropriate as a description of many contemporary "pentecostals." Therefore, diversity within both the Church of God and the large body of persons generally labeled "charismatic" or "pentecostal" has not permitted very many dependable generalizations and has generated a variety of approaches by Church of God people.

The volume of writing on this subject area by Church of God authors has not been substantial. Much of what has been written has been defensive in tone, written in response to experienced extremes in the teaching and practice of others rather than careful presentation of what was affirmed by Church of God people. Nonetheless, a reading of the published materials makes reasonably clear the following range of categories of approaches by Church of God people to the teaching/practice of glossolalia.

II. Range of Approaches

1. Avoid: It Causes Division

"Tongues" is something which historically the Church of God has avoided being identified with in practice or teaching because it has been believed to cause "pronounced confusion and division in our congregations." (Ohio General Assembly of the Church of God, March, 1985). To be more specific, "we believe Neo-Pentecostalism advocates unscriptural practices, intimidates sincere Christians and divides believers" (Winchester, KY. and Pryor, OK. Pastor's Fellowships, May, 1978). In summary, since the extremes are so obvious, the results so negative, wisdom lies with strict avoidance.

2. Permit: But Approach With Caution

Church of God historian John W. V. Smith (*The Quest for Holiness and Unity*, p. 425) noted that the doctrine of tongues received considerable attention and evoked some dissension among Church of God people during the 1970's. He concluded: "The attitude of most ministers was to permit but not to encourage glossolalia and, above all, not to allow the issue to become divisive either in congregations or in the movement." Such an attitude was and is supported by the feeling of many that (1) the Bible is not totally clear on this subject and (2) the Movement's stance against creedalism precludes an exclusive position on a subject about which equally sincere and biblically-oriented Christians differ. But because of the perceived high potential for abuse, the permission typically was accompanied by considerable caution.

3. Welcome: If Authentic and Not Demanded of All

Pastor Benjamin Reid (*V.C.*, June 30, 1985) stated that tongues is a valid New Testament gift of the Spirit and belongs in the New Testament church today. "As long as the gift of tongues is used in an authentic and spiritual manner, no one can forbid its operation in the

Church of God. God's word says clearly, 'Forbid not to speak with tongues' (I Cor. 14:39). The only thing I insist upon is that you cannot ever teach biblically that everybody has to speak in tongues." Others, such as R.R. Byrum, *Christian Theology*, pp. 484-487, and F. G. Smith in "The Gift of Tongues", c. 1923, have at least implied a similar point of view. If it is a valid gift, it must serve some important purpose and therefore should be welcomed. The welcome, however, always assumes the discipline of biblical guidelines, particularly that this gift is not essential, inevitable, to be expected of all sincere believers.

III. Points of Consensus

Despite the range of approaches just described, there appears to have been substantial consensus among most Church of God writers in all decades that:

1. A gift of tongues, biblically understood and practiced, is a valid gift of the Spirit.

2. This gift is not given to all believers and is not the evidence of the baptism of the Holy Spirit.

3. This gift, like the others, can easily be abused and become a destructive force in the life of the church. It, therefore, must be remembered that it is the "least" of the gifts and should never be allowed to divert Christians from the central purpose of the Holy Spirit's work, which is "to pour out the power and love of God into the hearts of all Christians—the power to witness to Christ, and the love that wins sinners and binds Christians together into

the mighty Church of God" (Kenneth Jones in "What About the Gift of Tongues").

4.   When this gift is exercised in a public assembly, it always should be disciplined by biblical guidelines. Lists of these guidelines are found in R.R. Byrum, *Christian Theology* (485-487), Barry L. Callen (*V.C.*, February 11, 1979) and Gene Miller, ("Speaking in Tongues in the New Testament," final paragraph).

IV. A Central Point of Difference

A central point of apparent <u>difference</u> among those Church of God leaders who have addressed this subject in writing over the decades has been varying understandings of the Bible's <u>definition</u> of the gift of tongues. These understandings might be grouped into two general categories, namely:

1.   Limited to a Real Human Language (Witness Orientation)

   a.   <u>Charles E. Brown</u>: ". . . the gift of tongues is the miraculous gift of God whereby the gifted one may speak, and does speak, in another earthly historic language which he has not learned naturally in any manner."

   b.   <u>Albert F. Gray</u>: "This gift is declared to be the least valuable of all. It is the power given by the Spirit to speak in a language not previously known. It has no practical value except as a sign to unbelievers."

   c.   <u>Boyce W. Blackwelder</u>: "'Unknown' tongues are not given by the Holy Spirit. . . . The modern phenomenon of ecstatic utterance is not identical with the New Testament gift of glossolalia. . . . The genuine gift of glossolalia is not manifest outside the sphere of intelligibility—it is always expressed in words that convey meaning. There is not a 'prayer language' in which a worshiper prays in utterances he does not understand."

d. <u>Kenneth E. Jones</u>: "Luke (in Acts) makes it abundantly clear that he meant that the men were speaking foreign languages, which they had never learned, under the inspiration of the Holy Spirit. . . . Alford consistently maintains that all of the New Testament references, in Mark, Acts, and I Corinthians, describe exactly this same speaking in foreign languages which one has never studied."

2. Not Necessarily Limited to a Real Human Language
(Witness And/Or Personal Edification Purpose)

a. <u>Russell R. Byrum</u>: "The New Testament speaking in tongues may be defined as an endowment by the Spirit of God with ability to speak a real language unknown to the speaker, but only as the Spirit operates through him. . . . There is also a speaking in tongues as described in I Cor. 14:2 which is forbidden in the public assembly unless there be an interpreter, and which therefore be exercised in private only (v. 28). A failure to clearly distinguish between the public and private phases of speaking in tongues has led to much misunderstanding."

b. Frederick G. Smith: "Christian glossolalia, or tongues, is a gift of God bestowed upon an individual whereby, through the operation of the Holy Spirit, he is enabled to speak UNTO GOD in a language which the Spirit chooses and which 'no man understands' or to speak UNTO MEN the mysteries of God in a language unknown to him (the speaker) but understood by his hearers . . . The private phase of tongues is designed as a special means of spirit communication, a language of the spirit and of the emotions, in the exercise of which the soul of man overflows in rapturous praise and thanksgiving to God."

c. Gene Miller: "Some commentators have held that all references to 'speaking in tongues' refer to the use of known human languages. The considerations above, however, particularly those regarding I Cor. 14, point definitely to the conclusion that the 'gift of tongues' and 'speaking in tongues', as exercised and known in the early Church, consist of the manifestation of spiritual or 'ecstatic' language or utterances, rather than known human languages or dialects. In 14:2, Paul points out that one who speaks in a tongue 'speaks not to men, but God; for no one understands him, but he utters mysteries—in the Spirit.' If there is no one to interpret, 'tongues' are not to be spoken at all in the church, but reserved for 'speaking to himself and to God.' "

V. Personal Observations

To the degree that the Church of God Movement has operated with a "consensus theology", speaking in tongues in the classical pentecostal sense has not been part of that generally agreed upon and proclaimed consensus.

Many ministers have been very negative toward such a phenomenon because of a particular understanding of biblical teaching and/or experience with or fear of extremism and division resulting in the church's life from exercising a gift of tongues. Others have been less negative, some even positive toward a tongues gift seen as both biblically taught and potentially strengthening to the life of the individual involved and/or the church addressed.

There clearly has not been uniformity within the Church of God in understanding of the biblical definition of "tongues", although, as listed above, there have been several positions about the gift of tongues which have been accepted almost universally within the Church of God.

One way to highlight the dilemma now faced by the Church of God in regard to the gift of tongues is to state again those often quoted words of Andrew L. Byers about the posture which always should characterize the true church:

"Disposition to obey all Scripture and to let the Spirit have his way and rule. This constitutes her [the church's] safety in matters of doctrine and government." (Found in Callen, *The First Century,* p.314).

The challenge, then, seems to lie in:

1. Clarifying, or settling for lack of clarity, regarding what Scripture teaches about tongues, particularly about how restrictive should be the definition of its nature. Is a private phase, a personal edification function to be accepted as potentially legitimate, although not essential or mandatory?

2. Remaining genuinely open and obedient to the Spirit of God so that our definitions and fear of abuses do not work to limit what He may wish to do in and through some of His children.

3. Determining again whether any move in the direction of a creedalistic doctrinal stance can be tolerated in the Church of God, particularly when there is honest disagreement about what the Bible teaches on a given subject. When there is perceived danger to the church's life from what is felt by some to be false teaching, do we yet believe that the church's "safety in matters of doctrine and government" resides in our common "disposition to obey all Scripture and to let the Spirit have his way and rule," or are we more inclined to establish formally a particular stance which hopefully will be accepted by and will regulate the church's life? If we are so inclined, we thereby would be challenging much which is central to the reasons classically stated for the very existence of this movement.

4. The well-being of the church obviously is a legitimate and major concern of those responsible for church leadership. Beginning with the congregation in Corinth and continuing in the

experience of many other congregations since, history has shown that the "least" of the gifts (tongues) is potentially troublesome and needful of careful disciplining in the church's life. On the other hand, the church is best equipped for its life and mission when there exist in its midst all of the gifts which the Spirit chooses to give to one or many in the fellowship. Wisdom seems to lie in a careful balance between the necessary discipline and the equally necessary openness. This discipline/openness tension is critical both for approaching the issue of the gift of tongues and for maintaining the integrity of the Church of God Movement itself. To state it another way, the heritage of the Church of God Movement has and does affirm in principle the "disposition to obey all Scripture and to let the Spirit have his way and rule." But there is ambiguity in practice resulting from lack of uniformity in interpreting Scripture and experiencing the leading of the Holy Spirit. It is vitally important how the Movement reacts to this ambiguity between principle and practice. To some extent it will always exist, particularly in a movement which does not equate Christian unity with the necessity of strict uniformity in thought and action.

Barry L. Callen
Anderson, Indiana
January 27, 1986

[Included by permission of the author.]

The Gift of Tongues.
By Dr. Jerry C. Grubbs

The June 30, 1985 issue of *Vital Christianity* published by Warner Press and edited by Dr. Arlo Newell has been a subject of discussion in recent months. The theme of that issue was a question: "Is the Tongues Movement Dividing the Church?"

Dr. Newell is to be commended for an editorial policy that allows for the confronting of crucial issues in the church's primary publication. He follows in a long tradition of editors who have expressed in practice the spirit expressed in the words of F.G. Smith in his May 15, 1930, *Gospel Trumpet* editorial:

> We have sought to maintain a middle ground between these extremes. It has been our desire not to make the *Trumpet* the organ of any one man, nor of any single group within the Church, but truly representative of the Church itself as a whole.

The gift of tongues is a "hot issue" in some circles. At times it is difficult to deal with the real biblical issues because of the passion and emotional fervor with which the issue is approached.

Some persons confront the issue of the gift of tongues as though it is a new phenomenon just lately arising in the church. In fact, between December 1, 1885, when D.S. Warner wrote on the subject in the *Gospel Trumpet* and 1923, when F.G. Smith released his sixty-one page tract there were no less than ten major articles in the *Gospel Trumpet* on the subject.

I have always been convinced that an informed historical perspective is valuable. More than once I have heard a person speak "authoritatively" about the past only to discover that they really were not informed—passionate, but not informed!

The question came to me not long ago: "What does the Church of God believe about the gift of tongues?" Of course I had to give the obvious response. The Church of God has no official position that can be put forth as an authoritative response. Our commitment to a non-creedal stance has led us to shy away from official pronouncements.

The more appropriate question from the standpoint of our heritage is, "What have Church of God folks believed about the gift of tongues across these years?" Even that is difficult to answer since all too few have taken time to preserve their beliefs in writing. Some have—witness the June 30, 1985, *Vital Christianity* issue. That issue illustrates an obvious diversity among us.

In doing a search of the written record, one major document stands out from among all the rest. Many articles have been written on the gift of tongues. But the 1923 (c.) sixty-one page tract by F.G. Smith is one of the better representations of the level of discussion of this issue by an early Church of God writer.

In 1921, F.G. Smith preached a sermon titled; "The Gift of Tongues." This sermon was preached at the Ministerial Assembly of the Church of God in Anderson, Indiana. A copy of his sermon outline can be found in the School of Theology Archives where his sermon collection is housed.

His sermon was so well received that a request was made for its publication and general distribution. His sermon was developed into a sixty-one page document and published by the Gospel Trumpet Company as Tract No. 154, c. 1923. A copy of the original is housed in the School of Theology.

Since the tract is out of print and not available for general reading, it is being reprinted for general distribution. Permission was received from Warner Press and it is printed in this issue in its entirety.

F.G. Smith has done us a good service in presenting his view of the biblical background for the gift of tongues. He goes one step further and offers pastoral guidance in dealing with the gift of tongues in the local church.

The reprint of this tract offers each of us a broader basis for further discussion about the issues involved. Smith does not have the answer for all the church, but he does give us a place to begin our discussion.

[Included by permission of the author. The original article appeared in the Winter 1986 Volume 11, Number 2 edition of *Centering on Ministry.* Published by The Center for Pastoral Studies, Anderson College - School of Theology Anderson, Indiana]

Annotated Resource List

A Selection of Church of God Publications Referencing
the Subject of Glossolalia

I. Books

1. Beck, Edward N. The Gift of Tongues and Other
   Tongues. Prestonsburg, KY: Reformation Publishers, 2006.

2. Boyer, Harold W. Gifts of the Spirit. Houston, TX:
   Gospel Outreach, 1983. Chapter Four, "The Gift of
   Tongues."

3. Bradley, Richard. The Bible and Today's Tongues.
   Anderson, IN: Warner Press, 1987.

4. Byrum, Russell R. Christian Theology. Anderson,
   IN: Gospel Trumpet Company, 1925. "The Gift of
   Tongues," pages 476-487.

5. Byrum, Russell R. Christian Theology. Revised Edition. Revision Editor Arlo F. Newell. Anderson,
   IN: Warner Press, 1982. "Chapter VI Baptism with
   the Holy Spirit," pages 386-404.

6. Callen, Barry L. The First Century. Anderson, IN:
   Warner Press, 1979.

7. Gray, Albert F. Christian Theology. Anderson, IN:
   Gospel Trumpet Company, 1946. Part Four, Chapter 5, "The Holy Spirit Baptism."

8. Hale, Mabel. Emma Bailey Seeks Truth. Anderson,
   IN: Gospel Trumpet Company. N.d.

9. Jones, Kenneth E. Commitment to Holiness. Anderson, IN: Warner Press, 1985. Chapter 12, "The Spirit in the Church." Pages 141-163.

10. Jones, Kenneth E. Theology of Holiness and Love. Lanham, MD: University Press of America, Inc., 1995. Pages 281-285.

11. Konstantopoulos, Bill C. The Holy Spirit Within Us. Anderson, IN. Warner Press, 2010. Chapter 7. "A Closer Look at the Gift of Tongues."

12. Linn, Otto F. Studies in the New Testament. Anderson, IN: Warner Press, 1942. Commentary series of three volumes.

13. Martin, Fay C. The Holy Spirit Versus Modern Tongues. Nappanee, IN: E.V. Publishing House, 1932.

14. Neace, Donald. A Challenge for Clarity. Prestonsburg, KY: Reformation Publishing Co. 2004.

15. Newell, Arlo F. Receive the Holy Spirit. Anderson, IN: Warner Press, 1978. "Charismata: The Gifts of the Spirit." Pages 91-102.

16. Reid, Benjamin F. Glory to the Spirit. Anderson, IN: Warner Press Inc., 1990.

17. Riggle, Herbert M. The Two Works of Grace. Moundsville, WVA: Gospel Trumpet, 1900. Chapter VII, Examples of Two Works.

18. Smith, Frederick G. What the Bible Teaches. Anderson, IN: Gospel Trumpet Company, 1914. Pages 182-193.

19. Smith, John W.V. The Quest for Holiness and Unity. Anderson, IN: Warner Press, 1980. Page 425.

20. Stafford, Gilbert W. Theology for Disciples. Anderson, IN: Church of God Ministries, 1996. Page 359ff. "Issue 1: Holy Spirit Baptism and the Indwelling of the Spirit."

21. Strege, Merle D. *I Saw the Church: The Life of the Church of God told Theologically.* Anderson, In.: Warner Press, 2002.

22. Teasley, D.O. The Holy Spirit and Other Spirits. Gospel Trumpet Company, 1903. Chapters 17 and 18.

23. Tippin, Kenneth R. ed., *Powerful Words: Radical Words Then and Now.* Sturgis, MI.: Douglas Carr, Gateway River of Life Ministries, 2001.

II. Magazine Articles –
Gospel Trumpet/Vital Christianity and
Reformation Witness Articles

1. Blackwelder, Boyce, W. "Baptism of the Holy Spirit." Gospel Trumpet, May 19, 1956.

2. Blackwelder, Boyce W. "Paul's Attitude Toward Glossolalia." Vital Christianity. Sept. 8, 1963.

3. Bradley, Richard. "Bible Truth About Today's Tongues." Vital Christianity, June 30, 1985.

4. Byers, Andrew L. "The Tongues-Evidence Theory Versus Scriptural Deduction." The Gospel Trumpet, December 11, 1930.

5. Byers, J. W. "The Gift of Tongues." Moundsville, WV: The Gospel Trumpet, Vol. 26, No. 10, March 8, 1906. [This is a duplicate of the article below.]

6. Byers, J.W. "The Gift of Tongues." Gospel Trumpet, June 23, 1898.

7. Byers, J.W. "The Tongues Spirit." The Gospel Trumpet, June 30, 1910.

8. Byers, J.W. "Spiritual Gifts." Grand Junction, MI: Gospel Trumpet. Vol. 17 No. 4. Jan. 28, 1897. Page 2.

9. Byrum, Enoch E. "A Craze for Tongues." The Gospel Trumpet, January 17, 1907.

10. Byrum, Russell R. "Sources and Nature of Speaking in Tongues." The Gospel Trumpet, September 16, 1920.

11. Callen, Barry L. "A Biblical Perspective on Tongues" Vital Christianity, January 21, 1979 (Part One.

12. Callen, Barry L. "A Biblical Perspective on Tongues" Vital Christianity, February 11, 1979 (Part Two).

13. Coon, Zula Evelyn. "Worship Services from the Hymns." Fleming H. Revell Co.as quoted in Gospel Trumpet Volume 79. May 2, 1959. Number 18.

14. Forrest, J. E. "The Gift of Tongues." Moundsville, W V: The Gospel Trumpet, April 7, 1904. Vol. XXIV. No. 14

15. Gospel Trumpet. "The Gifts of the Spirit." Moundsville, WV: The Gospel Trumpet. Vol. XXII NO. 6. Feb. 6, 1902. Page 4

16. Gospel Trumpet. Bible Teaching About Speaking with Tongues.

17. Gospel Trumpet. "Seeking Pentecost." Anderson, IN: Gospel Trumpet, Vol. XXVI, No. 51. Pages 8-9

18. Gospel Trumpet. "These Signs Shall Follow." Moundsville, WVA: Gospel Trumpet. Vol. XVIII NO. 48. December 1, 1898. Page 8.

19. Jones, Kenneth E. "Was Luke Mistaken?" Vital Christianity, April 21, 1963.

20. Jones, Kenneth E. "What Did Paul Mean?" Vital Christianity, Sept. 8, 1963.

21. Konstantopolous, Bill. "The Manifestations of the Holy Spirit." Reformation Witness. Winter 2002/03. Church of God Pastors Fellowship.

22. Lawrence, Robert R. "Questions for Charismatics." Reformation Witness.

23. M'Creary, James. "The Baptism of Fire." The Gospel Trumpet, Vol. 18 No. 6, Grand Junction, MI: February 10, 1898. Pages 5-6.

24. Means, William P. "Counterfeit Gifts of the Spirit." Reformation Witness. May 2010. Volume 26 Number 1.

25. Meyer, Lydia. "Bear Ye One Another's Burdens." Moundsville, WVA: The Gospel Trumpet. June 14, 1906. Volume NO. XXVI. Number 23. Page 3.

26. Miller, Milburn H. "What Happened in the Upper Room." Gospel Trumpet. Volume 79. May 16, 1959, No. 20.

27. Morton, Ralph D. "Fire!" Gospel Trumpet. Volume 79. February 14, 1959. No. 7.

28. Neace, Donald W. "Slain, But by What Spirit?" Reformation Witness. February 2001. Reformation Publishers; Prestonsburg, KY.

29. Newell, Arlo F. "Doctrine, Desire, and Deception." Vital Christianity, June 30, 1985.

30. Phillips, Harold L. "Editorial." Vital Christianity, March 24, 1963. Page 5.

31. Reid, Benjamin F. "The Gift of Tongues and Its Place in the Church." Vital Christianity, June 30, 1985.

32. _____. Letter to Executive Council. May 4, 1978.

33. Rice, Hillery C. "The Baptism of the Holy Spirit," The Gospel Trumpet. May 16, 1959.

34. Rupert, J. H. "From the Field." The Gospel Trumpet, Vol. 18 No. 6, Grand Junction, MI: February 10, 1898, p. 6.

35. Rutty, Jennie C. "The Gifts of Tongues." Moundsville, WV: The Gospel Trumpet, Vol. XXII. September 18, 1902. Page 3.

36. Schell, William G. "Questions Answered." Grand Junction, MI: Gospel Trumpet Vol. 16 No 39.. Oct. 1, 1896. Page 2

37. Seaton, William T. "Is Speaking in Tongues an Evidence?" The Gospel Trumpet, December 28, 1940.

38. Stewart, George N. "Babel and Pentecostal Tongues." The Gospel Trumpet, March 29, 1917.

39. Tufts, Jr G. "A Deceptive Fraud." The Gospel Trumpet, Vol. 18 No. 4, Grand Junction, MI: January 20, 1898. Pages 5-6.

III. Tracts/Booklets/Papers

1. Barber, Harold. The Baptism of The Holy Ghost. n.d.

2. Barber, Harold. The True Holy Spirit Gift of Tongues. n.d

3. Blackwelder, Boyce W. The Gifts of the Spirit. Anderson, IN: Warner Press. n.d.

4. Blackwelder, Boyce W. Thirty Errors of Modern Tongues Advocates. Anderson, IN: Warner Press, n.d.

5. Brown, Charles E. "The Confusion of Tongues." Anderson, IN: Gospel Trumpet Company, nd.

6. Byers, Andrew L. "The Tongues Evidence Theory in the Light of the Scriptures" Gospel Trumpet Company, n.d.

7. Caudill, R. C. The Bible Gift of Tongues.

8. Caudill, R. C. Why the Church of God Does Not Speak in an Unknown Tongue.

9. Chesnut, Lawrence. True Bible Tongues.

10. Conley, John. Confusion Clarified.

11. Gaulke, Max R. "Some Clear Statements About the 'Tongues' Issue." Gulf Coast Bible College, n.d.

12. Good, Virgil L. "The Modern Tongues Experience." Gospel Trumpet Company, n.d.

13. Gunter, Ruth Cochran. Do All Speak with Tongues.

14. Harmon, George. The Gift of Tongues.

15. Hazen, Robert. A Word of Warning About Tongues. Camrose, Alberta: Gospel Contact Press. 1979.

16. Heffren, H.C. From Babel to Pentecost.

17. Heffren, H.C. "The Holy Spirit and the Charismatic Movement." Gospel Contact Press, 1974.

18. Heffren, H.C. Rethinking Biblical Tongues. Camrose, Alberta, Canada: Bible Lovers' Correspondence School.

19. Hughes, Will. Speaking in Tongues.

20. Jones, Kenneth E. "What About the Gift of Tongues?" Anderson, IN: Warner Press, n.d.

21. Lewis, James W. The Phenomena of the Spirit. A Paper Prepared for the Doctrinal Dialogue. 119th North American Convention of the Church of God. Anderson, Indiana. June 29, 2005.

22. Ludwig, Charles. Book Review. Anderson, IN: Warner Press, 1987.

23. Lynch, J. W. A Challenge Answered. An Open Letter to the Church of God Reformation Movement, Anderson, Indiana. Detroit, MI. Truth and Tract Depot.

24. Martin, Fay C. An Experience with Demons in "Pentecostal Tonguism."

25. McCutcheon, Lillie. Speaking in Tongues. Anderson, IN: Warner Press, n.d.

26. Miller, Gene. " 'Speaking in Tongues' in the New Testament" (Gulf Coast Bible College, 1986).

27. Naylor, Charles W. "What Paul Taught About Tongues." Anderson, IN: Gospel Trumpet Company, n.d.

28. Naylor, Charles W. "Baptized with the Holy Spirit." Anderson, IN: Gospel Trumpet Company, n.d.

29. Neece, William C. The Gift of the Spirit and the Spirit's Gifts.

30. Ratzlaff, Leslie. "A Biblical Position in Respect to Tongues" Lake Wales, FL: Warner Southern College, n.d.

31. Shultz, Clair. Learning About the Holy Spirit.

32. Shultz, Clair. What a Christian Should Know About the Gift of Tongues. Mwihila, Yala: Church of God Publications, n.d.

33. Selected. Modern Pentecostalism.

34. Smith, Frederick G. "The Gift of Tongues." Anderson, IN: Gospel Trumpet Company, 1923.

35. Tasker, George P. An Open Letter on the Tongues-Evidence Teaching. Bangalore, India: L. S. Press, n.d.

36. Washington, Cecil. The Truth About Speaking in Tongues.

37. Washington, Cecil. The Modern Tongues Theory Exposed.

38. Washington, Cecil. What the Bible Teaches About Speaking in Tongues.

39. Washington, Cecil. Undeniable Facts About Speaking in Tongues.

IV. Other Sources

1. Boyer, Harold. "Guest Editorial." The Ohio Messenger. 1963.

2. Callen, Barry. "Glossolalia."

3. Callen, Barry and James Fleming. "Bibliography."

4. General Assembly of the Church of God. An Excerpt from the Minutes of the 1985 General Assembly of the Church of God. June 1985.

5. Grubbs, Jerry. "The Gift of Tongues." The Center for Pastoral Studies. Winter 1986.

6. Miller. Adam W. The Biblical Doctrine of the Holy Spirit. n.p. March 1975

7. Ohio General Assembly of the Church of God. Resolution, Ohio General Assembly of the Church of God. March, 1985.

8. Pastors Fellowship. Resolution, Winchester, Kentucky and Pryor, Oklahoma Pastor's Fellowships. May 1, 1978.

9. Study Committee on Glossolalia. Biblical Guidelines for the Local Church. 1986.

10. Susag, S. O. Personal Experiences of S. O. Susag. Guthrie, OK: Standard Printing Company, 1948, p. 62.

11. Unsigned. The Doctrine of the Holy Spirit. n.p. n.d.

—Compiled by
Barry L. Callen, and
James L. Fleming
January, 1986 & 2011.